Cases and Classics
in marketing management

Cases and Classics
in marketing management

DENNIS H. TOOTELIAN
California State University, Sacramento

RALPH M. GAEDEKE
California State University, Sacramento

HARCOURT BRACE JOVANOVICH, PUBLISHERS
San Diego   New York   Chicago   Atlanta   Washington, D.C.
London   Sydney   Toronto

Preface

This text is designed to give senior and graduate level students the opportunity to identify marketing problems, analyze them in depth, and develop viable strategies for their solution. These abilities are the very essence of successful marketing management. The readings and cases presented here are intended to help students understand the processes involved.

The readings and cases are carefully coordinated— each set of readings is followed by a set of cases that call on the students to apply the theories and skills they have just learned.

The readings are established classics in marketing, carefully selected for their focus on problem-solving and for their currency with modern marketing thought. From these selections, students will learn to recognize the necessary components of a marketing program and to understand the relationships between them.

The cases are selected to be of high topical interest to students. By covering a variety of issues and industries, they provide a mix of large and small, profit and nonprofit organizations. Retailing, wholesaling, and manufacturing functions are represented. The cases examine marketing decisions in their complexity and, most important, are complete for purposes of analysis. The latter criterion is especially significant because the case-study method has frequently been hampered by shallow cases that do not give students the opportunity to evaluate fully an organization's internal and external environments. The cases in this text avoid that pitfall and include the financial and managerial information pertinent to marketing programs.

All of the cases have been included for class discussion purposes only—not to illustrate either appropriate or inappropriate, effective or ineffective, handling of administrative situations.

The text begins with a discussion (written in collaboration with Leete A. Thompson) of the process of case analysis. The book is then organized in eight sections. Section One ("The Philosophy and Scope of Marketing") is designed to give students a broad perspective on what marketing is and what it can do for the firm. For many students, this section will serve as an important refresher on marketing thought.

Section Two ("Marketing Planning") focuses on marketing strategies and sets out the basic framework for developing a marketing plan.

Section Three ("Market Identification and Environments") deals with issues of buying behavior, both in consumer and in industrial settings, and with the methods used to collect and process pertinent market information.

Sections Four ("Product Strategies"), Five ("Price Strategies"), Six ("Channel Strategies"), and Seven ("Promotion Strategies") treat the major marketing strategy areas.

Section Eight ("Marketing Assessment and Control") examines the techniques used to evaluate and control the marketing program—including review of marketing strategies while they are in use and assessment of their performance at specific intervals.

An Instructor's Manual contains questions and answers for each of the readings, as well as case summaries, alternative programs to meet the challenges presented in the cases, and detailed discussion of the best alternatives.

Preparing a textbook is an involved process, demanding the coordinated and supportive efforts of many people. The authors who contributed their cases and articles to this work lent highly valued expertise. Christine Bolt provided much-needed assistance in many areas, and we especially thank her for her work on the Instructor's Manual. The staff of Harcourt Brace Jovanovich deserves special recognition for its support and encouragement. Ken Rethmeier, acquisitions editor, and Mike McKinley, Helen Triller, Merilyn Britt, Maggie Porter, and Lesley Lenox were most helpful throughout the production of the book.

Our wives (Virginia and Johanna) and children (Traci, Carrie, Jolene, and Michael) encouraged and coped with us throughout the writing process, and to them we are truly grateful.

Finally, we owe special appreciation to our friend and colleague Leete A. Thompson. His guidance over the years was most important to us, and we dedicate this book to his memory.

Contents

Cases and Classics
in marketing management

INTRODUCTION

Case Analysis

The process of analyzing and discussing actual cases can be a valuable adjunct to traditional methods of marketing education. By assuming the role of a surrogate marketing manager, the case analyst can apply and test the principles, theories, and practices he or she has studied. Moreover, analyzing marketing cases, then communicating and defending one's analysis, provides vicarious experience in managing the marketing function.

Each of the cases in the following chapters involves a real firm or nonprofit organization, which, at the time the case study was posed, faced some issue of concern to its top marketing managers.[1] These are complex cases rather than mere incidents. Most of them include information about an organization's operations, policies, and systems, liberally sprinkled with opinions, estimates, reports, or financial statements, plus other data selected by the casewriters.

Whether you are preparing for a class discussion or for a formal written analysis, plan to read the assigned case more than once. Begin with a fast skimming to get acquainted with the organization, its size, age, location, principal products, and other major characteristics. Take time to calculate a few critical financial ratios if the case includes balance sheets and income statements.[2] Comparing such ratios and their trends with those of the firm's industry sometimes reveals symptoms that are not mentioned specifically in the case.[3] Two or three additional readings of the case, some reflection, and, perhaps, a little outside research are likely to be needed to complete a comprehensive analysis. While much of the analysis will have to be done alone, you may want to discuss the case before class with two or three students in a sort of brainstorming atmosphere. Such sessions tend to expand and clarify one's thinking.

Your overall analysis will be addressed to finding the most critical problem and recommending appropriate executive action to deal with it. The scientific method of reasoning

---

1. In some of the cases, names or locations have been changed to protect the principals.

2. The authors suggest computing the following ratios as a minimum: current ratio, profit after taxes on sales, profit after taxes on equity, total debt to tangible net worth (leverage), inventory turnover, and receivables turnover (or collection period, which is 365/turnover). These are in addition to calculation of break-even points, contribution of products, markups, or other variables of significance in marketing cases.

3. *Dun's Review* and Robert Morris Associates' *Annual Statement Studies* each publish actual financial ratios for a wide variety of retail, wholesale, and manufacturing lines or industries. They are found in most business libraries.

can be an effective and convenient framework for such analysis if you proceed as follows:

1. isolate the problem,
2. accumulate and organize facts relevant to the problem,
3. consider alternative solutions,
4. choose a solution, and
5. implement the solution you choose.

Let us examine each of these steps in more detail.

ISOLATE THE SALIENT PROBLEM

Identifying exactly what problem you want to attack is one of the most frustrating tasks in case analysis. The problem should be significant in terms of achieving the organization's objectives. Top managers and staff experts in marketing earn substantial salaries; their time is valuable. Your time, in your role as surrogate manager, is also valuable—much too valuable to spend solving the organization's "paper clip" problems. The problem also should be solvable; the probability of success should warrant the executive effort.

Problems aren't easily identified, however. Distinguishing between a problem and symptoms of the problem is one of the first hurdles. In many respects, a physician faced with a patient's vague complaint is in a position analogous to that of the case analyst. He tries to determine the patient's (organization's) objectives; he examines any quantitative gauges of the patient's health (sales, share of market, turnover, costs, profits, and so forth) for trends or signs of weakness; and he estimates what deficiencies are likely to keep the patient from achieving wanted objectives in the environment forecast for future years. A headache or an elevated temperature (falling sales, high costs, low profits, or other gauges of an organization's vitality) usually should be looked upon as symptoms of some under-lying disease or deficiency rather than as the real problem, especially if the patient's long-run survival is paramount (the objective). Otherwise, a serious problem may grow worse while the symptom is being treated. In an emergency, however, either the physician or the case analyst is justified in treating such gauges of health as problems to be solved directly. What would ordinarily be a symptom can sometimes become a serious problem in the short run. Falling sales or rising costs, like headaches or elevated temperature, can quickly debilitate the patient; moreover, there are alternate choices of short-run remedies for each. Recognition of such emergencies can require careful judgment.

Now, suppose that you see multiple problems in the case situation. This is not at all unusual. Generally, it is recommended that you rank the problems in order and solve the most critical one first. Presumably, the other problems will be solved in order, but our model considers only one problem at a time. Another possibility is that the multiple problems you see really are part of a cluster. Thus, the problem statement can be broad-ened (generalized) to encompass all, or most, of the case problems. Be careful in making this assumption, though. Lumping unrelated problems into a single problem statement is a favorite tactic of a decision maker who is unwilling to stick his neck out. He tries to avoid the risk of ranking one problem as most crucial and solving it first, for fear that his peers or bosses will disagree. Unfortunately, alternatives to an overly broad problem state-ment are difficult to find, and recommended decisions tend to be vapid. Again, judgment becomes a factor in isolating the salient problem.

If you have chosen your major problem properly, you will be able to state it succinct-ly—probably in three to five sentences at the most.

ACCUMULATE AND ORGANIZE RELEVANT FACTS

Whether you are preparing a written analysis or just getting ready for class discussion of the case, facts and assumptions relevant to the problem you propose to solve should be accumulated gradually. This process may involve reclassifying information, searching for data outside the case, and analyzing data by both qualitative and quantitative techniques. The validity of information in the case, especially opinions, should always be questioned. Here, as in real life, not all information is equally reliable or equally relevant.

Your assumptions are bound to enter the analysis of complex cases. Your situation, as a case analyst, is similar to that of the real marketing manager. Each wants as much information as possible about finances, products, customers, distributors, competitors, or other variables in the case. Thus, there is a tendency to stall or complain, "I can't decide without more data." However, time and/or cost constraints set limits—invariably, assumptions must be substituted for some of the unknowns before the deadline. Decisions are made with less than perfect information. In fact, real executives have much less complete information than most students realize. So make your assumptions. But be sure that you recognize them as assumptions and not facts and that they are reasonable under the case circumstances.

Experienced case instructors are not in complete agreement as to how much or what kind of information should appear in written case analyses. Some favor inclusion of a company assessment—a short section which reorganizes the most critical facts and assumptions to show the organization's existing position with respect to finances, management capabilities, market position, or other variables. Such a section should not restate facts; rather it should interpret case material and show its implications. The section then becomes a logical transition between the problem statement and the listing of alternatives. Unfortunately, there seems to be a natural tendency to rehash facts in company assessments. Perhaps this is why other case instructors prefer that any critical facts or assumptions be dispersed and incorporated wherever appropriate throughout the case analysis.

CONSIDER ALTERNATIVE SOLUTIONS

If you have chosen your major problem properly, there should be at least two, but not more than perhaps seven, viable alternative solutions. Each alternative should be at least conceivably possible. Case analyses are exercises in pragmatism. Pragmatically, the organization should not waste resources considering ridiculous alternatives or alternatives that clearly violate organizational objectives.

Another important qualification for the alternatives is that they be mutually exclusive. This means that no two of them could possibly be implemented at the same time. If they meet the definition of *alternatives*, then any choice from among them would be limited to one, not some combination of two or more. Students often find this restriction difficult to live with, but mutual exclusivity is a very important requisite of a sound analysis. As a matter of fact, the most common reason for listing alternatives that are not mutually exclusive is that the problem statement has not been narrowed sufficiently—the student is trying to solve too many problems at the same time.

You may be tempted to list alternatives that shift your risk to others or push your risk into the longer future. One of the most common ploys is to recommend hiring a consultant. Lazy or disinterested executives may occasionally get away with passing the buck in such a manner. Indeed, some of the best managers do hire consultants *if the organization lacks the expertise required to solve this problem.* However, when instructors assign a case, they assume that you are ambitious and that you do have adequate expertise to solve the case's problems. In effect, you are the consultant who was hired. This does not, of course, preclude the possibility of your suggesting an alternative that would be implemented by a hired consultant.

A somewhat more controversial question is whether or not "do nothing" should be considered as a viable alternative. Generally, deciding to take no action couldn't possibly solve a problem, therefore it couldn't be a viable alternative. Cases tend to be action oriented, with problems that only some kind of executive action can solve. But exceptions are possible. In the short-run, doing nothing can occasionally be an effective delaying strategy for handling problems in which the organization occupies a risky adversary relationship with competitors, customers, employees, stockholders, suppliers, or government units. The presumption is that today's decision will be followed by others in a sequence or, perhaps, in a decision tree.

For most cases, a very effective way to start a list of alternatives is to select one at each extreme of viability. These extreme alternatives then become the limits for a spectrum, with one to five alternatives arrayed between them. The spectrum may be based on cost, risk, size, time, markets, or some variable critical to the case. Obviously, a considerable amount of judgment is involved in listing alternatives. The process also involves creativity; selecting alternatives to the problems that arise is one of the most creative of all management activities.

Once the alternatives have been listed, begin enumerating the advantages and the disadvantages of each. These pros and cons will form the basis for choosing one of your alternatives over the others. They also will serve as your support in class discussions, where your ideas may be challenged. If possible, assign weights, probabilities, and/or dollar values to each alternative.

RECOMMEND A SOLUTION TO THE PROBLEM

Choose one alternative over all of your others and explain the basis for your choice. If the analysis is written, there is little reason to repeat all of the advantages of the alternative chosen or all of the disadvantages of the alternatives rejected, but it is helpful to inform your reader which variables you weighted most heavily in making the choice and why.

Do not be frustrated if there seems to be no single right answer. This is typical. The quality of most executive decisions is relative; just when you think you have a perfect answer, along comes someone with a better alternative—a decision that no one had previously thought of. Moreover, the quality of a decision is difficult to judge until after it has been implemented. You, like the real marketing executive, aren't expected to make perfect decisions every time. The chances are good that you'll make some relatively weak decisions. However, you are expected to maintain a good batting average toward helping the organization achieve its objectives.

IMPLEMENT YOUR DECISION

Finally, you are expected to explain the steps, the resources that will be employed, and other details of carrying out your recommended solution to the problem. A sound decision, badly executed, may be worse than a well-implemented mediocre decision. In effect, the implementation plan proves that your solution is both possible and practical. Such details as who will be involved, when and where the money will come from, and how you will handle disadvantages or objections to the decision, should be anticipated.

Any minor or subsidiary problems that you encountered in the case should be considered in your implementation of the primary problem. Will they be minimized or altered by solving the major problem? If not, when should they be attacked and how? Suggested solutions are not at all out of order here.

THE WRITTEN ANALYSIS

Your instructor may or may not specify a model, a framework to use in your written analysis of cases. Such models will vary with the level of student sophistication, the emphasis of the course, and the resources available to participants.

The authors favor a model which emphasizes brevity in written case analysis—a range of 500 to 2,000 words has proven to be quite satisfactory. There are several reasons for such constraints. First, people, including bosses and instructors, tend to either put off or neglect to read long reports. Lengthy reports require extended periods of uninterrupted concentration, and managers just don't have many long periods of time without interruption. If you want your report to be read quickly and thoroughly, you had best keep it short. Consultants, who are well aware of this problem, often write two reports—one long one to show how much work they did, and one condensed version for their clients to read. Another reason for brevity is that it forces the writer to focus attention on those matters of greatest import. Cynics have observed that anyone who talks or writes long enough is certain to say something important; unfortunately, there is no assurance that either he or others will recognize that importance. The brevity requirement probably is an effective training device if, for no other reason, then that it stresses organization of one's presentations with a minimum of duplication and extraneous materials.

A relatively complete summary of a complex case analysis can be quickly presented in phrase-outline (or clause-outline) form. For example:

I. Problem statement
    A. Major problem
    B. Subsidiary or minor problems
       1.
       2.
II. Company assessment (when applicable)
    A. Financial situation
       1. Ratios and industry comparisons (current trends)
       2. Break-even or other quantitative analysis
       3. General assessment
    B. The organization
       1. Management capabilities
       2. Structure of authority and communications
       3. Attitudes
    C. Marketing assessment
       1. Product(s)
       2. Target markets
       3. Promotion strategy
       4. Pricing strategy
       5. Distribution and logistics strategy
       6. Competitive position
       7. Environmental climate
III. Alternatives
    A. First alternative
       1. Advantages (pro)
          a.
          b.
          c.
       2. Disadvantages (con)
          a.
          b.
    B. Second alternative
       1. Advantages
       2. Disadvantages
IV. Recommended solution
V. Implementation
    A. Who, how, when, where?
    B. Secondary problems and their solutions.

Philosophy and Scope of Marketing

DEFINING MARKETING

The American Marketing Association defines marketing as "the process of planning and executing the conception, pricing, promotion, and distribution of ideas, goods, and services to create exchanges that satisfy individual and organizational objectives."[1] This definition shows that marketing is not limited to activities in which businesses sell products. It can also involve the activities of private and public nonprofit organizations, or the marketing of an idea or a service, as well as a product. The core concept of this definition is that of *exchange*.

An exchange requires participation by two or more parties, each possessing something of value that the other party desires. Each party must be willing to give up "something of value" in order to receive "something of value" from the other party. The parties to the exchange must be able to communicate with each other in order to know what each party's "something of value" is and how it can be obtained. An exchange that has been consummated is called a transaction.

The "something of value" that is being exchanged must be capable of satisfying needs and wants. As such, marketing exchange transactions can involve physical goods, services, and financial resources such as money or credit. Transactions do not have to require monetary payment, however, since the "something of value" can be anything capable of satisfying the desires of the parties involved. Figure 1 shows examples of diverse marketing exchange transactions.

MARKETING MANAGEMENT PHILOSOPHIES

A change in marketing thinking has resulted from the growing recognition that if a firm is to survive, marketing should be the basic motivating force for the entire organization. Typically, business firms and nonprofit organizations evolve from being product oriented, to being sales oriented, to being marketing oriented. The evolution of Pillsbury Company's business philosophy from a production orientation to a sales orientation to a marketing orientation is traced by Robert Keith in the article, "The Marketing Revolution."

A product orientation is a philosophy emphasizing efficiency in producing and distributing products. Underlying this emphasis is the belief that customers are primarily interested in quality products per se.

A sales orientation concentrates on selling products through aggressive advertising and personal selling. This orientation implies that the primary emphasis in marketing is to sell.

1. "AMA Board Approves New Marketing Definitions," *Marketing News,* March 1, 1985, p. 1.

FIGURE 1
Examples of Marketing Exchange Transactions

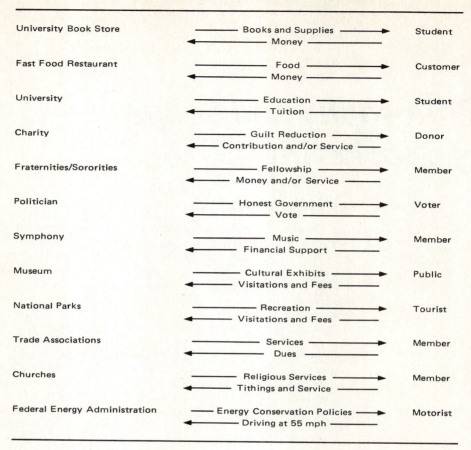

The marketing philosophy, also known as the marketing concept, implies that the major task of an organization is to satisfy customers' needs and wants and at the same time to achieve organizational objectives. Providing customer satisfaction is the thrust of the marketing concept. To provide maximum satisfaction, marketing executives must have a thorough understanding of customer needs, wants, and behavior. In the article, "Marketing Myopia," Theodore Levitt criticizes management for being shortsighted, that is, for being product oriented rather than customer oriented. Levitt notes that marketing should begin with the consumer by recognizing that customers buy benefits that are gained from products, rather than the products themselves.

The philosophy of the marketing concept calls for the coordination and integration of marketing with all other functional areas of the organization, including production, finance, accounting, and personnel. Focusing on customer needs and integrating all organizational activities to satisfy these needs is the best way to achieve organizational goals and assure long-term survival.

A commitment to being customer oriented does not imply that management must respond to every customer wish. It does, however, imply that management should make a sincere commitment to determine customer needs and wants and then determine whether a response to satisfy them will meet organizational objectives. An organization must, of course, adapt its "something of value" offering to keep pace with changes in the environment, notably with evolving consumer desires and preferences.

The marketing philosophy is applicable to all organizations, not only to those seeking a monetary profit. In the article, "Broadening the Concept of Marketing," Philip Kotler and Sidney J. Levy discuss the opportunities associated with applying the marketing concept to nonbusiness organizations. The authors show that those who manage private or public nonprofit organizations cannot avoid marketing. The choice is only whether to do it well or poorly.

CONCEPTS FOR EFFECTIVE MARKETING MANAGEMENT

A useful set of concepts for guiding those responsible for marketing in a forward-looking organization has been delineated by Kotler and Levy in "Broadening the Concept of Marketing." These concepts are:

- Generic product definition
- Target groups definition
- Differentiated marketing
- Customer behavior analysis
- Differential advantages
- Multiple marketing tools
- Integrated marketing planning
- Continuous marketing feedback
- Marketing audits

These concepts will be addressed throughout this book and should serve as an overall framework for analyzing the cases.

Robert J. Keith

The Marketing Revolution

The consumer, not the company, is in the middle.

In today's economy the consumer, the man or woman who buys the product, is at the absolute dead center of the business universe. Companies revolve around the customer, not the other way around.

Growing acceptance of this consumer concept has had, and will have, far-reaching implications for business, achieving a virtual revolution in economic thinking. As the concept gains ever greater acceptance, marketing is emerging as the most important single function in business.

A REVOLUTION IN SCIENCE

A very apt analogy can be drawn with another revolution, one that goes back to the sixteenth century. At that time astronomers had great difficulty predicting the movements of the heavenly bodies. Their charts and computations and celestial calendars enabled them to estimate the approximate positions of the planets on any given date. But their calculations were never exact—there was always a variance.

Then a Polish scientist named Nicolaus Copernicus proposed a very simple answer to the problem. If, he proposed, we assume that the sun, and not the earth, is at the center of our system, and that the earth moves around the sun instead of the sun moving around the earth, all our calculations will prove correct.

The Pole's idea raised a storm of controversy. The earth, everyone knew, was at the center of the universe. But another scientist named Galileo put the theory to test—and it worked. The result was a complete upheaval in scientific and philosophic thought. The effects of Copernicus' revolutionary idea are still being felt today.

Source: From the *Journal of Marketing,* Vol. 2, No. 3 (January 1960), pp. 35–38. Reprinted by permission of the American Marketing Association.

A REVOLUTION IN MARKETING

In much the same way American business in general—and Pillsbury in particular—is undergoing a revolution of its own today: a marketing revolution.

This revolution stems from the same idea stated in the opening sentence of this article. No longer is the company at the center of the business universe. Today the customer is at the center.

Our attention has shifted from problems of production to problems of marketing, from the product we *can* make to the product the consumer *wants* us to make, from the company itself to the market place.

The marketing revolution has only begun. It is reasonable to expect that its implications will grow in the years to come, and that lingering effects will be felt a century, or more than one century, from today.

So far the theory has only been advanced, tested, and generally proved correct. As more and more businessmen grasp the concept, and put it to work, our economy will become more truly marketing oriented.

PILLSBURY'S PATTERN: FOUR ERAS

Here is the way the marketing revolution came about at Pillsbury. The experience of this company has followed a typical pattern. There has been nothing unique, and each step in the evolution of the marketing concept has been taken in a way that is more meaningful because the steps are, in fact, typical.

Today in our company the marketing concept finds expression in the simple statement, "Nothing happens at Pillsbury until a sale is made." This statement represents basic reorientation on the part of our management. For, not too many years ago, the ordering of functions in our business placed finance first, production second, and sales last.

How did we arrive at our present point of view? Pillsbury's progress in the marketing revolution divides neatly into four separate eras—eras which parallel rather closely the classic pattern of development in the marketing revolution.

1st ERA—PRODUCTION ORIENTED

First came the era of manufacturing. It began with the formation of the company in 1869 and continued into the 1930s. It is significant that the *idea* for the formation of our company came from the *availability* of high-quality wheat and the *proximity* of water power—and not from the availability and proximity of growing major market areas, or the demand for better, less expensive, more convenient flour products.

Of course, these elements were potentially present. But the two major elements which fused in the mind of Charles A. Pillsbury and prompted him to invest his modest capital in a flour mill were, on the one hand, wheat, and, on the other hand, water power. His principal concern was with production, not marketing.

His thought and judgment were typical of the business thinking of his day. And such thinking was adequate and proper for the times.

Our company philosophy in this era might have been stated this way: "We are professional flour millers. Blessed with a supply of the finest North American wheat, plenty of water power, and excellent milling machinery, we produce flour of the highest quality. Our basic function is to mill high-quality flour, and of course (and almost incidentally) we must hire salesmen to sell it, just as we hire accountants to keep our books."

The young company's first new product reveals an interesting example of the thinking of this era. The product was middlings, the bran left over after milling. Millfeed, as the product came to be known, proved a valuable product because it was an excellent nutrient for cattle. But the impetus to launch the new product came not from a consideration of the nutritional needs of cattle or a marketing analysis. It came primarily from the desire to dispose of a by-product! The new product decision was production oriented, not marketing oriented.

2nd ERA—SALES ORIENTED

In the 1930s Pillsbury moved into its second era of development as a marketing company. This was the era of sales. For the first time we began to be highly conscious of the consumer, her wants, and her prejudices, as a key factor in the business equation. We established a commercial research department to provide us with facts about the market.

We also became more aware of the importance of our dealers, the wholesale and retail grocers who provided a vital link in our chain of distribution from the mill to the home. Knowing that consumers and dealers as well were vital to the company's success, we could no longer simply mark them down as unknowns in our figuring. With this realization, we took the first step along the road to becoming a marketing company.

Pillsbury's thinking in this second era could be summed up like this: "We are a flour-milling company, manufacturing a number of products for the consumer market. We must have a first-rate sales organization which can dispose of all the products we can make at a favorable price. We must back up this sales force with consumer advertising and market intelligence. We want our salesmen and our dealers to have all the tools they need for moving the output of our plants to the consumer."

Still not a marketing philosophy, but we were getting closer.

3rd ERA—MARKETING ORIENTED

It was at the start of the present decade that Pillsbury entered the marketing era. The amazing growth of our consumer business as the result of introducing baking mixes provided the immediate impetus. But the groundwork had been laid by key men who developed our sales concepts in the middle forties.

With the new cake mixes, products of our research program, ringing up sales on the cash register, and with the realization that research and production could produce literally hundreds of new and different products, we faced for the first time the necessity for selecting the best new products. We needed a set of criteria for selecting the kind of products we would manufacture. We needed an organization to establish and maintain these criteria, and for attaining maximum sale of the products we did select.

We needed, in fact, to build into our company a new management function which would direct and control all the other corporate functions from procurement to production to advertising to sales. This function was marketing. Our solution was to establish the present marketing department.

This department developed the criteria which we would use in determining which products to market. *And these criteria were, and are, nothing more nor less than those of the consumer herself.* We moved the mountain out to find out what Mahomet, and Mrs. Mahomet, wanted. The company's purpose was no longer to mill flour, nor to manufacture a wide variety of products, but to satisfy the needs and desires, both actual and potential, of our customers.

If we were to restate our philosophy during the past decade as simply as possible, it would read: "We make and sell products for consumers."

The business universe, we realized, did not have room at the center for Pillsbury or any other company or groups of companies. It was already occupied by the customers.

This is the concept at the core of the marketing revolution. How did we put it to work for Pillsbury?

The Brand-Manager Concept

The first move was to transform our small advertising department into a marketing department. The move involved far more than changing the name on organizational charts. It required the introduction of a new, and vitally important, organizational concept—the brand-manager concept.

The brand-manager idea is the very backbone of marketing at Pillsbury. The man who bears the title, brand manager, has total accountability for results. He directs the marketing of his product as if it were his own business. Production does its job, and finance keeps the profit figures. Otherwise, the brand manager has total responsibility for marketing his product. This responsibility encompasses pricing, commercial research, competitive activity, home service and publicity coordination, legal details, budgets, advertising plans, sales promotion, and execution of plans. The brand manager must think first, last, and always of his sales target, the consumer.

Marketing permeates the entire organization. Marketing plans and executes the sale—all the way from the inception of the product idea, through its development and distribution, to the customer purchase. Marketing begins and ends with the consumer. New product ideas are conceived after careful study of her wants and needs, her likes and dislikes. Then marketing takes the idea and marshals all the forces of the corporation to translate the idea into product and the product into sales.

In the early days of the company, consumer orientation did not seem so important. The company made flour, and flour was a staple—no one would question the availability of a market. Today we must determine whether the American housewife will buy lemon pudding cake in preference to orange angel food. The variables in the equation have multiplied, just as the number of products on the grocers' shelves have multiplied from a hundred or so into many thousands.

When we first began operating under this new marketing concept, we encountered the problems which always accompany any major reorientation. Our people were young and frankly immature in some areas of business; but they were men possessed of an idea and they fought for it. The idea was almost too powerful. The marketing concept proved its worth in sales, but it upset many of the internal balances of the corporation. Marketing-oriented decisions resulted in peaks and valleys in production, schedules, labor, and inventories. But the system worked. It worked better and better as maverick marketing men became motivated toward tonnage and profit.

4th ERA—MARKETING CONTROL

Today marketing is coming into its own. Pillsbury stands on the brink of its fourth major era in the marketing revolution.

Basically, the philosophy of this fourth era can be summarized this way: "We are moving from a company which has the marketing concept to a marketing company."

Marketing today sets company operating policy short-term. It will come to influence long-range policy more and more. Where today consumer research technical research, procurement, production, advertising, and sales swing into action under the broad canopy established by marketing, tomorrow capital and financial planning, ten-year volume and profit goals will also come under the aegis of marketing. More than any other function, marketing must be tied to top management.

Today our marketing people know more about inventories than anyone in top management. Tomorrow's marketing man must know capital financing and the implications of marketing planning on long-range profit forecasting.

Today technical research receives almost all of its guidance and direction from marketing. Tomorrow marketing will assume a more creative function in the advertising area, both in terms of ideas and media selection.

Changes in the Future

The marketing revolution has only begun. There are still those who resist its basic idea, just as there are always those who will resist change in business, government, or any other form of human institution.

As the marketing revolution gains momentum, there will be more changes. The concept of the customer at the center will remain valid; but business must adjust to the shifting tastes and likes and desires and needs which have always characterized the American consumer.

For many years the geographical center of the United States lay in a small Kansas town. Then a new state, Alaska, came along, and the center shifted to the north and west. Hawaii was admitted to the Union and the geographical mid-point took another jump to the west. In very much the same way, modern business must anticipate the restless shifting of buying attitudes, as customer preferences move north, south, east, or west from a liquid center. There is nothing static about the marketing revolution, and that is part of its fascination. The old order has changed, yielding place to the new—but the new order will have its quota of changes, too.

At Pillsbury, as our fourth era progresses, marketing will become the basic motivating force for the entire corporation. Soon it will be true that every activity of the corporation—from finance to sales to production—is aimed at satisfying the needs and desires of the consumer. When that stage of development is reached, the marketing revolution will be complete.

Theodore Levitt

Marketing Myopia

Every major industry was once a growth industry. But some that are now riding a wave of growth enthusiasm are very much in the shadow of decline. Others which are thought of as seasoned growth industries have actually stopped growing. In every case the reason growth is threatened, slowed, or stopped is *not* because the market is saturated. It is because there has been a failure of management.

Fateful Purposes. The failure is at the top. The executives responsible for it, in the last analysis, are those who deal with broad aims and policies. Thus:

- The railroads did not stop growing because the need for passenger and freight transportation declined. That grew. The railroads are in trouble today not because the need was filled by others (cars, trucks, airplanes, even telephones), but because it was *not* filled by the railroads themselves. They let others take customers away from them because they assumed themselves to be in the railroad business rather than in the transportation business. The reason they defined their industry wrong was because they were railroad-oriented instead of transportation-oriented; they were product-oriented instead of customer-oriented.
- Hollywood barely escaped being totally ravished by television. Actually, all the established film companies went through drastic reorganizations. Some simply disappeared. All of them got into trouble not because of TV's inroads but because of their own myopia. As with the railroads, Hollywood defined its business incorrectly. It thought

Note: Theodore Levitt's "Marketing Myopia" was first published in 1960. This reprint, published by the *Harvard Business Review* in 1975, includes a retrospective commentary by Levitt about the original article and its consequences.

it was in the movie business when it was actually in the entertainment business. "Movies" implied a specific, limited product. This produced a fatuous contentment which from the beginning led producers to view TV as a threat. Hollywood scorned and rejected TV when it should have welcomed it as an opportunity—an opportunity to expand the entertainment business.

Today TV is a bigger business than the old narrowly defined movie business ever was. Had Hollywood been customer-oriented (providing entertainment), rather than product-oriented (making movies), would it have gone through the fiscal purgatory that it did? I doubt it. What ultimately saved Hollywood and accounted for its recent resurgence was the wave of new young writers, producers, and directors whose previous successes in television had decimated the old movie companies and toppled the big movie moguls.

There are other less obvious examples of industries that have been and are now endangering their futures by improperly defining their purposes. I shall discuss some in detail later and analyze the kind of policies that lead to trouble. Right now it may help to show what a thoroughly customer-oriented management *can* do to keep a growth industry growing, even after the obvious opportunities have been exhausted; and here there are two examples that have been around for a long time. They are nylon and glass—specifically, E. I. duPont de Nemours & Company and Corning Glass Works.

Both companies have great technical competence. Their product orientation is unquestioned. But this alone does not explain their success. After all, who was more pridefully product-oriented and product-conscious than the erstwhile New England textile companies that have been so thoroughly massacred? The DuPonts and the Cornings have succeeded not primarily because of their product or research orientation but because they have been thoroughly customer-oriented also. It is constant watchfulness for opportunities to apply their technical knowhow to the creation of customer-satisfying uses which accounts for their prodigious output of successful new products. Without a very sophisticated eye on the customer, most of their new products might have been wrong, their sales methods useless.

Aluminum has also continued to be a growth industry, thanks to the efforts of two wartime-created companies which deliberately set about creating new customer-satisfying uses. Without Kaiser Aluminum & Chemical Corporation and Reynolds Metals Company, the total demand for aluminum today would be vastly less.

Error of Analysis. Some may argue that it is foolish to set the railroads off against aluminum or the movies off against glass. Are not aluminum and glass naturally so versatile that the industries are bound to have more growth opportunities than the railroads and movies? This view commits precisely the error I have been talking about. It defines an industry, or a product, or a cluster of know-how so narrowly as to guarantee its premature senescence. When we mention "railroads," we should make sure we mean "transportation." As transporters, the railroads still have a good chance for very considerable growth. They are not limited to the railroad business as such (though in my opinion rail transportation is potentially a much stronger transportation medium than is generally believed).

What is railroads lack is not opportunity, but some of the same managerial imaginativeness and audacity that made them great. Even an amateur like Jacques Barzun can see what is lacking when he says:

> I grieve to see the most advanced physical and social organization of the last century go down in shabby disgrace for lack of the same comprehensive imagination that built it up. [What is lacking is] the will of the companies to survive and to satisfy the public by inventiveness and skill.[1]

Shadow of Obsolescence

It is impossible to mention a single major industry that did not at one time qualify for the magic appellation of "growth industry." In each case its assumed strength lay in the apparently unchallenged superiority of its product. There appeared to be no effective substitute for it. It was itself a runaway substitute for the product it so triumphantly replaced. Yet one after another of these celebrated industries has come under a shadow. Let us look briefly at a few more of them, this time taking examples that have so far received a little less attention:

Dry Cleaning. This was once a growth industry with lavish prospects. In an age of wool garments, imagine being finally able to get them safely and easily clean. The boom was on.

Yet here we are 30 years after the boom started and the industry is in trouble. Where has the competition come from? From a better way of cleaning? No. It has come from synthetic fibers and chemical additives that have cut the need for dry cleaning. But this is only the beginning. Lurking in the wings and ready to make chemical dry cleaning totally obsolescent is that powerful magician, ultrasonics.

Electric Utilities. This is another one of those supposedly "no-substitute" products that has been enthroned on a pedestal of invincible growth. When the incandescent lamp came along, kerosene lights were finished. Later the water wheel and the steam engine were cut to ribbons by the flexibility, reliability, simplicity, and just plain easy availability of electric motors. The prosperity of electric utilities continues to wax extravagant as the home is converted into a museum of electric gadgetry. How can anybody miss by investing in utilities, with no competition, nothing but growth ahead?

But a second look is not quite so comforting. A score of nonutility companies are well advanced toward developing a powerful chemical fuel cell which could sit in some hidden closet of every home silently ticking off electric power. The electric lines that vulgarize so many neighborhoods will be eliminated. So will the endless demolition of streets and service interruptions during storms. Also on the horizon is solar energy, again pioneered by nonutility companies.

Who says that the utilities have no competition? They may be natural monopolies now, but tomorrow they may be natural deaths. To avoid this prospect, they too will have to develop fuel cells, solar energy, and other power sources. To survive, they themselves will have to plot the obsolescence of what now produces their livelihood.

Grocery Stores. Many people find it hard to realize that there ever was a thriving establishment known as the "corner grocery store." The supermarket has taken over with a powerful effectiveness. Yet the big food chains of the 1930s narrowly escaped being completely wiped out by the aggressive expansion of independent supermarkets. The first genuine supermarket was opened in 1930, in Jamaica, Long Island. By 1933 supermarkets were thriving in California, Ohio, Pennsylvania, and elsewhere. Yet the established chains pompously ignored them. When they chose to notice them, it was with such derisive descriptions as "cheapy," "horse-and-buggy," "cracker-barrel storekeeping," and "unethical opportunists."

The executive of one big chain announced at the time that he found it "hard to believe that people will drive for miles to shop for foods and sacrifice the personal service chains have perfected and to which Mrs. Consumer is accustomed."[2] As late as 1936, the National Wholesale Grocers convention and the New Jersey Retail Grocers Association said there was nothing to fear. They said that the supers' narrow appeal to the price buyer limited the size of their market. They had to draw from miles around. When imitators came, there would be wholesale liquidations as volume fell. The current high sales of the supers was said to be partly due to their novelty. Basically people wanted convenient neighborhood grocers. If the neighborhood stores "cooperate with their suppliers, pay attention to their costs, and improve their service," they would be able to weather the competition until it blew over.[3]

It never blew over. The chains discovered that survival required going into the supermarket business. This meant the wholesale destruction of their huge investments in corner store sites and in established distribution and merchandising methods. The companies with "the courage of their convictions" resolutely stuck to the corner store philosophy. They kept their pride but lost their shirts.

Self-deceiving Cycle

But memories are short. For example, it is hard for people who today confidently hail the twin messiahs of electronics and chemicals to see how things could possibly go wrong with these galloping industries. They probably also cannot see how a reasonably sensible businessman could have been as myopic as the famous Boston millionaire who 50 years ago unintentionally sentenced his heirs to poverty by stipulating that his entire estate be forever invested exclusively in electric streetcar securities. His posthumous declaration, "There will always be a big demand for efficient urban transportation," is no consolation to his heirs who sustain life by pumping gasoline at automobile filling stations.

Yet, in a casual survey I recently took among a group of intelligent business executives, nearly half agreed that it would be hard to hurt their heirs by tying their estates forever to the electronics industry. When I then confronted them with the Boston streetcar example, they chorused unanimously, "That's different!" But is it? Is not the basic situation identical?

In truth, *there is no such thing* as a growth industry, I believe. There are only companies organized and operated to create and capitalize on growth opportunities. Industries that assume themselves to be riding some automatic growth escalator invariably descend into stagnation. The history of every dead and dying "growth" industry shows a self-deceiving cycle of bountiful expansion and undetected decay. There are four conditions which usually guarantee this cycle:

1. The belief that growth is assured by an expanding and more affluent population.

2. The belief that there is no competitive substitute for the industry's major product.
3. Too much faith in mass production and in the advantages of rapidly declining unit costs as output rises.
4. Preoccupation with a product that lends itself to carefully controlled scientific experimentation, improvement, and manufacturing cost reduction.

I should like now to begin examining each of these conditions in some detail. To build my case as boldly as possible, I shall illustrate the points with reference to three industries—petroleum, automobiles, and electronics—particularly petroleum, because it spans more years and more vicissitudes. Not only do these three have excellent reputations with the general public and also enjoy the confidence of sophisticated investors, but their managements have become known for progressive thinking in areas like financial control, product research, and management training. If obsolescence can cripple even these industries, it can happen anywhere.

Population Myth

The belief that profits are assured by an expanding and more affluent population is dear to the heart of every industry. It takes the edge off the apprehensions everybody understandably feels about the future. If consumers are multiplying and also buying more of your product or service, you can face the future with considerably more comfort than if the market is shrinking. An expanding market keeps the manufacturer from having to think very hard or imaginatively. If thinking is an intellectual response to a problem, then the absence of a problem leads to the absence of thinking. If your product has an automatically expanding market, then you will not give much thought to how to expand it.

One of the most interesting examples of this is provided by the petroleum industry. Probably our oldest growth industry, it has an enviable record. While there are some current apprehensions about its growth rate, the industry itself tends to be optimistic.

But I believe it can be demonstrated that it is undergoing a fundamental yet typical change. It is not only ceasing to be a growth industry, but may actually be a declining one, relative to other business. Although there is widespread unawareness of it, I believe that within 25 years the oil industry may find itself in much the same position of retrospective glory that the railroads are now in. Despite its pioneering work in developing and applying the present-value method of investment evaluation, in employee relations, and in working with backward countries, the petroleum business is a distressing example of how complacency and wrongheadedness can stubbornly convert opportunity into near disaster.

One of the characteristics of this and other industries that have believed very strongly in the beneficial consequences of an expanding population, while at the same time being industries with a generic product for which there has appeared to be no competitive substitute, is that the individual companies have sought to outdo their competitors by improving on what they are already doing. This makes sense, of course, if one assumes that sales are tied to the country's population strings, because the customer can compare products only on a feature-by-feature basis. I believe it is significant, for example, that not since John D. Rockefeller sent free kerosene lamps to China has the oil industry done anything really outstanding to create a demand for its product. Not even in product improvement has it showered itself with eminence. The greatest single improvement—namely, the development of tetraethyl lead—came from outside the industry, specifically from General Motors and DuPont. The big contributions made by the industry itself are confined to technology of oil exploration, production, and refining.

Asking for Trouble. In other words, the industry's efforts have focused on improving the *efficiency* of getting and making its product, not really on improving the generic product or its marketing. Moreover, its chief product has continuously been defined in the narrowest possible terms, namely, gasoline, not energy, fuel, or transportation. This attitude has helped assure that:

- Major improvements in gasoline quality tend not to originate in the oil industry. Also, the development of superior alternative fuels comes from outside the oil industry, as will be shown later.
- Major innovations in automobile fuel marketing are originated by small new oil companies that are not primarily preoccupied with production or refining. These are the companies that have been responsible for the rapidly expanding multipump gasoline stations, with their successful emphasis on large and clean layouts, rapid and efficient driveway service, and quality gasoline at low prices.

Thus, the oil industry is asking for trouble from outsiders. Sooner or later, in this land of hungry inventors and entrepreneurs, a threat is sure to come. The possibilities of this will become more apparent when we turn to the next dangerous belief of many managements. For the sake of continuity, because this second belief is tied closely to the first, I shall continue with the same example.

Idea of Indispensability. The petroleum industry is pretty much persuaded that there is no competitive substitute for its major product, gasoline—or if there is, that it will continue to be a derivative of crude oil, such as diesel fuel or kerosene jet fuel.

There is a lot of automatic wishful thinking in this assumption. The trouble is that most refining companies own huge amounts of crude oil reserves. These have value only if there is a market for products into which oil can be converted—hence the tenacious belief in the continuing competitive superiority of automobile fuels made from crude oil.

This idea persists despite all historic evidence against it. The evidence not only shows that oil has never been a superior product for any purpose for very long, but it also shows that the oil industry has never really been a growth industry. It has been a succession of different businesses that have gone through the usual historic cycles of growth, maturity, and decay. Its overall survival is owed to a series of miraculous escapes from total obsolescence, of last-minute and unexpected reprieves from total disaster reminiscent of the Perils of Pauline.

Perils of Petroleum. I shall sketch in only the main episodes.

First, crude oil was largely a patent medicine. But even before that fad ran out, demand was greatly expanded by the use of oil in kerosene lamps. The prospect of lighting the world's lamps gave rise to an extravagant promise of growth. The prospects were similar to those the industry now holds for gasoline in other parts of the world. It can hardly wait for the underdeveloped nations to get a car in every garage.

In the days of the kerosene lamp, the oil companies competed with each other and against gaslight by trying to improve the illuminating characteristics of kerosene. Then suddenly the impossible happened. Edison invented a light which was totally nondependent on crude oil. Had it not been for the growing use of kerosene in space heaters, the incandescent lamp would have completely finished oil as a growth industry at that time. Oil would have been good for little else than axle grease.

Then disaster and reprieve struck again. Two great innovations occurred, neither originating in the oil industry. The successful development of coal-burning domestic central-heating systems made the space heater obsolescent. While the industry reeled, along came its most magnificent boost yet—the internal combustion engine, also invented by outsiders. Then when the prodigious expansion for gasoline finally began to level off in the 1920s, along came the miraculous escape of a central oil heater. Once again, the escape was provided by an outsider's invention and development. And when that market weakened, wartime demand for aviation fuel came to the rescue. After the war the expansion of civilian aviation, the dieselization of railroads, and the explosive demand for cars and trucks kept the industry's growth in high gear.

Meanwhile, centralized oil heating—whose boom potential had only recently been proclaimed—ran into severe competition from natural gas. While the oil companies themselves owned the gas that now competed with their oil, the industry did not originate the natural gas revolution, nor has it to this day greatly profited from its gas ownership. The gas revolution was made by newly formed transmission companies that marketed the product with an aggressive ardor. They started a magnificent new industry, first against the advice and then against the resistance of the oil companies.

By all the logic of the situation, the oil companies themselves should have made the gas revolution. They not only owned the gas; they also were the only people experienced in handling, scrubbing, and using it, the only people experienced in pipeline technology and transmission, and they understood heating problems. But, partly because they knew that natural gas would compete with their own sale of heating oil, the oil companies pooh-poohed the potentials of gas.

The revolution was finally started by oil pipeline executives who, unable to persuade their own companies to go into gas, quit and organized the spectacularly successful gas transmission companies. Even after their success became painfully evident to the oil companies, the latter did not go into gas transmission. The multibillion dollar business which should have been theirs went to others. As in the past, the industry was blinded by its narrow preoccupation with a specific product and the value of its reserves. It paid little or no attention to its customers' basic needs and preferences.

The postwar years have not witnessed any change. Immediately after World War II the oil industry was greatly encouraged about its future by the rapid expansion of demand for its traditional line of products. In 1950 most companies projected annual rates of domestic expansion of around 6% through at least 1975. Though the ratio of crude oil reserves to demand in the Free World was about 20 to 1, with 10 to 1 being usually considered a reasonable working ratio in the United States, booming demand sent oil men searching for more without sufficient regard to what the future really promised. In 1952 they "hit"

in the Middle East; the ratio skyrocketed to 42 to 1. If gross additions to reserves continue at the average rate of the past five years (37 billion barrels annually), then by 1970 the reserve ratio will be up to 45 to 1. This abundance of oil has weakened crude and product prices all over the world.

Uncertain Future. Management cannot find much consolation today in the rapidly expanding petrochemical industry, another oil-using idea that did not originate in the leading firms. The total United States production of petrochemicals is equivalent to about 2% (by volume) of the demand for all petroleum products. Although the petrochemical industry is now expected to grow by about 10% per year, this will not offset other drains on the growth of crude oil consumption. Furthermore, while petrochemical products are many and growing, it is well to remember that there are nonpetroleum sources of the basic raw material, such as coal. Besides, a lot of plastics can be produced with relatively little oil. A 50,000-barrel-per-day oil refinery is now considered the absolute minimum size of efficiency. But a 5,000-barrel-per-day chemical plant is a giant operation.

Oil has never been a continuously strong growth industry. It has grown by fits and starts, always miraculously saved by innovations and developments not of its own making. The reason it has not grown in a smooth progression is that each time it thought it had a superior product safe from the possibility of competitive substitutes, the product turned out to be inferior and notoriously subject to obsolescence. Until now, gasoline (for motor fuel, anyhow) has escaped this fate. But, as we shall see later, it too may be on its last legs.

The point of all this is that there is no guarantee against product obsolescence. If a company's own research does not make it obsolete, another's will. Unless an industry is especially lucky, as oil has been until now, it can easily go down in a sea of red figures—just as the railroads have, as the buggy whip manufacturers have, as the corner grocery chains have, as most of the big movie companies have, and indeed as many other industries have.

The best way for a firm to be lucky is to make its own luck. That requires knowing what makes a business successful. One of the greatest enemies of this knowledge is mass production.

Production Pressures

Mass-production industries are impelled by a great drive to produce all they can. The prospect of steeply declining unit costs as output rises is more than most companies can usually resist. The profit possibilities look spectacular. All effort focuses on production. The result is that marketing gets neglected.

John Kenneth Galbraith contends that just the opposite occurs.[4] Output is so prodigious that all effort concentrates on trying to get rid of it. He says this accounts for singing commercials, desecration of the countryside with advertising signs, and other wasteful and vulgar practices. Galbraith has a finger on something real, but he misses the strategic point. Mass production does indeed generate great pressure to "move" the product. But what usually gets emphasized is selling, not marketing. Marketing, being a more sophisticated and complex process, gets ignored.

The difference between marketing and selling is more than semantic. Selling focuses on the needs of the seller, marketing on the needs of the buyer. Selling is preoccupied with the seller's need to convert his product into cash, marketing with the idea of satisfying the needs of the customer by means of the product and the whole cluster of things associated with creating, delivering, and finally consuming it.

In some industries the enticements of full mass production have been so powerful that for many years top management in effect has told the sales departments, "You get rid of it; we'll worry about profits." By contrast, a truly marketing-minded firm tries to create value-satisfying goods and services that consumers will want to buy. What it offers for sale includes not only the generic product or service, but also how it is made available to the customer, in what form, when, under what conditions, and at what terms of trade. Most important, what it offers for sale is determined not by the seller but by the buyer. The seller takes his cues from the buyer in such a way that the product becomes a consequence of the marketing effort, not vice versa.

Lag in Detroit. This may sound like an elementary rule of business, but that does not keep it from being violated wholesale. It is certainly more violated than honored. Take the automobile industry.

Here mass production is most famous, most honored, and has the greatest impact on the entire society. The industry has hitched its fortune to the relentless requirements of the annual model change, a policy that makes customer orientation an especially urgent necessity. Consequently the auto companies annually spend millions of dollars on consumer research. But the fact that the new compact cars are selling so well in their first year indicates that Detroit's vast researches have for a long time failed to reveal what the customer really wanted. Detroit was not persuaded that he wanted anything different from what he had

been getting until it lost millions of customers to other small car manufacturers.

How could this unbelievable lag behind consumer wants have been perpetuated so long? Why did not research reveal consumer preferences before consumers' buying decisions themselves revealed the facts? Is that not what consumer research is for—to find out before the fact what is going to happen? The answer is that Detroit never really researched the customer's wants. It only researched his preferences between the kinds of things which it had already decided to offer him. For Detroit is mainly product-oriented, not customer-oriented. To the extent that the customer is recognized as having needs that the manufacturer should try to satisfy, Detroit usually acts as if the job can be done entirely by product changes. Occasionally attention gets paid to financing, too, but that is done more in order to sell than to enable the customer to buy.

As for taking care of other customer needs, there is not enough being done to write about. The areas of the greatest unsatisfied needs are ignored, or at best get stepchild attention. These are at the point of sale and on the matter of automotive repair and maintenance. Detroit views these problem areas as being of secondary importance. That is underscored by the fact that the retailing and servicing ends of this industry are neither owned and operated nor controlled by the manufacturers. Once the car is produced, things are pretty much in the dealer's inadequate hands. Illustrative of Detroit's arm's-length attitude is the fact that, while servicing holds enormous sales-stimulating, profit-building opportunities, only 57 of Chevrolet's 7,000 dealers provide night maintenance service.

Motorists repeatedly express their dissatisfaction with servicing and their apprehensions about buying cars under the present selling setup. The anxieties and problems they encounter during the auto buying and maintenance processes are probably more intense and widespread today than 30 years ago. Yet the automobile companies do not *seem* to listen to or take their cues from the anguished consumer. If they do listen, it must be through the filter of their own preoccupation with production. The marketing effort is still viewed as a necessary consequence of the product, not vice versa, as it should be. That is the legacy of mass production, with its parochial view that profit resides essentially in low-cost full production.

What Ford Put First. The profit lure of mass production obviously has a place in the plans and strategy of business management, but it must always *follow* hard thinking about the customer. This is one of the most important lessons that we can learn from the contradictory behavior of Henry Ford. In a sense Ford was both the most brilliant and the most senseless marketer in American history. He was senseless because he refused to give the customer anything but a black car. He was brilliant because he fashioned a production system designed to fit market needs. We habitually celebrate him for the wrong reason, his production genius. His real genius was marketing. We think he was able to cut his selling price and therefore sell millions of $500 cars because his invention of the assembly line had reduced the costs. Actually he invented the assembly line because he had concluded that at $500 he could sell millions of cars. Mass production was the *result* not the cause of his low prices.

Ford repeatedly emphasized this point, but a nation of production-oriented business managers refuses to hear the great lesson he taught. Here is his operating philosophy as he expressed it succinctly:

> Our policy is to reduce the price, extend the operations, and improve the article. You will notice that the reduction of price comes first. We have never considered any costs as fixed. Therefore we first reduce the price to the point where we believe more sales will result. Then we go ahead and try to make the prices. We do not bother about the costs. The new price forces the costs down. The more usual way is to take the costs and then determine the price; and although that method may be scientific in the narrow sense, it is not scientific in the broad sense, because what earthly use is it to know the cost if it tells you that you cannot manufacture at a price at which the article can be sold? But more to the point is the fact that, although one may calculate what a cost is, and of course all of our costs are carefully calculated, no one knows what a cost ought to be. One of the ways of discovering...is to name a price so low as to force everybody in the place to the highest point of efficiency. The low price makes everybody dig for profits. We make more discoveries concerning manufacturing and selling under this forced method than by any method of leisurely investigation.[5]

Product Provincialism. The tantalizing profit possibilities of low unit production costs may be the most seriously self-deceiving attitude that can afflict a company, particularly a "growth" company where an apparently assured expansion of demand already tends to undermine a proper concern for the importance of marketing and the customer.

The usual result of this narrow preoccupation with so-called concrete matters is that instead of growing, the industry declines. It usually means that the product fails to adapt to the constantly changing patterns of consumer needs and tastes, to new and modified marketing institutions and practices, or to product developments in competing or complementary industries. The industry has its eyes so firmly on its own specific product that it does not see how it is being made obsolete.

The classical example of this is the buggy whip industry. No amount of product improvement could stave off its death sentence. But had the industry defined itself as being in the transportation business rather than the buggy whip business, it might have survived. It would have done what survival always entails, that is, changing. Even if it had only defined its business as providing a stimulant or catalyst to an energy source, it might have survived by becoming a manufacturer of, say, fanbelts or air cleaners.

What may some day be a still more classical example is, again, the oil industry. Having let others steal marvelous opportunities from it (e.g., natural gas, as already mentioned, missile fuels, and jet engine lubricants), one would expect it to have taken steps never to let that happen again. But this is not the case. We are now getting extraordinary new developments in fuel systems specifically designed to power automobiles. Not only are these developments concentrated in firms outside the petroleum industry, but petroleum is almost systematically ignoring them, securely content in its wedded bliss to oil. It is the story of the kerosene lamp versus the incandescent lamp all over again. Oil is trying to improve hydrocarbon fuels rather than develop *any* fuels best suited to the needs of their users, whether or not made in different ways and with different raw materials from oil.

Here are some things which nonpetroleum companies are working on:

- Over a dozen such firms now have advanced working models of energy systems which, when perfected, will replace the internal combustion engine and eliminate the demand for gasoline. The superior merit of each of these systems is their elimination of frequent, time-consuming, and irritating refueling stops. Most of these systems are fuel cells designed to create electrical energy directly from chemicals without combustion. Most of them use chemicals that are not derived from oil, generally hydrogen and oxygen.
- Several other companies have advanced models of electric storage batteries designed to power automobiles. One of these is an aircraft producer that is working jointly with several electric utility companies. The latter hope to use off-peak generating capacity to supply overnight plug-in bat-

tery regeneration. Another company, also using the battery approach, is a medium-size electronics firm with extensive small-battery experience that it developed in connection with its work on hearing aids. It is collaborating with an automobile manufacturer. Recent improvements arising from the need for high-powered miniature power storage plants in rockets have put us within reach of a relatively small battery capable of withstanding great overloads or surges of power. Germanium diode applications and batteries using sintered-plate and nickel-cadmium techniques promise to make a revolution in our energy sources.

- Solar energy conversion systems are also getting increasing attention. One usually cautious Detroit auto executive recently ventured that solar-powered cars might be common by 1980.

As for the oil companies, they are more or less "watching developments," as one research director put it to me. A few are doing a bit of research on fuel cells, but almost always confined to developing cells powered by hydrocarbon chemicals. None of them are enthusiastically researching fuel cells, batteries, or solar power plants. None of them are spending a fraction as much on research in these profoundly important areas as they are on the usual run-of-the-mill things like reducing combustion chamber deposit in gasoline engines. One major integrated petroleum company recently took a tentative look at the fuel cell and concluded that although "the companies actively working on it indicate a belief in ultimate success...the timing and magnitude of its impact are too remote to warrant recognition in our forecasts."

One might, of course, ask: Why should the oil companies do anything different? Would not chemical fuel cells, batteries, or solar energy kill the present product lines? The answer is that they would indeed, and that is precisely the reason for the oil firms having to develop these power units before their competitors, so they will not be companies without an industry.

Management might be more likely to do what is needed for its own preservation if it thought of itself as being in the energy business. But even that would not be enough if it persists in imprisoning itself in the narrow grip of its tight product orientation. It has to think of itself as taking care of customer needs, not finding, refining, or even selling oil. Once it genuinely thinks of its business as taking care of people's transportation needs, nothing can stop it from creating its own extravagantly profitable growth.

Creative Destruction. Since words are cheap and deeds are dear, it may be appropriate to indicate what this kind of thinking involves and leads to. Let us start at the beginning—the customer. It can be shown that motorists strongly dislike the bother, delay, and experience of buying gasoline. People actually do not buy gasoline. They cannot see it, taste it, feel it, appreciate it, or really test it. What they buy is the right to continue driving their cars. The gas station is like a tax collector to whom people are compelled to pay a periodic toll as the price of using their cars. This makes the gas station a basically unpopular institution. It can never be made popular or pleasant, only less unpopular, less unpleasant.

To reduce its unpopularity completely means eliminating it. Nobody likes a tax collector, not even a pleasantly cheerful one. Nobody likes to interrupt a trip to buy a phantom product, not even from a handsome Adonis or a seductive Venus. Hence, companies that are working on exotic fuel substitutes which will eliminate the need for frequent refueling are heading directly into the outstretched arms of the irritated motorist. They are riding a wave of inevitability, not because they are creating something which is technologically superior or more sophisticated, but because they are satisfying a powerful customer need. They are also eliminating noxious odors and air pollution.

Once the petroleum companies recognize the customer-satisfying logic of what another power system can do, they will see that they have no more choice about working on an efficient, long-lasting fuel (or some way of delivering present fuels without bothering the motorist) than the big food chains had a choice about going into the supermarket business, or the vacuum tube companies had a choice about making semiconductors. For their own good the oil firms will have to destroy their own highly profitable assets. No amount of wishful thinking can save them from the necessity of engaging in this form of "creative destruction."

I phrase the need as strongly as this because I think management must make quite an effort to break itself loose from conventional ways. It is all too easy in this day and age for a company or industry to let its sense of purpose become dominated by the economies of full production and to develop a dangerously lopsided product orientation. In short, if management lets itself drift, it invariably drifts in the direction of thinking of itself as producing goods and services, not customer satisfactions. While it probably will not descend to the depths of telling its salesmen, "You get rid of it; we'll worry about profits," it can, without knowing it, be practicing precisely that formula for withering decay. The historic fate of one growth industry after another has been its suicidal product provincialism.

Dangers of R&D

Another big danger to a firm's continued growth arises when top management is wholly transfixed by the profit possibilities of technical research and development. To illustrate I shall turn first to a new industry —electronics—and then return once more to the oil companies. By comparing a fresh example with a familiar one, I hope to emphasize the prevalence and insidiousness of a hazardous way of thinking.

Marketing Shortchanged. In the case of electronics, the greatest danger which faces the glamorous new companies in this field is not that they do not pay enough attention to research and development, but that they pay *too much* attention to it. And the fact that the fastest growing electronics firms owe their eminence to their heavy emphasis on technical research is completely beside the point. They have vaulted to affluence on a sudden crest of unusually strong general receptiveness to new technical ideas. Also, their success has been shaped in the virtually guaranteed market of military subsidies and by military orders that in many cases actually preceded the existence of facilities to make the products. Their expansion has, in other words, been almost totally devoid of marketing effort.

Thus, they are growing up under conditions that come dangerously close to creating the illusion that a superior product will sell itself. Having created a successful company by making a superior product, it is not surprising that management continues to be oriented toward the product rather than the people who consume it. It develops the philosophy that continued growth is a matter of continued product innovation and improvement.

A number of other factors tend to strengthen and sustain this belief:

1. Because electronic products are highly complex and sophisticated, managements become top-heavy with engineers and scientists. This creates a selective bias in favor of research and production at the expense of marketing. The organization tends to view itself as making things rather than satisfying customer needs. Marketing gets treated as a residual activity, "something else" that must be done once the vital job of product creation and production is completed.

2. To this bias in favor of product research, development, and production is added the bias in favor of dealing with controllable variables. Engineers and scientists are at home in the world of concrete things like machines, test tubes, production lines, and even balance sheets. The abstractions to which

they feel kindly are those which are testable or manipulatable in the laboratory, or, if not testable, then functional, such as Euclid's axioms. In short, the managements of the new glamour-growth companies tend to favor those business activities which lend themselves to careful study, experimentation, and control—the hard, practical realities of the lab, the shop, the books.

What gets shortchanged are the realities of the *market.* Consumers are unpredictable, varied, fickle, stupid, shortsighted, stubborn, and generally bothersome. This is not what the engineer-managers say, but deep down in their consciousness it is what they believe. And this accounts for their concentrating on what they know and what they can control, namely, product research, engineering, and production. The emphasis on production becomes particularly attractive when the product can be made at declining unit costs. There is no more inviting way of making money than by running the plant full blast.

Today the top-heavy science-engineering-production orientation of so many electronics companies works reasonably well because they are pushing into new frontiers in which the armed services have pioneered virtually assured markets. The companies are in the felicitous position of having to fill, not find markets; of not having to discover what the customer needs and wants, but of having the customer voluntarily come forward with specific new product demands. If a team of consultants had been assigned specifically to design a business situation calculated to prevent the emergence and development of a customer-oriented marketing viewpoint, it could not have produced anything better than the conditions just described.

Stepchild Treatment. The oil industry is a stunning example of how science, technology, and mass production can divert an entire group of companies from their main task. To the extent the consumer is studied at all (which is not much), the focus is forever on getting information which is designed to help the oil companies improve what they are now doing. They try to discover more convincing advertising themes, more effective sales promotional drives, what the market shares of the various companies are, what people like or dislike about service station dealers and oil companies, and so forth. Nobody seems as interested in probing deeply into the basic human needs that the industry might be trying to satisfy as in probing into the basic properties of the raw material that the companies work with in trying to deliver customer satisfactions.

Basic questions about customers and markets seldom get asked. The latter occupy a stepchild status. They are recognized as existing, as having to be taken care of, but not worth very much real thought or dedicated attention. Nobody gets as excited about the customers in his own backyard as about the oil in the Sahara Desert. Nothing illustrates better the neglect of marketing than its treatment in the industry press.

The centennial issue of the *American Petroleum Institute Quarterly*, published in 1959 to celebrate the discovery of oil in Titusville, Pennsylvania, contained 21 feature articles proclaiming the industry's greatness. Only one of these talked about its achievements in marketing, and that was only a pictorial record of how service station architecture has changed. The issue also contained a special section on "New Horizons," which was devoted to showing the magnificent role oil would play in America's future. Every reference was ebulliently optimistic, never implying once that oil might have some hard competition. Even the reference to atomic energy was a cheerful catalogue of how oil would help make atomic energy a success. There was not a single apprehension that the oil industry's affluence might be threatened or a suggestion that one "new horizon" might include new and better ways of serving oil's present customers.

But the most revealing example of the stepchild treatment that marketing gets was still another special series of short articles on "The Revolutionary Potential of Electronics." Under that heading this list of articles appeared in the table of contents:

- "In the Search for Oil"
- "In Production Operations"
- "In Refinery Processes"
- "In Pipeline Operations"

Significantly, every one of the industry's major functional areas is listed, *except* marketing. Why? Either it is believed that electronics holds no revolutionary potential for petroleum marketing (which is palpably wrong), or the editors forgot to discuss marketing (which is more likely, and illustrates its stepchild status).

The order in which the four functional areas are listed also betrays the alienation of the oil industry from the consumer. The industry is implicitly defined as beginning with the search for oil and ending with its distribution from the refinery. But the truth is, it seems to me, that the industry begins with the needs of the customer for its products. From that primal position its definition moves steadily backstream to areas of progressively lesser importance, until it finally comes to rest at the "search for oil."

Beginning & End. The view that an industry is a customer-satisfying process, not a goods-producing process, is vital for all businessmen to understand. An industry begins with the customer and his needs, not with a patent, a raw material, or a selling skill. Given the customer's needs, the industry develops backwards, first concerning itself with the physical *delivery* of customer satisfactions. Then it moves back further to *creating* the things by which these satisfactions are in part achieved. How these materials are created is a matter of indifference to the customer, hence the particular form of manufacturing, processing, or what-have-you cannot be considered as a vital aspect of the industry. Finally, the industry moves back still further to *finding* the raw materials necessary for making its products.

The irony of some industries oriented toward technical research and development is that the scientists who occupy the high executive positions are totally unscientific when it comes to defining their companies' overall needs and purposes. They violate the first two rules of the scientific method—being aware of and defining their companies' problems, and then developing testable hypotheses about solving them. They are scientific only about the convenient things, such as laboratory and product experiments.

The reason that the customer (and the satisfaction of his deepest needs) is not considered as being "the problem" is not because there is any certain belief that no such problem exists, but because an organizational lifetime has conditioned management to look in the opposite direction. Marketing is a stepchild.

I do not mean that selling is ignored. Far from it. But selling, again, is not marketing. As already pointed out, selling concerns itself with the tricks and techniques of getting people to exchange their cash for your product. It is not concerned with the values that the exchange is all about. And it does not, as marketing invariably does, view the entire business process as consisting of a tightly integrated effort to discover, create, arouse, and satisfy customer needs. The customer is somebody "out there" who, with proper cunning, can be separated from his loose change.

Actually, not even selling gets much attention in some technologically minded firms. Because there is a virtually guaranteed market for the abundant flow of their new products, they do not actually know what a real market is. It is as if they lived in a planned economy, moving their products routinely from factory to retail outlet. Their successful concentration on products tends to convince them of the soundness of what they have been doing, and they fail to see the gathering clouds over the market.

Conclusion

Less than 75 years ago American railroads enjoyed a fierce loyalty among astute Wall Streeters. European monarchs invested in them heavily. Eternal wealth was thought to be the benediction for anybody who could scrape a few thousand dollars together to put into rail stocks. No other form of transportation could compete with the railroads in speed, flexibility, durability, economy, and growth potentials.

As Jacques Barzun put it, "By the turn of the century it was an institution, an image of man, a tradition, a code of honor, a source of poetry, a nursery of boyhood desires, a sublimest of toys, and the most solemn machine—next to the funeral hearse—that marks the epochs in man's life."[6]

Even after the advent of automobiles, trucks, and airplanes, the railroad tycoons remained imperturbably self-confident. If you had told them 60 years ago that in 30 years they would be flat on their backs, broke, and pleading for government subsidies, they would have thought you totally demented. Such a future was simply not considered possible. It was not even a discussable subject, or an askable question, or a matter which any sane person would consider worth speculating about. The very thought was insane. Yet a lot of insane notions now have matter-of-fact acceptance—for example, the idea of 100-ton tubes of metal moving smoothly through the air 20,000 feet above the earth, loaded with 100 sane and solid citizens casually drinking martinis—and they have dealt cruel blows to the railroads.

What specifically must other companies do to avoid this fate? What does customer orientation involve? These questions have in part been answered by the preceding examples and analysis. It would take another article to show in detail what is required for specific industries. In any case, it should be obvious that building an effective customer-oriented company involves far more than good intentions or promotional tricks; it involves profound matters of human organization and leadership. For the present, let me merely suggest what appear to be some general requirements.

Visceral Feel of Greatness. Obviously the company has to do what survival demands. It has to adapt to the requirements of the market, and it has to do it sooner rather than later. But mere survival is a so-so aspiration. Anybody can survive in some way or other, even the skid-row bum. The trick is to survive gallantly, to feel the surging impulse of commercial mastery; not just to experience the sweet smell of success, but to have the visceral feel of entrepreneurial greatness.

No organization can achieve greatness without a vigorous leader who is driven onward by his own pulsating *will to succeed*. He has to have a vision of grandeur, a vision that can produce eager followers in vast numbers. In business, the followers are the customers.

In order to produce these customers, the entire corporation must be viewed as a customer-creating and customer-satisfying organism. Management must think of itself not as producing products but as providing customer-creating value satisfactions. It must push this idea (and everything it means and requires) into every nook and cranny of the organization. It has to do this continuously and with the kind of flair that excites and stimulates the people in it. Otherwise, the company will be merely a series of pigeonholed parts, with no consolidating sense of purpose or direction.

In short, the organization must learn to think of itself not as producing goods or services but as *buying customers,* as doing the things that will make people *want* to do business with it. And the chief executive himself has the inescapable responsibility for creating this environment, this viewpoint, this attitude, this aspiration. He himself must set the company's style, its direction, and its goals. This means he has to know precisely where he himself wants to go, and to make sure the whole organization is enthusiastically aware of where that is. This is a first requisite of leadership, for *unless he knows where he is going, any road will take him there.*

If any road is okay, the chief executive might as well pack his attaché case and go fishing. If an organization does not know or care where it is going, it does not need to advertise that fact with a ceremonial figurehead. Everybody will notice it soon enough.

RETROSPECTIVE COMMENTARY

Amazed, finally, by his literary success, Isaac Bashevis Singer reconciled an attendant problem: "I think the moment you have published a book, it's not any more your private property.... If it has value, everybody can find in it what he finds, and I cannot tell the man I did not intend it to be so." Over the past 15 years, "Marketing Myopia" has become a case in point. Remarkably, the article spawned a legion of loyal partisans—not to mention a host of unlikely bedfellows.

Its most common and, I believe, most influential consequence is the way certain companies for the first time gave serious thought to the question of what businesses they are really in.

The strategic consequences of this have in many cases been dramatic. The best-known case, of course, is the shift in thinking of oneself as being in the "oil business" to being in the "energy business." In some instances the payoff has been spectacular (getting into coal, for example) and in others dreadful (in terms of the time and money spent so far on fuel cell research). Another successful example is a company with a large chain of retail shoe stores that redefined itself as a retailer of moderately priced, frequently purchased, widely assorted consumer specialty products. The result was a dramatic growth in volume, earnings, and return on assets.

Some companies, again for the first time, asked themselves whether they wished to be masters of certain technologies for which they would seek markets, or be masters of markets for which they would seek customer-satisfying products and services.

Choosing the former, one company has declared, in effect, "We are experts in glass technology. We intend to improve and expand that expertise with the object of creating products that will attract customers." This decision has forced the company into a much more systematic and customer-sensitive look at possible markets and users, even though its stated strategic object has been to capitalize on glass technology.

Deciding to concentrate on markets, another company has determined that "we want to help people (primarily women) enhance their beauty and sense of youthfulness." This company has expanded its line of cosmetic products, but has also entered the fields of proprietary drugs and vitamin supplements.

All these examples illustrate the "policy" results of "Marketing Myopia." On the operating level, there has been, I think, an extraordinary heightening of sensitivity to customers and consumers. R&D departments have cultivated a greater "external" orientation toward uses, users, and markets—balancing thereby the previously one-sided "internal" focus on materials and methods; upper management has realized that marketing and sales departments should be somewhat more willingly accommodated than before; finance departments have become more receptive to the legitimacy of budgets for market research and experimentation in marketing; and salesmen have been better trained to listen to and understand customer needs and problems, rather than merely to "push" the product.

A Mirror, Not a Window

My impression is that the article has had more impact in industrial-products companies than in consumer-products companies—perhaps because the former had lagged most in customer orientation. There are at least two reasons for this lag: (1) industrial-products companies tend to be more capital intensive, and (2) in the past, at least, they have had to rely heavily on communicating face-to-face the technical character of what they made and sold. These points are worth explaining.

Capital-intensive businesses are understandably preoccupied with magnitudes, especially where the capital, once invested, cannot be easily moved, manipulated, or modified for the production of a variety of products—e.g., chemical plants, steel mills, airlines, and railroads. Understandably, they seek big volumes and operating efficiencies to pay off the equipment and meet the carrying costs.

At least one problem results: corporate power becomes disproportionately lodged with operating or financial executives. If you read the charter of one of the nation's largest companies, you will see that the chairman of the finance committee, not the chief executive officer, is the "chief." Executives with such backgrounds have an almost trained incapacity to see that getting "volume" may require understanding and serving many discrete and sometimes small market segments, rather than going after a perhaps mythical batch of big or homogeneous customers.

These executives also often fail to appreciate the competitive changes going on around them. They observe the changes, all right, but devalue their significance or underestimate their ability to nibble away at the company's markets.

Once dramatically alerted to the concept of segments, sectors, and customers, though, managers of capital-intensive businesses have become more responsive to the necessity of balancing their inescapable preoccupation with "paying the bills" or breaking even with the fact that the best way to accomplish this may be to pay more attention to segments, sectors, and customers.

The second reason industrial products companies have probably been more influenced by the article is that, in the case of the more technical industrial products or services, the necessity of clearly communicating product and service characteristics to prospects results in a lot of face-to-face "selling" effort. But precisely because the product is so complex, the situation produces salesmen who know the product more than they know the customer, who are more adept at explaining what they have and what it can do than learning what the customer's needs and problems are. The result has been a narrow product orientation rather than a liberating customer orientation, and "service" often suffered. To be sure, sellers said, "We have to provide service," but they tended to define service by looking into the mirror rather than out the window. They *thought* they were looking out the window at the customer, but it was actually a mirror —a reflection of their own product-oriented biases rather than a reflection of their customers' situations.

A Manifesto, Not a Prescription

Not everything has been rosy. A lot of bizarre things have happened as a result of the article:

- Some companies have developed what I call "marketing mania"—they've become obsessively responsive to every fleeting whim of the customer. Mass production operations have been converted to approximations of job shops, with cost and price consequences far exceeding the willingness of customers to buy the product.
- Management has expanded product lines and added new lines of business without first establishing adequate control systems to run more complex operations.
- Marketing staffs have suddenly and rapidly expanded themselves and their research budgets without either getting sufficient prior organizational support or, thereafter, producing sufficient results.
- Companies that are functionally organized have converted to product, brand, or market-based organizations with the expectation of instant and miraculous results. The outcome has been ambiguity, frustration, confusion, corporate infighting, losses, and finally a reversion to functional arrangements that only worsened the situation.
- Companies have attempted to "serve" customers by creating complex and beautifully efficient products or services that buyers are either too risk-averse to adopt or incapable of learning how to employ—in effect, there are now steam shovels for people who haven't yet learned to use spades. This problem has happened repeatedly in the so-called service industries (financial services, insurance, computer-based services) and with American companies selling in less-developed economies.

"Marketing Myopia" was not intended as analysis or even prescription; it was intended as manifesto. It did not pretend to take a balanced position. Nor was it a new idea—Peter F. Drucker, J. B. McKitterick, Wroe Alderson, John Howard, and Neil Borden had each done more original and balanced work on "the

marketing concept." My scheme, however, tied marketing more closely to the inner orbit of business policy. Drucker—especially in *The Concept of the Corporation* and *The Practice of Management*—originally provided me with a great deal of insight.

My contribution, therefore, appears merely to have been a simple, brief, and useful way of communicating an existing way of thinking. I tried to do it in a very direct, but responsible, fashion, knowing that few readers (customers), especially managers and leaders, could stand much equivocation or hesitation. I also knew that the colorful and lightly documented affirmation works better than the tortuously reasoned explanation.

But why the enormous popularity of what was actually such a simple preexisting idea? Why its appeal throughout the world to resolutely restrained scholars, implacably temperate managers, and high government officials, all accustomed to balanced and thoughtful calculation? Is it that concrete examples, joined to illustrate a simple idea and presented with some attention to literacy, communicate better than massive analytical reasoning that reads as though it were translated from the German? Is it that provocative assertions are more memorable and persuasive than restrained and balanced explanations, no matter who the audience? Is it that the character of the message is as much the message as its content? Or was mine not simply a different tune, but a new symphony? I don't know.

Of course, I'd do it again and in the same way, given my purposes, even with what more I now know —the good and the bad, the power of facts and the limits of rhetoric. If your mission is the moon, you don't use a car. Don Marquis's cockroach, Archy, provides some final consolation: "an idea is not responsible for who believes in it."

NOTES

1. Jacques Barzun, "Trains and the Mind of Man," *Holiday*, February 1960, p. 21.

2. For more details see M. M. Zimmerman, *The Super Market: A Revolution in Distribution* (New York, McGraw-Hill Book Company, Inc., 1955), p. 48.

3. Ibid., pp. 45–47.

4. *The Affluent Society* (Boston, Houghton Mifflin Company, 1958), pp. 152–160.

5. Henry Ford, *My Life and Work* (New York, Doubleday, Page & Company, 1923), pp. 146–147.

6. Jacques Barzun, "Trains and the Mind of Man," *Holiday*, February 1960, p. 20.

Philip Kotler and Sidney J. Levy

Broadening the Concept of Marketing

The term "marketing" connotes to most people a function peculiar to business firms. Marketing is seen as the task of finding and stimulating buyers for the firm's output. It involves product development, pricing, distribution, and communication; and in the more progressive firms, continuous attention to the changing needs of customers and the development of new products, with product modifications and services to meet these needs. But whether marketing is viewed in the old sense of "pushing" products or in the new sense of "customer satisfaction engineering," it is almost always viewed and discussed as a business activity.

It is the authors' contention that marketing is a pervasive societal activity that goes considerably beyond the selling of toothpaste, soap, and steel. Political contests remind us that candidates are marketed as well as soap; student recruitment by colleges reminds us that higher education is marketed; and fund raising reminds us that "causes" are marketed. Yet these areas of marketing are typically ignored by the student of marketing. Or they are treated cursorily as public relations or publicity activities. No attempt is made to incorporate these phenomena in the body proper of marketing thought and theory. No attempt is made to redefine the meaning of product development, pricing, distribution, and communication in these newer contexts to see if they have a useful meaning. No attempt is made to examine whether the principles of "good" marketing in traditional product areas are transferable to the marketing of services, persons, and ideas.

The authors see a great opportunity for marketing people to expand their thinking and to apply their skills to an increasingly interesting range of social activity. The challenge depends on the attention given to it; marketing will either take on a broader social

Source: From the *Journal of Marketing*, Vol. 33 (January 1969), pp. 10–15. Reprinted by permission of the American Marketing Association.

meaning or remain a narrowly defined business activity.

The Rise of Organizational Marketing

One of the most striking trends in the United States is the increasing amount of society's work being performed by organizations other than business firms. As a society moves beyond the stage where shortages of food, clothing, and shelter are the major problems, it begins to organize to meet other social needs that formerly had been put aside. Business enterprises remain a dominant type of organization, but other types of organizations gain in conspicuousness and in influence. Many of these organizations become enormous and require the same rarefied management skills as traditional business organizations. Managing the United Auto Workers, Defense Department, Ford Foundation, World Bank, Catholic Church, and University of California has become every bit as challenging as managing Procter and Gamble, General Motors, and General Electric. These nonbusiness organizations have an increasing range of influence, affect as many livelihoods, and occupy as much media prominence as major business firms.

All of these organizations perform the classic business functions. Every organization must perform a financial function insofar as money must be raised, managed, and budgeted according to sound business principles. Every organization must perform a production function in that it must conceive of the best way of arranging inputs to produce the outputs of the organization. Every organization must perform a personnel function in that people must be hired, trained, assigned, and promoted in the course of the organization's work. Every organization must perform a purchasing function in that it must acquire materials in an efficient way through comparing and selecting sources of supply.

When we come to the marketing function, it is also clear that every organization performs marketing-like activities whether or not they are recognized as such. Several examples can be given.

The police department of a major U.S. city, concerned with the poor image it has among an important segment of its population, developed a campaign to "win friends and influence people." One highlight of this campaign is a "visit your police station" day in which tours are conducted to show citizens the daily operations of the police department, including the crime laboratories, police lineups, and cells. The police department also sends officers to speak at public schools and carries out a number of other activities to improve its community relations.

Most museum directors interpret their primary responsibility as "the proper preservation of an artistic heritage for posterity."[1] As a result, for many people museums are cold marble mausoleums that house miles of relics that soon give way to yawns and tired feet. Although museum attendance in the United States advances each year, a large number of citizens are uninterested in museums. Is this indifference due to failure in the manner of presenting what museums have to offer? This nagging question led the new director of the Metropolitan Museum of Art to broaden the museum's appeal through sponsoring contemporary art shows and "happenings." His marketing philosophy of museum management led to substantial increases in the Met's attendance.

The public school system in Oklahoma City sorely needed more public support and funds to prevent a deterioration of facilities and exodus of teachers. It recently resorted to television programming to dramatize the work the public schools were doing to fight the high school dropout problem, to develop new teaching techniques, and to enrich the children. Although an expensive medium, television quickly reached large numbers of parents whose response and interest were tremendous.

Nations also resort to international marketing campaigns to get across important points about themselves to the citizens of other countries. The junta of Greek colonels who seized power in Greece in 1967 found the international publicity surrounding their cause to be extremely unfavorable and potentially disruptive of international recognition. They hired a major New York public relations firm and soon full-page newspaper ads appeared carrying the headline "Greece Was Saved From Communism," detailing in small print why the takeover was necessary for the stability of Greece and the world.[2]

An anti-cigarette group in Canada is trying to press the Canadian legislature to ban cigarettes on the grounds that they are harmful to health. There is widespread support for this cause but the organization's funds are limited, particularly measured against the huge advertising resources of the cigarette industry. The group's problem is to find effective ways to make a little money go a long way in persuading influential legislators of the need for discouraging cigarette consumption. This group has come up with several ideas for marketing anti-smoking to Canadians, including television spots, a paperback book featuring pictures of cancer and heart disease patients, and legal research on company liability for the smoker's loss of health.

What concepts are common to these and many other possible illustrations of organizational marketing? All of these organizations are concerned about their "product" in the eyes of certain "consumers" and are seeking to find "tools" for furthering their acceptance. Let us consider each of these concepts in general organizational terms.

Products

Every organization produces a "product" of at least one of the following types:

Physical Products. "Product" first brings to mind everyday items like soap, clothes, and food, and extends to cover millions of *tangible* items that have a market value and are available for purchase.

Services. Services are *intangible* goods that are subject to market transaction such as tours, insurance, consultation, hairdos, and banking.

Persons. Personal marketing is an endemic *human* activity, from the employee trying to impress his boss to the statesman trying to win the support of the public. With the advent of mass communications, the marketing of persons has been turned over to professionals. Hollywood stars have their press agents, political candidates their advertising agencies, and so on.

Organizations. Many organizations spend a great deal of time marketing themselves. The Republican Party has invested considerable thought and resources in trying to develop a modern look. The American Medical Association decided recently that it needed to launch a campaign to improve the image of the American doctor.[3] Many charitable organizations and universities see selling their *organization* as their primary responsibility.

Ideas. Many organizations are mainly in the business of selling *ideas* to the larger society. Population organizations are trying to sell the idea of birth control, and the Women's Christian Temperance Union is still trying to sell the idea of prohibition.

Thus the "product" can take many forms, and this is the first crucial point in the case for broadening the concept of marketing.

Consumers

The second crucial point is that organizations must deal with many groups that are interested in their products and can make a difference in its success. It is vitally important to the organization's success that it be sensitive to, serve, and satisfy these groups. One set of groups can be called the *suppliers. Suppliers* are those who provide the management group with the inputs necessary to perform its work and develop its product effectively. Suppliers include employees, vendors of the materials, banks, advertising agencies, and consultants.

The other set of groups are the *consumers* of the organization's product, of which four sub-groups can be distinguished. The *clients* are those who are the immediate consumers of the organization's product. The clients of a business firm are its buyers and potential buyers; of a service organization those receiving the services, such as the needy (from the Salvation Army) or the sick (from County Hospital); and of a protective or a primary organization, the members themselves. The second group is the *trustees* or *directors,* those who are vested with the legal authority and responsibility for the organization, oversee the management, and enjoy a variety of benefits from the "product." The third group is the active *publics* that take a specific interest in the organization. For a business firm, the active publics include consumer rating groups, governmental agencies, and pressure groups of various kinds. For a university, the active publics include alumni and friends of the university, foundations, and city fathers. Finally, the fourth consumer group is the *general public.* These are all the people who might develop attitudes toward the organization that might affect its conduct in some way. Organizational marketing concerns the programs designed by management to create satisfactions and favorable attitudes in the organization's four consuming groups: clients, trustees, active publics, and general public.

Marketing Tools

Students of business firms spend much time studying the various tools under the firm's control that affect product acceptance: product improvement, pricing, distribution, and communication. All of these tools have counterpart applications to nonbusiness organizational activity.

Nonbusiness organizations to various degrees engage in product improvement, especially when they recognize the competition they face from other organizations. Thus, over the years churches have added a host of nonreligious activities to their basic religious activities to satisfy members seeking other bases of human fellowship. Universities keep updating their curricula and adding new student services in an attempt to make the educational experience relevant to the students. Where they have failed to do this, students have sometimes organized their own courses and publications, or have expressed their dissatisfac-

tion in organized protest. Government agencies such as license bureaus, police forces, and taxing bodies are often not responsive to the public because of monopoly status; but even here citizens have shown an increasing readiness to protest mediocre services, and more alert bureaucracies have shown a growing interest in reading the user's needs and developing the required product services.

All organizations face the problem of pricing their products and services so that they cover costs. Churches charge dues, universities charge tuition, governmental agencies charge fees, fund-raising organizations send out bills. Very often specific product charges are not sufficient to meet the organization's budget, and it must rely on gifts and surcharges to make up the difference. Opinions vary as to how much the users should be charged for the individual services and how much should be made up through general collection. If the university increases its tuition, it will have to face losing some students and putting more students on scholarship. If the hospital raises its charges to cover rising costs and additional services, it may provoke a reaction from the community. All organizations face complex pricing issues although not all of them understand good pricing practice.

Distribution is a central concern to the manufacturer seeking to make his goods conveniently accessible to buyers. Distribution also can be an important marketing decision area for nonbusiness organizations. A city's public library has to consider the best means of making its books available to the public. Should it establish one large library with an extensive collection of books, or several neighborhood branch libraries with duplication of books? Should it use bookmobiles that bring the books to the customers instead of relying exclusively on the customers coming to the books? Should it distribute through school libraries? Similarly the police department of a city must think through the problem of distributing its protective services efficiently through the community. It has to determine how much protective service to allocate to different neighborhoods; the respective merits of squad cars, motorcycles, and foot patrolmen; and the positioning of emergency phones.

Customer communication is an essential activity of all organizations although many nonmarketing organizations often fail to accord it the importance it deserves. Managements of many organizations think they have fully met their communication responsibilities by setting up advertising and/or public relations departments. They fail to realize that *everything about an organization talks.* Customers form impressions of an organization from its physical facilities, employees, officers, stationery, and a hundred other company surrogates. Only when this is appreciated do the members of the organization reorganize that they all are in marketing, whatever else they do. With this understanding they can assess realistically the impact of their activities on the consumers.

Concepts for Effective Marketing Management in Nonbusiness Organizations

Although all organizations have products, markets, and marketing tools, the art and science of effective marketing management have reached their highest state of development in the business type of organization. Business organizations depend on customer goodwill for survival and have generally learned how to sense and cater to their needs effectively. As other types of organizations recognize their marketing roles, they will turn increasingly to the body of marketing principles worked out by business organizations and adapt them to their own situations.

What are the main principles of effective marketing management as they appear in most forward-looking business organizations? Nine concepts stand out as crucial in guiding the marketing effort of a business organization.

Generic Product Definition

Business organizations have increasingly recognized the value of placing a broad definition on their products, one that emphasizes the basic customer need(s) being served. A modern soap company recognizes that its basic product is cleaning, not soap; a cosmetics company sees its basic product as beauty or hope, not lipsticks and makeup; a publishing company sees its basic product as information, not books.

The same need for a broader definition of its business is incumbent upon nonbusiness organizations if they are to survive and grow. Churches at one time tended to define their product narrowly as that of producing religious services for members. Recently, most churchmen have decided that their basic product is human fellowship. There was a time when educators said that their product was the three R's. Now most of them define their product as education for the whole man. They try to serve the social, emotional, and political needs of young people in addition to intellectual needs.

Target Groups Definition

A generic product definition usually results in defining a very wide market, and it is then necessary for the organization, because of limited resources, to limit its product offering to certain clearly defined groups within the market. Although the generic product of an automobile company is transportation, the company typically sticks to cars, trucks, and buses, and stays away from bicycles, airplanes, and steamships. Furthermore, the manufacturer does not produce every size and shape of car but concentrates on producing a few major types to satisfy certain substantial and specific parts of the market.

In the same way, nonbusiness organizations have to define their target groups carefully. For example, in Chicago the YMCA defines its target groups as men, women and children who want recreational opportunities and are willing to pay $20 or more a year for them. The Chicago Boys Club, on the other hand, defines its target group as poorer boys within the city boundaries who are in want of recreational facilities and can pay $1 a year.

Differentiated Marketing

When a business organization sets out to serve more than one target group, it will be maximally effective by differentiating its product offerings and communications. This is also true for nonbusiness organizations. Fund-raising organizations have recognized the advantage of treating clients, trustees, and various publics in different ways. These groups require differentiated appeals and frequency of solicitation. Labor unions find that they must address different messages to different parties rather than one message to all parties. To the company they may seem unyielding, to the conciliator they may appear willing to compromise, and to the public they seek to appear economically exploited.

Customer Behavior Analysis

Business organizations are increasingly recognizing that customer needs and behavior are not obvious without formal research and analysis; they cannot rely on impressionistic evidence. Soap companies spend hundreds of thousands of dollars each year researching how Mrs. Housewife feels about her laundry, how, when, and where she does her laundry, and what she desires of a detergent.

Fund raising illustrates how an industry has benefited by replacing stereotypes of donors with studies of why people contribute to causes. Fund raisers have learned that people give because they are getting something. Many give to community chests to relieve a sense of guilt because of their elevated state compared to the needy. Many give to medical charities to relieve a sense of fear that they may be struck by a disease whose cure has not yet been found. Some give to feel pride. Fund raisers have stressed the importance of identifying the motives operating in the marketplace of givers as a basis for planning drives.

Differential Advantages

In considering different ways of reaching target groups, an organization is advised to think in terms of seeking a differential advantage. It should consider what elements in its reputation or resources can be exploited to create a special value in the minds of its potential customers. In the same way Zenith has built a reputation for quality and International Harvester a reputation for service, a nonbusiness organization should base its case on some dramatic value that competitive organizations lack. The small island of Nassau can compete against Miami for the tourist trade by advertising the greater dependability of its weather; the Heart Association can compete for funds against the Cancer Society by advertising the amazing strides made in heart research.

Multiple Marketing Tools

The modern business firm relies on a multitude of tools to sell its product, including product improvement, consumer and dealer advertising, salesman incentive programs, sales promotions, contests, multiple-size offerings, and so forth. Likewise nonbusiness organizations also can reach their audiences in a variety of ways. A church can sustain the interest of its members through discussion groups, newsletters, news releases, campaign drives, annual reports, and retreats. Its "salesmen" include the religious head, the board members, and the present members in terms of attracting potential members. Its advertising includes announcements of weddings, births and deaths, religious pronouncements, and newsworthy developments.

Integrated Marketing Planning

The multiplicity of available marketing tools suggests the desirability of overall coordination so that these tools do not work at cross purposes. Over time, business firms have placed under a marketing vice-president activities that were previously managed in a semi-autonomous fashion, such as sales, advertising, and marketing research. Nonbusiness organizations typically have not integrated their marketing activ-

ities. Thus, no single officer in the typical university is given total responsibility for studying the needs and attitudes of clients, trustees, and publics, and undertaking the necessary product development and communication programs to serve these groups. The university administration instead includes a variety of "marketing" positions such as dean of students, director of alumni affairs, director of public relations, and director of development; coordination is often poor.

Continuous Marketing Feedback

Business organizations gather continuous information about changes in the environment and about their own performance. They use their salesmen, research department, specialized research services, and other means to check on the movement of goods, actions of competitors, and feelings of customers to make sure they are progressing along satisfactory lines. Nonbusiness organizations typically are more casual about collecting vital information on how they are doing and what is happening in the marketplace. Universities have been caught off guard by underestimating the magnitude of student grievance and unrest, and so have major cities underestimated the degree to which they were failing to meet the needs of important minority constituencies.

Marketing Audit

Change is a fact of life, although it may proceed almost invisibly on a day-to-day basis. Over a long stretch of time it might be so fundamental as to threaten organizations that have not provided for periodic reexaminations of their purposes. Organizations can grow set in their ways and unresponsive to new opportunities or problems. Some great American companies are no longer with us because they did not change definitions of their businesses, and their products lost relevance in a changing world. Political parties become unresponsive after they enjoy power for a while and every so often experience a major upset. Many union leaders grow insensitive to new needs and problems until one day they find themselves out of office. For an organization to remain viable, its management must provide for periodic audits of its objectives, resources, and opportunities. It must reexamine its basic business, target groups, differential advantage, communication channels, and messages in the light of current trends and needs. It might recognize when change is needed and make it before it is too late.

Is Organizational Marketing a Socially Useful Activity?

Modern marketing has two different meanings in the minds of people who use the term. One meaning of marketing conjures up the terms selling, influencing, persuading. Marketing is seen as a huge and increasingly dangerous technology, making it possible to sell persons on buying things, propositions, and causes they either do not want or which are bad for them. This was the indictment in Vance Packard's *Hidden Persuaders* and numerous other social criticisms, with the net effect that a large number of persons think of marketing as immoral or entirely self-seeking in its fundamental premises. They can be counted on to resist the idea of organizational marketing as so much "Madison Avenue."

The other meaning of marketing unfortunately is weaker in the public mind; it is the concept of sensitively *serving and satisfying human needs*. This was the great contribution of the marketing concept that was promulgated in the 1950s, and that concept now counts many business firms as its practitioners. The marketing concept holds that the problem of all business firms in an age of abundance is to develop customer loyalties and satisfaction, and the key to this problem is to focus on the customer's needs.[4] Perhaps the short-run problem of business firms is to sell people on buying the existing products, but the long-run problem is clearly to create the products that people need. By this recognition that effective marketing requires a consumer orientation instead of a product orientation, marketing has taken a new lease on life and tied its economic activity to a higher social purpose.

It is this second side of marketing that provides a useful concept for all organizations. All organizations are formed to serve the interest of particular groups: hospitals serve the sick, schools serve the students, governments serve the citizens, and labor unions serve the members. In the course of evolving, many organizations lose sight of their original mandate, grow hard, and become self-serving. The bureaucratic mentality begins to dominate the original service mentality. Hospitals may become perfunctory in their handling of patients, schools treat their students as nuisances, city bureaucrats behave like petty tyrants toward the citizens, and labor unions try to run instead of serve their members. All of these actions tend to build frustration in the consuming groups. As a result some withdraw meekly from these organizations, accept frustration as part of their condition, and find their satisfactions elsewhere. This used to be the common reaction of ghetto Negroes and college students in the face of indifferent city and university bureaucracies. But new possibilities have arisen, and now the same consumers refuse to withdraw so readily. Organized dissent and protest are seen to be an answer, and many organizations thinking of themselves as responsible have been stunned into recognizing that they have lost touch with their constituencies. They had grown unresponsive.

Where does marketing fit into this picture? Marketing is that function of the organization that can keep in constant touch with the organization's consumers, read their needs, develop "products" that meet these needs, and build a program of communications to express the organization's purposes. Certainly selling and influencing will be large parts of organizational marketing; but, properly seen, selling follows rather than precedes the organization's drive to create products to satisfy its consumers.

Conclusion

It has been argued here that the modern marketing concept serves very naturally to describe an important facet of all organizational activity. All organizations must develop appropriate products to serve their sundry consuming groups and must use modern tools of communication to reach their consuming publics. The business heritage of marketing provides a useful set of concepts for guiding all organizations.

The choice facing those who manage nonbusiness organizations is not whether to market or not to market, for no organization can avoid marketing. The choice is whether to do it well or poorly, and on this necessity the case for organizational marketing is basically founded.

NOTES

1. This is the view of Sherman Lee, Director of the Cleveland Museum, quoted in *Newsweek,* Vol. 71 (April 1, 1968), p. 55.

2. "PR for the Colonels," *Newsweek,* Vol. 71 (March 18, 1968), p. 70.

3. "Doctors Try an Image Transplant," *Business Week,* No. 2025 (June 22, 1968), p. 64.

4. Theodore Levitt, "Marketing Myopia," *Harvard Business Review,* Vol. 38 (July-August, 1960), pp. 45–56.

CASES

THE KNEADERY

The Kneadery is a health food bakery located in the Southwest. Its products include a variety of bakery items and health food sandwiches that are made and sold at the bakery. The Kneadery also wholesales its bakery items to other health food stores within the city and as far as one hundred miles away.

IRON MOUNTAIN SKI AREA

Iron Mountain Ski Area has had an erratic history as a Sierra ski resort. Industry trends, changing market conditions, and increased competition face the ski resort. Iron Mountain's particular characteristics and facilities require the right kind of marketing program to assure long-run survival.

MIDDLETON CHEMICALS

Middleton Chemicals is a subsidiary of Johnson Manufacturing, a large supplier of products and services for the aerospace-defense industry. Having served primarily as a supplier to the parent company, Middleton Chemicals is now in the process of expanding into other markets and not relying solely on its parent company for sales and profits.

COMMUNITY HEALTH PLAN

This organization is located in Rhode Island and was the first nonprofit health maintenance service in the state. Its overall mission is to provide a multipart health service delivery system so that total family health care would be available under one roof.

THE KNEADERY

In January of 1986, Mr. John MacHenry, owner of the Kneadery, was preparing his annual assessment of the operations of his health food bakery. Although sales had increased over the last two years, he had expected a faster rate of growth in both sales and profits. He was also concerned about possible expansions in his product lines since they had not progressed as he had hoped. Finally, Mr. MacHenry was worried about the competition he faced. The health food market was expanding rapidly and thereby bringing in much stronger competition. Local bakeries were introducing more natural foods; nationally franchised bakers were starting to make significant penetrations; and retail grocery stores were opening bake shops and coming out with health food products of their own.

HISTORY

The Kneadery was established in a medium-size city in the Southwest in early 1981 by Mr. William Kraus for the purpose of supplying whole grain breads to health food stores in the area. First year sales increased nearly month-by-month, and at a rate that even surprised Mr. Kraus. However, as the typical business day grew longer due to increased demand, cleanliness and quality control began to suffer. Customers became dissatisfied and sales began to decline. By August 1982, Mr. Kraus became disillusioned with the baking business and decided to sell out.

The purchasers of the Kneadery were a commune of nine people in the immediate area. After the first month of operation, this group dwindled to three members who took active charge of the operation of the business. Not only did they continue to sell to health food stores, but they also began to sell bread and made-to-order sandwiches on the premises. Business lost by the previous owner was regained and

This case was prepared by Professor Dennis H. Tootelian, California State University, Sacramento.

sales began to increase again at a rapid pace. Once the novelty wore off, however, and the workload increased, two of the remaining group dropped out. By May 1983, Mr. John Marsh became the sole proprietor of the business.

For the next eight months, Mr. Marsh continued to run the bakery. Over the course of this time, he too became tired of handling all facets by himself. His primary interest was in baking and all else was done on a time-available basis. Records were not kept, management became that of instinct, and the breakdown of two key pieces of equipment convinced him to sell the business.

In December 1983, Mr. MacHenry purchased the Kneadery and began operations in January 1984. Having no experience in baking or in running a business, he was faced with a number of problems. The main ones were the complete absence of records upon which to base operations and the lingering ill-will created by the past owners. Although Mr. MacHenry discussed the various aspects of the operations with Mr. Marsh, he was essentially starting the business anew.

PRODUCTS

The Kneadery produced whole grain breads for health food stores in the area and for its own retail sales. Completely organic whole wheat bread was the backbone of its product mix. This product outsold all other products combined. Other breads included: Russian rye, vegetable seed, cinnamon, carrot-raisin, herb, and sour rye. In addition, the product mix included buns made in the same varieties as the breads, date bars, cookies of various kinds, and banana-nut cake.

The retail operation of the Kneadery included the sale of all bakery products produced as well as other assorted natural food items. A refrigeration unit was stocked with a variety of cheeses, yogurts, and cold drinks. Mr. MacHenry also continued to make and sell made-to-order sandwiches which were composed entirely of natural ingredients.

Product characteristics focused mainly on the special organically grown ingredients used. No sugar or preservatives were added to any of the breads, cakes, or cookies. Honey and molasses were substituted as sweeteners. Although the recipes were obtained from Mr. Marsh, Mr. MacHenry had been experimenting with some existing and new product lines.

Main expansion efforts centered on producing health food cakes and pastries. Although pastries were still in the concept and testing stages, a banana-nut cake was the only cake success so far. Most of the problems encountered in product development centered on the baking process. With health food cakes, for example, the exterior tended to burn before the interior was fully cooked. Despite these problems, Mr. MacHenry wanted to continue in these two particular areas (cakes and pastries) since they tended to have higher markups than the other product lines.

PRODUCTION

Planning and control of daily operations were carried out through the use of production forms which also doubled as order forms. Orders were received from customers over the telephone or by Mr. MacHenry during his normal deliveries. Orders were taken over the telephone on Monday, Wednesday, Friday, and Saturday. Rush orders were also accepted the morning of a baking day if received early enough. Baking days at the Kneadery were Tuesday, Thursday, and Sunday.

Baking days usually began around 10:30 a.m., depending on when Mr. MacHenry completed the day's deliveries and any other work needing attention. The baking process, for a single batch of bread, usually took a total of three and one-half hours to complete. The baking process centered around the mixing, panning, baking, and slicing operations. Between mixing and panning, a one-half hour waiting period was required to allow the bread to rise. This slack time was used to complete or begin additional operations in the process.

Normally, it took seven hours to produce all of the scheduled loaves. Mr. MacHenry only did the mixing and panning processes and used a part-time employee to do the baking, slicing, and wrapping. Each loaf was individually wrapped and labeled with the Kneadery's specially designed label. Two female employees prepared and baked all of the cookies and

date bars scheduled. Everybody helped in the preparation of the banana-nut cake.

Quality control over the product centered mainly around the quality of ingredients used. Baking times and recipes acquired from the previous owner were based on trial and error, but not subject to much variation. Occasionally, a bad batch of bread was made and sold, but was immediately replaced when discovered. The only reason for the occasional bad batch was that for some reason the bread did not rise enough before baking. Mr. MacHenry had yet to discover why this occurred. Regarding the returned loaves, the Kneadery gave away this bread as "ducky bread" to be used by people to feed the ducks in the park across the street. The Kneadery had developed increasing goodwill with the children and senior citizens in the neighborhood through this policy.

Purchases of supplies were established by the independent distributors who serviced the Kneadery. Small order sizes make it impossible to take advantage of bulk discounts, and cash discounts for early payment were not given by the independent distributors. Because of this, Mr. MacHenry was negotiating with the local co-op over the use of the Kneadery's flour mill. Since the Kneadery had no room available to operate the mill, Mr. MacHenry was willing to lend it to the co-op in return for which the Kneadery would purchase freshly ground flour at cost. This was especially favorable to Mr. MacHenry since he was presently buying flour from one of the Kneadery's major competitors. In addition to these efforts, Mr. MacHenry also completed negotiations to rent out the Kneadery's baking facilities several nights a week to a local restaurant so that it could bake pies and pastries for its own use.

COMPETITION

Although competition in the local market was fragmented, it was becoming increasingly keen due to greater public interest in natural foods and the "return to nature" movement. While health foods had enjoyed a popularity with members of various cults for years, the newer interest in whole grain breads had a much broader base. Mr. MacHenry thought that although all age groups were possible buyers, the

EXHIBIT 1
Kneadery Price List

	Wholesale			Retail		
	1 lb.	1½ lb.	2¼ lb.	1 lb.	1½ lb.	2¼ lb.
Whole Wheat	$ .52	$ .65	$ .90	$ .62	$ .78	$1.13
Sour Rye	.80	.96	—	.96	1.08	—
Specialties:	.60	.75	—	.72	.89	—
Herb, Vegetable Seed, Russian Rye, Cinnamon						
Whole Wheat Buns	—	.75	—	—	.89	—
Specialty Buns	—	.85	—	—	.99	—
Rolled Loaves	—	.96	—	—	1.08	—
Date Bars	.20 each			.25 each		
Cookies	.10 each			.12 each		
Cakes (Banana-Nut)	$2.75			$3.25		

primary purchasers of these products were young adults and senior citizens.

Within the city, there were only two major bakers of health food products, one of which was the Kneadery. Two other competitors worked the area, however, with one being thirty-five miles away and the other more than one hundred miles away. None of the four could really claim a hold on the market, and all were about equal in terms of size and quality of output. In addition to these independent bakeries, large nationally franchised bakers began to enter the whole grain bread market. These breads could not be sold in health food stores because of their inferior ingredients, but they were able to capture the purchasers who wanted the convenience of buying these products in their grocery stores.

Mr. MacHenry thought that one of the more serious threats was from the increasing number of bakeries being placed in larger supermarkets. Not only did they produce a wide range of traditional products, but they also extended into health foods since many of the stores maintained distinct health food sections. Pushing the freshness and convenience, many of the would-be buyers from health food stores were finding it advantageous to buy at the same time they were doing their normal shopping. Prices at the supermarkets, furthermore, tended to be lower due to bulk buying and the ability to spread costs over the entire bakery operations.

PRICING

Mr. MacHenry used the same wholesale and retail price schedules for baked goods as the previous owner. As the Kneadery's products were competitively priced with other suppliers of similar products, he was somewhat leery of changing them. A price list is presented in exhibit 1.

Most owners of health food stores carried bread only as a convenience to their customers, due to the low markup of ten cents to twelve cents per loaf and the high perishability. Brand loyalty was not thought to be overly strong, although people look for quality products with healthful ingredients, and not necessarily for lower prices. Therefore, Mr. MacHenry felt that reducing the wholesale price of the bread would do little to increase the sales of the Kneadery's products.

DISTRIBUTION

Bread and other baked goods were either delivered by Mr. MacHenry the day following baking, or picked up by the wholesale customer at the store. Even though there were only five deliveries, the time involved typically ranged from two to three hours, depending on traffic conditions. The same wholesale prices were charged regardless of the distribution method. Indirectly, the Kneadery also reached some of the

EXHIBIT 2
List of Wholesale Customers' Weekly Sales

Delivered Bread	
American Food Company	$109
General Food Co-op	96
Leonard's	82
Nutritional Products	56
Williamson's	24
Total	$367
Non-Delivered Bread	
Mandy's (70 miles away)	$ 81
Health Food City (70 miles away)	61
King's Health Foods (96 miles away)	48
Back to Nature (25 miles away)	24
Nature's Delite (95 miles away)	21
Total	$235

EXHIBIT 3
Location of Buyers

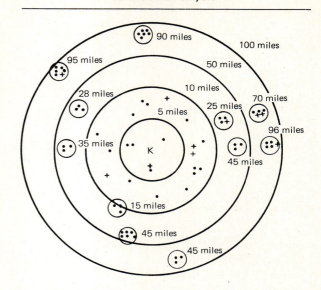

"•" denotes health food store (non-customer)
"+" denotes Kneadery customer
Circles denote towns and cities within 100 miles of Kneadery
Anticipated costs of delivery are $25 per 100 miles.

outlying regions by selling its products to the co-op, which in turn sold to health food stores in these areas. The breakdown in sales on a delivered versus non-delivered basis is presented in exhibit 2.

In April 1984, a restaurant owner asked that bread be delivered on a regular basis to his restaurant some thirty miles from the Kneadery. The sale was lost because Mr. MacHenry felt it was too much trouble to deliver bread beyond a ten-mile radius and because his time was at a premium. Of the twenty-two health food stores located in the area, all carried breads of the whole grain health food variety. Only five, however, carried bread from the Kneadery. The stores not carrying Kneadery products were divided about equally among the competition. The primary reason for the small number of outlets carrying its products was the delivery policy of the bakery. Since most wholesale deliveries were for relatively small orders and delivered three times a week, Mr. MacHenry felt that the distribution costs would be prohibitive and would consume too much of his time. See exhibit 3 for a schematic of the location of health food stores and the anticipated costs of distribution.

PROMOTION

The Kneadery had no advertising budget nor did Mr. MacHenry expect to allocate much, if any, money for advertising in the future. Most of the promotional

effort centered on word-of-mouth advertising and the distinctive labels placed inside each loaf of bread. Because the retail operations had become quite successful, some attention was directed at product placement and the overall appearance of the facilities. A few point-of-purchase displays were used, but were not considered especially important.

FINANCE

Financial aspects of the Kneadery were somewhat encouraging. No debt was incurred in the purchase of the company nor has any been needed since. It was anticipated that cash would be used to cover all future expenses or capital investments. The major liabilities were accounts payable and salary taxes payable. Financial statements are presented in exhibits 4 and 5.

EXHIBIT 4
Kneadery Income Statement

	Last Year	This Year
Sales		
Wholesale	$34,267	$31,304
Retail	35,666	41,246
Facilities Rental	–	250
Total	$69,933	$72,800
Cost of Goods Sold	35,176	37,856
Gross Profit	$34,757	$34,944
Controlled Expenses		
Salaries	$ 8,675	$ 9,352
Store Gas	250	291
Transportation	2,037	1,919
Labels, Molds, Baking Utensils, etc.	2,997	2,012
Total	$13,959	$13,574
Fixed Expenses		
Rent	$ 3,100	$ 3,540
Electricity	250	291
Telephone	981	728
Insurance	270	291
Employer Tax	631	655
Total	$ 5,232	$ 5,505
Net Profit Before Taxes	$15,666	$15,865

EXHIBIT 5
Kneadery Balance Sheet

	Last Year	This Year
Current Assets		
Cash in Bank	$ 2,198	$ 4,759
Petty Cash	250	222
Accounts Receivable	319	809
Prepaid Insurance	200	238
Inventory	831	2,078
Paper Supplies	450	476
Total	$ 4,248	$ 8,582
Fixed Assets		
Office Equipment	143	130
Baking Equipment	6,996	6,663
Refrigeration and Display Equipment	1,378	1,253
Bread Racks and Utensils	2,189	1,824
Stone Mill	1,100	1,000
Misc. Equipment	972	1,602
Total	$12,778	$12,472
Total Assets	$17,026	$21,054
Current Liabilities		
Accounts Payable	$ 3,173	$ 3,753
Salary Taxes Payable	78	95
Misc. Taxes Payable	37	48
Advances from Customers	781	535
Total	$ 4,069	$ 4,431
Capital Account	12,957	16,623
Total Liabilities and Capital	$17,026	$21,054

FUTURE OUTLOOK

In making his assessment, Mr. MacHenry noted that the retail section of the store was growing at a much faster rate than the wholesale bakery operation. The retail part had increased from about 51 percent to 57 percent of total sales. Mr. MacHenry attributed most of the increase to his made-to-order sandwich business. This market was composed largely of staff members of a hospital located two blocks away and to visitors to the park across the street.

Despite the success of the retail section, he was somewhat disappointed with overall sales and profits and was unsure of a course of action to pursue. Of added concern was the exterior appearance of his store. While the yearly lease had become more and more expensive, normal maintenance by the owner had all but ceased. Mr. MacHenry was worried about the possible effect of this on retail sales. He knew, however, that no other facilities were available within a reasonable distance and price range.

IRON MOUNTAIN SKI AREA

Iron Mountain Ski Area was a family-oriented Sierra ski resort, located approximately forty-five miles east of Jackson, California. The area had an erratic operating history, evidenced by the fact that ownership had changed three times since its opening in 1970. The area had operated as Silver Basin Ski Area (1971–74), and most recently as Ski Sundown (1977–79).

New owners purchased and renamed the area as Iron Mountain Ski Area. The goal of Iron Mountain Ski Area was to provide a winter sports area, primarily ski oriented, to be supplemented by a program of summer activities for family participation and enjoyment. At the time of this case (1982), Iron Mountain Ski Area was not yet in operation. Management had not decided how to "position" Iron Mountain Ski Area and what marketing strategy to pursue.

HISTORY

In the mid-1960s, John B. Allen of Sutter Creek, California, approached the United States Forest Service about the feasibility of developing a winter sports complex at the present site of Iron Mountain Ski Area. Allen owned approximately ninety acres of land in this area, while the remaining land belonged to the Forest Service. Allen's proposal was approved in 1970, and in June of that year he began development of Phase I of Silver Basin Winter Sports Development. The first phase consisted of two chair lifts and associated runs, one surface lift, a day lodge, a five-acre parking lot, and a motel/dormitory building, the majority of which was completed in

This case was prepared by Professor Ralph M. Gaedeke, California State University, Sacramento.

EXHIBIT 1
Silver Basin Ski Area
Skier Days for Selected Years

Year	Skier Days
1970/71	5,123
1971/72	13,187
1972/73	14,400
1973/74	10,500

October 1970, and Silver Basin Ski Area opened for business that December. Skier visitation data for the first season, along with the three seasons which followed, is shown in exhibit 1.

The drop in use during the 1973/74 season was attributed to two factors. First, the area lost several key weekends during the season due to equipment breakdowns and other problems. Second, after three seasons of steadily increasing use, a leveling off could be expected because of the limited facilities and terrain available. Area expansion seemed to be necessary for Silver Basin to grow and survive.

In 1974, the Silver Basin Market Development Plan, which outlined plans for expansion onto Forest Service property, was approved by the United States Forest Service. The Phase II plan proposed a winter sports development of six chair lifts and support facilities to serve 3,000 people at one time (including 2,700 skiers) on approximately 65 acres of private land and 1,040 acres of Forest Service Land. The 1974 Environmental Impact Report (USDA, 1974) states that the following conclusions and considerations resulted in the Forest Service's approval at that time:

1. Studies by the Outdoor Recreational Resources Review Commission showed that the number of Californians participating in snow skiing was five times greater than the national average. In addition, increasing numbers of Californians were skiing at non-California ski sites as a result of limited opportunities closer to home.
2. The unsettled energy supply had resulted in Californians utilizing nearby ski areas which were within one gas tank range of home.

3. Existing ski areas within comparable driving distances in the Central Sierra had been over-crowded for several years.
4. A smaller, more personal ski area, the size of Silver Basin, would complement the newly developed Kirkwood area on Highway 88.
5. The Forest Service agreed that the direct effects of the project would create little or no adverse aesthetic impacts outside the developmental area.
6. The need for and the desirability of a medium-sized, "family" ski area was apparent from the success of developments such as Sierra Ski Ranch, Incline Village, Homewood, and Boreal Ridge.

Unfortunately, the master plan approval came too late for Allen. Hurt by the unsuccessful 1973/74 season at Silver Basin, Allen's financial situation worsened, and the property was ultimately conveyed to William E. Crowder, et al., of Upland, California.

Under Crowder's ownership, the area was renamed Ski Sundown and operated during the 1977/78 and 1978/79 seasons. While both seasons resulted in significant losses for the ski area, the new owners continued area expansion by constructing a third chair lift during the summer of 1979. In addition, plans were made for construction of a fourth lift.

While Crowder's intentions were in the best interest of the area, his unprofitable record could be attributed to his failure to adhere to warnings that previous management had documented. Nathan Norman, general manager of the area under the Allen ownership, had warned the Forest Service in a letter of the potential problems which might result if expansion of the area was not approved:

> *Although you discuss the economics of the Central Sierras (in the Environmental Impact Statement Proposal), you fail to note that by denying further expansion, Silver Basin would go bankrupt. As pointed out in the Master Plan, Phase I was projected to be a loss type of operation and only in Phase II and beyond could Silver Basin become economically profitable.*

Crowder's decision to go ahead and operate Ski Sundown without expansion of facilities to the governmentally approved Phase II level resulted for a second time in the closure of the area.

In 1979, a Southern California-based family corporation acquired Ski Sundown and began immediate plans for expansion. The new owners, Pacific Western Ski Resorts, Inc., renamed the area Iron Mountain Ski Area since it lies at the intersection of Highway 88 and Iron Mountain Road. Recognizing the need for expansion of capacity if Iron Mountain Ski Area is to operate profitably, the new owners chose to cease operations during the 1980/81 and 1981/82 seasons so that construction could be completed on a fourth and fifth lift prior to reopening. In addition, the existing lodge was to be expanded from 10,300 to 26,300 square feet, while expanded parking facilities would provide 485 spaces for day-skier parking and 54 spaces for motel and dormitory parking.

The United States Forest Service was optimistic about the progress and future of Iron Mountain Ski Area. Citing managerial and financial problems as the major reasons for the area's past failures, the new owners felt they had learned from the previous owners' mistakes. The new owners retained the highly regarded ski area consulting firm of Sno-Engineering to prepare an updated master plan for area development. In addition, the new owners recognized the importance of a well-defined, sound marketing program for the success of Iron Mountain.

SKI INDUSTRY TRENDS

Skiing in the United States had become a big business. Resorts, retail ski shops, transportation, and real estate had all become a part of making skiing a major winter recreation industry. Recent studies put the number of United States residents who ski at over fourteen million. The industry was estimated to be growing at approximately 7.5 to 9.0 percent per year. In addition, the A. C. Nielson Company's *Sports Participation Survey* conducted in 1979 showed an overall increase in the number of skiers of approximately 40 percent from 1976. A 1976 study indicated an increase of approximately the same amount over 1973.

Several trends relevant to the operations of Iron Mountain Ski Area pointed to potential opportunities and problems. Notable industry trends included the following:

1. Demographic trends favored the continued growth of the ski industry:

   - Key age segments (that is, the young adult segment, 35 to 49-year-olds) of the population were increasing at significant rates.
   - The United States was becoming a more affluent society, with significant increases in income among the lower socioeconomic strata.
   - The United States was becoming a more highly educated population.
   - Percentage growth in the professional/managerial occupational segment was increasing twice as fast as that for the labor force as a whole.
   - The United States society was moving from a "work ethic" to a "leisure ethic."
   - The amount of free time available for leisure activities was growing at a significant rate.
   - There continued to be a dramatic increase in the number of single Americans.

2. Growth in the skier market was possible through the activation of potential skiers, the reactivation of skier market dropouts, and an increase in the rate of participation by active skiers.

3. Negative images associated with skiing (such as crowding and expense) could be minimized through constructive, informative marketing programs.

4. The automobile continued to be the major mode of transportation to the ski area, favoring resorts closer to home.

5. Evidence suggested that the rapid growth in cross-country skiing would complement the growth of downhill skiing.

6. Downhill skiing would continue to grow by 7 to 10 percent per year between 1982 and 1987.

7. The West was the most highly used ski region in the country and needed to expand capacity and facilities if growth in demand was to be satisfied.

8. Unless ski area utilization could be increased, the demand for skiing would continue to outstrip supply.

These trends reflected the overall healthy state of the skiing industry and had significant implications for ski area market planners.

THE MARKET

Market Characteristics

The Northern California ski market was a prime example of a regional competitive ski market, with over seventeen ski areas located within close proximity of the Lake Tahoe Basin (exhibit 2). This market was unique in that it offered the greatest variety of skiing terrain and capacity in the entire United States.

Very few of the Northern California ski areas had extensive guest lodging facilities directly adjacent to the resort. As a result, the weekend skier made a daily choice as to which particular ski area to visit. Even the most experienced Tahoe skiers, who favor certain areas a majority of the time, admitted to enjoying a variety of resorts depending upon their mood, the crowds, and the snow conditions. Therefore, the decision of when and where to go skiing could be thought of as a two-step process: (1) the decision to spend a weekend or a weekday skiing in Northern California, and, once there (2) the decision of where to spend each day.

Past capacity increases had averaged 8 to 10 percent per year between 1960 and 1975 at the Northern California ski areas. However, this rate had slowed down substantially between 1975 and 1980 due to declining land availability and increasing chair-lift costs. As a result, Northern California ski area capacity had not kept pace with demand. Industry forecasts predicted between 3.9 and 4.7 million skier visits in this area by 1990, with attendance then leveling off by the year 2000 (exhibit 3).

The overall growth in skiing in the Sierra/Tahoe Region had been approximately 15 percent per year in the last ten years. This was about 5 percent greater than growth in the skiing industry as a whole. This growth was attributed to four major factors:

1. The excellent accessibility from major population centers, with a combined population of over 5 million people, provided for attractive place utility.

2. An increase in spendable and/or discretionary income provided added dollars for recreational pursuits.

EXHIBIT 2
Northern California Ski Areas

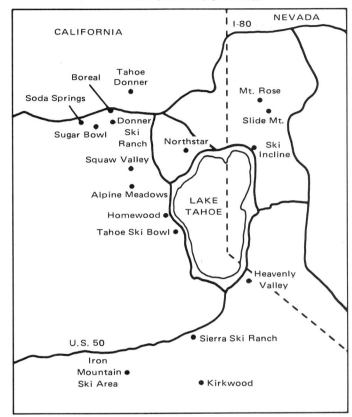

EXHIBIT 3
Northern California Skier Visit and Participation Rate
Projections, 1980 to 2000
(including three "most likely scenarios"*)

	Scenarios		
Year	No new ski developments[1]	Large ski area developments[2]	Small ski area developments[3]
1980	3,262,000	3,897,000	3,262,000
1985	3,663,000	4,432,000	3,832,000
1990	3,991,000	4,704,000	4,307,000
1995	4,062,000	4,787,000	4,384,000
2000	4,070,000	4,794,000	4,365,000

*The three scenarios would each result in different attendance rates. These scenarios are:

[1] Continuation of current trends: 2 percent per year uphill capacity growth between 1982 and 1990; 1.5 percent uphill capacity growth between 1990 and 2000.

[2] Large new development: assuming a large development which adds twenty VTF/hr.

[3] Several new middle-sized ski area developments: a 2 percent VTF/hr. yearly growth rate.

Source: John D. Landis, *The Skier Report: Forecasting the Demand for Skiing in the Western United States* (Research for the United States Forest Service, Pacific Southwest Forest and Range Experiment Station; University of California, Berkeley, 1979), p. 34.

3. A substantial increase in downhill skiing facilities throughout the region (with additions such as Kirkwood and Northstar) provided the skier with a wide variety of areas from which to choose.
4. Since most resorts in this region enjoyed a 135 to 145-day average operating season, skiers enjoyed a much longer season than most other ski areas in the United States.

Market Size

The Northern California ski market catered almost entirely to Californians. Historically, out of state "destination" skiers (with the exception of Nevada residents from the Carson City and Reno areas) had been rare. However, this trend could change as a result of improved air service into Reno and the large overnight housing facilities at South Lake Tahoe. For example, Heavenly Valley had recently organized a central reservation service which handled package sales for over fifty lodging suppliers in the South Lake Tahoe vicinity, in hopes of attracting the "destination skier."

The California Origin-Destination surveys conducted by the United States Forest Service between 1967 and 1970 revealed the importance of the San Francisco Bay Area as the primary demand pool for Northern California ski resorts. At the time of the case, over 54 percent of the Tahoe Basin's skier demand came from the Bay Area counties of Alameda, Contra Costa, San Francisco, San Mateo, and Santa Clara. The Bay Area skiers were evenly distributed across the Tahoe ski areas, with no one area attracting more than the others.

The Central Valley area, including the major metropolitan areas of Stockton and Sacramento, also provided attractive markets for Sierra ski resorts. The Central Valley skiers were drawn in greater numbers to ski areas on the fringe of the Tahoe Basin rather than those in the heart of the Tahoe area.

Population estimates for 1980 for those counties that were within two hundred miles of Iron Mountain Ski Area are presented in exhibit 4. These estimates indicated that the total population market, within a reasonable driving distance for a day of skiing, was in excess of eight million people.

Market Segmentation

Iron Mountain had segmented the market in the past solely on the basis of geographic variables. The primary target markets in its past seasons of operation were the South Bay counties of San Mateo and Santa Clara. The previous management made no effort to segment this market further.

Accessibility

Iron Mountain Ski Area was located immediately northwest of California State Highway 88, approximately 85 to 165 miles north and east of the metropolitan areas of Sacramento, Stockton, and San Francisco. The use of Highway 88 as an all-weather highway since 1972 placed the resort in a prime location in terms of accessibility.

Iron Mountain was located in a portion of the north central Sierra that has long been known for its summer recreational attributes. Silver Lake, a popular summer recreational area, was five miles northeast of the area. In addition, there were several reservoirs and streams to the west on Highway 88 that were popular for boating and fishing.

IRON MOUNTAIN

Climatic Conditions

Iron Mountain was a unique area in the Sierra in that wind conditions were not a major problem. It was visually evident through the tree cover and its conformation that extreme prevailing winds were nonexistent. In addition, the lifts and runs were protected by the surrounding terrain, with the exception of a small area in the northwest shoulder of the resort.

In its six years of operations, the area experienced no major lift problems as a result of wind conditions. Past records indicated that other ski areas, which were not wind protected, had to cease operations at certain times. For example, during the 1972/73 season, winds were recorded at Kirkwood at seventy miles per hour. During this storm, all lifts were closed at Kirkwood, Heavenly Valley and Mt. Reba, while operations at Iron Mountain were normal.

EXHIBIT 4
Population of Counties Within a Two-Hundred-Mile Radius of Iron Mountain, 1980

County	Population	County	Population
California		Sacramento	783,381
Alameda	1,105,379	San Benito	25,005
Alpine	1,097	San Francisco	678,974
Amador	19,314	San Mateo	588,164
Butte	143,851	Santa Clara	1,295,071
Calaveras	20,710	San Joaquin	347,342
Colusa	12,791	Sierra	3,073
Contra Costa	657,252	Solano	235,203
El Dorado	85,812	Sonoma	299,827
Fresno	515,013	Stanislaus	265,902
Glenn	21,350	Sutter	52,246
Lake	36,366	Tehama	38,888
Madera	63,116	Tuolumne	33,920
Marin	222,952	Yolo	113,374
Mariposa	11,108	Yuba	49,733
Merced	134,560		
Mono	8,577	Nevada	
Napa	99,199	Douglas	19,421
Nevada	51,645	Lyon	13,594
Placer	117,247	Storey	22,569
Plumas	17,340	Washoe	193,623

Topography and Land Characteristics

The land which comprises Iron Mountain Ski Area varies from fairly level to very steep, conforming generally to intermediate terrain. About 10 percent was beginner, 10 to 15 percent advanced, and the remaining 75 to 80 percent was intermediate.

The majority of the terrain lay in four north-facing bowls, with lodge facilities located on the ridges above. This terrain exposure assured ideal snow conditions. Although the slopes varied widely, their excellent accessibility and gradient allowed mechanized grooming on a major portion of the mountain.

Snow Conditions

Adjacent ski areas in the vicinity of the Lake Tahoe Basin operated very successfully between elevations of 6,200 and 10,000 feet. Iron Mountain would operate at an elevation of approximately 7,400 feet.

Snow depths had been recorded in the area since 1938. The average depth during this period in April was 7 feet, 9 inches; in March the depth was 6 feet,

8 inches; and in February it was 5 feet, 10 inches. During the past 44-year period, 1963 was the only year that the snow depth was less than 4 feet.

Facilities and Capacity

Winter Recreation. While downhill skiing was only one phase of winter recreation, it was the prime attraction to Iron Mountain during the winter months. The area had five lifts, which could accommodate a total of 2,700 skiers at one time.

Iron Mountain was classified as a small to moderate-sized "family type" resort, which offered terrain best suited for the intermediate skier. The area served a segment of the skier population which desired a smaller, more personal ski area.[1] In addition

---

[1] Because many of these skiers were adults whose children accompanied them, certain types of ski runs and services, as well as after-ski accommodations, were required. These included beginning and intermediate runs, ski instruction, and family-oriented dining and lodging facilities.

to the need for more ski areas of this type, Iron Mountain had additional attributes that gave it a competitive advantage over similarly sized resorts in the Tahoe Basin:

- altitude of 7,400 feet (compared to Tahoe Basin at 6,200 feet);
- average operating season of 140 days, as compared to a Tahoe Basin average of 120 days;
- consistently superior snow conditions;
- close proximity to the market area;
- excellent mix of terrain;
- scenic area;
- natural protection; and
- surrounding areas conducive to other summer/winter recreational activities.

In addition to downhill skiing, the areas around Iron Mountain were well suited to other popular winter sports, namely cross-country skiing and snowmobiling.

The major weaknesses of Iron Mountain were:

- the relatively limited vertical slope provided by the mountain;
- the regional setting and lack of support services within a reasonable travel distance;
- the negative image that skiers may associate with Iron Mountain as a result of its erratic operating history.

Summer Recreation. Many people who wished to escape the extreme valley heat in the summer time took advantage of the enjoyable cooler mountain atmosphere. There was considerable summer activity in the vicinity of Iron Mountain, centering around Silver Lake, Kirkwood Lake, Caples Lake, and Sly Park Reservoir. Silver Lake, the closest, was five miles northeast of the ski area and offered public and private camping facilities, horseback riding, fishing, boating, and hiking.

Since the mountain area in which Iron Mountain lay was in the two to four-hour travel zone from the nearest metropolitan areas, the assumption was that in order for summer recreational activities to succeed, overnight accommodations had to be provided. The lodging facilities at the area would be able to meet this criterion.

The top three summer activities were: (1) driving for pleasure, (2) swimming outdoors, and (3) walking for pleasure. Iron Mountain fared well with respect to each activity.

Iron Mountain planned to inaugurate an active summer program, utilizing the lodge, lifts, accommodations, and parking facilities. The possible summer programs to be implemented included camper parking, childrens' camps, health-related camps, and seminars and conferences. These programs were not intended to result in large profits, but would provide two important benefits: (1) allow fixed overhead to be amortized over ten months instead of six, and (2) enable management to hire key personnel on a yearly basis.

COMPETITION

The Northern California ski region was centered at Lake Tahoe and included a broad variety of ski areas, from the nationally known Squaw Valley to the purely local Granlibakken. Many people assumed that all ski areas in the Lake Tahoe area were competitive with each other. This assumption was somewhat simplistic because the market could be grouped into smaller submarkets on the basis of size and location.

Submarket Analysis by Size

The stratification of the Northern California Ski Market according to size yielded the following subgroups:

1. "The Big Three"—Squaw Valley, Heavenly Valley, Alpine Meadows;
2. "The Middle Seven"—Boreal, Dodge Ridge, Kirkwood, Northstar, Mt. Reba-Bear Valley, Sierra Ski Ranch, Sugar Bowl; and
3. "The Little Eight"—Donner Ski Ranch, Homewood, Ski Reno, Soda Springs, Tahoe Donner, Tahoe Ski Bowl, Iron Mountain.

Iron Mountain could compete in the smaller ski area segment and, to some degree, with the medium-sized resorts. A complicating factor in Iron Mountain's attempt to compete with the "Middle Seven," however, was the fact that Kirkwood was in this group. Kirkwood was only twelve miles east of Iron Mountain and was a larger, more attractive ski resort, catering primarily to young adult singles and couples.

Submarket Analysis by Location

The Lake Tahoe area ski resorts could be conveniently grouped into six geographical areas:

1. Truckee Area—Boreal, Sugar Bowl, Donner Ski Ranch, Tahoe Donner, Northstar;
2. West Lake Tahoe—Squaw Valley, Alpine Meadows, Homewood, Tahoe Ski Bowl;
3. Route 50—Heavenly Valley, Sierra Ski Ranch;
4. Highway 88—Kirkwood, Iron Mountain;
5. Nevada-Incline, Ski Reno; and
6. Other—Dodge Ridge, Bear Valley (not shown on exhibit 2).

Geographical considerations played a major role in skier choice processes. An analysis of the geographic submarkets revealed a competitive advantage for Iron Mountain in that it was the only small-to-moderate-sized area on Highway 88. The success of Kirkwood in attracting skiers to this area was evidenced by a 100 percent increase in utilization over the past five years. In light of this, the outlook for Iron Mountain appeared favorable. It was not known, however, if Iron Mountain Ski Area should position itself as a resort to complement Kirkwood or directly compete with it.

MIDDLETON CHEMICALS

Robert Morley, General Manager of Middleton Chemicals, was pondering the recent decision to change the company's entire business orientation. Having been primarily a supplier for the aerospace-defense industry, it was now going to focus on supplying chemicals to other markets.

Middleton Chemicals was just entering its fourth year of operation, and Mr. Morley had been with the company as General Manager since it was started as a subsidiary of Johnson Manufacturing, Inc. Middleton was originally organized by the parent company to be a producer of custom chemicals for government markets, but Johnson Manufacturing executives decided on this change as the future of government spending became questionable. Mr. Morley noted:

Ending our reliance on the government to compete in the private sector is like starting a whole new

This case was prepared by Professor Dennis H. Tootelian, California State University, Sacramento.

company. Before, we just had to be good in research and development and basic chemical production. Now, we have to do all the things other firms have to do. We have to re-establish this company, redefine our goals, possibly reorganize our management, and rethink virtually everything we do. It may be wise and profitable, but it's not going to be fun.

According to Mr. Morley, about one-third of Middleton's sales continued to be to the parent company:

Our problem is to convert from an internal supplier to a custom manufacturer and supplier of proprietary and specialty chemicals. For the long-term security of our company, we have to get into these two areas. Proprietary chemicals are those which no one else can produce because of size, handling problems, or patent restrictions. Specialty chemicals are formulations developed and made for others, who don't want to or cannot produce such chemicals themselves. Our major assets are our somewhat remote plant location and our unique technical capabilities. Very few of our competitors could match this combination since most other firms are located in highly populated areas. So, this helps, but I still am not sure where to go from here. It's difficult to get this change going the way it should.

HISTORY

Johnson Manufacturing was founded just before World War II, but achieved its most significant growth during the late 1950s and early 1960s, and then again in the late 1970s. It was extensively involved in research and development and production in such fields as electronics, systems for guided missiles, space exploration equipment, medical instrumentation, and various nuclear energy applications. Accordingly, its principle customers were National Aeronautics and Space Administration (NASA), the military, and miscellaneous other federal agencies.

In order to meet its commitments during the "boom" years, Johnson Manufacturing often had to extend the state-of-the-art in various areas of metallurgy and chemistry. As a result, several advanced laboratory and pilot-plant facilities were constructed on company property. Due to the hazardous nature of many of the compounds being processed, however, the facilities were widely spaced, and extensive precautions were taken in construction to protect personnel and prevent environmental pollution due to accidental spills or explosions. Provisions were also made for disposal of normal wastes without polluting the atmosphere or water systems (whether surface or underground). All of this occurred before legislation on environmental protection was enacted.

With the maturation of the big ICBM programs in the mid-1960s and the subsequent decline in space expenditures until the Space Shuttle program, sales of all such firms as Johnson Manufacturing were sharply reduced. Some companies began to contract their operations, others were extensively reorganized, and still others failed.

Executives at Johnson Manufacturing wanted to capitalize on the firm's strong combination of facilities and experience with high technology chemistry. Accordingly, Middleton Chemicals was created to enter the commercial chemical industry as a manufacturer of synthetic compounds and as a custom manufacturer of hazardous or dangerous chemicals. According to Mr. Morley, who was a Vice President of Johnson Manufacturing at the time this decision was made:

Although there was some initial disagreement about the creation of Middleton, all agreed that for it to be a success, it would have to be a fully self-sufficient specialty chemical operation. I was appointed General Manager, and operations began with ten people. One year later, there were ninety-six people on board and the company was growing vigorously. Our sales forecast for the first year was $700,000, but actual sales were around $2 million. And in the next year, our sales were approximately $3.5 million.

Middleton Chemicals was specifically oriented to proprietary chemicals, protected either by patents or secret processes. And as a beginning, the company sold chemicals to Johnson Manufacturing, and was supplemented by contracts for special research projects for the government.

INDUSTRY

Although there were numerous firms in the "chemical industry," it was difficult to determine how large a segment of the overall industry was involved in the sort of custom manufacture in which Middleton Chemicals specialized. There were no listings in *The Thomas Register of American Manufacturers* for custom chemicals specifically, but there were over 500 chemical manufacturers, some of which were very large while others were very small.

Thus, no breakdown of industry sales could be found which would permit a ready evaluation of the market available to Middleton Chemicals. Furthermore, many of the large manufacturers produced their own speciality chemical compounds. Nevertheless, Mr. Morley believed that custom chemical research and production easily accounted for over $1 billion in sales annually.

MANAGEMENT

The management team at Middleton Chemicals consisted of Robert Morley (General Manager), Jack Butler (Manager of Production), Pam Wynn (Marketing Manager), Bill Berle (Controller), and David Frazier (Manager of Research). An organizational chart is

EXHIBIT 1
Middleton Chemicals Organization Chart

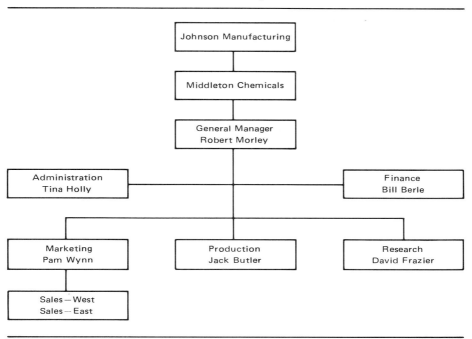

shown in exhibit 1. All of these managers had offices in one building, although Mr. Butler and Mr. Frazier had their "working" offices in buildings located near their operations.

Middleton Chemicals was divided into five major departments. The Administration Department, managed by Ms. Tina Holly, was responsible for training management, reviewing wage rates and salary ranges, designing employment forms, educating and training employees, reviewing and writing policies and procedures, and for some labor relations work in collaboration with the parent company's labor relations experts.

Bill Berle was the Controller, and was in charge of the Finance Department. Although Mr. Berle and Middleton Chemicals did not have authority from the parent company to make capital acquisitions, Mr. Morley considered him one of the more important members of the management team. The routine responsibilities of the department included making

up the payroll, maintaining the accounts receivable and accounts payable records, and doing general ledger work. It also had to prepare production records in such a way that costs could be accurately determined and prices correctly set. In addition, Mr. Berle was involved in pricing decisions, and forecasting the future impact of capital expenditures and new projects on the company's profitability.

Jack Butler was manager of the Production Department, and was responsible for procurement, and the scheduling and carrying out of production. According to Mr. Morley:

Jack had been interviewed along with five outside men for the Production Manager's job. I felt that one of the other men interviewed might have been better trained for the job, but Jack already knew something about Johnson Manufacturing systems and the people. Executives at the parent decided that his knowledge was important enough to overcome the other men's advantages in training. Unfortunately, as it has turned out, this has been our weakest link.

Middleton had been known to have difficulties with meeting time lines and technical specifications. Occasional lapses in quality control had caused problems with some of its government contracts. Despite these difficulties, however, Middleton Chemicals had a fair-to-good reputation. The highly complex nature of the work, coupled with normal frustrations associated with working on government contracts, made part of these production problems understandable to others in the industry.

The Research and Development Department was thought to be the strongest aspect of Middleton Chemicals. David Frazier, manager of the department, was regarded as one of the leading authorities on toxic chemicals. His staff of nine specialists and eleven technicians were given considerable latitude in experimenting in new areas, irrespective of whether there were existing contracts for the work. Johnson Manufacturing executives believed that such freedom was essential if the company were to make technological breakthroughs and earn a reputation for R&D excellence. As Mr. Morley noted, however, there often were conflicts between Mr. Frazier and Mr. Butler, each blaming the other for technical failures.

Pam Wynn, manager of the Marketing Department, was responsible for selling manufacturing services and special products to potential commercial customers, and for selling research services to the government. In addition to Ms. Wynn, the department was expanded to include George Actman as Sales Manager–West and Jerry Stacy as Sales Manager–East. They were in charge of commercial development. Ms. Wynn was also responsible for company advertising and public relations.

Regarding policy matters, Mr. Morley indicated that there were two levels of policy by which the company operated. First, there were a "considerable number" of detailed policies established by the parent company; and second, a "small number" of policies generated within the company. Of particular concern, however, was the parent company's policy regarding performance standards, which required a 15 percent return on investment (ROI). While Middleton had

been able to meet this requirement during the time it was oriented to government work, Mr. Morley was unsure this could continue with the new direction Middleton was taking. He felt the company should be rated more on the basis of growth. The parent company, however, had consistently resisted adding a growth factor to its evaluation criteria for Middleton.

Johnson Manufacturing was also involved in other aspects of Middleton's management. It took care of most maintenance work, purchasing, and quality control measurement. Since employees of Middleton Chemicals were members of the same union as those for Johnson Manufacturing, the parent handled most all of the labor relations. Although Mr. Morley hoped to eventually have all management activities performed internally, he did not think it was feasible in the near future, especially with the new orientation Middleton would take.

Management planning, although initiated internally, was also controlled by the parent company. The planning process began with the Marketing Department predicting product sales, typically in pounds. Then, the Production Department would estimate the costs to produce the products, including materials, research and development, engineering, and operator costs. From there, the Finance Department would estimate the overhead costs, and Mr. Morley would add a profit margin sufficiently high to ensure the 15 percent ROI required by the parent company. According to Mr. Morley:

> Pam is not authorized to consider any orders which do not provide a 15 percent ROI. She can appeal this policy to me, and if we think it is a real hot prospect for future business, we take it to the parent. But, the policy is that you don't buy contracts (i.e., take them at low profit margins), and so we have not planned for anything like this.

All operating and capital budgets were prepared internally by department managers and reviewed by Mr. Morley. Once they were complete, he would take them to Johnson Manufacturing's Finance Committee. This committee would review the budget and issue a final budget after making desired modifications. At that point, Mr. Morley was authorized to spend the money for approved items, but could not modify the budget in any manner—such as spending approved funds for other purposes, or increasing expenditures for one approved item at the expense of another.

OPERATIONS

Jack Butler transferred from the parent company to Middleton Chemicals shortly after it was formed in order to become Manager of Production. According to Mr. Butler, there were substantial facility and personnel problems:

I prefer to remember them as challenges. We were taking a relatively old pilot plant, built for a specific purpose, and transforming it into a flexible production facility. Also, we had to change the orientation of the people from experimental to production, while maintaining strict safety and quality-control procedures. There always has been a tremendous safety factor with toxic chemicals, and the rapid growth presented more problems in personnel training. Great changes in the concepts of the people were involved in working with the detailed paperwork requirements for government contracts which the parent company had always handled for us.

The batch plant (Plant A) had been built nearly twenty years ago, and Johnson Manufacturing owned the land and building. About 95 percent of the equipment and the storage buildings, however, were owned by the government. According to Mr. Butler:

This had been a serious problem until we came to some long-term arrangement. We now have agreements for commercial jobs such that we pay rental fees of 6 percent of the direct man-hour costs for the use of government equipment. This is fair, but expensive.

Approximately $750,000 was budgeted for Plant A expansion and new equipment. This was the only production facility actually operated by Middleton Chemicals prior to the reorientation. Plant B, a true chemical plant wholly owned by Johnson Manufacturing, was being reactivated for both commercial and government work. It was expected to start up early next year. Until then, some facilities were being made available in the parent's plant should the need for extra capacity arise. Plant B was expected to primarily supply processing chemicals for the parent company for the next ten years, with about 35 percent of its capacity available for making commercial products.

Mr. Butler also was in charge of procurement, buying raw materials from all over the country. No one vendor dominated supply, and Mr. Butler maintained a very small inventory level because there were no long-run contracts at the time—except for those from the parent company. To prepare for growth under the reorientation program, however, the company had just acquired an option on a storage facility from the parent. Although both Mr. Morley and Mr. Butler had thought this was somewhat premature, the decision had been made by the parent.

Overall, the production department employed 10 salaried people and 34 hourly operators. These people were responsible for performing all manufacturing work. In addition, the department included 14 engineers and draftsmen for manufacturing design, estimating, and set-up.

Closely related to the production department was research and development. David Frazier managed this department, and employed 9 Ph.D. chemists, 6 other chemists, and 11 laboratory technicians. These people did the research and development work required for new products, including research on the best processes for making each compound. There was some natural overlap between these activities and those undertaken by the engineers in Mr. Butler's department, and this had been a source of irritation between the two managers for some time.

Mr. Frazier spent most of his time investigating new custom or specialty chemicals. Ideas for them came from a variety of sources, including the company, the parent, potential customers (provided through the marketing department), universities' publications, and other specialty chemical companies (through trade and professional publications). Once the characteristics of a compound were understood, an evaluation would begin. It would start with a literature search, then lab tests would be conducted to determine which of several possible processes would be best for making the desired product. Weekly product screening meetings were held with Mr. Morley, Mr. Frazier, Ms. Wynn, and Mr. Butler. This group reviewed each new product idea in terms of what they knew about it and what steps to take from there. It was from this process that many new products were developed for Middleton Chemicals.

MARKETING

Pam Wynn had come to Middleton Chemicals three years ago, after working for the federal government for over ten years. She had been involved in various aspects of procurement, and was hired by Mr. Morley because of her technical expertise in government purchasing. In assessing her approach, she noted:

We are using a 'shotgun' approach to marketing. We are not mature enough to fully evaluate all the opportunities and decide where we want to concentrate our future efforts. For the same reason, we haven't pursued any external acquisitions. We do know we must not concentrate on military work. More and more, the public will demand fewer destructive products and products that contaminate the environment. We plan to keep away from halogenated products, which have lasting after-effects, and emphasize the nitrogenous products which are biodegradable. Also, the company must concentrate heavily on chemicals which are hazardous to make or to handle due to toxicity, flammability, or an explosive nature. This is where we really excelled in our government contracts.

According to parent company directives, Middleton Chemicals was to place more emphasis on volume production for industrial customers instead of short-term research and development. As Ms. Wynn noted:

We are not supposed to be interested in building up the kind of marketing organization needed to sell drugs in the consumer market. But, we are supposed to get some longer-run production jobs in the industrial market. It's a little confusing. I thought that the government policies and procedures were strange, but this place is even worse right now.

Ms. Wynn defined the primary strengths of Middleton Chemicals as its technological expertise in the engineering and handling of explosive and toxic materials. The competition, she felt, was an indeterminant number of small manufacturers who could do good jobs, given complete processes to follow. These firms sold their manufacturing services and probably operated on lower margins. Ms. Wynn commented:

There are lots of firms just as competent, and probably better at quickly reacting to customer requests. But, we can offer better than average research and development service, and we don't have the safety problems of most of the competition.

The principle weakness of the company, according to Ms. Wynn, was that the employees were oriented more towards government contract work than to commercial sales. Furthermore, she did not agree with the parent company's reorientation directives:

Government contracting and commercial work are not compatible. Government contractors lean toward increasing their costs since their profits are computed as a percentage of cost. On the other hand, commercial firms increase profits by cutting costs. For example, when I worked for the government, I saw a bid based on an estimated cost of 48 hours for preparation of the process procedure. The same thing was proposed for 8 to 16 hours at a commercial chemical firm.

In describing the sales approach she proposed for Middleton Chemicals, Ms. Wynn said:

We'll sell from a catalog that has wide distribution. We also have a brochure that describes our equipment and the services we can offer. Our salespeople will have to do a lot of calling too, to keep the company's name in the minds of possible customers.

Ms. Wynn employed two sales managers, who she felt would be critical to the proposed marketing effort. Jerry Stacy was located in New York and was assigned

CASE

EXHIBIT 2
Middleton Chemicals
Income Statement (in hundreds)

	Actual	Planned	Variance
Sales			
Government	$1,290	$1,320	($ 30)
Commercial	321	405	(84)
Internal	2,829	2,400	429
Total	$4,440	$4,125	$315
Cost of Sales			
Direct Material	$ 880	$ 908	$ 28
Direct Labor	1,037	922	(44)
Other Direct	1,073	1,029	(115)
Total	$2,990	$2,859	($131)
G & A Overhead	$ 948	$ 734	($214)
Total Costs	$3,938	$3,593	($345)
Net Profit	$ 502	$ 532	($ 30)

EXHIBIT 3
Middleton Chemicals
Balance Sheet (in hundreds)

Current Assets		
Cash		$ 1
Accounts Receivable		380
Government	316	
Commercial	64	
Inventory		166
Raw Materials	47	
In-Progress & Finished	119	
Prepaid Expenses		374
Total		$ 920
Property & Equipment		$1,255
Total Assets		$2,175
Current Liabilities		
Accounts Payable		$ 289
Salaries & Wages		162
Intercompany Accounts		1,205
Other Current Liabilities		28
Total		$1,684
Retained Earnings		$ 491
Total Liabilities & Retained Earnings		$2,175

everything east of the Mississippi. She anticipated that this initially would account for 85 percent of sales. The area to the west was assigned to George Actman in San Francisco. Since the company had done little in the western part of the United States, Ms. Wynn expected it to account for only 15 percent of company sales in the early period.

Ms. Wynn had plans to add one sales manager in the Midwest once sales in the commercial sector had grown to the point where she could recommend it to the parent company. In summarizing her thoughts, she commented:

Right now, the lab people are busy and have a backlog, so we have to delay the new hiring in sales until the lab needs work. Each of our sales managers have two salespeople, and that should be adequate. I hope that our outside commercial sales will account for between 35 percent and 40 percent of total sales, and will rise to around 50 percent within the next two years.

FINANCE

The Finance Department employed two accountants who processed the payroll, kept the accounts payable and accounts receivable, and did the general ledger work. An industrial engineer was responsible for the cost accounting system used by the company.

Regular accounting reports were prepared for internal use, and included a monthly Income Statement which showed actual and planned values plus variances—both for the month and for the year to date (see exhibit 2). A second report was a General and Administrative Overhead Analysis itemizing controllable and fixed costs. A third report was a Production Overhead Analysis with controllable and fixed costs identified for that department. Finally, there was a Balance Sheet prepared both for internal use and for the parent company (see exhibit 3).

Middleton Chemicals had its own bank account for operating funds, but once each month Mr. Berle would call the finance people in the parent company to tell them how much money the company would need for operating funds for the coming month. The parent company would then have the necessary funds transferred into Middleton Chemicals' bank account.

Mr. Berle's responsibilities were largely that of contract administration. About 95 percent of the work performed in the department was required to fulfill government contracts, either directly or through Johnson Manufacturing. As Mr. Berle noted:

There are reams of paperwork involved in every government job, but for a commercial sale we only issue two pieces of paper. Upon receipt of a customer's order, an internal Purchase Order is issued, which assigns a charge number and authorizes the work to be done. When the product is shipped, an Invoice is prepared. One of our biggest problems will be getting the people to accept the more simplistic records system needed for commercial work.

Mr. Berle also thought that the government ownership of equipment in Plant A was a problem. However, he identified three ways that Middleton Chemicals could obtain ownership of this equipment:

1. They could propose to buy the facilities outright. This would be the quickest, but they would probably have to pay more than the equipment was worth. Most of it was twelve years old, and the industry standard for useful life was ten years.
2. If Middleton Chemicals indicated it did not need the equipment, it would go up for bid. But, most of it couldn't be removed without destroying some of the parts. Only if no outsider bid on the equipment could Middleton buy it for a minimum, or scrap value.
3. The government could abandon the facilities in place, and Middleton could then just assume ownership. This would be the most desirable

process, except that it was also the most time-consuming to wait and hope for.

FUTURE

In considering the new direction Middleton Chemicals was taking, Mr. Morley realized that a whole new set of operating strategies might be needed—especially those related to marketing. He felt that the company would not be successful in competing on products where there was an established market price. He thought that plant size restrictions, shipping costs, and high internal costs would prevent Middleton from ever being able to compete in the high-volume, low-cost chemical business.

Consequently, he proposed that Middleton Chemicals concentrate on low volume, expensive products. Potential customers would be those involved in technically complicated products—companies that knew something about a particular chemical and needed further research completed, and that needed actual production of reasonable commercial quantities. He also proposed that the company concentrate on firms which wanted high purity and quality, and were not especially cost sensitive.

Over the long term, Mr. Morley hoped that an organization could be built which would support future sales rather than just current sales. He wanted to hire more scientists for the labs in order to extend the company's research capacity. Currently, the lab was 100 percent involved in custom chemical work and had no time for experimental research—an activity that could enhance the company's technical reputation.

COMMUNITY HEALTH PLAN

The Community Health Plan, Inc., known as CHP, is Rhode Island's first nonprofit health maintenance organization (HMO), established in June of 1971.

With the support and assistance of local organized labor leadership, CHP became the first viable alternative to sometimes costly and piecemeal medical coverage and services. For the first time in Rhode Island, families were offered the opportunity to obtain total family care at a reasonable cost under one roof.

THE BASIC HMO MODEL

The term HMO has been used to designate a variety of health care delivery systems. But the most commonly accepted definition is that of "a medical care delivery system which accepts responsibility for the organization, financing, and delivery of health care services for a defined population." The HMO is characterized by the combination of a financing mechanism—prepayment—with a particular mode of delivery—group practice—by means of a managerial-administrative organization responsible for insuring the availability of health services for a subscriber-population.

The principles of operation of HMOs may be divided into six primary characteristics:

1. Responsibility for organizing and delivering health services—the HMO is not merely a financing mechanism but is concerned with obtaining,

This case was prepared by Professor David Loudon and Professor Albert Della Bitta, both of the University of Rhode Island, as a basis for class discussion rather than to illustrate effective or ineffective handling of an administrative situation. Presented at the Northwestern University Case Workshop of the Intercollegiate Case Clearing House, October 28–30. Copyright © 1973 by Loudon and Della Bitta.

through contracts with providers, an assured source of supply of health services for its members.
2. Prepayment—costs of the organization are met through fixed periodic payments from subscribers. Many plans, however, supplement the prepayment income with co-payments charged at the time treatment is incurred, e.g., a $2.00 charge for an office call.
3. Group practice—physicians are organized into multi-specialty groups of sufficient size to maintain facilities which are capable of providing comprehensive, continuous care. In the early stages, a developing HMO may include only primary care physicians in the group and depend on referrals to outside specialists for those services beyond their capabilities.
4. Comprehensive benefits—although comprehensiveness varies, most plans offer a complete range of medical services, including some forms of preventive care.
5. Compensation of physicians—the physicians are usually compensated through the capitation principle (the payment of an amount of money equal to a fixed per capita sum for each subscriber, multiplied by the number of subscribers enrolled). In addition, most physician groups participate in any savings generated through effective management of the plan.
6. Voluntary enrollment—most HMOs enroll through a dual choice mechanism under which employees may choose between an indemnity plan or the HMO.

Group practice prepayment was initiated in this country in a small clinic in Elk City, Oklahoma, in 1932, and first implemented on a large scale by the Kaiser Foundation Health Plan on the west coast. Since then, plans have been organized by diverse groups, e.g., consumers at Puget Sound, physicians at Ross-Loos, a medical school at the Harvard Community Health Plan, and an insurance company at Columbia, Maryland—and in equally diverse forms. In 1970, approximately 75 HMOs provided health care for over eight million people nationally. The data derived from those participants indicate that HMOs have been able to supply health care for substantially less dollar outlay than has the predominant fee-for-service system.

COMMUNITY HEALTH PLAN

CHP embraces all of the concepts which make up the HMO definition—prepayment, group practice, and the organizational responsibility for insuring the availability of health services for the defined service populations.

The prepaid premium covers all benefits outlined in the CHP contract and precludes any additional expense to the subscriber except for items excluded under that contract. By and large, it can be said that all routine medical expenses are covered by the prepayment mechanism, as are most unexpected major medical eventualities—e.g., surgery, hospitalizations, specialty consultations required by CHP physicians, and so forth.

Although CHP has been widely respected in its two years of service to the Rhode Island community, the same problems experienced by other HMOs have also presented themselves in this setting. Group practice remains a fairly new and innovative concept about which some individuals remain skeptical, given long-standing relationships with private physicians. The newness of the organization also presented questions, at first, concerning its stability as compared to older, more established methods of health care delivery and insurance.

CHP started with 1,200 members (subscribers and their families), although the opening enrollment was forecasted to be 6,000. In January 1973, the organization had 12,000 subscribers who had been offered the CHP plan on a dual choice basis through their particular group setting—usually at their place of employment. CHP's marketing team was responsible for tapping the available group resources and arranging for dual choice to be offered to those groups.

Because of insufficient enrollment, CHP found it necessary to secure large loans from the Prudential Insurance Company. The organization was nearing its operational break-even point, which was estimated at 16,000 members. However, at that point CHP will not be retiring its debt, or setting money aside for expansion or replacement of capital equipment.

CHP has also had problems administratively. The fourth director of the organization, Mr. Philip Nelson, was recently brought in by Prudential in an effort to strengthen the organization and insure its success. As CHP enters its third year of operation, Nelson is looking forward to refining the organization's existing services and operations. He hopes to expand the organization to include new markets, additional medical capabilities, and larger, more numerous treatment facilities.

One of Mr. Nelson's first tasks as director was to evaluate the marketing facets of CHP. In order to familiarize himself with the proposed marketing thrust of the organization, Nelson requested a copy of the association's 1973 marketing plan, which had been prepared by Mr. Ralph Wilbur, director of marketing. Prior to receiving the plan, Mr. Nelson was reviewing CHP's past marketing strategies and decisional inputs. He expected that this review would suggest directions for future marketing activities.

Product

A principal marketing advantage of prepaid group practice programs over traditional health insurance is their comprehensive benefit package. In addition, they have the potential to deliver broader benefits for less than the cost of similar benefits under a fee-for-service plan.

In designing an HMO benefit package, a primary consideration is given to mandatory elements, that is, those which are essential to provide flexibility for the medical group treating patients. Any additions to this package must take into account the attractiveness of benefits to potential subscribers, the cost-effectiveness of such benefits, and the nature and price of competitive benefit packages in the community. Although most programs include co-payments and deductibles, CHP has none (except for a house call provision). The CHP benefit package is described in a brochure distributed to prospective members. A copy of part of this brochure is shown in exhibit 1.

Promotion

A substantial part of the work of an HMO is involved with promotion. For example, the community must be educated about prepaid group practice; management and union leadership must be sold on the idea of dual choice for the firm's employees; individuals must be enrolled in the program.

EXHIBIT 1
Medical, Surgical and Hospital Services

IN THE COMMUNITY HEALTH CENTER	Visits to Doctor's office	No Charge
Diagnosis and Treatment—Specialists' Care—Continued Care of Chronic Conditions—	Laboratory Tests—X-ray—Physical Therapy	No Charge
Eye Examinations—	Casts and Dressings	No Charge
Pediatric Checkups for Children—Physical Checkups—No Limit on Number of Visits	Injections—Allergy Injections	No Charge
IN THE HOSPITAL	Services of Physicians and Surgeons and Other Health Personnel—Including Operations.	No Charge
Unlimited Days at No Charge for semi-private care when arranged by CHP physician	Room and Board—General Nursing—Use of Operating Room—Anesthesia.	No Charge
Private Room Fully Paid when medically needed	X-ray and Laboratory Examinations—X-ray Therapy.	No Charge
	Dressings—Casts—Blood Transfusions if Blood is Replaced.	No Charge
AMBULANCE SERVICE		Provided Without Charge if Authorized by CHP Personnel
IN YOUR HOME	House Calls by CHP Physicians	$5 for first visit for each Acute Illness. No charge after first visit for the Same Illness. House Calls will be made at the judgment of a CHP Physician.
MATERNITY CARE	Full Physician's Services Including Pre-Natal Care	No Charge
	Hospital Care—Full Hospital Care is provided to a member after 180 days continuous family membership in CHP—or when continued combined membership in an alternate plan and CHP totals 180 days of family coverage.	No Charge

CASE

The marketing department at CHP consists of four employees. Mr. Wilbur is the director, with previous experience in marketing, but not in the health field. The three other personnel had no previous experience in marketing prior to joining CHP. These four individuals act as marketing representatives for CHP, calling on employees and employers in an effort to sell the concept of prepaid group practice.

Prospective subscribers appear to respond best to three sales themes: (1) comprehensive services are delivered at one place; (2) services are completely prepaid; and (3) very high quality medical care is obtained.

In addition to personal selling efforts, CHP has utilized newspaper advertising twice. Physicians are bound by professional codes of conduct which consider it unethical to directly or indirectly solicit patients. Thus, any promotion must be handled delicately so that no charges of unethical conduct arise. In addition, HMOs have been subjected to charges of socialized medicine and on occasion have suffered from the stigma associated with these charges. For these reasons, prepaid group practice programs generally have been very conservative in advertising and promoting. Some groups do not aggressively seek out new business but rely upon their reputations to attract new group accounts. However, for new prepaid programs in their infancy, there is pressure to meet enrollment quotas and educate the citizenry; thus, promotion is sometimes more aggressive.

In November 1972, CHP ran a newspaper advertisement, the copy of which appears in exhibit 2. As a result, the Rhode Island Medical Society lodged a complaint against CHP over its merchandising tactics.

Pricing

A 1964 study compared out-of-pocket costs in a prepaid group practice with two traditional health insurance plans. It was found that the premium of the prepaid program covered 76 percent of costs of physician services, prescription drugs, and hospitalization while the other programs covered 55 percent and 59 percent of these costs. Thus, price can be a significant marketing advantage in terms of out-of-pocket costs associated with prepaid programs.

Although co-payments are a feature of most prepaid plans, CHP has only one. A reason for the use of co-payments is that they allow prepaid premiums to be set more competitively. Many programs include small charges for office visits ($1 to $3). With such an approach, Nelson believes that CHP could reduce its price below its major competitor, which presently writes about 85 percent of the health insurance in the state.

CHP's primary competitor offers a low-option benefit package which fits the needs of a particular group of employees in the state, namely, low-pay, low-fringe-benefit industries such as jewelry and textiles. The competitor's plan pays only 60 percent of health care expenses but costs substantially less than CHP's only plan, a high option benefit package.

Another variable influenced by competition concerns the number of price steps. The major competitor and CHP both have two price steps—one rate for a single person and another rate for families (regardless of size). However, Mr. Nelson has considered adding another price step, so that the rates would be categorized three ways—for one person, two, and three or more. The result, if implemented, should be to skew CHP's membership more to one- and two-person enrollees since their rates would be lower than at present. However, large families would have a greater incentive to subscribe to the competitor's plan, because their rate would increase with CHP. Although Mr. Nelson was considering such a move, he was unsure what ramifications this might have on employer's acceptance, membership size, CHP's break-even point, or competitive reaction.

Location

CHP is located adjacent to a medium-size hospital in North Providence, one of the most heavily populated areas of the state. It is convenient to the main traffic arteries in the northern part of the state.

Mr. Nelson estimates that CHP will exhaust the capacity of the present facility when it reaches 16,000 enrollees, and thus thought must be given to expanded facilities and their location.

One of the current barriers to greater enrollment is the distance some members may have to travel in order to reach the facility for care. Studies of other HMO programs indicate that distances of ten or more miles from the facility significantly retard membership and utilization of the facility by existing members. However, because CHP presently lacks precise knowledge of the geographic distribution of its membership, Nelson is uncertain of the extent to which this could be a problem at CHP.

If CHP were to open additional locations, there are a number of areas in the state to which it might expand. Exhibit 3 presents a map of the state and population data. Two appealing locations to Nelson are Warwick and South Kingstown. Warwick's population has expanded very rapidly. The city offers a central location in the state and it features the state's two major regional shopping centers. The other area considered would be near the state university, which is located in South Kingstown and has a student and employee population of over 15,000. In fact, preliminary negotiations had been undertaken in the past between CHP and the university concerning the possibility of CHP's assuming a major role in the student health service.

A short time after Nelson had reviewed these aspects of CHP's marketing situation, Mr. Wilbur submitted the proposed marketing plan for 1973. The plan is presented in exhibit 4. Mr. Nelson looked forward to learning from the report what marketing directions were planned for CHP during the coming year.

EXHIBIT 3
Population of Rhode Island Counties, Cities and Towns
(Cities in Capitals)

	Population	
	1960 (Census)	1970 (Census)
BRISTOL COUNTY	37,146	45,937
Barrington	13,826	17,554
Briston	14,570	17,850
Warren	8,750	10,523
KENT COUNTY	112,619	142,382
Coventry	15,432	22,947
East Greenwich	6,100	9,577
WARWICK	68,504	83,694
West Greenwich	1,169	1,841
West Warwick	21,414	24,323
NEWPORT COUNTY	81,405	94,228
Jamestown	2,267	2,911
Little Compton	1,702	2,385
Middletown[1]	12,675	29,621
NEWPORT[1]	47,049	34,231
Portsmouth	8,251	12,521
Tiverton	9,461	12,559
PROVIDENCE COUNTY	568,778	581,470
Burrillville	9,119	10,087
CENTRAL FALLS	19,858	18,716
CRANSTON	66,766	74,287
Cumberland	18,792	26,605
EAST PROVIDENCE	41,955	48,207
Foster	2,097	2,626
Glocester	3,397	5,160
Johnston	17,160	22,037
Lincoln	13,551	16,182
North Providence	18,220	24,337
North Smithfield	7,632	9,349
PAWTUCKET	81,001	76,984
PROVIDENCE	207,498	179,116
Scituate	5,210	7,489
Smithfield	9,442	13,468
WOONSOCKET	47,080	46,820
WASHINGTON COUNTY	59,540	85,706
Charlestown	1,966	2,863
Exeter	2,298	3,245
Hopkinton	4,174	5,392
Narragansett	3,444	7,138
New Shoreham	486	489
North Kingstown[1]	18,977	29,793
Richmond	1,986	2,625
South Kingstown	11,942	16,913
Westerly	14,267	17,248
STATE TOTALS	858,488	949,723

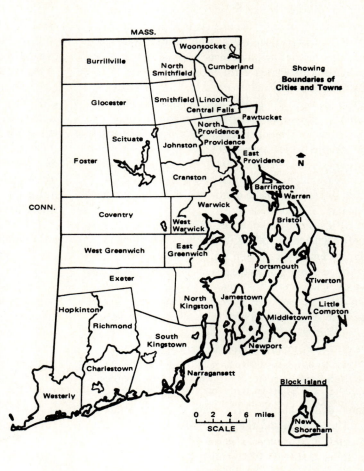

[1]Areas with extensive Navy facilities and housing. In Newport 10,281 shipboard naval personnel were counted in the city in 1960, but none in 1970.

CASE

PREFACE

The following recommended marketing program is based on the premise that the prepaid, group practice health care concept offered by the Rhode Island Community Health Plan is a highly marketable program. This is not to say that it is absolutely perfect and that *no* improvements could be made in the plan. Slight improvements may be made.

We face certain problems . . . some of which come under the category of demographics. Our market is unlimited by age. Every employed individual and adult family member with or without children is a prospective enrollee. However, at our present stage of growth and development, with one Health Care Center located in North Providence, CHP is somewhat limited geographically. While we are located almost in the heart of the Providence metropolitan area and the extension of Route 295 will place us in close proximity to a major expressway, our present facility is still far removed from southern areas of the State, both on the east and west sides of Narragansett Bay. Obviously, the answer is the future establishment of a family health care facility somewhere south of Warwick, which is the fastest growing city in the State. With this as a future goal, we still have the advantage of being located in an area with the greatest mass concentration of population in Rhode Island. Even a modest share of enrollees out of the potential in our present location could flood the CHP Center.

Based on a successful marketing program, the initial CHP planning grant projected an enrollment of 17,500 persons by June 1973, and 20,000 by June 1974. If these enrollments are attained, it leads to immediate consideration of a larger facility in the metropolitan area and/or a second facility in southern Rhode Island, plus expansion of the medical staff. We call your attention to goals and objectives later in this presentation.

A problem we will always face under our present concept is the disruption of previously established doctor-patient relationships. This is a particularly difficult problem with a segment of the female population. We see no simple solution to this problem. The Marketing Department's job will be to "sell" the CHP concept, the high degree of competence, experience and professionalism and on-going availability and accessibility of our staff physicians, as well as the importance of containment of the cost of health care.

In presenting a marketing "game plan," it is necessary to discuss some basic marketing techniques:

1. It is absolutely essential that the general public be totally aware of and familiarized with the existence of the product or service (Community Health Plan). We have made great strides in this direction during the past two months. However, *much* remains to be done. To coin a very hackneyed expression, CHP must become a "household word."

2. After CHP is known to the mass public, we must educate the people to accept the CHP concept of prepaid, group practice health care . . . the total health care . . . the preventive health care available under the plan.

3. Finally, we must break down old associations, market the acceptability of the CHP plan and *MOTIVATE* the individual to enroll. Once he is enrolled, we must provide the highest quality of health care, thereby creating satisfied customers, each of whom in a sense becomes a member of our Marketing Department, spreading the word of his satisfaction and the CHP concept. Once we have acquisition, we must have a very concentrated effort in retention . . . and this objective must permeate the entire CHP staff in their dealings with our membership. This is an extremely important area of the CHP marketing program . . . the constant liaison with the employer contacts and union representatives. It is through them that we gain the entree to the employee groups and the growth of our membership. This requires constant telephone and personal contact, *especially personal contact,* with visual presentations and/or visits to the CHP Family Health Care Center. Through good advertising and public relations, we hope to gain total public awareness of the CHP plan and the entree to management and unions.

How do we accomplish these objectives? Without high public mass media exposure, success will be slow in coming. It is essential that we establish a firm advertising and public relations budget. This can be formulated by setting an enrollment goal and a cost of acquisition of each individual enrollee. During the Blue Cross–Blue Shield Open Enrollment period in

(Continued)

EXHIBIT 4 (Continued)

October 1972, we have learned that their cost of acquisition was $5.00 per enrollee. (Blue Cross–Blue Shield spends in excess of $250,000 per year in advertising and public relations. They spent $40,000 during the open enrollment period to attract about 8,000 new members [total individuals].) Figuring our cost of acquisition at $2.50 and now projecting a total membership of *25,000* by December 31, 1973, or an increase of approximately 1,000 per month, we arrive at an advertising and public relations budget of $30,000 for 1973. We propose to spend this money in the following manner:

Advertising and Public Relations Budget

1. Outdoor Advertising.... A "roving," painted, high-quality 14 × 48-foot billboard. Such an illuminated billboard would be moved and the copy changed every two months, with the board facing north on Route 95 in the downtown Providence area, south on the expressway, at the intersection of Route 146 and other choice locations. It is estimated (in fact guaranteed) that such a board delivers 18,250,000 impressions a year.

   TOTAL COST including production for year $7,800.00

2. *Providence Sunday Journal,* Business and Industry Section...600-line ad once a month for 12 months. Directed toward employers and unions. Total estimated impressions...4,800,000 a year.

   TOTAL COST including production for year $5,400.00

3. Balance of advertising would be spread over television, radio, and other daily and weekly newspapers at selected times during the year. (Heavy concentration during November as they are Federal and State Re-opening Enrollment Periods, etc.).

   TOTAL COST including production for year $10,000.00

4. Public Relations Budget for year . . . . $ 2,000.00

5. Printing (new brochure, newsletter, 'including photography,' etc.) . . . . $ 4,400.00

6. Mimeograph machine (used) . . . . $ 400.00

   TOTAL 1973 Advertising and Public Relations Budget $30,000.00

Other Activities

1. It is the Marketing Department's opinion that a new CHP general purpose brochure is needed. Generally, the brochure should be more colorful, with more graphic art work to attract the eye and the reader's attention. We are securing estimates of the cost of printing.

2. Also underway is the preparation of a CHP Newsletter to be mailed to the entire membership three or four times a year. This can be an invaluable tool in the education and retention of our membership.

3. What can we get free? In the months of November and December, 1972, CHP was highly successful in gaining a large amount of free public service and news coverage in all the media. This increased our public image and visibility enormously. Because we are a nonprofit organization, we are in a better position to secure such coverage than a commercial, profit-making organization. Every effort will be made to secure free public exposure in all the mass media.

System for Follow-up of New and Old Marketing Group Leads

In order to guard against the possibility that any Marketing Representative might neglect the proper follow-up with a particular group at a future date, each representative should maintain a "tickler file" divided by months. At our weekly Marketing meeting, we shall continue to discuss the prospective groups with which each representative is in contact so that there is no unnecessary duplication. I do not feel it would be advantageous to establish any geographical territories to be assigned to our representatives since all of us have hundreds of contacts all over the state and established entrees with business and industry. However, we should all be aware of each other's activities in order to preclude the possibility that two of us would be pounding on different doors in the same plant at the same time.

OUR GOAL:

25,000 MEMBERS BY DECEMBER 31, 1973

Marketing Planning

Planning forces the marketing executive to think about the future, thereby helping to ensure that changing market conditions are dealt with. Formal planning leads to more disciplined thinking within the firm, better coordination of company-wide effort, increased interdepartmental communication, clearer understanding of goals and objectives, and improved monitoring procedures.

An organization's long-term survival and prosperity depend on its ability to determine where it is now, where it wants to go, and how it is going to get there. This is the essence of marketing planning. The process requires analysis of existing market characteristics and marketing programs, decisions on the direction of future marketing efforts, and formulation of marketing strategies with appropriate monitoring procedures.

BASIC ELEMENTS OF A MARKETING PLAN

Companies which routinely prepare some kind of formal marketing plans and put them in writing typically incorporate the following features in their plans:[1]

1. Situation analysis
   a. Product sales
   b. Market situation and competitive environment
   c. Problems and opportunities
   d. Planning assumptions and constraints
2. Forecasts
3. Objectives and strategies
   a. Mission
   b. Objectives
   c. Strategies
4. Action programs
5. Monitoring procedures

The *situation analysis* consists of a review of the current market status and outlook for the products covered by the plan. This review usually focuses on the company's existing product offerings, including such factors as trends in sales and profitability, advertising and other promotional support, competitive position, major market strengths and weaknesses, and threats and opportunities facing the product mix.

Much of the internal data gathered focuses on *product sales:* total sales, bookings, marketing expenses, and profit measures. Sales figures may be broken down by factors such as product type, sales and distribution features, market segments served, and profiles of major customers.

Common kinds of vital information about the *market situation* and *competitive environment* sought by many marketing planners include: size of the market, dynamics of

[1]See David S. Hopkins, *The Marketing Plan* (New York: The Conference Board, Inc., 1981), pp. 16–29.

the market environment (changes in market demand, shifts in customer tastes and preferences, changes in customer purchasing behavior, pricing trends, and so on, market share for the company and its major competitors, strengths and weaknesses of each competitor, technological developments, and pending governmental regulations.

Prospective *problems and opportunities* are identified after the market information has been obtained and analyzed. Alternative ways to deal with the problems and opportunities are then considered.

Planning assumptions and constraints are often noted throughout or in a separate section of the marketing plan. Since every marketing plan is based on various assumptions, companies may emphasize the internal and external assumptions that are considered to have the greatest impact on the viability of the plan.

Forecasts of total demand and expected sales for the company's product offerings are essential components of every marketing plan. Even though there are numerous difficulties involved in making accurate forecasts, the forecasts are essential because many company decisions, such as those concerning production, marketing, finance, and personnel, hinge on these estimates.

The establishment of marketing *objectives* and determination of marketing *strategies* for a specific time frame is a focal point of the marketing plan. Before determining objectives, a number of companies require that planners first define the *mission* of the firm. The fundamental question that should be answered is: "What is our business?" The answer to this question provides management with a sense of direction and growth for its products and markets. As Levitt emphasized in the article, "Marketing Myopia" (see Section One), the definition of a business should be stated in terms of a customer-satisfying process, rather than a goods-producing process.

Marketing *objectives* are an essential part of any marketing plan because a plan must have direction. Unless objectives are realistically obtainable, stated in quantifiable terms, and the eventual results measurable, planning would have little practical purpose.

Sales-volume objectives are found in almost all product marketing plans. In addition to statements of objectives pertaining to sales volume, specific objectives relating to profit margins, sales effort, new-product development, pricing, sales promotion, advertising expenditures, and marketing research are often stated in a marketing plan.

The marketing *strategies* describe how the objectives will be achieved. Formulating strategies requires the development of an appropriate marketing mix for each market segment served.

The *action program* spells out the actual steps involved in implementing the marketing strategy. This component of the marketing plan assigns responsibility for each strategy element and establishes schedules for completing marketing activities.

Monitoring procedures spell out the specific methods to be used in reviewing the marketing plan's progress throughout the planning period. They provide a means of assessing whether the objectives and/or strategies need to be altered or whether a different action program is called for.

MARKETING STRATEGIES

Developing a marketing strategy requires selection of target markets and formulation of appropriate marketing mix guidelines. The target market is a specific group of customers toward which the marketing strategy is directed. (Selection of target markets and the process of market segmentation are addressed in Section Three.)

The marketing mix consists of controllable marketing components used to satisfy the target market. These components are commonly classified into four categories: product, price, distribution or place, and promotion. The mnemonic "4 Ps" is often used to refer to these elements, which are explored in detail in Section Four through Section Eight.

A list of elements of the marketing mix covers the principal areas of marketing activities which call for management decisions. In the article, "The Concept of the Marketing

Mix," Neil H. Borden indicates that the concept of the "mix" delineates the areas in which facts should be assembled. These facts should serve as a guide to management in developing an appropriate marketing mix for a target market.

PRODUCT PORTFOLIO ANALYSIS

The determination of marketing objectives and strategies is subject to the guidelines of overall corporate strategies. At the corporate level, management makes long-range strategic plans designed to develop and maintain a viable fit between corporate strengths and market opportunities.

Through the use of product portfolio analysis, management can decide how best to allocate resources among all of its products—that is, it can determine which individual product or product lines to build (increase market share), hold (maintain market share), phase down, or phase out. The application of product portfolio analysis across all products marketed by the firm helps ensure that no single marketing plan will be based solely on the merits of an individual item considered in isolation from others.

A product portfolio analysis suggests specific marketing strategies to achieve a balanced mix of products for maximum long-run gains. It is a useful tool to demonstrate that the strategic issues facing the firm justify a considerable amount of centralized control over the planning and resource allocation process.

In the article, "Diagnosing the Product Portfolio," George S. Day shows how the product portfolio concept provides a useful synthesis of the analyses and judgments during the initial steps of the planning process, and how it is a provocative source of strategy alternatives. Inappropriate and misleading applications will result, however, when the basic assumptions are violated, the measurements are wrong, or the strategies are not feasible.

In Derek F. Abell's article, "Strategic Windows," the author notes that strategic market planning involves the dual tasks of anticipating and responding to changes which affect the marketplace for a firm's products. The "strategic window" concept focuses attention on the fact that there are only limited periods during which the "fit" between the key requirements of a market and the particular competencies of a firm competing in that market is at an optimum.

Abell cautions users of the product portfolio chart analysis to consider the dynamic as opposed to the static implications in designating a particular business. He emphasizes that marketing planning should be based upon predictions of future patterns of market evolution.

Neil H. Borden

The Concept of the Marketing Mix

I have always found it interesting to observe how an apt or colorful term may catch on, gain wide usage, and help to further understanding of a concept that has already been expressed in less appealing and communicative terms. Such has been true of the phrase "marketing mix," which I began to use in my teaching and writing some 15 years ago. In a relatively short time it has come to have wide usage. This note tells of the evolution of the marketing mix concept.

The phrase was suggested to me by a paragraph in a research bulletin on the management of marketing costs, written by my associate, Professor James Culliton (1948). In this study of manufacturers' marketing costs he described the business executive as a

"decider," an "artist"—a "mixer of ingredients," who sometimes follows a recipe prepared by others, sometimes prepares his own recipe as he goes along, sometimes adapts a recipe to the ingredients immediately available, and sometimes experiments with or invents ingredients no one else has tried.

I liked his idea of calling a marketing executive a "mixer of ingredients," one who is constantly engaged in fashioning creatively a mix of marketing procedures and policies in his efforts to produce a profitable enterprise.

For many years previous to Culliton's cost study, the wide variations in the procedures and policies employed by managements of manufacturing firms in their marketing programs and the correspondingly wide variation in the costs of these marketing functions, which Culliton aptly ascribed to the varied "mixing of ingredients," had become increasingly evident as we had gathered marketing cases at the Harvard Business School. The marked differences in

Source: Reprinted from the *Journal of Advertising Research*, Vol. 4, No. 2, pp. 2–7. Copyright © 1964 by the Advertising Research Foundation. Used by permission.

the patterns or formulae of the marketing programs not only were evident through facts disclosed in case histories, but also were reflected clearly in the figures of a cost study of food manufacturers made by the Harvard Bureau of Business Research in 1929. The primary objective of this study was to determine common figures of expenses for various marketing functions among food manufacturing companies, similar to the common cost figures which had been determined in previous years for various kinds of retail and wholesale businesses. In this manufacturer's study we were unable, however, with the data gathered to determine common expense figures that had much significance as standards by which to guide management, such as had been possible in the studies of retail and wholesale trades, where the methods of operation tended toward uniformity. Instead, among food manufacturers the ratios of sales devoted to the various functions of marketing such as advertising, personal selling, packaging, and so on, were found to be widely divergent, no matter how we grouped our respondents. Each respondent gave data that tended to uniqueness.

Culliton's study of marketing costs in 1947–48 was a second effort to find out, among other objectives, whether a bigger sample and a more careful classification of companies would produce evidence of operating uniformities that would give helpful common expense figures. But the result was the same as in our early study: there was wide diversity in cost ratios among any classifications of firms which were set up, and no common figures were found that had much value. This was true whether companies were grouped according to similarity in product lines, amount of sales, territorial extent of operations, or other bases of classification.

Relatively early in my study of advertising, it had become evident that understanding of advertising usage by manufacturers in any case had to come from an analysis of advertising's place as one element in the total marketing program of the firm. I came to realize that it is essential always to ask: what overall marketing strategy has been or might be employed to bring about a profitable operation in light of the circumstances faced by the management? What combination of marketing procedures and policies has been or might be adopted to bring about desired behavior of trade and consumers at costs that will permit a profit? Specifically, how can advertising, personal selling, pricing, packaging, channels, warehousing, and the other elements of a marketing program be manipulated and fitted together in a way that will give a profitable operation? In short, I saw that every advertising management case called for a consideration of the strategy to be adopted for the total marketing program, with advertising recognized as only one element whose form and extent depended on its careful adjustment to the other parts of the program.

The soundness of this viewpoint was supported by case histories throughout my volume, *The Economic Effects of Advertising* (Borden, 1942). In the chapters devoted to the utilization of advertising by business, I had pointed out the innumerable combinations of marketing methods and policies that might be adopted by a manager in arriving at a marketing plan. For instance, in the area of branding, he might elect to adopt an individualized brand or a family brand. Or he might decide to sell his product unbranded or under private label. Any decision in the area of brand policy in turn has immediate implications that bear on his selection of channels of distribution, sales force methods, packaging, promotional procedure, and advertising. Throughout the volume the case materials cited show that the way in which any marketing function is designed and the burden placed upon the function are determined largely by the overall marketing strategy adopted by managements to meet the market conditions under which they operate. The forces met by different firms vary widely. Accordingly, the programs fashioned differ widely.

Regarding advertising, which was the function under focus in the economic effects volume, I said at one point:

> In all the above illustrative situations it should be recognized that advertising is not an operating method to be considered as something apart, as something whose profit value is to be judged alone. An able management does not ask, "Shall we use or not use advertising," without consideration of the product and of other management procedures to be employed. Rather the question is always one of finding a management formula giving advertising its due place in the combination of manufacturing methods, product form, pricing, promotion and selling methods, and distribution methods. As previously pointed out, different formulae, i.e., different combinations of methods, may be profitably employed by competing manufacturers.

From the above it can be seen why Culliton's description of a marketing manager as a "mixer of ingredients" immediately appealed to me as an apt and easily understandable phrase, far better than my previous references to the marketing man as an empiricist seeking in any situation to devise a profitable "pattern" or "formula" of marketing operations from among the many procedures and policies that were open to him. If he was a "mixer of ingredients," what he designed was a "marketing mix."

It was logical to proceed from a realization of the existence of a variety of "marketing mixes" to the development of a concept that would comprehend not only this variety, but also the market forces that cause managements to produce a variety of mixes. It is the problems raised by these forces that lead marketing managers to exercise their wits in devising mixes or programs which they hope will give a profitable business operation.

To portray this broadened concept in a visual presentation requires merely:

1. a list of the important elements or ingredients that make up marketing programs:
2. a list of the forces that bear on the marketing operation of a firm and to which the marketing manager must adjust in his search for a mix or program that can be successful.

The list of elements of the marketing mix in such a visual presentation can be long or short, depending on how far one wishes to go in his classification and subclassification of the marketing procedures and policies with which marketing managements deal when devising marketing programs. The list of elements which I have employed in my teaching and consulting work covers the principal areas of marketing activities which call for management decisions as revealed by case histories. I realize others might build a different list. Mine is as follows:

Elements of the Marketing Mix of Manufacturers

1. *Product Planning*—policies and procedures relating to:
   a. Product lines to be offered—qualities, design, etc.
   b. Markets to sell: whom, where, when, and in what quantity.
   c. New product policy—research and development program.
2. *Pricing*—policies and procedures relating to:
   a. Price level to adopt.
   b. Specific prices to adopt (odd-even, etc.).
   c. Price policy, e.g., one-price or varying price, price maintenance, use of list prices, etc.
   d. Margins to adopt—for company; for the trade.
3. *Branding*—policies and procedures relating to:
   a. Selection of trade marks.
   b. Brand policy—individualized or family brand.
   c. Sale under private label or unbranded.
4. *Channels of Distribution*—policies and procedures relating to:

a. Channels to use between plant and consumer.
b. Degree of selectivity among wholesalers and retailers.
c. Efforts to gain cooperation of the trade.
5. *Personal Selling*—policies and procedures relating to:
  a. Burden to be placed on personal selling and the methods to be employed in:
    1. Manufacturer's organization.
    2. Wholesale segment of the trade.
    3. Retail segment of the trade.
6. *Advertising*—policies and procedures relating to:
  a. Amount to spend—i.e., the burden to be placed on advertising.
  b. Copy platform to adopt:
    1. Product image desired.
    2. Corporate image desired.
  c. Mix of advertising: to the trade; through the trade; to consumers.
7. *Promotions*—policies and procedures relating to:
  a. Burden to place on special selling plans or devices directed at or through the trade.
  b. Form of these devices for consumer promotions, for trade promotions.
8. *Packaging*—policies and procedures relating to:
  a. Formulation of package and label.
9. *Display*—policies and procedures relating to:
  a. Burden to be put on display to help effect sale.
  b. Methods to adopt to secure display.
10. *Servicing*—policies and procedures relating to:
  a. Providing service needed.
11. *Physical Handling*—policies and procedures relating to:
  a. Warehousing.
  b. Transportation.
  c. Inventories.
12. *Fact Finding and Analysis*—policies and procedures relating to:
  a. Securing, analysis, and use of facts in marketing operations.

Also if one were to make a list of all the forces which managements weigh at one time or another when formulating their marketing mixes, it would be very long indeed, for the behavior of individuals and groups in all spheres of life have a bearing, first, on what goods and services are produced and consumed, and, second, on the procedures that may be employed in bringing about exchange of these goods and services. However, the important forces which bear on marketers, all arising from the behavior of individuals or groups, may readily be listed under four heads, namely the behavior of consumers, the trade, competitors, and government.

The outline below contains these four behavioral forces with notations of some of the important behavioral determinants within each force. These must be studied and understood by the marketer, if his marketing mix is to be successful. The great quest of marketing management is to understand the behavior of humans in response to the stimuli to which they are subjected. The skillful marketer is one who is a perceptive and practical psychologist and sociologist, who has keen insight into individual and group behavior, who can foresee changes in behavior that develop in a dynamic world, who has creative ability for building well-knit programs because he has the capacity to visualize the probable response of consumers, trade, and competitors to his moves. His skill in forecasting response to his marketing moves should well be supplemented by a further skill in devising and using tests and measurements to check consumer or trade response to his program or parts thereof, for no marketer has so much prescience that he can proceed without empirical check.

Below, then, is the suggested outline of forces which govern the mixing of marketing elements. This list and that of the elements taken together provide a visual presentation of the concept of the marketing mix.

Market Forces Bearing on the Marketing Mix

1. *Consumers' Buying Behavior,* as determined by their:
  a. Motivation in purchasing.
  b. Buying habits.
  c. Living habits.
  d. Environment (present and future, as revealed by trends, for environment influences consumers' attitudes toward products and their use of them).
  e. Buying power.
  f. Number (i.e., how many).
2. *The Trade's Behavior*—wholesalers' and retailers' behavior, as influenced by:
  a. Their motivations.
  b. Their structure, practices, and attitudes.
  c. Trends in structure and procedures that portend change.
3. *Competitors' Position and Behavior,* as influenced by:
  a. Industry structure and the firm's relation thereto.
    1. Size and strength of competitors.
    2. Number of competitors and degree of industry concentration.
    3. Indirect competition—i.e., from other products.

b. Relation of supply to demand—oversupply or undersupply.

c. Product choices offered consumers by the industry—i.e., quality, price, service.

d. Degree to which competitors compete on price vs. nonprice bases.

e. Competitors' motivations and attitudes—their likely response to the actions of other firms.

f. Trends technological and social, portending change in supply and demand.

4. *Governmental Behavior—Controls over Marketing:*

a. Regulations over products.

b. Regulations over pricing.

c. Regulations over competitive practices.

d. Regulations over advertising and promotion.

When building a marketing program to fit the needs of his firm, the marketing manager has to weigh the behavioral forces and then juggle marketing elements in his mix with a keen eye on the resources with which he has to work. His firm is but one small organism in a large universe of complex forces. His firm is only a part of an industry that is competing with many other industries. What does the firm have in terms of money, product line, organization, and reputation with which to work. The manager must devise a mix of procedures that fit these resources. If his firm is small, he must judge the response of consumers, trade, and competition in light of his position and resources and the influence that he can exert in the market. He must look for special opportunities in product or method of operation. The small firm cannot employ the procedures of the big firm. Though he may sell the same kind of product as the big firm, his marketing strategy is likely to be widely different in many respects. Innumerable instances of this fact might be cited. For example, in the industrial goods field, small firms often seek to build sales on a limited and highly specialized line, whereas industry leaders seek patronage for full lines. Small firms often elect to go in for regional sales rather than attempt the national distribution practiced by larger companies. Again, the company of limited resources often elects to limit its production and sales to products whose potential is too small to attract the big fellows. Still again, companies with small resources in the cosmetic field not infrequently have set up introductory marketing programs employing aggressive personal selling and a "push" strategy with distribution limited to leading department stores. Their initially small advertising funds have been directed through these selected retail outlets, with the offering of the products and their story told over the signatures of the stores. The strategy has been to borrow kudos for their products from the leading stores' reputations and to gain a gradual radiation of distribution to smaller stores in all types of channels, such as often comes from the trade's follow-the-leader behavior. Only after resources have grown from mounting sales has a dense retail distribution been aggressively sought and a shift made to place the selling burden more and more on company-signed advertising.

The above strategy was employed for Toni products and Stoppette deodorant in their early marketing stages when the resources of their producers were limited (cf. case of Jules Montenier, Inc. in Borden and Marshall, 1959, pp. 498–518). In contrast, cosmetic manufacturers with large resources have generally followed a "pull" strategy for the introduction of new products, relying on heavy campaigns of advertising in a rapid succession of area introductions to induce a hoped-for, complete retail coverage from the start (cf. case of Bristol-Myers Company in Borden and Marshall, 1959, pp. 519–533). These introductory campaigns have been undertaken only after careful programs of product development and test marketing have given assurance that product and selling plans had high promise of success.

Many additional instances of the varying strategy employed by small versus large enterprises might be cited. But those given serve to illustrate the point that managements must fashion their mixes to fit their resources. Their objectives must be realistic.

Long vs. Short Term Aspects of Marketing Mix

The marketing mix of a firm in large part is the product of the evolution that comes from day-to-day marketing. At any time the mix represents the program that a management has evolved to meet the problems with which it is constantly faced in an ever changing, ever challenging market. There are continuous tactical maneuvers: a new product, aggressive promotion, or price change initiated by a competitor must be considered and met; the failure of the trade to provide adequate market coverage or display must be remedied; a faltering sales force must be reorganized and stimulated; a decline in sales share must be diagnosed and remedied; an advertising approach that has lost effectiveness must be replaced; a general business decline must be countered. All such problems call for a management's maintaining effective channels of information relative to its own operations and to the day-to-day behavior of consumers, competitors, and the trade. Thus, we may observe that short range forces play a large part in the fashioning of the mix to be used at any time and in determining the allocation of expenditures among the various functional accounts of the operating statement.

But the overall strategy employed in a marketing mix is the product of longer range plans and procedures dictated in part by past empiricism and in part, if the management is a good one, by management foresight as to what needs to be done to keep the firm successful in a changing world. As the world has become more and more dynamic, blessed is that corporation which has managers who have foresight, who can study trends of all kinds—natural, economic, social, and technological—and, guided by these, devise long-range plans that give promise of keeping their corporations afloat and successful in the turbulent sea of market change. Accordingly, when we think of the marketing mix, we need to give particular heed today to devising a mix based on long-range planning that promises to fit the world of five or ten or more years hence. Provision for effective long-range planning in corporate organization and procedure has become more and more recognized as the earmark of good management in a world that has become increasingly subject to rapid change.

To cite an instance among American marketing organizations which has shown foresight in adjusting the marketing mix to meet social and economic change, I look upon Sears Roebuck and Company as an outstanding example. After building an unusually successful mail order business to meet the needs of a rural America, Sears management foresaw the need to depart from its marketing pattern as a mail order company catering primarily to farmers. The trend from a rural to an urban United States was going on apace. The automobile and good roads promised to make town and city stores increasingly available to those who continued to be farmers. Relatively early, Sears launched a chain of stores across the land, each easily accessible by highway to both farmer and city resident, and with adequate parking space for customers. In time there followed the remarkable telephone and mail order plan directed at urban residents to make buying easy for Americans when congested city streets and highways made shopping increasingly distasteful. Similarly, in the areas of planning products which would meet the desires of consumers in a fast changing world, of shaping its servicing to meet the needs of a wide variety of mechanical products, of pricing procedures to meet the challenging competition that came with the advent of discount retailers, the Sears organization has shown a foresight, adaptability, and creative ability worthy of emulation. The amazing growth and profitability of the company attest to the foresight and skill of its management. Its history shows the wisdom of careful attention to market forces and their impending change in devising marketing mixes that may assure growth.

Use of the Marketing Mix Concept

Like many concepts, the marketing mix concept seems relatively simple, once it has been expressed. I know that before they were ever tagged with the nomenclature of "concept," the ideas involved were widely understood among marketers as a result of the growing knowledge about marketing and marketing procedures that came during the preceding half century. But I have found for myself that once the ideas were reduced to a formal statement with an accompanying visual presentation, the concept of the mix has proved a helpful device in teaching, in business problem solving, and, generally, as an aid to thinking about marketing. First of all, it is helpful in giving an answer to the question often raised as to "what is marketing?" A chart which shows the elements of the mix and the forces that bear on the mix helps to bring understanding of what marketing is. It helps to explain why in our dynamic world the thinking of management in all its functional areas must be oriented to the market.

In recent years I have kept an abbreviated chart showing the elements and the forces of the marketing mix in front of my classes at all times. In case discussion it has proved a handy device by which to raise queries as to whether the student has recognized the implications of any recommendation he might have made in the areas of the several elements of the mix. Or, referring to the forces, we can question whether all the pertinent market forces have been given due consideration. Continual reference to the mix chart leads me to feel that the students' understanding of "what marketing is" is strengthened. The constant presence and use of the chart leaves a deeper understanding that marketing is the devising of programs that successfully meet the forces of the market.

In problem solving the marketing mix chart is a constant reminder of:

1. The fact that a problem seemingly lying in one segment of the mix must be deliberated with constant thought regarding the effect of any change in that sector on the other areas of marketing operations. The necessity of integration in marketing thinking is ever present.
2. The need of careful study of the market forces as they might bear on problems in hand.

In short, the mix chart provides an ever ready checklist as to areas into which to guide thinking when considering marketing questions or dealing with marketing problems.

Marketing: Science or Art?

The quest for a "science of marketing" is hard upon us. If science is in part a systematic formulation and arrangement of facts in a way to help understanding, then the concept of the marketing mix may possibly be considered a small contribution in the search for a science of marketing. If we think of a marketing science as involving the observation and classification of facts and the establishment of verifiable laws that can be used by the marketer as a guide to action with assurance that predicted results will ensue, then we cannot be said to have gotten far toward establishing a science. The concept of the mix lays out the areas in which facts should be assembled, these to serve as a guide to management judgment in building marketing mixes. In the last few decades American marketers have made substantial progress in adopting the scientific method in assembling facts. They have sharpened the tools of fact finding—both those arising within the business and those external to it. Aided by these facts and by the skills developed through careful observation and experience, marketers are better fitted to practice the art of designing marketing mixes than would be the case had not the techniques of gathering facts been advanced as they have been in recent decades. Moreover, marketers have made progress in the use of the scientific method in designing tests whereby the results from mixes or parts of mixes can be measured. Thereby marketers have been learning how to subject the hypotheses of their mix artists to empirical check.

With continued improvement in the search for and the recording of facts pertinent to marketing, with further application of the controlled experiment, and with an extension and careful recording of case histories, we may hope for a gradual formulation of clearly defined and helpful marketing laws. Unitl then, and even then, marketing and the building of marketing mixes will largely lie in the realm of art.

BIBLIOGRAPHY

Borden, Neil H. *The Economic Effects of Advertising*. Homewood, Ill.: Richard D. Irwin, 1942.

Borden, Neil H., and M. V. Marshall. *Advertising Management: Text and Cases*. Homewood, Ill.: Richard D. Irwin, 1959.

Culliton, James W. *The Management of Marketing Costs*. Boston: Division of Research. Graduate School of Business Administration, Harvard University, 1948.

George S. Day

Diagnosing the Product Portfolio

The product portfolio approach to marketing strategy formulation has gained wide acceptance among managers of diversified companies. They are first attracted by the intuitively appealing concept that long-run corporate performance is more than the sum of the contributions of individual profit centers or product strategies. Secondly a product portfolio analysis suggests specific marketing strategies to achieve a balanced mix of products that will produce the maximum long-run effects from scarce cash and managerial resources. Lastly the concept employs a simple matrix

Source: From the *Journal of Marketing*, Vol. 41, No. 2 (April 1977), pp. 35–38. Reprinted by permission of the American Marketing Association.

representation which is easy to communicate and comprehend. Thus it is a useful tool in a headquarters campaign to demonstrate that the strategic issues facing the firm justify more centralized control over the planning and resource allocation process.

With the growing acceptance of the basic approach has come an increasing sensitivity to the limitations of the present methods of portraying the product portfolio, and a recognition that the approach is not equally useful in all corporate circumstances. Indeed, the implications can sometimes be grossly misleading. Inappropriate and misleading applications will result when:

- The basic assumptions (especially those concerned with the value of market share dominance and the product life cycle) are violated.
- The measurements are wrong, or
- The strategies are not feasible.

This article identifies the critical assumptions and the measurement and application issues that may distort the strategic insights. A series of questions are posed that will aid planners and decision-makers to better understand this aid to strategic thinking, and thereby make better decisions.

WHAT IS THE PRODUCT PORTFOLIO?

Common to all portrayals of the product portfolio is the recognition that the competitive value of market share depends on the structure of competition and the stage of the product life cycle. Two examples of this approach have recently appeared in this journal.[1] However, the earliest, and most widely implemented is the cash quadrant or share/growth matrix developed by the Boston Consulting Group.[2] Each product is classified jointly by rate of present or forecast *market growth* (a proxy for stage in the product life cycle) and a measure of *market share dominance*.

The arguments for the use of market share are familiar and well documented.[3] Their basis is the cumulation of evidence that market share is strongly and positively correlated with product profitability. This theme is varied somewhat in the BCG approach by the emphasis on relative share—measured by the ratio of the company's share of the market to the share of the largest competitor. This is reasonable since the strategic implications of a 20% share are quite different if the largest competitor's is 40% or if it is 5%. Profitability will also vary, since according to the experience curve concept the largest competitor will be the most profitable at the prevailing price level.[4]

The product life cycle is employed because it highlights the desirability of a variety of products or services with different present and prospective growth rates. More important, the concept has some direct implications for the cost of gaining and/or holding market share:

- During the rapid growth stage, purchase patterns and distribution channels are fluid. Market shares can be increased at "relatively" low cost by capturing a disproportionate share of incremental sales (especially where these sales come from new users of applications rather than heavier usage by existing users).
- By contrast, the key-note during the maturity stage swings to stability and inertia in distribution and purchasing relationships. A substantial growth in share by one competitor will come at the expense of another competitor's capacity utilization, and will be resisted vigorously. As a result, gains in share are both time-consuming and costly (unless accompanied by a breakthrough in product value or performance that cannot be easily matched by competition).

PRODUCT PORTFOLIO STRATEGIES

When the share and growth rate of each of the products sold by a firm are jointly considered, a new basis for strategy evaluation emerges. While there are many possible combinations, an arbitrary classification of products into four share/growth categories (as shown in figure 1) is sufficient to illustrate the strategy implications.

Low Growth/Dominant Share (Cash Cows)

These profitable products usually generate more cash than is required to maintain share. All strategies should be directed toward maintaining market dominance—including investments in technological leadership. Pricing decisions should be made cautiously with an eye to maintaining price leadership. Pressure to over-invest through product proliferation and market expansion should be resisted unless prospects for expanding primary demand are unusually attractive. Instead, excess cash should be used to support research activities and growth areas elsewhere in the company.

High Growth/Dominant Share (Stars)

Products that are market leaders, but also growing fast, will have substantial reported profits but need a lot of cash to finance the rate of growth. The appropriate strategies are designed primarily to protect the existing share level by reinvesting earnings in the form of price reductions, product improvement, better market coverage, production efficiency increases, etc. Particular attention must be given to obtaining a large share of the new users or new applications that are the source of growth in the market.

Low Growth/Subordinate Share (Dogs)

Since there usually can be only one market leader and because most markets are mature, the greatest number of products fall in this category. Such products are usually at a cost disadvantage and have few opportunities for growth at a reasonable cost. Their markets are not growing, so there is little new business to compete for, and market share gains will be resisted strenuously by the dominant competition.

The slower the growth (present or prospective) and the smaller the relative share, the greater the need for positive action. The possibilities include:

1. Focusing on a specialized segment of the market that can be dominated, and protected from competitive inroads.
2. Harvesting, which is a conscious cutback of all support costs to some minimum level which will maxi-

mize the cash flow over a foreseeable lifetime—which is usually short.

3. Divestment, usually involving a sale as a going concern.
4. Abandonment or deletion from the product line.

High Growth/Subordinate Share
(Problem Children)

The combination of rapid growth and poor profit margins creates an enormous demand for cash. If the cash is not forthcoming, the product will become a "Dog" as growth inevitably slows. The basic strategy options are fairly clear-cut; either invest heavily to get a disproportionate share of the new sales or buy existing shares by acquiring competitors and thus move the product toward the "Star" category or get out of the business using some of the methods just described.

Consideration also should be given to a market segmentation strategy, but only if a defensible niche can be identified and resources are available to gain dominance. This strategy is even more attractive if the segment can provide an entrée and experience base from which to push for dominance of the whole market.

OVERALL STRATEGY

The long-run health of the corporation depends on having some products that *generate* cash (and provide acceptable reported profits), and others that *use* cash to support growth. Among the indicators of overall health are the size and vulnerability of the "Cash Cows" (and the prospects for the "Stars," if any), and the number of "Problem Children" and "Dogs." Particular attention must be paid to those products with large cash appetites. Unless the company has abundant cash flow, it cannot afford to sponsor many such products at one time. If resources (including debt capacity) are spread too thin, the company simply will wind up with too many marginal products and suffer a reduced capacity to finance promising new product entries or acquisitions in the future.

The share/growth matrix displayed in figure 2 shows how one company (actually a composite of a number of situations) might follow the strategic implications of the product portfolio to achieve a better balance of sources and uses of cash. The *present* position of each product is defined by the relative share and market growth rate during a representative time *period*. Since business results normally fluctuate, it is important to use a time period that is not distorted by rare events. The *future* position may be either (a) a momentum forecast of the results of continuing the

present strategy, or (b) a forecast of the consequences of a change in strategy. It is desirable to do both, and compare the results. The specific display of figure 2 is a summary of the following strategic decisions.

- Aggressively support the newly introduced product A, to ensure dominance (but anticipate share declines due to new competitive entries).
- Continue present strategies of products B and C to ensure maintenance of market share.
- Gain share of market for product D by investing in acquisitions.
- Narrow and modify the range of models of product E to focus on one segment.
- Divest products F and G.

PITFALLS IN THE ASSUMPTIONS

The starting point in the decision to follow the implications of a product portfolio analysis is to ask whether the underlying assumptions make sense. The most fundamental assumptions relate to the role of market share in the businesses being portrayed in the portfolio. Even if the answers here are affirmative one may choose to not follow the implications if other objectives than balancing cash flows take priority, or there are barriers to implementing the indicated strategies.

What Is the Role of Market Share?

All the competitors are assumed to have the same overhead structures and experience curves, with their position on the experience curve corresponding to their market share position. Hence market share dominance is a proxy for the *relative* profit performance (e.g., GM vs. Chrysler). Other factors beyond market share may be influential in dictating *absolute, profit performance (e.g., calculators versus cosmetics).*

The influence of market share is most apparent with high value-added products, where there are significant barriers to entry and the competition consists of a few, large, diversified corporations with the attendant large overheads (e.g., plastics, major appliances, automobiles, and semi-conductors). But even in these industrial environments there are distortions under conditions such as:

- One competitor has a significant technological advantage which can be protected and used to establish a steeper cost reduction/experience curve.
- The principal component of the product is produced by a supplier who has an inherent cost advantage because of an integrated process. Thus

FIGURE 1
The Cash Quadrant Approach to Describing the Product Portfolio*

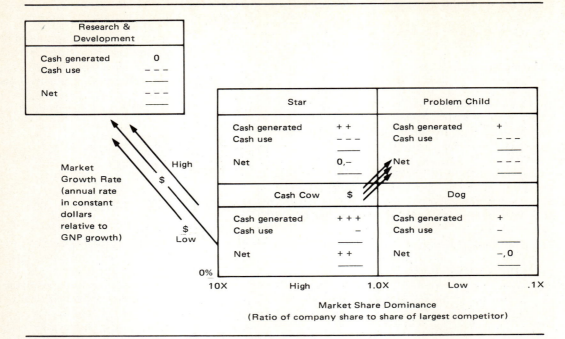

*Arrows indicate principal cash flows.

Dupont was at a cost disadvantage with Cyclo-hexane vis-à-vis the oil companies because the manufacture of the product was so highly integrated with the operations of an oil refinery.[5]

- Competitors can economically gain large amounts of experience through acquisitions or licensing, or shift to a lower (but parallel) cost curve by resorting to off-shore production or component sourcing.
- Profitability is highly sensitive to the rate of capacity utilization, regardless of size of plant.

There are many situations where the positive profitability and share relationship becomes very tenuous, and perhaps unattainable. A recent illustration is the building industry where large corporations—CNA with Larwin and ITT with Levitt—have suffered because of their inability to adequately offset their high overhead charges with a corresponding reduction in total costs.[6] Similar problems are also encountered in the service sector, and contribute to the many reasons why services which are highly labor-intensive and involve personal relationships must be approached with extreme caution in a product portfolio analysis.[7]

There is specific evidence from the Profit Impact of Market Strategies (PIMS) study[8] that the value of market share is not as significant for consumer goods as for industrial products. The reasons are not well understood, but probably reflect differences in buying behavior, the importance of product differentiation and the tendency for proliferation of marginally different brands in these categories. The strategy of protecting a market position by introducing line extensions, flankers, and spin-offs from a successful core brand means that product class boundaries are very unclear. Hence shares are harder to estimate. The individual brand in a category like deodorants or powdered drinks may not be the proper basis for evaluation. A related consequence is that joint costing problems multiply. For example, Unilever in the U.K. has 20 detergent brands all sharing production facilities and marketing resources to some degree.

When Do Market Shares Stabilize?

The operating assumption is that shares tend toward stability during the maturity stage, as the dominant competitors concentrate on defending their existing position. An important corollary is that gains in share

FIGURE 2
Balancing the Product Portfolio

(Diameter of circle is proportional to products contribution to total company sales volume)

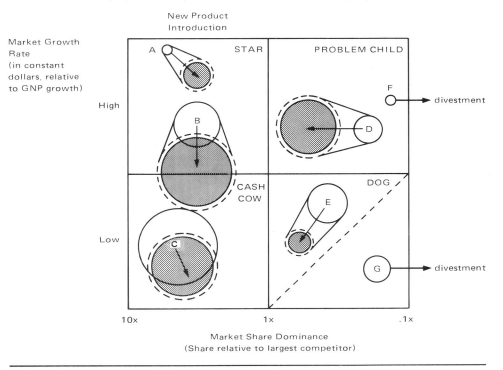

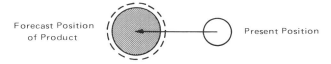

are easier and cheaper to achieve during the growth stage.

There is scattered empirical evidence, including the results of the PIMS project, which supports these assumptions. Several qualifications must be made before the implications can be pursued in depth:

- While market share *gains* may be costly, it is possible to mismanage a dominant position. The examples of A&P in food retailing, and British Leyland in the U.K. automobile market provide new benchmarks on the extent to which strong positions can erode unless vigorously defended.
- When the two largest competitors are of roughly equal size, the share positions may continue to be fluid until one is finally dominant.

- There are certain product categories, frequently high technology oriented, where a dominant full line/full service competitor is vulnerable if there are customer segments which do not require all the services, technical assistance, etc., that are provided. As markets mature this "sophisticated" segment usually grows. Thus, Digital Equipment Corp. has prospered in competition with IBM by simply selling basic hardware and depending on others to do the applications programming.[9] By contrast, IBM provides, for a price, a great deal of service backup and software for customers who are not self-sufficient. The dilemma for the dominant producer lies in the difficulty of serving both segments simultaneously.[10]

WHAT IS THE OBJECTIVE OF A PRODUCT PORTFOLIO STRATEGY?

The strategies emerging from a product portfolio analysis emphasize the balance of cash flows, by ensuring that there are products that use cash to sustain growth and others that supply cash.

Yet corporate objectives have many more dimensions that require consideration. This point was recognized by Seymour Tilles in one of the earliest discussions of the portfolio approach.[11] It is worth repeating to avoid a possible myopic focus on cash flow considerations. Tilles' point was that an investor pursues a balanced combination of risk, income, and growth when acquiring a portfolio of securities. He further argued that "the same basic concepts apply equally well to product planning." The problem with concentrating on cash flow to maximize income and growth is that strategies to balance risks are not explicitly considered.

What must be avoided is excessive exposure to a specific threat from one of the following areas of vulnerability:

- The economy (e.g., business downturns).
- Social, political, environmental pressures.
- Supply continuity.
- Technological change.
- Unions and related human factors.

It also follows that a firm should direct its new product search activities into several different opportunity areas, to avoid intensifying the degree of vulnerability. Thus, many companies in the power equipment market, such as Brown Boveri, are in a quandry over whether to meet the enormous resource demands of the nuclear power equipment market, because of the degree of vulnerability of this business compared to other possibilities such as household appliances.

The desire to reduce vulnerability is a possible reason for keeping, or even acquiring, a "Dog." Thus, firms may integrate backward to assure supply of highly leveraged materials.[12] If a "Dog" has a high percentage of captive business, it may not even belong as a separate entity in a portfolio analysis.

A similar argument could be used for products which have been acquired for intelligence reasons. For example, a large Italian knitwear manufacturer owns a high-fashion dress company selling only to boutiques to help follow and interpret fashion trends. Similarly, because of the complex nature of the distribution of lumber products, some suppliers have acquired lumber retailers to help learn about patterns of demand and changing end-user requirements. In both these cases the products/businesses were acquired for rea-

sons outside the logic of the product portfolio, and should properly be excluded from the analysis.

Can the Strategies Be Implemented?

Not only does a product portfolio analysis provide insights into the long-run health of a company; it also implies the basic strategies that will strengthen the portfolio. Unfortunately, there are many situations where the risks of failure of these strategies are unacceptably high. Several of these risks were identified in a recent analysis of the dangers in the pursuit of market share.[13]

One danger is that the company's financial resources will not be adequate. The resulting problems are enormously compounded should the company find itself in a vulnerable financial position if the fight were stopped short for some reason. The fundamental question underlying such dangers is the likelihood that competitors will pursue the same strategy, because they follow the same logic in identifying and pursuing opportunities. As a result, there is a growing premium on the understanding of competitive responses, and especially the degree to which they will be discouraged by aggressive action.

An increasingly important question is whether government regulations will permit the corporation to follow the strategy it has chosen. Antitrust regulations—especially in the U.S.—now virtually preclude acquisitions undertaken by large companies in related areas. Thus the effort by ITT to acquire a "Cash Cow" in Hartford Fire and Indemnity Insurance was nearly aborted by a consent decree, and other moves by ITT into Avis, Canteen Corp., and Levitt have been divested by court order at enormous cost. Recent governmental actions—notably the *ReaLemon* case—may even make it desirable for companies with very large absolute market share to consider reducing that share.[14]

There is less recognition as yet that government involvement can cut both ways; making it difficult to get in *or out of* a business. Thus, because of national security considerations large defense contractors would have a difficult time exiting from the aerospace or defense businesses. The problems are most acute in countries like Britain and Italy where intervention policies include price controls, regional development directives and employment maintenance which may prevent the replacement of out-moded plants. Unions in these two countries are sometimes so dedicated to protecting the employment status quo that a manager may not even move employees from one product line to another without risking strike activity.

The last implementation question concerns the viability of a niche strategy, which appears at the outset to be an attractive way of coping with both "Dogs" and "Problem Children." The fundamental problem, of course, is whether a product or market niche can be isolated and protected against competitive inroads. But even if this can be achieved in the long-run, the strategy may not be attractive. The difficulties are most often encountered when a full or extensive product line is needed to support sales, service and distribution facilities. One specialized product may simply not generate sufficient volume and gross margin to cover the minimum costs of participation in the market. This is very clearly an issue in the construction equipment business because of the importance of assured service.

PITFALLS IN THE MEASURES

The "Achilles' Heel" of a product portfolio analysis is the units of measure; for if the share of market and growth estimates are dubious, so are the interpretations. Skeptics recognize this quickly, and can rapidly confuse the analysis by attacking the meaningfulness and accuracy of these measures and offering alternative definitions. With the present state of the measurements there is often no adequate defense.

What Share of What Market?

This is not one, but several questions. Each is controversial because they influence the bases for resource allocation and evaluation within the firm:

- Should the definition of the product-market be broad (reflecting the generic need) or narrow?
- How much market segmentation?
- Should the focus be on the total product-market or a portion served by the company?
- Which level of geography: local versus national versus regio-centric markets?

The answers to these questions are complicated by the lack of defensible procedures for identifying product-market boundaries. For example, four-digit SIC categories are convenient and geographically available but may have little relevance to consumer perceptions of substitutability which will influence the long-run performance of the product. Furthermore, there is the pace of product development activity which is dedicated to combining, extending, or otherwise obscuring the boundaries.

Breadth of Product-Market Definition?
This is a pivotal question. Consider the following extremes in definitions:

- Intermediate builder chemicals for the detergent industry *or* Sodium Tri-polyphosphate.
- Time/information display devices *or* medium-priced digital-display alarm clocks.
- Main meal accompaniments *or* jellied cranberry.

Narrow definitions satisfy the short-run, tactical concerns of sales and product managers. Broader views, reflecting longer-run, strategic planning concerns, invariably reveal a larger market to account for (a) sales to untapped but potential markets, (b) changes in technology, price relationships, and supply which broaden the array of potential substitute products, and (c) the time required by present and prospective buyers to react to these changes.

Extent of Segmentation? In other words, when does it become meaningful to divide the total market into sub-groups for the purpose of estimating shares? In the tire industry it is evident that the OEM and replacement markets are so dissimilar in behavior as to dictate totally different marketing mixes. But how much further should segmentation be pushed? The fact that a company has a large share of the high-income buyers of replacement tires is probably not strategically relevant.

In general the degree of segmentation for a portfolio analysis should be limited to grouping those buyers that share situational or behavioral characteristics that are strategically relevant. This means that different marketing mixes must be used to serve the segments that have been identified, which will be reflected in different cost and price structures. Other manifestations of a strategically important segment boundary would be a discontinuity in growth rates, share patterns, distribution patterns and so forth when going from one segment to another.

These judgments are particularly hard to make for geographic boundaries. For example, what is meaningful for a manufacturer of industrial equipment facing dominant local competition in each of the national markets in the European Economic Community? Because the company is in each market, it has a 5% share of the total EEC market, while the largest regional competitor has 9%. In this case the choice of a regional rather than national market definition was dictated by the *trend* to similarity of product requirements throughout the EEC and the consequent feasibility of a single manufacturing facility to serve several countries.

The tendency for trade barriers to decline for countries within significant economic groupings will increasingly dictate regio-centric rather than nationally oriented boundaries. This, of course, will not happen where transportation costs or government efforts to protect sensitive industry categories (such as electric power generation equipment), by requiring local vendors, creates other kinds of barriers.

Market Served versus Total Market?

Firms may elect to serve only just a part of the available market; such as retailers with central buying offices or utilities of a certain size. The share of the market served is an appropriate basis for tactical decisions. This share estimate may also be relevant for strategic decisions, especially if the market served corresponds to a distinct segment boundary. There is a risk that focusing only on the market served may mean overlooking a significant opportunity or competitive threat emerging from the unserved portion of the market. For example, a company serving the blank cassette tape market only through specialty audio outlets is vulnerable if buyers perceive that similar quality cassettes can be bought in general merchandise and discount outlets.

Another facet of the served market issue is the treatment of customers who have integrated backward and now satisfy their own needs from their own resources. Whether or not the captive volume is included in the estimate of total market size depends on how readily this captive volume can be displaced by outside suppliers. Recent analysis suggests that captive production—or infeeding—is "remarkably resilient to attack by outside suppliers."[15]

WHAT CAN BE DONE?

The value of a strategically relevant product-market definition lies in "stretching" the company's perceptions appropriately—far enough so that significant threats and opportunities are not missed, but not so far as to dissipate information gathering and analysis efforts on "long shots." This is a difficult balance to achieve, given the myriad of possibilities. The best procedure for coping is to employ several alternative definitions, varying specificity of product and market segments. There will inevitably be both points of contradiction and consistency in the insights gained from portfolios constructed at one level versus another. The process of resolution can be very revealing, both in terms of understanding the competitive position and suggesting strategy alternatives.[16]

Market Growth Rate

The product life cycle is justifiably regarded as one of the most difficult marketing concepts to measure—or forecast.

There is a strong tendency in a portfolio analysis to judge that a product is maturing when there is a forecast of a decline in growth rate below some specified cut-off. One difficulty is that the same cut-off level does not apply equally to all products or economic climates. As slow growth or level GNP becomes the reality, high absolute growth rates become harder to achieve for all products, mature or otherwise. Products with lengthy introductory periods, facing substantial barriers to adoption, may never exhibit high growth rates, but may have an extended maturity stage. Other products may exhibit precisely the opposite life cycle pattern.

The focus in the product portfolio analysis should be on the long-run growth rate forecast. This becomes especially important with products which are sensitive to the business cycle, such as machine tools, or have potential substitutes with fluctuating prices. Thus the future growth of engineered plastics is entwined with the price of zinc, aluminum, copper and steel; the sales of powdered breakfast beverages depends on the relative price of frozen orange juice concentrate.

These two examples also illustrate the problem of the self-fulfilling prophecy. A premature classification as a mature product may lead to the reduction of marketing resources to the level necessary to defend the share in order to maximize net cash flow. But if the product class sales are sensitive to market development activity (as in the case of engineered plastics) or advertising expenditures (as is the case with powdered breakfast drinks) and these budgets are reduced by the dominant firms then, indeed, the product growth rate will slow down.

The growth rate is strongly influenced by the choice of product-market boundaries. A broad product type (cigarettes) will usually have a longer maturity state than a more specific product form (plain filter cigarettes). In theory, the growth of the individual brand is irrelevant. Yet, it cannot be ignored that the attractiveness of a growth market, however defined, will be diminished by the entry of new competitors with the typical depressing effect on the sales, prices and profits of the established firms. The extent of the reappraisal of the market will depend on the number, resources, and commitment of the new entrants. Are they likely to become what is known in the audio electronics industry as "rabbits," which come racing into the market, litter it up, and die off quickly?

PITFALLS FROM UNANTICIPATED CONSEQUENCES

Managers are very effective at tailoring their behavior to the evaluation system, *as they perceive it.* Whenever market share is used to evaluate performance, there is a tendency for managers to manipulate the product-market boundaries to show a static or increasing share. The greater the degree of ambiguity or compromise in the definition of the boundaries the more tempting these adjustments become. The risk is that the resulting narrow view of the market may mean overlooking threats from substitutes or the opportunities within emerging market segments.

These problems are compounded when share dominance is also perceived to be an important determinant of the allocation of resources and top management interest. The manager who doesn't like the implications of being associated with a "Dog," may try to redefine the market so he can point to a larger market share or a higher than average growth rate. Regardless of his success with the attempted redefinition, his awareness of how the business is regarded in the overall portfolio will ultimately affect his morale. Then his energies may turn to seeking a transfer or looking for another job, and perhaps another prophecy has been fulfilled.

The forecast of market growth rate is also likely to be manipulated, especially if the preferred route to advancement and needed additional resources is perceived to depend on association with a product that is classified as "Star." This may lead to wishful thinking about the future growth prospects of the product. Unfortunately the quality of the review procedures in most planning processes is not robust enough to challenge such distortions. Further dysfunctional consequences will result if ambitious managers of "Cash Cows" actually attempt to expand their products through unnecessary product proliferation and market segmentation without regard to the impact on profits.

The potential for dysfunctional consequences does not mean that profit center managers and their employees should not be aware of the basis for resource allocation decisions within the firm. A strong argument can be made to the effect that it is worse for managers to observe those decisions and suspect the worst. What will surely create problems is to have an inappropriate reward system. A formula-based system, relying on achievement of a target for return on investment or an index of profit measures, that does not recognize the differences in potential among businesses, will lead to short-run actions that conflict with the basic strategies that should be pursued.

ALTERNATIVE VIEWS OF THE PORTFOLIO

This analysis of the share/growth matrix portrayal of the product portfolio supports Bowman's contention that much of what now exists in the field of corporate or marketing strategy can be thought of as contingency theories. "The ideas, recommendations, or generalizations are rather dependent (contingent) for their truth and their relevance on the specific situational factors."[17] This means that in any specific analysis of the product portfolio there may be a number of factors beyond share and market growth with a much greater bearing on the attractiveness of a product-market or business; including:

- The contribution rate.
- Barriers to entry.
- Cyclicality of sales.
- The rate of capacity utilization.
- Sensitivity of sales to change in prices, promotional activities, service levels, etc.
- The extent of "captive" business.
- The nature of technology (maturity, volatility, and complexity).
- Availability of production and process opportunities.
- Social, legal, governmental, and union pressures and opportunities.

Since these factors are situational, each company (or division) must develop its own ranking of their importance in determining attractiveness.[18] In practice these factors tend to be qualitatively combined into overall judgments of the attractiveness of the industry or market, and the company's position in that market. The resulting matrix for displaying the positions of each product is called a "nine-block" diagram or decision matrix.[19]

Although the implications of this version of the product portfolio are not as clear-cut, it does overcome many of the shortcomings of the share/growth matrix approach. Indeed the two approaches will likely yield different insights. But as the main purpose of the product portfolio analysis is to help guide—but not substitute for—strategic thinking, the process of reconciliation is useful in itself. Thus it is desirable to employ both approaches and compare results.

SUMMARY

The product portfolio concept provides a useful synthesis of the analyses and judgments during the preliminary steps of the planning process, and is a provocative source of strategy alternatives. If nothing else, it demonstrates the fallacy of treating all businesses or profit centers as alike, and all capital investment decisions as independent and additive events.

There are a number of pitfalls to be avoided to ensure the implications are not misleading. This is especially true for the cash quadrant or share/growth matrix approach to portraying the portfolio. In many situations the basic assumptions are not satisfied. Further complications stem from uncertainties in the definitions of product-markets and the extent and timing of competitive actions. One final pitfall is the unanticipated consequences of adopting a portfolio approach. These may or may not be undesirable depending on whether they are recognized at the outset.

Despite the potential pitfalls it is important to not lose sight of the concept; that is, to base strategies on the perception of a company as an interdependent group of products and services, each playing a distinctive and supportive role.

NOTES

1. Bernard Catry and Michel Chevalier, "Market Share Strategy and the Product Life Cycle," *Journal of Marketing,* Vol. 38 No. 4 (October 1974), pp. 29–34; and Yoram Wind and Henry J. Claycamp, "Planning Product Line Strategy: A Matrix Approach," *Journal of Marketing,* Vol. 40 No. 1 (January 1976), pp. 2–9.

2. Described in the following pamphlets in the *Perspectives* series, authored by Bruce D. Henderson, "The Product Portfolio" (1970), "Cash Traps" (1972) and "The Experience Curve Reviewed: The Growth-Share Matrix or the Product Portfolio" (Boston Consulting Group, 1973). By 1972 the approach had been employed in more than 100 companies. See "Mead's Technique to Sort Out the Losers," *Business Week* (March 11, 1972), pp. 124–30.

3. Sidney Schoeffler, Robert D. Buzzell and Donald F. Heany, "Impact of Strategic Planning on Profit Performance," *Harvard Business Review* Vol. 52 (March–April 1974), pp. 137–45; and Robert D. Buzzell, Bradley T. Gale and Ralph G. M. Sultan, "Market Share—A Key to Profitability," *Harvard Business Review,* Vol. 53 (January–February 1975), pp. 97–106.

4. Boston Consulting Group, *Perspectives on Experience* (Boston: 1968 and 1970), and "Selling Business a Theory of Economics," *Business Week,* September 8, 1974, pp. 43–44.

5. Robert B. Stobaugh and Philip L. Towsend, "Price Forecasting and Strategic Planning: The Case of Petrochemicals,"
Journal of Marketing Research, Vol. XII (February 1975), pp. 19–29.

6. Carol J. Loomis, "The Further Misadventures of Harold Geneen," *Fortune,* June 1975.

7. There is incomplete but provocative evidence of significant share-profit relationships in the markets for auto rental, consumer finance, and retail securities brokerage.

8. Same as reference 3 above.

9. "A Minicomputer Tempest," *Business Week* January 27, 1975, pp. 79–80.

10. Some argue that the dilemma is very general, confronting all pioneering companies in mature markets. See Seymour Tilles, "Segmentation and Strategy," *Perspectives* (Boston: Boston Consulting Group, 1974).

11. Seymour Tilles, "Strategies for Allocating Funds," *Harvard Business Review,* Vol. 44 (January–February 1966), pp. 72–80.

12. This argument is compelling when $20,000 of Styrene Monomer can affect the production of $10,000,000 worth of formed polyester fiberglass parts.

13. William E. Fruhan, "Pyrrhic Victories in Fights for Market Share," *Harvard Business Review,* Vol. 50 (September–October 1972), pp. 100–107.

14. See Paul N. Bloom and Philip Kotler, "Strategies for High Market-Share Companies," *Harvard Business Review,* Vol. 53 (November–December 1975), pp. 63–72.

15. Aubrey Wilson and Bryan Atkin, "Exorcising the Ghosts in Marketing," *Harvard Business Review,* Vol. 54 (September–October 1976), pp. 117–27. See also, Ralph D. Kerkendall, "Customers as Competitors," *Perspectives* (Boston: Boston Consulting Group, 1975).

16. George S. Day and Allan D. Shocker, *Identifying Competitive Product-Market Boundaries: Strategic and Analytical Issues* (Boston: Marketing Science Institute, 1976).

17. Edward H. Bowman, "Epistemology, Corporate Strategy, and Academe," *Sloan Management Review* (Winter 1974), pp. 35–50.

18. The choice of factors and assessment of ranks is an important aspect of the design of a planning system. These issues are described in Peter Lorange, "Divisional Planning: Setting Effective Direction," *Sloan Management Review* (Fall 1975), pp. 77–91.

19. William E. Rothschild, *Putting It All Together: A Guide to Strategic Thinking* (New York: AMACOM, 1976).

Derek F. Abell

Strategic Windows

Strategic market planning involves the management of any business unit in the dual tasks of *anticipating* and *responding* to changes which affect the marketplace for their products. This article discusses both of these tasks. Anticipation of change and its impact can be substantially improved if an organizing framework can be used to identify sources and directions of change in a systematic fashion. Appropriate responses to change require a clear understanding of the alternative strategic options available to management as a market evolves and change takes place.

DYNAMIC ANALYSIS

When changes in the market are only incremental, firms may successfully adapt themselves to the new situation by modifying current marketing or other functional programs. Frequently, however, market changes are so far-reaching that the competence of the firm to continue to compete effectively is called into question. And it is in such situations that the concept of "strategic windows" is applicable.

The term "strategic window" is used here to focus attention on the fact that there are only limited periods during which the "fit" between the key requirements of a market and the particular competencies of a firm competing in that market is at an optimum. Investment in a product line or market area should be timed to coincide with periods in which such a strategic window is open. Conversely, disinvestment should be contemplated if what was once a good fit has been eroded—i.e., if changes in market requirements outstrip the firm's capability to adapt itself to them.

Among the most frequent questions which management has to deal with in this respect are:

Source: From the *Journal of Marketing,* Vol. 11, No. 1 (July 1978), pp. 21–26. Reprinted by permission of the American Marketing Association.

- Should funds be committed to a proposed new market entry? Now? Later? Or not at all? If a commitment is to be made, how large should it be?
- Should expenditure of funds of plant and equipment or marketing to support existing product lines be expanded, continued at historical levels, or diminished?
- When should a decision be made to quit and throw in the towel for an unprofitable product line or business area?

Resource allocation decisions of this nature all require a careful assessment of the future evolution of the market involved and an accurate appraisal of the firm's capability to successfully meet key market requirements. The strategic window concept encourages the analysis of these questions in a dynamic rather than a static framework, and forces marketing planners to be as specific as they can about these future patterns of market evolution and the firm's capability to adapt to them.

It is unfortunate that the heightened interest in product portfolio analysis evident in the last decade has failed to adequately encompass these issues. Many managers routinely classify their various activities as "cows," "dogs," "stars," or "question marks" based on a *static* analysis of the *current* position of the firm and its market environment.

Of key interest, however, is the question not only of where the firm is today, but of how well equipped it is to deal with *tomorrow*. Such a *dynamic* analysis may foretell non-incremental changes in the market which work to disqualify market leaders, provide opportunities for currently low share competitors, and sometimes even usher in a completely new cast of competitors into the marketplace. Familiar contemporary examples of this latter phenomenon include such products as digital watches, women's pantyhose, calculators, charter air travel, office copiers, and scientific instrumentation.

In all these cases existing competitors have been displaced by new contenders as these markets have evolved. In each case changing market requirements have resulted in a *closing* strategic window for incumbent competitors and an *opening* window for new entrants.

MARKET EVOLUTION

The evolution of a market usually embodies more far-reaching changes than the relatively systematic changes in customer behavior and marketing mix due to individual product life cycles. Four major categories of change stand out:

1. The development of new primary demand opportunities whose marketing requirements differ radically from those of existing market segments.
2. The advent of new competing technologies which cannibalize the existing ones.
3. Market redefinition caused by changes in the definition of the product itself and/or changes in the product market strategies of competing firms.
4. Channel changes.

There may be other categories of change or variants in particular industries. That doesn't matter; understanding of how such changes may qualify or disqualify different types of competitors can still be derived from a closer look at examples within each of the four categories above.

New Primary Demand

In a primary demand growth phase, decisions have to be reached by existing competitors about whether to spend the majority of the resources fighting to protect and fortify market positions that have already been established, or whether to seek new development opportunities.

In some cases, it is an original entrant who ploughs new territory—adjusting his approach to the emergent needs of the marketplace; in other cases it is a new entrant who, maybe basing his entry on expertise developed elsewhere, sees a "strategic window" and leapfrogs over the original market leader to take advantage of the new growth opportunity. Paradoxically, pioneering competitors who narrowly focus their activities in the early stages of growth may have the most difficulty in making the transition to new primary demand growth opportunities later. Emery Air Freight provides an example of a company that did face up to a challenge in such a situation.

Emery Air Freight. This pioneer in the air freight forwarding business developed many of the early applications of air freight in the United States. In particular, Emery's efforts were focused on servicing the "emergency" segment of the market, which initially accounted for a substantial portion of all air freight business. Emery served this market via an extensive organization of regional and district offices. Among Emery's major assets in this market was a unique nationwide, and later worldwide, communications network; and the special competence of personnel located in the district offices in using scheduled carriers in the most efficient possible way to expedite deliveries.

As the market evolved, however, many new applications for air freight emerged. These included regular planned shipments of high value-low weight merchandise, shipments of perishables; "off-line" service to hard-to-reach locations, and what became known as the TCC (Total Cost Concept) market. Each of these new applications required a somewhat different approach than that demanded by the original emergency business.

TCC applications, for example, required detailed logistics planning to assess the savings and benefits to be obtained via lower inventories, quicker deliveries and fewer lost sales through the use of air freight. Customer decisions about whether or not to use air freight required substantially more analysis than had been the case for "emergency" use; furthermore, decisions which had originally been made by traffic managers now involved marketing personnel and often top management.

A decision to seek this kind of business thus implied a radical change in Emery's organization—the addition of capability to analyze complex logistics systems and to deal with upper echelons of management.

New Competing Technologies

When a fundamental change takes place in the basic technology of an industry, it again raises questions of the adaptability to new circumstances of existing firms using obsolete technology.

In many cases established competitors in an industry are challenged, not by another member of the same industry, but by a company which bases its approach on a technology developed outside that industry. Sometimes this results from forward integration of a firm that is eager to develop applications for a new component or raw material. Texas Instrument's entry into a wide variety of consumer electronic products from a base of semi-conductor manufacture, is a case in point. Sometimes it results from the application by firms of a technology developed in one market to opportunities in another. Or sometimes a breakthrough in either product or process technology may remove traditional barriers to entry in an industry and attract a completely new set of competitors. Consider the following examples:

- Watchmakers have recently found that a new class of competitor is challenging their industry leadership—namely electronic firms who are seeking end market applications for their semi-conductors, as well as a new breed of assemblers manufacturing digital watches.

- Manufacturers of mechanical adjustable speed drive equipment found their markets eroded by electrical speed drives in the early 1900's. Electrical drives were based on rotating motor-generator sets and electronic controls. In the late 1950s, the advent of solid state electronics, in turn, virtually obsoleted rotating equipment. New independent competitors, basing their approach on the assembly of electronic components, joined the large electrical equipment manufacturers in the speed drive market. Today, yet another change is taking place, namely the advent of large computer controlled drive systems. This is ushering yet another class of competitors into the market—namely, companies whose basic competence is in computers.

In each of these cases, recurrent waves of new technology fundamentally changed the nature of the market and usually ushered in an entirely new class of competitors. Many firms in most markets have a limited capability to master all the technologies which might ultimately cannibalize their business. The nature of technological innovation and diffusion is such that most *major* innovations will originate outside a particular industry and not within it.

In many cases, the upheaval is not only technological; indeed the nature of competition may also change dramatically as technology changes. The advent of solid state electronics in the speed drive industry, for example, ushered in a number of small, low overhead, independent assemblers who based their approach primarily on low price. Prior to that, the market had been dominated by the large electrical equipment manufacturers basing their approach largely on applications engineering coupled with high prices and high margins.

The "strategic window" concept does not preclude adaption when it appears feasible, but rather suggests that certain firms may be better suited to compete in certain technological waves than in others. Often the cost and the difficulty of acquiring the new technology, as well as the sunk-cost commitment to the old, argue against adaption.

MARKET REDEFINITION

Frequently, as markets evolve, the fundamental definition of the market changes in ways which increasingly disqualify some competitors while providing opportunities for others. The trend towards marketing "systems" of products as opposed to individual pieces of equipment provides many examples of this phenomenon. The situation of Docutel illustrates this point.

Docutel. This manufacturer of automatic teller machines (ATM's) supplied virtually all the ATM's in use up to late 1974. In early 1975, Docutel found itself losing market share to large computer companies such as Burroughs, Honeywell, and IBM as these manufacturers began to look at the banks' total EFTS (Electronic Funds Transfer System) needs. They offered the bank a package of equipment representing a complete system of which the ATM was only one component. In essence their success may be attributed to the fact that they redefined the market in a way which increasingly appeared to disqualify Docutel as a potential supplier.

Market redefinition is not limited to the banking industry; similar trends are underway in scientific instrumentation, process control equipment, the machine tool industry, office equipment, and electric control gear, to name but a few. In each case, manufacturers basing their approach on the marketing of individual hardware items are seeing their "strategic window" closing as computer systems producers move in to take advantage of emerging opportunities.

CHANNEL CHANGES

Changes in the channels of distribution for both consumer and industrial goods can have far reaching consequences for existing competitors and would-be entrants.

Changes take place in part because of product life cycle phenomena—the shift as the market matures to more intensive distribution, increasing convenience, and often lower levels of channel service. Changes also frequently take place as a result of new institutional development in the channels themselves. Few sectors of American industry have changed as fast as retail and wholesale distribution, with the result that completely new types of outlets may be employed by suppliers seeking to develop competitive advantage.

Whatever the origin of the change, the effect may be to provide an opportunity for a new entrant and to raise questions about the viability of existing competitors. Gillette's contemplated entry into the blank cassette tape market is a case in point.

Gillette. As the market for cassettes evolved due to increased penetration and new uses of equipment for automotive, study, business, letter writing, and home entertainment, so did distribution channels broaden into an increasing number of drug chains, variety stores, and large discount stores.

Presumably it was recognition of a possible "strategic window" for Gillette that encouraged executives in the Safety Razor Division to look carefully at ways in which Gillette might exploit the cassette market at this particular stage in its evolution. The question was whether Gillette's skill in marketing low-priced, frequently purchased package goods, along with its distribution channel resources, could be applied to marketing blank cassettes. Was there a place for a competitor in this market to offer a quality, branded product, broadly distributed and supported by heavy media advertising in much the same way that Gillette marketed razor blades?

Actually, Gillette decided against entry, apparently not because a "strategic window" did not exist, but because profit prospects were not favorable. They did, however, enter the cigarette lighter business based on similar analysis and reportedly have had considerable success with their *Cricket* brand.

PROBLEMS & OPPORTUNITIES

What do all these examples indicate? *First,* they suggest that the "resource requirements" for success in a business—whether these be financial requirements, marketing requirements, engineering requirements, or whatever—may change radically with market evolution. *Second,* they appear to suggest that, by contrast, the firm's resources and key competencies often cannot be so easily adjusted. The result is a *predictable* change in the fit of the firm to its market—leading to defined periods during which a "strategic window" exists and can be exploited.

The "strategic window" concept can be useful to incumbent competitors as well as to would-be entrants into a market. For the former, it provides a way of relating future strategic moves to market evolution and of assessing how resources should be allocated to existing activities. For the latter, it provides a framework for diversification and growth.

Existing Businesses

Confronted with changes in the marketplace which potentially disqualify the firm from continued successful participation, several strategic options are available:

1. An attempt can be made to assemble the resources needed to close the gap between the new critical marketing requirements and the firm's competences.

2. The firm may shift its efforts to selected segments, where the "fit" between requirements and resources is still acceptable.
3. The firm may shift to a "low profile" approach—cutting back severely on all further allocation of capital and deliberately "milking" the business for short-run profit.
4. A decision may be taken to exit from that particular market either through liquidation or through sale.

All too frequently, however, because the "strategic window" phenomenon is not clearly recognized, these strategic choices are not clearly articulated. Instead, "old" approaches are continued long after the market has changed with the result that market position is lost and financial losses pile up. Or, often only half-hearted attempts are made to assemble the new resources required to compete effectively; or management is simply deluded into believing that it can adapt itself to the new situation even where this is actually out of the question.

The four basic strategic choices outlined above may be viewed hierarchically in terms of *resource commitment,* with No. 1 representing the highest level of commitment. Only the company itself can decide which position on the hierarchy it should adopt in particular situations, but the following guideline questions may be helpful:

- To what extent do the changes call for skills and resources completely outside the traditional competence of the firm? A careful analysis has to be made of the gap which may emerge between the evolving requirements of the market and the firm's profile.
- To what extent can changes be anticipated? Often it is easier to adapt through a series of minor adjustments—a stepping stone approach to change—than it is to be confronted with a major and unexpected discontinuity in approach.
- How rapid are the changes which are taking place? Is there enough time to adjust without forfeiting a major share of the market which later may be difficult to regain?
- How long will realignment of the functional activities of the firm take? Is the need limited to only some functions, or are all the basic resources of the firm affected—e.g., technology, engineering, manufacturing, marketing, sales, and organization policies?
- What existing commitments—e.g., technical skills, distribution channels, manufacturing approaches, etc.—constrain adaption?
- Can the new resources and new approaches be developed internally or must they be acquired?

- Will the changes completely obsolete existing ways of doing business or will there be a chance for coexistence? In the case of new technologies intruding from outside industry, the decision often has to be made to "join-em rather than fight-em." Not to do so is to risk complete obsolescence. In other cases, coexistence may be possible.
- Are there segments of the market where the firm's existing resources can be effectively concentrated?
- How large is the firm's stake in the business? To the extent that the business represents a major source of revenues and profit, a greater commitment will probably need to be made to adapt to the changing circumstances.
- Will corporate management, in the event that this is a business unit within a multi-business corporation, be willing to accept different goals for the business in the future than it has in the past? A decision not to adapt to changes may result in high short-run returns from that particular business. Looking at the problem from the position of corporate planners interested in the welfare of the total corporation, a periodic market-by-market analysis in the terms described above would appear to be imperative prior to setting goals, agreeing on strategies, and allocating resources.

New Entrants

The "strategic window" concept has been used implicitly by many new entrants to judge the direction, timing, and scale of new entry activities. Gillette's entry into cigarette lighters, major computer manufacturers entry into ATM's, and Procter & Gamble's entry into many consumer markets *after* pioneers have laid the groundwork for a large scale, mass market approach to the specific product areas, all are familiar examples.

Such approaches to strategic market planning require two distinctly different types of analysis:

1. Careful assessment has to be made of the firm's strengths and weaknesses. This should include audits of all the key resources of the company as well as its various existing programs of activity.
2. Attention should be directed away from the narrow focus of familiar products and markets to a search for opportunities to put unique competencies to work. This requires a broader appreciation of overall environmental, technical and market forces and knowledge of many more markets, than is encountered in many firms today. It puts a particular burden on marketing managers,

general managers, and business planners used to thinking in terms of existing activities.

Analysis of patterns of market evolution and diagnosis of critical market requirements in the future can also be of use to incumbent competitors as a forewarning of potential new entry. In such cases, adjustments in strategy can sometimes be made in advance, which will ultimately deter would-be new competitors. Even where this is not the case, resource commitments may be adjusted to reflect the future changes in structure of industrial supply.

CONCLUSION

The "strategic window" concept suggests that fundamental changes are needed in marketing management practice, and in particular in strategic market planning activities. At the heart of these changes is the need to base marketing planning around predictions of future patterns of market evolution and to make assessments of the firm's capabilities to deal with change. Such analyses require considerably greater strategic orientation than the sales forecasting activities which underpin much marketing planning today. Users of product portfolio chart analysis, in particular, should consider the dynamic as opposed to the static implications in designating a particular business.

Entry and exit from markets is likely to occur with greater rapidity than is often the case today, as firms search for opportunities where their resources can be deployed with maximum effectiveness. Short of entry and exit, the allocation of funds to markets should be timed to coincide with the period when the fit between the firm and the market is at its optimum. Entering a market in its early stages and evolving with it until maturity may, on closer analysis, turn out to be a serious management error.

It has been said that while the life of the product is limited, a market has greater longevity and as such can provide a business with a steady and growing stream of revenue and profit if management can avoid being myopic about change. This article suggests that as far as any one firm is concerned, a market also is a temporary vehicle for growth, a vehicle which should be used and abandoned as circumstances dictate—the reason being that the firm is often slower to evolve and change than is the market in which it competes.

BIBLIOGRAPHY

Abell, Derek F., "Business Definition as an Element of the Strategic Decision," presented at the American Marketing Association/Marketing Science Institute Conference on Product and Market Planning, Pittsburgh, November 1977.

——. "Competitive Market Strategies: Some Generalizations and Hypotheses," Marketing Science Institute, April 1975, Report No. 75-107.

Boston Consulting Group. "The Product Portfolio, Boston Consulting Group Perspective." See also, "A Note on the Boston Consulting Group Concept of Competitive Analysis and Corporate Strategy," Intercollegiat Case Clearing House No. 9-175-175; and George S. Day, "Diagnosing the Product Portfolio," *Journal of Marketing,* Vol. 41 No. 2 (April 1977), pg. 29.

Cooper, A. C., E. DeMuzzio, K. Hatten, E. J. Hicks, D. Tock, "Strategic Responses to Technological Threats," Proceedings of the Business Policy and Planning Division of the Academy of Management, Paper #2, Boston, Academy of Management, August 1974.

Enis, Ben M., Raymond LaGarce, and Arthur E. Prell, "Extending the Product Life Cycle." *Business Horizons,* June 1977, pg. 46.

Foote, Nelson N., "Market Segmentation as a Competitive Strategy," presented at the Consumer Market Segmentation Conference, American Marketing Association, Chicago, February 24, 1967.

Also see the following cases: Emery Air Freight Corporation (B); Gillette Safety Razor Division: The Blank Cassette Project; and Docutel Corporation; Intercollegiate Case Clearing House Nos. 9-511-044, 9-574-058 and 9-578-073 respectively.

CASES

FAR EAST NAUTICAL IMPORTS

Far East Nautical Imports, a Los Angeles-based company, is an importer and wholesaler of brass items of a nautical nature. These include ship bells, lanterns, anchors, and other decorative products. Some lines are especially designed and manufactured in Taiwan, while others are standard items carried by most competitors. Sales are made primarily through trade shows and the company's mail-order catalogue.

SUBURBAN CENTRE

This regional shopping center is located in a major Northwestern city. With competition from a similar shopping center directly across the street, and with a much larger center situated on the eastern edge of the city, the Suburban Centre has lost a number of stores and is presently trying to develop a proper mix of shops for its market area.

TOM KLINE PROPERTY MANAGEMENT

As a small property management firm, Tom Kline Property Management has enjoyed significant growth during the first two years of operation. To maintain revenue growth and profitability, Mr. Kline was faced with the tasks of establishing objectives and formulating appropriate marketing strategies in light of potentially adverse legislation and economic conditions.

ARIZONA SOCCER CAMP (PART A)

Located in the Phoenix, Arizona area, Arizona Soccer Camp was the idea of two individuals who loved soccer and wanted to start a local youth camp. They are in the process of developing a marketing program for this proposed venture.

FAR EAST NAUTICAL IMPORTS

Mr. Frank Claussen, president of Far East Nautical Imports, and Mr. Jack Haley, the company's vice-president, were in the process of reviewing operations for the last three years, and they were concerned. Sales and profits for the first eight months of the current fiscal year were up slightly over the previous one. It was apparent, however, that the 133 percent and 200 percent growth rates in sales and profits respectively of two years ago were not going to be replicated (see exhibits 1 and 2).

Since its beginnings, Far East Nautical Imports (FENI) has been plagued by sporadic growth. Over time, efforts to stabilize progress have resulted in changes in the firm's target market and in the various marketing strategies employed. In light of the current revelations concerning the slowdown in growth, Mr. Claussen was wondering whether the overall marketing program again needed to be revamped.

EXHIBIT 1
FENI Income Statement

	1980	1981	1982
Sales	$432,497	$1,007,363	$1,265,248
Cost of Goods Sold	213,576	472,038	593,807
Gross Profit	$218,921	$ 535,325	$ 671,441
Selling and Admin. Expenses	185,126	429,679	555,322
Income Before Taxes	$ 33,795	$ 105,646	$ 116,119

This case was prepared by Professor Dennis H. Tootelian, California State University, Sacramento.

EXHIBIT 2
FENI Balance Sheet

	1980	1981	1982
Current Assets			
Cash	$ 12,244	$140,222	$126,182
Accounts Receivable	54,661	123,721	176,321
Inventory	148,078	299,539	320,100
Prepaid Expenses	29,364	24,539	21,192
Total	$244,347	$588,021	$643,795
Fixed Assets (Net)			
Equipment	$ 12,441	$ 60,948	$ 63,210
Building & Land	39,885	32,128	29,268
Total	$ 52,326	$ 93,076	$ 92,478
Total Assets	$296,673	$681,097	$736,273
Current Liabilities			
Accounts Payable	$ 16,116	$206,235	$211,317
Customer's Deposits	11,295	2,128	3,129
Current Debt Due	47,570	119,198	133,481
Taxes	4,834	34,412	39,213
Total	$ 79,815	$361,973	$387,140
Long Term Liabilities	160,427	257,743	263,111
Total Liabilities	$240,242	$619,716	$650,251
Stockholders Equity			
Common Stock	$ 3,000	$ 3,000	$ 3,000
Retained Earnings	53,431	58,381	83,022
Total	$ 56,431	$ 61,381	$ 86,022
Total Liabilities & Stockholders Equity	$296,673	$681,097	$736,273

HISTORY

Located in an industrial park in southwest Los Angeles, the company specialized in the importing and wholesale distributing of antique and manufactured nautical brass merchandise, including ships' compasses, lanterns, divers' helmets, and portholes. Formation of the company began in late 1975, when Mr. Claussen visited an old friend from his Air Force days, Mr. John Willowby, who had been trading quite extensively in the Far East. During the course of conversation, Mr. Willowby, a collector of nautical antiques, raised the question of whether there would be a market for nautical brass items in the United States. Shortly thereafter, the two men purchased $10,000 worth of inventory and incurred $3,000 in expenses, and entered the San Francisco Boat Show in January 1976. Mr. Claussen remembered this first experience:

> We had absolutely no idea what to expect and our plan at that time was that we were going to do this once a year. We were going to have an excuse to go to the Far East two or three times a year on buying trips and stick what we bought in storage and once a year sell it at the San Francisco Boat Show. That was our total plan.

Despite several problems, the Boat Show was an immense success, generating $10,000 in revenue in five days. Follow-up telephone calls from all over the United States produced another $8,000 in sales, and the two men cleared a profit with about half of their goods still in inventory. Almost as amazing to them as their success was the fact that the newly manufactured brass items sold faster than the brass antiques.

Overall, the firm grew rapidly from the start, with Mr. Claussen and Mr. Willowby attending a number of trade shows on the West Coast and in the South. Merchandise lines also expanded to take advantage of market opportunities, and a large warehouse facility had to be purchased. By 1978, the pace became too hectic for Mr. Willowby, who wanted to retire anyway. At that point, Mr. Claussen purchased his share of the business.

MANAGEMENT

Frank Claussen, 60, attended the University of Southern California and received a bachelor's degree in Business Administration in 1944. After graduating from USC, he entered the United States Air Force, and served part of his military career at the Pentagon developing Air Force advertising. During that period, the Air Force was one of the largest advertisers in the country, with a budget in excess of $12 million.

Upon his retirement in 1969, Mr. Claussen began looking for a small business venture. His dislike for large firms and working for others was intense:

> I didn't want to go into a big corporation. I had had enough of a large outfit. I had several offers which scared me to death. After some soul searching, I found that I didn't want to work for anybody.

Between 1970 and 1975, Mr. Claussen developed two successful enterprises. The first was a chain of five care washes located in the Northeast. Although highly profitable, he became disenchanted with living in the cold and snow, and decided to sell the chain and move back to Los Angeles. After returning to the West Coast, Mr. Claussen entered the insurance field and founded an agency in which he was a partner. It, too, prospered, but after two years, he became bored with all the detail work and sold out his interest in the agency. It was at this point that Mr. Claussen and Mr. Willowby developed the prospect of importing nautical brass products.

Jack Haley, 51, was the other main decision maker within the company. He joined FENI in 1977 as its general manager, and became vice-president when Mr. Willowby retired in 1978. In 1981, he purchased a 10 percent interest in the firm from Mr. Claussen. Mr. Haley, too, was retired from the Air Force and had been a close associate of Mr. Claussen's for twelve years while in military service. Although Mr. Haley was not a college graduate, he had studied accounting and finance in his spare time. His primary responsibility was, according to Mr. Claussen:

> ... to determine how much money we have, where we have it, how much money we need, when we need it, and that sort of thing.

MARKETING

In 1976, the firm's three target markets were nautical and gift shops, marine and boat dealers, and antique dealers. The marketing effort was limited almost exclusively to operating booths at public boat and gift trade shows in Seattle, San Francisco, Long Beach, and Dallas. While this generated considerable revenue, Mr. Claussen believed that this was the reason for the highly volatile nature of sales and profits. Thus, Mr. Claussen and Mr. Haley decided that it was necessary to go to the potential buyers rather than wait for buyers to attend the trade shows.

Sales

By 1981, FENI had completed the transformation into strictly a wholesaling operation, and in 1982 over 95 percent of gross sales were generated from 300 to 400 small retail stores. About 50 percent of these stores were located in California, and 25 percent in Oregon and Washington. The remaining 25 percent of sales were dispersed over the rest of the United States.

To service the dealers in the three West Coast states, FENI employed two salesmen, one covering California, and the other handling Oregon and Washington. The salesmen were paid a flat rate of $300 per month for expenses and a 25 percent commission on sales. Buyers not on the West Coast were serviced through a mail order catalogue only, with relatively little effort going into selling to them. Mr. Claussen had often thought about enlarging the territory and adding new salesmen. Each time he started to seriously consider the possibilities, however, some crisis arose and distracted him.

Although both salesmen had been with FENI since 1980, they frequently complained about the large territories they had to cover and some of the company policies. In particular, they objected to Mr. Claussen's requirement that they sell only to small firms. Mr. Claussen, however, was quite strict about that one:

I originally tried to be nice to them (corporations), but I found out otherwise in the insurance business where I sold a lot of corporate pension plans. I went and presented a plan to the board of directors and they thought it was a great idea, but it took them a year to make up their minds. I want people-types of businesses, multi-partners, or sole proprietorships, or smaller corporations. I want the guy that sees you to make the decisions and buy right now. They are more loyal to you and appreciate you for many years.

Product Creation

FENI maintained a merchandise line of which approximately 50 percent of the products were standard items also carried by competition or already made and manufactured in the Far East. The other 50 percent were uniquely designed by Mr. Claussen, either in primary design or by modification:

Take a regular lamp, for example, that was selling in gift stores; I put a gimbel on it and made it into a ship's lamp. We take a big bell, put an anchor on it, add a hook and twist it around, and make a unique and super good seller out of it.

Those products which sold especially well would oftentimes be copied in competing catalogues the following year. On occasion, too, competing product lines would be replicated by FENI. Mr. Claussen's main product policy was to create twenty-five new products each year, giving the company the distinction of being the exclusive dealer for nine to twelve months before imitations were introduced.

Most products were manufactured in Taiwan because of the lower labor costs and more economical production processes. This permitted economies of scale to be reached with a relatively small number of units in production. In the United States, a minimum of 5000 units had to be manufactured to reach a reasonable cost level per unit. In Taiwan, a similar level could be achieved with lots of well under 2000 units.

Although this offered a distinct advantage, there were some problems too. According to Mr. Claussen, manufacturers oftentimes played one importer against another:

One manufacturer had my order ready to go and a competitor happened to be over there. They showed him a copy of it and he said, "I would like to have some. When can I get 500?" They said you can have them in two weeks and so they sold him my order and I had to wait until they manufactured 500 more.

Such practices at times made it possible for competitors to beat FENI to market with their own products.

EXHIBIT 3
Product Line Breakdown

	Number of Items	Percent of Sales
Helm Wheels	18	4.2
Lamps	19	7.8
Divers' Helmets	6	2.7
Plaques	42	35.6
Nautical Hooks	32	5.9
Bells	8	4.8
Special, Limited Offers	76	16.6
Nautical Decor	29	21.6
Antiques	Varies	.8
		100.0

No legal recourse was possible, and both Mr. Claussen and Mr. Haley believed that the only solution was to quit buying from a manufacturer once that happened.

Overall, Mr. Claussen thought his product policy was sound. Mr. Haley, however, was concerned about the rate of expansion. Although twenty-five new products a year had been added, few older ones had been eliminated (see the product list in exhibit 3). According to Mr. Haley, this has increased the inventory costs. Mr. Claussen agreed that the line was becoming quite large, but was unsure which products, if any, should be eliminated.

Promotion

Nearly all of the promotion for FENI was through its ten-page color catalogue. This was sent to all existing and potential retail buyers identified by the salesmen. Other dealers wrote directly to the company and were provided a catalogue.

In 1980, an attempt was made to increase sales through magazine advertising. Escalating overhead costs and increased inventory provided the impetus for the decision to advertise. Even with Mr. Claussen's extensive background in advertising, this effort proved unsuccessful, as Mr. Claussen noted:

We went to the wrong people and got the wrong ad and the wrong publication at the wrong time and advertised the wrong things. The cost was about $10,000, running a slick, multi-color institutional type ad in a national magazine instead of a head-on, clip-the-coupon, make-your-order-right-now type of thing.

In light of the present high inventory levels, both Mr. Claussen and Mr. Haley agreed that some form of promotional effort might again be needed to clear out some of the excessive merchandise. Mr. Claussen, however, was quite leery of normal catalogue and magazine advertising:

What we need is something really unique; something that will shake the socks off the buyers.

Pricing

Most products sold by FENI were priced at two to three times their cost. Increasing competition through price cutting by a few firms had forced FENI to reduce prices during the last fiscal year. At the present time, Mr. Claussen and Mr. Haley were somewhat reluctant to engage in a price war with their competitors. Although FENI was as large as any and had about the same cost and capital structure, they were unsure of whether large price decreases would greatly stimulate demand or would be matched by the competition.

Mr. Haley recalled that on two occasions in the past three years, severe price competition erupted. On the first occasion, prices fell by 30 percent and sales increased by 18 percent. The second time, FENI took the initiative and suddenly reduced prices by 25 percent; competitors were caught unaware, and sales quickly rose by 47 percent. Once competition began reacting, however, the sales increase fell to 15 percent.

FUTURE

Both Mr. Claussen and Mr. Haley felt confident that FENI was not facing a life-or-death crisis. Yet, Mr. Claussen was concerned that the firm was losing its progressiveness:

We have been operating in the same manner for several years now, and our position seems to be stagnating somewhat. If we don't create some new flair, we might find ourselves on the outside looking in.

Mr. Haley, on the other hand, held the view that the slowdown in growth was natural:

We cannot really expect to continue indefinitely

to grow as we have. We both want to have some stability in our growth, and I know Frank is concerned now that we may not be growing at all. What we need to do is evaluate our programs and modify them as necessary—but not to radically—to continue our growth.

THE SUBURBAN CENTRE

Nearing the end of the fiscal year, Mr. Larry Jacobs, manager of the Suburban Centre, was assessing the past performance of the regional shopping center (see exhibit 1) and trying to develop a plan for the future. Faced with rather poor performance several years ago, and increasing competition at the present time, Mr. Jacobs wanted to prepare a plan to present to the Centre's Board of Trustees. Of particular concern was

This case was prepared by Professor Dennis H. Tootelian, California State University, Sacramento.

identifying what types of retail outlets to bring into the mall and a program for attracting them. Mr. Jacobs noted:

Our best point is our location. If we come up with the right tenant mix, we'll have a good tenant mix AND a good location. This is a sure-fire formula.

CENTER PROFILE

The Suburban Centre, a regional shopping center located in a large Northwestern city, housed fifty-one tenants on about forty acres of land. There were 680,790 square feet of leasable space and 3,500 parking spaces (see exhibit 2). In 1978, the mall was enclosed, and the conversion allowed customers to enter any store either from the mall entrance or from the individual store's entrance on the parking lot. Mr. Jacobs commented on the enclosed mall conversion and the recent history of Suburban Centre:

EXHIBIT 1
Shopping Center Definitions

For case purposes, a shopping center is a group of retail businesses integrated in such a manner that customers can be provided one-stop shopping for their daily needs of goods and services. Three types of centers are included in this case.

SR—Super Regional Shopping Center	Provides goods and services in full depth and variety, includes three or more full-line department stores as principal tenants, and a total area of 1,000,000 or more square feet with parking for 5,000 or more cars.
R—Regional Shopping Center	Provides goods and services in full depth and variety, includes one or more major department stores as principal tenants and one or more large supermarkets; total area exceeds 300,000 square feet with parking for 1,000 or more cars.
C—Community Shopping Center	Provides a wide variety of goods and services in hard and soft lines, in addition to convenience goods and services. Principal tenants are generally a junior department store or large variety store and a supermarket. Total area usually ranges from 60,000 to 300,000 square feet with parking for 400 or more cars.

EXHIBIT 2
The Suburban Centre

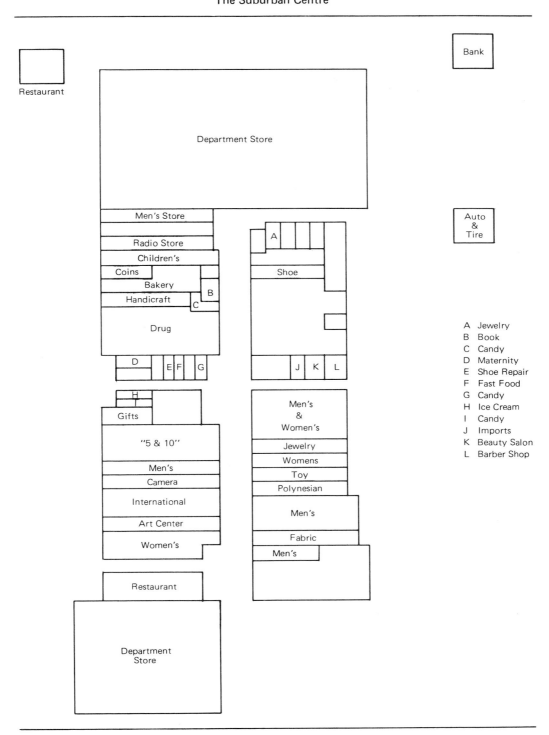

This fact that we're a conversion is a strike against us. The stores can be full, but the mall can be empty, giving the impression that the center is dead. In reality, many stores are doing excellently, have been in overage (paying percentage of sales over minimum rent) for years, and are still growing.

Seven years ago, Suburban Centre was extremely active with a 100 percent occupancy rate. The anchor store was one of the highest volume-per-square foot producers in the entire country, despite its small size.

It was at that time that we decided to enclose the mall because of competition. We had been an open mall for about twenty years.

In 1978, we also signed a lease with a big department store. Because of this commitment, we could no longer lease to Apex Supermarket, a twenty-year tenant, and they left. At the same time, the anchor store, also a long-time tenant, wanted to expand. We turned them down, too, because we really wanted the big department store. The anchor store went across the street to what is now Suburban Plaza, which started as a small strip center in 1964, and they built a beautiful 160,000-square-foot store. The Plaza became enclosed shortly thereafter.

The deal with the big department store fell through. They just pulled out. That action started the deterioration of the Suburban Centre. Another store left, a discount drugstore did not renew—overnight we had many vacancies. Stores either closed down or went across the street... some still even paid rent over here for years, even though they had closed long ago. We've had steady decreases in volume since then. The bottom literally fell out, until two years ago when a big department store signed with us. It opened in March of 1984 and a new discount drugstore just opened.

We've invested over $10,000,000 in the last year and a half, and we've put a lot of thought into our planning. It's sure to pay off. (See exhibits 3, 4, 5, and 6.)

EXHIBIT 3
Suburban Centre Growth Rate

	1982	1983	1984	1985
Sales	100.0	103.7	106.1	106.4
Total Store Net Profit	100.0	101.1	100.5	99.8
Percent of Stores Profitable	88.6	89.1	88.9	87.8
Number of Stores in Centre	41	47	48	51

EXHIBIT 4
Suburban Centre Projections

Tenant Group	Percent GLA*	Percent Sales	Percent Total Charges
Food	1.31	1.99	3.38
Food Services	2.19	2.27	3.9
General Merchandise	48.4	47.39	23.92
Clothing and Shoes	16.63	24.6	33.35
Dry Goods	4.53	5.79	4.37
Furniture	0	0	0
Other Retail	12.18	17.39	26.61
Financial	1.65	0	2.45
Offices	0.65	0	0
Services	0.51	0.49	1.21
Other	0.64	0	0.8
Vacant Space	11.31	0	0
Total	100.00	100.00	100.00

*GLA = Gross Leasable Area

MANAGEMENT

In 1969, Suburban Centre was purchased by a large investment company located on the East Coast. This firm bought the property from the original developers and leased it back to them for a period of eleven years. At the end of the lease, the investment company began operating the center through a professional management company which received a management fee plus a commission based on lease volume.

Suburban Centre was governed by a Board of Trustees, comprised of members of the professional management company and the owners. Policy was

CASE

EXHIBIT 5
Financial Data for Enclosed Regional Shopping Centers Over 10 Years Old
Based on GLA*
Suburban Centre 1976

Expected Suburban Centre Figures Based on Average Size Store			
Items	Median	Lower Decile	Upper Decile
Sales	$25,569,064	$14,856,294	$33,948,749
Operating Receivables	1,184,343	832,060	1,737,931
Operating Expenses	352,283	174,464	583,784
Operating Balance	852,190	637,465	1,097,111
Net Operating Income	362,349	23,486	832,060
Funds, After Debt Service	348,928	110,718	932,712

Expected Figures, Based on Actual GLA National Average			
Items	Median	Lower Decile	Upper Decile
Sales	$51,833,005	$30,145,381	$68,460,666
Operating Receivables	2,403,189	1,688,359	3,526,492
Operating Expenses	714,830	354,011	1,184,575
Operating Balance	1,729,207	1,293,501	2,226,183
Net Operating Income	735,253	47,655	1,683,354
Funds, After Debt Service	708,022	255,661	1,892,596

*GLA = Gross Leasable Area

Source: The Urban Land Institute, *Dollars and Cents of Shopping Centers, 1975.* The Urban Land Institute: Washington, 1975.

largely determined by a subgroup of the board which met biweekly on the West Coast. Mr. Jacobs had some input, but only of a suggestive nature.

Resident Management

Mr. Jacobs was formerly the shopping center's promotion director for the original developers. When the professional management company took over in 1980, he became the center's manager. Prior to his eight years with the Centre, he was promotion director with three other regional shopping centers on the West Coast and in the Midwest. Concerning his perception of his current responsibilities, Mr. Jacobs commented:

The basic reason for a resident manager is to make sure that the center stays clean, that mall floors are waxed, and so forth.

Mr. Jacobs was also the spokesman for the Merchants Association, to which all Suburban Centre tenants belonged. This association conducted the advertising in media and mall events, such as sidewalk sales and moonlight sales. Ms. Linda Schmidt was its promotion director.

Tenant Policy

Each lease was different. Negotiations for basic rent and percentage of sales for rent were based on the desirability of the tenant to the center and vice versa. Each tenant paid a certain cost per square foot. The larger the leased space, the lower the cost per foot. In addition, each tenant paid a common area fee for parking lot facilities and mall maintenance. When a predetermined sales volume was reached, a certain percentage of each dollar was paid for additional rent

EXHIBIT 6
Regional Shopping Center Store Size by Tenant Classification vs. Suburban Centre 1976

Average National Regional Shopping Center

Tenant Group	Percent GLA*	Percent Sales	Percent Total Charge†
Food	5.5	7.9	6.0
Food Service	2.9	3.6	5.2
General Merchandise	53.4	48.5	32.0
Clothing and Shoes	16.9	20.4	26.3
Dry Goods	1.4	1.5	2.5
Furniture	1.4	1.7	1.8
Other Retail	10.1	13.3	16.6
Financial	1.6	0	2.7
Offices	0.4	0	0.6
Services	1.2	1.1	2.7
Other	3.0	2.0	3.6
Vacant Space	2.2	0	0
Total	100.0	100.0	100.0

Suburban Centre

Tenant Group	Percent GLA	Percent Sales	Percent Total Charge
Food	0.75	1.17	2.19
Food Service	2.19	2.54	4.1
General Merchandise	48.4	48.69	25.15
Clothing and Shoes	15.48	23.94	32.98
Dry Goods	4.53	5.97	4.6
Furniture	0	0	0
Other Retail	11.34	17.1	26.29
Financial	1.65	0	2.58
Offices	0.65	0	0
Services	0.51	0.59	1.27
Other	0.84	0	0.84
Vacant Space	13.66	0	0
Total	100.00	100.00	100.00

*Gross Leasable Area

†Includes Rent, Overage (if any), Common Area Fees and Misc.

Source: Dollars and Cents of Shopping Centers, 1975.

charges (overages). Even though specific rental fee comparisons between shopping centers were difficult to assess, Mr. Jacobs knew that the costs at Suburban Centre were at the higher range. Only Blueridge Mall and Suburban Plaza had higher costs per square foot.

COMPETITION

Although the number of competing shopping centers had not increased appreciably within the last several years, the opening of a super regional—Blueridge Mall—about fifteen miles from Suburban Centre had hurt the sales of nearly all other malls within the city. Housing four major department stores and nearly one hundred other specialty stores, Blueridge Mall was especially popular.

One result of the opening of Blueridge was increased competition among the others to attract both customers and desirable retail stores. The major malls competing with Suburban Centre are identified in exhibit 7. Mr. Jacobs discussed the competition:

> *Suburban Plaza, across the street, is not competition. We are partners, more or less. We work together. We promote both sides of the street in what we call Suburban City. It seems like no one realizes that there are two different centers. In order, our competition is Blueridge Mall, Manor Fair, Southwest Center, and maybe the Downtown Mall which is under reconstruction.*

Despite Mr. Jacobs's contention that Suburban Plaza was not a competitor, most retailers within the Centre felt differently. Suburban Plaza was second only to Blueridge Mall in terms of retail sales even though it was no bigger than the others. Because of its tenant mix and success in its promotional efforts, the members of the Merchant Association rated Suburban Plaza its biggest threat. At times, this difference of opinion caused some friction between Mr. Jacobs and the association members.

CITY MARKET SURVEY

In order to make recommendations to the board, Mr. Jacobs gathered data on the metropolitan area and on the buying habits of the various shopping mall customers. A local newspaper recently published the results of a shopping center analysis it made, and Ms. Schmidt followed up on some aspects of the report with a study of her own sponsored by the Merchants Association. Mr. Jacobs hoped that this information would help him to better identify the types of retailers desired to best complete the tenant mix.

EXHIBIT 7
Competing Malls

Downtown Mall (Open and Enclosed)

Type . . . . Regional
Selling Space . . . . 127,000 sq. ft. (Enclosed)
Parking Capacity . . . . None Free
Total Units . . . . 63 Occupied
Year Opened 1965

Suburban Plaza (Enclosed)

Type . . . . Regional
Selling Space . . . . 600,000 sq. ft.
Parking Capacity . . . . 3,500 cars
Total Units . . . . 48 Occupied
Year Opened 1960

Suburban Centre (Enclosed)

Type . . . . Regional
Selling Space . . . . 580,000 sq. ft.
Parking Capacity . . . . 2,800 cars
Total Units . . . . 40 Occupied
Year Opened 1952

Remarks: Addition of 180,000 sq. ft. planned, including a major department store and its auto service center, plus 40,000 sq. ft. of new mall shops.

Manor Fair (Enclosed)

Type . . . . Regional
Selling Space . . . . 750,000 sq. ft.
Parking Capacity . . . . 8,000 cars
Total Units . . . . 69 Occupied
Year Opened 1959

Remarks: Space currently available, 27,000 sq. ft.

Blueridge Mall (Enclosed)

Type . . . . Super Regional
Selling Space . . . . 1,148,046 sq. ft.
Parking Capacity . . . . 6,500 cars
Total Units . . . . 103 Occupied
Year Opened 1972

Southwest Center (Enclosed)

Type . . . . Regional
Selling Space . . . . 680,000 sq. ft.
Parking Capacity . . . . 7,000 cars
Total Units . . . . 80 Occupied
Year Opened 1963

Remarks: Space currently available.

EXHIBIT 8
Market Profile of The City

	1960	1977	% Increase Since 1960
Population	625,603	918,600	47
Households	187,820	351,300	87
Effective Buying Income (in thousands)	$1,565,708	$4,664,122	198
Total Retail Sales (in thousands)	$ 903,352	$2,876,659	218
Total Retail Outlets	11,760	21,206	80

Shopper Characteristics

The sixteen shopping districts comprising the city contained 918,000 residents (see exhibits 8, 9, and 10). According to Ms. Schmidt's study, 30 percent of the population within Suburban Centre's district lived within a five-mile radius of the Centre, and accounted for 61 percent of its shoppers. The population within this five-mile radius was predominantly white (87 percent), with a median family income of $28,157. Most, furthermore, were white-collar workers (66 percent), and 36 percent of the adult population had at least some college education.

The local newspaper study of Suburban Centre and its major competitors identified two comparative characteristics regarded as highly significant in its findings. First, the Suburban Centre customers were found to be older than those of other shopping centers. Sixty-two percent of the other mall shoppers surveyed by the newspaper were under thirty-five years of age, whereas only 41 percent of Suburban Centre's customers fell into that age group.

Second, the Centre's patrons tended to be more affluent than those of the other shopping malls. In comparison to other malls, Suburban Centre had 27 percent more shoppers from families earning over $50,000 per year, and 20 percent fewer shoppers who came from families making $25,000 or less. Additionally, the Centre's customers ranked first in the number of credit cards possessed. Of nine local and national credit cards identified by the newspaper, the average Centre customer held eight.

CASE

EXHIBIT 9
Where They Come From, Where They Shop

Shoppers at each of the shopping center parking lots were asked to identify where they live by zip code number. Interviewers were trained in this technique. This survey was prepared by the marketing department of the local newspaper.

Populations and Households by Districts

No.		Population	Households	% of Households
1	....	59,000	19,800	6.5
2	(Manor Fair)	153,000	51,000	17.5
3	(Suburban Centre, Suburban Plaza)	126,000	39,100	13.4
4	....	21,000	6,400	2.2
5	....	22,600	7,100	2.4
6	....	28,300	9,000	3.1
7	(Downtown Mall)	29,600	16,600	5.7
8	....	23,400	10,000	3.4
9	(Blueridge Mall)	69,500	20,500	7.1
10	....	87,500	29,000	10.0
11	....	102,000	34,500	11.9
12	....	13,500	3,900	1.3
13	....	14,500	5,100	1.8
14	....	61,400	21,000	7.2
15	....	31,000	10,500	3.6
16	....	25,500	8,500	2.9
	Total	867,800	292,100	100.0

EXHIBIT 10
Retail Sales and Effective Buying Income
Comparison Increases: City, State, United States

	1973 (in thousands) City	% Increase 4 Years City	% Increase 4 Years State	% Increase 4 Years United States
Effective Buying Income	$3,664,122	39	37	41
Total Retail Sales	2,335,659	56	43	48
Food Store Sales	505,017	47	39	47
Super Markets (1)	422,103	45	37	56
General Merchandise Stores	292,894	36	19	21
Department Stores (1)	261,805	64	31	38
Apparel Store Sales	107,001	49	37	47
Furn. Hsld. Appliances	120,756	53	43	51
Furn. Home Furnish. (1)*	76,968	64	57	67
Automotive Dealers†	476,963	57	44	55
Gasoline Stations/Garages	194,964	54	44	58
Lumber/Bldg./Hardware	120,783	111	78	41
Drug Stores	99,292	31	22	36
Eating, Drinking Places	238,169	83	69	72

*3-Year Increase

†Includes dealers selling autos (new or used, motorcycles, house trailers, boats, and bicycles. New or used commercial dealers not included.

(1) Sales included in above category.

Source: Sales Management's Survey of Buying Power, 1974.

Although the greater affluence did not bother Mr. Jacobs at all, the age factor did. Catering to an older group, Mr. Jacobs thought, could be problematical. The newspaper cited city population estimates showing that the eighteen to thirty-five age group had been the fastest growing segment through the early 1980s. The newspaper also noted that the youth population (defined as under thirty years) was moving into the city's suburbs at a rate three times as fast as any other age group.

Shopping Patterns

In terms of shopping patterns, the newspaper characterized the average Suburban Centre shopper as a "hit and run" shopper. It found that the Centre had nearly twice as many patrons who spent less than thirty minutes in the mall as any competing shopping center. The Centre also tied with Manor Fair for the lowest percentage of customers who shopped for one hour or more.

The newspaper study additionally showed that 62 percent of Suburban Centre shoppers rated store selection as good to excellent. This was the lowest rating given by shoppers of all centers. Overall, nearly 85 percent of the shoppers at other malls rated the mall they were in as having a good to excellent selection of stores. Much the same rating was given to eating facilities. Nearly twice as many patrons at Manor Fair, Southwest Center, and Blueridge Mall evaluated their eating facilities as good to excellent as compared to those at Suburban Centre. One of the few attractions to the Centre was found to be the special promotions (art shows, craft exhibits, and the like) it used on occasion. Over 70 percent of the patrons in Suburban Centre said this was an appealing aspect of the mall.

As a follow-up to this particular issue of appeal, Ms. Schmidt's study addressed the question of what could be done to improve the Centre. Her findings are presented in exhibit 11.

MR. JACOBS'S RECOMMENDATION

In light of the stiff competition and of the shoppers' characteristics and buying patterns, Mr. Jacobs was trying to decide on the right mix. Many of the suggestions provided by Ms. Schmidt seemed sound, but he was wondering whether any special effort was necessary. After all, he thought, the rebuilding process took time, and perhaps competition had peaked.

EXHIBIT 11
Suburban Centre
Shopper's Comments

Suggested Improvements for Centre

Need More Stores	Should Remain Open Longer
More Eating Facilities	More Varied Merchandise
Furniture Store	Better Selection of Young Girls' Shoes
Wine Shop	Stores Need Clerks Who Know Their Merchandise and
Need a Supermarket	Care About Customers
Foxy Lady Clothing Store	More Junior Shops Like Casual Corner
Connect Plaza and Centre with Underground Walkway	Need a Macy's
More Ladies' Specialty Shops	More Art and Craft Shows
More Shoe Stores	More Parking for Moonlight Sales
A Good All-Hours Eating Place or Cafeteria	Office Supply Store
Public Restrooms	Need 15–20 Minute Parking for Rush Buying and
Drinking Fountains	Pickups
More Parking	More Clothing Stores

(Continued)

EXHIBIT 11 (Continued)

Stores, Services, or Restaurants to Add to the Centre

Large Music Store	Fast Food Place (Ice Cream and Popcorn)
Mr. Steak	Dress Shops
More Eating Places	Frank Moore's
Furniture Store	Orange Julius
More Department Stores	Pie Shop
Macy's	Expensive Restaurant
Inexpensive Shoe Store	Sandwich Shop
Wine Shop	Fashion Conspiracy
Quick Snack Facility	Movie Theatre
Fabric Store	Leed's Shoes
Music Center (pianos, organs)	Payless Drug
Good Clothing Store for Women	Mervyn's
Foxy Lady	Clothing Store for Large Women
Baby Shops	Book Store
Foxmoor	Good Cheap Coffee Shop
Chess King	Junior Apparel Shop
Buffet-Style Restaurant	Office Supply Store
Drug Store	Novelty Shop
Specialty Shops	Ladies Ready-to-Wear
Sporting Goods Store	Farrell's
Discount Store	Bible Book Store
Plant Store	Pet Shop
Craft Store	Record and Poster Shop

TOM CLINE PROPERTY MANAGEMENT

Tom Cline Property Management was a real estate management firm, located in a Northeastern city, that managed twenty-six apartment complexes and two condominiums. Net income for the most recent fiscal year had been $19,191. This was a significant increase over the net income for the previous (first) fiscal year which had been only $184. (For additional financial information, see exhibits 1 and 2.)

This case was prepared by Professor Ralph M. Gaedeke, California State University, Sacramento.

As he assessed the future for his company, Mr. Tom Cline, owner and chief operating/executive officer, reflected on its past performance:

People buy income property for three main reasons: (1) income, (2) depreciation—as a tax shelter for other income, (3) appreciation—resale value of the land and the building. The job of a good property management firm is to: (1) increase the income from the property, (2) control the vacancy/turnover rates, (3) reduce costs, and (4) maintain the property's appearance. My company has tried to do this, and I think we have done a good job. In the last year, we have increased the number of complexes managed from seventeen to twenty-eight and increased our profits while maintaining a high quality of service to our clients.

Regarding the future of his company, Mr. Cline was concerned with establishing objectives and formulating strategies to ensure further growth and

CASE

	Previous Year	Last Year
Income:		
Property management fees	$33,309	$71,882
Expenses:		
Salaries	$23,629	$28,053
Payroll taxes and workman's compensation	3,416	5,186
Automobile maintenance	2,175	3,549
Insurance	123	2,695
Rent	424	2,644
Office expense	33	2,386
Automobile leasing	914	2,296
Telephone	390	1,559
Office supplies	660	1,315
Photocopying service	48	640
Dues and subscriptions	198	616
Promotion and entertainment	302	494
Postage	257	413
Miscellaneous	246	374
Donations	10	370
Depreciation	—	126
Legal and accounting	300	75
Total expenses	$33,125	$52,791
Net Income	$ 184	$19,191

profit in the face of potentially unfavorable legislation and adverse economic conditions. There was a possibility of rent control at the local level; forty-two cities in the state would have rent control propositions on their November ballots. Also, the interest rates had been increasing; it was predicted that the prime rate would increase by 3 to 5 percent in the next six months. Both these factors would adversely affect the property management business.

In addition, Mr. Cline was concerned with how to better utilize the company's skills and resources, whether or not to incorporate his business, and what his future role in the company would be.

THE REAL ESTATE MANAGEMENT INDUSTRY

Prior to 1890, expert management of income properties in America was limited to that of the com-mercial hotel and the downtown business property. Residential property was mostly the single-family residence; large multi-family dwellings were rare at that time. After 1890, there began a shift from the single-family house to the multi-family apartment complex and from downtown business activity to the outlying areas. This shift brought into being the need for property management experts. Owners of buildings turned to their local real estate agent and asked if he would collect the rents, order the supplies, pay the bills, and forward the net income. Most real estate agents first entered into this new relationship as a favor to a potential future customer. Modern property management was born when the real estate profession recognized that here was a real field for the future.

Before the Great Depression of the Thirties, however, most of America's buildings were owned by individuals. After the stock market crash, much of the income property was controlled by banks,

EXHIBIT 2
Tom Cline Property Management
Balance Sheet (last fiscal year)

Assets

Current assets		
Petty cash		$ 100
Cash in bank—operating account		1,337
Cash in bank—payroll account		6,505
Properties receivable		296
Project supplies receivable		472
Total current assets		$ 8,710
Fixed assets—at cost		
Office furniture and equipment	$ 1,780	
Less: accumulated depreciation	162	
Total fixed assets		$ 1,618
Total Assets		$10,328

Liabilities and Capital

Current liabilities		
Accrued payroll taxes and work-man's compensation insurance		$ 6,505
Capital		
Capital as of January 1, 1985	$ 732	
Net income for period	19,091	
Withdrawals	(16,000)	
Total capital		$ 3,823
Total Liabilities and Capital		$10,328

insurance companies, trust companies, and other commercial firms. It was from this time that today's property management had its birth—since for the first time, a large volume of properties was gathered together under one ownership, one policy, and one common perspective.

There are three major types of buildings that are managed: commercial, industrial, and residential. Commercial buildings may be subdivided into office buildings, hotels (the oldest and best-developed phase of property management), and "store" buildings (where one structure contains several units for lease to a variety of businesses). Industrial buildings are those in which the majority of the business activities are conducted in unfinished space—that is, space which is neither plastered nor decorated on its interior surfaces. Residential buildings make up the largest group of the three major classifications and may be subdivided into single-family dwellings, multi-family apartment complexes, cooperative condominiums, and public housing.

In 1934, a group of people formed the Institute of Real Estate Management (IREM) and established ethical standards of practice for property management, to enable the public to identify qualified real estate managers. This new professional association was organized as an affiliate of the National Association of Real Estate Boards, which is now known as the National Association of Realtors (NAR).

By 1980, the IREM had over four thousand professional property managers who had met its stringent requirements in education, experience, and ethical conduct, and who therefore qualified for the designation of Certified Property Manager (CPM). They managed over seventy-seven billion dollars worth of America's income producing property. The residential units managed by CPMs totaled almost three million.

The IREM also designated management firms that met its qualifications, as Accredited Management Organizations (AMOs), and on-site managers as Accredited Resident Managers (ARMs). Besides identifying these professionals, the IREM also educated, organized, and provided services to them by sponsoring courses and seminars and by publishing programs of real estate-related literature.

The Modern Professional Real Estate Management Organization

Most property management firms have three key personnel: a chief operating executive officer, a property manager, and a resident manager. The chief operating executive officer's responsibilities include supervising other personnel, analyzing operating statements, reviewing cost programs, setting fee structures, developing the budget, establishing salary rates and fringe benefit programs, overseeing marketing strategies, and making long-term plans.

EXHIBIT 3

Company	Property Management Experience (in years)	Number of Units Managed	Fee Structure (percent of gross income)
Bailey Management Corp.	48	2,000	3–6
Jones-Wellin	10	2,000	5–9
Tom Cline Property Management	7	1,350	4–7
Perrall Management Co.	12	1,100	5
Michael Stern, Inc.	12	2,700	5
Golden City Property Management	20	1,000	5

The property manager's responsibilities include training resident managers, supervising rent collections and legal actions against delinquent tenants, supervising the flow of paperwork, ascertaining that resident managers keep the apartment complexes rented, checking that the buildings and grounds are properly maintained, seeing that tenant complaints are handled effectively, helping to control costs, generating creative advertising themes, and assisting in budget preparation.

The resident manager's responsibilities include renting the apartments, maintaining a high occupancy level, collecting and depositing rents and security deposits, ascertaining that the tenants are satisfied and are abiding by the terms of the rental agreement, performing minor maintenance and repairs, maintaining tenant records, and purchasing supplies.

THE LOCAL TRADE AREA

There were approximately ninety companies in the local trade area that were engaged in real estate management. About 77 percent of these were real estate companies that also managed a few income properties; the other 23 percent were primarily property management companies. This represented a 50 percent increase in the last five years.

Characteristics of the major firms in the local trade area that managed income properties last year are shown in exhibit 3.

HISTORY AND ORGANIZATION

Mr. Cline graduated in 1972 with a Bachelor of Science degree in Business Administration from Ohio State University. His major in finance helped him to obtain a position with Sears and Roebuck as a management trainee. He began his real estate management career as a property management trainee with the Westmark Investments, Inc., a subsidiary of Transpacific Industries. In 1978, when Westmark decided not to manage income properties anymore, he was hired by Transpacific Industries as a member of their property management department, where he was responsible for searching out and developing new apartment projects. Within a year, he was hired by Northeastern Property Consultants as a vice president and property manager. Two years later, Mr. Cline met the IREM's qualifications and became a Certified Property Manager.

Three years ago, Mr. Cline joined forces with Mr. Abel and formed a new partnership: Abel-Cline Property Management. Mr. Cline was primarily responsible for management and operations, while Mr. Abel was responsible for sales and syndications. During the next year, the number of units managed grew to 1,600. Mr. Cline was responsible for 90 percent of the growth. Believing that the partners' contributions and efforts were unequal, Mr. Cline left to form his own company, "Tom Cline Property Management." An organization chart of his new company is shown in exhibit 4.

Ms. Cheryl Brown, property manager, was previously associated with a public relations firm, an insurance company, and, most recently, Coldwell-Banker Real Estate Management Services. She did not yet have the CPM title but planned to start attending the necessary classes soon. Ms. Margaret Orr, who had three years of previous experience as a bookkeeper, was recently hired as head bookkeeper.

CASE

EXHIBIT 4
Tom Cline Property Management
Organizational Chart

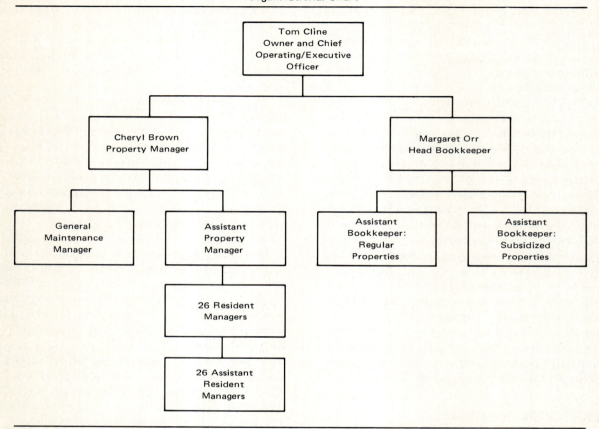

At the time of the case, Mr. Cline was also associated with the David Whitehead Company. He rented two offices of their suite (one for himself, one for his bookkeepers), and paid "office overhead" for the telephone, the secretary, the Xerox machine, and postage. Whereas Mr. Cline's company managed residential buildings, the David Whitehead Company managed commercial buildings in addition to other real estate-related activities.

OPERATIONS

Managing income property, specifically residential property, required many diversified talents in various areas, including accounting, advertising, budgeting, complaints, employee and tenant relations, fire prevention, government reports, insurance, landscaping, maintenance, marketing, parking, purchasing, renovation, and security. Final authority on extraordinary items rested with Mr. Cline, but his property manager had the authority to handle all routine matters. All policy determination and long-term planning decisions were the responsibility of Mr. Cline.

The property management business was highly public relations oriented. While Mr. Cline, along with his competitors, advertised his services in the local newspapers and the yellow pages of the telephone book, most new clients were referred to him by current/previous clients, business associates, and friends. Mr. Cline was well suited for this role. A local mortgage banker who had referred some prospective clients to him described him as "an experienced, knowledgeable, and very capable property manager" who was "one hell of a nice guy." Mr. Cline was also well liked by his employees, one of whom described him as being "sincere, understanding, perceptive, and well respected in the community." He was currently serving a term as the vice president of the local chapter of the Institute of Real Estate Management.

Financially, the company was doing fairly well. Profits had increased over the previous year, occupancy levels were high, and expenses had remained relatively constant. The rates charged for the company's services varied from 4 to 7 percent of adjusted gross income from apartment complexes, and a flat rate of $4 to $6 per unit for condominium projects. The rate varied according to the client, the project size, and the project location. The average rate was 5 percent throughout the industry. Mr. Cline was concerned, however, that he had very little working capital. He would like to see an increase in returns and an increase in working capital. No new major investments were under consideration at this time, but he wanted to increase the company's cash position to provide a "safety margin."

ENVIRONMENT

There was a possibility of rent control in communities throughout the state, although no specific measure would be on the local ballot in November. If passed, rent control might mean that rents would be fixed at their current levels; expenses, however, would continue to increase, and net income, therefore, would decrease. The real estate industry was engaged in extensive lobbying against rent control proposals.

There was also a possibility that apartment projects with mortgages insured by the Department of Housing and Urban Development would soon be governed by a set property-management fee schedule to be determined by HUD. Most of Mr. Cline's projects were in this category. The fee schedule would be based on the experience of the management company, the location

of the project, and the size of the project. If passed, property management fees would no longer have a hedge against inflation because they could not be raised. In addition, with the fee no longer based on the project's income, the management company would have no real incentive to keep the project fully rented. Property managers throughout America were fighting against this, and the outcome looked favorable.

In addition, the interest rates had been steadily increasing. This would tend to decrease the development of new apartment buildings. A local mortgage banker commented that the long term growth of apartments and condominiums in the local area looked very good because they were becoming a more popular choice as the price of a new house kept rising. He also expressed a belief that now and in the future more emphasis would be placed on the use of professional property managers due to the increased legal requirements and other complexities of managing income property.

FUTURE PLANS

At this time, Mr. Cline was seriously considering turning the day-to-day control of the company over to his property manager, Ms. Brown. Within the next three years he could become a consultant to her regarding major problems and continue to do most of the public relations work.

Since his association with the David Whitehead Company, Mr. Cline had expressed an increased interest in becoming more involved in the sales, syndications, leasing, and investment areas of real estate. He wanted to see his company remain medium sized, managing between 1,500 and 2,000 units. Increasing the size to more than 2,000 units would make it necessary to hire another property manager. He wanted to see the number of projects decrease, because it would be easier and more profitable to manage a few projects with many units than many projects with only a few units each.

There was also a problem with a lack of office space. The property manager did not have an office and worked out of her home. If and when she took over day-to-day control, she would need her own office near those of Mr. Cline and the bookkeepers. In addition, there was a need for some clerical assistance, perhaps on a part-time basis, to help with paperwork.

Finally, Mr. Cline was also trying to decide whether or not he should change his status from a single proprietorship to a corporation. Preliminary research indicated the following advantages to incorporation:

1. Incorporation would create a separate legal entity with:
   a. broad powers to do business,
   b. continuity of life,
   c. limited liability for stockholders/owners,
   d. transferable shares,
   e. better access of capital,
   f. income tax advantages in some cases.
2. Incorporation would qualify the company for fringe benefits for employees (who may also be stockholders/owners), including:
   a. deferred income plans,
   b. stock options,
   c. pension plans,
   d. life insurance.

Mr. Cline wanted, however, to investigate possible disadvantages to incorporation for a small business.

ARIZONA SOCCER CAMP

The game of soccer is thought to have originated with the Romans during their occupation of Britain. Contemporary historians state that the first soccer ball used was the head of a Dane who had been captured and slain, and whose head was kicked around for sport.[1]

The game was forbidden in England as far back as the 14th Century. In 1314, Edward II issued a proclamation which threatened imprisonment if anyone was caught playing soccer in the city. Edward III objected to the game because it discouraged the practice of archery, upon which the military strength of the nation was based. "Tenise and other games" were also banned.[2]

As the British colonized America, their pastimes were brought with them to the New World. Some

This case was prepared by John Schlacter, Professor of Marketing, Richard F. Beltramini, Assistant Professor of Marketing and Advertising, and Thomas Harkless, Research Assistant, all at Arizona State University. Copyright © Richard F. Beltramini, 1980; used by permission.

form of football, a forerunner of modern soccer and rugby, was played in the colony of Virginia as early as 1609. Football in Virginia was forbidden by ordinance, and it was not until nearly two centuries later that descriptions of the game appeared in colleges in the Northeast. "Bloody Monday" was the name given to the annual soccer game between Harvard freshmen and sophomores played on the first Monday of the new school year. This event was marked by much violence and was banned by Harvard officials in 1860.[3]

Though the sport of soccer experienced a decline in popularity on college campuses in the late 1800s, it continued to be a popular pastime among ethnic groups.[4] Cities populated by large numbers of Scotch, Irish, and English immigrants saw the sport gain in popularity through the late 1800s and early 1900s. New York, Philadelphia, the West Hudson section of New Jersey, and St. Louis were considered hotbeds of soccer around this time. These areas are still known for their strong soccer following.

In the early part of the twentieth century, soccer diminished in popularity in the United States. America's isolationist attitude at this time caused the country to shun foreign games such as soccer, and attention turned toward baseball and football. Disagreement between the two soccer leagues (the American Football Association and the American Amateur Football Association) created problems in scheduling matches, and thus contributed to the slow growth of soccer in the early 1900s. World War II also interrupted the advancement of the sport as attention in both the United States and Europe was directed toward the war effort.

The sport experienced moderate growth following the war until the 1960s. Then, in 1966, a televised broadcast of the World Cup finals brought high Nielsen ratings and soccer experienced a renewed interest. Investors formed two leagues, the United Soccer Association and the National Professional Soccer League, in an attempt to cash in on the rediscovered sport of soccer. Later the two leagues merged to form the North American Soccer League (NASL). The NASL has been able to steadily increase its attendance figures since its founding in 1968.

Soccer as a spectator sport has long been a big business in Europe and South America. Attendance for Cup finals in England and Scotland often exceeds 100,000 persons. The largest soccer stadiums in South America are built to hold nearly 200,000 persons.[5]

The growth in the popularity of soccer in the United States has been slow when compared with other countries, however. A number of reasons have been offered as an explanation of this. Soccer was regarded as a foreign game by many in the past because of its popularity in ethnic regions. Also, the game's continuous action does not lend itself to the breaks needed for the commercialization typically associated with American sports.

Though gate receipts in the United States have not reached the levels evidenced in Europe, soccer's popularity as a participant sport has grown in recent years. One reason for this could be the relatively low cost to play the game. The only equipment needed is a pair of tennis shoes, a soccer ball, and two goals. The comparatively low cost of soccer makes soccer attractive to all income levels. Skills basic to a good soccer player are speed, coordination, and endurance. Size is not an important factor, and thus, the sport can be played by people of all ages. One can easily see why participation in soccer on the amateur and scholastic levels has been increasing in recent years in the United States.[6] There are few schools that do not have soccer squads. Many schools even rate soccer as a major letter sport and some schools even have several soccer teams.

This increasing development of soccer in schools throughout the country has created a number of business opportunities for the alert investor. Among these opportunities would be a soccer camp designed to develop the soccer skills common to all successful players on both the amateur and professional levels.

In October 1978, Alan Meeder and Ron Walters began scanning the external and internal environments in an attempt to determine the attractiveness of a soccer camp for children as a business venture. The entrepreneurs considered opening the camp in the summer of 1979.

EXTERNAL ENVIRONMENT

Walters and Meeder first looked to the external environment in their analysis. The leisure industry, market, customer, and competition were all examined in their assessment of the external environment.

The Leisure Industry

Time and money are generally thought to be the two most important factors affecting the leisure industry. Having stayed fairly constant at about forty hours for the last thirty years, the work week has not grown shorter, nor does it seem likely to do so. It is the work year that has shrunk through the 1960s and 70s because of longer vacations and more holidays. The average leisure year (that time available for leisure activities) is now 123 days, a full one-third of a year. The longer leisure year has been a key force in the past growth of the leisure entertainment industry, but most agree it does not seem likely to grow from here.

America's favorite way to spend their leisure time continues to be watching television as shown in exhibit 1. Reading placed a distant second in this survey conducted by the Bureau of the Census. However, participation in outdoor recreational activities has increased in the 1970s. Exhibit 2 shows that although bicycling continues to have the largest percent of the population participation, tennis has shown the largest increase in popularity between the years 1973 and 1977. One can readily see that though Americans still consider watching television as their favorite recreational activity, participation in many

CASE

EXHIBIT 1
Favorite Leisure Activities, Selected Years: 1938–1977

			(Percent)		
Activity	1938	1960	1966	1974	1977
Reading	21	10	15	14	15
Movies and theater	17	6	5	9	6
Watching television	(NA)	28	46	46	30
Dancing	12	3	2	4	(^{1})
Listending to radio and records	9	(^{1})	2	5	4
Playing cards and games	9	6	5	8	4
Staying home with family	7	17	5	10	11
Visiting friends	4	10	5	8	4

Note: Other types of leisure activities less frequently mentioned by the respondents included resting or relaxing, dining out, sewing, participating in sports, and indoor hobbies. Percents are not additive because of multiple responses.

NA = Not available.

[1] Less than 1 percent.

Source: American Institute of Public Opinion, *The Gallup Poll: Public Opinion, 1972–1977, The Gallup Opinion Index,* report no. 146, 1977. Copyright; used by permission.

outdoor recreation activities is on the increase in the 1970s.

Many spectator sports have gained in popularity over the last twenty years as shown in exhibit 3. More specifically, attendance at North American Soccer League games has increased steadily since its beginning.

Money is the second variable affecting the leisure industry. Seemingly, an increase in revenue for the overall leisure-time industry can only come through a rise in consumer spending, which depends on Americans having money available to pursue their interests. The leisure market grew rapidly in the 1960s and early 1970s when real disposable income (that portion of income beyond the amounts needed for the essentials of everyday life) advanced significantly. Real disposable income adjusts this computation for inflation. In 1974, real disposable income dropped sharply, as the U.S. economy tumbled into a recession, and the profits of many companies associated with the leisure field also declined. Since then, real disposable income has risen steadily as seen in exhibit 4. This is important to companies in the industry, since consumer recreational expenditures invariably track the path of disposable income.

Figures from the Department of Commerce show that spending on recreation has increased from

$17.9 billion in 1960 to $101 billion in 1979, nationally. Expressed in other terms, recreation as a percent of total personal consumption has gone from 5.5 percent in 1960 to 6.8 percent in 1978 (see exhibit 5).

As exhibit 5 shows, the total dollars spent on recreational activities has continued to rise, though the percent of total personal consumption spent on recreation has remained fairly constant throughout the 1970s.

The Market

The market is defined as Maricopa County, Arizona. Over half the state's population lives in Maricopa County, and metropolitan Phoenix is the commercial and governmental center for the entire state. The county's population more than doubled in size between 1960 and 1979 and is expected to increase over the next twenty years (see exhibit 6).

Leading economic indicators all show an increase for Maricopa County between the years of 1969 and 1979. In fact, Maricopa County leads the state in terms of personal income. The county is racially mixed with Mexican Americans and Whites comprising most of the population. Additional information pertaining to the market may be seen in exhibit 7.

EXHIBIT 2
Participation in Selected
Outdoor Recreation Activities:
1973, 1976, and 1977

Activity	(Percent)		
	1973	1976	1977
Bicycle	32	36	39
Fish	30	30	36
Tennis	13	14	24
Boat[1]	16	17	20
Hunt	10	10	14
Golf	8	8	11
Ice skate	12	12	9
Water ski	7	8	8
Snowmobile	4	4	5
Sail	3	3	5
Downhill ski	4	5	4

Note: Data for 1973 and 1976 are based on nationwide surveys conducted by the A. C. Nielsen Company. In each of these surveys, 9,600 persons were asked if they participated in selected outdoor activities from time to time. Data for 1977 are based on a national telephone survey of the general population. There were 7,865 total households with eligible respondents, of which 4,029 resulted in completed interviews. In each instance, the respondent was asked if he or she had participated in selected outdoor activities more than four times in the last year.

[1] Excluding sail boating.

Source: Surveys by the A. C. Nielsen Company (copyright; used by permission) and U.S. Department of the Interior, Heritage Conservation and Recreation Service, 1977 National Outdoor Recreation Survey.

The Customer

The customer may be defined in terms of two components: (1) the participants, and (2) the parents of the participants.

The participants. The participants at the soccer camp would be both boys and girls between the ages of eight and sixteen, inclusive. In a 1977 survey conducted by the Maricopa County Youth Service Bureau, Phoenix-area youngsters were asked how they spend their free time. "Activities with friends" was the most frequent response to this question of 590 respondents. Television/radio/music/athletics, and staying around the house followed in order of

frequency. Boys spent more time in physically oriented activities, as compared to girls who preferred quieter pursuits. Boys' interests were centered around athletics, biking, camping, and hiking, while girls preferred television viewing, listening to the radio, and participating in church functions, hobbies, or activities around the house. Minority and lower-income youth expressed a high interest in activities charging no fee, such as home-centered entertainment.[7] Thus, boys in the Phoenix area are more interested in athletics than are Phoenix-area girls, and minorities and lower-income youths are price-sensitive when choosing their entertainment.

On a more specific level, the Tempe (a Phoenix area suburb) YMCA estimates that 25,000 children are currently enrolled in youth soccer clubs in the Maricopa County area. Girls compose an estimated twenty to twenty-five percent of the active participants in the valley's youth soccer programs. Of those involved in youth soccer, family incomes range from very affluent to poor. Because of the relatively low cost to play the game, soccer youth programs are popular in ethnic enclaves in Phoenix as well as in the suburbs. Thus, it becomes difficult to determine the demographics of the average child involved in youth soccer in Phoenix.

The participants' parents. Parents are likely to be the group that would actually pay for the youngsters to attend the soccer camp. Within this customer group, a sports awareness apparently already exists as is evidenced by the fact that 47 percent of the people in the valley attended either a professional or amateur sporting event in 1979. This activity was most common among households making $20,000 to $30,000 a year. Additional activities common to Phoenix residents are shown in exhibit 8.

People in the valley enjoy an active lifestyle. Participator sports are becoming more popular as society is placing a greater emphasis on health and physical fitness. Jogging and tennis are two examples of participator sports that have become popular in recent years. The warm climate Phoenix residents enjoy and the changing lifestyles caused by a longer leisure year have certainly combined to make valley residents sports enthusiasts.

Potentially large numbers of both customer groups

EXHIBIT 3
Selected Spectator Sports: 1960 to 1979

Sport	Unit	1960	1965	1970	1975	1976	1977	1978	1979
Baseball, major leagues: [1/2]									
Attendance	1,000	20,261	22,806	29,191	30,373	31,974	39,523	41,402	44,262
Regular season	1,000	19,911	22,442	28,747	29,789	31,318	38,710	40,637	43,550
National League	1,000	10,685	13,581	16,662	16,600	16,661	19,070	20,107	21,178
American League	1,000	9,227	8,861	12,085	13,189	14,658	19,640	20,530	22,372
Playoffs	1,000	(X)	(X)	191	276	432	475	428	344
World Series	1,000	350	364	253	308	223	338	337	368
Basketball: [3]									
College: [4] Teams	Number	(NA)	(NA)	(NA)	(NA)	(NA)	1,214	1,253	1,240
Attendance	1,000	(NA)	(NA)	(NA)	(NA)	(NA)	29,041	29,104	30,025
Professional, attendance [1/5]	1,000	1,986	2,750	7,113[6]	10,954[6]	8,494	10,706	10,672	10,665
Football:									
College: [4] Teams	Number	620	616	617	634	637	638	643	643
Attendance	1,000	20,403	24,683	29,466	31,688	32,012	32,905	34,252	35,020
Pro: [7] Total attendance	1,000	4,154[8]	6,547[8]	9,992	10,689	11,563	11,552	13,395	13,812
Regular season	1,000	4,054[8]	6,416[8]	9,533	10,213	11,071	11,018	12,771	13,182
Postseason games [9]	1,000	100[8]	131[8]	458	476	493	534	624	630
N. American Soccer League: [10]									
Teams	Number	(X)	(X)	6	20	20	18	24	24
Attendance	1,000	(X)	(X)	(NA)	1,825	2,748	3,674	5,351	5,800
National Hockey League: [3/11]									
Regular season attendance	1,000	2,387	2,823	5,992	9,522	9,104	8,564	8,526	8,333
Playoffs attendance	1,000	187	304	462	784	727	646	686	694
World Hockey Association: [3/12]									
Regular season attendance	1,000	(X)	(X)	(X)	4,096	4,123	3,625	2,890	2,193
Playoffs attendance	1,000	(X)	(X)	(X)	336	446	401	231	186
Professional boxers [13/14]	Number	2,920[15]	2,202	5,071	7,647	8,327	8,872	9,143	9,461
Boxing receipts, gross [13/16]	$1,000	5,902[15]	8,264	10,642	13,179	18,000[17]	19,036[17]	24,785	28,653
Horseracing: [18/19] Racing days	Number	6,099	8,051	9,962	13,110	13,570	13,300	13,147	13,083[20]
Attendance	1,000	46,879	62,887	69,704	78,662	79,307	75,987	75,324	73,818[20]
Parimutuel turnover	Mil. dol	3,358	4,615	5,977	7,862	9,421	9,698	10,029	10,580[20]
Revenue to States	Mil. dol	258	370	486	582	616	700	673	707[20]
Greyhound: [18] Racing days	Number	2,478	3,443	3,023	3,960	4,589	5,218	5,501	5,813
Attendance	1,000	7,924	10,865	12,660	17,458	18,978	19,985	20,272	21,155
Parimutuel turnover	Mil. dol	322	460	730	1,261	1,429	1,591	1,746	1,987
Revenue to States	Mil. dol	22	33	53	91	107	119	128	140

NA = Not available.   X = Not applicable.   [1] Excludes Alaska and Hawaii.   [2] Source: The National League of Professional Baseball Clubs, New York, N.Y., *National League Green Book;* and The American League of Professional Baseball Clubs, New York, N.Y., *American League Red Book.*   [3] Season ending in year shown.   [4] Source: National Collegiate Athletic Assn., Shawnee Mission, Kans.   [5] Source: National Basketball Assn., New York, N.Y. Includes playoffs.   [6] Includes American Basketball Assn., which, beginning 1977, ceased operation.   [7] Source: National Football League, New York, N.Y.   [8] Includes American Football League. Beginning 1970, American Football League merged with National Football League.   [9] Beginning 1970, includes Pro Bowl, a non-championship game.   [10] Source: North American Soccer League, New York, N.Y.   [11] Source: National Hockey League, Montreal, Quebec.   [12] The World Hockey Assn., Hartford, Conn.   [13] Source: The Ring Publishing Corp., New York, N.Y., *The Ring Magazine* (copyright).   [14] Boxers listed for one or more bouts.   [15] Excludes Alaska.   [16] Excludes closed-circuit TV receipts.   [17] Unpublished unofficial estimate.   [18] Source: National Assn. of State Racing Commissioners, Lexington, Ky.   [19] Includes thoroughbred, harness, quarter horse, and fairs.   [20] Estimate.

Source: U.S. Dept. of Commerce, Bureau of the Census, *Statistical Abstract of the United States,* 1980, p. 248.

EXHIBIT 4
Spending for Recreation in the United States
(in billions of dollars)

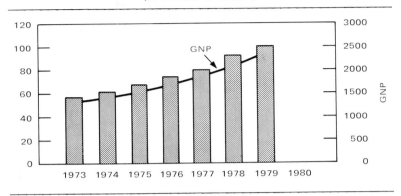

Source: Standard and Poors, *Industry Surveys,* 1980, p. L-9.

EXHIBIT 5
Personal Consumption Expenditures For Leisure and Cultural Activities

	1960	1965	1970	1975	1978
Personal Consumption Expenditures for leisure and cultural activities	$17,855	$25,907	$40,999	$66,527	$91,244
Expenditures for leisure and cultural activities as a percent of GWP	3.5	3.8	4.2	4.4	4.3
Expenditures for leisure and cultural activities as a percent of all personal consumption expenditures	5.5	6.0	6.6	6.8	6.8

Source: U.S. Dept. of Commerce, Bureau of the Census, *Statistical Abstract of the United States,* 1980, p. 245.

(soccer participants and their parents) exist. Exhibits 9 and 10 show the breakdown of the population by age and by sex. We see from these figures that while both the 6–17 and the 25–44 age groups are increasing in numbers, only the latter group increased as a percentage of the population over the 1970s.

The Competition

The assessment of the competition that a soccer camp would face may be viewed on two levels. Level 1 is defined as any camp offering an educational or social experience. Level 2 is camps intended to improve soccer skills in youngsters.

Level one. In a broad sense, a soccer camp would be competing for dollars of disposable income spent on sending a child to a camp of any sort. This category would include any camp offering social interaction that would help to make a youngster a well-rounded individual. Summer camps offer the opportunity for a child to develop friendships that they can maintain for many years. Band camps, golf camps, tennis camps, and camps run by the Boy Scouts and Girl Scouts would all be examples of competition faced at this level.

The Boy Scouts currently operate five camps in the Maricopa County area. The largest of these camps is Camp Geronimo, located north of Phoenix in

CASE

EXHIBIT 6
Arizona Population Projections by County
Selected Years: 1985–2000

County	1985	1990	1995	2000
Apache	57,513	65,931	73,509	81,160
Cochise	104,317	116,197	126,308	134,814
Coconino	99,974	117,620	134,656	150,062
Gila	42,391	44,518	45,989	46,964
Graham	29,280	32,698	34,427	36,190
Greenlee	12,809	13,722	14,451	14,516
Maricopa	1,621,941	1,831,559	2,077,239	2,352,335
Mohave	57,871	64,720	71,261	78,006
Navajo	77,495	89,340	103,214	116,896
Pima	555,411	608,907	672,450	744,786
Pinal	101,391	109,220	119,041	127,527
Santa Cruz	22,935	26,297	29,296	32,091
Yavapai	69,123	77,506	85,151	95,195
Yuma	88,245	95,722	105,323	116,967
State Total	2,940,697	3,293,956	3,692,315	4,127,510

Source: Statistical Abstract of Arizona, University of Arizona, Division of Economic and Business Research, 1979, p. 21.

EXHIBIT 7
Maricopa County Statistics

Population	Racial Breakdown	Leading Cities—Population
1970 Census 971,228	White 1,170,405	Phoenix 716,100
1979 Estimate 1,453,500	Spanish Heritage 212,175	Mesa 130,000
	Indian 16,625	Tempe 106,765
	Black 45,595	Scottsdale 85,070
	Oriental 5,345	Glendale 80,000
	Other 3,355	Sun City 45,125

Economic Indicators

Indicator	1969	1979	% Change
Population	946,000	1,453,500	+ 53.6
Retail Sales	$2,126,026,000	$7,854,996,000	+269.5
Bank Deposits	$1,985,290,000	$6,705,628,000	+237.8
Vehicle Registrations	672,347	1,095,774	+ 63.0
Motor Fuel Consumption (gal)	433,976,000	740,598,000	+ 70.7

Principal Industries

Manufacturing (high technology products), agriculture (largest producer of crops and livestock in the state), tourism and travel (over $2 billion in annual expenditures).

Source: "The Arizona Statistical Review," Valley National Bank, 1979, pp. 5–8.

EXHIBIT 8
Leisure Activities of Metro Phoenix Residents

Activities—Past 30 Days—By Income

	Under $5,000	$5,000–$9,999	$10,000–$14,999	$15,000–$19,999	$20,000–$24,999	$25,000–$29,999	$30,000–$34,999	$35,000–$39,999	$40,000–$44,999	$45,000–$49,999	$50,000 & Over	Total Area	Projected Households	MEDIAN INCOME
Dined at restaurant	5%	9%	10%	13%	16%	13%	10%	6%	5%	3%	9%	77%	458,000	$23,979
Purchased food at a fast-food operation	5	8	10	14	16	14	10	7	5	3	9	68	405,000	24,209
Attended drive-in/in-door movie theater	3	7	10	12	15	14	11	7	6	3	11	35	208,000	25,772
Played golf	2	6	8	13	13	12	11	7	8	5	15	13	77,000	28,198
Played tennis	2	5	8	9	12	13	11	9	8	5	18	10	60,000	30,334
Played racquetball	1	4	7	11	15	15	14	6	10	4	13	11	65,000	28,805
Gone bowling	7	6	12	12	16	18	17	19	22	10	19	14	83,000	25,982
Had an outdoor barbecue	3	5	8	14	15	15	11	7	6	4	12	40	238,000	26,551
Gone swimming	4	6	8	14	13	13	11	6	8	4	12	34	202,000	26,653
Gone bicycling for health or recreation	3	7	8	14	14	14	11	7	7	4	11	29	173,000	26,473
Gone horseback riding for recreation	3	6	6	11	11	13	14	6	9	5	17	6	36,000	30,114

Activities—Past 12 Months—By Income

	Under $5,000	$5,000–$9,999	$10,000–$14,999	$15,000–$19,999	$20,000–$24,999	$25,000–$29,999	$30,000–$34,999	$35,000–$39,999	$40,000–$44,999	$45,000–$49,999	$50,000 & Over	Total Area	Projected Households	MEDIAN INCOME
Camped out	4%	5%	10%	15%	16%	14%	11%	8%	6%	3%	9%	39%	232,000	$25,296
Gone fishing	4	6	9	14	15	14	11	7	5	3	11	35	208,000	25,688
Gone hunting	3	4	7	15	14	17	12	7	6	3	12	15	89,000	26,979
Gone boating	3	5	9	12	14	14	13	8	7	3	13	24	143,000	31,803
Visited Big Surf	3	5	5	13	15	15	11	7	5	5	15	12	71,000	28,021
Visited Turf Paradise	3	7	6	13	12	16	8	9	6	3	16	7	42,000	27,349
Visited Phoenix Greyhound Park	3	12	10	15	8	13	14	7	6	2	10	9	54,000	27,143
Visited Phoenix Zoo	4	7	8	14	17	14	11	7	6	2	10	25	149,000	24,856
Visited Phoenix Art Museum	4	6	6	10	15	11	11	7	9	5	17	12	71,000	28,939
Visited Heard Museum	5	6	7	13	15	11	11	5	8	4	14	10	60,000	26,466
Visited Phoenix Public Library (including branches)	3	6	9	13	18	12	11	7	6	3	12	25	149,000	25,382

(Continued)

EXHIBIT 8 (Continued)

Activities—Past 12 Months—By Income

	Under $5,000	$5,000–$9,999	$10,000–$14,999	$15,000–$19,999	$20,000–$24,999	$25,000–$29,999	$30,000–$34,999	$35,000–$39,999	$40,000–$44,999	$45,000–$49,999	$50,000 & Over	Total Area	Projected Households	MEDIAN INCOME
Visited other community public library in Valley	3	7	8	13	15	14	10	7	8	3	12	23	137,000	$26,559
Attended Phoenix Symphony Concert	5	6	4	13	10	10	11	5	8	4	25	6	36,000	31,528
Attended event at Phoenix Civic Plaza	3	6	7	12	15	13	12	8	8	4	12	21	125,000	27,500
Attended event at Grady Gammage Auditorium	4	4	6	12	13	12	11	7	8	4	17	15	89,000	28,959
Attended Phoenix Little Theater performance	5	5	6	8	15	9	12	10	8	2	21	5	30,000	31,964
Attended community theater production in Valley	3	4	8	11	13	13	10	5	7	6	20	8	48,000	29,327
Attended professional sports event	2	4	4	10	14	15	13	9	8	5	16	22	131,000	30,469
Attended amateur sports event	2	5	5	11	15	14	12	9	8	5	13	25	149,000	29,000
Bought a hard-back book (other than text)	3	6	6	12	18	13	11	7	8	4	14	36	214,000	27,320
Taken 1–2 day recreation trip by car, outside Maricopa County	3	7	10	14	15	14	10	7	7	3	10	53	315,000	25,588

Source: *Inside Phoenix 1979*, Phoenix Newspapers, Inc., p. 73.

EXHIBIT 9
Age Breakdowns—Metro Phoenix

	1960 U.S. Census		1970 U.S. Census		1979 Consumer Survey	
Age Group	Number of Persons	Percent	Number of Persons	Percent	Number of Persons	Percent
Under 2	33,178	5.0	34,302	3.5	59,000	4.1
2–5	65,054	9.8	68,967	7.1	97,000	6.7
6–11	88,203	13.3	123,024	12.7	151,000	10.5
12–13	28,102	4.2	41,520	4.3	50,000	3.5
14–17	42,917	6.5	77,255	8.0	111,000	7.7
18–24	59,354	8.9	112,942	11.6	176,000	12.2
25–29	42,910	6.5	66,460	6.9	115,000	8.0
30–34	45,243	6.9	56,312	5.8	101,000	7.0
35–39	49,080	7.4	54,262	5.6	86,000	6.0
40–44	43,501	6.5	55,512	5.7	68,000	4.7
45–49	39,223	5.9	56,775	5.9	63,000	4.4
50–54	32,058	4.8	49,525	5.1	63,000	4.4
55–59	26,017	3.9	43,297	4.5	69,000	4.8
60–64	21,215	3.2	39,205	4.0	68,000	4.7
65–74	33,686	5.1	59,889	6.2	107,000	7.4
75 & Over	13,769	2.1	30,178	3.1	56,000	3.9
Total	663,510	100.0	969,425	100.0	1,440,000[1]	100.0
Median Age	26.7 years		27.0 years		28.2 years	

Source: *Inside Phoenix 1979,* Phoenix Newspapers, Inc., p. 10.

EXHIBIT 10
Male-Female Proportion by Age, 1979

Age Group	Male Percent	Female Percent
Under 2	50	50
2–5	53	47
6–11	53	47
12–13	50	50
14–17	49	51
18–24	51	49
25–29	48	52
30–34	49	51
35–39	51	49
40–44	47	53
45–49	50	50
50–54	49	51
55–59	45	55
60–64	46	54
65–74	46	54
75 & Over	50	50
Total Area	50	50

Source: *Inside Phoenix 1979,* Phoenix Newspapers, Inc., p. 11.

Payson, Arizona. The majority of the campers attending Camp Geronimo each summer are in the 11–15 age group. Phoenix area Girl Scouts report that approximately 2,000 girls attend their camps each year, also. Currently nearly 20,000 girls are involved in Girl Scouts in Maricopa County.

Level two. On a more specific level, a soccer camp would be competing with other camps in the area designed to improve soccer skills. Day camps as well as boarding camps would be considered competition at this level.

No other soccer boarding camps are currently being offered in the Phoenix area. However, it is rumored that a Phoenix-area entrepreneur plans to open a soccer camp next summer to be called the Camp of Champions. This camp has been seeking highly-touted foreign players to serve as coaches. It is also rumored that the Camp of Champions is planning heavy promotional spending to publicize their entry into the market.

One day camp is already offered at this time in

Phoenix. A day camp differs from a boarding camp in that those attending day camps are only there from morning until afternoon. Under a boarding camp concept, the youngsters do not go home at night, but instead stay on the premises. Additional facilities would then become necessary for the campers to sleep and eat if Meeder and Walters want to operate a boarding camp. Twenty-four-hour supervision would also be necessary.

Phoenix's only soccer day camp runs two one-week sessions for youngsters between the ages of seven and thirteen. An advanced session lasting one week is also offered for the more experienced players between the ages of fourteen and seventeen. The lessons begin at 9:00 A.M. and are finished by 4:00 P.M. Instruction is provided by Phoenix area soccer professionals. The beginning sessions are designed to teach youngsters the basic skills of a good soccer player, and the skills are refined in the advanced session. Both the beginning and the advanced lessons stress good sportsmanship. One week of lessons at this day camp costs the student $70. Attendance in 1977 totaled about 150 children per week for the beginning lessons and 75 children at the advanced lessons.

INTERNAL ENVIRONMENT

After completing their scan of the external environment, Meeder and Walters next turned their attention to the internal environment. The management, personnel, location, and finances were the resources examined as part of the assessment of the internal environment.

The Management

The two entrepreneurs who are considering opening the soccer camp have different backgrounds, but are alike in that they both love soccer. Alan Meeder was attending college on a track scholarship when he first became interested in soccer. After an injury forced him to give up track, he played soccer for the school. Meeder went on to play semi-pro soccer in California and later to become headmaster at a private boy's school in Ojai, California. Meeder presently owns soccer camps in Washington and California. His

knowledge of soccer and experience in working with youngsters would provide an excellent background for running a soccer camp.

Ron Walters has been actively involved in youth sports programs at the Tempe YMCA for a number of years. Walters is an excellent salesman and immediately becomes excited when asked about his ideas for the proposed soccer camp. Walters originally saw the opportunity for a soccer school in the Phoenix area in 1977. After leaving his job as a life insurance salesman, Walters put together a trip to a soccer camp in California for twenty Phoenix area children. Ron's plans went sour when a travel agent absconded with his deposit, leaving him with no reservations and twenty children ready to go to California. With a great deal of luck and a few phone calls the trip went off as scheduled.

Walters later contacted Meeder with his idea of a soccer camp in Arizona and the partnership was formed. These two men will serve as principal spokesmen for the camp, and will organize, staff, plan, and direct the camp. Walters and Meeder believe the time is right to open a soccer camp in the Phoenix area.

Personnel

Alan Meeder's soccer background should provide enough contacts to obtain qualified players to staff the camp. Players from West Germany, England, and Spain are highly respected in the sports community for their soccer skills. Though they would be located nearer to the camp, players from Arizona are not as well known for their skills. However, California soccer players have the advantage of being close to the proposed camp and are well-regarded in the United States for their soccer abilities.

The location becomes a key factor because soccer camps generally pay the transportation expense of the coaches. Meeder and Walters estimate this cost to run hopefully not more than $2,000. European players would be easy to attract to a soccer camp in Arizona since they often seek coaching jobs during the off season as a vacation in the United States. The camp will pay the coaches a salary that is expected to amount to about $200 a week.

Coaches would be expected to perform night time

EXHIBIT 11
Meeders & Walters Soccer Camp
Proposed Job Description

Job Title:	Instructor
Supervisor:	Alan Meeder
Location:	Orme School, Bisbee, Arizona or Cochise College, Douglas, Arizona

Job is that of a soccer coach for youngsters between the ages of eight and sixteen. Applicant should have soccer coaching and playing experience and enjoy working with children. Duties to be performed include:

1. Soccer instruction through the use of films, chalk talks, and demonstrations.
2. Lead the students in basic soccer drills and conditioning exercises.
3. Referee scrimages.
4. Supervise students during their free time in the afternoon and evening.
5. Evaluate performance of students.

supervisory duties in addition to day time instruction. It is important that the coaches enjoy working with children, have good verbal skills, and a strong soccer background. A proposed job description has been drawn up and is shown in exhibit 11.

Location

The cost of renting a facility large enough to accommodate between 100 and 200 people is expected to be the major cost incurred by Meeder and Walters. Two sites are presently available for the location of the soccer camp. Either location would be suitable.

Orme School. One proposed site for the soccer camp is a private boarding school located about ninety miles north of Phoenix. This location offers the advantage of a higher altitude and lower temperatures than one would find in Phoenix during the summer. Orme School is known throughout the Phoenix area for its picturesque setting. Complete recreational facilities including five soccer fields, a swimming pool, and recreation room are available for the campers' use. The profit potential of the camp would be limited by the size of the Orme facility. It has been estimated that the facility can

accommodate 150 youngsters plus staff at one time. The camp is available for three weeks during the summer months. Negotiations were started with the owners of the school, and Meeder and Walters believe the facility could be rented for about $44,000 for the three week period.

Cochise College. The second proposed site for the camp is located southeast of Phoenix near Douglas, Arizona at a small college. The Cochise College facility is available for five weeks during the summer months, and will hold 200 youngsters plus staff at one time. Complete recreational facilities are also offered at this location. Cochise College is farther from Phoenix than Orme School, and temperatures are likely to be higher in Douglas, Arizona. However, Walters and Meeder estimate the facility could be rented for less than the Orme facility.

Financial

To conclude their internal analysis Walters and Meeder developed a pro-forma income statement for the camp's first year of operations (see exhibit 12). As was expected, rent expense is the largest cost associated with such a venture (note the difference in rent for the two facilities). Payroll was the next largest cost estimated at $5,600. Meeder and Walters estimated that they would need about one coach for each fifteen youngsters. Payroll was thus determined to be a variable cost since the number of coaches would reflect this 15 to 1 student to teacher ratio. In addition, they plan to have a supervisor to child ratio of 1 to 6.

Meeder and Walters noted that the break-even point for their soccer camp would be high due to the high level of fixed costs required for such a venture. Thus, we see that the camp would be exposed to a great deal of operating risk. However, assuming demand estimates are correct, the potential returns from operating the camp for a three-week period could be very attractive.

Mission Statement

With their analysis of the external and internal environment complete, the entrepreneurs developed a mission statement for their proposed camp:

CASE

EXHIBIT 12
Meeders & Walters Soccer Camp
Pro Forma Income Statement, 1979

	Orme		Cochise	
Sales				
150 @ $150 each for 3 weeks		$67,500		$67,500
Variable cost of goods sold				
Payroll	$ 5,600		$ 5,600	
Travel	1,350		1,350	
Camp supplies	1,300		1,300	
		$ 8,250		$ 8,250
Marginal Income		$59,450		$59,450
Fixed costs and expenses				
Rent	$43,875		$37,125	
Insurance	675		675	
Advertising	700		700	
Postage	560		560	
Legal and accounting	500		500	
Office expense	2,360		2,360	
Video expense	600		600	
		$49,270		$42,520
Net Income From Operations		$10,180		$16,930

We want to profitably operate a live-in soccer camp that will:

1. Teach soccer skills, and
2. Provide a beneficial social experience for children between the ages of eight and sixteen (inclusive) living in Maricopa County, Arizona.

REFERENCES

1. Menke, Frank G. *Encyclopedia of Sports,* A. S. Barnes & Co., New York, 1978, pp. 871–879.
2. Ibid.
3. Henshaw, Richard. *Encyclopedia of World Soccer,* New Republic Books, Washington, D.C., 1979, pp. 739–748.
4. Ibid.
5. Menke, *Encyclopedia of Sports.*
6. Ibid.
7. Maricopa County Youth Service Bureau, "Needs Assessment: A Survey of Youth Needs in Metropolitan Phoenix," 1977, pp. 9–19.

Market Identification and Environments

The market environments for most companies are highly complex and dynamic. A variety of forces affect the marketplace, and if the firm is to successfully compete, the marketing manager must remain attuned to those forces and to the variations in behavior exhibited by potential buyers. To do this, marketing research is often needed to better define what is going on within the market, to identify the various market alternatives, and to analyze the attractiveness of each for the firm.

ENVIRONMENTAL FORCES IN THE MARKETPLACE

Although the forces operating within a market environment can be classified in many ways, they are usually grouped into the following categories:

1. Social & Cultural Forces
2. Political & Legal Forces
3. Economic Forces
4. Competitive Forces
5. Technological Forces

Among the more important social and cultural forces affecting modern market environments are population demographics, styles and qualities of life, social awareness, and sex roles. Shifts in demographics resulting from advancing life expectancies and the aging of the huge "baby boom" group born in the 1940's have altered the overall market structure in the United States. The manners in which people work and spend their leisure time, and the changing roles of men and women, also have created and closed numerous markets. And, greater concern for protection of the environment, the problems of the poor and elderly, and other social issues, have extended the scope of the marketing efforts of many firms.

While social and cultural forces tend to change relatively slowly, political and legal factors can cause rapid shifts in the marketplace. Laws governing competitive practices and consumer protection, procedures for obtaining patent protection, regulations concerning the importing of foreign goods, policies governing the safety of new products, and a variety of other political and legal matters, can open or close markets quickly.

Economic factors also can affect the firm's market environment quite rapidly. Consumer ability and willingness to spend will change dramatically depending on whether the economy is in a period of prosperity or recession. Accordingly, interest rates, employment levels, growth in GNP, and other variables must be considered when making an assessment of the marketplace.

The nature and extent of competition in the market is one of the more important environmental factors the marketing manager must examine. The number of competitors, the quality of their operations, and their propensities for growth will significantly affect development of the firm's marketing program.

Advances in technology are some of the most difficult environmental forces to assess. Changes in product and service offerings, the manner in which goods are produced, and the methods used to deliver products to the end consumer, can make the difference between market success and failure. If obsolescence is to be avoided, the marketing manager must be able not only to identify impending changes in technology, but also to understand the direction the technology will take in the next five to ten years.

CONSUMER AND INDUSTRIAL MARKETS

A key part of the overall examination of the environment within which the firm operates is the behavior of potential buyers. Whether operating in consumer or industrial markets, the marketing manager must be attuned to the unique processes buyers go through in making their purchase decisions. The article by Philip Kotler, "Behavioral Models for Analyzing Buyers," describes one approach to the issue of consumer buying behavior. Frederick E. Webster, Jr.'s article, "Modeling the Industrial Buying Process," considers the nature of industrial buying behavior.

Generally, the buying processes for consumer goods can be examined in terms of three stages: pre-purchase behavior, purchase behavior, and post-purchase behavior. The amount of effort going into buying depends, of course, on many factors. Among the more critical external factors are the individual's cultural and social standing (including social class and reference groups). Factors internal to the individual include his or her needs, perceptions, past learning, personality, and self-concept. All of these variables influence the individual's needs and the process the individual uses to identify and evaluate alternatives, make decisions, and purchase and use products and services.

There are some distinct differences between consumer and industrial markets. Industrial markets—consisting of manufacturing, agriculture, middlemen, and government segments—tend to contain buyers that are more sophisticated and rational. They are more knowledgeable about the products and services they purchase, and are less likely to be affected by nonfunctional product attributes. This is especially true in instances of modified rebuys and straight rebuys—situations where purchases have previously been made from the firm.

MARKETING RESEARCH AND INFORMATION SYSTEMS

To examine the many attributes of the environment, the marketing manager typically uses some form of marketing information system. One of the more popular descriptions of an information system is presented in Philip Kotler's article, "A Design for the Firm's Marketing Nerve Center." Designed to collect primary and secondary data and process it into usable sets of information for decision-making purposes, the information system relies heavily on marketing research. To ensure that the collection of data is made in an unbiased and efficient manner, the marketing research process typically follows a series of well-defined steps:

1. Determine the information needed to solve the problem.
2. Make a preliminary investigation of the general issue to better identify the nature and scope of the particular problem.
3. Conduct an analysis to determine if the benefits to be derived from collecting data are worth the costs involved.
4. Develop the research design (i.e., survey, observation, or experimental method).
5. If appropriate, determine the size of the sample to be used for data collection.
6. If appropriate, develop a method for sample selection (i.e., probability or nonprobability sampling technique).

7. Develop a questionnaire or other data-collection instrument.
8. Conduct the market study.
9. Analyze the data.
10. Prepare a report in usable form for the decision-maker.

MARKET SEGMENTATION AND PRODUCT DIFFERENTIATION

The collection and processing of information can be extremely helpful to the marketing manager in better identifying and assessing the potential of possible target markets, and in developing a set of competitive strategies. One of the first decisions a marketing manager must make is whether to take a product differentiation or market segmentation approach to the marketing effort. With a product differentiation approach (sometimes called the whole market method) the marketing manager elects not to recognize diverse facets of the market. Instead, the market is treated as a single entity, and the firm's product will be essentially the same as all others with which it is competing. The main strategy of this approach is to use various forms of promotion to create an *image* of difference between the products.

A market segmentation strategy is quite different. With this approach, the marketing manager recognizes that a "market" is really composed of a number of submarkets, or segments, each of which has unique characteristics. Accordingly, the firm will develop a product to specifically serve the needs of a particular segment. This approach relies more on product development than on promotion, and is based on the premise that an improved product-to-market match can be created. The resulting product is more likely to be successful since it should better satisfy the particular needs of a particular market. The segmentation approach is preferred to the product differentiation method, although both have been used successfully.

Markets can be segmented on many bases, depending on the specific product. Among the more common methods for segmenting markets are geography, population demographics, psychographics, and product use. Certainly the two most common methods are based on geography and demographics. Most firms do not have the resources to make their products available nationwide.

Thus, they need to limit their marketing efforts to those geographic areas that offer the greatest opportunities. In addition, geographic segmentation is appropriate in many instances because there are variations in market needs in different parts of the country.

Demographics are often used as bases for segmenting markets for two main reasons. First, peoples' needs for products and services vary with such factors as sex, age, and income. Second, it is relatively easy to segment on this basis since population data is readily available on the demographic characteristics of nearly all possible segments.

Psychographics and product use also have served as bases for segmenting markets. Psychographic factors relate to how people live their lives, and include such variables as lifestyle and social class. Segmenting on the basis of product use typically concerns such patterns as how and when people use the product, and whether they are heavy or light users. Both of these approaches to segmenting have proven to be difficult to quantify and use for the identification of actual markets.

The selection of a target market(s) is one of the most important decisions a marketing manager will make. A thorough understanding of the environment and of the buyer's characteristics is essential to ensuring that there are enough people with money to spend, and a willingness to spend it. With such an understanding, the marketing manager can begin to formulate product, price, distribution, and promotional strategies for the desired market.

Philip Kotler

Behavioral Models for Analyzing Buyers

In times past, management could arrive at a fair understanding of its buyers through the daily experience of selling to them. But the growth in the size of firms and markets has removed many decision-makers from direct contact with buyers. Increasingly, decision-makers have had to turn to summary statistics and to behavioral theory, and are spending more money today than ever before to try to understand their buyers.

Who buys? How do they buy? And why? The first two questions relate to relatively overt aspects of buyer behavior, and can be learned about through direct observation and interviewing.

But uncovering *why* people buy is an extremely difficult task. The answer will tend to vary with the investigator's behavioral frame of reference.

The buyer is subject to many influences which trace a complex course through his psyche and lead eventually to overt purchasing responses. This conception of the buying process is illustrated in figure 1. Various influences and their modes of transmission are shown at the left. At the right are the buyer's responses in choice of product, brand, dealer, quantities, and frequency. In the center stands the buyer and his mysterious psychological processes. The buyer's psyche is a "black box" whose workings can be only partially deduced. The marketing strategist's challenge to the behavioral scientist is to construct a more specific model of the mechanism in the black box.

Unfortunately no generally accepted model of the mechanism exists. The human mind, the only entity in nature with deep powers of understanding, still remains the least understood. Scientists can explain planetary motion, genetic determination, and molecular behavior. Yet they have only partial, and often partisan, models of *human* behavior.

Source: From the *Journal of Marketing,* Vol. 29 (October 1965), pp. 37–45. Reprinted by permission of the American Marketing Association.

Nevertheless, the marketing strategist should recognize the potential interpretative contributions of different partial models for explaining buyer behavior. Depending upon the product, different variables and behavioral mechanisms may assume particular importance. A psychoanalytic behavioral model might throw much light on the factors operating in cigarette demand, while an economic behavioral model might be useful in explaining machine-tool purchasing. Sometimes alternative models may shed light on different demand aspects of the same product.

What are the most useful behavioral models for interpreting the transformation of buying influences into purchasing responses? Five different models of the buyer's "black box" are presented in the present article, along with their respective marketing applications: (1) the Marshallian model, stressing economic motivations; (2) the Pavlovian model, learning; (3) the Freudian model, psychoanalytic motivations; (4) the Veblenian model, social-psychological factors; and (5) the Hobbesian model, organizational factors. These models represent radically different conceptions of the mainsprings of human behavior.

THE MARSHALLIAN ECONOMIC MODEL

Economists were the first professional group to construct a specific theory of buyer behavior. The theory holds that purchasing decisions are the result of largely "rational" and conscious economic calculations. The individual buyer seeks to spend his income on those goods that will deliver the most utility (satisfaction) according to his tastes and relative prices.

The antecedents for this view trace back to the writings of Adam Smith and Jeremy Bentham. Smith set the tone by developing a doctrine of economic growth based on the principle that man is motivated by self-interest in all his actions.[1] Bentham refined this view and saw man as finely calculating and weighing the expected pleasures and pains of every contemplated action.[2]

Bentham's "felicific calculus" was not applied to consumer behavior (as opposed to entrepreneurial behavior) until the late 19th century. Then, the "marginal-utility" theory of value was formulated independently and almost simultaneously by Jevons[3] and Marshall[4] in England, Menger[5] in Austria, and Walras[6] in Switzerland.

Alfred Marshall was the great consolidator of the classical and neoclassical tradition in economics; and his synthesis in the form of demand-supply analysis constitutes the main source of modern micro-economic thought in the English-speaking world. His

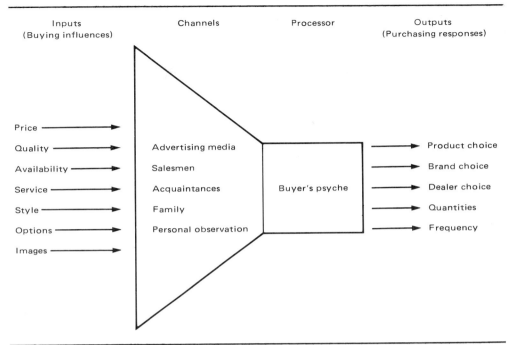

theoretical work aimed at realism, but his method was to start with simplifying assumptions and to examine the effect of a change in a single variable (say, price) when all other variables were held constant.

He would "reason out" the consequences of the provisional assumptions and in subsequent steps modify his assumptions in the direction of more realism. He employed the "measuring rod of money" as an indicator of the intensity of human psychological desires. Over the years his methods and assumptions have been refined into what is now known as *modern utility theory:* economic man is bent on maximizing his utility, and does this by carefully calculating the "felicific" consequences of any purchase.

As an example, suppose on a particular evening that John is considering whether to prepare his own dinner or dine out. He estimates that a restaurant meal would cost $2.00 and a home-cooked meal 50 cents. According to the Marshallian model, if John expects less than four times as much satisfaction from the restaurant meal as the home-cooked meal, he will eat at home. The economist typically is not concerned with how these relative preferences are formed by John, or how they may be psychologically modified by new stimuli.

Yet John will not always cook at home. The principle of diminishing marginal utility operates. Within a given time interval—say, a week—the utility of each additional home-cooked meal diminishes. John gets tired of home meals and other products become relatively more attractive.

John's efficiency in maximizing his utility depends on the adequacy of his information and his freedom of choice. If he is not perfectly aware of costs, if he misestimates the relative delectability of the two meals, or if he is barred from entering the restaurant, he will not maximize his potential utility. His choice processes are rational, but the results are inefficient.

Marketing Applications of Marshallian Model

Marketers usually have dismissed the Marshallian model as an absurd figment of ivory-tower imagination. Certainly the behavioral essence of the situation is omitted, in viewing man as calculating the marginal utility of a restaurant meal over a home-cooked meal.

Eva Mueller has reported a study where only one-fourth of the consumers in her sample bought with any substantial degree of deliberation.[7] Yet there are a number of ways to view the model.

From one point of view the Marshallian model is tautological and therefore neither true nor false. The model holds that the buyer acts in the light of his best "interest." But this is not very informative.

A second view is that this is a *normative* rather than a *descriptive* model of behavior. The model provides logical norms for buyers who want to be "rational." Although the consumer is not likely to employ economic analysis to decide between a box of Kleenex and Scotties, he may apply economic analysis in deciding whether to buy a new car. Industrial buyers even more clearly would want an economic calculus for making good decisions.

A third view is that economic factors operate to a greater or lesser extent in all markets, and, therefore, must be included in any comprehensive description of buyer behavior.

Furthermore, the model suggests useful behavioral hypotheses such as: (a) The lower the price of the product, the higher the sales. (b) The lower the price of substitute products, the lower the sales of this product; and the lower the price of complementary products, the higher the sales of this product. (c) The higher the real income, the higher the sales of this product, provided that it is not an "inferior" good. (d) The higher the promotional expenditures, the higher the sales.

The validity of these hypotheses does not rest on whether *all* individuals act as economic calculating machines in making their purchasing decisions. For example, some individuals may buy *less* of a product when its price is reduced. They may think that the quality has gone down, or that ownership has less status value. If a majority of buyers view price reductions negatively, then sales may fall, contrary to the first hypothesis.

But for most goods a price reduction increases the relative value of the goods in many buyers' minds and leads to increased sales. This and the other hypotheses are intended to describe average effects.

The impact of economic factors in actual buying situations is studied through experimental design or statistical analyses of past data. Demand equations have been fitted to a wide variety of products—including beer, refrigerators, and chemical fertilizers.[8] More recently, the impact of economic variables on the fortunes of different brands has been pursued with significant results, particularly in the case of coffee, frozen orange juice, and margarine.[9]

But economic factors alone cannot explain all the variations in sales. The Marshallian model ignores the fundamental question of how product and brand preferences are formed. It represents a useful frame of reference for analyzing only one small corner of the "black box."

THE PAVLOVIAN LEARNING MODEL

The designation of a Pavlovian learning model has its origin in the experiments of the Russian psychologist Pavlov, who rang a bell each time before feeding a dog. Soon he was able to induce the dog to salivate by ringing the bell whether or not food was supplied. Pavlov concluded that learning was largely an associative process and that a large component of behavior was conditioned in this way.

Experimental psychologists have continued this mode of research with rats and other animals, including people. Laboratory experiments have been designed to explore such phenomena as learning, forgetting, and the ability to discriminate. The results have been integrated into a stimulus-response model of human behavior, or as someone has "wisecracked," the substitution of a rat psychology for a rational psychology.

The model has been refined over the years, and today is based on four central concepts—those of *drive, cue, response,* and *reinforcement.*[10]

Drive. Also called needs or motives, drive refers to strong stimuli internal to the individual which impels action. Psychologists draw a distinction between primary physiological drives—such as hunger, thirst, cold, pain, and sex—and learned drives which are derived socially—such as cooperation, fear, and acquisitiveness.

Cue. A drive is very general and impels a particular response only in relation to a particular configuration of cues. Cues are weaker stimuli in the environment and/or in the individual which determine when, where, and how the subject responds. Thus, a coffee advertisement can serve as a cue which stimulates the thirst drive in a housewife. Her response will depend upon this cue and other cues, such as the time of day, the availability of other thirst-quenchers, and the cue's intensity. Often a relative change in a cue's intensity can be more impelling than its absolute level. The housewife may be more motivated by a 2-cents-off sale on a brand of coffee than the fact that this brand's price was low in the first place.

Response. The response is the organism's reaction to the configuration of cues. Yet the same configuration of cues will not necessarily produce the same response in the individual. This depends on the degree to which the experience was rewarding, that is, drive-reducing.

Reinforcement. If the experience is rewarding, a

particular response is reinforced; that is, it is strengthened and there is a tendency for it to be repeated when the same configuration of cues appears again. The housewife, for example, will tend to purchase the same brand of coffee each time she goes to her supermarket so long as it is rewarding and the cue configuration does not change. But if a learned response or habit is not reinforced, the strength of the habit diminishes and may be extinguished eventually. Thus, a housewife's preference for a certain coffee may become extinct if she finds the brand out of stock for a number of weeks.

Forgetting, in contrast to extinction, is the tendency for learned associations to weaken, not because of the lack of reinforcement but because of nonuse.

Cue configurations are constantly changing. The housewife sees a new brand of coffee next to her habitual brand, or notes a special price deal on a rival brand. Experimental psychologists have found that the same learned response will be elicited by similar patterns of cues; that is, learned responses are *generalized*. The housewife shifts to a similar brand when her favorite brand is out of stock. This tendency toward generalization over less similar cue configurations is increased in proportion to the strength of the drive. A housewife may buy an inferior coffee if it is the only brand left and if her drive is sufficiently strong.

A counter-tendency to generalization is *discrimination*. When a housewife tries two similar brands and finds one more rewarding, her ability to discriminate between similar cue configurations improves. Discrimination increases the specificity of the cue-response connection, while generalization decreases the specificity.

Marketing Applications of Pavlovian Model

The modern version of the Pavlovian model makes no claim to provide a complete theory of behavior—indeed, such important phenomena as perception, the subconscious, and interpersonal influence are inadequately treated. Yet the model does offer a substantial number of insights about some aspects of behavior of considerable interest to marketers.[11]

An example would be in the problem of introducing a new brand into a highly competitive market. The company's goal is to extinguish existing brand habits and form new habits among consumers for its brand. But the company must first get customers to try its brand; and it has to decide between using weak and strong cues.

Light introductory advertising is a weak cue compared with distributing free samples. Strong cues, although costing more, may be necessary in markets characterized by strong brand loyalties. For example, Folger went into the coffee market by distributing over a million pounds of free coffee.

To build a brand habit, it helps to provide for an extended period of introductory dealing. Furthermore, sufficient quality must be built into the brand so that the experience is reinforcing. Since buyers are more likely to transfer allegiance to similar brands than dissimilar brands (generalization), the company should also investigate what cues in the leading brands have been most effective. Although outright imitation would not necessarily effect the most transference, the question of providing enough similarity should be considered.

The Pavlovian model also provides guide lines in the area of advertising strategy. The American behaviorist, John B. Watson, was a great exponent of repetitive stimuli; in his writings man is viewed as a creature who can be conditioned through repetition and reinforcement to respond in particular ways.[12] The Pavlovian model emphasizes the desirability of repetition in advertising. A single exposure is likely to be a very weak cue, hardly able to penetrate the individual's consciousness sufficiently to excite his drives above the threshold level.

Repetition in advertising has two desirable effects. It "fights" forgetting, the tendency for learned responses to weaken in the absence of practice. It provides reinforcement, because after the purchase the consumer becomes selectively exposed to advertisements of the product.

The model also provides guide lines for copy strategy. To be effective as a cue, an advertisement must arouse strong drives in the person. The strongest product-related drives must be identified. For candy bars, it may be hunger; for safety belts, fear; for hair tonics, sex; for automobiles, status. The advertising practitioner must dip into his cue box—words, colors, pictures—and select that configuration of cues that provides the strongest stimulus to these drives.

THE FREUDIAN PSYCHOANALYTIC MODEL

The Freudian model of man is well known, so profound has been its impact on 20th century thought. It is the latest of a series of philosophical "blows" to which man has been exposed in the last 500 years. Copernicus destroyed the idea that man stood at the center of the universe; Darwin tried to refute the idea that man was a special creation; and Freud attacked the idea that man even reigned over his own psyche.

According to Freud, the child enters the world driven by instinctual needs which he cannot gratify by himself. Very quickly and painfully he realizes his separateness from the rest of the world and yet his dependence on it.

He tries to get others to gratify his needs through a variety of blatant means, including intimidation and supplication. Continual frustration leads him to perfect more subtle mechanisms for gratifying his instincts.

As he grows, his psyche becomes increasingly complex. A part of his psyche—the id—remains the reservoir of his strong drives and urges. Another part —the ego—becomes his conscious planning center for finding outlets for his drives. And a third part—his super-ego—channels his instinctive drives into socially approved outlets to avoid the pain of guilt or shame.

The guilt or shame which man feels toward some of his urges—especially his sexual urges—causes him to repress them from his consciousness. Through such defense mechanisms as rationalization and sublimation, these urges are denied or become transmuted into socially approved expressions. Yet these urges are never eliminated or under perfect control; and they emerge, sometimes with a vengeance, in dreams, in slips-of-the-tongue, in neurotic and obsessional behavior, or ultimately in mental breakdown where the ego can no longer maintain the delicate balance between the impulsive power of the id and the oppressive power of the super-ego.

The individual's behavior, therefore, is never simple. His motivational wellsprings are not obvious to a casual observer nor deeply understood by the individual himself. If he is asked why he purchased an expensive foreign sports-car, he may reply that he likes its maneuverability and its looks. At a deeper level he may have purchased the car to impress others, or to feel young again. At a still deeper level, he may be purchasing the sports-car to achieve substitute gratification for unsatisfied sexual strivings.

Many refinements and changes in emphasis have occurred in this model since the time of Freud. The instinct concept has been replaced by a more careful delineation of basic drives; the three parts of the psyche are regarded now as theoretical concepts rather than actual entities; and the behavioral perspective has been extended to include cultural as well as biological mechanisms.

Instead of the role of the sexual urge in psychic development—Freud's discussion of oral, anal, and genital stages and possible fixations and traumas— Adler[13] emphasized the urge for power and how its thwarting manifests itself in superiority and inferiority complexes; Horney[14] emphasized cultural mechanisms; and Fromm[15] and Erickson[16] emphasized the role of existential crises in personality development. These philosophical divergencies, rather than debili-

tating the model, have enriched and extended its interpretative value to a wider range of behavioral phenomena.

Marketing Applications of Freudian Model

Perhaps the most important marketing implication of this model is that buyers are motivated by *symbolic* as well as *economic-function*al product concerns. The change of a bar of soap from a square to a round shape may be more important in its sexual than its functional connotations. A cake mix that is advertised as involving practically no labor may alienate housewives because the easy life may evoke a sense of guilt.

Motivational research has produced some interesting and occasionally some bizarre hypotheses about what may be in the buyer's mind regarding certain purchases. Thus, it has been suggested at one time or another that:

- Many a businessman doesn't fly because of a fear of posthumous guilt—if he crashed, his wife would think of him as stupid for not taking a train.
- Men want their cigars to be odoriferous, in order to prove that they (the men) are masculine.
- A woman is very serious when she bakes a cake because unconsciously she is going through the symbolic act of giving birth.
- A man buys a convertible as a substitute "mistress."
- Consumers prefer vegetable shortening because animal fats stimulate a sense of sin.
- Men who wear suspenders are reacting to an unresolved castration complex.

There are admitted difficulties of proving these assertions. Two prominent motivational researchers, Ernest Dichter and James Vicary, were employed independently by two separate groups in the prune industry to determine why so many people dislike prunes. Dichter found, among other things, that the prune aroused feelings of old age and insecurity in people, whereas Vicary's main finding was that Americans had an emotional block about prunes' laxative qualities.[17] Which is the more valid interpretation? Or if they are both operative, which motive is found with greater statistical frequency in the population?

Unfortunately the usual survey techniques—direct observation and interviewing—can be used to establish the representativeness of more superficial characteristics—age and family size, for example—but are not feasible for establishing the frequency of mental states which are presumed to be deeply "buried" within each individual.

Motivational researchers have to employ time-consuming projective techniques in the hope of throwing individual "egos" off guard. When carefully administered and interpreted, techniques such as word association, sentence completion, picture interpretation, and role-playing can provide some insights into the minds of the small group of examined individuals; but a "leap of faith" is sometimes necessary to generalize these findings to the population.

Nevertheless, motivation research can lead to useful insights and provide inspiration to creative men in the advertising and packaging world. Appeals aimed at the buyer's private world of hopes, dreams, and fears can often be as effective in stimulating purchase as more rationally-directed appeals.

THE VEBLENIAN SOCIAL-PSYCHOLOGICAL MODEL

While most economists have been content to interpret buyer behavior in Marshallian terms, Thorstein Veblen struck out in different directions.

Veblen was trained as an orthodox economist, but evolved into a social thinker greatly influenced by the new science of social anthropology. He saw man as primarily a *social animal*—confirming to the general forms and norms of his larger culture and to the more specific standards of the subcultures and face-to-face groupings to which his life is bound. His wants and behavior are largely molded by his present group-memberships and his aspired group-memberships.

Veblen's best-known example of this is in his description of the leisure class.[18] His hypothesis is that much of economic consumption is motivated not by intrinsic needs or satisfaction so much as by prestige-seeking. He emphasized the strong emulative factors operating in the choice of conspicuous goods like clothes, cars, and houses.

Some of his points, however, seem overstated by today's perspective. The leisure class does not serve as everyone's reference group; many persons aspire to the social patterns of the class immediately above it. And important segments of the affluent class practice conspicuous underconsumption rather than overconsumption. There are many people in all classes who are more anxious to "fit in" than to "stand out." As an example, William H. Whyte found that many families avoided buying air conditioners and other appliances before their neighbors did.[19]

Veblen was not the first nor the only investigator to comment on social influences in behavior; but the incisive quality of his observations did much to stimulate further investigations. Another stimulus came from Karl Marx, who held that each man's world-view was determined largely by his relationship to the "means of production."[20] The early field-work in primitive societies by social anthropologists like Boas[21] and Malinowski[22] and the later field-work in urban societies by men like Park[23] and Thomas[24] contributed much to understanding the influence of society and culture. The research of early Gestalt psychologists—men like Wertheimer,[25] Köhler,[26] and Koffka[27]—into the mechanisms of perception led eventually to investigations of small-group influence on perception.

Marketing Applications of Veblenian Model

The various streams of thought crystallized into the modern social sciences of sociology, cultural anthropology, and social psychology. Basic to them is the view that man's attitudes and behavior are influenced by several levels of society—culture, subcultures, social classes, reference groups, and face-to-face groups. The challenge to the marketer is to determine which of these social levels are the most important in influencing the demand for his product.

Culture

The most enduring influences are from culture. Man tends to assimilate his culture's mores and folkways, and to believe in their absolute rightness until deviants appear within his culture or until he confronts members of another culture.

Subcultures

A culture tends to lose its homogeneity as its population increases. When people no longer are able to maintain face-to-face relationships with more than a small proportion of other members of a culture, smaller units or subcultures develop, which help to satisfy the individual's needs for more specific identity.

The subcultures are often regional entities, because the people of a region, as a result of more frequent interactions, tend to think and act alike. But subcultures also take the form of religions, nationalities, fraternal orders, and other institutional complexes which provide a broad identification for people who may otherwise be strangers. The subcultures of a person play a large role in his attitude formation and become another important predictor of certain values he is likely to hold.

Social Class

People become differentiated not only horizontally but also vertically through a division of labor. The society becomes stratified socially on the basis of wealth, skill, and power. Sometimes castes develop in which the members are reared for certain roles, or social classes develop in which the members feel empathy with others sharing similar values and economic circumstances.

Because social class involves different attitudinal configurations, it becomes a useful independent variable for segmenting markets and predicting reactions. Significant differences have been found among different social classes with respect to magazine readership, leisure activities, food imagery, fashion interests, and acceptance of innovations. A sampling of attitudinal differences in class is the following:

Members of the *upper-middle* class place an emphasis on professional competence; indulge in expensive status symbols; and more often than not show a taste, real or otherwise, for theater and the arts. They want their children to show high achievement and precocity and develop into physicists, vice-presidents, and judges. This class likes to deal in ideas and symbols.

Members of the *lower-middle* class cherish respectability, savings, a college education, and good housekeeping. They want their children to show self-control and prepare for careers as accountants, lawyers, and engineers.

Members of the *upper-lower* class try to keep up with the times, if not with the Joneses. They stay in older neighborhoods but buy new kitchen appliances. They spend proportionately less than the middle class on major clothing articles, buying a new suit mainly for an important ceremonial occasion. They also spend proportionately less on services, preferring to do their own plumbing and other work around the house. They tend to raise large families and their children generally enter manual occupations. This class also supplies many local businessmen, politicians, sports stars, and labor-union leaders.

Reference Groups

There are groups in which the individual has no membership but with which he identifies and may aspire to—reference groups. Many young boys identify with big-league baseball players or astronauts, and many young girls identify with Hollywood stars. The activities of these popular heroes are carefully watched and

frequently imitated. These reference figures become important transmitters of influence, although more along lines of taste and hobby than basic attitudes.

Face-to-Face Groups

Groups that have the most immediate influence on a person's tastes and opinions are face-to-face groups. This includes all the small "societies" with which he comes into frequent contact: his family, close friends, neighbors, fellow workers, fraternal associates, and so forth. His informal group memberships are influenced largely by his occupation, residence, and stage in the life cycle.

The powerful influence of small groups on individual attitudes has been demonstrated in a number of social psychological experiments.[28] There is also evidence that this influence may be growing. David Riesman and his coauthors have pointed to signs which indicate a growing amount of *other-direction*, that is, a tendency for individuals to be increasingly influenced by their peers in the definition of their values rather than by their parents and elders.[29]

For the marketer, this means that brand choice may increasingly be influenced by one's peers. For such products as cigarettes and automobiles, the influence of peers is unmistakable.

The role of face-to-face groups has been recognized in recent industry campaigns attempting to change basic product attitudes. For years the milk industry has been trying to overcome the image of milk as a "sissified" drink by portraying its use in social and active situations. The men's-wear industry is trying to increase male interest in clothes by advertisements indicating that business associates judge a man by how well he dresses.

Of all face-to-face groups, the person's family undoubtedly plays the largest and most enduring role in basic attitude formation. From them he acquires a mental set not only toward religion and politics, but also toward thrift, chastity, food, human relations, and so forth. Although he often rebels against parental values in his teens, he often accepts these values eventually. Their formative influence on his eventual attitudes is undeniably great.

Family members differ in the types of product messages they carry to other family members. Most of what parents know about cereals, candy, and toys comes from their children. The wife stimulates family consideration of household appliances, furniture, and vacations. The husband tends to stimulate the fewest purchase ideas, with the exception of the automobile and perhaps the home.

The marketer must be alert to what attitudinal configurations dominate in different types of families, and also to how these change over time. For example, the parent's conception of the child's rights and privileges has undergone a radical shift in the last 30 years. The child has become the center of attention and orientation in a great number of households, leading some writers to label the modern family a "filiarchy." This has important implications not only for how to market to today's family, but also on how to market to tomorrow's family when the indulged child of today becomes the parent.

The Person

Social influences determine much but not all of the behavioral variations in people. Two individuals subject to the same influences are not likely to have identical attitudes, although these attitudes will probably converge at more points than those of two strangers selected at random. Attitudes are really the product of social forces interacting with the individual's unique temperament and abilities.

Furthermore, attitudes do not automatically guarantee certain types of behavior. Attitudes are predispositions felt by buyers before they enter the buying process. The buying process itself is a learning experience and can lead to a change in attitudes.

Alfred Politz noted at one time that women stated a clear preference for G.E. refrigerators over Frigidaire, but that Frigidaire continued to outsell G.E.[30] The answer to this paradox was that preference was only one factor entering into behavior. When the consumer preferring G.E. actually undertook to purchase a new refrigerator, her curiosity led her to examine the other brands. Her perception was sensitized to refrigerator advertisements, sales arguments, and different product features. This lead to learning and a change in attitudes.

THE HOBBESIAN ORGANIZATIONAL-FACTORS MODEL

The foregoing models throw light mainly on the behavior of family buyers.

But what of the large number of people who are organizational buyers? They are engaged in the purchase of goods not for the sake of consumption, but for further production or distribution. Their common denominator is the fact that they (1) are paid to make purchases for others and (2) operate within an organizational environment.

How do organizational buyers make their decisions? There seem to be two competing views. Many marketing writers have emphasized the predominance of rational motives in organizational buying.[31] Organizational buyers are represented as being most impressed by cost, quality, dependability, and service factors. They are portrayed as dedicated servants of the organization, seeking to secure the best terms. This view has led to an emphasis on performance and use characteristics in much industrial advertising.

Other writers have emphasized personal motives in organizational buyer behavior. The purchasing agent's interest to do the best for his company is tempered by his interest to do the best for himself. He may be tempted to choose among salesmen according to the extent they entertain or offer gifts. He may choose a particular vendor because this will ingratiate him with certain company officers. He may shortcut his study of alternative suppliers to make his work day easier.

In truth, the buyer is guided by both personal and group goals; and this is the essential point. The political model of Thomas Hobbes comes closest of any model to suggesting the relationship between the two goals.[32] Hobbes held that man is "instinctively" oriented toward preserving and enhancing his own well-being. But this would produce a "war of every man against every man." This fear leads men to unite with others in a corporate body. The corporate man tries to steer a careful course between satisfying his own needs and those of the organization.

Marketing Applications of Hobbesian Model

The import of the Hobbesian model is that organizational buyers can be appealed to on both personal and organizational grounds. The buyer has his private aims, and yet he tries to do a satisfactory job for his corporation. He will respond to persuasive salesmen and he will respond to rational product arguments. However, the best "mix" of the two is not a fixed quantity; it varies with the nature of the product, the type of organization, and the relative strength of the two drives in the particular buyer.

Where there is substantial similarity in what suppliers offer in the way of products, price, and service, the purchasing agent has less basis for rational choice. Since he can satisfy his organizational obligations with any one of a number of suppliers, he can be swayed by personal motives. On the other hand, where there are pronounced differences among the competing vendors' products, the purchasing agent is held more accountable for his choice and probably pays more attention to rational factors. Short-run personal gain becomes less motivating than the long-run gain which comes from serving the organization with distinction.

The marketing strategist must appreciate these goal conflicts of the organizational buyer. Behind all the ferment of purchasing agents to develop standards and employ value analysis lies their desire to avoid being thought of as order-clerks, and to develop better skills in reconciling personal and organizational objectives.[33]

SUMMARY

Think back over the five different behavioral models of how the buyer translates buying influences into purchasing responses:

Marshallian man is concerned chiefly with economic cues—prices and income—and makes a fresh utility calculation before each purchase.

Pavlovian man behaves in a largely habitual rather than thoughtful way; certain configurations of cues will set off the same behavior because of rewarded learning in the past.

Freudian man's choices are influenced strongly by motives and fantasies which take place deep within his private world.

Veblenian man acts in a way which is shaped largely by past and present social groups.

And finally, *Hobbesian* man seeks to reconcile individual gain with organizational gain.

Thus, it turns out that the "black box" of the buyer is not so black after all. Light is thrown in various corners by these models. Yet no one has succeeded in putting all these pieces of truth together into one coherent instrument for behavioral analysis. This, of course, is the goal of behavioral science.

NOTES

1. Adam Smith, *An Inquiry into the Nature and Causes of the Wealth of Nations,* 1776 (New York: The Modern Library, 1937).

2. Jeremy Bentham, *An Introduction to the Principles of Morals and Legislation,* 1780 (Oxford, England: Clarendon Press, 1907).

3. William S. Jevons, *The Theory of Political Economy* (New York: The Macmillan Company, 1871).

4. Alfred Marshall, *Principles of Economics,* 1890 (London: The Macmillan Company, 1927).

5. Karl Menger, *Principles of Economics,* 1871 (Glencoe, Illinois: Free Press, 1950).

6. Leon Walras, *Elements of Pure Economics,* 1874 (Homewood, Illinois: Richard D. Irwin, Inc., 1954).

7. Eva Mueller, "A Study of Purchase Decisions," Part 2, *Consumer Behavior, The Dynamics of Consumer Reaction,* edited by Lincoln H. Clark (New York: New York University Press, 1954), pp. 36–87.

8. See Erwin E. Nemmers, *Managerial Economics* (New York: John Wiley & Sons, Inc., 1962), Part II.

9. See Lester G. Telser, "The Demand for Branded Goods as Estimated from Consumer Panel Data," *Review of Economics and Statistics,* Vol. 44 (August, 1962), pp. 300–324; and William F. Massy and Ronald E. Frank, "Short Term Price and Dealing Effects in Selected Market Segments," *Journal of Marketing Research,* Vol. 2 (May, 1965), pp. 171–185.

10. See John Dollard and Neal E. Miller, *Personality and Psychotherapy* (New York: McGraw-Hill Book Company, Inc., 1950), Chapter III.

11. The most consistent application of learning-theory concepts to marketing situations is found in John A. Howard, *Marketing Management: Analysis and Planning* (Homewood, Illinois: Richard D. Irwin, Inc., revised edition, 1963).

12. John B. Watson, *Behaviorism* (New York: The People's Institute Publishing Company, 1925).

13. Alfred Adler, *The Science of Living* (New York: Greenberg, 1929).

14. Karen Horney, *The Neurotic Personality of Our Time* (New York: W. W. Norton & Co., 1937).

15. Erich Fromm, *Man For Himself* (New York: Holt, Rinehart & Winston, Inc., 1947).

16. Erik Erikson, *Childhood and Society* (New York: W. W. Norton & Co., 1949).

17. L. Edward Scriven, "Rationality and Irrationality in Motivation Research," in Robert Ferber and Hugh G. Wales, editors, *Motivation and Marketing Behavior* (Homewood, Illinois: Richard D. Irwin, Inc., 1958), pp. 69–70.

18. Thorstein Veblen, *The Theory of the Leisure Class* (New York: The Macmillan Company, 1899).

19. William H. Whyte, Jr., "The Web of Word of Mouth," *Fortune,* Vol. 50 (November, 1954), pp. 140 ff.

20. Karl Marx, *The Communist Manifesto,* 1848 (London: Martin Lawrence, Ltd., 1934).

21. Franz Boas, *The Mind of Primitive Man* (New York: The Macmillan Company, 1922).

22. Bronislaw Malinowski, *Sex and Repression in Savage Society* (New York: Meridian Books, 1955).

23. Robert E. Park, *Human Communities* (Glencoe, Illinois: Free Press, 1952).

24. William I. Thomas, *The Unadjusted Girl* (Boston: Little, Brown and Company, 1928).

25. Max Wertheimer, *Productive Thinking* (New York: Harper & Brothers, 1945).

26. Wolfgang Köhler, *Gestalt Psychology* (New York: Liveright Publishing Co., 1947).

27. Kurt Koffka, *Principles of Gestalt Psychology* (New York: Harcourt, Brace and Co., 1935).

28. See, for example, Solomon E. Asch, "Effects of Group Pressure Upon the Modification & Distortion of Judgments," in Dorwin Cartwright and Alvin Zander, *Group Dynamics*

(Evanston, Illinois: Row, Peterson & Co., 1953), pp. 151–162; and Kurt Lewin, "Group Decision and Social Change," in Theodore M. Newcomb and Eugene L. Hartley, editors, *Readings in Social Psychology* (New York: Henry Holt Co., 1952).

29. David Riesman, Reuel Denney, and Nathan Glazer, *The Lonely Crowd* (New Haven, Connecticut: Yale University Press, 1950).

30. Alfred Politz, "Motivation Research—Opportunity or Dilemma?", in Ferber and Wales, same reference as footnote 17, at pp. 57–58.

31. See Melvin T. Copeland, *Principles of Merchandising* (New York: McGraw-Hill Book Co., Inc., 1924).

32. Thomas Hobbes, *Leviathan,* 1651 (London: G. Routledge and Sons, 1887).

33. For an insightful account, see George Strauss, "Tactics of Lateral Relationship: The Purchasing Agent." *Administrative Science Quarterly,* Vol. 7 (September, 1962), pp. 161–186.

Frederick E. Webster, Jr.

Modeling the Industrial Buying Process

The aim of the industrial marketer is to influence the industrial buying process to his advantage. To accomplish this objective, he tries to create an awareness of his product offering, and to develop favorable attitudes toward his offering at certain key points within the buying organization. For a favored competitive position, the marketer must offer a combination of product quality, service, and price which provides the most effective solution to customer company problems. The success of the marketer's efforts depends upon his understanding of how the buying decision is made, including the location of responsibility and authority for buying, the processes by which alternatives are identified and decision criteria are established, and how alternatives are evaluated and selected.

Industrial buying decisions are made by individuals functioning as part of an organization. To understand the industrial buying process, therefore, one must study both individual and organizational decision making. Virtually all studies of industrial buying patterns and processes have been of the descriptive, case study variety. With a few notable exceptions [see references 3, 4, 5, and 8] there has been no attempt to *analyze* the industrial buying process, i.e., to identify and assign priorities to the variables which are important in the buying decision and to find causal relationships among them. This article presents an analytical description of the industrial buying process, an identification of the critical variables, and some statements about their interrelationships. By advancing a four-part descriptive model, a way of viewing the industrial buying process is suggested which has been found useful as a guide to research in industrial marketing.

While this model of the industrial buying process has not been tested empirically for its descriptive validity or predictive ability, it is based upon interviews with approximately 135 individuals in 75 companies, representing a cross-section of organizational responsibilities and SIC classifications. The model has not been developed as a vehicle for presenting research findings, but as an expository device which attempts to structure the buying process in a manner which suggests specific research needs and opportunities. As a general model, it may also be productive of insights into the buying process which have significance for the marketer by highlighting the need for particular kinds of information as the basis for strategy decisions.

PROBLEMS IN DESCRIPTION, ANALYSIS, AND GENERALIZATION

To be effective, an industrial marketing program must mesh closely with the buying process of the customer organization. It would be convenient if similar buying processes were used by all customers or even by those customers in a particular segment. Such is not the

Source: From the *Journal of Marketing Research,* Vol. II (November 1965), pp. 370–76. Reprinted by permission of the American Marketing Association.

case. Available research evidence strongly suggests that prevailing generalizations about buying patterns characterizing particular industry segments or types of companies are likely to be misleading. For example, during participation in a recent study of the markets for a particular group of chemical products, not only were eight distinct market segments (classified on the basis of products bought and industry affiliation) found, but within each segment there were from two to five subsegments, each of which followed markedly different purchasing patterns. These subsegments were identified on the basis of the organizational responsibilities of the people who actively participated in the buying process. In one subsegment, the purchasing agent exercised the major influence, but relied heavily upon laboratory personnel for analysis and recommendations. In another subsegment, major influence was exercised by the foreman of the production process who relied upon production engineering for advice and recommendations.

Unfortunately, no consistent and predictable relationship has been found to exist between particular subsegments in terms of who influences the decision process and more tangible descriptive variables, such as size of company or the customer company's industry affiliation. The strongest research findings are still incomplete. For example, one of the studies revealed that as reciprocity becomes more important, top management becomes more actively involved in the buying decision. And, as top management becomes more involved, technical people become less involved and a bias is created against technological innovation in purchased products. The direction of causation is uncertain. Does reciprocity cause a bias against innovation, or is the lack of an innovative attitude conducive to reciprocity? Or, is there a common underlying element in both, such as a low tolerance of risk? What factors in an organization contribute to low tolerance of risk? In short, available research is more productive of questions than answers.

The problem may be that *too much* is "known" about industrial buying. There is probably little information of a descriptive and factual nature about the details and nuances of the industrial buying process that has not been reported in one form or another. Industrial advertising media provide a continual stream of studies describing the buying process in those industry segments which are their audiences. A conceptual structure is lacking to provide direction to research and analysis, and much of the research is, therefore, duplicative. Without an analytical structure it is difficult to identify the critical factors and relationships which need explanation.

The first step in building an analytical structure, or model, is to simplify the problem so that it is manageable. Any model is nothing more than a simplified representation of a more complex situation, and is an attempt to state the variables which will affect the situation being studied [1]. Preliminary research results suggest a dissection of the industrial buying process into four elements: (1) problem recognition; (2) organizational assignment of buying responsibility and authority; (3) search procedures for identifying product offerings and for establishing selection criteria; and (4) choice procedures for evaluating and selecting among alternatives.

The following section attempts to describe some dimensions of the four elements of the buying process. There is no attempt to describe all of the details and ramifications which characterize each stage. Several generalizations are advanced, but these may not be valid for all industrial buying situations. Nonetheless, it is possible to make some statements about the nature of the buying process in terms broader than those applying to a particular company. While these statements provide shaky ground upon which to build a marketing strategy, they may be productive of insights into the nature of the buying process for both the researcher and the practitioner.

PROBLEM RECOGNITION

Industrial organizations purchase goods and services to solve a particular problem. While there is little that could be called impulse buying in industrial organizations, there appears to be more subjective evaluation and persuasion in the industrial buying process than some writers have indicated. To view the industrial buying process as completely objective and rational is to ignore the essential fact that industrial buyer-seller relationships involve interaction among people. Likewise, some companies may buy goods and services because of something like pride of possession, just as an individual may buy a new car when he does not really need one. The company-owned computer, the modern glass and steel office building, the services of a consultant, and the "institutional" advertisement in a prestigious business publication all may be purchased for reasons not related to strict economic considerations.

However, most purchases are made in response to a particular need or problem which can be solved by the purchase of products or services, a buying situation. Industrial customers are concerned with profits and budgets. A company cannot spend a large sum of money, regardless of the benefits which might be derived, if it does not have (or cannot obtain) the money. Furthermore, if the industrial marketer cannot persuade his potential customers that the purchase of his offering can result in greater profits, either through reducing costs or providing the opportunity for greater revenues, he stands little chance of making the sale.

Industrial organizations develop an awareness of the need to buy products from outside vendors in a wide variety of ways. While much additional research is needed on the problem-recognition process, the following factors have been found to create buying situations:

1. regularly scheduled review of vendor performance;
2. the initiative of product development and design departments;
3. the marketing initiative of potential suppliers;
4. difficulty in maintaining the production process due to slow delivery, inadequate quality control, or unavailability of desired quantities from present suppliers;
5. value analysis programs;
6. new construction, or renovation of existing facilities;
7. reaching reorder points for items purchased routinely.

Problem recognition can be rephrased as dissatisfaction with the present level of goal attainment. Like consumer marketing, industrial marketing presents opportunities for persuasion and for creating dissatisfaction with the ability of presently used products to perform a given function. That is, industrial marketers can cause potential customers to raise their goals, to expect a higher level of satisfaction. In this case, buying motivation is the result of the seller increasing the buyer's aspiration level.

In other cases, goals are raised by the buyer as a result of his own initiative. The buyer is under constant pressure to do better, to deliver more value, generally defined as the ratio of quality to price. Engineering personnel frequently improve products and methods of production, to improve saleability, productive efficiency, or to reduce costs. This desire to do better is stimulated by such factors as new competitors, price cutting, pressures created by managers, and personal ambitions of the individuals involved. Despite the apparent rationality of the industrial buying process, any thorough model must explicitly recognize the host of personal, organizational, and environmental factors which influence the level of aspiration of individual buying influences and bring about reappraisal and redefinition of goals. There is

no doubt that marketing efforts provide a major input to the goal-setting stage of the industrial buying, decision-making process [3].

These goals do not reflect the maximum level attainable, but rather an acceptable level. The postulate of acceptable level goals is a major building block of the behavioral theory of the firm developed by Cyert, March, Simon, and others [2, 6]. One of the basic hypotheses of the behavioral theory of the firm is that satisfactory profits, not maximum profits, provide the criterion against which decision makers evaluate alternatives. Individuals within the firm do not try to find *the best* alternative, but rather any alternative that meets these acceptable level goals which provide criteria for evaluation of alternatives.

Thus, the first part of a model of the industrial buying process must be a model of the problem-recognition or need-definition stage. A problem or need presents a potential buying situation when a purchased item can help solve the problem. A problem is generally defined as the perception of a difference between the desired and actual level of goal attainment; a problem can result either from a change in goals or a change in performance. Because of the large number of vendors and products available in most market segments, and the low probability of finding all of them, the use of acceptable level goals seems to be particularly necessary for the industrial buyer.

ASSIGNMENT OF BUYING AUTHORITY

As noted, industrial purchasing decisions are made by individuals functioning within formal organizations (whose functioning is facilitated by informal organizations) which define the individual's responsibility for the purchasing decision on a specific product or products. Preliminary research results indicate that an individual's responsibility in a given buying situation will be a function of the technical complexity of the product, its importance to the firm either in dollar terms or in terms of its relationship with the firm's production process, the product-specific technical knowledge which the individual has, and the individual's centrality in the production process.* An individual's influence on the purchase decision is directly determined by his organizationally defined responsibility.

*The term *production process,* is defined in broadest terms to include such functions as office procedures and maintenance; in short, any process or system which uses a procured product.

The assignment of responsibility for the purchase decision to a central purchasing department reflects a basic change in purchasing philosophy. Centralization of purchasing responsibility is based upon an assumption that knowledge of the market, *not* knowledge of the physical product is of major importance in the buying decision. Purchasing agents tend to concentrate on price, vendor performance, delivery, and similar variables which are determined by market and competitive pressures, rather than upon the technical and physical aspects of the product.

These distinctions between product and market variables, and the importance attached to them by purchasing decision makers, are very hard to make in practice. The purchasing agent may be acutely sensitive to product quality as a variable. Or, the assignment of responsibility for a group of products to a buyer may reflect that individual's strong technical competence and knowledge as it applies to those products. Conflicts between the purchasing department and the using department are often the result of disagreement about the relative importance of product variables vs. market variables.* Both types of variables must be taken into account in a model of industrial buying behavior. Therefore, our model of the assignment of responsibility for the industrial buying process consists of the following propositions derived from our preliminary studies of the buying situation:

1. The relative importance of product variables vs. market variables in the buying decision increases as:
   a. the technical complexity of the product increases;
   b. the importance of the product to the firm's production process increases;
   c. the number and size of firms on the supply side of the market decreases.
2. The relative importance of the influence of the central purchasing department on the buying decision increases as:
   a. market variables become more important relative to product variables;
   b. the size of the firm and the spatial separation of its activities increases;
   c. the organization assigns specific responsibility to the purchasing department, in a formal sense.

*For conflict to exist, the following conditions must exist: (1) a perceived need for joint decision making, (2) divergent goals, or (3) divergent perception of outcomes. The first is a necessary condition, the second and third are sufficient conditions.

3. Conversely, the relative importance of the using or operating department in the buying decision increases as:
   a. product variables become more important relative to market variables;
   b. the experience of the firm in buying and using the product decreases.
4. Top management personnel influence the buying decision:
   a. more, as the dollar value of the purchase increases;
   b. less, as the size of the firm increases.

Further research is needed to identify the variables which determine the assignment of responsibility, and to measure their influence.

THE SEARCH PROCESS

Industrial buyers have two tasks which require the collection and analysis of information. First, the criteria against which to evaluate potential vendors must be established, based on a judgment as to what is needed and what is available. Second, alternative product offerings must be identified in the market.

The search process starts with an evaluation of goals. If the present state of goal attainment is satisfactory, there is no need for search. However, even if the present goals are being attained, evaluation of the goals may suggest the possibility of raising the goals and the level of attainment. If the goals are raised, the level of attainment may thereby become unsatisfactory and the search for new alternatives must be initiated. Furthermore, the search process itself may also indicate the need to raise or lower the goals which initially were set in the buying situation. Goal evaluation in actual buying practices is most clearly seen in such activities as value analysis programs within companies, in periodic requests for competitive bids on regularly purchased items ("to keep our present suppliers honest"), and in purchasing agents' seminars. Vendors' marketing efforts, as previously stated, can also provide the stimulus for goal evaluation.

Because most industrial buyers have imperfect knowledge of the market, it is impossible for the buyer to continue his search until he is sure he has found *the* best alternative. This is so simply because he could never be certain that he had identified *all* available alternatives, and therefore could identify that which was best. As suggested by Marschak [7], it might be possible for the buyer to estimate the *expected* value of additional information, and to stop the search when this value was less than the cost of gathering that information. While some kind of intuitive judgment may be exercised which resembles this quasi-marginal calculus, it is unlikely that most buyers consciously apply this process. Here again, present data and understanding are incomplete.

The established criteria may not (and probably will not) be the optimal levels available in the market, because the buyer does not have complete information. Rather, the criteria represent the acceptable level goals for the purchase decision to achieve. During the search for available alternatives, the buyer may find that: (1) one or more of the goals is unattainable; (2) two or more of the goals are in conflict; or (3) the goals have been set too low. As a result of this new information, the buyer will revise the goals, thus setting new criteria against which to evaluate alternatives.

Even if search were costless (which it is not) and if the buyer had access to information about all markets (which he does not), the time factor places a limitation upon the amount of search and, hence, upon the number of alternatives identified and considered. Most purchase decisions have time constraints, dates when orders must be placed, deliveries received, and when the material will actually be used. Likewise, the buyer has a time constraint in the number of hours in the day which must be allocated over several buying actions and responsibilities. Time is a major constraint upon the amount of market information which can be obtained.

Once the goals have been defined, and preliminary screening criteria established, the buyer searches for product offerings (product-vendor combinations, or brands) available in the market. The first step in the search process is the identification of information sources, focal points for information about one or more alternatives which might be available. These information sources would include vendors' salesmen (both manufacturers and distributors), catalogs, trade journal advertising, company personnel, purchasing personnel in other companies, industrial trade shows, and so on. The procedures followed in this search of information sources are not well understood, and little is known about how these information sources are sought out and used. It is likely, however, that the search process is largely routinized (or programmed) for the individual buyer and that he follows more or less fixed and habitual patterns in his search of the market. These routines, or search rules, involve *selective perception,* simply stated as a tendency to rely upon certain sources of information and to ignore others. For example, a given buyer may tend to rely more or less exclusively on catalogs for a major portion of his search, to request visits from salesmen after he has identified their product offerings through

catalogs, and to ignore trade journal advertising altogether.

It also seems likely that these search rules change over time and are modified as the result of success or failure of the rules in helping the buyer to achieve his goals. This can be called *organizational learning.* More specifically, we would expect that unsuccessful search would result in a change of search rules, mainly the consideration of new sources of information.

It is hypothesized that search continues until a sufficiently large number of alternatives have been identified. What constitutes a sufficiently large number of alternatives is determined by the particular buying situation and the search rules invovled. (This is an obvious opportunity for further research.) One dimension of the search rule is the number of alternatives which must be identified before the search is stopped. This parameter frequently expresses itself in the size of a vendor list. There is evidence to suggest that one alternative offers enough in many procurement situations. Charles G. Moore, Jr., has conducted some research investigations which suggest that buyers have rigorous definitions of the acceptable size of the vendor list, which usually contains no fewer than three and no more than five alternatives [8].

The rules of search may further specify the order in which particular information sources are to be used. From the work of Cyert, Simon, March, and others, it would be hypothesized that the search process would move from the consideration of familiar alternatives, especially present vendors, toward the consideration of new and unfamiliar alternatives. Cyert and March have characterized this as "constrained" or "simpleminded search," which is defined by a tendency to search in the neighborhood of known alternatives and, when search is not successful, to use increasingly complex search and to consider increasingly radical alternatives [2, pp. 121–2]. In the case of the industrial buyer, this is seen (from the research evidence) in a tendency to consider present vendors first in meeting new requirements, then to consider familiar information sources, such as trade publications and acquaintances or identify new alternatives, and finally to search for new information sources which might suggest new alternatives. One reason for this sequence is that as search becomes more complex, it also becomes more costly.

It would be expected that a large amount of adaptive behavior would be exhibited in the industrial buying process. Both goals and search rules (as well as decision rules), are likely to be modified to reflect the extent of the organization's success in achieving its goals.

While there is ample evidence that buyers do use

routine search procedures, a need exists for information and conceptualization on *how* the search is conducted. This need is suggested by the following questions, for which available evidence can provide only partial answers:

1. How do buyers establish or learn routines for searching the market?
2. What is the value of various information sources to buyers?
3. How efficiently do buyers use available information and information sources?
4. What organizational and market pressures influence the rate of search?
5. What is the relative frequency of buyer-initiated vs. seller-initiated contact?
6. How and when are search procedures modified as the result of "learning" during the search?
7. What are the specific factors that trigger the search procedures?
8. How are the results of search communicated back to decision centers within the organizations?

There are literally hundreds of similar questions about buyer search which need answers. These answers would not only be of interest to students of marketing and purchasing, but would also have direct applicability for the marketing executive in making a better response to market opportunities. They also would undoubtedly show how the industrial marketing process could be more efficient, with direct benefits for both buyers and sellers.

The industrial marketer's promotional decisions should be based on the process by which buyers identify available product-vendor combinations. Just as buyers are seeking sellers in the market, so are sellers seeking buyers. They will find one another more easily if they are aware of each other's activities. Industrial marketing efficiency can be measured, in part, by the precision with which the two search procedures overlap.

THE RELATIONSHIP BETWEEN SEARCH AND CHOICE

Having identified some alternative product offerings, the buyer must choose among alternatives. The choice process is guided by the use of decision rules provided by objectives, policies, and procedures established for buying actions by management and specific criteria for evaluating the variables of the product offering. *Parameters* are those factors which are assumed to be given, or uncontrollable by the decision maker; *variables* are those factors which can be influenced or controlled by the decision maker. The buyer may

assume, for example, that he will have to accept the going price in the market, in which case price would be a *parameter* in his decision making. On the other hand, he might try to change the price through negotiation, thus treating it as a *variable* in his decision process, as a factor which can be influenced (or controlled) by his action. Whether price is a parameter or a variable depends on the buyer's perception of the market.

Decision rules must be applied to real alternatives, however, and it is relatively meaningless to make abstract generalizations about decision rules in the absence of specific alternatives. This position is taken for two reasons. First, it is quite likely that the search process itself will reveal which factors must be taken as parameters and which can be treated as variables. For example, the buyer may find that he cannot change the fact that only one quality level is available (a parameter), but he can influence the price he will pay (a variable). Second, the sequential nature of the search process provides the alternatives with which the choice process must be performed. Consequently, the way search is conducted and the specific alternatives which are identified determine the final choice as much as the decision rules employed.

This is not to deny that choice procedures are firmly established and followed. Decision rules *do* exist; but, because goal setting, the search process, and the decision process are so closely related, it is dangerous to discuss the decision process in the absence of the search process. For example, a decision rule may be embodied in a search rule: Continue searching until a feasible alternative is identified, then stop.

The above points have been summarized by Cyert and March:

it is awkward to assume perfect knowledge in the theory of the firm, and introducing expected value calculations in the case of risk solves only some of the problems. In particular, Simon and others have argued that information is not given to the firm but must be obtained, that alternatives are searched for and discovered sequentially, and that the order in which the environment is searched determines to a substantial extent the decisions that will be made. In this way, the theory of choice and the theory of search become closely intertwined and take on prime importance in a general theory of decision making [2, p. 10].

THE CHOICE PROCESS

The last element of the proposed descriptive model of

the industrial buying process is choosing among those identified alternative product-vendor combinations. The following description of the choice process consists of three stages: vendor qualification, comparing offerings with specifications, and comparing offerings with each other. While this formulation lacks completeness, it is not intended as a complete description of how buyers select sellers in actual practice. Rather, it summarizes the important classes of variables which may be considered by the buyer, and which the analyst will want to consider in describing or analyzing the buyer's behavior.

The first step in selecting a vendor to fulfil a given requirement is to determine whether the vendor is qualified as an approved source. A qualified vendor is one approved as a source of supply, based upon evaluation of such factors as credit rating, financial strength, management ability, years in business, size and quality of production facilities, and (frequently) the ability of the product to pass certain laboratory, quality control, and performance test standards. For some kinds of purchases, some companies will not consider new, unproven suppliers, because it is too risky. Others will allow any potential supplier to submit to qualification procedures and, if these criteria are met, add him to the vendors' list.

The next step in the choice process is to compare the vendor's product with the criteria, or specifications that have been established. These criteria would include constraints such as: specific product features and quality levels; highest acceptable price; satisfactory availability—quantities and delivery time; and minimum acceptable service offerings, e.g., installation, application, maintenance, and repair. The third and final step is to compare those alternatives which meet all of the stated specifications and to select one (or more) which provides the greatest value to the buyer.

As a framework for research and analysis, this model is sufficiently general and simple to include most procurement decisions. It suggests the importance of the analyst's understanding the influence of the relative importance which the buyer assigns to three classes of variables—price, quality, and service. Obviously, it tells nothing about the process by which these priorities are determined, that must be a matter of empirical investigation. How does a buyer determine the trade-offs between quality, price, and service? Under what conditions does he simply try to optimize on *one* variable—for example, get the lowest possible price as opposed to trying to optimize the value of the *combination* of all three classes of variables? How does he relate differences in quality level to differences in price?

SUMMARY

With all the descriptive detail available about the industrial buying process, a way must be found for structuring this information to identify the important variables and causal relationships. The model proposed here presents an analytical structure that divides the buying process into four segments:

1. *Problem Recognition*—A buying situation is created by the recognition of a problem which can be solved by making a purchase. A problem exists when there is a perceived difference between goals and actual performance, and can be caused by a change in either goals or performance. Goal-setting and problem-recognition are influenced by personal and impersonal factors, both internal and external to the buying organization. Research is needed to identify the major factors and their influence on the buying decision.
2. *Buying Responsibility*—Buying decisions are made by individuals working as part of an organization. The assignment of buying responsibility is influenced by industry, company, market, product, and individual factors. Some propositions about the influence of these factors have been drawn from exploratory field studies.
3. *The Search Process*—Individuals have more or less routine methods for gathering information for the purposes of identifying alternative problem solutions and establishing criteria for evaluating buying alternatives. Search can result in a change in goals, and goals serve as selection criteria. As search becomes more complex and considers new information sources, it also becomes more costly. Cost and time factors constrain the amount of search.
4. *The Choice Process*—The final stage in the industrial buying decision is the selection of one or more suppliers. The choice process is closely related to the search process—the order in which alternatives are identified influences the final decision. The relationship between three classes of variables (price, quality, and service) and the influence of priorities assigned to each, are important areas for empirical investigation.

This model is only the start toward rationalization of the industrial buying process. There is a need for greater specificity and measurement of variables and causal relationships. Improved efficiency in industrial marketing can result from a more effective response to the buying process. For the researcher in marketing, the industrial buying process is full of opportunities. Communication, organization, and decision theorists all have a major role to play in furthering an understanding of the industrial buying process.

BIBLIOGRAPHY

1. Seymour Banks, *Experimentation in Marketing,* New York: McGraw-Hill Book Co., Inc., 1965.
2. Richard M. Cyert and James G. March, *A Behavioral Theory of the Firm,* Englewood Cliffs, N.J.: Prentice-Hall, Inc., 1963.
3. –––, H. A. Simon and D. B. Trow, "Observation of a Business Decision," *Journal of Business,* 29, No. 4 (October 1956), 237–48.
4. John A. Howard and Charles G. Moore, Jr., *A Descriptive Model of the Purchasing Function,* unpublished monograph. Graduate School of Business, University of Pittsburgh, 1963.
5. Theodore Levitt, *Industrial Purchasing Behavior: A Study of Communications Effects,* to be published in 1965 by the Division of Research, Graduate School of Business Administration, Harvard University.
6. James G. March and Herbert A. Simon, *Organizations,* New York: John Wiley and Sons, Inc., 1958.
7. Jacob Marschak, "Remarks on the Economics of Information," in *Contributions to Scientific Research in Management,* Los Angeles: Division of Research, Graduate School of Business Administration, University of California at Los Angeles, 1959, 79–97.
8. Charles G. Moore, Jr., "A Model of the Industrial Purchasing Process," unpublished and undated working paper, Administrative Science Center, University of Pittsburgh.

Philip Kotler

A Design for the Firm's Marketing Nerve Center

As company operations expand in size and complexity, company executives grow further removed from first-hand contact with the scenes of marketing action. They have to rely increasingly on second-hand information for their picture of what is happening in the marketplace, and, on the basis of highly fragmented and typically tenuous information, must make decisions that have profound consequences. The company's effectiveness in the marketplace is increasingly at the mercy of the executive's marketing information.

It is hard to find executives who are satisfied with the quality of their marketing information. Their complaints fall into a number of categories:

There is too much marketing information of the wrong kind, and not enough of the right kind.

Marketing information is so dispersed throughout the company that a great effort is usually necessary to locate simple facts.

Source: From *Business Horizons,* Vol. 9, No. 3 (Fall 1966), pp. 63–74. Reprinted by permission of Indiana University.

Important information is sometimes suppressed by other executives or subordinates, for personal reasons.

Important information often arrives too late to be useful.

Information often arrives in a form that leaves no idea of its accuracy, and there is no one to turn to for confirmation.

Despite these serious complaints, few companies have taken the trouble to consider basic alternatives to their present marketing information arrangements. They are surprisingly slow to take advantage of new information-management concepts and technology. The typical attitude seems to be that important marketing information eventually flows to the right executives, that each executive can gather best the information he needs, and that a system of information management carries the danger of manipulation.

My work with companies convinces me that these premises are wrong. Key executives are often abysmally ignorant of important marketing developments; they do not always make optimal use of existing information; and they frequently distort information in passing it on. A systematic solution to these problems is absolutely necessary if executives are to make effective and swift marketing decisions in an age characterized by intensifying competition, frequent product change, and complex and shifting customer wants.

The literature on total management information systems is singularly uninformative on the specific subject of marketing, and, while a small handful of progressive companies are conducting their own experiments, these are either undisclosed or revealed in a form too fragmentary to provide concrete guidance. This article will present a coherent view of the major concepts and design steps in developing a modern marketing information system.

PRESENT INADEQUACIES

The marketing information requirements of the modern executive have changed radically in the postwar period while the basic information arrangements have remained essentially the same.

On the one hand, the firm is involved in many more markets and products than ever before; the competitors are able to move more swiftly and deftly; and the environment of surrounding law, technology, economics, and culture is undergoing faster change.

On the other hand, executives must still hunt for their information from highly dispersed sources within and outside the company. The marketing research department typically supplies only a fraction of what is needed. The executive must also seek and receive information from the controller, the research and development department, the long-range corporate planning department, the legal department, the economic research department, and other parts of the company. He must supplement these findings by scanning hundreds of salesmen and dealer reports, and by reading half a dozen magazines and newspapers for possible items of significance. In short, he is on a perpetual information safari.

The marketing research department's primary obligations are to conduct special field studies, generate some routine reports and analyses of current sales, and send occasional clippings that might interest particular executives. On the other hand, it does not actively search for all sorts of marketing intelligence that might be needed by executives; it does not typically develop computer programs to aid in marketing analysis and decision making; and it generally does not render information evaluation, indexing, storage, and retrieval services, which would be the mark of a real information center. The marketing research department generally lacks—both in spirit and form—a conception of itself as the total information arm of the modern marketing executive.

One aspect of the insufficiency of information arrangements is dramatized in a planned experiment by Albaum. Albaum set out to study how well information flowed from the customers of a large decentralized company through company salesmen to company executives. He arranged with a sample of company customers to pass on six fabricated pieces

of market information to company salesmen. The intelligence told of the changing requirements of customers, the building of a new factory by a competitor, the price being quoted by a competitor, the availability of a new material that might be used in making the product, and the development of a competitive product made from a new material. Clearly, all of these constitute useful marketing information in the right hands. Albaum wanted to discover how far, how fast, and how accurately this information would travel within the company.

Of the six pieces of market information, only two ever traveled beyond the company salesmen! For one reason or another, the majority of the salesmen chose not to pass on their intelligence to anyone in their company. Of the two reports that reached company executives, one arrived in three days but was seriously distorted; the other arrived in about ten days in fairly accurate form, although its usefulness could have been impaired by its tardiness.[1]

Three Information Problems

Albaum's report suggests that at least three different problems arise in an unmanaged information system. They are information disappearance: the salesmen may forget to relay information, may not know who can use it, or may purposely suppress it for personal reasons; information delay: intelligence takes longer than necessary to travel from the original relay point to the decision center; information distortion: the message becomes distorted in the process of being encoded, transmitted and decoded many times. The likelihood of disappearance, delay, and distortion tends to increase with the number of relay points between the source and the final decision center.

Attempts at Correction

There are signs here and there that a few companies have recognized that these problems are sufficiently serious to warrant the development of new concepts and innovations. One such company is Du Pont:

> ... Du Pont is moving toward marketing information centers. Basically, it means storing in a computer a great deal of information about specific markets, your position and your competitor's in those markets, the vehicles which cover the markets, etc. When the time comes to make a move, all this information is at your fingertips, so you're working on facts, not hunches.[2]

Monsanto is another company that is taking steps to put marketing information on a technologically advanced footing. Wherever feasible, the computer has been harnessed to supply rapid information and complex marketing analysis. Computer programs have been developed to help the executive select the best warehouse from which to ship an order, the best means of shipment, and the best allocation of customer sales effort. Computer programs also are available to generate sales forecasts, customer profitability studies, analyses of sales call effectiveness, and pricing proposals.[3]

In addition, United Air Lines recently commissioned the Univac Division of Sperry Rand Corporation to build a $56 million on-line computerized system designed to provide United with a totally integrated reservations, operations, and management information capability. Applications will range from passenger reservations, complete name record storage, crew and aircraft scheduling, and flight and meal-planning data to air freight and cargo loading information.

Retailing is also showing signs of innovation in the area of marketing information. The Chicago department store of Carson Pirie Scott & Company recently installed an in-store system that enables its retail personnel to check a customer's credit in a matter of seconds by dialing the customer's number on a phone. The computer returns a spoken answer, either authorizing the sale or giving other instructions. Giant retailers are also experimenting with computerized inventory-ordering systems, direct computer lines to suppliers, and improved sales analysis systems.

Other companies, such as the Hotpoint Division of General Electric, the Mead Paper Company of Dayton, Ohio, and General Mills, are known to be developing a total systems approach to their marketing information needs. But these companies still number only a handful. Other companies are interested but lack a comprehensive understanding of the marketing information problem or how to proceed to solve it.

THE MAJOR INFORMATION FLOWS

Every company is involved in three distinct marketing information flows (see figure 1a). The first, the marketing intelligence flow, is the flow of information from the environment to relay points within the firm. Information on dealers, competitors, customers, government actions bearing on marketing, prices, advertising effectiveness, and so forth would be considered marketing intelligence. The second, the internal marketing information flow, is the flow between relay points within the firm. This includes intelligence as it

flows through the company and internally generated reports germane to marketing. The third, or marketing communications flow, is the flow of information from the firm outward to the environment. It consists of both straight information and product and company promotion. The importance of marketing communications cannot be overemphasized but, as an outward information flow, it will not concern us here.

The Marketing Intelligence Flow

The flow of information known as marketing intelligence consists of salient facts about institutions and developments in the environment that affect the company's opportunities and performance. Figure 1b shows the nine major institutions in the environment that the firm monitors for marketing intelligence. It represents an elaboration of the marketing intelligence flow in figure 1a.

Marketing intelligence is a broad term, embracing raw data, summary statistics, qualitative inferences, expert and lay opinions, impressions, and even rumors. Examples include figures showing that a certain important customer is beginning to divert some of his purchases to competitors; rumors that a competitor is developing a substantially improved product; and a survey indicating that many customers are dissatisfied with the service provided by the manufacturer's representative.

Each item constitutes marketing intelligence since it has potential action implications for one or more marketing executives in the firm. Information about a wavering customer is useful intelligence to a district sales manager, although it would be trivial to the new product manager. Reports about a competitor's development of a new product would be useful to the new product manager, and information about customer dissatisfaction with the manufacturer's representative would be useful to the trade relations manager.

The idea of marketing intelligence comes from the military. The high level military decision maker is usually far removed from the battlefield and therefore totally dependent upon second-hand information in directing the battle. He requires continuous data on the current position of his troops, the occurrence and outcomes of skirmishes, and the plans of the enemy. He needs hunches and rumors as well as hard facts.

The marketing executive is in an analogous situation. He fights for terrain (markets) with allies (channels) against an enemy (competitors) for a prize (sales). Because he is remote from the battle scenes, he needs reports on the positions and effectiveness of his salesmen, on the resistances they are encountering,

FIGURE 1
What is Meant by Marketing Information

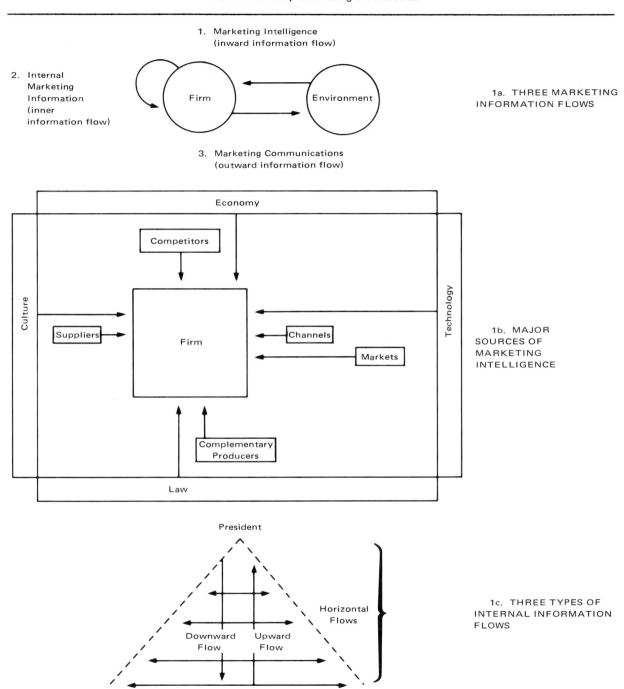

1. Marketing Intelligence
(inward information flow)

2. Internal Marketing Information (inner information flow)

Firm

Environment

1a. THREE MARKETING INFORMATION FLOWS

3. Marketing Communications
(outward information flow)

Economy

Competitors

Culture

Suppliers

Firm

Channels

Markets

Technology

Complementary Producers

Law

1b. MAJOR SOURCES OF MARKETING INTELLIGENCE

President

Horizontal Flows

Downward Flow

Upward Flow

Rank-and-file Employees

1c. THREE TYPES OF INTERNAL INFORMATION FLOWS

Source: Copyright 1966 by the Foundation for the School of Business at Indiana University. Reprinted by permission.

and on the activities of competitors. He needs current and accurate facts as well as some of the talk and gossip of the marketplace.

Marketing intelligence varies in its availability. Information about broad characteristics of the market —such as the number of buyers or their geographical dispersion—is the easiest to obtain. The information is public and often can be drawn routinely from secondary sources—government and trade associations. Information about present and potential customer preferences and attitudes is a little more difficult to acquire. Generally, it does not exist in published form, and, since it may have to be gathered as primary information, its value must be considered carefully in relation to its cost. Most difficult to collect is information related to the marketing expenditures and plans of competitors. Such facts are tightly controlled for security reasons. The firm that wants it may have to develop an industrial espionage unit within the marketing intelligence unit. This, however, raises fundamental issues in business ethics.

The Internal Information Flow

A crucial point about marketing intelligence is that it must reach the right executive to be useful; the information must flow not only to the firm but through it. The internal flow is made up of downward, upward, and horizontal flows. The three are illustrated in figure 1c where a pyramid form of organization is assumed. The downward flow consists of communications from higher company officials to subordinates. The upward flow consists of requisitioned as well as unsolicited information moving from lower to higher levels in the organization. The horizontal flow consists of information passing among company employees who occupy approximately the same levels.

In the typical company, these internal flows are left to take place in a natural unmediated way. It is assumed that employees generally will know where to find needed information within the company and will receive vital intelligence from others in the company as a matter of course. But these assumptions about the free flow of internal information in an unmanaged communications system are not justified, as Albaum's earlier cited study shows.

EXAMINING INFORMATION NEEDS

At least three steps must be taken by the company that is serious about a total systems approach to marketing information. The first step is to appoint a responsible committee; the second is for this committee to develop studies of present information

arrangements and needs. Third, the committee must design the new system on the basis of its studies and carry out its gradual implementation.

The Committee

Responsibility for the quality of marketing information should rest ultimately with the vice-president of marketing and his top ranking executives. This group must define the objectives that are to guide the supply of marketing information; it is also their responsibility to review the workings of the system and to institute desirable reforms.

These same men, however, are not equipped with either the time or training to play a first-hand role in studying, designing, or implementing the improved system. The actual work must be done by a special team usually consisting of the following personnel: the marketing research director, the economic research director, a company sales force executive, a representative from the long-range corporate planning office, a representative from the controller's office, a company computer center specialist, and a company operations researcher (see figure 2). Each man is on this committee, either because of his special concern for the quality of marketing information or because of his special skills in helping design efficient information systems.

Committee Studies

At its initial meetings, the committee will want to develop a consensus on broad objectives regarding the marketing information system and a general strategy for improvement. It will find, however, that substantial information is lacking on the present system, and that information must be collected. Two studies in particular will loom large in the future recommendations of this committee.

Internal Information Flow Characteristics Elementary study of the flow of basic information through the company often leads to substantial improvements. For example, what happens after the receipt of a customer purchase order? How long does the customer credit check take? What procedures are used to check inventory, and how long does this take? How soon does manufacturing hear of new stock requirements? How long does it take for sales executives to learn of daily or weekly total sales?

Ringer and Howell reported a study of one company's order routing, which resulted in cutting down the elapsed time between the receipt of an order and the issuance of the order to be filled from sixty-two

FIGURE 2
The Marketing Information Systems Committee

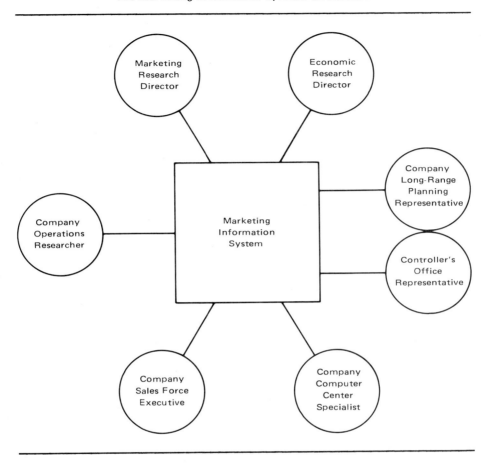

hours to thirty hours without any change in costs.[4] Evans and Hague showed how advanced information flow charting techniques could be used to describe and improve interoffice and intraoffice information flows.[5]

The effect of information delays on marketing and manufacturing efficiency has been studied most intensively by Forrester at M.I.T. Using simulation techniques, Forrester is able to show how various delays in the processing and transmission of information lead to marketing decisions that often accentuate production fluctuations beyond those caused by forecasting errors and resource immobilities. His technique enables an estimate to be made of the cost-benefit effects of proposed alterations in the speed of information transmission through the organization.[6]

Executive Marketing Information Needs The committee also will want direct feedback from executives on their satisfactions and dissatisfactions with current marketing information. Sampling of a small but representative group of executives from different levels and parts of the organization is adequate. The purpose is not to find out individual needs at this stage since information appetites and decision-making styles differ from executive to executive. Rather, the purpose is to determine how the information needs of product managers, territorial sales managers, customer account executives, advertising managers, salesmen, and other types of executives differ from each other.

Executive attitudes can be surveyed in a number of ways, including interoffice mail or the telephone. The best technique, however, is through personal in-

1. What types of decisions are you regularly called upon to make?
2. What types of information do you need to make these decisions?
3. What types of information do you regularly get?
4. What types of special studies do you periodically request?
5. What types of information would you like to get which you are not now getting?
6. What information would you want daily? weekly? monthly? yearly?
7. What magazines and trade reports would you like to see routed to you on a regular basis?
8. What specific topics would you like to be kept informed of?
9. What types of data analysis programs would you like to see made available?
10. What do you think would be the four most helpful improvements that could be made in the present marketing information system?

terviews. Figure 3 suggests the major types of executive responses sought. The questionnaire covers the executive's information sources, attitudes, needs, and suggestions. The questions are stated mainly in an open-end fashion to encourage more involvement and frankness on the part of executives. Results will be more difficult to tabulate, but open-end surveys lead to deeper insights into the problem being studied.

Developing a Long-Range Plan

The studies of the present information flows and executives' needs provide the basis for developing a long-range plan for improving the marketing information system. The committee will not accept all suggestions because the value of additional or faster information must always be measured against the costs of providing it. The committee's task is to rate the various information needs against their probable contributions to better decision making and control. The resulting long-range plan would be submitted to the executive committee for comment and approval, and would be implemented in a series of steps over a number of years.

THE MARKETING INFORMATION AND ANALYSIS CENTER

This section will describe a blueprint for an organizational unit that promises to improve the accuracy, timeliness, and comprehensiveness of executive marketing information services. This unit is a generalization of the marketing research department into something infinitely more effective known as the Marketing Information and Analysis Center (MIAC). MIAC will function as the marketing nerve center for the company and will not only provide instantaneous information to meet a variety of executive needs but also will develop all kinds of analytical and decision aids for executives—ranging from computer forecasting programs to complex simulations of the company's markets.

The concept of this center can be understood best if we view its functions as being completely user oriented. It is designed to meet the total planning, implementational, and control needs of the modern marketing executive. Figure 4 shows the flow of marketing information from ultimate sources to and through MIAC to those who use this information. The ultimate sources consist of parties outside the firm, such as customers, dealers, suppliers, and competitors (see figure 1b), and parties inside the firm, such as the accounting department, the economic and forecasting department, and the field sales force. The ultimate users consist of company executives, such as product managers, sales force managers, advertising managers, traffic managers, and production scheduling personnel. The MIAC stands between these two groups and performs over a dozen different services to enhance and expedite the marketing information and decision-making process. These information services break down into three major types: gathering, processing, and utilization.

Information Gathering

Gathering involves the effort to develop or locate information sought by company executives or deemed to be relevant to their needs. This function is made up of three constituent services.

The first is search, which is activated by requests for specific marketing information. Search projects can range from quick "information please" inquiries to large-scale field marketing studies. Marketing research departments traditionally spend a substantial portion of their time in search activity.

The second information gathering service is scanning. This describes MIAC's responsibility for assem-

FIGURE 4
A Schematic Diagram of MIAC's Information Services

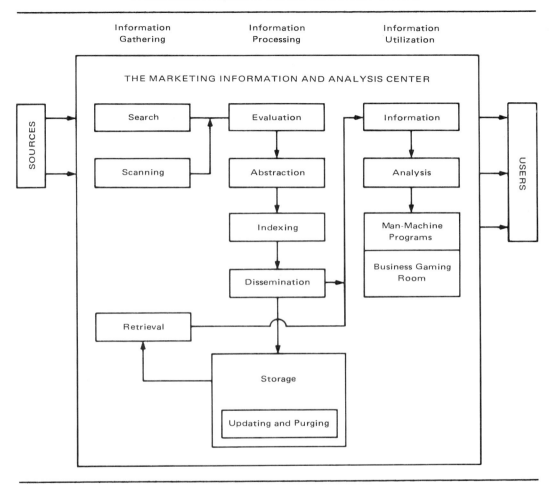

bling general marketing intelligence. Intelligence specialists in MIAC will regularly scan newspapers, magazines, trade journals, special reports, and specific individuals to uncover any developments that might have import for one or more company executives. This partially relieves executives from the necessity to scan endless reams of written material for the sake of finding only a few items of interest. Because executives have overlapping information interests, the centralization of this function and its delegation to MIAC is likely to save considerable executive time. Its effectiveness, however, depends on how well MIAC personnel really understand the differing and specific information needs.

The third information gathering service is retrieval. When the needed information is already on file, the

problem is to locate the information efficiently and speedily. This depends on the extent to which MIAC adopts advanced information storage and retrieval techniques, such as computer systems, microfilm devices, display consoles, and the like.

Information Processing

MIAC will also offer a variety of processing services designed to enhance the over-all quality of the information. Five major services can be distinguished.

The first service is evaluation. One or more MIAC staffers trained in techniques of data validation would offer a technical opinion as to how much confidence might be placed in a piece of information. The amount of confidence depends upon how the information was gathered, the size of the sample, the reliability of the source, and other considerations that the data evaluator would immediately recognize as pertinent. This service would offset the tendency to treat all information as equally valid. The data evaluator may show that a particular consumer panel market share figure may vary 20 percent from the true value (at the 95 percent confidence level), and that a magazine readership estimate may vary by as much as 50 percent from the true figure. These opinions on the reliability and credibility of information will temper executive judgments in making decisions.

A second important service is information abstraction. Marketing information comes to MIAC in highly discursive forms. Many executives do not want to read pages and pages of reports to get a kernel of information. Trained abstracters on MIAC's staff condense and edit incoming information; they may omit important material, but this risk must be balanced against the gains accruing from a service that sharpens up information and supplies the executive with an immediate sense of what is relevant.

A third important service is that of indexing the information. This involves devising a set of descriptors that will permit its efficient classification for storage and retrieval purposes, and a ready identification of which executives might be interested in it. For example, information about a proposed merger of two supermarket chains in California might be assigned the descriptors "supermarkets," "mergers," and "California," so that marketing executives interested in either supermarkets, mergers, or California would find this information readily. Developing a good indexing system is the key to the rapid dissemination of marketing information among the right parties and to its easy retrieval.

Dissemination is a fourth important information processing service. Dissemination involves getting information to the right people in the right form in the shortest feasible time. Among the devices used are periodic newsletters, telephone calls, teletype services, and interconnected company computers. Companies are experimenting with new and bolder dissemination procedures, as the following two examples show.

A large chemical company compiles during the week news of special interest to its salesmen, records the news on magnetic tapes, and sends the tapes to them. Each salesman's car is equipped with a tape recorder, and the salesmen pass many otherwise idle driving hours assimilating relevant marketing and company information.

A large supermarket chain is considering the idea of preparing up-to-the-minute reports of news affecting store operations, which its managers around the country can dial into.

MIAC's final information processing service is that of storage. Every company must find an efficient way to store and compress the mountains of information that come in yearly; otherwise, it is storage without utility. Executives should be able to put their fingers on past sales figures, costs, dealer data, and other information with minimum effort. The engineering of an efficient system is a problem for the technicians. Each company must determine the economically desirable life of different types of information so that it can be periodically updated and purged.

Information Utilization

MIAC must offer more than information gathering and processing services if it is to add substantial leverage to the executive's planning and control capabilities. The executive basically needs three types of staff assistance.

His first need is for information itself. Under this heading fall periodic reports, special market studies, and general marketing intelligence. We have seen how MIAC represents an improved vehicle for these services over the traditional marketing research department.

The second major need is for assistance in analysis. In this connection, MIAC's staff would include research specialists in statistical analysis, econometric analysis, psychometric analysis, and operations research, as well as research generalists to gauge needs and interpret results. These analysts would assist the decision maker in formulating problems and developing models for a solution. They would be able to specify the data needed and analyze the gathered data for important relationships and parameters. In this way, complex marketing decisions such as dropping a price, revising sales territories, or increasing the advertising expenditure level can be preevaluated and postevaluated through the scientific analysis of available data. These analysts would also help make periodic analyses of distribution costs, sales trends, expense records, and product and salesman performances.

The third major need of the executive is for computer programs, which will enhance his power to make decisions and to control operations. Future management gains in decision-making effectiveness will depend on the development of "man-computer" systems of decision making. Cohen and Miller have defined this type of system in the following way:

> ... it makes use of mathematical models (processed by a computer) to arrive at many decisions, but requires management to monitor these decisions and

make others that are less subject to programming. The computer not only relieves the firm of much clerical work in handling and compiling the data, but it permits the use of mathematical techniques for optimizing certain decisions which involve large quantities of data and numerous calculations. Where models are not available, the computer often can produce information, from data on hand, to permit more efficient decisions.[7]

The nature of this new and growing service area is best conveyed by several examples.

A large paper company is developing a computer hookup among its plants and warehouses, which will permit salesmen to obtain quick answers to customers' questions concerning how soon they might receive the goods if they placed an order. The inquiry is entered at a console and transmitted to the central computer system where a determination is made as to whether the item is in stock. If it is not in stock, the computer indicates how long it would take to schedule its production and ship it to the customer. The salesman can give the customer his answer in a number of minutes.

At a large chemical company, an executive can have a statistical demand analysis made for any product or product item by entering its past sales into the console. The computer program selects the economic and other variables (from a set of 200), which are most highly correlated with the product's past sales and prints out the resulting demand equation.

At a large packaged food company, sales executives get weekly reports on deliveries to retail trade with a red asterisk after those figures showing unusual variances from norms. The red asterisks alert the executives to look into these situations and determine if any special measures are needed.

A large department store is experimenting with a computer program that can make ordering, pricing and markdown decisions on some staple items and thus free buyers' time for the less routine decisions.

A major advertising agency uses the computer to develop an initial media plan, which will optimize on the clients' objectives, given the available information and constraints. The computer's proposed plan is then refined by changing certain assumptions or information, or by modifying it according to more intangible considerations.

A large chemical company uses a computer program to help evaluate each new product's promise at any point in its development. The executive

enters the best information at his disposal regarding probable price, advertising, size of market, competitive strength, cost of development, and so forth, and the computer prints out possible rates of return and their respective probabilities.

A major electrical manufacturer uses a large and complex computer model of the company's markets for one of its products to pretest the likely effects of alternative trade promotions on competitors, customers, and final sales.

All of these are contemporary examples of the possibilities that lie in the exploitation of the man-machine interface. The ultimate implication is the development of a business gaming room, as part of MIAC where information comes in continuously on field operations, and is evaluated, indexed, abstracted, and disseminated; important developments lead to speedily arranged executive meetings to decide on marketing defensive or offensive actions. Information can be retrieved instantly as the meeting progresses, and the executives can pretest proposed moves on a simulation model of the relevant markets.

There is considerable evidence that executives are dissatisfied with the quality and quantity of their marketing information. Contemporary information systems are usually inadequate to supply the information and analysis needed by marketing and other company executives to respond rapidly and optimally to changing opportunities and challenges. Only a handful of companies are presently pioneering an assortment of innovations, which promise to synthesize one day into the outlines of a new and more effective marketing information system.

A look at the nature and types of information flows provides perspective on planning an improved system. The plan of attack for an organization serious about improving its system calls for the formation of a systems committee, studies of present information flows and executive information needs, and a long-range plan for progressive improvement of the information services. The nerve center of such a system, MIAC, carries out information gathering, processing, and utilization services, which go far beyond those observed in traditional marketing research departments.

The description of MIAC is more a blueprint for the future than a feasible system for the present. Marketing information systems cannot be overhauled overnight. Yet present systems can be guided to evolve in the direction of this blueprint. Difficult questions have to be answered concerning the proper relation between MIAC and other company information centers; the proper relation between MIAC and grass roots marketing research efforts by company personnel; the proper administrative arrangements within MIAC; the cost of MIAC; and so forth.

It must also be asked what the dangers may be in the centralized management of marketing information, and whether this system could make a fetish of information, causing more to be gathered than is economically justifiable. There are no general answers to these questions. They call for inventiveness and good judgment on the part of individual firms. The only judgment to be ventured here is that companies now have it within their power to make substantial improvements in their marketing information system —and can ill afford to neglect them.

NOTES

1. Gerald S. Albaum, "Horizontal Information Flow: An Exploratory Study," *Journal of the Academy of Management,* VII (March, 1964), pp. 21–33.

2. Malcolm McNiven, "An Interview with Malcolm McNiven," *Sales Management* (April 19, 1963), p. 42.

3. William A. Clark, "Monsanto Chemical Company: A Total Systems Approach to Marketing," in Alan D. Meacham and Van B. Thompson, eds., *Total Systems* (Detroit: American Data Processing Inc., 1962), pp. 130–42.

4. Jurgen F. Ringer and Charles D. Howell, "The Industrial Engineer and Marketing," in Harold Bright Maynard, ed., *Industrial Engineering Handbook* (2nd ed.; New York: McGraw-Hill Book Co., Inc., 1963), pp. 10, 102–3.

5. Marshall K. Evans and Lou R. Hague, "Master Plan for Information System," *Harvard Business Review* (January-February, 1962), pp. 92–104.

6. Jay W. Forrester, "Advertising—A Problem in Industrial Dynamics," *Harvard Business Review* (March-April, 1959), pp. 100–110.

7. Kalman J. Cohen and Merton H. Miller, "Management Games, Information Processing, and Control," *Management International,* III (1963), p. 168.

CASES

AMERICAN PARK GOLF CENTER

This privately owned golf course is located in northern California. After purchasing the land and developing the course, the owners lost a condemnation suit to the city. As a result, they were given only a forty-year lease on the property. Throughout its existence, American Park Golf Center has been faced with uncooperative city officials and environmentalists, especially in its efforts to expand course utilization and sales.

SOUTHWEST MONTANA COORS, INC.

In preparing his application for a Coors beer distributorship for southwestern Montana, the entrepreneur was attempting to choose between several possible research studies, all of which were designed to assess the market potential and feasibility of such a distributorship.

AMERICAN RECREATION CENTERS, INC.

Based in Sacramento, California, American Recreation Centers is a chain of bowling alleys, one of the largest such chains on the West Coast. Changing trends in population characteristics and in the bowling industry in general have created long-range planning problems for its management.

MASSACHUSETTS STATE LOTTERY

In 1971, the state of Massachusetts enacted a law to begin a state-operated lottery. The Massachusetts Lottery Commission was created and given the assignment to determine what ticket buyers expect from such a sweepstakes and how it would compete with similar lotteries in other northeastern states.

AMERICAN PARK GOLF CENTER

In June 1979, Mr. Jeffrey Robbins, president of American Park Golf Center, was evaluating the past operations of his golf course and trying to determine what future actions he should take. Mr. Robbins opened his golf center on December 26, 1976, after approximately six years of planning, development, and legal battles with the city. Although the course was privately owned, it was open to the public and, in Mr. Robbins's opinion, had been reasonably successful.

THE GOLF CENTER

Located in a large metropolitan area in northern California, the American Park Golf Center (APGC) was an executive style nine-hole golf course, with two par-four holes and seven par-three holes. While the course was only 1,635 yards long, the golfer could use woods on occasion and was faced with a multitude of water hazards, trees, and sand traps. Providing further obstacles, and enhancing the beauty of the course, was a large river bordering the west side of the course. During the summer months (May through September), the course was open for twelve hours per day, and during the winter for ten hours per day (hours open are equivalent to hours available for starting times, which are at five minute intervals).

In addition to the course itself there was a practice putting green, a practice chipping area, and a temporary clubhouse. The clubhouse was actually a converted mobile home which contained vending machines for snacks and beverages, and a small pro shop operated independently by the course pro, Mr. James Kilgore.

This case was prepared by Professor Dennis H. Tootelian, California State University, Sacramento.

To staff this golf center, Mr. Robbins hired one full-time employee and one part-time employee to work in the clubhouse. In addition, one full-time and two part-time employees were hired to maintain the course. Mr. Robbins prided himself in keeping the course as well maintained and litter free as was physically possible.

BACKGROUND

Although Mr. Robbins, forty-six, enjoyed golf, he was not an avid golfer himself. His previous work experience included merchandising and site location studies for a large retail chain, ownership of a doughnut shop, and the development of a similar golf center in southern California. He principally enjoyed the challenge of starting new ventures and tried to maintain more of a business than a golfing orientation in this operation.

After deciding to pursue this venture, Mr. Robbins took one year in looking for a suitable location for a golf center. He wanted to locate in a high traffic area close to the center of the city so as to appeal to the afternoon businessperson. As he stated: "I travelled up and down many streets around the city until I found this site. It was worth it, however, since I found just what I wanted, despite the legal troubles I ran into."

After purchasing the land (twenty-five acres) in 1967, Mr. Robbins began planning for the construction of the course itself. In 1974, however, the city filed a condemnation suit which it won in 1975. Because the land bordered a river and was adjacent to a public bikeway, the city wanted to obtain ownership of the land for "public use for the public good." As a result, the land was resold to the city and Mr. Robbins was given a forty-year lease on it. When the lease expires, the golf center will be operated by the city. The terms of the lease were such that Mr. Robbins paid $6,000 per year rent and the taxes on the land (currently $6,500 per year).

According to Mr. Robbins, his troubles with the city did not end with the disposition of the condemnation suit.

They have fought me on virtually everything I have tried to do. The taxes should be roughly

8 percent of expenses instead of the current 13 percent. I am fighting this now. I have made every effort possible to make this course a beautiful one which fits into its surroundings. I have no intention of altering the landscape in any significant way. You would think the city would help me build up business since it will be theirs someday, but for some reason they give me a bad time.

APGC was incorporated in 1974. With respect to the disposition of the common stock, Mr. Robbins held 65 percent, his son 20 percent, and the other 15 percent was held by individuals who had assisted in starting the business.

THE COMPETITION

Within the city and surrounding area (twenty-five miles), there were thirteen major golf courses open to the public, and five private ones. Of those open to the public, six were responsible for approximately 75 percent of the golf starts in the area (see exhibit 1).

Although there was one publicly owned nine-hole golf course within the city, it did not compare favorably to APGC in terms of beauty or difficulty of play. Mr. Robbins felt that the course most similar to American Park in terms of being relatively short and well maintained was located about twenty-five miles away, and was an eighteen-hole course (course F). The other major courses in the area (courses A through E) were of standard length, requiring four and one-half to five hours to play eighteen holes. The average player at APGC could play nine holes in approximately one and one-half hours.

Mr. Robbins felt that APGC had several advantages relative to the competition in the area. First, the course was close to highly populated areas and numerous business offices. With respect to housing, there were fifteen apartment complexes within a two-mile radius of the golf center, and two of these bordered the center itself (230 units). Within this area, therefore, there were well over 1500 apartment units. Accounting for a large part of this concentration of apartment units was a university with some 18,000 students, located approximately one mile from the APGC. In addition to the apartment com-

EXHIBIT 1

Golf Courses in Relevant Market

	Number of Holes	Par	Ownership	Distance from Central City
Course— High Volume				
A	18	72	County	8 miles
B	18	72	City*	20 miles
C	36	72 (per 18 holes)	City	5 miles
D	18	72	City*	25 miles
E	18	72	City*	25 miles
F	18	61	Private	25 miles
Course— Mid Volume				
G	18	72	City*	25 miles
H	18	72	City*	15 miles
I	18	71	City*	25 miles
J	18	70	City	9 miles
K	9	27	City	7 miles
L	18	72	Private	15 miles
APGC	9	29	Private	5 miles

*Not the same city in which American Park is located.

plexes, there were twelve relatively small professional centers (business offices) within this area also. The average professional center contained approximately twenty-five individual business offices. Because of this concentration, Mr. Robbins thought that this site was good for a golf center.

A second advantage of the APGC was its outstanding reputation. Because the course had been professionally designed and was so well maintained, it received excellent word of mouth advertising. In 1977, Mr. Robbins commissioned some university students to do a small market survey of golfers at his course and at two of the public courses (courses A and C). While the survey was not professional in nature, it did offer insights into the attitudes of the various golfers (see exhibits 2 and 3).

The third advantage Mr. Robbins felt he had was that while the course was busy (some 44,000 starts in 1977 and 47,000 starts in 1978), it was relatively easy

EXHIBIT 2
Market Study—Most Desirable Characteristics

What They Liked About the Course	APGC	Course A	Course C
Challenging Course	22%	12%	19%
Long Course	0	20	15
Short Course	9	0	0
Beauty of Course Surroundings	21	10	16
Well Kept Landscape (General)	11	5	3
Location	3	10	15
Well Maintained Greens	9	5	6
Course Well Laid Out	12	8	10
Other	13	30	16
	100%	100%	100%

EXHIBIT 3
Market Study—Least Desirable Characteristics

What They Disliked About the Course	APGC	Course A	Course C
No Rakes in Traps	16%	0%	2%
Lack of Sufficient Ball Washers	19	0	0
Debris on Course	0	10	10
Price	14	3	0
Poorly Maintained Greens	5	21	14
Overcrowded	0	32	24
Lack of Organization in Teeing Off	28	0	7
Too Many Children Playing Course	0	26	5
Other	18	8	38
	100%	100%	100%

to get a convenient starting time. Many of the high volume courses averaged anywhere from 175,000 to 250,000 starts per year, and golfers without advance reservations often waited one to two hours, whereas at APGC the golfer normally did not have to wait for more than fifteen to twenty minutes even during relatively busy times.

Consequently, for golfers who wanted to play with no advance starting time, the APGC was very appealing. Coupled with the fact that the course was close to the center of the city and challenging golf could be played in a shorter time period, Mr. Robbins thought that the course was ideally suited for businessmen and students.

Despite these advantages, however, there were several disadvantages. First, while the golf course was in a high traffic area, it could not be seen directly from the main cross streets. Golfers had to turn onto a relatively obscure side street in order to reach the clubhouse. Although there was a small sign stating "Golf" on one of the main cross streets, the clubhouse was not readily visible.

The second disadvantage was the fact that the green fees were somewhat higher for APGC than for the publicly owned golf courses (see exhibit 4). In assessing his pricing structure, Mr. Robbins did not believe his market to be overly price sensitive, except perhaps for the university students. To compensate for this, a $.50 discount was given to students with valid university identification cards for weekday

afternoon play. Publicly owned courses, however, gave $.70 reductions to players under eighteen and allowed those over seventy years of age to play free on weekday afternoons.

The final disadvantage recognized by Mr. Robbins was that the course was a short, nine-hole course. The "true" golfer normally preferred a regulation eighteen-hole course. Consequently, Mr. Robbins felt that his course had somewhat limited appeal. Even though some golfers played the course twice, most only played nine holes.

MARKETING ACTIVITIES

Mr. Robbins engaged in few marketing activities since he believed that location and word of mouth advertising sold the course itself. Other than the "Golf" sign, membership in a "Let's Dine Out" type of group, and an advertisement in the yellow pages of the telephone directory, no efforts were made to promote the golf center. Furthermore, knowing that most of the city- and county-owned golf courses operated at a loss, Mr. Robbins made no effort to compete with them on a price basis. He did, however, give free rounds of golf to some of his regular customers, but this was very sporadic. In addition, he made some price concessions to lure in local tournaments by giving $.25 off for nine holes of play.

EXHIBIT 4
Comparative Prices

Green Fees	APGC	City-County Owned	Private Course
Weekdays			
9 holes	$ 2.50	$1.75 to $2.00	$3.00 to $10.00
18 holes	$ 4.50	$3.25 to $4.00	$5.00 to $15.00
Weekends			
9 holes	$ 3.00	$2.50 to $3.00	$5.00 to $15.00
18 holes	$ 5.50	$4.00 to $5.00	$7.50 to $20.00
Special Prices			
Monthly Card	$20.00	$15.00	—
All Day Play			
Weekdays	$ 5.00	$4.00 to $4.50	—
Weekends	$ 6.00	—	—
Junior Players (under 18)			
9 holes (weekdays only)	$ 2.00	$1.50 to $2.00	—
18 holes (weekdays only)	$ 3.00	$2.00 to $2.75	—
All Day (weekdays only)	$ 3.50	$3.00 to $3.50	—
Senior Players (70 or over)			
Weekdays only	—	Free	—
Students (weekdays only)	$ .50 discount	$ .70 discount	—

FINANCIAL STATUS

The financial statements for APGC are presented in exhibits 5 and 6. Although the golf center had always been profitable, Mr. Robbins recognized that his costs could be lower. The care and maintenance of the course were of prime importance to him, and he was very reluctant to trim these costs.

I know that I go a little overboard on some things. For example, I use only the best fertilizer on the course, and I make sure the course is mown three times per week compared to city and county courses which are mown two times per week. In the winter when most courses close due to the excess moisture on the greens, I use highly absorbent sand so that the course can stay open and be playable. I believe, nevertheless, that these things are important for the reputation of the course. Over time these activities will pay off.

The lengthy delay and high legal costs involved in starting operations, furthermore, made it difficult for Mr. Robbins to put more of his personal wealth into the business. Although he was not opposed to bringing in outside investors, he did not want to lose control of the corporation.

FUTURE OPERATIONS

In reviewing his operations, Mr. Robbins wanted to increase the utilization of the course and maximize his profit position. Since the costs of operation did not vary significantly with the number of players, Mr. Robbins felt that by increasing the number of starts, profits would increase appreciably. In his deliberations, he had identified several possible courses of action.

While it was impossible to acquire enough additional land to add nine more holes to the course, Mr. Robbins had thought about putting lights on the existing nine holes to allow for night play. This would allow the APGC to stay open for three more hours in the summer and five more hours in the winter. No other course in the area had lights. He had approached the city with this idea about one year earlier, but met with strong resistance from a group of ecologists.

EXHIBIT 5
APGC Income Statement

	1978		1977	
Golf Starts (Sales)	$64,884	(90.1)	$60,742	(95.4)
Merchandise Sales (Net)	7,136	(9.9)	2,956	(4.6)
Total Sales	$72,020	(100.0)	$63,698	(100.0)
Variable Costs				
Labor	$14,685	(20.4)	$13,884	(21.8)
Fertilizer	3,500	(4.9)	3,750	(5.9)
Equipment Repair	1,200	(1.7)	750	(1.2)
Misc. (Sand, etc.)	400	(0.5)	650	(1.0)
Total	$19,785	(27.5)	$19,034	(29.9)
Fixed Costs				
Utilities				
Water	$ 4,000	(5.6)	$ 3,700	(5.8)
Electricity	800	(1.1)	775	(1.2)
Telephone	360	(0.5)	360	(0.6)
Misc. (Garbage, etc.)	180	(0.3)	180	(0.3)
Advertising	3,750	(5.2)	3,540	(5.5)
Supplies (Scorecards, etc.)	450	(0.6)	840	(1.3)
Loan Payments	3,992	(5.5)	3,992	(6.3)
Lease Payments	6,000	(8.3)	6,000	(9.4)
Property Taxes	6,500	(9.0)	6,500	(10.2)
Administrative Salaries	15,315	(21.3)	14,250	(22.4)
Depreciation	3,700	(5.1)	3,700	(5.8)
Total	$45,047	(62.5)	$43,837	(68.8)
Total Variable and Fixed Costs	$64,832	(90.0)	$62,871	(98.7)
Income Before Taxes	$ 7,188	(10.0)	$ 827	(1.3)

Given his past experience with the city, he was somewhat skeptical about carrying this effort further. He anticipated the costs of installing the lighting to be approximately $36,000. The other costs are presented in exhibit 7.

Mr. Robbins was also considering the feasibility of putting a driving range near the clubhouse. A church adjacent to the land had excess parking facilities, and Mr. Robbins thought they would lease some of this space to him at a yearly fee of $2,500. Although the costs of a driving range were relatively low (see exhibit 8), he was unsure of its profit potential. The one main limitation was that there was not enough space to allow the use of woods unless specially designed plastic golf balls were used. These were very

expensive, but would travel only about one-third the distance of regular golf balls. If plastic golf balls were not used, Mr. Robbins would have to limit the range to irons only.

A third idea Mr. Robbins had was to build a modern clubhouse to replace the temporary mobile home. He felt that this would provide for a better image and enhance the sales of merchandise. While all merchandise sales and lessons were handled by Mr. Kilgore, Mr. Robbins received a commission of 5 percent on gross sales (including lessons). He estimated the cost to build a clubhouse was approximately $22,000.

One other idea was to convert APGC to a private club and membership. Although Mr. Robbins was

EXHIBIT 6
APGC Balance Sheet

	1978	1977
Current Assets		
Cash	$ 2,300	$1,100
Net Accounts Receivable	3,415	595
Prepaid Expenses	2,875	268
Total	$ 8,590	$ 1,963
Net Fixed Assets		
Portable Clubhouse	$14,275	$15,050
Equipment for Course	2,800	2,410
Features on Course	750	300
Office Equipment	475	324
Golf Accessories	635	290
(Carts, Clubs, etc.)		
Leasehold Improvements	44,000	44,000
Total	$62,935	$62,374
Total Assets	$71,525	$64,337
Current Liabilities		
Accounts Payable	$ 3,725	$ 3,160
Wages Payable	1,285	350
Total	$ 5,010	$ 3,510
Long-term Liabilities		
Bank Loan	$38,500	$40,000
Total	$38,500	$40,000
Common Stock	$20,000	$20,000
Equity	$ 8,015	$ 827
Total Liabilities	$71,525	$64,337

EXHIBIT 7
Costs of Nightlights

Installation of Nightlights	$36,000

Additional Annual Costs:

Labor	$5,648
Electricity	6,000
Misc. Costs	2,000
Interest on Loan	2,400

EXHIBIT 8
Driving Range Costs

Initial Outlay

Machine to Pick Up Golf Balls (5-year life)	$2,500
Baskets—50 at $4 Per Basket (5-year life)	200
Golf Balls—75 Per Basket at $.20 Per Ball (3-year life)	750
Protective Screens Around Range	6,000
Labor Costs	2,190
General Maintenance	200
Insurance	300

Anticipated Loss of Golf Balls—20% Per Year

certain the city would object since his contract states the course will be open to the public, he felt that he could try to fight that battle. The anticipated miscellaneous costs of making such a switch were considered to be approximately $3,000 and would necessitate the building of a modern clubhouse with some added features like showers, lockers, etc. The costs of this clubhouse were thought to be about $60,000.

In his evaluations, Mr. Robbins could not decide whether to take one of these, or other alternatives, or whether he should stick with or improve his present operations.

SOUTHWESTERN MONTANA COORS, INC.

INTRODUCTION

Larry Brownlow was just beginning to realize the problem was more complex than he thought. The problem, of course, was giving direction to Manson and Associates regarding which research should be completed by February 20, 1976, to determine the market potential of a Coors beer distributorship for southwestern Montana. With data from this research, Larry would be able to estimate the feasibility of such an operation before the March 5 application deadline. Larry knew his decision of whether or not to apply for the distributorship was the most important career choice he had ever faced.

LARRY BROWNLOW

Larry was just completing his M.B.A., and, from his standpoint, the Coors announcement of expansion into Montana could hardly have been better timed. He had long ago decided the best opportunities and rewards were in smaller, self-owned businesses and not in the jungles of corporate giants.

Because of a family tragedy some three years ago, Larry found himself in a position to consider small business opportunities such as the Coors distributorship. Approximately $200,000 was held in trust for Larry, to be dispersed when he reached age thirty. Until then, Larry and his family lived on an annual trust income of about $8,000. It was because of this income that Larry decided to leave his sales engineering job and return to graduate school for his M.B.A.

The decision to complete a graduate program and operate his own business had been easy to make.

This case was prepared by Professor James E. Nelson, Montana State University.

While he could have retired and lived off investment income, Larry knew such a life would not be to his liking. Working with people and the challenge of making it on his own, Larry thought, were far preferable to enduring an early retirement.

Larry would be thirty in July, about the time money would actually be needed to start the business. In the meantime, he had access to about $2,500 for feasibility research. While there certainly were other places to spend the money, Larry and his wife agreed the opportunity to acquire the distributorship could not be overlooked.

COORS, INC.

Coors's history dates back to 1873 when Adolph Coors built a small brewery in Golden, Colorado. Since then, the brewery has prospered and has become the fifth largest seller of beer in the country. Coors's operating philosophy could be summed up as "hard work, saving money, devotion to the quality of the product, caring about the environment, and giving people something to believe in."

Company operation is consistent with this philosophy. All facilities are still located in Golden, which is centrally located to the eleven Western states in which Coors is marketed. Coors is still family operated and controlled. The company recently expanded into the Texas market and issued its first public stock, $127 million worth of nonvoting shares. The issue was enthusiastically received by the financial community despite its being offered at the bottom of the 1975 recession.

Coors's unwillingness to compromise on the high quality of its product is well known both to its suppliers and to its consuming public. Coors beer requires constant refrigeration to maintain this quality, and wholesalers' facilities are closely controlled to insure that proper temperatures are maintained. Wholesalers are also required to install and use aluminum can recycling equipment. Coors was one of the first breweries in the industry to recycle its cans.

Larry was aware of Coors's popularity with consumers. From both personal experience and published articles, Coors consumers were characterized as almost fanatically brand-loyal despite the beer's premium price. As an example, ticket counter employees at the Denver airport regularly report seeing out-of-state passengers carrying one or more cases of Coors on board for home consumption in non-Coors states. Local acceptance, Larry thought, would be no less enthusiastic.

Because of this high consumer acceptance, the Coors company spent less on advertising than did competitors. Consumer demand seemed to pull the product through the distribution channel.

MANSON RESEARCH PROPOSAL

Because of the press of studies, Larry contacted Manson and Associates in January for their assistance. The firm was a Spokane-based general research supplier that had conducted other feasibility studies in the Pacific Northwest.

Larry met John Rome, senior research analyst for Manson, and extensively discussed the Coors opportunity and appropriate research in the January meeting. Rome promised a formal research proposal (exhibit 1; with sample tables, exhibit 2) for the project that Larry now held in his hand. It certainly was extensive, Larry thought, and reflected the

professionalism he expected. Now came the hard part, choosing the more relevant research from the proposal, because he certainly couldn't afford to pay for it all. Rome had suggested a meeting for Friday which gave Larry only three more days to decide.

Larry was at first overwhelmed. All of the research would certainly be useful. He was sure he needed estimates of sales and costs in a form allowing managerial analysis, but what data in what form? Knowledge of competing operations' experience, retailer support, and consumer acceptance also seemed crucial for feasibility analysis. For example, what if consumers were excited about Coors but retailers were indifferent, or the other way around? Finally, several of the studies would provide information also useful in later months of operation in the areas of promotion and pricing, for example. The problem now appeared more difficult than before!

It would have been nice, Larry thought, if he only had some time to perform part of the suggested research himself. There just was too much in the way of class assignments and other matters to allow him that luxury. Besides, using Manson and Associates would give him research results from an unbiased source. Anyway, there would be plenty enough for him to do once he received the results.

EXHIBIT 1
Manson and Associates Research Proposal

January 16, 1976

Mr. Larry Brownlow
1198 West Lamar
Pullman, WA 99163

Dear Larry:

It was a pleasure meeting you last week and discussing your business and research interests in Coors wholesaling. From further thought and discussion with my colleagues, the Coors opportunity appears even more attractive than when we met.

Appearances can be deceiving, as you know, and I fully agree that some formal research is needed before you make application. Research that we recommend would proceed in two distinct stages and is described below:

Stage One Research Based on Secondary Data

Study A: National and Montana Per Capita Beer Consumption for 1973, 1974, and 1975
              Description: Per capita annual consumption of beer for the total population and population age twenty-one and over in gallons is provided.
              Source: Various publications
              Cost: $100

(continued on next page)

EXHIBIT 1 (continued)

Study B: Population Estimates for 1975 to 1980 for Five Montana Counties in Market Area
Description: Annual estimates of total population and population age twenty-one and over is provided for the period 1975 to 1980.
Source: U.S. Bureau of Census and Sales Management Annual Survey of Buying Power
Cost: $150

Study C: Coors Market Share Estimates for 1977 to 1980
Description: Coors market share based on total gallons consumed in the five-county market area is estimated for each year in the period 1977 to 1980. These data will be projected from Coors's experience in Idaho, Colorado, California, Oklahoma, and Texas.
Source: Various publications
Cost: $200

Study D: Estimated Liquor and Beer License for the Market Area 1976 to 1980
Description: Projections of the number of on-premise sale operations and off-premise sale operations is provided.
Source: Montana Department of Revenue, Liquor Division
Cost: $100

Study E: Beer Taxes Paid by Montana Wholesalers for 1974 and 1975 in the Market Area
Description: Beer taxes paid by each of the five currently operating competing beer wholesalers is provided. This can be converted to gallons sold by applying the state gallonage tax rate (10.5 cents per gallon).
Source: Montana Department of Revenue, Liquor Division
Cost: $400

Study F: Financial Statement Summary of Wine, Liquor, and Beer Wholesalers for 1975
Description: Composite balance sheets, income statements, and relevant measures of performance provided for 152 similar wholesaling operations are provided.
Source: Robert Morris Associates Annual Statement Studies, 1976 ed.
Cost: $13.50

Stage Two Research Based on Primary Data

Study G: Consumer Study
Description: Study G involves focus-group interviews and a mail questionnaire to determine consumer past experience, acceptance, and intention to buy Coors beer. Three interviews would be conducted in three counties in the market area. From these data, a mail questionnaire would be developed and sent to 1,000 adult residents in the market area utilizing direct questions and a semantic differential scale to measure attitudes towards Coors beer, competing beers, and an ideal beer.
Source: Manson and Associates
Cost: $1,100

Study H: Retailer Study
Description: Focus-group interviews would be conducted with six potential retailers of Coors beer in one county in the market area to determine their past beer sales and experience and their intention to stock and sell Coors. From these data, a mail questionnaire would be developed and sent to all appropriate retailers in the market area to determine similar data.
Source: Manson and Associates
Cost: $600

Study I: Survey of Retail and Wholesale Beer Prices
Description: Study I involves in-store interviews with a sample of fifteen retailers in the market area to determine retail and wholesale prices for Budweiser, Hamms, Michelob, Olympia, and a low-price beer.
Source: Manson and Associates
Cost: $500

(continued on next page)

EXHIBIT 1 (*continued*)

Examples of the form of final report tables are shown in Exhibit 2. This should give you a better idea of the data you will receive.

As you can see, the research is extensive and, I might add, not cheap. However, the research as outlined will supply you with sufficient information to make an estimate of the feasibility of a Coors distributorship, the investment for which is substantial.

I have scheduled 9:00 a.m. next Friday as a time to meet with you to discuss the proposal in more detail. Time is short, but we firmly feel the study can be completed by February 20, 1976. If you need more information in the meantime, please feel free to call.

Sincerely,

John Rome
Senior Research Analyst

EXHIBIT 2
Examples of Final Research Report Tables

TABLE A
National and Montana Resident Annual Beer Consumption, 1973–1975 (Gallons)

	U.S. consumption			Montana consumption	
Year	Based on entire population	Based on population over age 21		Based on entire population	Based on population over age 21
1973					
1974					
1975					

Source: Study A.

TABLE B
Population Estimates for 1975–1980 for Five Montana Counties in Market Area

	Projected entire population					
County	1975	1976	1977	1978	1979	1980
A						
B						
C						
D						
E						

	Projected population age 21 and over					
County	1975	1976	1977	1978	1979	1980
A						
B						
D						
C						
E						

Source: Study B.

(*continued on next page*)

EXHIBIT 2 (*continued*)

TABLE C
Coors Market Share Estimates for 1977–1980*

Year	Market share (%)
1977	
1978	
1979	
1980	

Source: Study C.

*Coors 1975 market shares for Idaho, Colorado, California, Oklahoma, and Texas are _____ %, _____ %, _____ %, _____ %, and _____ %, respectively.

TABLE D
Liquor and Beer License Estimates for Market Area for 1976–1980

Type of license	1976	1977	1978	1979	1980
All beverages					
Retail beer and wine					
Off-premise beer only					

Type of License	1976	1977	1978	1979	1980
Veterans beer and liquor					
Fraternal					
Resort beer and liquor					

Source: Study D.

TABLE E
Beer Taxes Paid By Beer Wholesalers in the Market Area, 1974 and 1975*

Wholesaler	1974 tax paid ($)	1975 tax paid ($)
A		
B		
C		
D		
E		

Source: Study E.

*Montana beer tax is 10.5 cents per gallon.

(*continued on next page*)

CASE

EXHIBIT 2 (*continued*)

TABLE F
Financial Statement Summary for 152 Wholesalers of Wine, Liquor, and Beer in 1975

Assets	%	Liabilities	%
Cash		Due to banks—short-term	
Marketable securities		Due to trade	
Receivables net		Income taxes	
Inventory net		Current maturities LT debt	
All other current		All other current	
Total current		Total current debt	
Fixed assets net		Noncurrent debt unsubordinated	
All other noncurrent		Total unsubordinated debt	
		Subordinated debt	
Total	100.0%	Tangible net worth	
		Total	100.0%

Income data	%	Ratios	
Net sales		Quick	
Cost of sales		Current	
Gross profit		Debts/worth	
All other expenses net		Sales/receivables	
Profit before taxes		Cost sales/inventory	
		% Profit before taxes	
		Based on total assets	

Source: Study F (Robert Morris Associates © 1976).

Note: Robert Morris Associates cannot emphasize too strongly that its figures *may not* be representative of the entire industry for the following reasons:

1. The only companies with a chance of being included in Table F are those for whom their submitting banks have recent figures.

2. Even from this restricted group of potentially includable companies, those which are chosen, and the total number chosen, are not determined in any random or otherwise statistically reliable manner.

3. Many companies in Table F have *varied* product lines. Bankers have categorized them by their *primary* product line and some "impurity" in the data will be introduced. Thus, the figures should not automatically be considered as representative norms.

(*continued on next page*)

EXHIBIT 2 (*continued*)

TABLE G
Consumer Questionnaire Results

	% Yes	% No	Total %		% Yes	% No	Total %
Consumed Coors in the past:							
Attitudes toward Coors:				**Usually buy beer at:**			
Strongly like				Liquor stores			
Like				Taverns and bars			
Indifferent/No opinion				Supermarkets			
Dislike				Corner grocery			
Strongly dislike							
Total			100.0%	Total			100.0%
Weekly beer consumption:				**Features considered important**			
Less than 1 can				**when buying beer:**			
1–2 cans				Taste			
3–4 cans				Brand name			
5–6 cans				Price			
7–8 cans				Store location			
9 cans and over				Advertising			
				Carbonation			
				Other			
Total			100.0%	Total			100.0%
Intention to buy Coors:							
Certainly will							
Maybe will							
Not sure							
Maybe will not							
Certainly will not							
Total			100.0%				

Semantic differential scale*

	Extremely	Very	Somewhat	Somewhat	Very	Extremely	
Masculine	___	___	___	___	___	___	Feminine
Healthful	___	___	___	___	___	___	Unhealthful
Cheap	___	___	___	___	___	___	Expensive
Strong	___	___	___	___	___	___	Weak
Old-fashioned	___	___	___	___	___	___	New
Upper-class	___	___	___	___	___	___	Lower-class
Good taste	___	___	___	___	___	___	Bad taste

Source: Study G.

*Profiles would be provided for Coors, three competing beers, and an ideal beer.

(*continued on next page*)

EXHIBIT 2 (*continued*)

TABLE H
Retailer Questionnaire Results

Brands of beer carried	%	1975 beer sales	%
Olympia		Olympia	
Budweiser		Budweiser	
Rainier		Rainier	
Hamms		Hamms	
Brand E		Brand E	
Brand F		Brand F	
Brand G		Brand G	
		Others	
Total	100.0%	Total %	100.0%

Semantic differential scale*

	Extremely	Very	Somewhat	Somewhat	Very	Extremely	
Masculine	____	____	____	____	____	____	Feminine
Healthful	____	____	____	____	____	____	Unhealthful
Cheap	____	____	____	____	____	____	Expensive
Strong	____	____	____	____	____	____	Weak
Old-fashioned	____	____	____	____	____	____	New
Upper-class	____	____	____	____	____	____	Lower-class
Good taste	____	____	____	____	____	____	Bad taste

Intention to sell Coors: Certainly will
Maybe will
Not sure
Maybe will not
Certainly will not

Total %   100.0%

Source: Study H.

*Profiles would be provided for Coors, three competing beers, and an ideal beer.

(*continued on next page*)

CASE

EXHIBIT 2 (*continued*)

TABLE I
Retail and wholesale prices for selected beers in the market area

Beer	Wholesale* six-pack price ($)	Retail† six-pack price ($)
Budweiser		
Hamms		
Michelob		
Olympia		
Low-price special		

Source: Study I.

*Price that the wholesaler sold to retailers.

†Price that the retailer sold to consumers.

NVESTMENT AND OPERATING DATA

Larry was not completely in the dark regarding investment and operating data for the distributorship. In the previous two weeks he had visited two beer wholesalers in his hometown of Pullman, Washington, who handled Olympia and Hamms beer to get a feel for their operation and market experience. It would have been nice to interview a Coors wholesaler, but Coors management had strictly informed all of their distributors to provide no information to prospective applicants.

While no specific financial data were discussed, general information had been provided in a near cordial fashion because of the noncompetitive nature of Larry's plans. Based on his conversations, Larry had made the following estimates:

Inventory		$120,000
Equipment		
Delivery trucks	$76,000	
Forklift	10,000	
Recycling and misc. equip.	10,000	
Office equipment	4,000	
Total equipment		100,000
Warehouse		160,000
Land		20,000
Total investment		$400,000

A local banker had reviewed Larry's financial capabilities and had seen no problem in extending a line of credit on the order of $200,000. Other family sources also might lend as much as $200,000 to the business.

As a rough estimate of fixed expenses, Larry planned on having four route salesmen, a secretary, and a general warehouseman. Salaries for these people and himself would run about $75,000 annually plus some form of incentive compensation he had yet to determine. Other fixed or semifixed expenses were estimated at:

Equipment depreciation	$20,000
Warehouse depreciation	8,000
Utilities and telephone	8,000
Insurance	6,000
Personal property taxes	5,000
Maintenance and janitorial	2,800
Miscellaneous	1,200
Total	$51,000

According to the two wholesalers, beer in bottles and cans outsold keg beer by a three-to-one margin. Keg beer prices at the wholesale level were about 45 percent of prices for beer in bottles and cans.

MEETING

The entire matter deserved much thought. Maybe it was a golden opportunity, maybe not. The only thing certain was that research was needed, Manson and Associates was ready, and Larry needed time to think. Today is Tuesday, Larry thought, only three days until he and John Rome get together for direction.

AMERICAN RECREATION CENTERS, INC.

In July 1975, Mr. Robert Feuchter, president and board chairman of American Recreation Centers, Inc. (ARC), proudly announced that fiscal 1975 had ended with the second best profits in that firm's history. Concurrently, he mentioned the establishment of an Employee Stock Ownership Trust and spoke of ARC's plans to open two new bowling centers in August for the current year.

American Recreation Centers, Inc., "largest publicly owned bowling chain in the West," owned and operated sixteen bowling centers, an office building in Corona, and a shopping center in Hayward, all in California. Fourteen of the bowling centers were in the northern half of the state, and headquarters were in Sacramento.

Although President Feuchter was optimistic about the future, he continued to be concerned about long-range planning, particularly in the areas of growth, diversification, and possible energy shortages. Bowling had reached its peak in 1962. It could no longer be regarded as a growth industry. Yet, Feuchter saw possibilities for profitable expansion. He believed that the firm could grow through careful selection of sites and make money by innovations in operating efficiency despite competition from the giant

This case was prepared by Professor Leete A. Thompson, California State University, Sacramento.

Brunswick Corporation. He also believed that some diversification probably was essential for long-term survival, though ARC had, so far, been unable to find synergistic partners or services. He expressed concern about the economy too. ARC would have to plan for possible energy shortages which could seriously affect bowling operations and their profitability. Inflation was a continuing threat. Only recently, ARC had decided to hedge against the threat by acquiring underlying real properties for all new centers.

Mr. Feuchter had joined ARC in 1959 as vice-president under ARC's founder, Elliot Jones, Jr. A group of the shareholders became dissatisfied with Mr. Jones's performance and instituted a proxy battle in 1963 which resulted in electing four new directors to the (then) nine-member board. Profits had declined to almost zero, and little could be accomplished because of conflicts and arguments. Although a majority of the board at first supported Mr. Jones, other stockholders teamed with dissidents to secure his resignation in 1964. Mr. Feuchter, who had been filling the void in general management, voluntarily tendered his resignation after Mr. Jones's dismissal.

A management consulting firm was brought in to "straighten out the firm's affairs," and their Mr. Hamman became board chairman and chief executive officer. In 1965, the consulting firm asked Mr. Feuchter to rejoin the firm as president and assume the general management duties he had performed in his former position as vice-president. In Mr. Feuchter's words:

I discussed the appointment with other directors and Mr. Jones. I was hopeful that Mr. Jones would be recalled by the directors, but they had voted him a separation payment and definitely would not reconsider the decision.

I thought that the offer was a good opportunity, and after much consideration, I decided to take the job. No one else in the company seemed to have the ability, competence, or desire to assume the duties. At a special meeting of the board on May 4, 1965, I was appointed president.

Mr. Hamman stayed on as board chairman for one additional year. At that point, the consulting firm felt that their services were no longer needed full-time, so Mr. Hamman resigned and the directors elected me chairman.

THE BOWLING INDUSTRY

The torrid growth in bowling that began in the 1950s was based, in part, upon its practicality as a participative sport. It provides vigorous exercise which can be started at an early age and continued into retirement. The necessary personal equipment is relatively inexpensive and long-lived. A bowling session does not require a great amount of time (as would golf) and, unlike outdoor sports, bowling is possible during evening hours, when most employees are free. Moreover, employers often pay all or part of a bowler's fees. In fact, more money probably is budgeted for employee bowling than for any other employee recreational activity. Employers tend to appreciate the fact that bowling is one of the few employee recreational activities for which supervision can be shifted outside the firm—virtually all scheduling and supervision of teams and leagues is taken care of by the bowling proprietor.

Bowling activity increased at a rapid pace until 1962, when it suddenly reached its zenith. Some industry sources estimate that the number of regular bowlers rose from 22 million in 1958 to 30 million in 1961–62. Thereafter, the approximately 3 percent annual decline in league bowlers (those who belong to teams which bowl regularly) was catastrophic to the industry, particularly when the decline was accompanied by over-capacity. Bowling centers had been built in anticipation of a rapid growth rate, and many folded, unable to continue lease payments or installment payments on the heavy capital investments. By 1965, 10,750 bowling centers with 159,000 lanes remained, and these numbers had declined to

8,674 centers with 138,562 lanes by 1973. In California, the State Department of Human Resources and the Franchise Tax Board reported that the number of "bowling and billiard centers" (approximately 60 percent of them bowling alleys) fell from 735 in 1962 to 597 in 1970, and 537 by June 1973.

The chief suppliers of bowling and billiard equipment—Brunswick Corporation and AMF, Inc.—also suffered greatly in the 1960s. According to Standard and Poor's "Industrial Surveys," Brunswick, which sold its bowling lanes and pinsetters, repossessed assets worth $17.7 million in 1966 and 1967. The firm even became an important competitor in operating bowling centers which they had repossessed. AMF, which leased its equipment to bowling centers, set aside $62.8 million to cover losses on receivables. By 1973, the reserve still totalled $40 million—14 percent of receivables. Both firms began programs of diversification which reduced their dependence on bowling, and the efforts to diversify were spurred again in 1972 when the Japanese bowling boom (nearly twice as many games bowled per capita as the U.S.) leveled out and the industry suddenly realized it had overbuilt. Only about 20 percent of AMF's revenues came from sales to the bowling industry in 1973.

Many of the bowling chains also decided to diversify. Charan Industries, which operated eleven bowling centers in the New York–New Jersey metropolitan area, increased its revenues nearly 58 percent by acquiring firms in the real estate and construction fields. Fair Lanes, Inc., a huge Baltimore–Washington area chain, diversified into commercial real estate development as well as into food and restaurant chains until bowling-related revenues constituted only 50 percent of its sales. However, Fair Lanes continued to acquire more bowling centers, particularly in Virginia and Florida. Great Lakes Recreation Co., a Detroit chain of eleven centers, diversified into motels, while Treadway Companies' acquisitions of motels, food distribution, and management services all but dwarfed their bowling center chain in size. Unfortunately, the chains did not find diversification to be as profitable as they anticipated.

There was much speculation about the cause of bowling's top out in the 1960s. Some industry sources viewed it as cyclical. They pointed out that league bowling had dropped off before, then it rose again. Certainly bowling had not lost its popularity with casual (non-league) bowlers by 1974. It remained the second most popular participative sport (after swimming). Data summarized in the U.S. Department of Commerce's *Statistical Abstract of the U.S.* show that the number of people in the U.S. who bowl at least a few times a year rose from 30 million in 1961 to 43 million in 1974. League bowling also had made a comeback since 1971. Membership in the American Bowling Congress, Women's Bowling Congress and American Junior Bowling Congress increased from approximately 7.7 million in 1971 to 8.9 million persons by 1974. Industry sources reported that the games bowled per lane also were increasing in 1975, although the number of lanes in operation continued to drop.

On the other hand, some saw bowling as a casualty of American affluence. Historically, the bowling industry has been little affected by booms and recessions in the economy, but it has had to contend with its traditional image as a "blue-collar" recreation. Although the number of women and junior Bowling Congress members rose steadily from about 35 percent of all Congress members in the 1960s to 49 percent in 1973, membership in the American Bowling Congress dropped during the 1960s, concurrent with increased disposable income per capita, and concurrent with the shift from blue-collar to white-collar or service employment of the labor force. Recreation expenditures increased relatively more for boats, camping equipment, and golf than for bowling. The view that regular bowling declines when people step up in income class seemed to be partially supported by a 1975 Louis Harris survey for the National Bowling Council. He found that among the more than 9 million league bowlers, 21 percent of those with family incomes of less than $10,000 per year bowled at least once a week, whereas only 17 percent of those with family incomes over $10,000 bowled that frequently. However, nearly one-third of all higher income families had casual bowlers (at least once a year), while only 21 percent of those families earning less than $9,999 bowled in 1974. Perhaps 1973–75 increases in league

bowling reflected little more than consumers' reaction to the recession—a shift from expensive physical recreation to bowling.

Owners and managers of bowling centers continued to face such imponderables in 1975. Expansion of facilities or diversification out of bowling called for long-range forecasting of consumer behavior as well as evaluating the effects of such distinct possibilities as inflation, fuel and energy shortages, or increased employment of women. Expansion of bowling facilities would involve considerable risks because it incurred very high fixed costs for relatively long periods of time. A modern alley in a favorable urban location had a practical annual capacity of approximately 15,000 games per lane, but the break-even point might be more than 9,000 games per lane. Improved automation of services, while desirable, tended to raise the break-even point, so decisions to stake a firm's life on the future of bowling activity had to rest upon assumptions that the number of bowlers would increase and/or that the 24-hour load-factor per lane could be improved in the long run. Women bowlers, who almost equalled men in numbers, had increased both the total market and the utilization of lanes during the formerly idle morning and early afternoon hours. Unfortunately, bowling activity was also highly seasonal. Utilization tended to be high from September through May—the traditional winter league season—and low during the late spring and summer months. The seasonality continued despite summer leagues, tournaments, and promotional specials employed by most operators during the off-season.

In 1975, approximately 85 percent of all bowling alleys in the U.S. continued to be small, family-owned businesses. Most owners were members of the Bowling Proprietors Association of America, paying dues and attending meetings at the state and national levels. Most of the 25 chains had dropped out rather than try to coordinate so many meetings. Furthermore, they feared government antitrust action if they participated in some proposed actions. In 1973, the chains formed the loosely structured Multi-Unit Bowling Information Group without incorporation or by-laws, with three meetings per year to exchange information and discuss common problems. ARC was a member.

ORGANIZATION AND MANAGEMENT

ARC employed approximately 650 people in 1975. President Feuchter, Vice-President—Treasurer—Assistant Secretary Bruce Elliot, and Paul Wagner, Vice-President—Sales and Marketing, were considered to be "key" officers. Both Mr. Feuchter and Mr. Elliott also served on the board of directors. A summary of their backgrounds follows:

Robert Feuchter, President and Chairman, Board of
    Directors
    B.A. in Bus. Adm., University of California at Los
      Angeles, 1949
    Hughes Aircraft Co., Culver City, CA—9 years
      8 years in finance, budgeting, cost control, and
        data processing
      1 year as General Accounting Manager,
        Commercial Products Division
    American Recreation Centers—15 years
      5 years as V.P. and Director and Asst. Secretary
      3 years as President and Director
      7 years as President and Chairman, Board of
        Directors

Bruce C. Elliott, Vice President—Treasurer, Assistant
    Secretary, Board Member
    B.A. in Bus. Adm., University of California, 1947
    C.P.A., 1950
    Hugh J. Peat & Co., public accounting—2 years
    Self Employed, C.P.A. practice in Monterey—7
      years
    State of California, Legislative Audit Committee—
      2 years
    American Recreation Centers—16 years
      6 years as Treasurer
      1 year as Treasurer and Assistant Secretary
      9 years as Treasurer, Asst. Secty. and Director

Paul Wagner, Vice President of Sales and Marketing
    B.S., Colorado State University, 1953
    U.S. Navy—3 years (special training, Navy
      Journalism School)
    Jos. Gamble Stations, Inc., KJOY, Stockton,
      program director—4 years
    KXOA, Sacramento, copy writer and promotion
      director—1 year

Gerth, Brown, Clark & Elkus, copy writer and
    account executive—2 years
Ferguson Advertising, account executive—1 year
Pettet Advertising, account executive—6 months
American Recreation Centers—11 years
    2 years as Marketing Aide to President Jones
    1 year as Director of Marketing
    8 years as Vice President for Sales and Marketing

*John Chartz, Director
    B.S. in Engineering, Santa Clara University, 1948
    Various firms as process engineer—3 years
    Dalmo-Victor, Belmont, CA as major stockholder,
      Vice-President, and General Manager—5 years
    Textron Corp., as Manager, Dalmo-Victor
      Division—6 years
    Randtron Corp., Redwood City, CA, V.P. and
      major stockholder—12 years
    American Recreation Centers—15 years as Director
    Major stockholder in two small firms manufac-
      turing industrial rubber and fiberglass products
    Member of El Monte Investment Group

*C. Gervaise Davis, III, Secretary and Director
    LL.D., Georgetown University, 1955
    A Washington D.C. law firm—2 years
    A San Francisco law firm—2 years
    A Monterey law firm as Partner—2 years
    Walker, Schroeder, Davis and Brehmer, a Monterey
      law firm, Senior Partner—13 years
    American Recreation Centers—10 years
    2 years as Legal Counsel
    3 years as Asst. Secretary and Legal Counsel
    5 years as Secretary, Legal Counsel, and Director

*Eliot Peck, Director
    B.S. in Engineering, University of California, 1936
    U.S. Armed Services—5 years
    Various firms as a process engineer—10 years
    U.S. Steel, Pittsburg, CA as Senior Staff Engineer—
      25 years
    Member of El Monte Investment Group with John
      Chartz

*Some data estimated or changed slightly at informants' request.

The board of directors, at Mr. Feuchter's urging, had adopted a policy of diversification into "other service industries," in 1968, his first year as board chairman. ARC's first luxury beauty salon was opened in April of that year, and they continued to seek other appropriate diversifications after brief ventures into a landscape and nursery business and a sporting goods supply store. The directors even discussed the possibility of entering the physical security business, but they were unable to acquire a going concern, with good management, at a reasonable price.

The diversification policy in no way implied abandonment of bowling. In fact, the directors always seemed to favor purchasing additional centers from individual proprietors who were nearing retirement age and, in 1972, they approved a policy of purchasing at least one new center each year. Apparently, they also agreed with Mr. Feuchter that survival would require adoption of the latest innovations in bowling facilities as well as sales to untapped segments of the bowling market. In this regard, they had approved the installation of ARC-developed fast-ball returns for all alleys.

Nonunion salaried employees were granted a profit-sharing and pension plan in 1971 to encourage their performance and, in 1975, the profit-sharing plan was replaced with a more expensive Employee Stock Ownership Trust which encompassed 190 employees.

Unfortunately, the board had little opportunity to plan for long-range needs, because two of its five members were harried executives, heavily involved in "crisis" decisions. Mr. Davis, who was retained as secretary and legal counsel, devoted most of the approximately 20 hours per week he spent with ARC (40 percent of his client billings), to the solution of immediate problems. The board usually held six formal meetings a year, but their agenda usually was filled with practical, current problems involving operations in one or more centers, acquisition proposals, reviews of projects, and declarations of dividends.

Mr. Feuchter was convinced that it would be beneficial for the firm to have additional outside directors with a broad spectrum of experience and competence. He was particularly pleased with

Mr. Chartz, with whom he consulted by phone or on weekend social visits. Unfortunately, high-quality outside directors were hard to find within the constraints. ARC paid only $25 per meeting, and they did not feel that they could afford the relatively high premiums for director liability insurance. The board had declined in size over the years—from fifteen to nine, then to the present five members.

In the course of the interviews, the case writer talked with all of the key officers about ARC's organization and management.

According to Mr. Elliott, treasurer and assistant secretary:

Each of the bowling centers has a general manager. The general managers report on line authority direct to the president, and they are responsible for all operations and employees at the centers. However, a maintenance director, who also reports to the president, is responsible for equipment at all the alleys and has authority to hire mechanics for any center with the permission of its general manager. The arrangement has caused no serious problems.

The financial and marketing divisions act as staff to the president. Every one of the staff officers and managers reports directly to the president. Theoretically, Mr. Feuchter has too many people—too wide a span of control—especially since he gets heavily involved in the details of the operations. However, with a company of this size, he doesn't have any alternative.

The general managers have leeway to do anything within reason at the centers. Nonmerchandise purchases up to $25 can be made without approval of the president.

As you can see, the organizational system really has fluid lines of authority and responsibility. Although it would be easy to outline, the company doesn't have a formal organization chart. If they had one, the lines would appear pretty awkward and unconventional to an outsider.

Mr. Elliott observed that his duties seemed to vary considerably from day to day:

Board meetings... take about 5 percent of my time. I have to travel occasionally to look at possible takeovers for expansion purposes, or to look at a company as a diversification candidate. The assessment problem takes up a lot of my time. I am continually traveling to the various counties to discuss property taxes with assessors. A running battle ... continued conflict over the exorbitant property tax rates on the centers.

I also supervise the corporate general office staff—the accountant, four bookkeepers, and two women in the reception area who perform clerical and typing work for all the officers.

The vice-president for sales and marketing, Mr. Wagner, discussed the organization and management at ARC in somewhat different terms. In his words:

I do not have any staff assigned directly to me, either at headquarters or the centers. Each center is staffed with two promotion specialists reporting to the managers. It's their responsibility to carry out ARC's marketing policies, but the policies aren't written down in a manual. I consider the sales staff to comprise the center managers, assistant managers, promotion specialists, and sales counter personnel. Counter salesmen are the important marketing element.

My key responsibilities include coordination of the program between the centers and training personnel to perform the various marketing functions. I don't feel, however, that the organizational structure poses any major weaknesses.

Mr. Wagner disclosed that he devoted six to ten hours weekly to training sales personnel. Also, he spent some time recruiting new employees or selecting employees to move up to assistant manager or manager's positions. On the average, the remainder of his week was taken up in sales management activities. However, during promotional campaigns each season, he tended to be fully occupied in his role of vice-president of sales and marketing.

Mr. Feuchter viewed the organization and management of ARC as primarily a problem of staffing. He observed.

A center's managers have to be carefully selected because it is the key management position. A

manager has to be very reliable ... a person I can trust and have confidence in, because the centers are too decentralized to keep on top of managers' performance ... Legally, we're a holding company. A few centers have to maintain a separate identity because of old loose provisions. But practically, we're all one.

I occasionally make a mistake in choosing a manager, and I've had to "deep six" a few in past years who didn't work out. A couple couldn't get along with the officers or the customers. Others got dictatorial with employees.

It's our policy to promote managers from the ranks of the center's sales staffs. Sales people start on the counter. Those who show the aptitude, are given a promotional specialist position. We generally want employees in these positions who like bowling themselves and enjoy long hours of work at the centers. Assistant managers are in charge of the evening bowling. If they show promise of performing in that capacity, some additional duties are delegated to them.

OPERATIONS

ARC attempted to purchase, build, or expand bowling centers only in areas where the population growth trend and competition were favorable. They also tried to drop centers which failed to show sufficient profit. For example, a contract to manage the Sea Bowl in Pacifica was dropped for this reason in 1969. In 1975, they were negotiating the sale of another disappointing center—the Jolly Roger Lanes in Grass Valley.

Most of the areas in which ARC competed continued to enjoy a favorable population trend, but there was some question about the growth rate in Grass Valley and Whittier (see exhibit 1). One of the difficulties in judging favorable population trends is that pockets of change exist in each city, county, or standard metropolitan area. Corona (population 28,000) and Whittier (population 73,000) locations, for example, are pockets in huge population districts. From the bowling center manager's point of view, the number of people within easy commuting distance is important. One firm, Bowl America, Inc., a large chain in southeastern U.S., was reported by *Barron's*

EXHIBIT 1
Population in Operating Locations 1970–1975

Location of Bowling Center	Population—Standard Metropolitan Area (in thousands)					
	Census			Estimated		
	1970	1971	1972	1973	1974	1975
Alameda	1,081	1,091	1,101	1,111	1,098	1,100
Mel's Southshore Bowl (40 lanes)						
Corona	1,380	1,425	1,467	1,505	1,530	1,572
Corona Bowl (24 lanes)						
Grass Valley	21	n.a.	n.a.	n.a.	n.a.	n.a.
Jolly Roger Lanes (12 lanes)						
Hayward	1,081	1,091	1,101	1,111	1,098	1,100
Fiesta Lanes (40 lanes)						
Monterey	250	253	256	258	263	266
Cypress Bowl (24 lanes)						
Oakland	1,081	1,091	1,101	1,111	1,098	1,100
Broadway Bowl (40 lanes)						
Palo Alto	557	559	562	564	575	577
Fiesta Lanes (32 lanes)						
Redwood City	557	559	562	564	575	577
Mel's Redwood Bowl (40 lanes)						
Sacramento	816	836	857	875	885	902
Alpine Alley (40 lanes)						
Mardi Gras Lanes (40 lanes)						
San Jose	1,090	1,123	1,157	1,190	1,189	1,209
Fiesta Lanes (40 lanes)						
Futurama Bowl (42 lanes)						
Oakridge Lanes (38 lanes)						
Plaza Lanes (40 lanes)						
Saratoga Lanes (32 lanes)						
Whittier	7,037	6,999	6,958	6,945	6,956	6,948
Friendly Hills Lanes (32 lanes)						
California Metropolitan Areas	18,800	19,019	19,230	19,441	20,216	20,406

NOTES: Metropolitan area data for: Alameda County (Alameda, Hayward and Oakland), San Diego County (Corona), Nevada County (Grass Valley), San Mateo County (Palo Alto and Redwood City), Sacramento-Placer-Yolo Counties, Santa Clara County (San Jose), and Los Angeles-Long Beach (Whittier). Estimates by United California Bank, "1973 Forecast" and "1975 Forecast."

to believe that a successful center must have 2,000 people within a three-mile radius for each lane. Certainly, the Grass Valley location would be suspect on this count. It seems obvious that many of the standard metropolitan areas have bowling center competitors who must share patrons in overlapping radii of three miles. Competitive factors, such as traffic density, price structures, and service, then become critical. The Whittier center might well overcome other disadvantages because it is considered to be "the prestige bowl in its market." Strong competitors often are able to draw patrons from a considerable distance.

Current data about the number and size of competitors in each of ARC's immediate locations were unavailable, but exhibit 2 suggests that competition probably varies considerably from one center to another.

CASE

EXHIBIT 2
Competition by Area—Number of Bowling Centers

Location of ARC Bowling Center(s)	1970 Population (in thousands)	Number of Bowling Centers*		1970 Population per Center
		1962	1970	
Alameda County (3)	1,081	33	29	32,000
Los Angeles-Long Beach (1)	7,037	n.a.	n.a.	n.a.
Nevada County (1)	21	2	1	21,000
Sacramento-Yolo-Placer Cos. (2)	816	19	17	48,000
Salinas-Seaside-Monterey (1)	250	17	16	17,000
San Diego County (1)	1,380	n.a.	n.a.	n.a.
San Mateo County (2)	557	18	16	35,000
Santa Clara County (5)	1,090	21	19	57,000
California Metropolitan Areas	18,800	440	360	52,200

*Research and Statistics Section, California State Department of Human Resources.

Mr. Wagner discussed ARC operations in considerable detail. He said that locations were specifically decided on to take advantage of market demand in an area. Population growth trends and lack of bowling facilities in the specific area indicated the best locations. When asked whether ARC was operating at full capacity, he replied:

Room for any volume increase during peak hours would exist in only two or three bowls. During the day and early morning hours, they have a substantial number of lanes open.... Housewives' leagues have improved this. Regular league times start at 6:00 p.m. Agreements for price and reservations are entered into with the teams in May and September.... The agreements aren't really binding on the teams. Bowling captains have been known to sign up for more than one league at the same time and then cancel.

He indicated that business slowed down severely during the last of April and first of September, when leagues are formed. Also, leagues did not play between Christmas and New Years. In reply to a question about promotional efforts, Mr. Wagner explained that promotional programs covering all locations were conducted several times a year. Campaigns before the start of a new league season stimulated business during slack periods and attracted new teams. During holiday weeks, they promoted student play by special

low rates per line, and in the newer facilities, special holiday fun packages on New Year's eve included dancing, food, liquor, and bowling for one ticket price ... "They have the run of the entire place."

He believed that direct sales were the most effective promotional method:

Repeat business from league teams must be solicited by the promotional staff, counter salesmen, and managers—by phone or direct contact. New league business comes from direct contact with employee "reps" or businesses with recreational programs. Promotional brochures are mailed out at random. We spend $10,000 or $15,000 a year on TV, radio, and newspaper media advertising—mainly to promote open play on holidays or during the slack, off-season.... It's hard to give a dollar amount, because broadcast stations do a lot of trading and bartering. For example, time can be purchased with free bowling tickets; then broadcasters use these to put together an advertising campaign for another client.

In response to a question about ARC's marketing research, Mr. Wagner answered that the firm had no formal marketing research program:

... attempts to promote new demand evolved over the years. Brunswick and AMF assist bowl operators by providing training materials, seminars,

and classroom instruction for sales people and managers. Also they supply data on marketing trends and industry developments.

Billiard rooms, coffee shops, and cocktail lounges were included in most of the centers. Beer, wine, and mixed drink sales were natural, and relatively profitable, adjuncts to bowling. Food service also was complementary, but ARC had not always found it to be profitable. A 1969–70 attempt to solve the problem by leasing all food service operations was aborted when the contractor suffered heavy losses. In 1971, ARC took over what appeared to be the most profitable food centers and leased facilities in the other centers to experienced food service firms. Losses continued, so additional food operations were leased out in 1974. Billiard parlors were quite profitable when patronized, because desk clerks could handle the play as part of their regular duties. Unfortunately, patronage had dwindled as more and more home tables were purchased. Revenues from billiards dropped $70,000 in fiscal 1969 alone. According to Mr. Feuchter: "Billiard activities have become a minor part of our business." By 1975, various coin-operated games were enticing patrons (particularly teenagers) in increasing numbers to most bowling centers.

Pricing was, of course, a significant factor in marketing ARC's bowling services. While the policy, according to Mr. Wagner, was to "set rates as high as possible without hurting demand," price competition was conceded to be a problem from time to time. League agreements seldom called for discounts, although ARC did pioneer in giving players who belonged to leagues at any of their centers substantial discounts on open play, during nonprime hours. Wagner explained that, "It was first tried as a promotion gimmick to attract league teams to the centers. . . . It has become very popular. Some competitors don't like the discounted rates. . . . They question the logic of the policy. But it has resulted in much more casual play by league members."

ARC always tried to raise prices enough to offset increased labor costs. Union contracts covering all employees below assistant managers were renegotiated every two years, usually with an across-the-board hike.

Contracts generally included cost-of-living escalation clauses which tended to raise wages in the interim. Mr. Wagner explained that ARC followed a policy of raising prices in 5¢ and 10¢ increments to a level which would at least provide enough income to offset the increased wages for the contract period. Some competitors adjusted prices more frequently, he said, "but our prices can't be too far out of line. It's easy to monitor, because prices are posted by all operators, and feedback is fast from regular bowlers."

FINANCES

At the end of fiscal 1975, ARC's 293,469 shares of common stock were widely distributed among northern California investors and were being traded in regional over-the-counter markets at about 7½ bid and 8 asked. Major stockholders included the three key officers (about 10 percent), outside directors (8 to 9 percent), former convertible debenture holders, and a federally qualified Employee Stock Ownership Trust (ESOT). The ESOT, which replaced a profitsharing plan for 50 nonunion employees, encompassed 190 of the firm's 650 employees and would almost certainly increase their future share of ownership (already about 25 percent).

ARC's financial statements for 1965, and 1970 through 1975, are shown on the following pages (exhibits 3 and 4).

Mr. Elliott had some reservations about the way ARC's balance sheets treated lease obligations. In his view, off-the balance-sheet financing tended to blind managers to the real fixed debt incurred. He illustrated the problem by ARC's acquisition of a center for $800,000, with a noncancelable lease requiring payments for 20 years. The acquisition did not change the long-term debt shown on the books; yet, the liability was just as real as a 20-year note for $800,000. A lease usually required minimum rental plus taxes, insurance, and additional rent based on sales volume above a minimum. In the past, ARC had tried to sell some unprofitable centers, he said, but buyers were not interested because they would be committed to existing long-term leases. The company would be much better off now if they had purchased

EXHIBIT 3
American Recreation Centers, Inc.
Consolidated Statement of Income—Fiscal Year Ending May 31st (in thousands)

	1965	1970	1971	1972	1973	1974	1975
Revenues:							
Bowling	$2,692	$3,256	$3,461	$3,823	$4,266	$5,192	$ 5,731
Restaurant*	1,480	1,051	224	419	772	1,385	1,860
Bar	1,132	1,475	1,516	1,625	1,854	2,343	2,550
Accessories, billiards & misc.	377	171	170	307	328	374	348
Total Revenues	$5,681	$5,953	$5,371	$6,174	$7,220	$9,294	$10,489
Operating Costs:							
Operating, Gen'l & Admin. Expense	$4,892	$5,199	$4,526	$5,172	$6,101	$7,797	$ 8,957
Depreciation & Amortization	467	470	475	466	446	426	436
Total Operating Costs	$5,359	$5,669	$5,001	$5,638	$6,547	$8,223	$ 9,393
Net Income Before Interest & Extra Items	$ 322	$ 284	$ 370	$ 536	$ 673	$1,071	$ 1,096
Interest	305	204	174	174	173	193	270
Extraordinary (income) or expenses		(33)	(35)				
Net Income Before Taxes	$ 17	$ 113	$ 231	$ 362	$ 500	$ 878	$ 826
Provision for Estimated Income Taxes	6	46	115	182	255	430	417
Net Income After Taxes	$ 11	$ 67	$ 116	$ 180	$ 245	$ 448	$ 409

*Most food service centers were taken over by private contractors in 1971; ARC reclaimed some in 1972 and leased others in 1973-75.

facilities, he said; unfortunately, they didn't have the money at that time.

ARC's equity base had tended to increase during the past several years, but President Feuchter still favored wider sale and distribution of the common stock. Toward this end, he had supported the board's decisions to grant stock options to key officers and to pay stock dividends. In 1974, ARC became a member of The Committee of Publicly Owned Companies, a national organization dedicated to attracting wider stock ownership. Additional employee ownership was encouraged when, in 1966, ARC adopted a stock purchase plan for employees and added 50¢ to each $1 an employee spent for ARC stock, within limits. In 1975, the ESOT was still another move to distribute stock more widely.

Debt service and other fixed charges still were high. However, the debt structure had improved significantly since 1965, cash flow had increased, profits had risen, all lanes had been modernized, and

acquisitions had continued. Since 1965, ARC had acquired 6 more bowling centers, the Southgate Shopping Center in Hayward, and an office building adjoining the Corona Bowl near San Diego. Birdcage Lanes, in Sacramento's newest shopping center, and Northridge Lanes in Los Angeles County's San Fernando Valley—both brand new—were scheduled to open in August, 1975.

THE FUTURE

Mr. Wagner saw a profitable future for the bowling industry, and he felt that ARC's place lay in bowling plus related services. In his view, the firm had never had much success with ventures into other industries. In bowling it was ARC's policy, until about 1971, to contain expansion within northern California. He said, "The president probably did this due to lack of capital and adequate personnel to branch over a wide geographical area. Then, in 1972, he went into

CASE

EXHIBIT 4
American Recreation Centers, Inc.
Consolidated Balance Sheet—Fiscal Year Ending May 31st (in thousands)

	1965	1970	1971	1972	1973	1974	1975
ASSETS							
Current Assets:							
Cash	$ 89	$ 120	$ 104	$ 29	$ 88	$ 26	$ 59
Marketable Securities (cost)		234	357	350	100	495	552
Accounts Receivable (less doubtful accounts)	71	52	45	52	63	77	106
Inventories	81	44	42	51	98	100	94
Prepaid Expenses	127	174	179	196	277	328	396
Total Current Assets	$ 368	$ 624	$ 727	$ 678	$ 626	$ 1,026	$ 1,207
Fixed Assets (cost):							
Land & Buildings	$ 103	$ 205	$ 205	$ 1,578	$ 1,762	$ 2,651	$ 3,285
Machinery & Equipment	5,890	6,469	6,511	6,704	6,808	7,385	7,495
Leaseholds & Improvement	1,840	1,933	1,967	2,023	2,123	2,157	2,236
Total	$7,833	$8,607	$8,683	$10,305	$10,693	$12,193	$13,016
Less Depr. & Amortization	2,277	4,610	5,085	5,517	5,961	6,362	6,793
Total Fixed Assets	$5,556	$3,997	$3,598	$ 4,788	$ 4,732	$ 5,831	$ 6,223
Deposits, Licenses & Deferred Expenses	388	226	284	302	245	253	298
TOTAL ASSETS	$6,312	$4,847	$4,609	$ 5,768	$ 5,603	$ 7,110	$ 7,728
LIABILITIES							
Current Liabilities:							
Accounts Payable	$ 301	$ 241	$ 221	$ 311	$ 385	$ 533	$ 681
Accrued Tax & Expenses	179	165	170	196	233	303	329
Income Taxes Payable		23	114	156	224	236	159
Dividends Payable		7	9	6	7	9	12
Total Current Liabilities*	$ 480	$ 436	$ 514	$ 669	$ 849	$ 1,081	$ 1,181
Long-term Debt	4,218	2,393	1,991	2,833	2,271	3,162	3,340
Deferred Income Taxes	251	420	420	396	349	305	286
TOTAL LIABILITIES	$4,949	$3,249	$2,925	$ 3,898	$ 3,469	$ 4,548	$ 4,807
STOCKHOLDERS' EQUITY							
Capital Stock (no par, Stated Value $2.50)	$ 539	$ 589	$ 601	$ 623	$ 668	$ 707	$ 734
Capital in Excess of Stated Value	517	520	517	562	633	681	714
Retained Earnings	307	489	566	685	833	1,174	1,473
TOTAL EQUITY	$1,363	$1,598	$1,684	$ 1,870	$ 2,134	$ 2,562	$ 2,921
TOTAL LIABILITIES & NET WORTH	$6,312	$4,847	$4,609	$ 5,768	$ 5,603	$ 7,110	$ 7,728

*Exclusive of current portion of long-term debt, which was $459 in 1965, $310 in 1970, and $325, $510, $410, $474 and $428 in subsequent years.

southern California. Now with business improving and some capital available... he would consider expanding into neighboring states.... We are looking at Arizona now," Wagner mentioned the popularity of bowling in Japan and other countries, but he was doubtful whether ARC had sufficient capital or personnel to expand internationally. "Occasionally, a national firm has voiced consolidation overtures," he said, "but none of the offers to date has been worth consideration."

Mr. Wagner emphasized that "the president is solely responsible for handling the diversification program, looking primarily for a service-oriented business, not involving manufacture of a product, and manageable by the ARC team." As for himself, Wagner explained: "My goals include providing the best possible marketing training for development of the sales staff. I am primarily concerned with developing a good sales management training program to improve management of existing centers and enable the company to expand when opportunities arise." Another of his goals, he said, was "to find ways to maximize utilization of the lanes. This is the main job of the sales and marketing staff. Right now we are considering low-cost child-care centers to encourage more daytime bowling by women."

Marketing policies, Wagner observed, were "formulated jointly by the key officers, based on inputs from the general managers and other sales staff in the centers." With regard to the board of directors, he said, "I am not aware of any marketing policies specifically established by the board."

Mr. Elliott seemed to feel that efficiency of operations was the only avenue to profits. He commented in some detail about the systems for controlling cash, payrolls, and inventories with budgets and daily or weekly feedback on expense and sales items from each center. One bar to efficiency, he thought, was the seasonality of bowling. Losses during the first two quarters of a fiscal year were usual.

President Feuchter appeared to be more concerned than other executives and directors about formulating goals and policies for the future, but he insisted that any goals or plans be pragmatic. In his words:

I have read with interest some elaborate goals stated in recent annual reports of companies.... Wordy goals related to ecology and environmental factors sound good to investors, but it's doubtful whether managers are really sincere in what is being proposed.

I could probably come up with a fancy society-related goal stating that ARC is interested in promoting wholesome recreation for the family. It'd be true... about 40,000 persons use the facilities weekly for recreation, and most of these customers are, of course, family members. But I don't see where stating such goals would add any real significance to our operations. In general, I don't feel that the effort of formulating intangible concepts is worthwhile to ARC or any other organization for practical day-to-day operations.

Mr. Feuchter mentioned that ARC had not established formal goals and policies, nor had he found a need to write down the ones key officers had practiced over the years.

I have my goals, and one of them is to gain growth for the company—both internally and by expansion. Diversification policies will be continued in the future.... Internally, profit margins must be widened still more to attract investors. The existing centers have substantial potential for unit sales expansion during weekdays until 6:00 p.m. and on weekends.

Mr. Feuchter indicated that the energy problem concerned him. He wondered: "Will the government say that bowling is an 'essential industry'? Should electricity be rationed or should the maximum hours a business can stay open during a day be determined by whether the business is 'essential'?"

In the future, Mr. Feuchter expected the problems of reducing debt and fighting Brunswick Corporation's dominance would occupy much of his time. He noted that independents throughout the U.S. were toying with the idea of banding together to keep Brunswick from further domination of the industry. Already, they owned about 250 bowling centers.

MASSACHUSETTS STATE LOTTERY

PRODUCT (PENDING)

In early February 1972, the lottery's director, assistant director, and deputy directors met to consider further steps to implement the recently enacted state lottery. They were under considerable time pressure because the bill passed by the legislature on September 27, 1971, had been designated an "emergency law" to indicate that the lottery should be made operational as soon as possible. Accordingly, a tentative decision was made to instigate the lottery in April of 1972. By the end of January, the main staff positions had been filled and a meeting was then called to decide what kind of marketing program should be followed. The commission had already set up headquarters in a new building, purchased computer equipment, selected an advertising agency, and visited other states that had lotteries in order to gain background information. Three other states—New Hampshire, New York, and New Jersey—had already been operating lotteries.

During the strategy formulation meeting various issues were raised, including whether the lottery administrators were ready to make specific marketing plans or whether they should try to generate some primary marketing data. Some of the administrators believed that they should go ahead and specify a marketing program. They pointed to the urgency of the situation as well as to the available data from the other state lotteries. Vern Fredericks, one of the deputy directors, strongly asserted, "We should copy the features of the other state lotteries, especially New Jersey which has been so successful. What worked well in New Jersey will work in Massachusetts.

This case was prepared by Professors Dharmendra T. Verma of Bentley College and Frederick Wiseman, Northeastern University.

We don't have time to go around doing marketing studies here. Besides, why should a ticket buyer in Boston be any different from someone buying a ticket in New York City or Newark?"

But others believed it was necessary to find out something about people's attitudes toward various aspects of a lottery. Donald Phillips, another deputy director, argued, "It is difficult to decide on specific aspects of a lottery, such as what price to charge and what kind of prize distribution to offer, unless we know how Massachusetts residents feel. The other states have made many changes or are considering changes in their initial programs. Also, how do we decide which features to copy when we're not sure what factors are responsible for a successful lottery? We should undertake a study to give us the kind of information we need to help design our marketing program."

FORMULATION AND ORGANIZATION OF THE STATE LOTTERY

The Massachusetts State Lottery was established by the "State Lottery Law" enacted by the Senate and the House of Representatives of the Commonwealth of Massachusetts on September 27, 1971.[1] The two major purposes of the lottery as stated by the majority whip of the Massachusetts House of Representatives, William Q. MacLean, Jr., were "to raise revenue for the cities and towns in Massachusetts and to decrease organized (illegal) gambling within the state."

The Massachusetts Lottery Law specified, among other things, that prizes should amount to no less than 45 percent of total revenues; that costs for operation and administration should not exceed 15 percent; and that a minimum of 40 percent should go to the state treasury for subsequent disbursement to the cities and towns. In addition, the legislative act designated the bill an "emergency law" which was to be implemented as soon as possible. The salient features of the legislation are reproduced in exhibit 1.

The lottery commission consisted of five members, with the state treasurer serving as chairman. The other members were the secretary of public safety, the state comptroller and two persons appointed by the

CASE

EXHIBIT 1
The Massachusetts State Lottery Act—Selected Sections

Section 23. There shall be, in the office of the state treasurer, a state lottery commission, hereinafter called the commission, consisting of the state treasurer, the secretary of public safety or his designee, the state comptroller or his designee, and two persons to be appointed by the governor for terms coterminous with that of the governor. No more than four members of the commission shall be of the same political party. The state treasurer shall be the chairman of the commission. . . .

Section 24. The commission is hereby authorized to conduct a state lottery and shall determine the type of lottery to be conducted, the price, or prices, of tickets or shares in the lottery, the numbers and sizes of the prizes on the winning tickets or shares, the manner of selecting the winning tickets or shares, the manner of payment of prizes to the holders of winning tickets or shares, the frequency of the drawings or selections of winning tickets or shares and the type or types of locations at which tickets or shares may be sold, the method to be used in selling tickets or shares, the licensing of agents to sell tickets or shares, provided that no person under the age of twenty-one shall be licensed as an agent, the manner and amount of compensation, if any, to be paid licensed sales agents, and such other matters necessary or desirable for the efficient and economical operation and administration of the lottery and for the convenience of the purchasers of tickets or shares and the holders of winning tickets or shares. . . .

The commission shall make a continuous study and investigation of the operation and administration of similar laws in other states or countries, of any literature on the subject which from time to time may be published or available, of any federal laws which may affect the operation of the lottery, and of the reaction of citizens of the commonwealth to existing and potential features of the lottery with a view to recommending or effecting changes that will tend to better serve and implement the purposes of the state lottery law. . . .

Section 25. The apportionment of the total revenues accruing from the sale of lottery tickets or shares and from all other sources shall be as follows: *(a)* the payment of prizes to the holders of winning tickets or shares which in any case shall be no less than forty-five percent of the total revenues accruing from the sale of lottery tickets; *(b)* the payment of costs incurred in the operation and administration of the lottery, including the expenses of the commission and the costs resulting from any contract or contracts entered into for promotional, advertising or operational services or for the purchase or lease of lottery equipment and materials which in no case shall exceed fifteen percent of the total revenues accruing from the sale of lottery tickets, subject to appropriation; and *(c)* the balance to be used for the purposes set forth in clause *(c)* of section thirty-five [. . . shall be credited to the Local Aid Fund. . . . and shall be distributed to the several cities and towns in accordance with preestablished provisions.].

Section 27. No person shall be licensed as an agent to sell lottery tickets or shares if such person engaged in business exclusively as a lottery sales agent. Before issuing such license the director shall consider the financial responsibility and security of each applicant for licenses, his business or activity, the accessibility of his place of business or activity to the public, the sufficiency of existing licenses to serve the public convenience, and the volume of expected sales. . . .

Section 29. No person shall sell a ticket or share at a price greater than that fixed by the commission. No person other than a licensed lottery sales agent shall sell lottery tickets or shares, except that nothing in this section shall be construed to prevent any person from giving lottery tickets or shares to another as a gift.

No ticket or share shall be sold to any person under age eighteen, provided that a person eighteen years of age or older may purchase a ticket or share for the purpose of making a gift to a person under age eighteen. . . .

Source: The Commonwealth of Massachusetts, Chapter 813, Act H 5925, 1971.

---

governor for terms coterminous with that of the governor. The specific responsibilities of the commission are also outlined in exhibit 1.

In November 1971, Dr. William E. Perrault, chairman of the mathematics department at Boston State College, was appointed director of the state lottery by the state treasurer with the approval of the governor. The director was responsible for the supervision and administration of the lottery.

The next few weeks were spent in setting up the organization structure and filling the administrative positions necessary to start the lottery operation. Computer equipment was purchased and a Boston advertising firm was appointed. The first-year

EXHIBIT 2
Partial Organization Chart

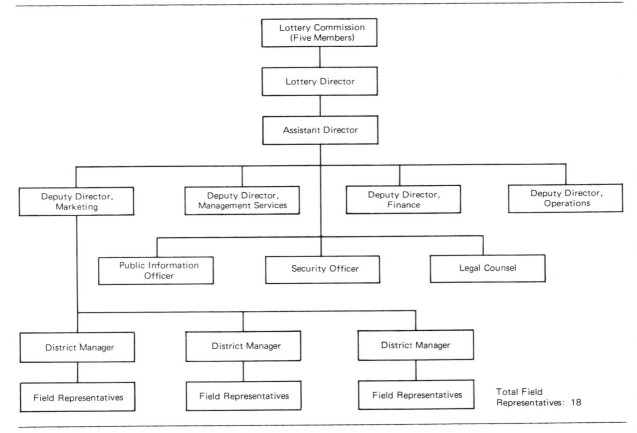

Source: Drawn from Massachusetts Lottery Commission records.

advertising and promotional budget was approximately $1 million. By the end of January, most of the staff had been appointed and operating plans were being formulated. A partial organization chart is presented in exhibit 2. Initial funding for the staffing requirements was provided by the state legislature with the stipulation that this money be returned to the state out of revenues from ticket sales.

The marketing staff consisted of Mr. Louis J. Totino, deputy director—marketing, three district managers, and eighteen field representatives. Each of the representatives was to service the various Massachusetts retail outlets which would be licensed to sell the lottery tickets. In addition, the commission entered into a $300,000 contract with a Cambridge-based major consulting firm, Arthur D. Little, Inc. The objective of the contract was to advise in the planning, design, and implementation of the lottery.

OTHER FORMS OF GAMBLING IN MASSACHUSETTS

In addition to the lottery there were several other types of legal gambling in Massachusetts. These were pari-mutuel horse and dog racing and beano. Total receipts to the Commonwealth from horse and dog racing had increased from $19.4 million in 1968 to almost $29 million in 1971.[2] Beano was expected to return at least $1.0 million (10 percent of gross receipts) to the state in 1972.

Recent changes had been made in the Massachusetts laws to allow Sunday horse racing and to increase the length of the racing season. Also, additional beano legislation was being considered which would increase the maximum allowable daily prize from $50 to $200, allow games on Sunday, and allow each licensee to hold more than one game per week.

Illegal gambling also thrived within the state, with the most well-known varieties being off-track betting and the "numbers" game. Officials of the state legislature believed that sales of the lottery tickets and the fact that no more local newspapers published the "number" would cut down revenues in the "numbers" by about 20 to 25 percent.

BACKGROUND ON OTHER STATE LOTTERIES
New Hampshire Sweepstakes

In 1963, the state legislature of New Hampshire passed the "New Hampshire Sweepstakes Law." This law set up a sweepstakes commission with responsibility to "conduct public drawings at such intervals and in such places within the state as it may determine."[3] The stated purpose of the sweepstakes, the first of modern times in the United States, was to provide New Hampshire's cities and towns with additional revenue to aid in defraying educational costs.

The state law limited participation in the sweepstakes to individuals over twenty-one years of age. The law also specified that tickets, priced at $3 by the sweepstakes commission, could be sold only at state-owned liquor stores and at state-regulated horse racetracks. Further, as part of the act creating the sweepstakes, the legislature included a provision which made it possible for any city or town, by referendum, to elect not to have tickets sold within its boundaries.

Only one sweepstakes drawing was held during each of the first two years of operation, 1964 and 1965. The exact prize distribution, which totalled

approximately 35–40 percent of gross revenue, was a direct function of tickets sold. Top prize was $50,000 and additional major prizes were set at $25,000, $12,500, and $10,000. In all, there were approximately 400 prizes awarded for each $500,000 worth of tickets sold, over 95 percent of these being consolation prizes between $100 and $500.

In 1964, gross revenue from the first sweepstakes drawing totalled $5.7 million. After accounting for operating expenses, the commission was able to return a total of $2.8 million to the cities and towns in which tickets were sold. Ticket sales for the following year declined almost 20 percent and there was approximately a $300,000 reduction in revenue returned by the state.

A consumer study, conducted by a University of New Hampshire professor in 1965, revealed a number of insights into the characteristics of the typical purchaser. Among these were that (1) 88 percent of all buyers came from out of state and (2) among neither residents nor nonresidents was the number of tickets purchased significantly related to family income. A more complete discussion of the findings of the New Hampshire consumer study is given in exhibit 3.

In an attempt to increase yearly gross revenue, the commission decided to have two drawings in 1966. The result of this change was unexpected as gross revenue again fell significantly. The following year brought about the first major change in the running of the sweepstakes. The state legislature granted permission for tickets to be sold at sweepstakes commission offices, at toll booths along the state highway and, most importantly, at retail business establishments. It was expected that with the increased number of ticket outlets, sales and interest in the sweepstakes would also increase. In anticipation of this, the commission decided to conduct three drawings in 1967. This marketing program remained in force through 1970. The result of this strategy was a substantial decline in sales during the first two years, followed by a leveling off at approximately $2.0 million during the next two years. The gross revenues, operating expenses, prizes paid, and educational aid contribution figures for the years 1964–1970 are given in exhibit 4.

CASE

EXHIBIT 3
New Hampshire Consumer Study

The characteristics of purchasers of New Hampshire tickets can be summarized as follows:

1. 88% come from out of state.
2. 67% are male.
3. 80% of the men and 60% of the women are married.
4. 82% support four persons or less.
5. 50% are between 40 and 60 years of age.
6. 75% purchased three tickets or less.
7. 50% obtained the ticket themselves.
8. 10% made a special trip to get the tickets.
9. 52% of the nonresidents are in New Hampshire for recreational purposes.
10. 65% completed high school and 11% have more than college training—levels of educational achievement which are significantly above the national average.
11. 31% have incomes of $10,000 or more, 75% have incomes over $5,000 and 10% have incomes below $3,000—the income pattern being significantly higher than the national average.
12. In terms of income and education levels, resident winners are not as different from the state population as nonresident winners are from the national population.
13. Residents tend to buy more tickets per purchaser than nonresidents.
14. Resident and nonresident winners are comparable in the relationship which exists between family incomes and the number of persons supported.
15. Among neither residents or nonresidents is the number of tickets purchased related significantly to family income.

These findings provide a picture of Sweepstakes participants which is quite different from that which might have been anticipated on the basis of historical precedent. If, as the analysis shows, the number of tickets purchased is unrelated to income, why are the poor not participating much more heavily in the Sweepstakes?

At least three intuitive explanations for these results can be offered. It is clear that the majority of the purchasers come from outside of New Hampshire. Federal statutes limiting the use of the mails for lottery purposes were enacted before the turn of this century and remain in full force. As a result, the buyer, or someone acting for him, must personally come to New Hampshire to obtain a ticket. For nonresidents to get a ticket, therefore, some travel will be required. However, travel is not something the poor or their friends can readily afford, particularly for recreational purposes.

A second factor, the price of the tickets, may also have an impact. At three dollars each, tickets are not easily obtained by those who prefer to do their gambling on the basis of a nickle, dime or quarter a day.

Finally, the Sweepstakes is essentially an "investment" form of gambling in that the results are not known until well after the ticket has been picked out. This lag has probably contributed to the noticeable lack of interest inveterate and professional gamblers have demonstrated in the Sweepstakes. Perhaps the poor who gamble do not like the deferred outcome this form of wager entails as much as they like gambling where results are known within 24 hours.

The "typical" Sweepstakes ticket purchaser appears from this study to be a middle-aged married man who has a good education and is earning a relatively high income with which he supports a small family. He has come to New Hampshire for the purpose of having a good time, which apparently includes buying a few Sweepstakes tickets.

As a means of raising public revenue, the New Hampshire Sweepstakes does not appear to be extracting a disproportionate amount of money from those in society who are least able to pay for government services.

Source: New Hampshire Sweepstakes Commission. Survey conducted by Professor S. Kenneth Howard, University of New Hampshire, 1965.

EXHIBIT 4
New Hampshire Sweepstakes, Operating Results, 1964–1970

Year	Gross Revenue	Operating Expenses	Prizes Paid	Net to Education
1964	$ 5,740,093	$1,172,010*	$1,799,995	$ 2,768,088
1965	4,566,044†	678,679	1,400,000	2,487,365
1966	3,889,056	633,447	1,414,993	1,840,616
1967	2,577,341	578,578	943,565	1,055,198
1968	2,054,434	364,162	800,150	890,122
1969	2,017,667	358,710	790,599	868,358
1970	2,019,367	391,208	791,596	836,563
Total	$22,864,002	$4,176,794**	$7,940,898	$10,746,310

*Includes $587,710 paid to Internal Revenue Service for 10 percent wagering tax.
†Includes $664,448 refund from Internal Revenue Service, including interest.
**Includes $580,876 paid to State Liquor Commission for sale of tickets, therefore, total revenue paid to state—$11,327,186.
Source: New Hampshire Sweepstakes Commission.

New York State Lottery

New York had considered having its own lottery for many years, but it was not until the initial success of the New Hampshire sweepstakes that the New York state legislature passed "The New York State Lottery Law" in 1965 and 1966.[4]

The New York law required that 45 percent of the gross receipts of lottery ticket sales be applied exclusively for the purpose of providing aid to primary, secondary, and higher education and for providing scholarships. It also provided that no more than 40 percent of the proceeds be awarded as prizes and no more than 15 percent be used for all administrative expenses including promotion and commissions to vendors.

New York's marketing program differed significantly from that of New Hampshire. Tickets were priced at $1 and drawings were scheduled monthly. The advertising campaign centered around the purpose of the lottery and used the theme: "Give a dollar to education." It was believed that people would not mind contributing to educational costs if they also had a chance of winning a large amount of money at the same time. This approach was also expected to minimize social criticism of the lottery.

Distribution, as in the New Hampshire plan, was very limited and tickets could be purchased only at about 4,000 banks and at government buildings. These outlets were chosen by the New York Lottery Commission in order to gain respectability for the lottery and to minimize the risk of underworld influence and other forms of corruption. The prize structure for the monthly lottery was established on the basis of each million tickets sold. A total of $400,000 was to be allocated among approximately 1,100 winners. The major prizes were $100,000, $50,000, $5,000, and $2,000. There were also ten $1,000 winners. The remainder of the prizes were for $500 and $100.

Ticket sales for the first ten drawings (June 1967 through March 1968) averaged 5.3 million tickets per month. This level was below expectations based on the performance of the New Hampshire Sweepstakes.[5]

On April 1, 1968, a law passed by the United States Congress took effect which restricted banks from being used as outlets for selling lottery or sweepstakes tickets in any state. This required the New York Commission to adopt a new distribution policy. Foremost consideration was given to those outlets which were reputable and willing to provide the necessary push in the selling of tickets. Hotels, motels, drug and variety stores were the types of stores that were sought. Licenses were granted to 13,000 business establishments and a 5 percent

EXHIBIT 5
Gross Receipts of New York State Lottery, by Month
(millions of dollars)

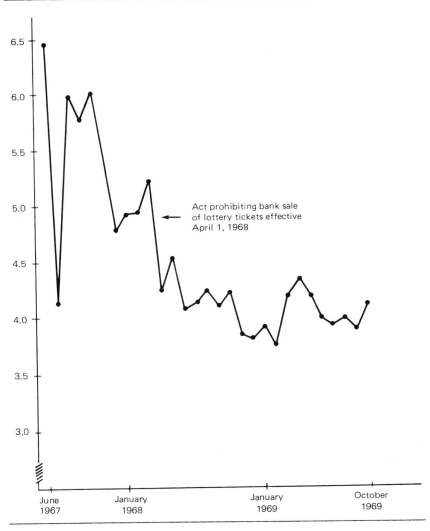

Act prohibiting bank sale
of lottery tickets effective
April 1, 1968

Source: New York State Lottery Commission records.

commission on ticket sales was to be paid to all vendors. (In New Hampshire, the sales commission was 4 percent for state stores and 8 percent for private vendors.) The immediate consequence of the required change in distribution policy was a reduction in ticket sales as is shown in exhibit 5.

New York, as well as New Hampshire, also came under the provisions of a second federal law. This one prohibited information regarding any aspect of a lottery or sweepstakes from being communicated in a media vehicle which crossed over state lines. Hence, no radio or television advertising of any sort was allowed. Even winners could not be identified or interviewed over radio or television networks. Further, only those newspapers that were distributed within the state could be used for transmission of lottery information. With such restriction, point of purchase displays, billboards, and in-state newspapers became heavily used as the means by which the lottery or sweepstakes commission communicated with their potential purchasers.

During the fiscal years April 1968 through March 1969 and April 1969 through March 1970, New York ticket sales totalled nearly $49 million and $47 million, respectively. Both years' sales were considerably below the average $5.3 million in ticket sales of the first ten months. During 1970–1971, bonus $2 and $3 lotteries were scheduled to be held on an alternating quarterly basis in an attempt to stimulate sales. Further details of these special lotteries are given in exhibit 6 which is the promotional piece displayed at outlets selling lottery tickets. Ticket sales increased during the fiscal year 1970–1971 to $70 million with the $3 summer special lottery contributing a record $17 million to gross revenues. Also, the New York commission held three special 50¢ weekly lotteries on a test basis in November, December, and January. Gross sales averaged approximately $900,000. The $2 lottery had not been started. Exhibit 7 shows the sales record, by month, for all drawings held between April 1970 and March 1971.

New Jersey State Lottery

In January 1971, New Jersey became the third state to commence lottery operations.[6] The New Jersey lottery differed from the New Hampshire and New York lotteries in a number of ways: tickets were priced at 50¢; drawings were held weekly; vending machines as well as sales personnel were used to sell tickets; supermarkets were emphasized heavily in the distribution network; and tickets could be purchased from vending machines up until the day of the drawing.

As in New York, New Jersey's prize distribution was based on the sale of one million tickets. For each

million tickets there were 1,000 prizes with the total prize money amounting to $158,000 to be distributed as follows:

Number of Winners	Prize
1	$50,000
9	4,000
90	400
900	40

Since, by state law, a minimum of 45 percent of gross revenue had to be returned in the form of prize money, $67,000 was left undistributed. This money was used to finance a special "millionaire's" drawing in which the prize distribution was as follows:

Number of Winners	Prize
1	$1,000,000
1	200,000
1	100,000
7	10,000
215	500
2025	100

New Jersey promoted its lottery heavily with the use of newspaper, billboard and point-of-purchase advertisements and promotional materials, such as placemats which were given to restaurant owners to be used on their tables (see exhibit 8).

Tickets were sold at approximately 6,000 retail establishments with the heaviest concentration being at large supermarkets. Vending machines were also placed at high traffic locations such as bus, train, and airport terminals. A 5 percent commission was paid to vendors for each ticket sold. In addition, bonus money totalling 1 percent of gross revenue was paid to outlets that sold prize winning tickets. For example, the outlet selling the "millionaire" winning ticket was given a $10,000 bonus.

In its initial year of operation, the New Jersey lottery sales totalled 282 million tickets (see exhibit 9 for weekly sales data). The New Jersey State Lottery Planning Commission in 1970 had said, "Our estimate of gross revenues for the first full year of operation will be about $30 million, although there is a substantial amount of possible error in this figure.

EXHIBIT 6
New York State Lottery Promotion

Somebody's always winning the New York State Lottery...
it might as well be you!

MORE THAN $80 MILLION IN PRIZES PAID TO OVER 200,000 WINNERS

(front)

Tickets are on sale at more than 13,000 business establishments licensed by the Division of the Lottery throughout the State.

Results of all drawings are published in newspapers throughout the State and posted by sales agents. Winners are notified by phone or wire.

BUY YOUR TICKETS IN COMBINATIONS

DL - 601 (7/71)

(back)

Can win you $100,000 !	Top Prize $25,000	Can make you a Millionaire!
or one of these other Grand Tier Prizes (for every million tickets sold)	**a year for life** $500,000 GUARANTEED	(payable $50,000 a year for 20 years)
• $50,000 • $5,000	Other Grand Tier Prizes	Other Grand Tier Prizes
• $2,000 • 10 at $1,000	• $75,000 • $40,000	• $100,000 • $50,000
	• $15,000 • 10 at $5,000	• $25,000 • 10 at $10,000
Consolation Prizes	Consolation Prizes	Consolation Prizes
• 300 at $500	• 500 at $1,000	• 10 at $5,000 • 10 at $4,000
(per million tickets sold)		• 10 at $3,000 • 10 at $2,000
plus thousands of $100 prizes	plus thousands of $300 prizes	• 100 at $1,000
		plus thousands of $500 prizes
Tickets on Sale Every Month	*Tickets on Sale Aug. - Sept. 1971*	*Tickets on Sale Oct. - Nov. 1971*

EXHIBIT 7
New York State Lottery Operating Results, 1970–1971

Sales Month*	Gross Sales	Commissions Retained	Net Revenues
April 1970	$ 3,948,275.00	$ 225,076.05	$ 3,723,198.95
May	3,785,567.00	215,748.37	3,569,818.63
June	3,688,096.00	208,424.99	3,479,671.01
July	3,309,573.00	188,538.28	3,121,034.72
August	3,220,801.00	182,954.10	3,037,846.90
September	3,169,871.00	179,665.78	2,990,205.22
Summer Special ($3)	16,747,581.00	940,210.68	15,807,370.32
October	3,606,144.00	205,326.78	3,400,817.22
November 50¢ Special	765,752.00	55,861.20	709,890.80
November	3,384,900.00	193,798.70	3,191,101.30
December 50¢ Special	1,001,995.50	74,312.91	927,682.59
December	3,276,925.00	188,588.16	3,088,336.84
Holiday Special ($3)	8,667,298.00	489,182.02	8,178,115.98
January 50¢ Special 1971	938,887.00	69,265.66	869,621.34
January	3,303,844.00	189,728.95	3,114,115.05
February	3,806,400.00	218,178.34	3,588,221.66
March	3,461,860.00	197,549.83	3,264,310.17
Total:	$70,083,769.50	$4,022,410.80	$66,061,358.70

*Net revenues are collected in the month following the sales month.
Source: New York State Lottery Commission.

The potential revenues, of course, may be somewhat higher, but some margin must be allowed for errors and experimentation in the initial stages." Thus, the first-year sales totalling $141 million far exceeded the planning commission's estimate.

Recent Developments

Both New Hampshire and New York reacted to the New Jersey success by changing many of the basic characteristics of their own lotteries.

New Hampshire New Hampshire, which had expanded its number of retail outlets to 850 in 1971, decided to institute a weekly 50¢ drawing in addition to its now quarterly $3 sweepstakes drawing. Drawings were held each Friday and tickets could be purchased as late as Tuesday. On Wednesday, tickets for the following week's drawing were put on sale. Also, a bonus drawing was scheduled in October of each year with the top prize being $100,000. A June 25, 1971,

news release by the sweepstakes commission concerning this new lottery is shown in exhibit 10. During the first week of the 50¢ ticket, 207,957 tickets were sold and for 1971, gross lottery revenue (which included the $3 sweepstakes and the 50¢ drawings beginning July 23) amounted to $4.3 million.

New Hampshire also added a new dimension to the purchase of lottery tickets which was called the "uniticket." This permitted any resident or visitor to the state to buy a 50¢ lottery ticket for a 12-, 24-, or 52-week period at a cost of $6, $12, or $25, respectively. Further, subscribers could select their own number and were also guaranteed renewal rights on this number. Advertisements suggested that residents and tourists purchase "unitickets" for themselves, or as gifts for friends, relatives, or associates.

Three further changes in this marketing program were made in 1971 to increase the number of winners. The first was that buyers of the 50¢ ticket were given

EXHIBIT 8

New Jersey State Lottery Promotion

HOW TO WIN IN THE NEW JERSEY LOTTERY

BUY A TICKET!

You can't win if you don't have a ticket. Buy as many as you want, each week. Tickets are 50¢ each. You have a chance to win $50,000, or other cash prizes . . . EVERY WEEK! Tickets can be purchased from any of the thousands of Licensed Agents throughout New Jersey. Look for the Official Lottery Sign in the window. There's an agent near you.

SIGN YOUR TICKET!

Very important! Write your name on the back of your ticket. Now, only you can collect if your ticket wins.

LOOK AT THE DRAWING DATE

Could be your lucky day. On that date, the WINNING NUMBER will be announced for the Lottery in which your ticket is entered. Winning number is published in New Jersey newspapers each week, and posted by all Licensed Agents.

CHECK YOUR LOTTERY TICKET NUMBER

See if all or part of your Lottery Ticket Number wins! For example—On Jan. 7, 1971, the Winning Number was 394584. Here were the winners:

Lottery Ticket No. 394584 . . . $50,000
Lottery Ticket No. *94584 . . . $4,000
Lottery Ticket No. **4584 . . . $400
Lottery Ticket No. ***584 . . . $40
Lottery Ticket No. ***84 . . . Entry Into a 50¢ Millionaire Semi-Final Drawing.

IF YOU'RE A CASH WINNER . . .

take your ticket in person to any N.J. State Motor Vehicle Agency. DO NOT MAIL. After your ticket is validated, you will receive your check.

Our Stakes are the greatest!

MAY WE RECOMMEND

Food for thought . . . bound to make your mouth water. We cooked it up to whet your appetite while you're waiting for your order. Eat hearty! Then treat yourself to lottery tickets on your way out.

Good luck!

Benefits State Education and Institutions

Important Information. All determinations of winners are subject to Lottery Commission rules and regulations. Winners must claim their prizes within one year following date of drawing. Ticket void if torn or altered. Valid only for drawing date shown on ticket. New Jersey State Lottery is not responsible or accountable for lost or stolen tickets.

HOW THE 50¢ MILLIONAIRE DRAWING WORKS . . .

If you're a winner with the last 2 correct digits in any Weekly Drawing you have a chance to become a millionaire! KEEP YOUR TICKET and watch for the announcement of the 50¢ Millionaire Semi-Final Drawing in which your ticket is entered. There will be several during the year—whenever the revenue from the sale of 50¢ Millionaire prizes warrants the awarding of 50¢ Millionaire prizes!

There are two parts to the 50¢ Millionaire prize. The Semi-Final Drawing and the Final Drawing. At the Semi-Final Drawing, the SERIAL NUMBER on your winning ticket is all important. A 3-digit number will be drawn as the Semi-Final Winning Number. Check to see if the last 3 digits of the Serial Number on your eligible ticket exactly matches the Semi-Final Number.

For example—On Feb. 25, 1971, the Semi-Final Number was 460. Serial Number—***460 (Last 3 digits matched) . . . became a Finalist, guaranteed at least $500.
Serial Number—****60 (Last 2 digits matched) . . . became a $100 winner.

Sample Winning Ticket!

Correct last 3 digits of Serial Number

Correct Drawing Date

Correct last 2 digits of Ticket Number

IF YOU'RE A SEMI-FINAL WINNER . . .

take your ticket to any N.J. State Motor Vehicle Agency. After your ticket has been validated, if you're a FINALIST, you will be invited to a Final Drawing. If you're a $100 winner a check will be forwarded to you.

NOW, THE FINAL DRAWING!

In this drawing, your name is used, so you must identify yourself within the published time limit before the drawing. You, or your representative, will take part in the Final Drawing process. As a Finalist, you can win prizes from $500 up to $1,000,000! First Prize $1,000,000 ($50,000 a year for 20 years), Second Prize $200,000 ($20,000 a year for 10 years), Third Prize $100,000 ($10,000 a year for 10 years), and seven Fourth Prizes of $10,000 each. All other Finalists receive $500 each.

PLAY NOW! PLAY OFTEN . . .

This is America's Most Rewarding Lottery. Every ticket you buy goes a long way toward the improvement of State Education and Institutions. Help yourself and others

EXHIBIT 9
New Jersey State Lottery Operating Results, 1971

1971 Drawing Date		Total Number of Tickets Sold (in millions)	1971 Drawing Date		Total Number of Tickets Sold (in millions)	1971 Drawing Date		Total Number of Tickets Sold (in millions)
January	7	4.7	May	6	5.9	September	2	5.3
	14	2.5		13	6.0		9	5.3
	21	3.7		20	5.9		16	5.2
	28	3.9		27	5.9		23	5.4
							30	5.5
February	4	4.9	June	3	5.9	October	7	5.5
	11	5.8		10	5.8		14	5.5
	18	5.8		17	5.9		21	5.4
	25	5.7		24	5.9		28	5.5
March	4	5.9	July	1	5.8	November	4	5.4
	11	6.1		8	5.6		11	5.5
	18	6.1		15	5.4		18	5.4
	25	6.0		22	5.4		24	5.3
				29	5.4			
April	1	6.0	August	5	5.3	December	2	5.4
	8	5.9		12	5.2		9	5.1
	15	5.9		19	5.2		16	5.3
	22	5.6		26	5.3		23	5.2
	29	5.8					30	5.0
						Total for 1971:		282.3

Source: New Jersey State Lottery Commission.

ten $3 sweepstakes tickets if their weekly ticket number was one more or one less than the winning number. The second change established a "scramble bonus" in which a ticket holder won $25 if his ticket contained the five digits of the winning ticket number in any order. The third change was to increase the number of prize winners for the $3 sweepstakes ticket. The new prize distribution for each 100,000 tickets sold was as follows:

Number of Winners	Prize
1	$50,000
1	10,000
1	5,000
5	2,000
20	500
100	100
300	50

New York New York, like New Hampshire, also changed its lottery substantially. The $1 monthly ticket was discontinued and replaced by a weekly 50¢ ticket; the prize structure was changed; and the distribution network was streamlined by dropping a number of outlets. A news release issued by the New York State Lottery Commission in January 1972 described the new 50¢ lottery:

New York State's 50¢ lottery offers the advantages of fast action and fast payoff. Drawings are held weekly on Thursday at various locations within New York State. Tickets may be purchased from any of approximately 7,200 licensed vendors. A new lottery begins each Wednesday. . . . For each series of one million 50¢ tickets sold, 10,000 prizes are offered weekly.

The prizes, for each million tickets sold, are:

CASE

EXHIBIT 10
New Hampshire State Lottery News Release

NEW HAMPSHIRE
SWEEPSTAKES COMMISSION
State House Annex, Concord, N.H.

NEWS RELEASE

FOR RELEASE

June 25, 1971

50/50 N. H. SWEEPS POISED FOR TAKEOFF

The Sweepstakes Commission announced today that tickets for the new 50/50 N. H. Sweeps will go on sale at all outlets on July 14. The ticket price has been set at 50¢ and provides a chance at a top prize of $50,000, as well as hundreds of other prizes.

Public drawings will be held every Friday morning beginning July 23. The first drawing will take place on the State House Plaza in Concord. Prizes will be determined by a randomly selected 5-digit number. Each ticket has a 5-digit Sweeps number. If a ticket matches the winning 5-digit Sweeps number for that drawing date, the holder of that ticket wins at least $5,000 and qualifies for a super drawing with a chance to win $50,000 or $10,000. It is estimated that super drawings will be held every 2 or 3 weeks, depending on ticket sales. A variety of additional prizes of varying amounts will be awarded. The prize schedule is best explained by example.

Selected Winning Sweeps Number	Your Sweeps Number	Prize
12345 12345	12345	— $5,000 Minimum. Chance at $10,000 or $50,000
12345 12345	X2345	— $500
12345 12345	XX345	— $50
12345 12345	XXX45	— Weekly Bonus Chance at $500 next week
12345 12345	XXXX5	— Hold for special BONANZA drawing to be held at least quarterly with minimum prize pool of $50,000.

Flyers will be distributed within the next several days explaining the prizes and drawings in greater detail. All existing sales outlets will be selling the 50/50 Sweeps tickets along with the regular $3.00 Sweeps tickets. It is anticipated about 200 additional private outlets will be authorized by the Commission.

The Commission explained that the new 50/50 N. H. Sweeps is patterned after the successful New Jersey Lottery; however, the Commission believes that the N. H. program provides a more exciting prize structure. In the New Jersey program there is an 8-day delay between the end of sales and the weekly drawing. This has been eliminated in the N. H. program since the drawing will take place during the same week. This improves the action. This is in harmony with one of the slogans for the new 50/50 N. H. Sweeps program, "Where the Action Is!"

Source: New Hampshire Sweepstakes Commission.

---

1 first prize — *$50,000* — *all six digits of winning number (in exact order)*

9 second prizes — *$5,000* — *last five digits*

90 third prizes — *$500* — *last four digits*

900 fourth prizes — *$50* — *last three digits*

Those holding the last two digits (9,000 per million tickets sold) will participate in the next bonus drawing and should retain their tickets to await the results of that drawing.... Of the more than 7,200

vendors licensed to sell lottery tickets, virtually every line of business is represented, including supermarkets, department stores, hotels and motels, restaurants, drugstores, variety stores, specialty shops, bars, liquor stores, and others.

The New York Commission decided against the policy of awarding large major prizes in its bonus drawing. Instead, they selected a prize distribution which featured a relatively large number of smaller prizes. For example, if $150,000 was available in the bonus pool,[7] the prize distribution would be:

CASE

EXHIBIT 11
Summary: Structure of State Lotteries, January, 1972

State	Price	Frequency of Drawing	Prize Distribution*		Number of Outlets
			Number	Amount	
New Hampshire	50¢	Weekly	1	$5,000 minimum— chance at $50,000 or $10,000	850
			9	$500	
			90	$50	
			900	Bonus chance of $500 in the next drawing	
			119†	25 (Scramble Bonus)	
	$3	Quarterly	1	$50,000	
			1	$10,000	
			1	$5,000	
			5	$2,000	
			20	$500	
			100	$100	
			300	$50	
New York	50¢	Weekly	1	$50,000	7,200
			9	$5,000	
			90	$500	
			900	$50	
	$3	Infrequent intervals	1	$50,000 a year for twenty years	
			1	$100,000	
			1	$50,000	
			1	$25,000	
			10	$10,000	
			10	$5,000	
			10	$4,000	
			10	$3,000	
			10	$2,000	
			100	$1,000	
				plus an unspecified amount of $500 prizes depending on the number of tickets sold	
New Jersey	50¢	Weekly	1	$50,000	6,000
			9	$4,000	
			90	$400	
			900	$40	

*Prize distribution is based on sales of 100,000 tickets for New Hampshire and 1,000,000 tickets for New York and New Jersey.
†Maximum number. The actual number of $25 prizes depends upon the number of different digits in the week's winning number.
Source: Various state lottery commissions.

CASE

Number of Winners	Prize	Number of Winners	Prize
1	$22,500	1	$1,000,000
1	7,500	1	200,000
6	1,500	1	100,000
79	379	27	10,000
945	85	443	500
		4252	100

The first 50¢ drawing took place on January 20, 1972, and sales of 3.2 million tickets were recorded. During the subsequent four weeks, sales of 3.6 million, 4.0 million, 4.2 million, and 4.8 million tickets, respectively, were achieved.

New Jersey As New Jersey entered into its second year of operation, two changes were announced by the New Jersey Lottery Commission. The first was to offer a subscription ticket which was identical to New Hampshire's "uniticket" except for the fact that an individual was assigned a number, rather than being able to select his own. The second was to double the total number of ways that buyers could qualify into the "millionaire" drawing. This was done by making all those with tickets whose first two numbers matched the winning number eligible for the drawing. A new prize distribution was also established creating 2,000 more cash prizes in the "millionaire" drawing which was held once every five or six weeks:

Present Situation In preparation for the February meeting, staff members of the Massachusetts Lottery Commission had prepared two summary tables showing comparative data on the other three states and their lottery operations. These are presented in exhibits 11 and 12. At this same time, two other states—Connecticut and Pennsylvania—had decided to start lotteries and were in the process of preparing plans for their newly created state lotteries. Also, New Hampshire, fearing lost sales from the soon-to-start Massachusetts lottery, had under consideration further changes in its sweepstakes. One such plan involved daily drawings with a 25¢ ticket price. It was in this general context of uncertainty and time pressure that the director of the Massachusetts lottery had called the February staff meeting.

EXHIBIT 12
Comparative Data—State Lotteries

State	First Year Lottery Revenues*		1971 Lottery Revenues		1971 Estimates		
	Total (in millions)	Per Capita	Total (in millions)	Per Capita	Population (in thousands)	Number of Households (in thousands)	Per Capita Income
New Hampshire	$ 5.7	$ 7.70	$ 4.3	$ 5.81	738	225	$3,608
New York	61.7	3.39	70.1	3.85	18,237	5,893	4,797
New Jersey	141.1	19.60	141.1	19.60	7,168	2,218	4,539
Massachusetts	—	—	—	—	5,689	1,760	4,294

*The first year of operation for the various state lotteries was as follows: New Hampshire, 1964; New York, 1967–1968; and New Jersey, 1971.

Source: Various state lottery commissions and the *Statistical Abstract of the United States: 1971.*

NOTES

1. The bill was passed by a two-thirds majority overriding the veto of the Governor: by a 171 to 33 vote in the State House of Representatives and a 26 to 13 vote in the State Senate. No public referendum was required in Massachusetts.

2. Total pari-mutuel handle from horse and dog racing was 308.9 million dollars; total attendance was 4.4 million during the 439 racing days.

3. Chapter 284:21:h New Hampshire Sweepstakes Law.

4. State law required passage by two successive sessions of the legislature in addition to a public referendum. The referendum, held at the general election in November, 1966, passed by a 2 to 1 margin.

5. See exhibit 11 for comparative data on the three states with lotteries.

6. The act creating the lottery was approved by residents at the general election on November 11, 1969 by a 4.5 to 1 margin.

7. The $150,000 would come from prize money that was undistributed in the 50¢ weekly prize distribution.

Product Strategies

The firm's product is one of the most important elements of its marketing mix. Developing the right product to satisfy the needs of the target market is essential to the overall success of the firm's marketing effort.

DEFINITION OF A PRODUCT

Critical to the development of an overall marketing strategy is the recognition that a product typically is much more than just the composite of its physical elements. One of the best definitions of a product is that it is a combination of tangible and intangible attributes that satisfy customer needs. The inclusion of "intangible" attributes is a key factor of this definition. The social-symbolic meaning of a product—generated by the brand name, advertising image, image of the middlemen who sell the item to consumers, and a variety of other factors—can be as important or even more important than its tangible attributes.

In many instances, the *image* of the product will be more important than its functional value—consumers buy products not only for what they do, but also for what they mean. Generally, the intangible aspects are more important for products that are highly visible to the public when being used—automobiles and wearing apparel, for example. For items that are consumed in private, such as canned green beans and electric blankets, the tangible attributes usually are of greater importance.

The other key factor in this definition of a product is that it satisfy the needs of the target market. Unfortunately, many firms have focused their attention on the technical aspects of product development and virtually ignored the issues of what needs are being satisfied. For what purpose do consumers want the product? This latter orientation is essential to the successful marketing of products and services and is discussed in G. L. Shostack's article, "Breaking Free From Product Marketing."

Products can be classified into three groups: convenience, shopping, and specialty goods. Convenience items are those that consumers know about and buy frequently, that are relatively low in cost, and for which buyers want to spend very little time in the market. Shopping goods, on the other hand, are items about which consumers are not very knowledgeable. Hence, they either want or need to "shop around" to better define their options before making a purchase. Specialty goods are those which carry very high brand recognition and loyalty, and for which consumers are willing to expend the effort to acquire.

NEW PRODUCT DEVELOPMENT

The development of new products and the strategies to be used in offering them to the target market can be a very complex process. Many firms organize expressly for the development of new products. The least formal process is where the product manager is given responsibility for not only marketing existing products, but for identifying new ones as well. A more structured effort to develop and market new products is made through the establishment of new-product departments, new-product committees, and venture teams. Whether established on a permanent or temporary basis, these latter forms of organizations have the express purposes of developing new products for the firm.

The processes that firms use to develop new products vary widely. Some firms do not have formal procedures leading to the creation of new products, while others have quite rigid steps for new product development. In general, the process, whether structured or not, will include the following series of steps:

1. Generate ideas for possible new products.
2. Conduct a preliminary screening of the ideas generated to initially assess their appropriateness for the firm and their potential for profits.
3. Test the product concept both internally and on small samples of consumers who might comprise an actual target market, to better define desired attributes and overall viability of the product idea.
4. Conduct a business analysis to evaluate the product's potential for success.
5. Develop the final product and the marketing strategies which will be used when it is introduced.
6. Test market the product in limited areas to assess consumer acceptance and the viability of the marketing strategies developed.
7. Introduce the product to the market for which it was designed.

THE PRODUCT LIFE CYCLE

Planning the marketing strategies to be used for the product over its life is another key activity for the marketing manager. For planning purposes, the product life-cycle concept can be especially useful, as described in John E. Smallwood's article, "The Product Life Cycle: A Key To Strategic Marketing Planning."

The issue of whether products actually go through a cycle described as a normal, or bell-shaped, curve has been the subject of much debate. However, the concept serves to recognize that a product will go through various stages in its life, appealing to different elements in the market and requiring different marketing strategies along the way. Furthermore, it emphasizes the fact that eventually the product will die, and will need to be replaced by others if the firm is to maintain a reasonable level of profits.

Most descriptions of the life cycle identify between four to six stages. The cycle generally accepted consists of four stages:

1. Introduction
2. Growth
3. Maturity
4. Decline

In the Introduction stage, the product is first made available to the target market on a regular basis. Characteristics of this stage include: limited distribution, high price, few competitors, some modification of the product to better match consumer needs, and low profits.

The Growth stage is characterized by increasing sales and profits as the product gains market acceptance. Even though more competitors enter the market, distribution becomes easier to obtain and the product's price remains high.

In the Maturity stage, sales grow for a time and then start to decline. Profits begin to decline almost from the beginning of the stage, as competition becomes intense and prices fall to low levels. Most firms in the market will introduce new models and styles of the product; before the end of this stage, some of the firms will leave the market.

The Decline stage is typified by the continued erosion of sales and profits. During this time, most of the firms leave the market, and the few firms that remain will cut back their offerings of models and styles. The product's price may increase in this stage as the remaining firms try to make profits from higher margins on low volume.

Some product life-cycle models contain a Pre-Introduction stage to illustrate the importance of all the efforts that go into the development of the product. Others divide the Maturity stage into two components—called the Maturity and Saturation stages—to describe the continued but slow growth in the early part of the stage and the start of its decline in the latter part.

Implicit in the consideration of the life cycle is the recognition that different types of buyers enter the market as the product progresses from its introduction to its decline. One well-quoted article by Everett M. Rogers and F. Floyd Shoemaker defined the adoption process as consisting of five groups of buyers:

1. Innovators: The first 2½ percent of the buyers.
2. Early Adopters: The next 13½ percent of the buyers.
3. Early Majority: The next 34 percent of the buyers.
4. Late Majority: The next 34 percent of the buyers.
5. Laggards: The last 16 percent of the buyers.[1]

Because different groups purchase the product over the course of its life, the firm's marketing strategies with respect to product, price, channel, and promotion must be adjusted accordingly.

PLANNING PRODUCT STRATEGIES

Planning for a product through its life cycle involves a great many important decisions. Not only will the physical product have to be created, but decisions will have to be made on such issues as what brand will be placed on the product, what label will be used, how will the product be packaged, what warranties will be given, and what support services (maintenance, credit, and so on) will be offered.

Over the life of the product, consideration also will have to be given to expanding the product line to include more models and styles in order to broaden its market base. As the product begins to appeal to different elements within the market, some repositioning of the product may also be called for to keep it appropriate for the desired target market.

Finally, the firm will find it necessary to reduce the product line as consumer needs change and the profit potential in the market declines. Eliminating a product can be a very difficult decision. Not only is it hard to identify just when a product should be eliminated, but the firm may encounter some resistance among middlemen and consumers who still want the product. R. A. Alexander's article "The Death and Burial Of Sick Products" describes the necessity and difficulties of product elimination.

[1]*Communication in Innovations,* Everett M. Rogers and F. Floyd Shoemaker, 2nd Edition, New York: The Free Press, 1971.

G. Lynn Shostack

Breaking Free from Product Marketing

New concepts are necessary if service marketing is to succeed. Service marketing is an uncharted frontier. Despite the increasing dominance of services in the U.S. economy, basic texts still disagree on how services should be treated in a marketing context.[1]

The heart of this dispute is the issue of applicability. The classic marketing "mix," the seminal literature, and the language of marketing all derive from the manufacture of physical goods. Practicing marketers tend to think in terms of products, particularly mass-market consumer goods. Some service companies even call their output "products" and have "product" management functions modeled after those of experts such as Procter and Gamble.

Marketing seems to be overwhelmingly product-oriented. However, many service-based companies are confused about the applicability of product marketing, and more than one attempt to adopt product marketing has failed.

Merely adopting product marketing's labels does not resolve the question of whether product marketing can be overlaid on service businesses. Can corporate banking services really be marketed according to the same basic blueprint that made *Tide* a success? Given marketing's historic tenets, there is simply no alternative.

Could marketing itself be "myopic" in having failed to create relevant paradigms for the service sector? Many marketing professionals who transfer to the services arena find their work fundamentally "different," but have a difficult time articulating how and why their priorities and concepts have changed. Often, they also find to their frustration and bewilderment that "marketing" is treated as a peripheral function or is confused with one of its components, such as

Source: From the *Journal of Marketing*, Vol. 41, No. 2 (April 1977), pp. 73–80. Reprinted by permission of the American Marketing Association.

research or advertising, and kept within a very narrow scope of influence and authority.[2]

This situation is frequently rationalized as being due to the "ignorance" of senior management in service businesses. "Education" is usually recommended as the solution. However, an equally feasible, though less comforting, explanation is that service industries have been slow to integrate marketing into the mainstream of decision-making and control because marketing offers no guidance, terminology, or practical rules that are clearly *relevant* to services.

Making Room for Intangibility

The American Marketing Association cites both goods *and* services as foci for marketing activities. Squeezing services into the procrustean phrase "intangible products,"[3] is not only a distortion of the AMA's definition but also a complete contradiction in terms.

It is wrong to imply that services are just like products "except" for intangibility. By such logic, apples are just like oranges, except for their "appleness." Intangibility is not a modifier; it is a state. Intangibles may come with tangible trappings, but no amount of money can buy physical ownership of such intangibles as "experience" (movies), "time" (consultants), or "process" (dry cleaning). A service is rendered. A service is experienced. A service cannot be stored on a shelf, touched, tasted or tried on for size. "Tangible" means "palpable," and "material." "Intangible" is an antonym, meaning "*im*palpable," and "*not* corporeal."[4] This distinction has profound implications. Yet marketing offers no way to treat intangibility as the core element it is, nor does marketing offer usable tools for managing, altering, or controlling this amorphous core.

Even the most thoughtful attempts to broaden the definition of "that which is marketed" away from product synonymity suffer from an underlying assumption of tangibility. Not long ago, Philip Kotler argued that "values" should be considered the end result of "marketing."[5] However, the text went on to imply that "values" were created by "objects," and drifted irredeemably into the classic product axioms.

To truly expand marketing's conceptual boundaries requires a framework which accommodates intangibility instead of denying it. Such a framework must give equal descriptive weight to the components of "service" as it does to the concept of "product."

The Complexity of Marketed Entities

What kind of framework would provide a new conceptual viewpoint? One unorthodox possibility can be drawn from direct observation of the marketplace and the nature of the market "satisfiers" available to it. Taking a fresh look, it seems that there are really very few, if any, "pure" products or services in the marketplace.

Examine, for instance, the automobile. Without question, one might say, it is a physical object, with a full range of tangible features and options. But another, equally important element is marketed in tandem with the steel and chrome—i.e., the service of transportation. Transportation is an *independent* marketing element; in other words, it is not car-dependent, but can be marketed in its own right. A car is only *one* alternative for satisfying the market's transportation needs.

This presents a semantic dilemma. How should the automobile be defined? Is General Motors marketing a *service*, a service that happens to include a *by*-product called a car? Levitt's classic "Marketing Myopia" exhorts businessmen to think in exactly this generic way about what they market.[6] Are automobiles "tangible services"? It cannot be denied that both elements—tangible and intangible—exist and are vigorously marketed. Yet they are, by definition, different qualities, and to attempt to compress them into a single word or phrase begs the issue.

Conversely, how shall a service such as airline transportation be described? Although the service itself is intangible, there are certain very real things that belong in any description of the total entity, including such important tangibles as interior decor, food & drink, seat design, and overall graphic continuity from tickets to attendants' uniforms. These items can dramatically affect the "reality" of the service in the consumer's mind. However, there is no accurate way to lump them into a one-word description.

If "either-or" terms (product vs. service) do not adequately describe the true nature of marketed entities, it makes sense to explore the usefulness of a new *structural* definition. This broader concept postulates that market entities are, in reality, *combinations of discrete elements* which are linked together in molecule-like wholes. Elements can be either tangible or intangible. The entity may have either a tangible or intangible nucleus. But the whole can only be described as having a certain dominance.

Molecular Model

A "molecular" model offers opportunities for visualization and management of a total market entity. It reflects the fact that a market entity can be partly tangible *and* partly intangible, without diminishing the importance of either characteristic. Not only can

the potential be seen for picturing and dealing with multiple *elements*, rather than *a thing*, but the concept of dominance can lead to enriched considerations of the priorities and approach that may be required of a marketer. Moreover, the model suggests the scientific analogy that if market entities have multiple elements, a deliberate or inadvertent change in a *single* element may completely alter the entity, as the simple switching of FE_3O_2 to FE_2O_3 creates a new substance. For this reason, a marketer must carefully manage all the elements, especially those for service-based entities, which may not have been considered previously within his domain.

DIAGRAMMING MARKET ENTITIES

A simplified comparison demonstrates the conceptual usefulness of a molecular modeling system. In figure 1, automobiles and airline travel are broken down into their major elements. As shown, these two entities have different nuclei. They also differ in dominance.

Clearly, airline travel is intangible-dominant; that is, it does not yield physical ownership of a tangible good. Nearly all of the other important elements in the entity are intangible as well. Individual elements and their combinations represent unique satisfiers to different market segments. Thus:

- For some markets—students, for example—pure transport takes precedence over all other considerations. The charter flight business was based on this element. As might be expected during lean economic times, "no frills" flights show renewed emphasis on this nuclear core.
- For business travelers, on the other hand, schedule frequency may be paramount.
- Tourists, a third segment, may respond most strongly to the combination of in-flight and post-flight services.

As the market entity of airline travel has evolved, it has become more and more complex. Ongoing re-weighting of elements can be observed, for example, in the marketing of airline food, which was once a battleground of quasi-gourmet offerings. Today, some airlines have stopped marketing food altogether, while others are repositioning it primarily to the luxury markets.

Airlines vs. Automobiles

In comparing airlines to automobiles, one sees obvious similarities. The element of transportation is common to both, as it is to boats, trains, buses, and bicycles.

FIGURE 1
Diagram of Market Entities

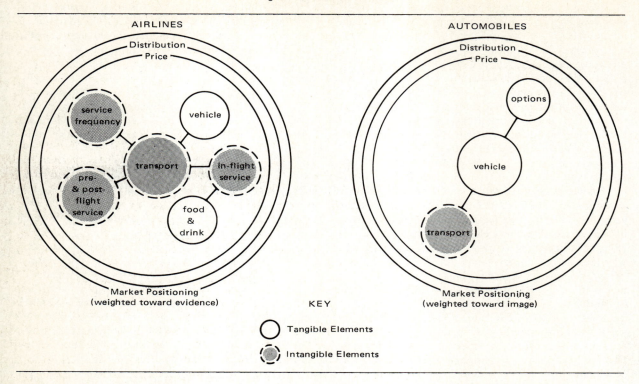

KEY

Tangible Elements

Intangible Elements

Tangible decor also plays a role in both entities. Yet in spite of their similarities, the two entities are not the same, either in configuration or in marketing implications.

In some ways, airline travel and automobiles are mirror opposites. A car is a physical possession that renders a service. Airline travel, on the other hand, cannot be physically possessed. It can only be experienced. While the inherent "promise" of a car is service, airline transportation often promises a Lewis Carroll version of "*product*," i.e., *destination,* which is marketed as though it were physically obtainable. If only tropical islands and redwood forests *could* be purchased for the price of an airline ticket!

The model can be completed by adding the remaining major marketing elements in a way that demonstrates their function vis-à-vis the organic core entity. First, the total entity is ringed and defined by a set value or price. Next, the valued entity is circumscribed by its distribution. Finally, the entire entity is encompassed, according to its core configuration, by its public "face," i.e., its positioning to the market.

The molecular concept makes it possible to describe and array market entities along a continuum, according to the weight of the "mix" of elements that comprise them. As figure 2 indicates, teaching services might be at one end of such a scale, *intangible or I-dominant,* while salt might represent the other extreme, *tangible or T-dominant.* Such a scale accords intangible-based entities a place and weight commensurate with their true importance. The framework also provides a mechanism for comparison and market positioning.

In one of the handful of books devoted to services, the author holds that "the more intangible the service, the greater will be the difference in the marketing characteristics of the service."[7] Consistent with an entity scale, this axiom might now be amended to read: *the greater the weight of intangible elements in a market entity, the greater will be the divergence from product marketing in priorities and approach.*

Implications of the Molecular Model

The hypothesis proposed by molecular modeling carries intriguing potential for rethinking and reshaping classic marketing concepts and practices. Recognition that service-dominant entities differ

FIGURE 2
Scale of Market Entities

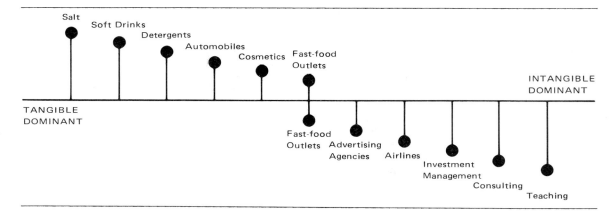

from product-dominant entities allows consideration of other distinctions which have been intuitively understood, but seldom articulated by service marketers.

A most important area of difference is immediately apparent—i.e., that service "knowledge" and product "knowledge" cannot be gained in the same way.

A *product* marketer's first task is to "know" his product. For tangible-dominant entities this is relatively straight-forward. A tangible object can be described precisely. It is subject to physical examination or photographic reproduction or quantitative measure. It can not only be exactly replicated, but also modified in precise and duplicate ways.

It is not particularly difficult for the marketer of *Coca-Cola,* for example, to summon all the facts regarding the product itself. He can and does make reasonable assumptions about the product's behavior, e.g., that it is consistent chemically to the taste, visually to the eye, and physically in its packaging. Any changes he might make in these three areas can be deliberately controlled for uniformity since they will be tangibly evident. In other words, the marketer can take the product's "reality" for granted and move on to considerations of price, distribution, and advertising or promotion.

To gain *service* "knowledge," however, or knowledge of a service element, where does one begin? It has been pointed out that intangible elements are dynamic, subjective, and ephemeral. They cannot be touched, tried on for size, or displayed on a shelf. They are exceedingly difficult to quantify.

Reverting to airline travel, precisely what *is* the service of air transportation to the potential purchaser? What "percent" of airline travel is comfort? What "percent" is fear or adventure? What *is* this

service's "reality" to its market? And how does that reality vary from segment to segment? Since this service exists only during the time in which it is rendered, the entity's true "reality" must be defined experientially, not in engineering terms.

A New Approach to Service Definition

Experiential definition is a little-explored area of marketing practice. A product-based marketer is in danger of assuming he understands an intangible-dominant entity when, in fact, he may only be projecting his *own* subjective version of "reality." And because there is no documented guidance on acquiring service-knowledge, the chances for error are magnified.

Case Example One short-lived mistake (with which the author is familiar) occurred recently in the trust department of a large commercial bank. The department head, being close to daily operations, understood "investment management" as the combined work of hundreds of people, backed by the firm's stature, resources, and long history. With this "reality" in mind, he concluded that the service could be better represented by professional salesmen, than through the traditional, but interruptive use of the portfolio manager as main client contact.

Three salesmen were hired, and given a training course in investments. They failed dismally, both in maintaining current client relationships and in producing new business for the firm. In hindsight, it became clear that the department head misunderstood the service's "reality" as it was being experienced by his clients. To the clients, "investment *management*" was found to mean "investment *manager*"—i.e., a single human being upon whom they depended for decisions and advice. No matter how well prepared, the professional salesman was not seen as an acceptable substitute by the majority of the market.

Visions of Reality   Clearly, more than one version of "reality" may be found in a service market. Therefore, the crux of service-knowledge is the description of the major *consensus realities* that define the service entity to various market segments. The determination of consensus realities should be a high priority for service marketers, and marketing should offer more concrete guidance and emphasis on this subject than it does.

To define the market-held "realities" of a service requires a high tolerance for subjective, "soft" data, combined with a rigidly objective attitude toward that data. To understand what a service entity is to a market, the marketer must undertake more initial research than is common in product marketing. More important, it will be research of a different kind than is the case in product marketing. The marketer must rely heavily on the tools and skills of psychology, sociology and other behavioral sciences—tools that in product marketing usually come into play in determining *image,* rather than fundamental "reality."

In developing the blueprint of a service entity's main elements, the marketer might find, for instance, that although tax return preparation is analogous to "accurate mathematical computation" within his firm, it means "freedom from responsibility" to one segment of the consuming public, "opportunity for financial savings" to another segment, and "convenience" to yet a third segment.

Unless these "realities" are documented and ranked by market importance, no sensible plan can be devised to represent a service effectively or deliberately. And in *new* service development, the importance of the service-research function is even more critical, because the successful development of a new service—a molecular collection of intangibles—is so difficult it makes new-product development look like child's play.

Image vs. Evidence—The Key

The definition of consensus realities should not be confused with the determination of "image." Image is a method of *differentiating* and *representing* an entity to its target market. Image is not "product," nor is it "service." As was suggested in figure 1, there appears to be a critical difference between the way tangible- and intangible-dominant entities are best represented to their markets. Examination of actual cases suggests a common thread among effective representations of services that is another mirror-opposite contrast to product techniques.

In comparing examples, it is clear that consumer product marketing often approaches the market by enhancing a physical object through abstract associations. *Coca-Cola,* for example, is surrounded with visual, verbal and aural associations with authenticity and youth. Although *Dr. Pepper* would also be physically categorized as a beverage, its *image* has been structured to suggest "originality" and "risk-taking;" while *7-Up* is "light" and "buoyant." A high priority is placed on linking these abstract images to physical items.

But a service is already abstract. To compound the abstraction dilutes the "reality" that the marketer is trying to enhance. Effective service representations appear to be turned $180°$ *away* from abstraction. The reason for this is that service images, and even service "realities," appear to be shaped to a large extent by the things that the consumer can comprehend with his five senses—tangible things. But a service itself cannot be tangible, so reliance must be placed on *peripheral* clues.

Tangible clues are what allow the detective in a mystery novel to surmise events at the scene of a crime without having been present. Similarly, when a consumer attempts to judge a service, particularly before using or buying it, that service is "known" by the tangible clues, the tangible evidence, that surround it.

The management of tangible evidence is not articulated in marketing as a primary priority for service marketers. There has been little in-depth exploration of the *range* of authority that emphasis on tangible evidence would create for the service marketer. In product marketing, tangible evidence is primarily the product itself. But for services, tangible evidence would encompass broader considerations in contrast to product marketing, *different* considerations than are typically considered marketing's domain today.

Focusing on the Evidence

In *product* marketing, many kinds of evidence are beyond the marketer's control and are consequently omitted from priority consideration in the market positioning process. Product marketing tends to give first emphasis to creating *abstract* associations.

Service marketers, on the other hand, should be focused on enhancing and differentiating "realities" through manipulation of *tangible* clues. The management of evidence comes first for service marketers, because service "reality" is arrived at by the consumer mostly through a process of deduction, based on the total impression that the evidence creates. Because of product marketing's biases, service marketers often fail to recognize the unique forms of evidence that they *can* normally control and fail to see that they should be part of marketing's responsibilities.

MANAGEMENT OF THE ENVIRONMENT

Environment is a good example. Since product distribution normally means shipping to outside agents, the marketer has little voice in structuring the environment in which the product is sold. His major controllable impact on the environment is usually product packaging. Services, on the other hand, are often fully integrated with environment; that is, the setting in which the service is "distributed" *is* controllable. To the extent possible, management of the physical environment should be one of a service marketer's highest priorities.

Setting can play an enormous role in influencing the "reality" of a service in the consumer's mind. Marketing does not emphasize this rule for services, yet there are numerous obvious examples of its importance.

Physicians' offices provide an interesting example of intuitive environmental management. Although the quality of medical service may be identical, an office furnished in teak and leather creates a totally different "reality" in the consumer's mind from one with plastic slipcovers and inexpensive prints. Carrying the example further, a marketer could expect to cause change in the service's image simply by painting a physician's office walls neon pink or silver, instead of white.

Similarly, although the services may be identical, the consumer's differentiation between "Bank A Service" and "Bank B Service" is materially affected by whether the environment is dominated by butcher-block and bright colors or by marble and polished brass.

By understanding the importance of evidence management, the service marketer can make it his business to review and take control of this critical part of his "mix." Creation of environment can be deliberate, rather than accidental or as a result of leaving such decisions in the hands of the interior decorators.

Integrating Evidence

Going beyond environment, evidence can be integrated across a wide range of items. Airlines, for example, manage and coordinate tangible evidence, and do it better than almost any large service industry.

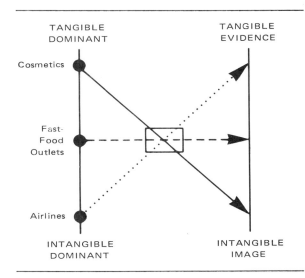

FIGURE 3
Principle of Market Positioning Emphasis

Whether by intuition or design, airlines do *not* focus attention on trying to explain or characterize the service itself. One never sees an ad that attempts to convey "the slant of takeoff," "the feel of acceleration," or "the aerodynamics of lift." Airline transport is given shape and form through consistency of a firm's identification, its uniforms, the decor of its planes, its graphics, and its advertising. Differentiation among airlines, though they all provide the same service, is a direct result of differences in "packages" of evidence.

Some businesses in which tangible and intangible elements carry equal weight emphasize abstractions and evidence in about equal proportions. McDonald's is an excellent example. The food *product* is associated with "nutritious" (two all-beef, etc.), "fun" (Ronald McDonald) and "helpful" ("We Do it All for You," "You Deserve a Break Today"). The main *service* element, i.e., fast food preparation, is tangibly distinguished by uniformity of environment, color, and style of graphics and apparel, consistency of delivery (young employees), and the ubiquitous golden arches.

Using the scale developed in figure 2, this concept can be postulated as a principle for service representation. As shown in figure 3, once an entity has been analyzed and positioned on the scale, the degree to which the marketer will focus on either tangible evidence or intangible abstractions for market positioning will be found to be *inversely related to the entity's dominance*.

The more intangible elements there are, the more the marketer must endeavor to stand in the consumer's shoes, thinking through and gaining control of *all* the inputs to the consumer's mind that can be classified as material evidence.

Some forms of evidence can seem trivial until one recognizes how great their impact can be on service perception. Correspondence is one example. Letters, statements, and the like are sometimes the main conveyers of the "reality" of a service to its market; yet often these are treated as peripheral to any marketing plan. From the grade of paper to the choice of colors, correspondence is visible evidence that conveys a unique message. A mimeographed, non-personalized, cheaply offset letter contradicts any words about service quality that may appear in the text of that letter. Conversely, engraved parchment from the local dry cleaner might make one wonder about their prices.

Profile as Evidence

As was pointed out in the investment management example, services are often inextricably entwined with their human representatives. In many fields, a person is perceived to *be* the service. The consumer cannot distinguish between them. Product marketing is myopic in dealing with the issue of *people as evidence* in terms of market positioning. Consumer marketing often stops at the production of materials and programs for salesmen to use. Some service industries, on the other hand, have long intuitively managed human evidence to larger ends.

Examples of this principle have been the basis for jokes, plays, and literature. "The Man in the Grey Flannel Suit," for example, was a synonym for the advertising business for many years. Physicians are uniformly "packaged" in smocks. Lawyers and bankers are still today known for pin-stripes and vests. IBM representatives were famous for adhering to a "White Shirt" policy. Going beyond apparel, as mentioned earlier, McDonald's even achieves age uniformity—an extra element reinforcing its total market image.

These examples add up to a serious principle when thoughtfully reviewed. They are particularly instructive for service marketers. None of the above examples were the result of deliberate market planning. McDonald's, for instance, backed into age consistency as a result of trying to keep labor costs low. Airlines are the single outstanding example of consciously-planned standards for uniformity in human representation. The power of the human evidence principle is obvious, and the potential power of more deliberately controlling or structuring this element is clear.

Lest this discussion be interpreted as an advocacy of regimentation, it should be pointed out that management of human evidence can be as basic as providing nametags to service representatives or as complex as the "packaging" of a political candidate, whose very words are often chosen by committee and whose hair style can become a critical policy issue. Or, depending upon what kind of service "reality" the marketer wishes to create, human representation can be encouraged to display *non*-conformity, as is the case with the "creative" departments of advertising agencies. The point is that service marketers should be charged with tactics and strategy in this area, and must consider it a management responsibility.

SERVICES AND THE MEDIA

As has been previously discussed, service elements are abstract. Because they are abstract, the marketer must work hard at making them "real," by building a case from tangible evidence. In this context, media advertising presents a particularly difficult problem.

The problem revolves around the fact that media (television, radio, print) are one step removed from tangibility. Media, by its McLuhanesque nature, abstracts the physical.

Even though product tangibility provides an anchor for media representation because a product can be *shown,* media still abstract products. A photograph is only a two-dimensional version of a physical object, and may be visually misleading. Fortunately, the consumer makes the mental connection between seeing a product in the media and recognizing it in reality. This is true even when a product is substantially distorted. Sometimes, only part of a product is shown. Occasionally, as in recent commercials for *7-Up,* the product is *not* shown. However, the consumer remembers past experience. He has little difficulty recognizing *7-Up* by name or remembered appearance when he sees it or wants to buy it.

Thus, media work *with* the creation of product image and *help* in adding abstract qualities to tangible goods. Cosmetics, for example, are often positioned in association with an airbrushed or soft-focus filmed *ideal* of beauty. Were the media truly accurate, the wrinkles and flaws of the flesh, to which even models are heir, might not create such an appealing product association.

Making Services More Concrete

Because of their abstracting capabilities, the media often make service entities more *hazy,* instead of more *concrete,* and the service marketer must work *against* this inherent effect. Unfortunately, many marketers are so familiar with product-oriented thinking that they go down precisely the wrong path and attempt to represent services by dealing with them in abstractions.

The pages of the business press are filled with examples of this type of misconception in services advertising. In advertisements for investment management, for instance, the worst examples attempt to describe the already intangible service with *more* abstractions such as "sound analysis," "careful portfolio monitoring," "strong research capability," etc. Such compounded abstractions do *not* help the consumer form a "reality," do *not* differentiate the service and do *not* achieve any credibility, much less any customer "draw."

The best examples are those which attempt to associate the service with some form of *tangible evidence,* working against the media's abstracting qualities. Merrill Lynch, for instance, has firmly associated itself with a clear visual symbol of bulls and concomitant bullishness. Where Merrill Lynch does not use the visual herd, it uses photographs of *tangible physical booklets,* and invites the consumer to write for them.

Therefore, the final principle offered for service marketers would hold that *effective media representation of intangibles is a function of establishing nonabstract manifestations of them.*

CONCLUSION

This article has presented several market-inspired thoughts toward the development of new marketing concepts, and the evolution of relevant service marketing principles. The hypotheses presented here do not by any means represent an exhaustive analysis of the subject. No exploration was done, for example, on product vs. service pricing or product vs. service distribution. Both areas offer rich potential for creative new approaches and analysis.

It can be argued that there are many grey areas in the molecular entity concept, and that diagramming and managing according to the multiple-elements schema could present considerable difficulties by virtue of its greater complexity. It might also be argued that some distinctions between tangible and intangible-dominant entities are so subtle as to be unimportant.

The fact remains that service marketers are in urgent need of concepts and priorities that are relevant to their actual experience and needs, and that marketing has failed in evolving to meet that demand. However unorthodox, continuing exploration of this area must be encouraged if marketing is to achieve stature and influence in the new post-Industrial Revolution services economy.

NOTES

1. See, for example, E. Jerome McCarthy, *Basic Marketing: A Managerial Approach,* 4th ed. (Homewood, IL: Richard D. Irwin, 1971) pg. 303 compared to William J. Stanton, *Fundamentals of Marketing,* 3rd ed. (New York: McGraw-Hill, 1971), pg. 567.

2. See William R. George and Hiram C. Barksdale, "Marketing Activities in the Service Industries," *Journal of Marketing,* Vol. 38 No. 4 (October 1974), pp. 65–70.

3. *The Meaning and Sources of Marketing Theory*—Marketing Science Institute Series (New York: McGraw-Hill, 1965), pg. 88.

4. *Webster's New Collegiate Dictionary* (Springfield, MA: G.&C. Merriam Company, 1974).

5. Philip Kotler, "A Generic Concept of Marketing," *Journal of Marketing,* Vol. 36 No. 2 (April 1972), pp. 46–54.

6. Theodore H. Levitt, "Marketing Myopia," *Harvard Business Review,* Vol. 38 (July-August 1960), pp. 45–46.

7. Aubrey Wilson, *The Marketing of Professional Services* (New York: McGraw-Hill, 1972), pg. 8.

John E. Smallwood

The Product Life Cycle: A Key to Strategic Marketing Planning

Modern marketing management today increasingly is being supported by marketing information services of growing sophistication and improving accuracy. Yet the task remains for the marketing manager to translate information into insights, insights into ideas, ideas into plans, and plans into reality and satisfactory programs and profits. Among marketing managers there is a growing realization of the need for concepts, perspectives, and for constructs that are useful in translating information into profits. While information flow can be mechanized and the screening of ideas routinized, no alternative to managerial creativity has yet been found to generate valuable marketing ideas upon which whole marketing programs can be based. The concept of the product life cycle has been extremely useful in focusing this creative process.

The product life cycle concept in many ways may be considered to be the marketing equivalent of the periodic table of the elements concept in the physical sciences; like the periodic table, it provides a framework for grouping products into families for easier predictions of reactions to various stimuli. With chemicals—it is a question of oxidation temperature and melting point; with products—it is marketing channel acceptance and advertising budgets. Just as like chemicals react in similar ways, so do like products. The product life cycle helps to group these products into homogeneous families.

The product life cycle can be the key to successful and profitable product management, from the introduction of new products to profitable disposal of obsolescent products. The fundamental concept of the product life cycle (PLC) is illustrated in figure 1.

Source: From *MSU Business Topics,* Winter 1973, pp. 29–35. Reprinted by permission of the Graduate School of Business, Michigan State University.

In application, the vertical scale often is measured in saturation of the product (percentage of customer units using), while the horizontal scale is calibrated to represent the passage of time. Months or years are usually the units of time used in calibration, although theoretically, an application along the same concept of much shorter or longer durations (milliseconds in physical sciences, millenia in archaeology) might be found. In figure 1 the breakdown in the time scale is shown by stages in the maturity of product life. The saturation scale, however, is a guide only and must be used accordingly. When comparing one product with another, it is sometimes best treated by use of qualitative terms, not quantitative units. It is important to the user of the product life cycle concept that this limitation be recognized and conceptual provisions be made to handle it. For example, if the basic marketing unit chosen is "occupied U.S. households," one cannot expect a product such as room air conditioners to attain 100 percent saturation. This is because many households already have been fitted with central air conditioning; thus, the potential saturation attainment falls well short of 100 percent of the marketing measurement chosen.

To overcome this difficulty, marketing managers have two basic options. They can choose a more restrictive, specific marketing unit such as "all occupied U.S. households that do not have forced air heating"; homes without forced air heating are unlikely candidates for central air conditioning. It can be anticipated that room air conditioners will saturate not only *that* market, but portions of other markets as well. On the other hand, on the basis of informed judgment, management can determine the *potential* saturation of total households and convert the PLC growth scale to a measurement representing the degree of attainment of potential saturation in U.S. households. The author has found the latter approach to be the more useful one. By this device, automatic washers are considered to be at 100 percent saturation when they are at their full potential of an arbitrarily chosen 80 percent.

Consider figure 1, where various products are shown positioned by life cycle stages: the potential saturations permit the grouping of products into like stages of life cycle, even when their actual saturation attainments are dissimilar. One can note that in figure 1 automatic washers (which are estimated at 58 percent saturation) and room air conditioners (30 percent) are positioned in the same growth stage in figure 1; freezers (29 percent) and refrigerators (99 percent), on the other hand, are in the maturity stage. This occurs because, *in our judgment,* freezers have a potential of only about one-third of "occupied households" and thus have attained almost 90 percent of

FIGURE 1
Life Cycle Stages of Various Products

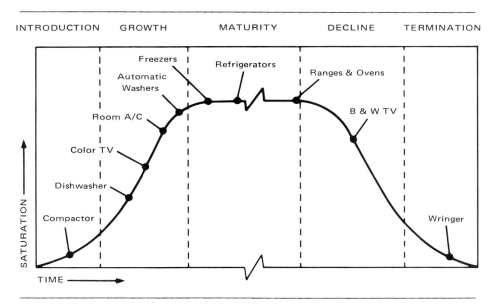

that market. Automatic clothes washers, however, have a potential of about four-fifths of the occupied households and at about 70 percent of their potential still show some of the characteristics of the growth stage of the PLC. General characteristics of the products and their markets are summarized in figure 2.

The product life cycle concept is illustrated as a convenient scheme of product classification. The PLC permits management to assign given products to the appropriate stages of acceptance by a given market; *introduction, growth, maturity, decline,* and *termination.* The actual classification of products by appropriate stages, however, is more art than science. The whole process is quite imprecise; but unsatisfactory as this may be, a useful classification can be achieved with management benefits that are clearly of value. This can be illustrated by examining the contribution of the PLC concept in the following marketing activities: sales forecasting, advertising, pricing, and marketing planning.

APPLICATIONS OF THE PLC TO SALES FORECASTING

One of the most dramatic uses of the PLC in sales forecasting was its application in explaining the violent decline in sales of color TV during the credit crunch recession of 1969–70. This occurred after the experience of the 1966–67 mini-recession which had almost no effect on color TV sales that could be discerned through the usual "noise" of the available product flow data. A similar apparent insensitivity was demonstrated in 1958, in 1961, and again in 1966–67, with sales of portable dishwashers. However, it too was followed by a noticeable sales reduction in the 1969–71 period, with annual factory shipments as shown in figure 3.

In early 1972 sales of both portable dishwashers and color TV sets showed a positive response to an improving economic climate, raising the question as to why both products had become vulnerable to economic contractions after having shown a great degree of independence of the business cycle during previous years. The answer to the question seems to lie in their stage in the product life cycle. In comparing the saturation of color TV and dishwashers, as shown in figure 3, consider first the case of color TV sales.

We can ascertain that as late as 1966, saturation of color TV was approximately 8 percent. By late in 1969, however, saturation had swiftly increased to nearly 40 percent.

The same observation is true in the case of dishwashers—considered a mass market appliance only since 1965. This is the key to the explanation of both situations. At the early, introductory stages of their

FIGURE 2
Product Life Cycle

	Introduction	Growth	Maturity	Decline	Termination
MARKETING					
Customers	Innovative/ High Income	High Income/ Mass Market	Mass Market	Laggards/ Special	Few
Channels	Few	Many	Many	Few	Few
Approach	Product	Label	Label	Specialized	Availability
Advertising	Awareness	Label Superiority	Lowest Price	Psychographic	Sparse
Competitors	Few	Many	Many	Few	Few
PRICING					
Price	High	Lower	Lowest	Rising	High
Gross Margins	High	Lower	Lowest	Low	Rising
Cost Reductions	Few	Many	Slower	None	None
Incentives	Channel	Channel/ Consumer	Consumer/ Channel	Channel	Channel
PRODUCT					
Configuration	Basic	Second Generation	Segmented/ Sophisticated	Basic	Stripped
Quality	Poor	Good	Superior	Spotty	Minimal
Capacity	Over	Under	Optimum	Over	Over

life cycles, both appliances were making large sales gains as the result of being adopted by consumers with high incomes. Later, when sales growth depended more upon adoption by the less affluent members of the mass market whose spending plans are modified by general economic conditions, the product sales began to correlate markedly to general economic circumstances.

It appears that big ticket consumer durables such as television sets and portable dishwashers tend to saturate as a function of customer income. This fact is illustrated by the data displayed in figure 4, concerning refrigerators and compactors, where one can note the logical relationship between the two products as to the economic status of their most important customers and as to their position in the product life cycle. The refrigerator is a mature product while the compactor is the newest product in the major appliance family.

The refrigerator once was in the introduction stage and had marketing attributes similar to the compactor. The refrigerator's present marketing characteristics are a good guide to proper expectations for the compactor as it matures from the *introductory* stage through *growth* to *maturity*. One can anticipate that the compactor, the microwave oven, and even nondurables such as good quality wines, will someday be included in the middle income consumption patterns, and we will find their sales to be much more coincident with general economic cycles.

PRODUCT LIFE STAGES AND ADVERTISING

The concept of a new product filtering through income classes, combined with long-respected precepts of advertising, can result in new perspectives for marketing managers. The resulting observations are both strategic and tactical. New advertising objectives and

FIGURE 3
Effect of Recession on Product Sales

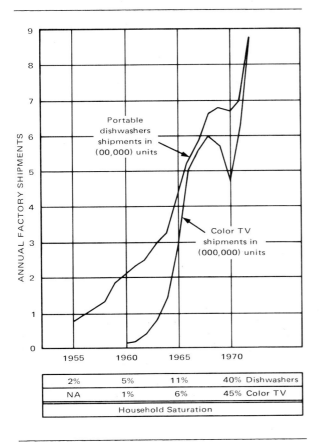

2%	5%	11%	40% Dishwashers
NA	1%	6%	45% Color TV
Household Saturation			

Sources: AHAM, EIA, Census

other "inferior" substitutes while, at the same time, to provide a rationalization that this purchase is not merely a wasteful, luxury indulging activity but that it will make the consumer a better *something*, a better husband, mother, accountant, driver, and so forth.

Phase 3

Maturity. A new rationalization, respectability, is added, besides an intensification of brand superiority ("don't buy substitutes; get the real *XYZ* original which incidentally, is *new* and *improved...*"). To a great extent, the *product* registration is dropped. Respectability is a strong requisite of the American lower class, which in this phase is the economic stratum containing the most important opportunities for sales gains. Companies do not abandon higher income customers, but they now match advertising to a variety of market segments instead of concentrating on only one theme for the market. Several distinct advertising programs are used. All elements of the marketing mix—product, price, sales promotion, advertising, trading and physical distribution channels—are focused on specific market segments.

Phase 4

Decline. Superior substitutes for a product generally will be adopted first by the people who before were the first to adopt the product in consideration. These people usually are from the upper economic and social classes. Advertising themes reflect this situation when they concentrate on special market segments such as West Coast families or "consumption societies" such as beer drinkers or apartment dwellers.

PRODUCT LIFE STAGES AND PRICING

As a product progresses through all five stages of the life cycle shown in figure 1, the price elasticity can be expected to undergo dramatic changes. Generally speaking, price elasticity of a relatively simple product will be low at first. Thus, when customers are drawn from the higher income classes, demand is relatively inelastic. Later, when most customers are in the lower income categories, greater price elasticity will exist.

Of course, increased price elasticity will not automatically lower prices during the growth stage of the PLC. It is in this growth stage, however, that per unit costs *are* most dramatically reduced because of the effect of the learning curve in engineering, production, and marketing. Rising volume and, more important, the *forecasts* of higher volumes, justify increased capital investments and higher fixed costs, which when

new insights for copy points and media selection may be realized. Consider the advertising tasks by the following phases:

Phase 1

Introduction. The first objective is to make the best customer prospects aware that the new product or service is now available; to tell him what it does, what are the benefits, why claims are to be believed, and what will be the conditions of consumption.

Phase 2

Growth. The next objective is to saturate the mass market with the same selling points as used in Phase 1. In addition, it is to recognize that a particular brand of the product is clearly superior to

FIGURE 4
Purchase Patterns
(by age and income of households)

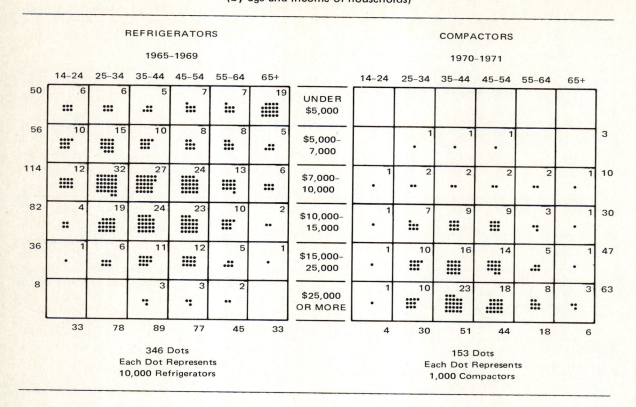

346 Dots
Each Dot Represents
10,000 Refrigerators

153 Dots
Each Dot Represents
1,000 Compactors

spread over a larger number of units, thereby reduce unit costs markedly. New competitors surface with great rapidity in this stage as profits tend to increase dramatically.

Pricing in the mature phase of the PLC usually is found to be unsatisfactory, with no one's profit margins as satisfactory as before. Price competition is keener within the distribution channel in spite of the fact that relatively small price differences seldom translate into any change in aggregate consumer activity.

PRODUCT PLANNING AND THE PLC

Curiously enough, the very configuration of the product takes on a classical pattern of evolution as it advances through the PLC. At first, the new device is designed for function alone; the initial design is sometimes crude by standards that will be applied in the future. As the product maturation process continues, performance sophistication increases. Eventually the product develops to the point where competitors are hardpressed to make meaningful differences which are perceptible to consumers.

As the product progresses through the product life cycle these modifications tend to describe a pattern of metamorphosis from "the ugly box" to a number of options. The adjustment cycle includes:

Part of house: the built-in look and function. Light fixtures, cooking stoves, wall safes, and furnaces are examples.

Furniture: a blending of the product into the home decor. This includes television, hi-fi consoles, radios, clocks, musical instruments, game tables, and so forth.

Portability: a provision for increased *presence* of the product through provisions for easier movement (rollers or compactness), or multiple unit ownership (wall clocks, radios, even refrigerators), or miniaturization for portability. Portability and *personalization*, such as the pocket knife and the wristwatch, can occur.

System: a combination of components into one

unit with compatible uses and/or common parts for increased convenience, lower cost, or less space. Home entertainment centers including television, radio, hi-fi, refrigerator-freezers, combination clothes washer dryers, clock radios, pocket knife-can-and-bottle openers are illustrative.

Similar changes can also be observed in the distribution channel. Products often progress from specialty outlets in the introductory stage to mass distribution outlets such as discount houses and contract buyers during the "maturity" and "decline" phases of the PLC. Interestingly enough, the process eventually is reversed. Buggy whips can still be found in some specialty stores and premium prices are paid for replicas of very old products.

CONCLUSION

The product life cycle is a useful concept. It is the equivalent of the periodic table of the elements in the physical sciences. The maturation of production technology and product configuration along with marketing programs proceeds in an orderly, somewhat predictable, course over time with the merchandising nature and marketing environment noticeably similar between products that are in the same stage of their life cycle. Its use as a concept in forecasting, pricing, advertising, product planning, and other aspects of marketing management can make it a valuable concept, although considerable amounts of judgment must be used in its application.

R. S. Alexander

The Death and Burial of "Sick" Products

Euthanasia applied to human beings is criminal; but aging products enjoy or suffer no such legal protection. This is a sad fact of business life.

The word "product" is used here not in its broad economic sense of anything produced—such as wheat, coal, a car, or a chair—but in its narrower meaning of an article made to distinct specifications and intended for sale under a separate brand or catalogue number. In the broader sense of the word, certain products may last as long as industrial civilization endures; in the narrow sense, most of them are playthings of change.

Much has been written about managing the development and marketing of new products, but business literature is largely devoid of material on product deletion.

This is not surprising. New products have glamor. Their management is fraught with great risks. Their

Source: From the *Journal of Marketing,* Vol. 28 (April 1964), pp. 1–7. Reprinted by permission of the American Marketing Association.

successful introduction promises growth in sales and profits that may be fantastic.

But putting products to death—or letting them die —is a drab business, and often engenders much of the sadness of a final parting with old and tried friends. "The portable 6-sided, pretzel polisher was the first product The Company ever made. Our line will no longer be our line without it."

But while deletion is an uninspiring and depressing process, in a changing market it is almost as vital as the addition of new products. The old product that is a "football" of competition or has lost much of its market appeal is likely to generate more than its share of small unprofitable orders; to make necessary short, costly production runs; to demand an exorbitant amount of executive attention; and to tie up capital that could be used more profitably in other ventures.

Just as a crust of barnacles on the hold of a ship retards the vessel's movement, so do a number of worn-out items in a company's product mix affect the company's progress.

Most of the costs that result from the lack of an effective deletion system are hidden and become apparent only after careful analysis. As a result, management often overlooks them. The need for examining the product line to discover outworn members, and for analysis to arrive at intelligent decisions to discard or to keep them, very rarely assumes the urgency of a crisis. Too often, management thinks of this as something that should be done but that can wait until tomorrow.

This is why a definite procedure for deletion of products should be set up, and why the authority and responsibility for the various activities involved should be clearly and definitely assigned. This is especially important because this work usually requires the cooperation of several functional groups within the business firm, including at least marketing, production, finance, and sometimes personnel.

Definite responsibility should be assigned for at least the following activities involved in the process: (1) selecting products which are candidates for elimination; (2) gathering information about them and analyzing the information; (3) making decisions about elimination; and (4) if necessary, removing the doomed products from the line.

SELECTION OF PRODUCTS
FOR POSSIBLE ELIMINATION

As a first step, we are not seeking the factors on which the final decision to delete or to retain turns, but merely those which indicate that the product's continuation in the product mix should be considered carefully with elimination as a possibility. Although removal from the product line may seem to be the prime aim, the result is not inevitably deletion from the line; instead, careful analysis may lead to changes in the product itself or in the methods of making or marketing it.

Sales Trend. If the trend of a product's sales is downward over a time period that is significant in relation to the normal life of others like it, its continuation in the mix deserves careful examination. There may be many reasons for such a decline that in no way point toward deletion; but when decline continues over a period of time the situation needs to be studied.

Price Trend. A downward trend in the price of a new product may be expected if the firm introducing it pursues a skimming-price policy, or if all firms making it realize substantial cost savings as a result of volume production and increased processing know-how. But when the price of an established product whose competitive pattern has been relatively stabilized shows a downward trend over a significant period of time, the future of that product should receive attention.

Profit Trend. A declining profit either in dollars or as a per cent of sales or investment should raise questions about a product's continued place in the product line. Such a trend usually is the result of a price-factory cost squeeze, although it may be the outcome of a loss in market appeal or a change in the method of customer purchase which forces higher marketing expenditures.

Substitute Products. When a substitute article appears on the market, especially if it represents an improvement over an old product, management must face the question of whether to retain or discard the old product. This is true regardless of who introduces the substitute. The problem is especially difficult when the new product serves the same general purpose as the old one but is not an exact substitute for it.

Product Effectiveness. Certain products may lose some of their effectiveness for the purposes they serve. For example, disease germs may develop strains that are resistant to a certain antibiotic. When this happens, the question of whether to keep or delete the drug involves issues not only of the interests of the firm but of the public welfare.

Executive Time. A possible tipoff as to the location of "illness" in a product mix lies in a study of the amount of executive time and attention devoted to each of the items in the product line. Sick products, like sick people, demand a lot of care; but one must be careful to distinguish the "growing pains" of a new product from the more serious disorders of one that has matured and is now declining.

The six indicators mentioned do not of themselves provide evidence justifying deletion. But they can help management to single out from a line of products those upon which it can profitably spend time and money in analyzing them, with elimination from the line as a *possibility.*

ANALYSIS AND DECISION MAKING
ABOUT "SICK" PRODUCTS

Although the work of analyzing a sick or decrepit product is usually done by people other than the management executives who decide what to do about it, the two processes are interdependent. Unless the right factors are chosen for analysis and unless the work is properly done, the decision is not likely to be an intelligent one. Accordingly, these two factors will be discussed together.

What information does a decision-maker need about a product, and what sort of analysis of it should he have in order to render a sound verdict as to its future? The deletion decision should not turn on the sole issue of profitability. Profit is the most important objective of a business; but individual firms often seek to achieve both long-run and short-run objectives other than profit.

So, in any individual case the critical factors and the weights assigned them in making a decision must be chosen in the light of the situation of the firm and the management objectives.

Profits

Profit management in a firm with a multi-product line (the usual situation in our economy) is not the simple operation generally contemplated in economic theory. Such a firm usually has in its product mix (1) items in various stages of introduction and development, some of which may be fantastically profitable and others deep "in the red"; (2) items which are mature but not "superannuated," whose profit rate is likely to be satisfactory; and (3) declining items which may yield a net profit somewhat less than adequate or may show heavy losses.

The task is to manage the whole line or mix so that it will show a satisfactory profit for the company. In this process, two questions are vital; What is a profit? How much profit is satisfactory?

Operating-statement accounting makes it possible to determine with reasonable accuracy the total amount of net profit a company earns on an overall basis. But when the management of a multi-product firm seeks to determine how much of this total is generated by its activities in making and marketing each product in its mix, the process is almost incredibly complex; and the results are almost certain to be conditioned on a tissue of assumptions which are so debatable that no management can feel entirely comfortable in basing decisions on them.

This is because such a large portion of the costs of the average multi-product firm are or behave like overhead or joint expense. Almost inevitably several of the items in the product mix are made of common materials, with the same equipment, and by manpower which is interchangeable. Most of the company's marketing efforts and expenses are devoted to selling and distributing the mix or a line within the mix, rather than individual items.

In general, the more varied the product mix of a firm, the greater is the portion of its total expense that must be classified as joint or overhead. In such a company, many types of cost which ordinarily can be considered direct tend to behave like overhead or joint expenses. This is particularly true of marketing costs such as advertising that does not feature specific items; personal selling; order handling; and delivery.

This means that a large part of a company's costs must be assigned to products on some arbitrary basis and that however logical this basis may be, it is subject to considerable reasonable doubt in specific cases. It also means that if one product is removed from the mix, many of these costs remain to be reassigned to the items that stay in the line. As a result, any attempt to "prune" the product mix entirely on the basis of

the profit contribution, or lack of it, of specific items is almost certain to be disappointing and in some cases disastrous.

But if a multi-product firm could allocate costs to individual items in the mix on some basis recognized as sound and thus compute product-profit accurately, what standard of profit should be set up, the failure to meet which would justify deletion?

Probably most managements either formally or unconsciously set overall company profit targets. Such targets may be expressed in terms of dollars, although to be most useful in product management they usually must be translated into percentages on investment, or money used. As an example, a company may have as its profit target 15 percent on investment before taxes.

Certainly *every* product in the mix should not be required to achieve the target, which really amounts to an average. To do so would be to deny the inevitable variations in profit potential among products.

Probably a practical minimum standard can be worked out, below which a product should be eliminated unless other considerations demand its retention. Such a standard can be derived from a balancing out of the profit rates among products in the mix, so as to arrive at the overall company target as an average. The minimum standard then represents a figure that would tip the balance enough to endanger the overall target.

What role, then, should considerations of product profit play in managerial decisions as to deletion or retention?

1. Management probably will be wise to recognize an overall company target profit in dollars or rate on investment, and to set in relation to it a minimum below which the profit on an individual product should not fall without marking that item for deletion (unless other special considerations demand its retention).

2. Management should cast a "bilious eye" on all arguments that a questionable product be kept in the mix because it helps to defray overhead and joint costs. Down that road, at the end of a series of decisions to retain such products, lies a mix entirely or largely composed of items each busily "sopping up" overhead, but few or none contributing anything to net profit.

3. This does not mean that management should ignore the effect of a product deletion on overhead or joint costs. Decision-makers must be keenly aware of the fact that the total of such costs borne

by a sick product must, after it is deleted, be reallocated to other products, and with the result that they may become of doubtful profitability. A detailed examination of the joint or overhead costs charged against an ailing product may indicate that some of them can be eliminated in whole or in part if it is eliminated. Such costs are notoriously "sticky" and difficult to get rid of; but every pretext should be used to try to find ways to reduce them.

4. If a deletion decision involves a product or a group of products responsible for a significant portion of a firm's total sales volume, decision-makers can assess the effects of overhead and joint costs on the problem, by compiling an estimated company operating statement after the deletion and comparing it with the current one. Such a forecasted statement should include expected net income from the use of the capital and facilities released by deletion if an opportunity for their use is ready to hand. Surviving joint and overhead expenses can even be reallocated to the remaining products, in order to arrive at an estimate of the effect that deletion might have, not only on the total company net income but on the profitability of each of the remaining products as well. Obviously such a cost analysis is likely to be expensive, and so is not justified unless the sales volume stakes are high.

Financial Considerations

Deletion is likely not only to affect the profit performance of a firm but to modify its financial structure as well.

To make and sell a product, a company must invest some of its capital. In considering its deletion, the decision-makers must estimate what will happen to the capital funds presently used in making and marketing it.

When a product is dropped from the mix, most or all of the circulating capital invested in it—such as inventories of materials, goods in process, and finished goods and accounts receivable—should drain back into the cash account; and if carried out in an orderly fashion, deletion will not disturb this part of the capital structure except to increase the ratio of cash to other assets.

This will be true, unless the deletion decision is deferred until product deterioration has gone so far that the decision assumes the aspect of a crisis and its execution that of a catastrophe.

The funds invested in the equipment and other facilities needed to make and market the "sick" product are a different matter. If the equipment is versatile and standard, it may be diverted to other uses. If the firm has no need of it and if the equipment has been properly depreciated, management may find a market for it at a price approaching or even exceeding its book value.

In either case, the capital structure of the company is not disturbed except by a shift from equipment to cash in the case of sale. In such a case management would be wise, before making a deletion decision, to determine how much cash this action promises to release as well as the chances for its reinvestment.

If the equipment is suited for only one purpose, it is highly unlikely that management can either find another use for it or sell it on favorable terms. If it is old and almost completely depreciated, it can probably be scrapped and its remaining value "written off" without serious impairment of the firm's capital structure.

But if it is only partly depreciated, the decision-makers must weigh the relative desirability of two possible courses of action: (1) to delete immediately, hoping that the ensuing improvement in the firm's operating results will more than offset the impairment in capital structure that deletion will cause; or (2) to seek to recapture as much as possible of its value, by continuing to make and market the product as long as its price is enough to cover out-of-pocket costs and leave something over to apply to depreciation.

This choice depends largely on two things: the relation between the amount of fixed and circulating capital that is involved; and the opportunities available to use the funds, executive abilities, manpower, and transferable facilities released by deletion for making profits in other ventures.

This matter of opportunity costs is a factor in every deletion decision. The dropping of a product is almost certain to release some capital, facilities, manpower skills, and executive abilities. If opportunities can be found in which these assets can be invested without undue risk and with promise of attractive profits, it may be good management to absorb considerable immediate loss in deleting a sick product.

If no such opportunities can be found, it is probably wise to retain the product so long as the cash inflow from its sales covers out-of-pocket costs and contributes something to depreciation and other overhead expenses. In such a case, however, it is the part of good management to seek actively for new ventures which promise satisfactory profits, and to be ready to delete promptly when such an opportunity is found.

Employee Relations

The effect which product elimination may have on the employees of a firm is often an important factor in decisions either to drop or to retain products.

This is not likely to be a deciding factor if new product projects are under development to which the people employed in making and marketing the doubtful product can be transferred, unless such transfer would deprive them of the earning power of special skills. But when deletion of a product means discharging or transferring unionized employees, the decision-makers must give careful thought to the effect their action is likely to have on company-union relations.

Even in the absence of union pressure, management usually feels a strong sense of responsibility for the people in its employ. Just how far management can go in conserving specific jobs at the expense of deferring or foregoing necessary deletions before it endangers the livelihood of all the employees of the firm is a nice question of balance.

Marketing Factors

Many multi-product firms retain in their marketing mixes one or more items which, on the basis of profits and the company financial structure, should be deleted. To continue to make and market a losing product is no managerial crime. It is reprehensible only when management does not know the product is a losing one or, knowing the facts, does not have sound reasons for retaining it. Such reasons are very likely to lie in the marketing area.

Deletions of products are often deferred or neglected because of management's desire to carry a "full line," whatever that means. This desire may be grounded on sound reasons of consumer patronage or on a dubious yearning for the "prestige" that a full line is supposed to engender. But there is no magic about a full line or the prestige that is supposed to flow from it. Both should be evaluated on the basis of their effects on the firm's sales volume, profits, and capacity to survive and grow.

Products are often associated in the marketing process. The sale of one is helped by the presence of another in the product mix.

When elimination of a product forces a customer who buys all or a large part of his requirements of a group of profitable items from the firm to turn to another supplier for his needs of the dropped product, he might shift some or all of his other patronage as well. Accordingly, it is sometimes wise for management to retain in its mix a no-profit item, in order to

hold sales volume of highly profitable products. But this should not be done blindly without analysis.

Rarely can management tell ahead of time exactly how much other business will be lost by deleting a product, or in what proportions the losses will fall among the remaining items. But in many cases the amount of sales volume can be computed that will be *hazarded* by such action; what other products will be subject to that hazard; and what portion of their volume will be involved. When this marketing interdependence exists in a deletion problem, the decision-makers should seek to discover the customers who buy the sick product; what other items in the mix they buy; in what quantities; and how much profit they contribute.

The firm using direct marketing channels can do this with precision and at relatively little cost. The firm marketing through indirect channels will find it more difficult, and the information will be less exact; but it still may be worth-while. If the stakes are high enough, marketing research may be conducted to discover the extent to which the customer purchases of profitable items actually are associated with that of the sick product. Although the results may not be precise, they may supply an order-of-magnitude idea of the interlocking patronage situation.

Product interrelationships in marketing constitute a significant factor in making deletion decisions, but should never be accepted as the deciding factor without careful study to disclose at least the extent of the hazards they involve.

Other Possibilities

The fact that a product's market is declining or that its profit performance is substandard does not mean that deletion is the *only* remedy.

Profits can be made in a shrinking market. There are things other than elimination of a product that can be done about deteriorating profit performance. They tend to fall into four categories.

1. *Costs.* A careful study may uncover ways of reducing factory costs. This may result from improved processes that either eliminate manpower or equipment time or else increase yield; or from the elimination of forms or features that once were necessary or worth-while but are no longer needed. The natural first recourse of allocating joint and overhead costs on a basis that is "kinder" to the doubtful product is not to be viewed with enthusiasm. After reallocation, these costs still remain in the business; and the general profit picture has not been improved in the least.

2. *Marketing.* Before deleting a product, management will be wise to examine the methods of market-

ing it, to see if they can be changed to improve its profit picture.

Can advertising and sales effort be reduced without serious loss of volume? A holding operation requires much less effort and money than a promotional one.

Are services being given that the product no longer needs?

Can savings be made in order handling and delivery, even at some loss of customer satisfaction? For example, customers may be buying the product in small orders that are expensive to handle.

On the other hand, by spending more marketing effort, can volume be increased so as to bring about a reduction in factory cost greater than the added marketing expense? In this attempt, an unexpected "assist" may come from competitors who delete the product and leave more of the field to the firm.

By remodeling the product, "dressing it up," and using a new marketing approach, can it be brought back to a state of health and profit? Here the decision-makers must be careful not to use funds and facilities that could be more profitably invested in developing and marketing new products.

3. *Price.* It is natural to assume that the price of a failing product cannot be raised. At least in part, its plight is probably due to the fact that it is "kicked around" by competition, and thus that competition will not allow any increases.

But competitors may be tired of the game, too. One company that tried increasing prices found that wholesalers and retailers did not resent a larger cost-of-goods-sold base on which to apply their customary gross profit rates, and that consumers continued to buy and competitors soon followed suit.

Although a price rise will not usually add to the sum total of user happiness, it may not subtract materially from total purchases. The decision-makers should not ignore the possibility of using a price reduction to gain enough physical volume to bring about a more-than-offsetting decline in unit costs, although at this stage the success of such a gambit is not likely.

4. *Cross Production.* In the materials field, when small production runs make costs prohibitive, arrangements may sometimes be made for Firm A to make the *entire* supply of Product X for itself and Competitor B. Then B reciprocates with another similar product. Such "trades," for instance, are to be found in the chemical business.

Summation for Decision

In solving deletion problems, the decision-makers must draw together into a single pattern the results of the analysis of all the factors bearing on the matter. Although this is probably most often done on an intangible, subjective basis, some firms have experimented with the formula method.

For example, a manufacturer of electric motors included in its formula the following factors:

Profitability

Position of growth curve

Product leadership

Market position

Marketing dependence of other products

Each factor was assigned a weight in terms of possible "counts" against the product. For instance, if the doubtful item promised no profits for the next three years, it had a count of 50 points against it, while more promising prospects were assigned lesser counts. A critical total for all factors was set in advance which would automatically doom a product. Such a system can include other factors—such as recapturability of invested capital, alternate available uses of facilities, effects on labor force, or other variables peculiar to the individual case.

The use of a formula lends an aura of precision to the act of decision-making and assures a degree of uniformity in it. But obviously the weights assigned to different factors cannot be the same in all cases. For example, if the deletion of a doubtful product endangers a large volume of sales of other highly profitable items, that alone should probably decide the matter.

The same thing is true if deletion will force so heavy a writeoff of invested funds as to impair the firm's capital structure. Certainly this will be true if all or most of the investment can be recaptured by the depreciation route if the product stays in the mix.

This kind of decision requires that the factors be weighted differently in each case. But when managers are given a formula, they may tend to quit thinking and do too much "weighing."

THE DELETION OF A PRODUCT

Once the decision to eliminate a product is made, plans must be drawn for its death and burial with the least disturbance of customer relations and of the other operations of the firm.

Such plans must deal with a variety of detailed problems. Probably the most important fall into four categories: timing; parts and replacements; stocks; and holdover demand.

Timing. It is desirable that deletion be timed so as to dovetail with the financial, manpower, and facilities needs for new products. As manpower and facilities are released from the dying product and as the capital devoted to it flows back into the cash account, it is ideal if these can be immediately used in a new venture. Although this can never be completely achieved, it may be approximated.

The death of a product should be timed so as to cause the least disturbance to customers. They should be informed about the elimination of the product far enough in advance so they can make arrangements for replacement, if any are available, but not so far in advance that they will switch to new suppliers before the deleting firm's inventories of the product are sold. Deletion at the beginning of a selling season or in the middle of it probably will create maximum customer inconvenience, whereas at the end of the season it will be the least disturbing.

Parts and Replacements. If the product to be killed off is a durable one, probably the deleting firm will find it necessary to maintain stocks of repair parts for about the expected life of the units most recently sold. The firm that leaves a trail of uncared-for "orphan" products cannot expect to engender much good will from dealers or users. Provision for the care and maintenance of the orphan is a necessary cost of deletion.

This problem is much more widespread than is commonly understood. The woman who buys a set of china or silverware and finds that she cannot replace broken or lost pieces does not entertain an affectionate regard for the maker. The same sort of thing is true if she installs draperies and later, when one of them is damaged, finds that the pattern is no longer available.

Stocks. The deletion plan should provide for clearing out the stocks of the dying product and materials used in its production, so as to recover the maximum amount of the working capital invested in it. This is very largely a matter of timing—the tapering off of purchase, production, and selling activities. However, this objective may conflict with those of minimizing inconvenience to customers and servicing the orphan units in use after deletion.

Holdover Demand. However much the demand for a product may decline, it probably will retain some following of devoted users. They are bound to be disturbed by its deletion and are likely to be vocal about it; and usually there is little that management can do to mitigate this situation.

Sometimes a firm can avoid all these difficulties by finding another firm to purchase the product. This should usually be tried before any other deletion steps are taken. A product with a volume too small for a big firm to handle profitably may be a money-maker for a smaller one with less overhead and more flexibility.

NEGLECT OR ACTION?

The process of product deletion is important. The more dynamic the business, the more important it is.

But it is something that most company executives prefer not to do; and therefore it will not get done unless management establishes definite, clearcut policies to guide it, sets up carefully articulated procedures for doing it, and makes a positive and unmistakable assignment of authority and responsibility for it.

Exactly what these policies should be, what form these procedures should take, and to whom the job should be assigned are matters that must vary with the structure and operating methods of the firm and with its position in the industry and the market.

In any case, though, the need for managerial attention, planning, and supervision of the deletion function cannot be overemphasized. Many business firms are paying dearly for their neglect of this problem, but unfortunately do not realize how much this is costing them.

CASES

TREE TOP SKI RESORT

Tree Top Ski Resort is a privately owned ski area in northwestern Colorado. To assess and systemize its development, the management commissioned a consulting team to recommend future additions and changes to its facilities. From its beginnings, Tree Top Ski Resort has maintained a family atmosphere and has emphasized this through available facilities and promotional efforts.

GILLETTE COMPANY

In 1978, the brand manager responsible for TRAC II was in the process of developing a marketing plan for the product. One of the key issues was how to position TRAC II in the razor market relative to Gillette's new product, Atra. In addition, the brand manager was concerned about the level of funding available to market the TRAC II appropriately.

NORTHERN MAMMOTH EQUIPMENT COMPANY

Northern Mammoth Equipment Company is a West Coast subsidiary of a large corporation based in the Midwest. This company sells, leases, and services high-quality heavy equipment used in major public and private construction projects. Although it is the second largest in the market area, its domestic sales have not exhibited the same growth as its foreign sales, even though it devotes very little effort to exports.

QUALITY FOODS

Quality Foods is one of the largest food processors in the United States. Having experienced great success with one of its new products, Wonder Dessert Cup, an individually packaged pudding-like dessert, management is in the process of deciding whether to expand this product line to include individually packaged cups of potato and macaroni salads.

INTERCOMMUNITY SPCA

The Intercommunity Society for the Prevention of Cruelty to Animals provides a shelter for the health and safety of animals. In addition to guaranteeing a home for animals that come to the Shelter, ICSPCA provides a spay and neuter clinic, shot clinic, ambulance service, animal cruelty investigations, and humane education programs. As a means of increasing revenue and providing more services, the Society is considering various options in its service strategy.

Before proceeding to take some action based on ARC's findings, Mr. Monroe thought he had better reassess the market opportunities and examine each recommendation personally since the costs were so high.

TREE TOP SKI RESORT

Norman A. Monroe, president of Tree Top Ski Resort, was in the process of examining a report prepared by a professional marketing research firm. A year earlier, Advanced Research Corporation (ARC) had been commissioned by Mr. Monroe to provide an assessment of the overall market for the ski resort and prepare a program of expansion for the next ten years. The specific recommendations for development over this time period were to:

1. Increase parking facilities to accommodate an additional 550 automobiles. Estimated cost: $300,000

2. Increase the day lodge space by 16,000 square feet. Estimated cost: $1,100,000

3. Expand cafeteria service capacity to accommodate 800 persons per hour. Estimated cost: $200,000

4. Construct a beverage lounge and restaurant with a motif conducive to after-ski activities. Estimated cost: $400,000

5. Increase ski terrain by 170 acres, with proportionally more area for advanced skiers. Estimated cost: $1,800,000

6. Add three chairlifts and one surface lift to the existing ski area. Estimated cost: $500,000

7. Develop an eighty-unit condominium-apartment complex for lease and rental purposes. Estimated cost: $1,600,000.

Due to the anticipated development cost of $5.9 million, ARC suggested that the project not begin until the resort had experienced at least two to three years of very profitable operations and that the lift capacity not increase until demand reached 90 percent of current capacity on at least twenty days of the season.

This case was prepared by Professor Dennis H. Tootelian, California State University, Sacramento.

BACKGROUND

Tree Top Ski Resort was a winter ski resort located in northwestern Colorado. Originally designed by Mr. Monroe to be a family recreation area for his relatives and their friends, he also realized that it had to be managed as a business given the costliness of the venture. Thus, Tree Top was organized (see exhibit 1) and incorporated ten years ago and began operating ski lifts two years thereafter.

Since its incorporation, Tree Top's facilities were expanded nearly continuously during its first three seasons. From then on, additions were somewhat sporadic and tended not to follow a single overall development plan. It was for this reason that Mr. Monroe hired ARC. For the next ten years he wanted all expansion to be based on a goal-oriented approach. Mr. Monroe and the Board of Directors had as their primary objective to make Tree Top Ski Resort into an internationally recognized facility while at the same time maintaining a "family atmosphere," rather than one for "swinging singles."

Beginning its first season, Tree Top had three ski lifts (one chair and two poma lifts), and by the end of its tenth year had twelve lifts (five chair, two T-bar, and five poma lifts). In addition to ski lifts, the company operated a day lodge, ski shop, bar, ski equipment rentals, ski school, and locker and office rentals. It also concessioned out a cafeteria and some vending machines to a separately owned firm (see exhibit 2).

At peak season, the resort employed well over one hundred workers. Included among these were thirty people who operated the various lifts, twenty members of a ski patrol, ten snow maintenance personnel, ten lodge workers, and two doctors. There were also twenty to thirty volunteer ski patrol workers. Beyond possessing the skills, knowledge, and abilities required to perform their duties satisfactorily, resort employees were required to maintain a clean-

EXHIBIT 1
Tree Top Ski Resort Organization Chart

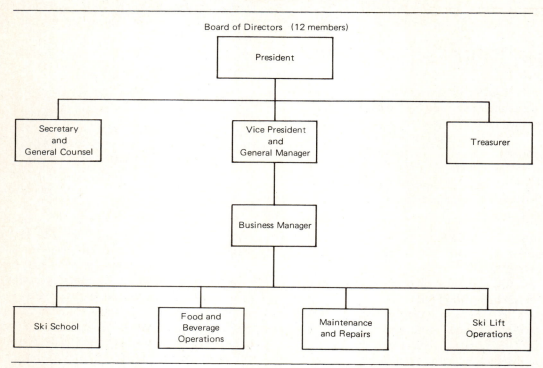

cut appearance to support the desired family atmosphere. Although some turnover of personnel was attributed to this requirement, Mr. Monroe did not consider it to be a major problem.

FACILITIES

Tree Top's average daily capacity was 3,912 skiers, up from 600 in the first year of operation. The resort's activities, however, were restricted to winter use (mid-November to early May) for skiing purposes only (see exhibit 3). While there were a large number of summer season visitors to the general area, estimated to be nearly 500,000 people annually, demand during that period was for accommodations and other commercial facilities at a nearby lakeshore. It was the opinion of ARC that Tree Top's relatively limited capacity for summer activities, other than

EXHIBIT 2
Tree Top Ski Resort—Characteristics

Daily Skier Capacity		3,912
Number of lifts		12
Chair	5	
Poma	5	
T-Bar	2	
Hourly Lift Capacity		8,900
Number of Ski Trails & Slopes		25
Total Acreage of Trails		396
Novice	38.6 (9.7%)	
Intermediate	313.7 (79.2%)	
Expert	43.7 (11.1%)	
Day Lodge (Total Square Footage)		12,000
Food Service		
Seating Capacity		160 + 40 in bar
Serving Capacity		180 persons per hour
Parking Capacity		
Number of Cars		1,350
Acreage		13.5

EXHIBIT 3
Monthly Usage in Skier Days

Month	3rd	8th	9th	10th
		Year		
November				
Midweek	0	0	420	209
Weekend/Holiday	103	4,380	8,724	5,161
December				
Midweek	0	962	1,804	4,213
Weekend/Holiday	751	24,035	9,520	32,753
January				
Midweek	8	5,082	6,360	8,406
Weekend/Holiday	1,772	16,576	24,043	27,270
February				
Midweek	638	8,779	12,726	10,470
Weekend/Holiday	6,410	20,735	26,749	34,710
March				
Midweek	2,623	7,586	8,792	4,140
Weekend/Holiday	10,400	25,042	19,991	23,071
April				
Midweek	2,416	1,835	2,572	4,778
Weekend/Holiday	15,352	8,174	20,604	19,549
May				
Midweek	341	0	0	132
Weekend/Holiday	4,730	362	572	1,961
Annual				
Midweek	6,026	24,244	32,674	32,348
Weekend/Holiday	39,518	99,304	110,203	144,475
Total	45,544	123,548	142,877	176,823

EXHIBIT 4
Ski Resort Usage in Skier Days
(thousands)

	8th	9th	10th
		Year	
Tree Top	123.5	142.9	176.8
Ski Bowl	174.7	284.3	301.2
Indian Meadows	123.6	171.8	232.2
West Ridge	57.0	56.4	73.2
Sky Valley	Not Open		42.2
Green Mountain	28.9	38.4	42.0
Alpine Ridge	10.8	30.2	35.4
Summit Bowl	18.1	25.0	27.7
Mountain Ranch	11.0	21.6	26.4
North Slope	Not Open		25.2
Big Slope	11.3	14.5	18.1
Total	558.9	785.1	1,000.4

facilities, however, were seldom used to capacity, so overcrowding of any set of trails had not as yet been a real problem.

An alpine-style, two-story day lodge was situated close to the main ski areas. It was also next to Tree Top's only parking facilities, which accommodated 1,350 automobiles. The lodge itself had nearly 12,000 square feet of space and housed the ski shop, offices, cafeteria, bar, and restrooms, but had no overnight facilities. The closest overnight accommodations were about fifteen minutes away.

Adjacent to the lodge was a locker room in which 296 lockers were available on a lease basis. Originally 200 were built, but within two years an additional 96 had to be constructed to meet skiers' needs. All lockers had been leased for a twenty-year period, and a waiting list was being maintained. Locker leases were set at a standard rate of $1,000 for twenty years.

To aid in supporting the family orientation, Tree Top offered ski classes for both adults and children. Additionally, a ski nursery was provided so that children could enjoy supervised activities in protected outdoor play areas while their parents were on the ski slopes. The most recent family-style innovation was to offer nondenominational church services every Sunday morning at 9:30 a.m. in the day lodge.

low-income producing ones (such as sightseeing, horseback riding, camping, and hiking), offered no economic justification for extending the resort's operations beyond the winter season.

Tree Top encompassed a total land area of approximately 4,500 acres with about 1,000 acres serviced by lift facilities. For the most recent season, there were nearly 396 acres of ski trails, of which 9.7 percent were for novice skiers, 79.2 percent for intermediate skiers, and 11.1 percent for expert skiers. This ratio indicated somewhat of an imbalance when compared to the general standard of 20 percent, 50 percent, and 30 percent, respectively. The

EXHIBIT 5
Ski Resort Facility Comparisons

	Ski Trails & Runs	Number of Lifts	Price of Lift Ticket	Other Facilities*
Tree Top	25	12	$10.00	1, 3, 5, 7, 9
Ski Bowl	55	25	$13.00	1, 2, 3, 4, 6, 7, 8, 9
Indian Meadows	14	13	$ 9.00	1, 3, 5, 7, 9
West Ridge	14	8	$ 9.00	2, 3, 4, 7, 9
Sky Valley	12	7	$ 6.50	1, 3, 5, 7
Green Mountain	8	4	$ 7.00	1, 3, 4, 9
Alpine Ridge	8	5	$ 7.00	3, 4, 7, 9
Summit Bowl	10	5	$ 6.50	1, 9
Mountain Ranch	10	5	$ 6.50	3, 6, 9
North Slope	8	4	$ 6.50	6, 9
Big Slope	10	4	$ 6.50	1, 5, 7, 9

*Facilities: 1 = Day Lodge   2 = Lodge   3 = Ski Shop   4 = Restaurant   5 = Cafeteria   6 = Snack Bar   7 = Bar   8 = Ice Rink   9 = Rentals

MARKETING

Including Tree Top, there are eleven winter ski resorts operating in the area. As shown in exhibits 4 and 5, Tree Top had the second largest skier capacity; but for the most recent season, it demonstrated only the third strongest drawing power of all the resorts. The leader, Ski Bowl, had a drawing power 1.7 times that of Tree Top, and Indian Meadows drew the same even though only half as large.

Mr. Monroe attributed the lower level of resort usage to the family atmosphere approach used at Tree Top as opposed to the more youthful image conveyed by most of the other resorts. The typical Tree Top skier was believed to be male, over thirty years of age, to have a higher than average income, and to be a family man skiing with at least one other member of his family. He did not have the interest in after-ski activities of the young, single, less affluent skier who frequented the other ski sites in the area. Despite the affluence, however, the average Tree Top skier spent $15.26 per day at Tree Top, while the average for the other ten resorts was more than twice that amount.

The price of lift tickets was considered to be a major component of daily skiing expenditures, particularly for families. Tree Top's $10 daily lift tickets were the second highest, with only Ski Bowl pricing its lift tickets higher ($13). The average in the area was $8. Although the price was somewhat high at Tree Top, certain discounts were offered. Skiers who leased lockers were given a $250 credit toward the purchase of lift tickets over the twenty-year lease period. These credits were redeemable at a maximum rate of $50 per year. Credits toward the purchase of lift tickets were also extended to several of the ski clubs in the area. In return, the clubs were asked to conduct official and nonofficial events at Tree Top. Since opening, the resort had hosted several national and many local events and had attracted competitors of international reputation.

Promotional expenditures for Tree Top have typically ranged from 1 percent to 4 percent of gross revenues, although the rate has varied depending on the monetary needs of the resort. In the most recent year, for example, expenditures were curtailed somewhat in order to pay for the research conducted by ARC. In the past, spot radio commercials had been purchased on Denver and other major city stations. These consisted of both straight advertising for Tree Top and weather reports on its skiing conditions.

Coupled with radio advertising, the resort used outdoor signs on a very limited basis. Unlike most of the resorts, Tree Top did not use billboards along the major thoroughfares which reach the resorts. Some sites used highway advertising at intervals nearly one hundred miles away, while Tree Top placed theirs within two miles of the ski area. A few resorts also advertised at the neastest airports, although Tree Top did not. To some extent, Mr. Monroe and some members of the Board of Directors believed that promotional efforts were wasteful. They felt that the key factor determining revenues was the weather.

FINANCIAL CONDITIONS

Company financial statements are presented in exhibits 6, 7, and 8. Tree Top's primary source of revenues was ski lift operations. Ski lift revenues represented about 70 percent of total revenues in recent years, increasing to approximately 79 percent of the total in the last season. Ski school and ski rental operations contributed from 12 to 14 percent of total revenues, and bar sales amounted to about 3 percent. The remainder came from the concessions, locker leasing, and other operations.

The land Tree Top operated on was leased for a seventy-five-year period from a land holding company. Under provisions of the lease, the rental rate was 7.5 percent of gross revenues until Tree Top's revenues reached the $2,000,000 level. After that point, the percentage increased to 9 percent.

Although the resort had been profitable for some time, Mr. Monroe was somewhat concerned that profits were not growing with any consistency. Of particular importance in determining which recommendations of ARC to pursue was the effect the actions would have on revenues and profits.

EXHIBIT 6
Tree Top Ski Resort
Income Statement—Year 10

Operating Income		
Bar	$ 121,309	
Less: Cost of Sales	39,680	$ 81,629
Sports Shop	217,408	
Less: Cost of Sales	152,586	64,822
Ski Lifts		2,157,258
Ski School and Rental Shop		345,820
Concession Income		
Cafeteria	27,334	
Vending Machines	4,330	31,664
Office Rent		3,395
Locker Leases		14,800
Sundry		9,632
Total Operating Income		$2,709,020
Operating Expenses		
Salaries	$1,167,529	
Maintenance	194,211	
Rent (Property and Lifts)	243,812	
Taxes and Licenses	87,675	
Interest	167,866	
Advertising	26,298	
Promotion and Special Events	21,372	
Insurance	72,729	
Utilities and Services	93,366	
Travel and Entertainment	30,162	
Legal and Accounting	22,844	
General and Administrative	24,532	
Total Operating Expenses		$2,152,396
Operating Income Before		
Depreciation and Amortization		$ 556,624
Depreciation and Amortization		402,355
Net Profit (Loss) Before Taxes		$ 154,269

CASE

EXHIBIT 7
Tree Top Ski Resort
Previous Years' Income Statements—Condensed

	Year 9	Year 8	Year 7
Income			
Ski Lifts	$1,881,893	$1,453,532	$1,200,737
Bar	113,414	104,832	80,773
Sports Shop	182,556	167,724	140,292
Ski School & Rental Shop	326,999	323,132	244,328
Office Rent	2,099	2,318	3,150
Locker Rent	14,800	14,800	14,800
Concession Income	22,147	21,395	16,780
Sundry	4,522	8,356	2,182
Total Income	$2,548,430	$2,096,089	$1,703,042
Operating Expenses			
Salaries & Wages	$ 727,196	$ 636,980	$ 476,626
Maintenance	64,800	65,095	86,447
Rent	229,359	188,648	127,728
Advertising & Promotion	67,983	68,158	26,183
Other	920,840	738,710	483,119
Total	$2,010,178	$1,697,591	$1,200,103
Income Before Depreciation & Amortization	$ 538,252	$ 398,498	$ 502,939
Depreciation & Amortization	313,139	321,744	342,435
Income Before Taxes	$ 225,113	$ 76,754	$ 160,504

CASE

EXHIBIT 8
Tree Top Ski Resort
Balance Sheet—Year 10

Assets			Liabilities & Capital		
Current Assets			**Current Liabilities**		
Cash	$ 92,425		Notes Payable	$ 149,232	
Accounts Receivable	14,648		Contracts Payable	67,901	
Inventories	10,817		Accounts Payable	304,350	
Prepaid Expenses	27,244		Accrued Expenses	84,145	
Deposits	8,220		Total		$ 605,628
Total		$ 153,354	**Long-Term Liabilities**		
Fixed Assets			Notes Payable	$1,314,416	
Buildings, Roads, Parking Lot,			Convertible Subordinated		
& Bridges	$1,794,361		Debentures	304,200	
Electrical & Telephone			Total		$1,618,616
Systems	36,048		Total Liabilities		$2,224,244
Ski Lifts	1,195,594				
Furnishings & Equipment	292,944		**Capital**		
Land Lease Improvements	20,705		Capital Stock	$ 699,485	
Construction in Progress	34,525		Paid-In Surplus	603,802	
Total		$3,374,177	Total Capital		$1,303,287
Total Assets		$3,527,531	Total Liabilities & Capital		$3,527,531

THE GILLETTE COMPANY—SAFETY RAZOR DIVISION

In July 1978, Mike Edwards, Brand Manager for TRAC II[1], is beginning to prepare his marketing plans for the following year. In preparing for the marketing plan approval process, he has to wrestle with some major funding questions.

The most recent sales figures show that TRAC II has continued to maintain its share of the blade and razor market. This has occurred even though the Safety Razor Division (SRD) has introduced a new product to its line, Atra. The company believes that Atra will be the shaving system of the future and, therefore, is devoting increasing amounts of marketing support to this brand. Atra was launched in 1977 with a $7 million advertising campaign and over 50 million $2 rebate coupons. In less than a year, the brand achieved a 7 percent share of the blade market and about one-third of the dollar razor market. Thus, the company will be spending heavily on Atra, possibly at the expense of TRAC II, still the number one shaving system in America.

Edwards is faced with a difficult situation, for he believes that TRAC II still can make substantial profits for the division provided the company

[1]TRAC II® is a registered trademark of The Gillette Company.

Sales, market share, advertising data, and other cost figures used in this case were taken from published and unpublished sources and are to be considered as estimates only. These data present a representative picture of the situation discussed in the case. This case was made possible by the cooperation of The Gillette Company.

This case was prepared by Charles M. Kummel, Research Assistant, under the supervision of Professor Jay E. Klompmaker, The University of North Carolina at Chapel Hill, School of Business Administration.

continues to support the brand. In preparing for 1979, the division is faced with two major issues:

1. What are TRAC II's and Atra's future potentials?
2. Most important of all, can SRD afford to support two brands heavily? If they can, is it sound marketing policy to do so?

COMPANY BACKGROUND

The Gillette Company was founded in 1903 by King C. Gillette, a 40-year-old inventor, utopian writer, and bottle-cap salesman in Boston, Massachusetts. Since marketing its first safety razor and blades, the Gillette Company, the parent of the Safety Razor Division, has been the leader in the shaving industry.

The Gillette safety razor was the first system to provide a disposable blade that could be replaced at low cost and that provided a good inexpensive shave. The early ads focused on a shave-yourself theme: "If the time, money, energy and brainpower which are wasted (shaving) in the barbershops of America were applied in direct effort, the Panama Canal could be dug in four hours."

The Pre-World War Years

With the benefit of a 17-year patent, Gillette was in a very advantageous position. However, it wasn't until the first World War that the safety razor began to gain wide consumer acceptance. One day in 1917 King Gillette came into the office with a visionary idea: present a Gillette razor to every soldier, sailor, and marine. Other executives modified this idea so that the government would do the presenting. In this way, millions just entering the shaving age would give the nation the self-shaving habit. In World War I, the government bought 4,180,000 Gillette razors as well as smaller quantities of competitive models.

Daily Shaving Development

While World War I gave impetus to self-shaving, World War II popularized frequent shaving—12 million American servicemen shaved daily. There were two results: (1) Gillette was able to gain consumer acceptance of personal shaving, and (2) the Company was able to develop an important market to build for the future.

Post-War Years

After 1948, the Company began to diversify through the acquisition of three companies that gave Gillette entry into new markets. In 1948, the acquisition of the Toni Company extended the company into the women's grooming aid market. Papermate, a leading maker of writing instruments, was bought in 1954, and the Sterilon Corporation, a manufacturer of disposable supplies for hospitals, was acquired in 1962.

Diversification also occurred through internal product development propelled by a detailed marketing survey conducted in the late 1950's. The survey found that the public associated the company as much or more with personal grooming as with cutlery and related products. Gillette's response was to broaden its personal care line. As a result, Gillette now markets such well-known brands as Adorn hairspray, Tame cream rinse, Right Guard anti-perspirant, Dry Look hairspray for men, Foamy shaving cream, Earth Borne and Ultra Max shampoos, Cricket lighters, and Pro Max hairdryers as well as Papermate, Erasermate, and Flair Pens.

Gillette Today

Gillette is divided into four principal operating groups (North America, International, Braun AG, Diversified Companies) and five product lines. As exhibit 1 indicates, the importance of blades and razors to company profits is immense. In just about all the 200 countries where its blades and razors are sold, Gillette remains the industry leader.

In 1977, Gillette reported increased worldwide sales of $1587.2 million with income after taxes of $79.7 million (see exhibit 2). Of total sales, $720.9 million were domestic and $866.3 million were international, with profit contributions of $109 million and $105.6 million, respectively. The Company employs 31,700 people worldwide with 8600 employees in the United States.

Statement of Corporate Objectives and Goals

At a recent stockholder's meeting, the Chairman of the Board outlined the Company's strategy for the future:

The goal of The Gillette Company is sustained growth. *To achieve this, the company concentrates on two major objectives: to maintain the strength of existing product lines and to develop at least two new significant businesses or product lines that can make important contributions to the growth of the Company in the early 1980's.*

In existing product lines, the Company broadens its opportunities for growth by utilizing corporate technology to create new products. In other areas, growth is accomplished through either internal development or the acquisition of new businesses.

The Company uses a number of guidelines to evaluate growth opportunities. Potential products or services must fulfill a useful function and provide value for the price paid; offer distinct advantages easily perceived by consumers; be based on technology available within, or readily accessible outside the Company; meet established quality and safety standards; and offer an acceptable level of profitability and attractive growth potential.

THE SAFETY RAZOR DIVISION

The Safety Razor Division has long been regarded as the leader in shaving technology. Building upon King Gillette's principle of using razors as a vehicle for blade sales, and of associating the name "Gillette" with premium shaving, the Division has been able to maintain its number one position in the U.S. market.

Share of Market

Market share is important in the shaving industry. The standard is that each share point is equivalent to approximately $1 million in pre-tax profits. Over recent history, Gillette has held approximately

CASE

EXHIBIT 1
Gillette Sales and Contributions to Profits (1973–1977)[1]
Business Segments

	Blades and Razors		Toiletries and Grooming Aids		Writing Instruments		Braun Products		Other	
Year	Net Sales	Contributions to Profits	Net Sales	Contributions to Profits	Net Sales	Contributions to Profits	Net Sales	Contributions to Profits	Net Sales	Contributions to Profits
1977	31%	75%	26%	13%	8%	6%	23%	13%	12%	(7)%
1976	29	71	28	15	7	6	21	10	15	(2)
1975	30	73	30	15	7	5	20	8	13	(1)
1974	30	69	31	17	7	6	20	5	12	3
1973	31	64	32	20	7	5	22	10	8	1

[1] *Source:* Gillette Annual Report for 1977, page 28.

EXHIBIT 2
The Gillette Company Annual Income Statements
(1963–1977)
(thousands of dollars)

Year	Net Sales	Gross Profit	Profit from Operations	Income Before Taxes	Federal and Foreign Income Taxes	Net Income
1977	$1,587,209	$834,786	$202,911	$158,820	$79,100	$79,720
1976	1,491,506	782,510	190,939	149,257	71,700	77,557
1975	1,406,906	737,310	184,368	146,954	67,000	79,954
1974	1,246,422	667,395	171,179	147,295	62,300	84,995
1973	1,064,427	600,805	155,949	154,365	63,300	91,065
1972	870,532	505,297	140,283	134,618	59,600	75,018
1971	729,687	436,756	121,532	110,699	48,300	62,399
1970	672,669	417,575	120,966	117,475	51,400	66,075
1969	609,557	390,858	122,416	119,632	54,100	65,532
1968	553,174	358,322	126,016	124,478	62,200	62,278
1967	428,357	291,916	101,153	103,815	47,200	56,615
1966	396,190	264,674	90,967	91,666	41,800	49,866
1965	339,064	224,995	75,010	75,330	33,000	42,330
1964	298,956	205,884	72,594	73,173	35,500	37,673
1963	295,700	207,552	85,316	85,945	44,400	41,545

EXHIBIT 3
Gillette Percentage of U.S. Blade Sales
(estimated market share)

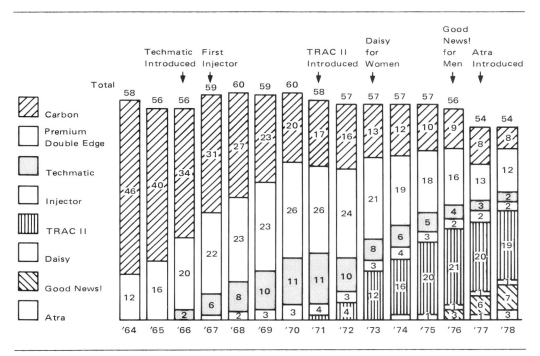

60 percent of the total dollar market. However, the Division has put more emphasis on increasing its share from its static level.

Product Line

During the course of its existence, Gillette has introduced many new blades and razors. In the last 15 years, the shaving market has evolved from a double-edged emphasis to twin-bladed systems (see exhibit 3). Besides Atra and TRAC II, Gillette markets Good News! disposables, Daisy for women, double-edge, injector, carbon and Techmatic band systems (see exhibit 4). Within their individual markets, Gillette sells 65 percent of all premium double-edge blades, 12 percent of injector sales, and almost all of the carbon and band sales.

Marketing Approach and Past Traditions

During 1977, the Gillette Company spent $207.9 million to promote all its products throughout the world, of which $133.1 million was spent for advertising, including couponing and sampling, and $74.8 million for sales promotion. In terms of the domestic operation, the Safety Razor Division uses an eight-cycle promotional schedule, whereby every six weeks a new program is initiated. During any one cycle, some but not all products and their packages are sold on promotion. Usually one of the TRAC II packages is sold on promotion during each of these cycles.

Gillette advertising is designed to provide information to consumers and motivate them to buy the Company's products. Sales promotion

EXHIBIT 4
Safety Razor Division Product Line
June 1978

	Package Sizes	Manufacturer's Suggested Retail Price
Blades		
TRAC II	5, 9, 14, Adjustable 4	$1.60, 2.80, 3.89, 1.50
Atra	5, 10	$1.70, 3.40
Good News!	2	$.60
Daisy	2	$1.00
Techmatic	5, 10, 15	$1.50, 2.80, 3.50
Double Edge:		
Platinum Plus	5, 10, 15	$1.40, 2.69, 3.50
Super-Stainless	5, 10, 15	$1.20, 2.30, 3.10
Carbon:		
Super Blue	10, 15	$1.50, 2.15
Regular Blue	5, 10	$.70, 1.25
Injector:		
Regular	7, 11	$1.95, 2.60
Twin-Injector	5, 8	$1.40, 2.20
Razors		
TRAC II	Regular	$3.50
	Lady	$3.50
	Adjustable	$3.50
	Deluxe	$3.50
Atra		$4.95
Double-Edge		
Super Adjustable		$3.50
Lady Gillette		$3.50
Super Speed		$1.95
Twin Injector		$2.95
Techmatic	Regular	$3.50
Three-Piece		$4.50
Knack		$1.95
Cricket Lighters		
	Regular	$1.49
	Super	$1.98
	Keeper	$4.49

ensures that these products are readily available, well located and attractively displayed in retail stores. Special promotion at the point of purchase offers consumers an extra incentive to buy Gillette products. [2]

[2]*Source:* 1977 Gillette Company Annual Report, p. 14.

In the past the Company has concentrated its advertising and promotion on its newest shaving product; reducing support for its other established lines. The theory is that growth must come at the expense of other brands. For example, when TRAC II was introduced, the advertising budget for other brands was cut such that the double-edge portion

CASE

EXHIBIT 5
Gillette Advertising Expenditures, 1965–1978
(percent of total dollar market)

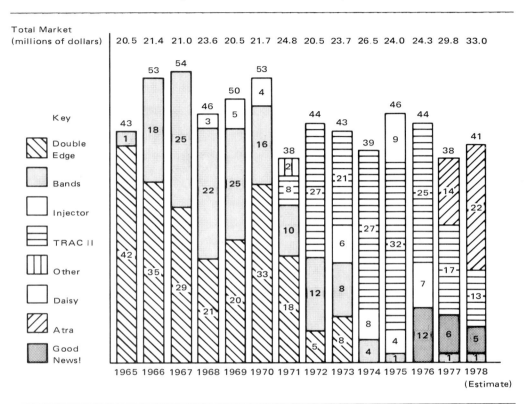

decreased from 47 percent in 1971 to 11 percent in 1972, while TRAC II received 61 percent of the Division budget (see exhibit 5).

A longstanding tradition has been that razors are used as a means for selling blades. Thus, with razors the emphasis is to induce the consumer to try the product by offering coupon discounts, mail samples, and heavy informational advertising. Blade strategy has been to emphasize a variety of sales devices—such as discounts, displays and sweepstakes at pharmacies, convenience stores, and supermarkets—to encourage point of purchase sales. In spite of this tradition, razor sales are a very significant portion of division sales and profits.

At the center of this marketing strategy has been the Company's identification with sports. The Gillette "Cavalcade of Sports" began with Gillette's radio sponsorship of the 1939 World Series and continues today with the World Series, the Super Bowl, professional and NCAA basketball, as well as boxing. During the 1950s and 60s, Gillette spent 60 percent of its ad dollar on sports programming. Influenced by research that showed prime-time entertainment offered superior audience potential, the early 1970s saw the Company switch to a prime-time emphasis. However, Gillette has recently returned in the last two years to its sports formula.

Marketing Research

Research has been a cornerstone to the success of the Company for it has been the means to retain a superior position in relation to its competitors. For example, Gillette was faced in 1917 with the expiration of its basic patents and the eventual flood of competitive models. Six months before the impending expiration, the Company came out with new razor models, including one for a dollar. As a result, the Company made more money than ever before. In fact, throughout the history of shaving, Gillette has introduced most of the improvements in shaving technology. The major exceptions are the injector, which was introduced by Schick, and the stainless steel double-edge blade introduced by Wilkinson.

The company spends $37 million annually on research and development of new products, product improvements, and consumer testing. In addition to Atra, a recent development is a new sharpening process called "Micro-smooth," which improves the closeness of the shave and the consistency of the blade. This improvement is to be introduced on all of the Company's twin blades by early 1979. Mike Edwards believes that this will help to insure TRAC II's retention of its market.

At the time of Atra's introduction, Gillette research found that users would come from TRAC II and from non-twin blade systems. This loss was estimated to be 60 percent of TRAC II users. Recent research indicates that with heavy marketing support in 1978, TRAC II's loss will be held to 40 percent.

THE SHAVING MARKET

The shaving market is divided into two segments: wet shavers and electric. Today, the wet shavers account for 75 percent of the market. In the United States alone, 1.9 billion blades and 23 million razors are sold annually.

Market Factors

There are a number of factors at work within the market: (1) the adult shaving population has increased in the past 15 years to 74.6 million men and 68.2 million women, (2) technological innovations have improved the quality of the shave as well as increased the life of the razor blade and (3) the volume of blades and razors has begun to level off after a period of declining and then increasing sales (see exhibit 6).

While the shaving market has increased slightly, there are more competitors. Yet Gillette has been able to maintain its share of the market—approximately two-thirds of the dollar razor market and a little over half of the dollar blade market.

Market Categories

The market is segmented into seven components: new systems, disposables, injector, premium double-edge, carbon double-edge, continuous bands, and single-edge systems. In the early 1900s the shaving market was primarily straight-edge. During the past 70 years, the market has evolved away from its single, then double-edge emphasis to the present market of 60 percent bonded systems (all systems where the blade is encased in plastic). Exhibit 7 shows the recent trends within the market categories.

Competitors

Gillette's major competitors are Warner-Lambert's Schick, Colgate-Palmolive's Wilkinson, American Safety Razor's Personna, and BIC.

Each has its own strongholds. Schick, which introduced the injector system, now controls 80 percent of that market. ASR's Personna sells almost all of the single-edge blades on the market. Wilkinson's strength is its bonded system which appeals to an older, wealthier market. BIC has developed a strong product in its inexpensive disposable.

Competitive pricing structure is comparable to Gillette within the different system categories. While all the companies have similar suggested retail prices, the differences found on the racks in the market are a function of the companies' off-invoice rates to the trade and their promotional allowances.

While it is not much of a factor at this time, private label competition covers the range of systems and continues to grow.

EXHIBIT 6
Razor & Blade Sales Volume, 1963–1979

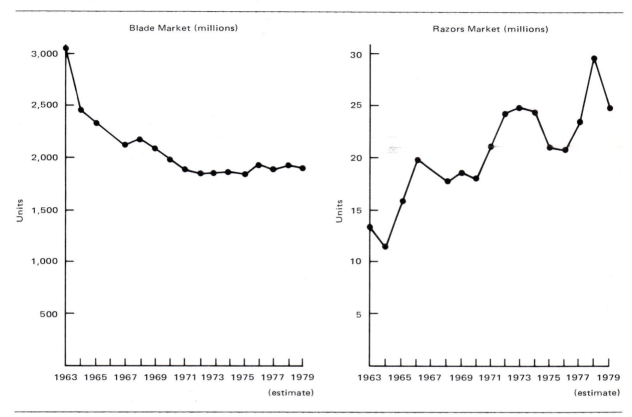

Blade Market (millions)

Razors Market (millions)

Market Segmentation

The success of Gillette's technological innovations can be seen in its effect on the total shaving market. While there are other factors at play in the market, new product introductions have contributed significantly to market expansion, as exhibit 8 indicates.

TWIN-BLADE MARKET

Research played a key role in the development of twin blades. Gillette had two variations—the current one where the blades were in tandem; the other where the blades' edges faced each other and required an up and down scrubbing motion. For marketing reasons and because the Atra swivel system had problems in testing development, TRAC II was launched first. The research department played a major role in the positioning of the product when it discovered hysteresis, the phenomenon of whiskers being lifted out and after a time receding into the follicle. Thus, the TRAC II effect was that the second blade cut the whisker before it receded.

Since its introduction in 1971, the twin-blade market has grown to account for almost 60 percent of all blade sales. The twin-blade market is defined as all bonded razors and blades (e.g., new systems: Atra and TRAC II; disposables: Good News! and BIC).

Exhibit 9 shows the trends in the twin-blade market.

EXHIBIT 7
Recent System Share Trends

	1972	1973	1974	1975	1976	1977	First half, 1978
Volume							
New systems	8.8%	20.6%	28.8%	36.2%	39.9%	40.8%	43.8%
Injector	20.2	17.6	17.1	16.3	15.7	14.2	12.8
Double-edge							
premium	39.4	34.9	30.8	27.4	24.5	21.1	19.0
carbon	12.0	10.6	9.4	8.1	7.3	7.6	6.6
Bands	13.1	10.3	8.0	6.4	4.7	3.7	2.7
Disposables	—	—	—	—	2.5	6.9	9.7
Single-edge	6.5	6.0	5.9	5.6	5.4	5.7	5.4
Total Market	100.0%	100.0%	100.0%	100.0%	100.0%	100.0%	100.0%
Dollars							
New systems	11.8%	26.9%	36.9%	46.0%	50.1%	50.1%	52.1%
Injector	21.8	18.6	17.8	16.4	15.0	13.8	12.5
Double-edge							
premium	41.5	34.2	28.7	24.0	20.8	18.1	16.1
carbon	6.1	5.4	4.7	4.2	4.0	4.1	3.5
Bands	15.4	11.8	8.7	6.5	4.8	3.6	2.8
Disposables	—	—	—	—	2.8	7.5	10.5
Single-edge	3.4	3.1	3.2	2.9	2.5	2.8	2.5
Total Market	100.0%	100.0%	100.0%	100.0%	100.0%	100.0%	100.0%

EXHIBIT 8
New Product Introductions and Their Effects on the Market, 1959–1977

Year	Product Segment	Dollar Sales: Blade/Razor Market (millions)	Change (percent)
1959	Carbon	$122.4	Base
1960	Super Blue	144.1	+17.7 over 1959
1963	Stainless	189.3	+31.3 over 1960
1965	Super Stainless	201.2	+ 6.3 over 1963
1966	Banded System	212.1	+ 5.4 over 1965
1969	Injector	246.8	+16.3 over 1966
1972	Twin Blades	326.5	+32.2 over 1969
1975	Disposable	384.0	+17.6 over 1972
1977	Pivoting Head	444.9	+15.9 over 1975

EXHIBIT 9
The Twin-Blade Market, 1972–1978
(millions of dollars)

	1972	1973	1974	1975	1976	1977	1978 (estimated)	1979 (estimated)
Razors	29.5	32.1	31.4	31.3	31.5	39.7	53.8	
Disposables	—	—	—	—	14.5	41.5	64.9	
Blades	31.6	72.0	105.7	147.5	176.3	183.7	209.2	
Total Twin	61.1	104.1	137.1	176.2	222.3	264.9	327.9	
Total Market	326.5	332.6	342.5	384.0	422.2	444.9	491.0	500.0

During this period there have been many products introduced. They include: 1971—Sure Touch; 1972—Deluxe TRAC II and Schick Super II; 1973—Lady TRAC II, Personna Double II, and Wilkinson Bonded; 1974—Personna Flicker, Good News!, and BIC Disposable; 1975—Personna Lady Double II; 1976—Adjustable TRAC II and Schick Super II.

Advertising

In the race for market share, the role of advertising is extremely important in the shaving industry. Of all the media expenditures, television is the primary vehicle in the twin blade market. For Gillette, this means an emphasis on maximum exposure and sponsorship of sports events. The Company's policy for the use of television advertising is based on the convictiion that television is essentially a family medium and that programs should be suitable for family viewing. Gillette tries to avoid programs that unduly emphasize sex or violence.

As the industry leader, TRAC II receives a great deal of competitive pressure in the form of aggressive advertising from competitors and other Gillette twin-blade brands (see exhibit 10). For example, the theme of recent Schick commercials was the "Schick challenge," while BIC emphasized its low cost and comparable clean shave in relation to other twin-blade brands. However, competitive media expenditures are such that their cost per share point is substantially higher than TRAC II.

Despite competitive pressures, TRAC II aggressively advertises too. As a premium product, it does not respond directly to competitive challenges or shifts in the challengers' media; rather, TRAC II follows a standard principle of emphasizing its own strengths.

As exhibits 11 and 12 indicate, the TRAC II media plan emphasizes diversity with a heavy emphasis on advertising, using prime time television and sports programs. In addition, TRAC II is continuously promoted to retain its market share.

For 1978, the Division budgeted $18 million for advertising with Atra and TRAC II receiving the major portion of the Division budget (see exhibit 13). The traditional Gillette approach has the newest brand receiving the bulk of the advertising dollars (see exhibit 5). Therefore, it is certain that Atra will receive a substantial increase in advertising for 1979; whether the Division will increase or decrease TRAC II's budget, as well as whether the Division will increase the total ad budget for 1979, is unknown at this time.

TRAC II

The 1971 introduction of TRAC II was the largest in shaving history. Influenced by the discovery of the hysteresis process, by the development of a clog-free dual-blade cartridge, and by consumer testing data which showed 9 to 1 preference for TRAC II over panelists' current razors, Gillette raced to get the product to market. Because the introduction involved so many people, and was so critical to reversing a leveling of corporate profits (see exhibit 2), the

CASE

EXHIBIT 10
Estimated Media Expenditures
(hundreds of dollars)

	1976	1977 1st Half	1977 2nd Half	Total 1977	1978 1st Half	Total 1978 Estimate
Companies:						
Gillette	$10,800	$ 4,800	$ 6,400	$11,200	$ 8,100	$13,800
Schick	7,600	3,700	4,300	8,000	4,300	8,900
Wilkinson	2,700	1,400	2,200	3,600	1,400	2,200
ASR	2,600	700	200	900	200	800
BIC	600*	4,300	1,800	6,100	4,000	7,300
Total Market	$24,300	$14,900	$14,900	$29,800	$18,000	$33,000
Brands:						
TRAC II	$ 6,000	$ 3,300	$ 1,700	$ 5,000	$ 2,400	$ 4,000
Atra	—	—	4,000*	4,000	4,500	7,500
Good News!	1,900	1,200	600	1,800	700	1,600
Super II	2,600	1,400	2,600	4,000	3,000	4,600

*Product Introduction

EXHIBIT 11
TRAC II Media Plan, 1976, 1977
(in $ hundreds)

| | Quarter | | | | |
	1	2	3	4	Total
1976					
Prime	935	575	1,200	550	3,160
Sports	545	305	450	1,040	2,440
Network total	1,480	880	1,650	1,590	5,650
Other	80	85	70	165	400
Total	1,560	965	1,720	1,755	6,000
1977					
Prime	1,300	900	300	—	2,500
Sports	500	400	400	400	1,700
Network total	1,800	1,300	700	400	4,200
Print	—	—	200	200	400
Black	75	75	75	75	300
Military, miscellaneous	25	25	25	25	100
Total	1,900	1,400	1,000	700	5,000

division president personally assumed the role of product development manager and lived with the project day and night throughout its development and introduction.[3]

Launched during the 1971 World Series promotion, TRAC II was the most frequently advertised shaving system in America during its introductory period. Supported by $10 million in advertising and promotion, TRAC II results were impressive: 1.7 million

razors and 5 million cartridges were sold in October; and during the first year, the introductory campaign made 2 billion impressions and reached 80 percent of all homes an average of 4.7 times per week. In addition, a multimillion unit sampling campaign, the largest of its kind, was implemented in 1972.

For five years TRAC II was clearly the fastest growing product on the market, and it helped to shape the switch to twin-blades. Its users are predominantly men who are young, college-educated, metropolitan, suburban, and upper-income.

The brand reached its peak in 1976 when it sold 485 million blades and 7 million razors. In comparison, projected TRAC II sales for 1978 are 433 million

[3] For an excellent account of the TRAC II introduction by the President of Gillette North America, see Salatich, William G., "Gillette's TRAC II: The Steps to Success," *Marketing Communications,* January 1972.

EXHIBIT 12
TRAC II Media Plan, 1978

Media	Jan.	Feb.	March	April	May	June	July	Aug.	Sept.	Oct.	Nov.	Dec.	Totals
Prime TV*		\$1,055M							\$115M				\$1,170M
		15 weeks							World Series promo				
Baseball†					\$1,278M								\$1,278M
					19 weeks + All Star, Playoffs, and World Series								
Miscellaneous sports†			\$1,062M										\$1,062M
			52 weeks										
Spot TV											\$230M		\$230M
											4 weeks		
Black, military,					\$260M								\$260M
Sunday newspaper, miscellaneous				40 weeks									\$400M

Note: M = \$1,000.

*Prime-time TV advertising:
KAZ	Love Boat
ABC Friday Movie	Different Strokes
Tuesday Big Event	Real People
ABC Sunday Movie	Duke
Roots Two	Rockford Files

†Sports TV advertising:
Wide World of Sports, Saturday	NBA Basketball
College Basketball	History of Baseball
NBA All Star Game	Game of the Week Day
International Teen Boxing	This Week Baseball
Wide World of Sports, Sunday	

EXHIBIT 13
Razor Division Marketing Budget, 1978

	Atra line	TRAC II line	Good News!	Double-edged blades	Double-edged razors	Techmatic line	Daisy	Injector line	Twin injector	Total blade/razor
Marketing expenses:										
Promotion*	42.3	69.4	65.2	92.2	75.4	52.7	58.4	77.5	48.3	60.7
Advertising†	55.6	28.8	31.2	4.6	—	—	39.0	—	26.3	36.5
Other	2.1	1.8	3.6	3.2	24.6	47.3	2.6	22.5	25.4	2.8
Total marketing	100.0	100.0	100.0	100.0	100.0	100.0	100.0	100.0	100.0	100.0
Percentage line/total direct marketing	34.1	38.4	14.9	7.6	.4	.3	3.4	.2	.7	100.0
Percentage line/total full revenue sales	20.5	41.8	13.4	16.8	1.4	2.1	2.2	.6	1.2	100.0

*Defined as off-invoice allowances, wholesale push money, cooperative advertising, excess cost, premiums, contests, and prizes.
†Defined as media, sampling, couponing, production, and costs.

blades and 4.2 million razors. During this period, TRAC II brand contribution decreased 10 percent (see exhibit 14).

Competitors' responsive strategies seem to be effective. The growth of Super II during the last two years is attributed to certain advantages that it has over TRAC II. Super II has higher trade allowances (20 percent vs. 15 percent), has gained valuable distribution, has increased media expenditures, and has generally lower everyday prices.

In preparing the 1979 marketing plans, the objective for TRAC II was to retain its consumer franchise, despite strong competitive challenges, through consumer-oriented promotions, and to market the brand aggressively year round. Specifically, TRAC II was:

1. to obtain a 20 percent share of the cartridge and razor market.
2. to deliver 43 percent of the division's profit.
3. to retain its valuable pegboard space at the checkout counters in convenience, food, and drug stores, and at supermarkets.

In 1978, Mike Edwards launched a new economy-size blade package (14 blades) and a heavy spending campaign to retain TRAC II's market share. He employed strong trade and consumer promotion incentives supported by (1) "new, improved" product claims for "Micro-smooth," (2) new graphics, and (3) a revised version of the highly successful "Sold Out" advertising campaign.

Mid-year results indicate that TRAC II's performance exceeded division expectations as it retained 21.6 percent of the blade market, and contribution exceeded budget by $2 million.

ATRA
Origin

Research for the product began in Gillette's United Kingdom Research and Development Lab in 1970. The purpose was to improve the high standards of performance of twin-blade shaving and specifically, to enhance the TRAC II effect. The Company's scientists discovered that instead of moving the hand and face to produce the best shaving angle for the blade, the razor head itself could produce a better shave if the razor head could 'pivot' in such a way as to maintain the most effective twin-blade shaving angle. Once the pivoting head was shown to produce

EXHIBIT 14
TRAC II Line Income Statement, 1972–1978

	1972*	1973	1974	1975	Base 1976	1977	Estimated 1978
Full revenue sales (FRS):							
Promotional	28	41	71	100	100	110	112
Nonpromotional	38	91	89	83	100	80	65
Total	32	60	78	93	100	99	95
Direct cost of sales:							
Manufacturing	63	77	93	111	100	88	83
Freight	51	80	91	106	100	82	80
Total	62	77	93	111	100	88	83
Standard profit contribution	26	56	75	89	100	101	97
Marketing expenses							
Promotional expenses:							
Lost revenue	26	39	72	100	100	114	126
Wholesale push money	455	631	572	565	100	562	331
Cooperative advertising	27	36	58	71	100	115	133
Excess cost	25	50	59	83	100	63	92
Premiums	3	29	16	28	100	78	217
Contests and prizes	7	21	110	115	100	215	109
Total	26	40	67	90	100	112	129
Advertising:							
Media	90	83	110	119	100	96	75
Production	96	128	130	104	100	196	162
Couponing and sampling	470	344	177	112	100	166	131
Other	19	120	68	78	100	54	54
Total	124	110	108	117	100	96	78
Other marketing expenses	108	120	847	617	100	242	86
Market research	122	65	47	34	100	134	91
Total assignable marketing expenses	67	69	87	102	100	106	108
Net contribution:	14	53	81	85	100	100	94
Percentage of promotional FRS/total FRS	56	43	58	76	63	70	74
Percentage of promotional expense/promo FRS	15	16	16	15	11	17	20
Percentage of promotional expenses/total FRS	9	7	9	10	11	12	15
Percentage of advertising expenses/total FRS	28	13	10	9	7	7	6
Percentage of Media expenses/total FRS	17	8	8	8	6	6	5

*Each year's data are shown as a percentage of 1976's line item. For example, 1972 sales were 32 percent of 1976 sales.

a better shave, test after test, research continued in the Boston headquarters on product design, redesign, and consumer testing.

The name "Atra" was selected after two years of intensive consumer testing of the various names which could be identified with this advanced razor. The name was designed to be easy to remember, and to communicate technology, uniqueness, and a feeling of the future. Atra stands for *Automatic Tracking Razor Action.*

Introduction

Atra was first introduced in mid-1977. The introduction stressed the new shaving system and was supplemented by heavy advertising coupled with $2 razor rebate coupons to induce trial and 50¢ coupons toward Atra blades to induce brand loyalty.

During its first year on the national market, Atra was expected to sell 9 million razors, although 85 percent of all sales were sold on a discount basis.

Early results showed that Atra sold at a faster rate than Gillette's previously most successful introduction, TRAC II.

The Atra razor retails for $4.95. Blade packages are sold in five- and ten-blade sizes. TRAC II and Atra blades are not interchangeable. Because of Gillette's excellent distribution system, Atra hasn't had much problem gaining valuable pegboard space.

CURRENT TRENDS AND COMPETITIVE RESPONSES IN THE TWIN-BLADE MARKET

There has been quite a bit of activity in the shaving market during the first half of 1978. Atra has increased total Gillette share in the razor and blade market. During the June period, Atra razors have continued to exceed TRAC II as the leading selling razor; Atra blades share was approximately 8 percent, accounting for most of Gillette's 4 percent share of growth since June 1977. Thus, the growth of Atra has put more competitive pressure on TRAC II.

In addition, the disposable segment (due to BIC and Good News!) has increased by 5 share points to a hefty 12 percent dollar share of the blade market. Compared with TRAC II's resiliency in maintaining share, competitive brands have lost share: Schick Super II, ASR, and Wilkinson were all down 2 points since June, 1977.

In response to these recent trends, the TRAC II team expects competition to institute some changes. In an effort to recover its sagging share, Edwards expects the Schick Muscular Dystrophy promotion in October to help bolster Super II with its special offer. The pressure may already be appearing with Schick's highly successful introduction of Personal Touch for women this year, currently about 10 percent of the razor market, which has to draw TRAC II female shavers. In addition, it appears inevitable that Schick will bring out an Atra-type razor. This will remove Atra's competitive advantage but increase pressure on TRAC II with the addition of a second pivoting head competitor.

Continuing its recent trends, it appears that the disposable segment of the market will continue to expand. The first indication of this is the BIC advertising campaign which offers 12 BIC disposables for $1. Good News! will receive additional advertising support in the latter half of the year and will be available in a new size package.

One of Edwards' major objectives is to emphasize the importance of TRAC II to upper management. Besides the "Micro-smooth" introduction, a price increase on TRAC II products will be implemented soon. It is unclear whether the price change will have an adverse effect on brand sales.

In preparing the 1979 TRAC II marketing plan, Edwards realizes that Atra will be given a larger share of the advertising dollars following a strong year, and that the disposable market will continue to grow. The TRAC II share remains questionable and is dependent upon the level of marketing support it receives. Whether TRAC II will be able to continue its heavy spending program and generate large revenues for the Division remains to be seen. All these factors, as well as the Company's support of Atra, make 1979 a potentially tough year for Mike Edwards and TRAC II.

1979 MARKETING PLAN PREPARATION

Edwards recently received the following memorandum from the Vice President of Marketing:

MEMO TO: *Brand Group*

FROM: *P. Meyers*

DATE: *July 7, 1978*

SUBJECT: *1979 Marketing Plans*

In preparation for the marketing plan approval process and in developing the division strategy for 1979, I would like a preliminary plan from each brand group by the end of the month. Please submit statements of objective, corresponding strategy and levels of dollar support requested for the following:

1. *overall brand strategy*—target market*
2. *blade and razor volume and share goals*
3. *sales promotion*
4. *advertising*
5. *couponing and sampling*
6. *miscellaneous—new packaging, additional marketing research, marketing cost-saving ideas, and so forth.*

See you at the weekly meeting on Wednesday.

*Brand strategy means positioning the brand in such a way that it appeals to a distinguishable target market.

In developing the TRAC II marketing plan, Edwards has to wrestle with some strategy decisions. To obtain significant funding, how should he position TRAC II? Can he enhance the likelihood of retaining current funding levels for TRAC II with the proper positioning strategy?

In addition, where do disposables fit into Gillette's overall marketing strategy? Are they a distinct segment? How does he convince the Vice President that dollars expended for TRAC II are more effectively spent than those allocated to a program for Good News!? What is Atra's current positioning strategy and does he anticipate changes? Given the strategies of TRAC II, Atra, and disposables, what problems will be created for the consumer and for the trade?

NORTHERN MAMMOTH EQUIPMENT COMPANY, INC.

Mr. Harold Walton, office manager of Northern Mammoth Equipment Company, at the request of the board of directors, was trying to decide what should be done with respect to company sales. Mammoth's profits had been declining steadily for the last three years because, as Mr. Walton stated: "There simply isn't much construction business in the area now; and we have to wait for contractors to obtain business before we can sell equipment to them."

COMPANY PRODUCTS

Northern Mammoth sold and serviced heavy

This case was prepared by Professor Dennis H. Tootelian, California State University, Sacramento. All company names, names of individuals, and facts and figures have been disguised to assure anonymity.

equipment used in large construction projects. They handled several makes of well-known equipment. Equipment the company sold included various sizes of end-dumps, crawlers, front-end loaders, scrapers, bell-dumps, shovels, cranes, backholders, miners, and paving equipment. The prices for Northern Mammoth's equipment ranged from $3,000 to about $170,000.

In addition to selling and servicing new equipment, Northern Mammoth rented equipment, sold parts, and sold and serviced used equipment. The sale of new equipment and parts accounted for approximately 68 percent of the company's total sales.

HISTORY

Northern Mammoth Equipment Company was founded in 1958 in northern California as a franchised dealer for Mammoth Equipment Company located in Cleveland, Ohio. Mammoth Equipment Company, in turn, is owned by General Equipment Company, one of the largest contractors in the world.

The board of directors for Northern Mammoth was composed of its general manager (Mr. Eugene Rayburn) and office manager (Mr. Harold Walton), two representatives from Mammoth Equipment

Company, and three representatives from General Equipment Company.

Northern Mammoth maintained a relatively stable market within the area almost from its inception. The main reason for this was that it handled equipment and parts which were well accepted in the construction industry. Thus, although it still had to compete with other equipment lines, its main product was already established. Mammoth had a franchised dealer in every state, and through them it also conducted foreign operations.

THE MARKET

In northern California, the relevant market area for Northern Mammoth, competition was very keen. Northern Mammoth competed with other companies which also sold well-known brands. For the most part these were, like Northern Mammoth, franchised dealers which had the exclusive rights to sell their respective brands. While franchise agreements placed restrictions on territorial expansion and types of products handled, no restrictions were placed on foreign operations.

Although Northern Mammoth had not made a study of its market position, the management felt that it was the second largest dealer in northern California. Management assumed that Northern Mammoth's largest and most important competitor was the Caterpillar dealership located in San Francisco. As one company member put it: "We are probably the second largest dealer in northern California, but CAT is way ahead of us."

San Francisco was considered to be the most important market area for heavy equipment, primarily because there were a large number of construction contractors located in and around the city. In general, contractors would bid for public and/or private contracts for construction projects. The winning bidder would then purchase whatever equipment and parts he needed from one of the dealers. Most dealers, such as Northern Mammoth, attempted to establish good working relations with as many contractors as possible to make them "established" customers.

ORGANIZATION

Northern Mammoth had forty-eight employees, including eight salesmen. The salesmen were located in various regions of northern California, and each maintained a small office there. For the forty-eight employees, there were four department managers plus a general manager who coordinated the entire operation (see exhibit 1). The departments were broken down into a sales department, service department, parts department, and an office department; and there was a manager for each of these departments. With the exception of the parts manager, all of the managers had been in their respective positions since the company began its operations.

Sales Manager. The sales manager, Mr. James Farrell, forty-eight years old, was responsible for supervising the eight salesmen. He had been in the heavy equipment business for almost seventeen years. Before coming to Northern Mammoth, Mr. Farrell worked as a sales manager for another company which sold heavy equipment. That company, however, did not sell lines that competed with Northern Mammoth.

Mr. Farrell was responsible for maintaining control over selling activities. Not only did he have to hire and fire salesmen, but he also had to approve all new and used equipment sales made for Northern Mammoth. In addition, he handled some of the company's larger accounts.

Service Manager. The service manager, Mr. Harold Wilman, was in charge of the service department where all repair and maintenance work was done. Although he ordinarily did not work on equipment himself, he was qualified to make repairs. Furthermore, he was directly in charge of customer relations for sales and service areas. Mr. Wilman, fifty-six years old, had been in the heavy equipment business for thirty-two years, fourteen of which were with Mammoth. Before Mr. Wilman came to work for Northern Mammoth, he worked as a shop foreman in the same company that previously employed Mr. Farrell.

CASE

EXHIBIT 1
Northern Mammoth Equipment
Organization Chart

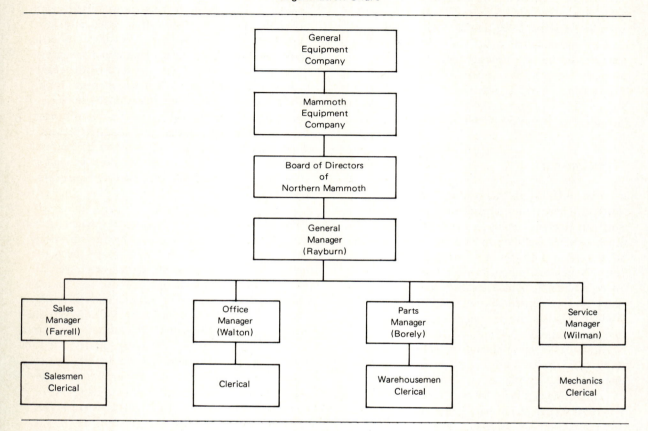

Parts Manager. The parts manager, Mr. William Borely, ordered and controlled all parts inventory, including shipping and receiving. In addition, he took care of all telephone orders for equipment for northern California. Mr. Borely, forty-one years old, had been in this field for twenty-one years and with Mammoth since 1958. Mr. Borely was a parts manager for an automobile dealership before he came to Northern Mammoth. He worked for Northern Mammoth for four years in the parts department before becoming the parts manager in 1962.

Office Manager. The office manager, Mr. Harold Walton, was the secretary-treasurer for the company.

He controlled the accounting, credit, and clerical work for day-to-day operations. Because he had been in this field for twenty-eight years, mostly with the Mammoth company, he had been instrumental in setting company policy. He was also considered by most of the employees of the company to be the most knowledgeable about the product line. He was sixty-two years old.

General Manager. The general manager, Mr. Eugene Rayburn, fifty-one years old, coordinated all company operations. He was primarily concerned with establishing goodwill with clients and potential customers. Seldom did he concern himself with the day-to-day operations of the company; he left that to Mr. Walton. Mr. Rayburn had an engineering degree and twenty years of experience in the business. He was the only one of the five managers who had a college education. When Northern Mammoth was founded, Mr. Rayburn became the General Manager after leaving one of Mammoth's principal competitors.

SALES

The market for Northern Mammoth extended from Eureka in the north to the Fresno and Monterey areas in the south. Although this total area had been quite busy with construction work, Mr. Walton felt that it was beginning to tail-off: "We have been involved in some of the largest projects in northern California, but now there doesn't seem to be much construction taking place."

Normally, Mr. Walton and others forecasted the potential demand for the area by reading about the contracts that were open for bid. They would try to determine who would bid for each contract, and who would make the winning bid. Since many of the bidders were established customers of one dealer, the company could frequently determine if they would be selling any equipment for the contract. They considered all contracts for the northern California area as potential sales.

Domestic Sales. To cover this area, Northern Mammoth employed eight salesmen who had, on the average, been with Northern Mammoth for eight years. Each lived in his respective area and conducted business from a small regional office located in his own area. The regional offices for these salesmen were in Modesto, San Jose, San Francisco, Martinez, Santa Rosa, Sacramento, Yuba City, and Eureka.

Each salesman worked for a salary plus a commission on his sales. While the salaries varied with the individual salesman, the commissions were fixed. On new equipment sales, the commission was 1½ percent of the *actual* sale price; and, on used equipment the commission was 3 percent of the sale price. If there was a trade-in with the sale, however, the commission was reduced to compensate for any overallowance given on the equipment turned in.

In addition to the salary and commission, the salesmen were given expense accounts and the use of a rented car. The expense accounts ranged between $125 and $200 per week for meals, gas, and lodging. Except for unusual conditions, the salesmen were not required to turn in any receipts except for gasoline. As Mr. Walton stated: "The cost of handling all the paperwork would be higher than it's worth." On the average, a salesman made about $18,000 each year.

The sales manager, Mr. Farrell, and the equipment salesmen accounted for all of the new and used equipment sales and rentals, and about 10 percent of the domestic parts sales. (Note: Northern Mammoth rents out both new and used equipment although this accounts for a small part of their total sales.) The remainder of the parts sales were made by the parts department manager, either over the telephone or by mail orders.

Northern Mammoth had about 300 steady customers which accounted for about 85 percent of their sales for both equipment and parts. Their orders were not definitely timed, nor were they for the same equipment or parts each time. Most customers did not stock parts, since Northern Mammoth was close by and stocked the parts for them. Even though orders varied considerably, sales over the years have tended to remain stable, except for the decline over the last three years. As Mr. Rayburn put it: "If our sales change very much on a yearly basis, the factory representatives who come by every so often want to know why." (See exhibits 2, 3, 4, and 5.)

Export Sales. In addition to domestic sales, Northern Mammoth exported parts and equipment to the Philippines, Indonesia, Ghana, Mexico, and Guatemala. The company did not keep records of the breakdown of domestic and foreign sales, but estimated that foreign sales accounted for about 50 percent of the company's parts sales. The amount of export sales of equipment was estimated to be about 10 percent of total equipment sales. These sales were not solicited.

Advertising. As far as other marketing aspects are concerned, Northern Mammoth did a little advertising in trade publications such as *Local Construction.*

EXHIBIT 2
Comparative Profit and Loss Statements
(in thousands)

	1977	1976	1975	1974	1973	1972	1971	1970
Sales:								
Equipment								
New	$2,038	$2,141	$2,196	$2,204	$2,187	$2,072	$1,939	$1,900
Rental	406	427	438	452	463	426	378	379
Used	1,031	1,103	1,093	1,130	1,001	1,013	989	904
Service								
Customers	158	162	171	182	170	163	150	138
Other	183	199	208	216	193	180	186	192
Parts	2,013	2,092	2,111	2,187	2,081	2,000	1,893	1,630
Total	$5,829	$6,124	$6,217	$6,371	$6,095	$5,854	$5,535	$5,143
Cost of Goods Sold								
Equipment								
New	$1,824	$1,863	$1,868	$1,871	$1,863	$1,792	$1,671	$1,620
Rental	377	397	404	409	413	404	347	330
Used	951	1,015	997	1,063	978	998	979	900
Service	161	187	190	194	187	205	207	212
Parts	1,496	1,536	1,595	1,667	1,560	1,390	1,293	1,150
Total	$4,809	$4,998	$5,054	$5,204	$5,001	$4,789	$4,497	$4,212
Gross Profit	$1,020	$1,126	$1,163	$1,167	$1,094	$1,065	$1,038	$ 931
Other Expenses								
Wages & Salaries	$ 315	$ 298	$ 291	$ 269	$ 257	$ 230	$ 213	$ 213
Other Operating Expenses	380	367	374	369	372	368	379	386
Fixed Expenses	109	109	109	109	109	109	109	109
Total	$ 804	$ 774	$ 774	$ 747	$ 738	$ 707	$ 701	$ 708
Net Profit Before Income Tax	$ 216	$ 352	$ 389	$ 420	$ 356	$ 358	$ 337	$ 223

Their total advertising budget ran around $18,000 annually, and had not changed much over the years. When Northern Mammoth advertised their main brand, they received a promotional allowance from the manufacturer which was set at a maximum of $750 per year. The only other advertising that Northern Mammoth did was to buy a spot in the yellow pages of the telephone directory. The management as a whole felt that the main method of promoting the company's products was by personal contact with the prospective contractors and with other customers who bought their parts from Northern Mammoth.

Pricing. Although the company had manufacturer's suggested retail price lists, they rarely used them except as a starting point for negotiations. Sales contracts were negotiated on an individual basis; and, in almost every case a discount was given on the retail price of the new equipment. In many cases, too, an overallowance was given on the equipment that was traded in; and sometimes both discounts and overallowances were given.

However, even with discounts and/or over-allowances, Northern Mammoth had a policy of pricing their equipment somewhat higher than their competitors. As Mr. Farrell put it: "Our prices are a

EXHIBIT 3
Comparative Balance Sheets
(in thousands)

	1977	1976	1975	1974	1973	1972	1971	1970
Current Assets								
Cash	$ 549	$ 567	$ 526	$ 575	$ 538	$ 498	$ 502	$ 478
Receivables	845	874	836	931	875	926	872	799
Inventory	1,751	1,646	1,701	1,662	1,741	1,599	1,638	1,621
Other	78	58	71	47	26	37	49	19
Total Current Assets	$3,223	$3,145	$3,134	$3,215	$3,180	$3,060	$3,061	$2,917
Fixed Assets	82	89	96	103	110	117	124	131
Total Assets	$3,305	$3,234	$3,230	$3,318	$3,290	$3,177	$3,185	$3,048
Current Liabilities	$ 678	$ 698	$ 702	$ 808	$ 825	$ 818	$ 831	$ 824
Notes Payable	372	372	372	372	372	372	372	372
Other Liabilities	45	11	20	36	50	9	46	23
Stockholders Equity	343	343	343	343	343	343	343	343
Retained Earnings	1,867	1,810	1,793	1,759	1,700	1,635	1,593	1,486
Total Liabilities	$3,305	$3,234	$3,230	$3,318	$3,290	$3,177	$3,185	$3,048

little higher because we feel that our equipment is of a better quality, and this is what we try to stress to the contractors." In conjunction, Mr. Walton added: "Our main products are sort of like the 'Cadillac' of the heavy equipment lines and most contractors know this. We don't want to sell lower quality lines."

Discounts and Credit Policies. Sales discounts on new and used equipment varied in size and type with each sale. Sometimes a straight percentage was taken off the list price, or payment periods were lengthened, or both. Since each sale was negotiated independently, the discount depended on what was needed to make the sale. As for parts, no discounts were given except for export sales. In these cases, usually a 5/10/net 30 discount was offered.

As for the credit policies, contracts for new and used equipment were made for each sale. Ordinarily either Mr. Farrell or Mr. Walton made an investigation of the credit rating of the potential buyer. Basically, Mr. Farrell or Mr. Walton checked Dun and Bradstreet reports, the Retail Credit Associations, and the relevant banks. On some occasions the investigator would analyze the buyer's financial statements before making the final decision on granting credit for the purchase; however, there was no set policy. By being quite cautious, company management felt that they had a very low bad debt loss, averaging approximately 0.9 percent of total sales, and 6.0 percent of the total accounts receivable.

Profitability. The profit on new and used equipment sales was set by the terms of the negotiation and contract. For new equipment, Northern Mammoth tried to make between 12 percent and 24 percent on their main lines, and between 7½ percent and 20 percent on the other lines. The company maintained specific mark-ups on its parts sales ranging from 24 percent to 30 percent. Overall, their main line parts accounted for about 65 percent of the total parts sales with all others making up the balance. In Northern Mammoth's parts department they had arranged their inventory into two separate divisions, one for their main line and one for other parts.

EXHIBIT 4
Common Size Profit and Loss Statements

	1977	1976	1975	1974	1973	1972	1971	1970
Sales								
Equipment								
New	35.1%	35.0%	35.4%	34.2%	35.9%	35.6%	35.2%	37.1%
Rental	7.0	7.0	7.0	6.2	7.5	7.2	6.7	7.2
Used	17.6	18.3	17.5	17.0	16.5	17.3	17.8	17.5
Service								
Customers	2.6	2.5	2.7	2.4	2.8	2.5	2.7	2.7
Other	3.1	3.1	3.3	6.2	3.2	3.1	3.2	3.7
Parts	34.6	34.1	34.1	34.0	34.1	34.3	34.4	31.8
Total	100.0%	100.0%	100.0%	100.0%	100.0%	100.0%	100.0%	100.0%
Cost of Goods Sold								
Equipment								
New	31.4%	30.5%	30.1%	29.2%	30.5%	30.1%	30.0%	31.8%
Rental	6.5	6.5	6.5	6.4	6.8	7.0	6.3	6.5
Used	16.4	16.6	12.8	16.6	16.0	17.2	17.8	17.6
Service	2.8	3.1	3.1	3.0	3.1	3.5	3.8	4.2
Parts	25.8	25.1	25.7	25.6	25.6	24.0	23.5	22.5
Total	82.9%	81.8%	78.2%	80.8%	82.0%	81.8%	81.4%	82.6%
Gross Profit	17.1%	18.2%	21.8%	19.2%	18.0%	18.2%	18.6%	17.4%
Other Expenses								
Wages & Salaries	5.4%	4.9%	4.7%	4.2%	4.2%	4.0%	3.9%	4.2%
Other Operating Expenses	6.6	6.0	6.0	5.8	6.1	6.3	6.9	7.6
Fixed Expenses	1.9	1.8	1.6	1.7	1.8	1.9	2.0	2.1
Total	13.9%	12.7%	12.3%	11.7%	12.1%	12.2%	12.8%	13.8%
Net Profit Before Income Tax	3.2%	5.5%	9.5%	7.5%	5.9%	6.0%	5.8%	3.5%

CUSTOMER SERVICE

Even though their prices were high, Northern Mammoth offered some services which were specifically designed to assist their customers. Two programs have been instituted in the last few years, the "Exchange Component Program," and the "Temporary Warehouse Program." Although none of the managers knew what these programs cost, they admitted that these two programs were expensive. They agreed, however, that they were justifiable expenditures.

Exchange Component Program. Under the Exchange Component Program, if a customer bought a tractor or any other piece of equipment from Northern Mammoth and the machine broke down in the field, Northern Mammoth would send a boom truck and a team of mechanics to the construction site to pull out the engine, transmission, differential, or other defective part, and replace it with a rebuilt one from the company's inventory. The broken part would then be returned to Northern Mammoth and repaired. The contractor paid only for parts and labor and kept the rebuilt part that was put in by the team of mechanics; the company kept the repaired part. It should be noted that the contractor was not charged for the service call. Mr. Wilman felt that the cost to Northern Mammoth to send a boom truck and a team of mechanics out to replace a broken part cost

EXHIBIT 5
Common Size Balance Sheets

	1977	1976	1975	1974	1973	1972	1971	1970
Current Assets								
Cash	16.6%	17.6%	16.2%	16.9%	16.3%	15.6%	15.7%	15.9%
Receivables	25.6	26.3	26.0	27.3	26.5	28.7	27.5	26.5
Inventory	53.2	51.3	52.6	51.3	53.1	50.8	51.4	52.8
Other	2.2	2.1	2.2	1.4	.8	1.3	1.5	.6
Total Current Assets	97.6%	97.3%	97.0%	96.9%	96.7%	96.4%	96.1%	95.8%
Fixed Assets	2.4	2.7	3.0	3.1	3.3	3.6	3.9	4.2
Total Assets	100.0%	100.0%	100.0%	100.0%	100.0%	100.0%	100.0%	100.0%
Current Liabilities	20.6%	21.8%	21.9%	24.2%	24.7%	26.2%	26.4%	27.2%
Notes Payable	11.4	11.5	11.5	11.4	11.4	11.5	11.5	12.3
Other Liabilities	1.2	—	.1	1.0	1.5	—	1.5	.6
Stockholders Equity	10.3	10.4	10.4	10.3	10.3	10.4	10.4	11.2
Retained Earnings	56.5	56.3	56.1	53.1	52.1	51.9	50.2	48.7
Total Liabilities	100.0%	100.0%	100.0%	100.0%	100.0%	100.0%	100.0%	100.0%

anywhere from $25 to $100, depending on the distance and part(s) replaced.

Temporary Warehouse Program. The second service, the Temporary Warehouse Program, was essentially a temporary parts warehouse set up at the site of a large construction project if the contractor(s) bought some of Northern Mammoth's equipment. Ordinarily, the warehouse was something like a large trailer with one or two employees from Northern Mammoth operating it. In addition, there were usually two or three field mechanics who moved from one site to another to assist in the repair of any Northern Mammoth equipment.

Both of these services normally were run at a loss, but were used to provide "a little extra" for the customers. All of the managers seemed quite pleased with the two programs, and considered them to be two of the most important actions they had initiated. As Mr. Walton explained: "These two programs are somewhat expensive to the company but they are needed. We couldn't meet competition without them."

PURCHASES

Northern Mammoth bought its equipment primarily from Mammoth's plant in Cleveland, Ohio. Mammoth also had set up depot areas across the country. For northern California, there were depots in Denver, Portland, Dallas, and Los Angeles. Although Northern Mammoth had made purchases from each of these, it more frequently bought from Denver or Los Angeles. These depots, for the most part, only handled parts, although some equipment was available at times. It should also be noted that Northern Mammoth maintained its own parts warehouses at San Leandro and Arcadia, although both warehouses were quite small.

On the average, Northern Mammoth tried to stick to making regular weekly orders, which averaged about $30,000 apiece. Northern Mammoth did not receive discounts on parts or equipment purchases; however, the shipping expenses from Cleveland were prepaid although the shipping expenses from the depots were not. When ordering equipment from Cleveland, Northern Mammoth usually had to wait one month. Delivery from there was most commonly by rail (piggyback). Although the company could order parts from Cleveland, this was done quite infrequently. The parts usually came from one of the depots by a special-order truck. In either case, when the shipments arrived they were unpacked immediately and inspected for damage, usually by a member of the parts department.

Special Orders. Because there are so many parts in this type of business, Northern Mammoth did not carry all of the parts that were desired by its clients and ran out of parts quite frequently. In these cases, they teletyped their orders to one of the depots and usually received delivery within two days. One employee in the parts department stated that the company made special orders on the average of four to five times a day, accounting for approximately 12 percent of its parts purchases. The cost of making a special purchase order was the costs of the teletype, a 5 percent emergency charge from the depot, and the extra freight costs involved since special orders were usually sent by bus or airplane. On the whole, management figured that they lost about 10 percent of their profits on a purchase order of this sort.

Regular Ordering. Since Northern Mammoth did not have a purchasing department, the parts manager signed all order forms. He was not held to a maximum limit (dollarwise) on what he could order. Ordinarily, he was the only one who made out purchase orders. In most cases, Mr. Borely tried to order so as to maintain a stock for about ninety days. All purchases were automatically insured by an insurance policy that the company carried.

INVENTORY

Although sales tended to be highest between May and December, Northern Mammoth kept extra inventory on hand over and above the estimated ninety-day supply during the January to April period. On the average, then, they tried to maintain a parts inventory valued at approximately $800,000, and an equipment inventory of approximately $1,200,000.

Northern Mammoth carried about 15,000 different parts which they classified as their "active" parts in their parts list system. They also handled about 5,000 parts which were "inactive" and not always carried in the supply room. Of the $800,000 in parts, approximately 10 to 15 percent were considered to be either extremely slow moving or obsolete. Some of this inventory included specially ordered parts which were not used and could not be returned (specially ordered goods could not be returned at any time). All of the extremely slow moving and obsolete parts were kept in a loft above the supply room. A few of these parts were used occasionally in repairing old machines. However, since management did not feel that they needed the extra space, no attempt had been made to dispose of them. No one in the company had investigated whether they could be sold.

Inventory Control. Inventory control was handled primarily by the parts manager, but occasionally Mr. Walton assisted in this area. All inventory information was maintained by the use of a Cardex file. Each active part type was listed on a card with the minimum and maximum quantities to keep on hand as well as the actual inventory available. Although this system gave a rough idea as to how much inventory was on hand, Northern Mammoth only made one actual inventory count per year. It was estimated by Mr. Walton that it cost Northern Mammoth about $8,000 a year to maintain its inventory control system.

Pilferage. Although management did not make estimates of pilferage, losses of this sort were thought to be considerable. As one employee stated: "A lot of these parts and tools can be used on cars and other trucks. This place gets robbed of everything from neon light filaments to engine parts." Management caught several of its mechanics stealing in the past and in most cases fired them.

ASSESSMENT

In assessing the company's development to date, Mr. Walton felt that on the whole Northern Mammoth had been fairly successful: "Sales have been somewhat steady except for 1975, 1976, and 1977. The factory representatives complain that we don't have enough penetration into different market areas, but the companies we buy from don't always have the size of equipment that the contractors need, and we do no product research and development ourselves."

Another member of the management team felt that Northern Mammoth could do considerably better if the factory left them alone. He stated: "They have training schools for each department and they make us use various accounting forms which just don't fit into our operations. The representatives are always coming around and questioning us; if they would let us run the company the way we wanted to, we would be much better off."

Although they did have to use specified accounting procedures, other managers did not feel that the factory was being overly domineering. The general consensus was that Northern Mammoth had done reasonably well, but they didn't know what actions they should take to increase sales and profitability.

QUALITY FOODS, INC.

Mr. Jason Hutchinson, vice-president of new product development for Quality Foods, Inc., had just received a preliminary report from his staff. Buoyed by the overwhelming success of the Wonder Dessert Cup, serious consideration was being given to expanding the line to include a new Wonder Salad Cup. The Wonder Dessert Cup was a ready-to-eat dessert that was packaged in a four-ounce metal can with a pull-tab lid. Available in grocery stores, they were sold individually and in six-packs that contained an equal number of fruit, pudding, and gelatin varieties. To evaluate this expansion possibility, the Wonder Salad Cup was put through a business analysis and then a test market. Provided with the results of these studies, Mr. Hutchinson was to make a go/no-go recommendation to the president of the company.

HISTORY

Quality Foods was one of the giants in the food processing industry, with sales in excess of $450

This case was prepared by Professor Dennis H. Tootelian, California State University, Sacramento.

million. From its beginnings in the mid-1950s, the company was oriented towards growth through new product development and acquisition, and corporate executives have continued to view this as one of the most important parts of Quality Foods' total competitive strategy.

To better synthesize its new product efforts, Quality Foods was partially restructured in 1971 to include a New Product Department (NPD). The purposes of this were threefold. First, by separating out new product development, Quality Foods could more readily identify and control the direct costs of individual projects as well as overall new product activities. Secondly, this approach allowed specialists to centralize in order to apply the lastest and most sophisticated testing and analytical techniques available. Finally, it was felt that excessive delays in the decision-making and introduction processes could be reduced. In previous periods, rather lengthy delays were attributed to individual department efforts to conceptualize, test, and introduce new products.

Within the NPD itself, all ideas were subjected to considerable scrutiny. Beginning with a preliminary screening, one of the key requirements was that any concept have a potential return of approximately 40 percent to be considered further. Over 60 percent of all ideas were dropped in this phase. Once passed through this first stage, the concept was put through a business analysis, then a development proposal (a more detailed analysis), and finally, if still in good

CASE

EXHIBIT 1
Report on Idea Flow

	Last Year	Two Years Ago	Three Years Ago
Inputs Received During Year	190	171	144
CURRENT STATUS			
Unscreened	30	33	24
Preliminary Screening	40	46	27
Available for Business Analysis	10	12	0
Available for Development Proposal	8	0	3
In Development Process	8	0	5
Available for Test Market	5	0	2
In Test Market	3	1	1
Adjustments	17	0	9
Rejected	69	79	73
Total	190	171	144

Source: Company records.

EXHIBIT 2
Wonder Dessert Cup Sales

Year	Case Sales	Market Share	Average Retail Price Per Case
1975	2.970M	45%	$ 9.35
1976	2.043M	39%	9.95
1977	2.326M	40%	10.75

Source: Fictionalized company records based on A. C. Nielsen report.

standing, an actual market test. Overall, between 1 percent and 2 percent of all new product concepts reached the test market stage. Historically, Quality Foods sought at least a 14 percent return on investment from its new products, and any that could not reach this were discontinued, unless there were extenuating circumstances. The stringency of this process is shown in exhibit 1, which indicates the status of new product ideas for the last three years.

ORIGIN OF THE WONDER DESSERT CUP

When the New Product Department was being organized, Quality Foods was in the final stages of test marketing its Wonder Cup line. This was considered by top management to be a new idea for individual packaging of portable desserts. Particularly appealing to Quality Foods executives were the convenience it offered and its overall possibilities for positioning. A Wonder Dessert Cup was an individual serving of fruit, pudding, or gelatin; it was sealed in a pull-tab can that needed no refrigeration, was easy to carry, and required no opening tools. As such, this product could be distributed through normal grocery

channels or vending machines. The only major concern which persisted prior to the market test was whether the relatively high costs of packaging could be passed on to the consumer.

Extensive analyses of the Wonder Dessert Cup proved extremely favorable. Market results, in fact, were even better than originally expected, and consumers did not appear resistant to the higher price resulting from the package. Company executives were especially enthused about this because increased sales would reduce production costs of packaging and thereby make this type of container economically feasible for other products.

In 1972, Mr. Hutchinson reported that the first year's marketing of Wonder Dessert Cup had exceeded anticipated sales by a comfortable margin. He also announced that these gains would have carry-over effects on the sales of other Quality Foods lines. By 1977, the market share had stabilized around the 39 percent to 45 percent level, as shown in exhibit 2. While this was quite acceptable, Mr. Hutchinson was somewhat concerned about the decline in case sales over the 1975 through 1977 period. He was unsure whether sales were about to stabilize, or whether this represented a weakness in the product itself.

DEVELOPMENT OF THE WONDER SALAD CUP

Given the success of the Wonder Dessert Cup, the NPD began examining various product additions. As originally developed, Quality Foods had planned to introduce a line of entrees along with the Wonder Dessert Cup. Department executives viewed the

CASE

EXHIBIT 3
Business Analysis on Wonder Salad Cup
(in thousands of dollars)

	Development	Projected Test Market	National Introduction
Gross Sales		$530.4	$22,610.0
Transportation		10.2	1,360.0
Promotion		27.2	1,105.0
Net Sales		$493.0	$20,145.0
Cost of Goods Sold		453.9	12,750.0
Gross Profit/(Loss)		$ 39.1	$ 7,395.0
Warehousing and Shipping		18.7	782.0
Advertising		153.0	2,380.0
Extra Promotion		28.9	765.0
Special Sales Expense		5.1	34.0
Marketing Research	$ 59.5	88.4	110.5
New Products	42.5	34.0	
Graphics	8.5	1.7	
Product & Process Technology	59.5	25.5	
Operations/Engineering	25.5	—	
Packaging Development	59.5	8.5	
Profit/(Loss)		($324.7)	($ 3,323.5)
Total Allocated Development Expenses	$255.0	$158.1	
Total Capital Investment			$ 7,310.0
Return on Total Investment			45%
Anticipated Growth Rate/Year			5%

Source: Company records, figures disguised.

Wonder Salad Cup as a logical extension of the line— provided, of course, that it passed the normal new product screening.

Under consideration were two offerings: potato salad and a macaroni and cheese salad. Initial screening and the business analysis both showed that this line had considerable potential (see exhibit 3). Of some concern, however, was whether the Wonder Salad Cup had to be chilled to be appealing to the consumer. Would they want a salad at room temperature? If consumers thought the product needed refrigeration, Mr. Hutchinson felt this could seriously jeopardize its attractiveness. Some consideration was being given to developing a container for better chilling the salad, although its impact on sales was not determined. Such a package would be considerably different in design and add to the product cost.

Despite expectations, the Wonder Salad Cup was not considered to be a great success in the test market (see exhibit 4). Not only did its profitability fall below desired levels, but some production problems were discovered with the macaroni and cheese salad. When stored for prolonged periods of time, the cheese separated from the macaroni. Production engineers, however, felt that this was only a minor problem and could be rectified rather easily. Since the test market stage only lasted a few months, this problem was not discovered by consumers and therefore was not thought to be a cause of its poor showing.

CASE

EXHIBIT 4
Wonder Salad Cup Test Market Results
(in thousands of dollars)

Gross Sales		$425.0
Cash Discounts	$ 8.5	
Transportation	25.5	
Promotion	22.1	
Net Sales	$ 56.1	$368.9
Cost of Goods Sold	374.0	
Gross Profit/(Loss)		($ 5.1)
Warehouse & Shipping	$ 15.3	
Advertising	187.0	
Extra Promotion	22.1	
Sales Expense	17.0	
Publicity	3.4	
Net Profit/(Loss)	($244.8)	($249.9)
Development Costs		
Marketing Research	170.0	
New Products	42.5	
Graphics	5.1	
Product & Process Technology	25.5	
Packaging	17.0	
Total Development Costs	$260.1	
Net Costs		($510.0)

Source: Company records, figures disguised.

THE DECISION

Although a poor test market would typically doom a new product, Mr. Hutchinson was reluctant to accept those findings at face value. While he did not doubt the validity of the study, he was wondering whether this was a time when extenuating circumstances should prevail.

Since the Wonder Dessert Cup was so well accepted, Mr. Hutchinson thought that its success might well pull the Wonder Salad Cup along too. Additionally, there was little question that this product fit appropriately into any line extension, and in fact might do well if marketed primarily through vending machines and mobile snack shops rather than the traditional grocery store. Finally, its introduction might heighten consumer interest in the entire line and thereby help stimulate Wonder Dessert Cup sales, which had been declining.

In preparing to make his recommendation, Mr. Hutchinson was unsure of the significance of these considerations, especially in light of the disappointing test market results. This decision, he thought, was not going to be as easy as he had originally expected.

INTERCOMMUNITY SOCIETY FOR THE PREVENTION OF CRUELTY TO ANIMALS

HISTORY AND BACKGROUND

The Intercommunity Society for the Prevention of Cruelty to Animals (ICSPCA), founded in 1925, was incorporated in a Northwestern state as a nonprofit charitable organization in 1930. The Society is not affiliated with any other SPCA organization, but it is a member of the American Humane Society and the Humane Society of the United States. Located in a town of approximately 185,000 people, the ICSPCA serves four counties that have a combined population of 1.4 million.

The ICSPCA has occupied an old building in the downtown area since 1947. This building provides administrative offices and shelter for animals. The Shelter has a capacity for housing two hundred animals. Due to its overcrowded conditions, the Society hopes to start construction of a new shelter capable of housing four hundred animals in one of the city's suburbs. Considering the financial condition of the Society, it appears unlikely that the new facility, estimated to cost $455,000, can be started any time soon.

Last year the Society experienced the most rapid growth in its history. Over 25,000 animals were processed—that is, either adopted or humanely disposed of; 2,755 animals were spayed; and several hundred complaints about cruelty to animals were investigated. This growth severely strained the Society's financial and human resources. Operating funds came largely from contributions and adoption

This case was prepared by Professor Ralph M. Gaedeke, California State University, Sacramento.

fees. The organization's nineteen full-time employees and a limited number of volunteers handled the case load.

To raise funds for the ICSPCA, the organization founded the Women's Guild in 1963. The Guild sponsors numerous events, such as the annual book sale and the poster contest for children. The Guild also operates a thrift shop, which sells clothes, children's games, garden tools, electrical appliances, and various household items. Although the Women's Guild has in the past been the backbone and strength of the Society, the director of the ICSPCA recently indicated:

Unfortunately, the Guild's strength is now a weakness in many respects. Traditionally, upper and middle-class women devoted themselves to a "cause" as a socially acceptable outlet for their talents and energies and the Society was just such a cause. This had been a major factor in the organization's longevity and stability, but it is now an obstacle in terms of improving management techniques and expanding the organization's goals. The Women's Guild has stagnated into a social club. It is resistant to change in either the structure or the purpose of the Society.

Purpose of the ICSPCA

The ICSPCA's purpose is to prevent and alleviate the suffering of animals. Its focus extends beyond pets to include all animal life. The Society operates a shelter to house animals which are picked up, on request, by the staff, as well as those brought in by owners who no longer can care for their pets. The Society does not handle animal control problems such as barking dogs and healthy strays. These are the responsibility of the City and County Animal Control departments.

SERVICES PERFORMED BY THE ICSPCA

The ICSPCA operates an animal shelter in which housing, handling, and adoption policies provide for the health and safety of animals and prevent the infliction of fear, pain, or distress. The Shelter is open to the public seven days a week, from 9:00 A.M. until 5:00 P.M. on Monday through Saturday, and from 10:00 A.M. until 4:00 P.M. on Sunday.

Adoption Policy

Adoption fees are set by the ICSPCA and can be waived for cause by the executive director. The ICSPCA does not guarantee that an animal brought to the Shelter will be adopted, but it attempts to place all of the animals that are suitable for adoption. This is emphasized in their literature:

> No animal that comes into this shelter is guaranteed a home. Some will not be placed for adoption, some will become sick while they are in the shelter or some will run out of time. We place as many animals as we are able, but we cannot promise to place yours.

Last year, over 25,000 animals were brought to the Shelter, but only 20 percent were placed in new homes. Injured and unplaced animals were euthanized.

Low-Cost Spay and Neuter Clinic

An adoption policy of the Shelter requires that all dogs and cats be spayed or neutered to prevent more unwanted pets from being born. The Society operates a low-cost spay and neuter clinic five days a week on an appointment basis. Initially, the spay and neuter clinic was established to provide services for indigent families, but it has become a major source of the Shelter's revenues.

Low-Cost Shot Service

A nonappointment, nonadvertised distemper and rabies shots service operates through the spay and neuter clinic, from 9:00 until 10:30 A.M., Monday through Friday.

There has been some discussion regarding the future of the low-cost shot service. During the past several years, the Shelter's relationship with the veterinary community has deteriorated. Both the spay and neuter clinic and the low-cost shot service compete with local veterinarians. The director feels

that it is important to maintain good relations with the veterinary community, but hesitates to lose the income generated by the clinics and the shot service. Discontinuing the shot service would result in a loss of $6000 in Shelter income.

In the past, injured animals were taken to the local emergency veterinary clinic and the ICSPCA was billed for one-half the cost of services. If the Shelter discontinues the low-cost shot service, these emergency services would be provided free by the veterinary clinic and by private veterinarians. This would result in savings in service costs, and also in gasoline costs, since injured animals would not have to be transported across town to the emergency clinic, but could be treated by a veterinarian in the immediate area.

Ambulance Service

The ICSPCA provides 24-hour emergency ambulance service for all sick or injured animals. Strays are rescued at no charge to the caller. Charges on services for owned animals are $15 for service within twenty miles of the Shelter and $20 for service outside a twenty-mile radius.

Services for Injured or Sick Animals

All abandoned, stray, or injured animals given to the ICSPCA are taken to the Central Valley Emergency Veterinary Clinic or to a veterinarian for treatment. If the animal only has a minor injury or a noncontagious illness, it is taken to the Shelter for adoption.

Animal Cruelty Investigation

The Shelter employs State Humane Officers who investigate animal cruelty complaints. The officers enforce the state penal code concerning housing, starvation, neglect, abuse, and poisoning of animals.

Humane Education

Students and other groups are invited to tour the ICSPCA facilities. The Society distributes materials at fairs and other events, and the executive director and other employees present information at schools and at civic meetings. It is envisioned that an auditorium for educational purposes will be included in the new building plans.

Wildlife Care Association

The Society is a constituent member of the Wildlife Care Association (WCA). All emergency calls to the ICSPCA involving exotic animals are referred to the WCA. The ICSPCA provides ambulance service and temporary care for injured wildlife. It is hoped that a facility for the care of wild animals would be established upon development of the new shelter.

PROPOSED SERVICES

Several proposals are being considered as means to increase revenues and provide more services to the community. While some members want to discontinue the low-cost spay and neuter clinic and the low-cost shot service, others feel that the ICSPCA should provide complete veterinary services to the community at competitive rates. This group feels that more money would be lost by closing the clinics than could be justified merely for the sake of improving relations with the veterinary community. The provision of complete veterinary care for the community, could increase revenue, utilize existing facilities more efficiently, and generate additional publicity for the Society.

Another proposal is to open a dog obedience school. The staff realizes that many people adopting pets do not know how to train their animals. Also, it has been discovered that people placing pets for adoption often do so because of problems created by untrained animals. It is felt that some of these problems could be avoided if more people used a dog obedience program. The dog obedience school would be competitively priced and would generate revenue and publicity.

Other suggestions are to offer pet grooming services and to operate a kennel to board pets while owners are on vacation.

ORGANIZATION AND MANAGEMENT

The Society's policy decisions are made by the fifteen member board of directors. The board makes important directional policy decisions and establishes the Society's rules and regulations, which are implemented by the executive director. Directors are nominated by the general membership or by the board. Each director is elected to a two-year term and cannot serve for more than two consecutive terms. In order to achieve some continuity, eight directors are elected in odd-numbered years and seven directors in even-numbered years. The president and vice-president are elected annually by the board. The president appoints a secretary and a treasurer, or a combined secretary-treasurer.

The composition of the board has changed over the past five years. For many years, it had consisted of retired individuals who were leaders of the community. But recently, young, professional individuals with business expertise have been elected to the board. Denise King, a local attorney, was president of the board last year. She described the reason for the transition: "It was felt that a more aggressive board was needed if the ICSPCA were to become an active, timely organization." Last year the board included two lawyers, an accountant, a schoolteacher, a school vice-president, a dentist, a business manager, and retirees.

The board of directors meets once a month. Ms. King has indicated that the board makes two major types of policy decisions—those involving philosophical issues, such as the Shelter's stand on euthanasia and policy decisions regarding operations. Committees play an important role in operational decisions. The committees research problems and make recommendations to the board. Philosophical issues are resolved by discussion among all board members.

Directors are asked to participate in one or more committees, which meet separately once a month. Three committees are required by the bylaws of the Society: the Nominating Committee, the Finance Committee, and the Shelter Committee. The Nominating Committee is responsible for submitting a list of candidates for the office of Board Director.

The Finance Committee informs the board of the financial status of the Society and reviews the Society's investment practices. The Shelter Committee reviews personnel policies and serves as an appeals board for employee grievances. Two additional committees, not required by the bylaws, are the Fund-Raising Committee and the Building Committee. The Fund-Raising Committee was established ten years ago to act as a liaison between the board and outside professional fundraisers. The responsibilities of the committee's members include decisions on the use of professional fundraisers, the development of fundraising drives, and decisions on budgetary matters. The Building Committee was established six years ago to locate a site for the new shelter. The committee located and purchased a ten-acre site four years ago, contracted with a local architect, and is in charge of overseeing contract responsibilities for the new shelter.

The Women's Guild

The Women's Guild operates as an auxiliary to the ICSPCA. Annual fundraising activities sponsored by the Guild include the December Boutique, the Annual Luncheon, and the January Book Sale. Last year's book sale raised $8,500. In addition, the Guild has operated a thirft shop for the past seven years. The thrift shop, open Monday through Saturday from 9:30 A.M. until 3:30 P.M., nets nearly $2,200 a month. It is staffed by approximately thirty women, each of whom donates six hours per week. The majority of items sold, which include clothes, dishes, utensils, books, and games, are purchased by dealers who resell the items at flea markets.

Executive Director

The day-to-day operations at the Shelter and in the Humane Investigation Department are conducted by a skilled and dedicated staff. Janet Pearsley heads the staff and is responsible for administration. She became executive director six months ago. She is responsible for advising and assisting the board, for conducting the activities and business of the Society, and for the operation of the Shelter in accordance

with the principles and the policies prescribed by the board of directors. Ms. Pearsley describes her relationship with the board as "excellent." Before she became director of the ICSPCA, Janet was employed at a state university where she worked in the agronomy and genetics departments and was a staff research associate for the animal science department. This entailed administrative responsibilities, researching and writing grant proposals, training graduate students, and overseeing budgetary matters for a laboratory engaged in stress research. Janet was in charge of the laboratory while its senior professor was on a year's sabbatical leave.

All previous executive directors had backgrounds and affiliations related to the care of animals. However, past directors lacked managerial effectiveness. Janet Pearsley is the fourth individual to assume the position in five years. Harry Stevens, her predecessor, had been fired. Basically, the executive director is free to handle day-to-day operations and administration of the Society. Mr. Stevens misused this privilege and this resulted in mismanaged funds and an inefficient Shelter. Ms. Pearsley has initiated control measures, because she feels that the Shelter must be operated like a business to maximize its efficiency.

Ms. King has said that the Board is very satisfied with Janet Pearsley's performance. She has the two most important qualifications: administrative experience and experience with animal care. Some members have found that her lack of affiliation with national organizations is an asset. As one member indicated, "Janet's primary interest is the Intercommunity Valley Shelter and its activities, rather than the much broader national humane focus."

Shelter Staff

The organization of the Shelter staff is shown in exhibit 1. Dr. Bailey, the Shelter's veterinarian during the past year, was appointed by the board of directors. Dr. Bailey receives half of the spay and neutering fees and also is free to keep his own hours. Some board members feel that the present agreement, arranged by the previous director, is too generous. Ms. Pearsley hopes that in the future the veterinarian, although appointed by the board, will be responsible

EXHIBIT 1
I.C.S.P.C.A.
Organization Chart

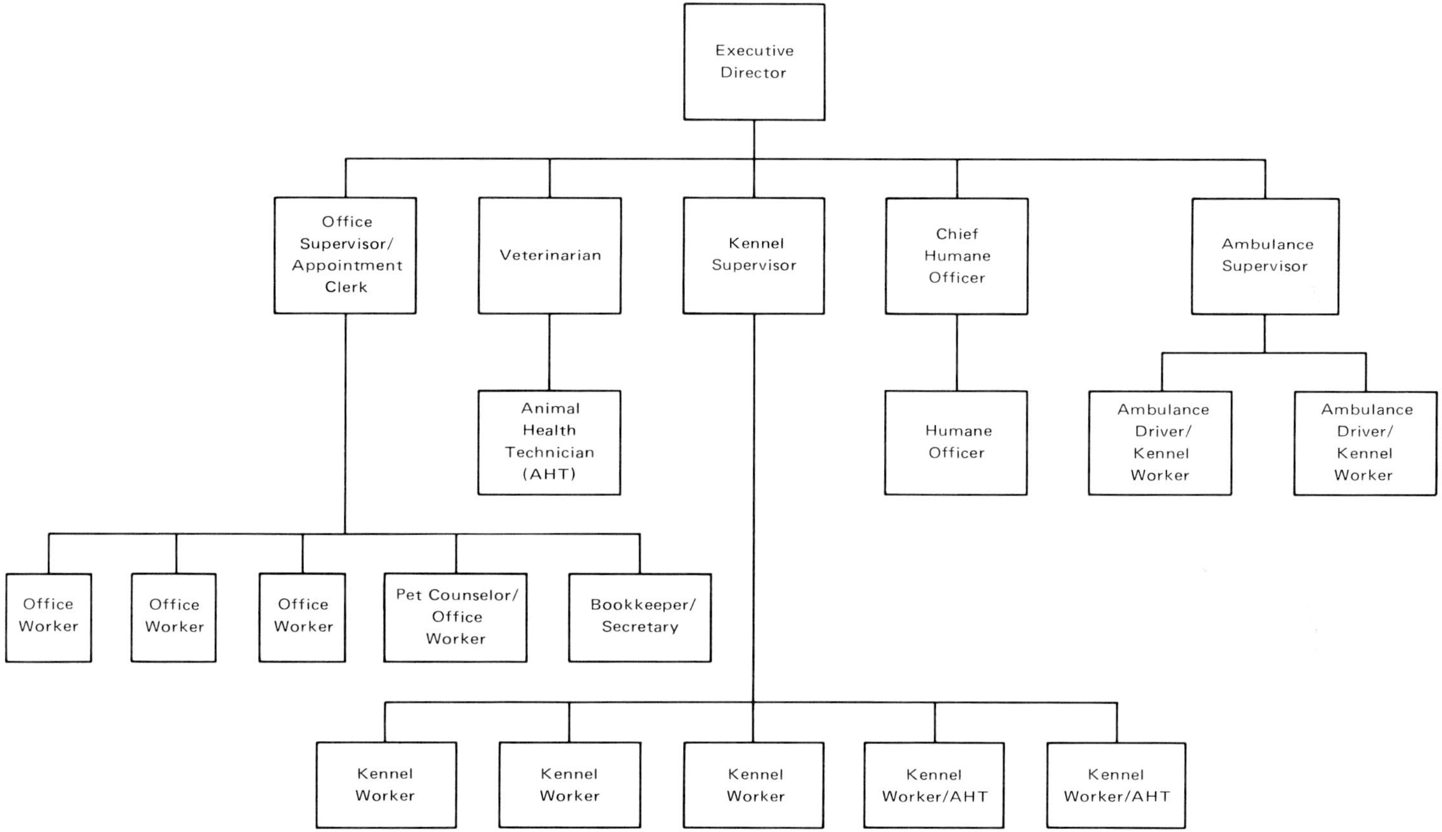

to the executive director. It seems unlikely that the present agreement with Dr. Bailey will be renewed.

Shelter supervisors train and instruct other animal care personnel and prepare employee work schedules. They are responsible for maintaining the inventory of supplies.

The office staff receives incoming animals, processes the adoptions, answers telephones, and dispatches emergency calls. The bookkeeper is in charge of payroll, purchases, and accounts payable and maintains all appropriate ledgers and membership files. An outside bookkeeper comes in once a month to help with problems and the Society is audited yearly at its own request.

Members of the kennel staff are responsible for receiving and taking care of animals. They maintain the proper identification records for the Shelter animals and are responsible for the cleanliness of the kennel. Emergency rescue services and ambulance maintenance are the responsibilities of the ambulance staff. The humane officer's duties are to conduct humane investigations and supervise the care of impounded animals. The spay and neuter clinic personnel assist in surgery, are in charge of the clinic and its patients, admit and release the animals, and keep the appropriate records for the clinic. All of the staff members, except the spay and neuter clinic personnel, assist with tours, lectures, and public education.

Since Janet Pearsley assumed the directorship, staff turnover has no longer been a problem. Previously, the average length of an employee's tenure with the Shelter was four and a half months. Ms. Pearsley is concerned about Intercommunity's inability to pay competitive salaries. Last year, the salary for an office worker was six hundred dollars per month. Consequently, the Shelter has had difficulty attracting highly qualified individuals.

Fundraising activities have been contracted to an advertising agency (the Harper Agency) which is paid a flat fee plus expenses. The Shelter is considering hiring a staff person to be responsible for fundraising activities. The staff is encouraged by the prospect of fundraising being carried out by the Shelter itself. If funding is increased, part of the additional funds will be utilized to raise salary levels.

FINANCIAL CHARACTERISTICS

The ICSPCA was incorporated in 1936 as a nonprofit charitable organization under Section 501(c)(3) of the Internal Revenue Code.

The Society does not receive funds from local, state, or federal government sources, or from any charitable fundraising organization. Its sources of funds are:

1. Personal donations and bequests
2. Contributions from those who adopted animals
3. ICSPCA memberships
4. The ICSPCA's Women's Guild fundraising activities.

Total revenue last year was $229,315. Revenue from bequests ($76,645) was the largest source of funds. Income from estates varies considerably from year to year and cannot be anticipated; budgeting is complicated due to this variability. Shelter revenue, which is derived largely from adoption fees and membership renewals, contributed $77,450. The Harper Agency raised $35,714. Together these three sources accounted for 75 percent of total revenue. The income statement and balance sheet for the ICSPCA General Fund are presented in exhibits 2 and 3.

An agreement was made two years ago with the Harper Agency to raise funds for the Society. Although the agency raised $35,714 last year, income generated by the Society from "mail donations" and "extra activities" dropped significantly from two years ago. The decrease was greater than the net contribution of the agency. Janet Pearsley feels that the agreement with the agency will not be renewed. The Society is considering hiring a fundraiser to be paid on a commission basis.

Membership fees brought in $7,698 last year. The schedule of fees were as follows:

Junior	$ 2.00
Senior Citizen	5.00
Regular	10.00
Organization	25.00
Life	100.00
Perpetual	250.00

EXHIBIT 2
ICSPCA General Fund
Income Statement, December 31

	Previous Year	Last Year
Revenues		
Shelter Income	$ 82,115	$ 77,450
Ambulance Service	2,010	2,419
New Building Donations		5,777
New Members	6,417	6,533
Life Members	2,350	950
Mail Donations	48,943	11,115
Business Members	385	215
Interest Income	5,010	5,714
Extra Activity Income	8,430	6,333
Donations From Estates	14,588	76,645
Harper Agency		35,714
Miscellaneous	1,205	450
Total Revenue	$171,453	$229,315
Transfer From Spay Clinic	7,000	21,500
Total	$178,453	$250,815
Expenses		
New Building Expenses		$ 3,455
Building Repairs and Maint.	$ 2,614	3,115
Telephone	1,985	2,314
Utilities	4,111	5,765
Depreciation Expenses	7,589	8,324
Vehicle Gas and Repair	10,314	7,605
Insurance	2,100	4,150
Office Supplies	2,791	4,030
Total Labor	135,600	140,050
Public Relations and Newsletter	4,440	3,950
Dues and Subscriptions	321	403
Postage	657	1,057
Internal Fundraising	14,650	3,252
Miscellaneous and Travel	2,100	1,550
Taxes	305	1,214
Audit Fees	2,330	1,772
Legal Fees and Bookkeeping	761	776
Bad Checks	977	638
Humane Activities Expense	3,200	1,850
Chemical Supplies	2,938	3,515
Medical Supplies	3,415	6,750
Pet Food	3,984	7,055
Disposal	1,000	1,100
Euthanasia	987	107
Uniforms	450	760
Harper Agency	8,100	27,415
Total Expenses	$217,719	$241,972
Gain (Loss)	($ 31,266)	$ 10,843

Adoption fees or shelter income provided 33.8 percent of revenue last year. The schedule of fees for adoption were as follows:

Puppy, kitten, or intact cat	$ 5.30
Intact dog, neutered cat	10.60
Neutered dog	15.90

The Society's two major expenses were labor ($140,050) and fees paid to the Harper Agency ($27,415), which together accounted for 69.2 percent of total expenses.

Half of the Society's assets were in cash and half in fixed assets. The Society had purchased land for $65,000 for a new facility that was expected to cost $455,000.

Capital accumulated from previous years was approximately $116,000. Other capital paid-in came from the spay clinic and the Women's Guild.

The accounts for the spay and neuter clinic were kept separately from the Shelter's general fund. A separate income statement and a balance sheet for the spay and neuter clinic are presented in exhibits 4 and 5.

The spay and neuter clinic had a net income of $10,342 last year. The schedule of fees were as follows:

Spaying and Neutering Fees	(Deposit)
Spaying dog	$25.00
Spaying cat	17.50
Neutering dog	20.00
Neutering cat	10.00

Note: Additional charge of $5 for pregnant, obese, excessively large animals, or other complications.

The schedule applied to deposits required of those adopting an intact animal. The deposit is refunded upon proof of spaying or neutering; otherwise the deposit is forfeited. This allows individual clients to have their animals spayed or neutered at other facilities. The adoption fees and spaying and neutering fees were changed last year. Before that time, adoption fees were set on a graduated scale based on the type of animal, and individuals were required to pay half of the spaying or neutering fee. After the fee change, the individual assumed the full

EXHIBIT 3
ICSPCA General Fund
Balance Sheet, December 31

	Previous Year		Last Year	
Current Assets:				
Cash*		$ 86,987		$ 83,164
Interest Receivable		172		―――
Total		$ 87,159		$ 83,164
Fixed Assets:				
Ambulance	$10,000		$10,200	
Less Accumulated Depreciation	0	10,000	2,040	8,160
Equipment	38,460		40,826	
Less Accumulated Depreciation	25,741	12,719	29,356	11,470
Cars	8,648		10,657	
Less Accumulated Depreciation	4,498	4,150	3,239	7,417
Land		―――		65,000
Total		$ 26,869		$ 92,047
Other Assets:				
Prepaid Insurance		$ 3,444		$ 4,079
Supplies		820		―――
Service Policies		274		234
Note Receivable		―――		375
Total Assets		$118,566		$179,899
Liabilities:				
Payroll Tax		$ 16		$ 1,324
Dental Plan		87		―――
Sales Tax Payable		―――		610
Accounts Payable		843		―――
Insurance		25		25
Total Liabilities		$ 971		$ 1,959
Capital				
Accumulated Savings		$ 47,301		―――
Gain Prior Years		87,001		$116,485
Current Gain (Loss)		(16,647)		28,556[†]
Capital Gain (Loss)		(60)		400
Transferred From Women's Guild		―――		32,500
Total Capital		$117,595		$117,941
Total Liabilities and Capital		$118,566		$179,900

*Cash was invested in the short term money market.
[†]Includes 21,500 transferred from Spay Clinic.

EXHIBIT 4
ICSPCA Spay Clinic
Income Statement, December 31

	Previous Year	Last Year
Revenues		
Income From Services	$61,569	$62,252
Shot Clinic	—	9,684
Forfeited Deposits	—	8,837
Miscellaneous Donations	114	—
Total Income	$61,683	$80,773
Expenses		
Veterinarians's Services	$30,706	$35,589
Assistant's Wages	8,539	10,153
Office Clerk's Wages	8,259	11,385
Materials and Supplies	3,511	6,419
Insurance	612	985
Payroll Taxes	1,831	2,064
Miscellaneous	58	258
Advertising	648	416
Office Expenses	663	1,362
Bad Checks	45	—
Licenses	5	—
Telephone	410	340
Medical and Dental Plans	—	925
Sales Tax	—	535
Total Expenses	$55,287	$70,431
Net Income	$ 6,396	$10,342

EXHIBIT 5
ICSPCA Spay Clinic
Balance Sheet, December 31

	Previous Year	Last Year
Assets		
Cash	$2,522	$10,919
Prepaid Insurance	373	951
Total	$2,895	$11,870
Liabilities		
Payroll Taxes Payable	—	$ 457
Spay Deposits Payable	(85)	19,371
Sales Tax Payable	—	220
Total Liabilities	($ 85)	$20,048
Capital		
Gain (Loss) Prior Year	$3,585	$ 2,980
Gain (Loss)	(604)	10,341
Transfer to General Fund	—	(21,500)
Total Capital	$2,980	$ 8,179
Total Liabilities and Capital	$2,895	$11,870

cost of the spaying and neutering fee, but paid less in adoption fees.

Major expenses last year for the spay and neuter clinic included: veterinarian's fees ($35,589), assistant's wages ($10,152) and office clerk's wages ($11,385). These expenses represented 81 percent of the Clinic's total expenses last year.

MARKETING ACTIVITIES

The ICSPCA uses advertising, membership drives, publicity, and fund raising campaigns. Advertising placed in a local newspaper appeals for donations, and a campaign called "The Pet of the Week" announces weekly drawings for a pet giveaway.

The local media has been generous in providing the Society with publicity. The newspaper carries announcements of various fund-raising activities, and one radio station announces Society activities and services. Other stations have been approached regarding similar announcements. The executive director of the Society has appeared on all three local television stations. This exposure had been quite effective both in placing pets for adoption and in informing the public of ICSPCA functions.

Public relations activities consist of presentations to schools and tours of the shelter. The Society provides qualified people to speak to civic clubs, schools, and other organizations.

Various fundraising activities are held by the Women's Guild. The Guild sponsors annual "Kindness to Animals" poster contests, an Intercommunity Cat Fanciers Show, an Intercommunity Dachshund Club Specialty Show, and an annual book sale.

The ICSPCA publishes a monthly and quarterly newsletter which is distributed free of charge to members and is available at the Shelter. Literature on the proper care of pets and on the services provided by the ICSPCA is distributed free.

The Harper Agency has acted as a fundraiser for the Society for two years. During its first year, the agency held a cocktail party hosted by two television personalities. It also held a crab feed and conducted a mail campaign which solicited donations from existing members. In the latest campaign year, the agency held another crab feed and was again working on a mail campaign. Due to the limited funds raised, it is unlikely that the contract with the agency will be renewed. The Society is considering hiring a staff person to be responsible for its fundraising activities. The fundraiser's duties would include investigating possible grants from local, state, and federal government agencies and identifying sources of funding in the private sector.

Ms. Pearsley and the staff have several ideas for future fundraising activities. These include a "Buy a Brick" campaign which would allow the public to contribute to construction costs; negotiations are under way to obtain the donation of an automobile to be raffled.

Price Strategies

One of the most difficult tasks for the marketing manager is to develop the pricing strategies for a product. In the exchange process, "price" represents the value placed on goods and services by both the seller and the buyer. But sellers and buyers place different values on a product, depending on their needs, characteristics, and alternatives for using the funds available to them. And, because these relationships can change rapidly, the values placed on a product can also change quickly.

As a result, there is no absolute "right" price for a product. Too much depends on the unique characteristics of the product and the potential customers. Yet, it is the marketing manager's job to arrive at a price that continually balances these dynamic forces.

SETTING PRICING OBJECTIVES

Developing a set of price strategies must begin with consideration of what the firm wants to achieve with its pricing. This process is described in the article by A. R. Oxenfeldt, "A Decision-Making Structure for Price Decisions." While it is commonly believed that profit maximization is the only objective, this is frequently not the case. A number of other objectives may be of equal or greater importance. These include:

1. Maximizing sales
2. Increasing market share
3. Increasing cash flow
4. Maximizing return on investment
5. Stabilizing pricing within the market
6. Discouraging competition from entering the market
7. Supporting the firm's other products

In cases where the marketing manager is attempting to gain a strong position in the marketplace, maximizing sales and/or increasing market share may be more important than increasing profits—at least in the short run. Or, if the firm was having problems with cash flow, prices could be set to increase the amount of cash coming into the company.

Although profit maximization (for either the short or long term) is an important goal of pricing, an equally critical issue is how much is earned on the amount of resources committed. Return on investment typically is a truer measure of profitability than is dollars of profit.

Among the less quantitative goals are stabilizing the market, discouraging competition, and supporting the firm's other products. One method of stabilizing the market is to set prices at the same level as competitors. When this is accomplished throughout a market, and no firm has a price advantage, price becomes a less critical component of the marketing mix. Accordingly, firms also compete on bases other than price (such as product design, image, and distribution).

Using price as a means of preventing or eliminating competition has been a somewhat risky strategy. Antitrust legislation has placed heavy penalties on attempts to monopolize markets and predatory pricing tactics are specifically prohibited. Nevertheless, to the extent that a firm maintains a very aggressive pricing policy, competitors may be discouraged from entering the market.

In some instances, the firm will set prices for one product in such a way as to help other products it offers for sale. When complementary goods are sold or when high or low prices are needed to build the overall image of the firm, the marketing manager's primary objective may be to maintain internal consistency in the pricing of the firm's products.

DEVELOPING PRICING STRATEGIES

Once the pricing goals are set, the marketing manager must choose from among alternative pricing strategies (see Joel Dean's article, "Pricing Policies for New Products"). The key strategies which should be considered are:

1. Skim versus penetration pricing
2. Fixed versus variable pricing
3. Price lining versus singular pricing
4. Customary pricing
5. Prestige pricing
6. Psychological pricing

For new products, one of the central issues is whether to use a skim or penetration pricing strategy. With a skim strategy, the firm sets the price for the product artificially high to take advantage of the initial purchasers' willingness to pay a high price when there is no alternative product on the market. Then, as competitors enter the market, prices are lowered to market levels. As would be expected, the large profit margins produced by the skim strategy attract competition to the marketplace, making this a short-term strategy. A penetration strategy, on the other hand, involves setting prices somewhat lower to discourage competitors from entering the market—thereby allowing the firm more time to entrench itself.

Another strategy issue is whether to use fixed or variable pricing. In using fixed prices, the firm does not allow for negotiations between the buyer and seller. The price is set, and the consumer has the choice of paying that price or not buying the product. With variable pricing, the price for each product is the subject of negotiation between the seller and the buyer. Because of the time and complexity of variable pricing, most firms prefer to use fixed prices. Only in selected industries (such as automobiles and home sales) has variable pricing proven to be worthwhile.

In instances where the firm has several products appealing to the same market, a choice must be made between price lining and singular pricing. With price lining, the firm establishes a limited number of prices, and all products are priced at one of those levels. For example, a retailer of women's dresses may set prices at $30, $50, $85, $120 and $150, and all dresses in the store will be priced at one of those five levels. This is easier for the retailer and simplifies the decision for the consumer—the choice will be among five prices rather than among individual prices for each specific item, as would be the case in singular pricing.

In some cases, the marketing manager will find that the prices charged for competing items have been consistently set at a certain price level, which the consumer has come to expect to pay. Since it is a "customary" price, there is no need to price below that level and consumers are likely to strongly resist higher prices. In these cases, a decision has to be made whether to accept the customary price or attempt to break with tradition.

Depending on the target market, the marketing manager may have to decide whether to use prestige pricing. For some classes of products, value resides as much in the high price as it does in the product's functional value. In these instances, prices must be set high to maintain an image of worth. Examples of these products would include jewelry, fur coats, and expensive sports cars.

Certainly one of the most critical strategy issues is whether to use psychological pricing, and in particular whether to watch price thresholds. Recognizing that consumers read from left to right and hear higher dollar levels before lesser levels, some prices may appear to be higher than they actually are when the consumer stops reading or listening. For example, a price of $2.01 may be unacceptably higher that a price of $1.98, while consumer sensitivity to the difference between $1.85 and $1.98 may be negligible. By considering possible thresholds, such as the $2.00 level in this example, the marketing manager can ensure that the price set for the product does not appear to be too high or low in the mind of the consumer.

APPROACHES TO SETTING PRICES

There are a variety of approaches to setting the actual price for a product, as described in Joel Dean's article, "Techniques for Pricing New Products and Services." Generally, the various techniques can be classified as being either cost or demand oriented.

As the name implies, cost-oriented approaches focus on the costs of manufacturing or buying the product and selling it to the consumer. Typically, some percentage mark-up is added to the cost to arrive at the selling price. In other cases, a target return on investment will be established, and the price needed to earn that level will be set. The advantages of these approaches are that they are easy to use, and they insure that most or all of the costs of the product are covered in the price depending on how fixed costs are allocated. The primary disadvantage of cost-oriented approaches is that in setting the final price for the product, little, if any, consideration is given to demand—to what consumers are able and willing to pay.

Demand-oriented approaches to pricing involve the analysis of consumer sensitivity to price. Measures of elasticity are commonly taken to better determine consumer trade-offs between the price and the quantity demanded. These techniques are difficult to use, though, and imprecise at best. Because consumer sensitivities are fluid, it is hard to determine what the price should be for any reasonable length of time.

The selling price of a product is a critical variable in the total pricing strategy used by the marketing manger. However, it is not the only one, nor the most important issue in many instances. Other factors may be much more significant to potential buyers, especially in industrial markets. These include: quantity discounts (both cumulative and noncumulative), cash discounts, trade discounts, seasonal pricing, promotional pricing, forward dating, transportation costs, and the quality of the warranty.

Because so many factors affect the appropriateness of a price, overall pricing strategies must be reevaluated frequently. Changes in the market environment, the costs of production, or the other marketing mix variables will necessitate adjustments in the firm's pricing strategy over time.

Alfred R. Oxenfeldt

A Decision-making Structure for Price Decisions

Until recently, almost all pricing decisions have either been highly intuitive, as in the case of new product introductions, or based on routine procedures, as in cost-plus or imitative pricing. The proportion of price decisions representing these extreme approaches seems to have declined substantially; yet, many business executives have not altered their pricing methods substantially.[1]

Research continues on how businesses should set prices. Most of these studies attempt to uncover the best methods rather than those in current practice. No researcher has completely overcome the enormous difficulties of learning the basis on which group decisions are made and the "sensitive" reasons underlying many price decisions.[2] This article examines some trends in pricing and the apparent gulf between pricing theory and practice. A pricing framework is presented to help practitioners structure their important pricing decisions.

THE GAP BETWEEN PRICING THEORY AND APPLICATION

The current pricing literature has produced few new insights or exciting new approaches that would interest most businessmen enough to change their present methods. Those executives who follow the business literature have no doubt broadened their viewpoint and become more explicit and systematic about their pricing decisions; however, few, if any, actually employ new and different goals, concepts, or techniques.

The gap between pricing literature and practice may exist because the authors lack extensive personal experience with the practical problems facing execu-

Source: From the *Journal of Marketing,* Vol. 37 (January, 1973), pp. 48–53. Reprinted by permission of the American Marketing Association.

tives in a highly competitive and complex business environment. Other explanatory factors include: the number of products for which executives are responsible, the lack of reliable information on product demand, the dynamic nature of technology, and the unpredictable responses from competitors. Because of the large number of highly uncertain and variable factors, executives responsible for pricing closely adhere to methods that they have found to be effective in the past. Economists and practitioners have long recognized that price is a dangerously explosive and complex marketing variable.

This discussion does not suggest that those responsible for pricing should always adhere to traditional methods of setting price, or that those writing about pricing have contributed little of value. The point is that a significant gap exists between the two areas and that this gap must be closed if pricing is to continue to develop as a crucially important area of marketing theory and practice. Pricing specialists have suggested many helpful methods that have not been implemented in practice even after they have demonstrated to be valid.

LITERATURE TRENDS: A CRITIQUE

The field of pricing remains largely the domain of economic theorists who discuss price primarily in relation to the analyses of specific market structures.

Much of the pricing literature deals with tactics and strategems for particular kinds of firms—wholesalers, manufacturers, franchisees, or joblot shops. Special corporate situations such as new product introductions, inflation, declining products, product-line pricing, price-structure problems, and price-cutting are also popular topics in the pricing literature.[3] The current literature on pricing, like that in most other areas of marketing, draws heavily on the behavioral sciences, quantitative tools, and detailed empirical research. Present-day writers employ simulation techniques and other computer applications much more than in the past, and are often concerned with cost computation and demand estimation. Pricing receives far more attention from marketing specialists today than it did when managerial economists such as Joel Dean, Jules Bachman, Arthur R. Burns, Donald Wallace, Edward Mason, Edwin Nourse, Walton Hamilton, Walter Adams, and Morris A. Adelman were the chief contributors to the field.

Recently, pricing specialists have channeled much of their research efforts into the development of approaches designed to aid the accuracy and efficiency of the decision maker. The most promising methods are: use of the computer;[4] simulation as a method for anticipating the effect of price changes on sales and for testing complex strategies;[5] research techniques for obtaining more reliable information about prospective customer responses to price change;[6] and the nature and determinants of price perception.[7]

Nevertheless, large gaps still remain in the pricing literature. Very little is said about reconciling the various price-optima; i.e., the prices that are best vis-à-vis costs, the ultimate customer, resellers, and rivals. Most authors deal with pricing problems unidimensionally, whereas businessmen must generally deal with price as one element in a multidimensional marketing program. Price is often dealt with as if it were completely separated from the other elements in the marketing mix. These authors tend to concentrate on the effect of price on immediate marketwide sales without adequately considering long-run or individual market effects. The writers dealing with pricing decisions typically identify variables that are sometimes not considered and suggest conceptual errors that are commonly made, but they typically treat only small, isolated parts of the problem faced by a business executive. Little has been written on innovative approaches to pricing—approaches designed to *increase* demand, rather than *adapt to existing* demand. This failing has been most common in writings that employ quantitative techniques. A price-setter must not merely view his responsibility as that of determining the various demand elasticities (price, promotion, assortment, quality, design, and place) and finding the price that best adapts to them. Attention must be given to measures that alter these elasticities in his firm's favor.

The setting of any price involves: (1) values that particular segments of customers place on a firm's offering; (2) consumer responses to price changes of the product; (3) competitive responses to any price changes; and (4) resellers' sensitivity to price changes. No one has yet developed a completely reliable method to measure the price elasticity of demand for a particular brand. Similarly, little is known about resellers' responses to margin changes or the sales support a brand will receive from distributors and retailers. The specific responses of competitors to both price and nonprice actions is still a matter of great uncertainty in almost all industries.

Pricing should be regarded as a field where the essential elements are quite clear and well known and where the concepts that need to be applied also are widely recognized and within reach of all executives. Practitioners face the problem of measuring a multitude of factors in many different specific situations; that is, they must attempt to quantify the response functions (elasticities) so they can be compared. One of the major problems in pricing is obtaining the data required to measure each of these response functions in different market contexts. Pricing specialists have made very few contributions to the solution of this problem.

CONSTRAINTS ON PRICING DECISIONS

Many vital price-related decisions made by top management deal with the following issues: Are we willing to drive competitors from business if we can? Should we inflict serious injury upon them when they have been struck by misfortune? Are we willing to violate the spirit or letter of the law to increase sales? At a different level of concern, pricing decisions are related to price strategy and general competitive policy by questions such as: "Should we seek price leadership for ourselves or foster a pattern of price leadership with some other firm as leader? Should we try to shake out the weak firms in the industry to achieve price stability and higher profitability? Should we foster a spirit of cooperativeness among rivals by an avoidance of price competition?

These decisions are properly made by top executives and do not require a frequent revision. When they are not made explicitly, the executive responsible for pricing decision implicitly makes many of these decisions by default. A complete discussion of these constraints goes beyond the scope of this article.

To manage the complex nature of price-setting, practitioners need an effective, multidimensional model to guide their analysis. Such a pricing model would not only explicitly encourage systemized thinking, but also underscore the differential advantage available to the firm which strategically sets the prices of all of its products.

A FRAMEWORK FOR
PRICING DECISIONS

The following discussion of price decisions employs a decision-making framework which identifies the following stages:

1. Recognize the need for a pricing decision.
2. Price determination.
3. Develop a model.
4. Identify and anticipate pricing problems.
5. Develop feasible courses of action.
6. Forecast the outcomes of each alternative.
7. Monitor and review the outcome of each action.

These seven stages overlap somewhat and are not strictly sequential.

Recognize the Need for a Pricing Decision

A firm's pricing difficulties and opportunities are related to its overall objectives. Only when a firm is explicit in defining its corporate objectives can the executive specifically evaluate the obstacles and opportunities confronting him. Table 1 provides a partial list of feasible pricing objectives. It is important to note that the objectives of profitability and growth constitute only a small part of this list. The pricing objectives of many different firms are listed below; however, *each firm* must evaluate and determine the priority of these objectives as they relate to the individual firm.

From this list of objectives, some of the pricing problems that firms face can readily be inferred. Among the more important are:

1. A decline in sales.
2. Prices are too high—relative to those charged by rivals, relative to the benefits of the product. (Prices might be too high in a few regional markets and very appropriate elsewhere.)
3. Price is too low, again in certain markets and not in others.
4. The company is regarded as exploitative of customers and not to be trusted.
5. The firm places excessive financial burdens on its resellers.
6. The price deferentials among items in the line are objectionable or unintelligible.
7. Its price changes are too frequent—or do not take account of major changes in market circumstances.
8. The firm's price reflects negatively on itself and on its products.
9. The price is unstabilizing the market which had finally become stabilized after great difficulty.
10. The first is offering its customers too many price choices and confusing its customers and resellers.
11. The firm's prices seem higher to customers than they really are.
12. The firm's price policy attracts undesirable kinds of customers which have no loyalty to any seller.
13. The firm's pricing behavior makes customers unduly price sensitive and unappreciative of quality differences.
14. The company has fostered a decline in market discipline among sellers in the industry.

The list of pricing objectives in Table 1 and the illustrative list of pricing difficulties above suggest that prices and price changes do not simply affect current sales, but have more far-reaching effects.

TABLE 1
Potential Pricing Objectives

1. Maximum long-run profits
2. Maximum short-run profits
3. Growth
4. Stabilize market
5. Desensitize customers to price
6. Maintain price-leadership arrangement
7. Discourage entrants
8. Speed exit of marginal firms
9. Avoid government investigation and control
10. Maintain loyalty of middlemen and get their sales support
11. Avoid demands for "more" from suppliers—labor in particular
12. Enhance image of firm and its offerings
13. Be regarded as "fair" by customers (ultimate)
14. Create interest and excitement about the item
15. Be considered trustworthy and reliable by rivals
16. Help in the sale of weak items in the line
17. Discourage others from cutting prices
18. Make a product "visible"
19. "Spoil market" to obtain high price for sale of business
20. Build traffic

TABLE 2
Data That Might be Used to Design a Price Monitoring System

1. Sales—in units and in dollars
   a. Previous year comparisons
   b. Different markets/channels comparisons
2. Rivals' prices
3. Inquiries from potential customers about the line
4. Company's sales at "off list" price
   a. Measured as a % of total sales
   b. Revenue as % of sales at full price
5. Types of customers getting the most and largest price reductions
6. Market shares—in individual markets
7. Marketing costs; production cost; production costs at nearly output
8. Price complaints
   a. From customers
   b. From salesmen
9. Inventories of finished goods at different levels
10. Customers' attitudes toward firm, prices, etc.
11. Number of lost customers (brand-switching)
12. Inquiries—and subsequent purchases
13. Marketing costs

To identify the problems listed, a firm requires a monitoring system or a means of empirically determining the existence of potential problems and opportunities. Table 2 presents indicators a firm might use to suggest the existence of pricing problems. It is evident that some of these indicators are very difficult to measure with accuracy.

Price Determination

A warning system will detect pricing problems and allow the manager to decide how much attention to give to each potential price problem and to whom to assign it. In assigning a problem for study, a decision-maker must determine whether to use his own staff or call upon outside resources. Some price problems are self-correcting, in which case the price setter should ignore the warning.

Develop a Model

The primary question that must be addressed here is: What models would help businessmen to best cope with pricing responsibilities? Models developed by economic theorists rarely direct a pricing executive's attention to the key variables. Behavioral science offers far more insight into the factors that determine how price changes will be perceived and reacted to by consumers. The influence of price extends far beyond current sales figures, and behavioral science helps us more fully understand the extensive effect of price decisions.

Some mathematical models deserve a brief mention, even though they are not widely used in practice. The multiple regression model is familiar to most economists and marketing specialists. Based on historical data, this technique determines a linear functional relationship between sales and factors such as price, advertising, personal selling, relative product quality, product design, distribution arrangements, and customer services.

Another technique is the experimental approach to pricing strategy. One type of experimental approach, which may be based on regression analysis, is simulation. Such models allow the pricing specialist to combine wide varieties of inputs (including price) to achieve desired results such as short- and long-run sales together with the costs incurred. The relative merits of different factor combinations can be tested and compared.

A third type of mathematical model emphasizes the situation-specific parameters of a strategy. This approach is referred to as adaptive modeling and combines historical analysis with different environmental situations. A given input mix may have widely diver-

gent results for each situation. This type of approach is particularly helpful in assessing the merits of market expansion, segmentation analysis, and other decisions where contextual analysis is important.

These last two models deal with some fundamental characteristics of price. First, the interdependence and synergy of related model components become key issues in their effective use. Second, the proper mix of variables will differ from occasion to occasion, even for the same product or brand. Third, the outcome of any combination of marketing actions may be perceived differently by different consumers.

To completely understand how and when price works, an executive must understand how potential customers perceive, interpret, and evaluate price changes in making their purchase decisions. These decisions vary with the individual; therefore, an executive must also consider different market segments.

Identify and Anticipate Pricing Problems

When a firm encounters a pricing problem, its manifestations are generally not subtle and obscure; however, executives still have difficulty obtaining information that identifies the source of the problem. Information about customer reactions to a product are extremely difficult to interpret because the responses must be related to their particular market segments. A seller primarily seeks the opinions of those customer segments he wishes to serve, rather than of all prospective customers. Most research data, however, do not match customer responses with the corresponding market segment to which they belong.

Price-setters require an information system to monitor the effects of their pricing arrangements and thus to help make prompt and specific adaptive action in a fast changing market environment. Salesmen's reports, current sales experience, and individual favorite customers are the primary sources of information available to most firms.

Develop Feasible Courses of Action

Traditionally, price setters have considered only a very limited number of alternatives when faced with pricing difficulties. If their price seemed high, they would lower it, and if it was too low, they would simply raise it. Much more complex behaviors are available to most pricers which provide opportunities for novel approaches. In addition to varying the price level, the executive responsible for pricing may also change the following factors: (1) The timing of the price change; (2) the number of price changes (he is not limited to a single change); (3) the time interval to which the price change applies; and (4) the number of items whose price he changes (he could raise some prices while lowering others). In addition, the executive can combine a price change with other marketing actions. For example, he might change the product's package, advertising, quality, appearance, or the after-sale customer service. Even more important, he can change price in some markets and not in others, or change them in different ways. The price-setter may even modify his discount arrangements in such a way as to increase the effectiveness of the price change.

A price-setter must not regard his actions as simply shifting prices on individual product offerings. He must recognize that his firm sells a line of products in a wide variety of geographic markets, and that its offerings embrace many benefits of varying importance to customers. Price is only one of those consumer benefits. A firm rarely makes its very best reaction to a pricing problem or opportunity by simply altering price.

Forecast the Outcome of Each Alternative Action

Once a price-setter has selected the most feasible actions available, he must forecast their consequences to determine which will best achieve his goals. At this stage, the price-setter must be as specific as possible about the expected short- and long-term consequences of his decision.

Successful management of pricing information requires an understanding of the possible consequences of price changes. The more important of these include the effect of price changes on: the customer's ability to buy; the brand image and customers' evaluations of a product's quality; the value of inventories held by resellers; the willingness of resellers to hold inventory; the attitude of ultimate customers and resellers who recently purchased the product at a different price; the company's cash flow; and the need to borrow capital. Price changes can also disrupt or improve market discipline; foster or retard the growth and power of a trade association; instill the trust or suspicion of competitors in the integrity of one's business practices; or increase or reduce the probability of government investigation and criminal prosecution.

The effects of most business actions are extremely difficult to forecast, but an executive must attempt to forecast them. Before selecting an alternative, the executive should consciously consider all possible effects.

If the concept of price elasticity of demand has any value to price-setters, it is in forecasting the effect of price changes. Therefore, the following questions should be asked: Can price elasticity of demand be measured accurately? How much do such measurements cost? How long are such measurements valid? Does price elasticity apply to all geographic markets or only represent an average of all regions? Do elasticity measurements apply equally to all items in a firm's line of products? Is the elasticity of demand the same for all brands of the same product? The emphatic answer is that it is impossible to measure accurately the price elasticity of demand for any brand or product. However, executives responsible for pricing must continue to improve their understanding of the effects of price changes on sales.

Can a measure of demand be developed that is a better indicator than the price elasticity of demand? As implied above, past experience is an unreliable guide to present relationships. Rather than seek a quantitative measure of price elasticity, perhaps a different concept is needed. Businessmen will rarely change price alone, but ordinarily adopt a marketing program coordinated around the proposed price change. A marketing executive wishes to forecast the effects of the total marketing program, rather than the effect of price change alone.

Since most markets are highly dynamic and extremely complex, one cannot expect to develop reliable quantitative measures of the effects of different marketing programs on unit sales. How can a marketing executive forecast the results of alternative price strategies and marketing programs? He must intuitively estimate the effects of the program; however, he will rarely find precisely comparable circumstances in either his own firm's experience or in that of other firms. Specifically, the executive should consider the extent to which his price change will be perceived; the possible interpretations that customers and resellers can attribute to his price change; and the effects of customers reactions to the price changes.

Select Among Alternative Outcomes

When a price-setter forecasts the outcomes of alternative actions, he selects that alternative which best achieves his objectives. As indicated earlier, an executive actually pursues many objectives; therefore, the selection among alternatives is quite difficult in practice, although it is simple in principle. An index should be developed to indicate the extent to which any set of outcomes achieves the executive's multiple goals—weighing each one according to its importance. Various outcomes of each feasible course of action can then be forecast by assigning probabilities to each one. The action selected should represent the alternative that best realizes product, department, and corporate goals, while reflecting an acceptable amount of risk.

SUMMARY

Pricing involves far more than arriving at a dollar and cents figure for a single product. A price-setter is responsible for managing a complex function, even though pricing involves relatively little effort for the implementation of decisions. To manage the pricing function, a firm must develop a detailed hierarchy of objectives; a monitor system; explicit mathematical models; and, most importantly, new approaches to pricing management.

The corporate pricing function within a decision-making structure is a very complex process. Many components must be integrated and managed as a unit if the firm is quickly to capitalize on its pricing opportunities.

NOTES

1. Professor F. E. Gillis writes in 1969, "Joel Dean opines that cost-plus pricing is the most common technique in the United States. The statement is too weak; it is almost universal." See his *Managerial Economics* (Reading, Mass.: Addison-Wesley, 1969), p. 254.

2. A. A. Fitzpatrick, *Pricing Methods of Industry* (Boulder, Colo.: Pruett Press, Inc., 1964); *Decision Making in Marketing—A Description of Decision Making Processes and Its Application to Pricing,* 1971, Report No. 525, National Industrial Conference Board; Kaplan, Dirlam and Lanzilotti, *Pricing in Big Business* (Washington, D.C.: The Brookings Institution, 1958); B. Fog, *Industrial Pricing Policies* (Amsterdam, Holland: North Holland Publishing Co., 1960); W. W. Haynes, *Pricing Decisions in Small Business* (Lexington, Ky.: University of Kentucky Press, 1962); and J. Fred Weston has been reported as directing a major study of this subject. See "The Myths and Realities of Corporate Pricing," *Fortune,* Vol. LXXXV (April, 1972), p. 85.

3. The best of these writings are to be found in several collections of articles and talks about pricing. These are: Elizabeth Marting, ed., *Creative Pricing* (New York: American Marketing Association, 1968); Almarin Phillips and O. E. Williamson, eds., *Prices: Issues in Theory, Practice and Public Policy* (Philadelphia: University of Pennsylvania Press, 1967); D. F. Mulviholl and S. Paranka, eds., *Price Policies and Practices: A Source Book of Readings* (New York: John Wiley, 1967); American Management Association, Management Report No. 17, *Competitive Pricing: Policies, Practices and Legal Considerations,* 1958; American Management Association, Management Report No. 66, *Pricing: The Critical Decision,* 1961; Donald Watson, ed., *Price Theory in Action: A Book of Readings* (Boston: Houghton Mifflin, 1965); and B. Taylor and G. Wills, eds., *Pricing Strategy* (London: 1969).

4. R. E. Good, "Using the Computer in Pricing," in *Creative Pricing,* Elizabeth Marting, ed. (New York: American Marketing Association, 1968), pp. 182–194.

5. Arnold E. Amstutz, *Computer Simulation of Competitive Market Response* (Cambridge, Mass.: M.I.T. Press, 1967); and D. Kollat, R. Blackwell and J. Robeson, *Strategic Marketing* (New York: Holt, Rinehart and Winston, 1972), Chapter 19.

6. A. Gabor and C. W. J. Granger, "On the Price Consciousness of Consumers," *Applied Statistics,* Vol. 10 (1961), pp. 170–188; idem, "Price as an Indicator of Quality: Report on an Enquiry," *Economica,* Vol. 33 (1966), pp. 43–70; and idem, "The Pricing of New Products," *Scientific Business,* Vol. 3 (1965), pp. 141–150.

7. Nystrom, *Retail Pricing: An Integrated Economic and Psychological Approach* (Stockholm: Economic Research Institute of Stockholm School of Economics, 1970), especially Chapters 7 and 8; Brown and Oxenfeldt, *Misperceptions of Economic Phenomena* (New York: Sperr and Douth, 1972).

Joel Dean

Pricing Policies
for New Products

How to price a new product is a top-management puzzle that is too often solved by cost-theology and hunch. This article suggests a pricing policy geared to the dynamic nature of a new product's competitive status. Today's high rate of innovation makes the economic evolution of a new product a strategic guide to practical pricing.

MARKET BEHAVIOR

New products have a protected distinctiveness which is doomed to progressive degeneration from competitive inroads. The invention of a new marketable specialty is usually followed by a period of patent protection when markets are still hesitant and unexplored and when product design is fluid. Then comes a period of rapid expansion of sales as market acceptance is gained. Next the product becomes a target for competitive encroachment. New competitors enter the field, and innovations narrow the gap of distinctiveness between the product and its substitutes. The seller's zone of pricing discretion narrows as his distinctive "specialty" fades into a pedestrian "commodity" which is so little differentiated from other products that the seller has limited independence in pricing, even if rivals are few.

Author's Note: For major assistance in preparing this article, I am indebted to Stephen Taylor of Joel Dean Associates. Professors James Bonbright and Carl Shoup and Mr. Samuel Richman of the Graduate School of Business, Columbia University, were kind enough to read the manuscript and make helpful suggestions.

Source: From the *Harvard Business Review,* Vol. 28, No. 6 (November 1950) pp. 45–53. Reprinted by permission of the *Harvard Business Review.* Copyright © 1975 by the President and Fellows of Harvard College; all rights reserved.

Throughout the cycle, continual changes occur in promotional and price elasticity and in costs of production and distribution. These changes call for adjustments in price policy.

Elements of Cycle. Appropriate pricing over the cycle depends on the development of three different aspects of maturity, which usually move in approximately parallel time paths: (1) technical maturity, indicated by declining rate of product development, increasing standardization among brands, and increasing stability of manufacturing processes and knowledge about them; (2) market maturity, indicated by consumer acceptance of the basic service idea, by widespread belief that the products of most manufacturers will perform satisfactorily, and by enough familiarity and sophistication to permit consumers to compare brands competently; and (3) competitive maturity, indicated by increasing stability of market shares and price structures.

Of course, interaction among these components tends to make them move together. That is, intrusion by new competitors helps to develop the market, but entrance is most tempting when the new product appears to be establishing market acceptance.

Speed of Degeneration. The rate at which the cycle of degeneration progresses varies widely among products. What are the factors that set its pace? An overriding determinant is technical—the extent to which the economic environment must be reorganized to use the innovation effectively. The scale of plant investment and technical research called forth by the telephone, electric power, the automobile, or air transport makes for a long gestation period, as compared with even such major innovations as cellophane or frozen foods. Development comes fastest when the new gadget fills a new vacuum made to order for it. Electric stoves, as one example, have risen to 50% market saturation in the fast-growing Pacific Northwest, where electric power has become the lowest cost energy. Products still in early developmental stages also provide rich opportunities for product differentiation, which with heavy research costs hold off competitive degeneration.

But aside from technical factors, the rate of degeneration is controlled by economic forces that can be subsumed under (1) rate of market acceptance and (2) ease of competitive entry.

By *market acceptance* is meant the extent to which buyers consider the product a serious alternative to other ways of performing the same service. Market acceptance is a frictional factor. The effect of cultural lags may endure for some time after quality and costs make products technically useful. The slow catch-on of the "electric pig" (garbage-disposal unit) is an example. On the other hand, the attitude of acceptance may exist long before any workable model can be developed; then the final appearance of the product will produce an explosive growth curve in sales. The antihistamine cold tablet, a spectacular example, reflects the national faith in chemistry's ability to vanquish the common cold. And, of course, low unit price may speed market acceptance of an innovation; ball-point pens and all-steel houses started at about the same time, but look at the difference in their sales curves.

Ease of competitive entry is a major determinant of the speed of degeneration of a specialty. An illustration is found in the washing machine business before the war, where with little basic patent protection the Maytag position was quickly eroded by small manufacturers who performed essentially an assembly operation. The ball-point pen cascaded from a $12 novelty to a 49-cent "price football," partly because entry barriers of patents and techniques were ineffective. Frozen orange juice, which started as a protected specialty of Minute Maid, is speeding through its competitive cycle, with competing brands now crowding into the market.

At the outset the innovator can control the rate of competitive deterioration to an important degree by nonprice as well as by price strategies. Through successful research in product improvement he can protect his specialty position both by extending the life of his basic patent and by keeping ahead of competitors in product development. The record of the International Business Machines punch-card equipment illustrates this potentiality. Ease of entry is also affected by a policy of stay-out pricing (so low as to make the prospects look uninviting), which under some circumstances may slow down the process of competitive encroachment.

STEPS IN PIONEER PRICING

Pricing problems start when a company finds a product that is a radical departure from existing ways of performing a service and that is temporarily protected from competition by patents, secrets of production, control at the point of a scarce resource, or by other barriers. The seller here has a wide range of pricing discretion resulting from extreme product differentiation.

A good example of pricing latitude conferred by protected superiority of product is provided by the McGraw Electric Company's "Toastmaster," which, both initially and over a period of years, was able to command a very substantial price premium over competitive toasters. Apparently this advantage resulted from (1) a good product that was distinctive and superior, and (2) substantial and skillful sales promotion. Similarly, Sunbeam priced its electric iron $2 above comparable models of major firms with considerable success. And Sunbeam courageously priced its new metal coffee-maker at $32, much above competitive makes of glass coffee-makers, but it was highly successful.

To get a picture of how a manufacturer should go about setting his price in the pioneer stage, let me describe the main steps of the process (of course the classification is arbitrary and the steps are interrelated): (1) estimate of demand, (2) decision on market targets, (3) design of promotional strategy, and (4) choice of channels of distribution.

Estimate of Demand. The problem at the pioneer stage differs from that in a relatively stable monopoly because the product is beyond the experience of buyers and because the perishability of its distinctiveness must be reckoned with. How can demand for new products be explored? How can we find out how much people will pay for a product that has never before been seen or used? There are several levels of refinement to this analysis.

The initial problem of estimating demand for a new product can be broken into a series of subproblems: (a) whether the product will go at all (assuming price is in a competitive range); (b) what range of price will make the product economically attractive to buyers; (c) what sales volumes can be expected at various points in this price range; and (d) what reaction will price produce in manufacturers and sellers of displaced substitutes.

The first step is an exploration of the *preferences and educability of consumers,* always of course in the light of the technical feasibility of the new product. How many potential buyers are there? Is the product a practical device for meeting their needs? How can it be improved to meet their needs better? What proportion of the potential buyers would prefer, or could be induced to prefer, this product to already existing products (prices being equal)?

Sometimes it is feasible to start with the assumption that all vulnerable substitutes will be fully displaced. For example, to get some idea of the maximum limits of demand for a new type of reflecting-sign material, a company started with estimates of the aggregate number and area of auto license plates, highway markers, railroad operational signs, and name signs for streets and homes. Next, the proportion of each category needing night-light reflection was guessed. For example, it was assumed that only rural and suburban homes could benefit by this kind of name sign, and the estimate of need in this category was made accordingly.

It is not uncommon and possibly not unrealistic for a manufacturer to make the blithe assumption at this stage that the product price will be "within a competitive range" without having much idea of what that range is. For example, in developing a new type of camera equipment, one of the electrical companies judged its acceptability to professional photographers by technical performance without making any inquiry into its economic value. When the equipment was later placed in an economic setting, the indications were that sales would be negligible.

The second step is marking out this *competitive range of price*. Vicarious pricing experience can be secured by interviewing selected distributors who have enough comparative knowledge of customers' alternatives and preferences to judge what price range would make the new product "a good value." Direct discussions with representative experienced industrial users have produced reliable estimates of the "practical" range of prices. Manufacturers of electrical equipment often explore the economic as well as the technical feasibility of a new product by sending engineers with blueprints and models to see customers, such as technical and operating executives.

In guessing the price range of a radically new consumers' product of small unit value, the concept of barter equivalent can be a useful research guide. For example, a manufacturer of paper specialties tested a dramatic new product in the following fashion: A wide variety of consumer products totally unlike the new product were purchased and spread out on a big table. Consumers selected the products they would swap for the new product. By finding out whether the product would trade even for a dish pan, a towel, or a hairpin, the executives got a rough idea of what range of prices might strike the typical consumer as reasonable in the light of the values she could get for her money in totally different kinds of expenditures.

But asking prospective consumers how much they think they would be willing to pay for a new product, even by such indirect or disguised methods, may often fail to give a reliable indication of the demand schedule. Most times people just do not know what they would pay. It depends partly on their income and on future alternatives. Early in the postwar period a manufacturer of television sets tried this method and got highly erratic and obviously unreliable results because the distortion of war shortages kept prospects from fully visualizing the multiple alternative ways of spending their money. Another deficiency, which may, however, be less serious than it appears, is that responses are biased by the consumer's confused notion that he is bargaining for a good price. Not until techniques of depth interviewing are more refined than they are now can this crude and direct method of exploring a new product's demand schedule hold much promise of being accurate.

One appliance manufacturer tried out new products on a sample of employees by selling to them at deep discounts, with the stipulation that they could if they wished return the products at the end of the experiment period and get a refund of their low purchase price. Demand for frozen orange juice was tested by placing it in several markets at three different prices, ranging around the price of fresh fruit; the result showed rather low price elasticity.

While inquiries of this sort are often much too short-run to give any real indication of consumer tastes, the relevant point here is that even such rough probing often yields broad impressions of price elasticity, particularly in relation to product variations such as styling, placing of controls, and use of automatic features. It may show, for example, that $5 of cost put into streamlining or chromium stripping can add $50 to the price.

The third step, a more definite inquiry into the *probable sales from several possible prices,* starts with an investigation of the prices of substitutes. Usually the buyer has a choice of existing ways of having the same service performed; an analysis of the costs of these alternatives serves as a guide in setting the price for a new way.

Comparisons are easy and significant for industrial customers who have a costing system to tell them the exact value, say, of a fork-lift truck in terms of warehouse labor saved. Indeed, chemical companies setting up a research project to displace an existing material often know from the start the top price that can be charged for the new substitute in terms of cost of the present material.

But in most cases the comparison is obfuscated by the presence of quality differences that may be important bases for price premiums. This is most true of household appliances, where the alternative is an unknown amount of labor of a mysterious value. In pricing a cargo parachute the alternatives are: (1) free fall in a padded box from a plane flown close to the ground, (2) landing the plane, (3) back shipment by land from the next air terminal, or (4) land shipment all the way. These alternatives differ widely in their service value and are not very useful pricing guides.

Thus, it is particularly hard to know how much good will be done by making the new product cheaper than the old by various amounts, or how much the market will be restricted by making the new product more expensive. The answers usually come from experiment or research.

The fourth step in estimating demand is to consider the *possibility of retaliation by manufacturers of displaced substitutes* in the form of price cutting. This development may not occur at all if the new product displaces only a small market segment. If old industries do fight it out, however, their incremental costs provide a floor to the resulting price competition and should be brought into price plans. For example, a manufacturer of black-and-white sensitized paper studied the possibility that lowering his price would displace blueprint paper substantially. Not only did he investigate the prices of blueprint paper, but he also felt it necessary to estimate the out-of-pocket cost of making blueprint paper because of the probability that manufacturers already in the market would fight back by reducing prices toward the level of their incremental costs.

Decision on Market Targets. When the company has developed some idea of the range of demand and the range of prices that are feasible for the new product, it is in a position to make some basic strategic decisions on market targets and promotional plans. To decide on market objectives requires answers to several questions: What ultimate market share is wanted for the new product? How does it fit into the present product line? What about production methods? What are the possible distribution channels? These are questions of joint costs in production and distribution, of plant expansion outlays, and of potential competition. If entry is easy, the company may not be eager to disrupt its present production and selling operations to capture and hold a large slice of the new market. But if the prospective profits shape up to a substantial new income source, it will be worth while to make the capital expenditures on plant needed to reap the full harvest.

A basic factor in answering all these questions is the expected behavior of production and distribution costs. The relevant data here are all the production outlays that will be made after the decision day—the capital expenditures as well as the variable costs. A go-ahead decision will hardly be made without some assurance that these costs can be recovered before the product becomes a football in the market. Many dif-

ferent projections of costs will be made, depending on the alternative scales of output, rate of market expansion, threats of potential competition, and measures to meet that competition that are under consideration. But these factors and the decision that is made on promotional strategy are interdependent. The fact is that this is a circular problem that in theory can only be solved by simultaneous equations.

Fortunately, it is possible to make some approximations that can break the circle: Scale economies become significantly different only with broad changes in the size of plant and the type of production methods. This narrows the range of cost projections to workable proportions. The effects of using different distribution channels can be guessed fairly well without meshing the alternatives in with all the production and selling possibilities. The most vulnerable point of the circle is probably the decision on promotional strategy. The alternatives here are broad and produce a variety of results. The next step in the pricing process is therefore a plan for promotion.

Design of Promotional Strategy. Initial promotion outlays are an investment in the product that cannot be recovered until some kind of market has been established. The innovator shoulders the burden of creating a market—educating consumers to the existence and uses of the product. Later imitators will never have to do this job; so, if the innovator does not want to be simply a benefactor to his future competitors, he must make pricing plans to recover his initial outlays before his pricing discretion evaporates.

His basic strategic problem is to find the right mixture of price and promotion to maximuze his long-run profits. He can choose a relatively high price in pioneering stages, together with extravagant advertising and dealer discounts, and plan to get his promotion costs back early; or he can use low prices and lean margins from the very outset, in order to discourage potential competiton when the barriers of patents, distribution channels, or production techniques become inadequate. This question is discussed further below.

Choice of Channels of Distribution. Estimation of the costs of moving the new product through the channels of distribution to the final consumer must enter into the pricing procedure, since these costs govern the factory price that will result in a specified consumer price, and since it is the consumer price that matters for volume. Distributive margins are partly pure promotional costs and partly physical distribution costs. Margins must at least cover the distributors' costs of warehousing, handling, and order taking. These costs are similar to factory production costs in being related to physical capacity and its utilization, i.e., fluctuations in production or sales volume. Hence these set a floor to trade-channel discounts. But distributors usually also contribute promotional effort— in point-of-sale pushing, local advertising, and display —when it is made worth their while.

These pure promotional costs are more optional. Unlike physical handling costs they have no necessary functional relation to sales volume. An added layer of margin in trade discounts to produce this localized sales effort (with retail price fixed) is an optional way for the manufacturer to spend his prospecting money in putting over a new product.

In establishing promotional costs, the manufacturer must decide on the extent to which the selling effort will be delegated to members of the distribution chain. Indeed, some distribution channels, such as house-to-house selling and retail store selling supplemented by home demonstrators, represent a substantial delegation of the manufacturer's promotional job, and these usually involve much higher distribution-channel costs than do conventional methods. Rich distributor margins are an appropriate use of promotion funds only when the producer thinks a high price plus promotion is a better expansion policy on the specialty than low price by itself. Thus there is an intimate interaction between the pricing of a new product and the costs and the problems of floating it down the distribution channels to the final consumer.

POLICIES FOR PIONEER PRICING

The strategic decision in pricing a new product is the choice between (1) a policy of high initial prices that skim the cream of demand and (2) a policy of low prices from the outset serving as an active agent for market penetration. Although the actual range of choice is much wider than this, a sharp dichotomy clarifies the issues for consideration.

Skimming Price. For products that represent a drastic departure from accepted ways of performing a service, a policy of relatively high prices coupled with heavy promotional expenditures in the early stages of market development (and lower prices at later stages) has proved successful for many products. There are several reasons for the success of this policy:

1. Demand is likely to be more inelastic with respect to price in the early stages than it is when the product is full grown. This is particularly true for consumers' goods. A novel product, such as the electric

blanket or the electric pig, is not yet accepted as a part of the expenditure pattern. Consumers are still ignorant about its value as compared with the value of conventional alternatives. Moreover, at least in the early stages, the product has so few close rivals that cross-elasticity of demand is low. Promotional elasticity is, on the other hand, quite high, particularly for products with high unit prices such as television sets. Since it is difficult for the customer to value the service of the product in a way to price it intelligently, he is by default principally interested in how well it will work.

2. Launching a new product with a high price is an efficient device for breaking the market up into segments that differ in price elasticity of demand. The initial high price serves to skim the cream of the market that is relatively insensitive to price. Subsequent price reductions tap successively more elastic sectors of the market. This pricing strategy is exemplified by the systematic succession of editions of a book, sometimes starting with a $50 limited personal edition and ending up with a 25-cent pocket book.

3. This policy is safer, or at least appears so. Facing an unknown elasticity of demand, a high initial price serves as a "refusal" price during the stage of exploration. How much costs can be reduced as the market expands and as the design of the product is improved by increasing production efficiency with new techniques is difficult to predict. One of the electrical companies recently introduced a new lamp bulb at a comparatively high initial price, but with the announcement that the price would be reduced as the company found ways of cutting its costs.

4. Many companies are not in a position to finance the product flotation out of distant future revenues. High cash outlays in the early stages result from heavy costs of production and distributor organizing, in addition to the promotional investment in the pioneer product. High prices are a reasonable financing technique for shouldering these burdens in the light of the many uncertainties about the future.

Penetration Price. The alternative policy is to use low prices as the principal instrument for penetrating mass markets early. This policy is the reverse of the skimming policy in which the price is lowered only as short-run competition forces it. The passive skimming policy has the virtue of safeguarding some profits at every stage of market penetration. But it prevents quick sales to the many buyers who are at the lower end of the income scale or the lower end of the preference scale and who therefore are unwilling to pay any substantial premium for product or reputation superiority. The active approach in probing possibilities for market expansion by early penetration pricing requires research, forecasting, and courage.

A decision to price for market expansion can be reached at various stages in a product's life cycle: before birth, at birth, in childhood, in adulthood, or in senescence. The chances for large-volume sales should at least be explored in the early stages of product development research, even before the pilot stage, perhaps with a more definitive exploration when the product goes into production and the price and distribution plans are decided upon. And the question of pricing to expand the market, if not answered earlier, will probably arise once more after the product has established an elite market.

Quite a few products have been rescued from premature senescence by pricing them low enough to tap new markets. The reissues of important books in the 25-cent pocket-book category illustrate this point particularly well. These have produced not only commercial but intellectual renascence as well to many authors. The pattern of sales growth of a product that had reached stability in a high-price market has been known to undergo sharp changes when it was suddenly priced low enough to tap new markets. A contrasting illustration of passive policy is the recent pricing experience of the airlines. Although safety considerations and differences in equipment and service cloud the picture, it is pretty clear that the bargain-rate coach fares of scheduled airlines were adopted in reaction to the cut rates of nonscheduled airlines. This competitive response has apparently established a new pattern of traffic growth for the scheduled airlines.

An example of penetration pricing at the initial stage of the product's market life, again from the book field, is Simon & Schuster's recently adopted policy of bringing out new titles in a $1, paper-bound edition simultaneously with the conventional higher priced, cloth-bound edition.

What conditions warrant aggressive pricing for market penetration? This question cannot be answered categorically, but it may be helpful to generalize that the following conditions indicate the desirability of an early low-price policy: (1) a high price-elasticity of demand in the short-run, i.e., a high degree of responsiveness of sales to reductions in price; (2) substantial savings in production costs as the result of greater volume—not a necessary condition, however, since if elasticity of demand is high enough, pricing for market expansion may be profitable without realizing production economies; (3) product characteristics such that it will not seem bizarre when it is first fitted into the consumers' expenditure pattern; (4) a strong threat of potential competition.

This threat of potential competition is a highly persuasive reason for penetration pricing. One of the major objectives of most low-pricing policies in the pioneering stages of market development is to raise entry barriers to prospective competitors. This is appropriate when entrants must make large-scale investments to reach minimum costs and they cannot slip into an established market by selling at substantial discounts.

In many industries, however, the important potential competitor is a large, multiple-product firm operating as well in other fields than that represented by the product in question. For such a firm, the most important consideration for entry is not existing margins but the prospect of large and growing volume of sales. Present margins over costs are not the dominant consideration because such firms are normally confident that they can get their costs down as low as competitors' costs if the volume of production is large. Therefore, when total industry sales are not expected to amount to much, a high-margin policy can be followed because entry is improbable in view of the expectation of low volume and because it does not matter too much to potential competitors if the new product is introduced.

The fact remains that for products whose market potential appears big, a policy of stay-out pricing from the outset makes much more sense. When a leading soap manufacturer developed an additive that whitened clothes and enhanced the brilliance of colors, the company chose to take its gains in a larger share of the market rather than in a temporary price premium. Such a decision was sound, since the company's competitors could be expected to match or better the product improvement fairly promptly. Under these circumstances, the price premium would have been short-lived, whereas the gains in market share were more likely to be retained.

Of course, any decision to start out with lower prices must take into account the fact that if the new product calls for capital recovery over a long period, the risk may be great that later entrants will be able to exploit new production techniques which can undercut the pioneer's original cost structure. In such cases, the low-price pattern should be adopted with a view to long-run rather than to short-run profits, with the recognition that it usually takes time to attain the volume potentialities of the market.

It is sound to calculate profits in dollar terms rather than in percentage margins and to think in terms of percentage return on the investment required to produce and sell the expanded volume rather than in terms of percentage markup. Profit calculation should also recognize the contributions that market-development pricing can make to the sale of other products and to the long-run future of the company. Often a decision to use development pricing will turn on these considerations of long-term impacts upon the firm's total operation strategy rather than on the profits directly attributable to the individual product.

An example of market-expansion pricing is found in the experience of a producer of asbestos shingles, which have a limited sale in the high-price house market. The company wanted to broaden the market in order to compete effectively with other roofing products for the inexpensive home. It tried to find the price of asphalt shingles that would make the annual cost per unit of roof over a period of years as low as the cheaper roofing that currently commanded the mass market. Indications were that the price would have to be at least this low before volume sales would come. Next, the company explored the relationship between production costs and volume, far beyond the range of its own volume experience. Variable costs and overhead costs were estimated separately, and the possibilities of a different organization of production were explored. Calculating in terms of anticipated dollars of profit rather than in terms of percentage margin, the company reduced the price of asbestos shingles and brought the annual cost down close to the cost of the cheapest asphalt roof. This reduction produced a greatly expanded volume and secured a substantial share of the mass market.

PRICING IN MATURITY

To determine what pricing policies are appropriate for later stages in the cycle of market and competitive maturity, the manufacturer must be able to tell when a product is approaching maturity. Some of the symptoms of degeneration of competitive status toward the commodity level are:

1. *Weakening in brand preference*—this may be evidenced by a higher cross-elasticity of demand among leading products, the leading brand not being able to continue demanding as much price premium as initially without losing position;
2. *Narrowing physical variation among products as the best designs are developed and standardized*—this has been dramatically demonstrated in automobiles and is still in process in television receivers;
3. *The entry in force of private-label competitors*—this is exemplified by the mail-order houses' sale of own-label refrigerators and paint sprayers;

4. *Market saturation*—the ratio of replacement sales to new equipment sales serves as an indicator of the competitive degeneration of durable goods, but in general it must be kept in mind that both market size and degree of saturation are hard to define (e.g., saturation of the radio market, which was initially thought to be one radio per home and later had to be expanded to one radio per room);
5. *The stabilization of production methods*—a dramatic innovation that slashes costs (e.g., prefabricated houses) may disrupt what appears to be a well-stabilized oligopoly market.

The first step for the manufacturer whose specialty is about to slip into the commodity category is to reduce real prices promptly as soon as symptoms of deterioration appear. This step is essential if he is to forestall the entry of private-label competitors. Examples of failure to make such a reduction are abundant. By and large, private-label competition has speeded up the inevitable evolution of high specialties into commodities and has tended to force margins down by making price reductions more open and more universal than they would otherwise be. From one standpoint, the rapid growth of the private-label share in the market is a symptom of unwise pricing on the part of the national-brand sector of the industry.

This does not mean that the manufacturer should declare open price war in the industry. When he moves into mature competitive stages, he enters oligopoly relationships where price slashing is peculiarly dangerous and unpopular. But, with active competition in prices precluded, competitive efforts may move in other directions, particularly toward product improvement and market segmentation. Product improvement at this stage, where most of the important developments have been put into all brands, practically amounts to market segmentation. For it means adding refinements and quality extras that put the brand in the elite category, with an appeal only to the top-income brackets. This is a common tactic in food marketing, and in the tire industry it was the response of the General Tire Company to the competitive conditions of the 1930's.

As the product matures and as its distinctiveness narrows, a choice must sometimes be made by the company concerning the rung of the competitive price ladder it should occupy—roughly, the choice between a low and a not-so-low relative price.

A price at the low end of the array of the industry's real prices is usually associated with a product mixture showing a lean element of services and reputation (the product being physically similar to competitive brands, however) and a company having a lower gross margin than the other industry members (although not necessarily a lower net margin). The choice of such a low-price policy may be dictated by technical or market inferiorities of the product, or it may be adopted because the company has faith in the long-run price elasticity of demand and the ability of low prices to penetrate an important segment of the market not tapped by higher prices. The classic example is Henry Ford's pricing decision in the 1920's.

SUMMARY

In pricing products of perishable distinctiveness, a company must study the cycle of competitive degeneration in order to determine its major causes, its probable speed, and the chances of slowing it down. Pricing in the pioneering stage of the cycle involves difficult problems of projecting potential demand and of guessing the relation of price to sales. The first step in this process is to explore consumer preferences and to establish the feasibility of the product, in order to get a rough idea of whether demand will warrant further exploration. The second step is to mark out a range of prices that will make the product economically attractive to buyers. The third step is to estimate the probable sales that will result from alternative prices.

If these initial explorations are encouraging, the next move is to make decisions on promotional strategy and distribution channels. The policy of relatively high prices in the pioneering stage has much to commend it, particularly when sales seem to be comparatively unresponsive to price but quite responsive to educational promotion. On the other hand, the policy of relatively low prices in the pioneering stage, in anticipation of the cost savings resulting from an expanding market, has been strikingly successful under the right conditions. Low prices look to long-run rather than short-run profits and discourage potential competitors.

Pricing in the mature stages of a product's life cycle requires a technique for recognizing when a product is approaching maturity. Pricing problems in this stage border closely on those of oligopoly.

Joel Dean

Techniques for Pricing New Products and Services

Pricing a new product or service is one of the most important and puzzling of marketing problems. The high proportion of new products which fail in the marketplace is partly due to the difficulty of pricing them correctly.

A *new* product (or service)* is here defined as one which incorporates a major innovation. It is new to the world, not just new to the company. This means that its market is, at the outset, ill defined. Potential applications cannot be foreseen with precision. Pricing decisions usually have to be made with little knowledge and with wide margins of error in the forecasts of demand, cost, and competitors' capabilities.

This section deals with the price level, not the price structure; e.g., the average price per ton-mile of air freight, not the structure of price differentials by size of shipment, density, distance, etc.

The difficulty of pricing new products is enhanced by the dynamic deterioration of the competitive status of most new products, which is speeded by today's high rate of innovation. This makes the evolution of a new product's economic status a strategic consideration in practical pricing.

DYNAMIC COMPETITIVE SETTING

A product which is new to the world, as opposed to being merely new to the company, passes through distinctive competitive stages in its life cycle. The appropriate pricing policy is likely to be different for each stage.

New products have a protected distinctiveness which is doomed to progressive degeneration from competitive inroads. As new competitors enter the

*Hereafter, the term "new product" will encompass new services as well.

Source: From *Handbook of Modern Marketing,* Victor P. Buell, ed. Copyright © 1970 by McGraw-Hill Book Company. Used by permission.

field and innovations narrow the gap of distinctiveness between the product and its substitutes, the seller's zone of pricing discretion narrows. His distinctive "specialty" fades into a pedestrian "commodity" which is so little differentiated from other products that the seller has limited independence in pricing, even if rivals are few.

Throughout the cycle, continual changes occur in promotional and price elasticity and in costs of production and distribution. These changes call for adjustments in price policy.

Appropriate pricing over the cycle depends on the development of three different aspects of maturity which usually move in approximately parallel time paths: (1) *technical maturity,* indicated by declining rate of product development, increasing uniformity of competing brands, and increasing stability of manufacturing processes and knowledge about them; (2) *market maturity,* indicated by consumer acceptance of the basic service idea, by widespread belief that the products of most manufacturers will perform satisfactorily, and by enough familiarity and sophistication to permit consumers to compare brands competently; and (3) *competitive maturity,* indicated by increasing stability of market shares and price structures.

The rate at which the cycle of degeneration progresses varies widely among products. What are the factors that set its pace? An overriding determinant is technical—the extent to which the economic environment must be reorganized to use the innovation effectively. The scale of plant investment and technical reaction called forth by the telephone, electric power, the automobile, or the jet airplane makes for a long gestation period as compared with even such major innovations as cellophane or frozen foods. Development comes fastest when the new gadget fills a new vacuum.

Monopoly Pricing. New product pricing, if the product is truly novel, is in essence monopoly pricing. Stark monopoly pricing, which is the core of new product pricing, considers only what the traffic will bear—the price which will maximize profits, taking into account the price sensitivity of demand and the incremental promotional and production cost of the seller. What the product is worth to the buyer, not what it costs the seller, is the controlling consideration.

The competitive setting of the new product has, however, peculiar features that modify monopoly pricing. The monopoly power of the new product is (1) restricted (i.e., buyers have alternatives in the form of products that compete indirectly), (2) ephemeral (i.e., subject to inevitable erosion by imitation and obsolescence), and (3) controllable (i.e., capable of some degree of expansion and prolongation by actions of the seller).

For example, Quanta Welding's new diffusion bonding system, based on a millisecond-shaped power pulse, is a patented monopoly. But its pricing power is restricted by alternatives. For supersonic aircraft, these are resistance-welding or riveting, which are candidate pricing benchmarks. The market power of Quanta's superior metals-joining process will be eventually eroded. Solid-state devices may make obsolete the mercury vapor tube that supplies the controllable massive pulses of electrical energy on which the process depends. Penetration pricing might discourage this competitive entry.

These peculiarities of the new-product monopoly introduce dynamism and uncertainty which call for dynamic modifications of monopoly pricing. Examples include:

1. Substitute ways to get the service. These set limits on the market power of a new product and hence serve as benchmarks for pricing it.
2. The perishability of the new product's wanted distinctiveness. This makes the timing of price, promotion, and capacity competiton crucial (e.g., choice between skimming and penetration pricing).
3. The ability to influence the amount and the durability of the new product's market power in some degree by specially planned pricing and promotion actions. This gives added weight to the effect of today's pricing upon tomorrow's demand.

DEMAND: SENSITIVITY OF VOLUME TO PRICE

Profitable monopoly pricing of a new product, even with these dynamic competitive modifications, requires an estimate of how price will affect sales. This relationship can be explored in two steps, by (1) finding what range of price will make the product economically attractive to buyers, and (2) estimating what sales volumes can be expected at various points in this price range.

Price Range. The price range is determined by the indirect competition of substitutes, which sets limits to the monopoly power of the new product. In this sense, no product is really new; the most novel product merely plugs an abnormally large gap in the chain of substitutes. This gap marks out the potential range of its price.

For industrial products, a relatively quick and cheap

way to find this range is to "pick the brains" of professionals experienced in looking at comparative product performance in terms of buyers' costs and requirements—for example, distributors, prime contractors, and consulting engineers, as well as purchasing analysts and engineers of prospect companies.

For consumers' goods, different methods are needed. In guessing the price range of a radically novel product of small unit value, the concept of barter equivalent can be useful. For example, a manufacturer of paper specialties tested a dramatic new product this way: A wide variety of consumer products totally unlike the new product were purchased and spread out on a big table. Consumers selected the products they would swap for the new product.

Price-Volume Relationship. The effect of the price of the new product upon its volume of sales is the most important and most difficult estimate in pricing. We know in general that the lower the price, the greater the volume of sales and the faster its rate of growth. The air-freight growth rate is about 18 per cent; priced higher, it will grow more slowly. But to know the precise position and shape of the price-quantity demand schedule or how much faster sales will grow if the price is 20 per cent lower is not possible. But we must estimate.

The best way to predict the effect of price on sales volume for a new product is by controlled experiments: offering it at several different prices in comparable test markets under realistic sales conditions. For example, frozen orange juice was thus tested at three prices. When test marketing is not feasible, another method is to braoden the study of the cost of buyers' alternatives and include forecasts of the sales volume of substitutes (and other indications of the volume to customers of different categories). This approach is most promising for industrial customers, because performance comparisons are more explicit and measurable and economics more completely controls purchases. When buyers' alternatives differ widely in service value, the difficulty of translating this disparity into superiority premiums adds to the imprecision of this method of estimating price-volume relationships.

PRICING BENCHMARKS

The buyers' viewpoint should be controlling in pricing. For every new product there are alternatives. Buyers' best alternatives are usually products already tested in the marketplace. The new product will, presumably, supply a superior solution to the problem of some categories of buyers. The superiority differential over existing products differs widely among new products. The degree of superiority of any one new product over its substitutes usually also differs widely as viewed by different buyers.

Buyers' Alternatives. The prospective buyer of any new product does have alternatives. These indirectly competitive products are the benchmark for his appraisal of the price-performance package of a new product. This comparison with existing products determines its relative attractiveness to potential buyers. Such an analysis of demand can be made in the following steps:

1. Determine the major uses for the new product. For each application, determine the product's performance characteristics.
2. For each important usage area, specify the products that are the buyer's best alternative to the new product. Determine the performance characteristics and requirements which buyers view as crucial in determining their product selection.
3. For each major use, determine how well the product's performance characteristics meet the requirements of customers compared with the performance of these buyers' alternative products.
4. Forecast the prices of alternative products in terms of transaction prices, adjusted for the impact of the new product and translated into units of use. Estimate from the prices of these benchmark substitutes the alternative costs to the buyer per unit of the new product. Real transactions prices (after all discounts), rather than list prices, should be the benchmark in order to reflect marketplace realities. Prices should be predicted, after the introduction of the new product, so as to reflect probable competitive adaptation to the new product. Where eventual displacement of existing substitutes appears likely, short-run incremental cost supplies a Jeremiah forecast of defender's pricing retaliation.
5. Estimate the superiority premium; i.e., price the performance differential in terms of what the superior solution supplied by the new product is worth to buyers of various categories.
6. Figure a "parity price" for the product relative to the buyer's best alternative product in each use, and do this for major categories of customers. Parity is a price which encompasses the premium a customer would be willing to pay for comparative superiority in performance characteristics.

Pricing the Superiority Differential. Determining this price premium over benchmark products which the new product's superiority will most profitably warrant is the most intricate and challenging problem of new-product pricing.

The value to the customer of the innovational superiority of the new product is surrounded by uncertainties: whether the product will work, whether it will attain its designed superiorities, what its reliability and durability performance will be, and how soon it in turn will become obsolete. These uncertainties influence the price a customer would pay and the promotional outlay that would be required to persuade him to buy. Thus, customers' uncertainties will cost the seller something, either in price or promotion.

In essence, the superiority premium requires translation of differential performance characteristics into dollars, based on value analysis from the buyer's viewpoint. The premium will differ among uses, among alternative products, and among categories of customers. For some, it will be negative. Unless it proves practical to segment the market by application and to have widely discriminatory prices, the new product is likely to be priced out of some markets.

A simplistic, single-point premium reflecting "what the product can command in the marketplace" will not do. The customer-response pattern that is needed is the relationship between (1) a series of prospective superiority premiums and (2) the corresponding potential volumes.

What matters is superiority as *buyers* value it, not superiority as calibrated by technicians' measurements or by the sellers' costs. This means that more and better promotion can raise the premium-volume schedule and make a higher superiority premium achieve the same sales volume or rate of sales growth as would a lower premium without the promotion. This premium-volume schedule will be kicked about by retaliatory pricing of displaceable substitutes as well as by the imitative and innovative new-product competition of rivals.

The optimizing premium—i.e., the price that would maximize profits in any specified time period—will depend upon future costs as well as upon the hazy and dynamic demand schedule. It will be hard to find. Uncertainty about the future thus makes the appropriate pricing strategy for the long run a matter of sophisticated judgment.

RATE-OF-RETURN PRICING

Application of the principles of economic pricing is illustrated by rate-of-return pricing of new capital equipment. Industrial goods are sold to businessmen in their capacity as profit-makers. The technique is different for a producer's good (e.g., a truck) than for a consumer's good (e.g., a sports car).

The difference is caused by the fact that the essential service purchased if a product is a producer's good is added profits. A product represents an investment by the customer. The test of whether or not this investment is a desirable one should be its profitability to the customer. The pricing guide that this suggests is rate of return on the capital a customer ties up by his investment in a product.

Rate of Return on Customer's Investment. Rate-of-return pricing looks at a price through the investment eyes of the customer. It recognizes that the upper limit is the price which will produce the minimum acceptable rate of return on the customer's investment. The added profits obtainable from the use of equipment differ among customers and among applications for the same customer.

Cutoff criteria of required return also differ, so prospective customers differ in the rate of return which will induce them to invest in a given product. Thus, the rate-of-return approach opens up a new kind of demand analysis for industrial goods. This analysis consists of inquiry into (a) the costs to buyers from displaceable alternative ways to do the job; (b) the cost-saving and profit-producing capability of equipment in different applications and for different prospects; and (c) the capital budgeting policies of customers, with particular emphasis on their cost-of-capital and their minimum rate-of-return requirements.

The rate-of-return analysis just outlined is particularly useful in the pioneering stages of new products when the competition consists of only obsolescent ways of doing the job. At more mature stages in the life cycle of a new product, competitive imitation improves prospective customers' alternatives. These rival investment alternatives must then be taken explicitly into the analysis.

One way is to use a competitor's product as the benchmark in measuring the rate of return which a given product will produce for specified categories of prospects. The profitability from the product is measured in terms of its superiority over the best alternative new equipment offered by rivals rather than by its superiority over the customer's old equipment. Rate-of-return pricing translates this competitive superiority into dollars of added profit for the customer and relates this added profit to the added investment. In effect, one would say: "To be sure, buying my competitor's product will give you a 25 per cent rate of return, and that is better than keeping your old equipment; but buying *my* product will give you a 30 per cent rate of return." For each customer category, rate-of-return analysis reveals a price for a given product that makes it an irresistibly good investment to the customer in view of his alternatives and at the same time extracts from the customer all that can safely be demanded.

Investigation of (1) the productivity of the buyers' capital invested in your new product and (2) the required rate of return of prospective customers has proven a practical way to predict the demand for industrial goods. It must be coupled with forecasts of costs to find the immediately most profitable price, and with considerations of competitive strategy for the longer run.

THE ROLE OF COST

To get maximum practical use from costs in new product pricing, three questions of theory must be answered: (1) Whose cost? (2) Which cost? and (3) What role? As to whose cost, three classes of costs are important: (1) those of prospective buyers, (2) those of existent and potential competitors, and (3) those of the producer of the new product. Cost should play a different role for each of the three, and the pertinent concept of cost will differ accordingly.

Buyers' Cost. How should costs of prospective customers be used in setting the price of a new product? By applying value analysis to prices and performance of alternative products to find the superiority premium that will make the new product attractive from an economic standpoint to buyers of specified categories. Rate-of-return pricing of capital goods illustrates this buyer's-cost approach, which is applicable in principle to all new products.

Competitors' Costs. Competitors' costs are usually the crucial estimate in appraisal of competitors' capabilities.

Costs of two kinds of competitive products can be helpful. The first kind are products already in the marketplace. The objectives are to estimate (1) their staying power and (2) the floor of retaliation pricing. For the first objective, the pertinent cost concept is the competitor's long-run incremental cost. For the second, his short-run incremental cost.

The second kind is the unborn competing product that could blight a new product's future or eventually displace it. Forecasts of competitors' costs for such products can help assess this crucial dimension of capability of prospective competitors and estimate the

effectiveness of a strategy of pricing the new product so as to discourage entry. For this purpose, the cost behavior to forecast is the relationship between unit production cost and plant size as the new producer and his rivals move from pilot plant to small-scale test production plant to large-scale mass production. The cost forecasts should take into account technological progress and should be spotted on a time scale that reflects the potential head-start cost advantages that could be attained under a policy of penetration pricing and under skimming pricing.

Estimates of cost of unborn competitive products are necessarily rough, but evaluation of major differences between competitors' costs and the new producer's costs can nevertheless be useful. Thus cost estimates can help forecast a defending product's retaliation pricing and an invading product's conquest pricing.

Producer's Costs. The cost of the producer plays several roles in pricing a new product. The first is birth control. A new product must be prepriced provisionally early in the R&D stage and then again periodically as it progresses toward market. Forecasts of production and promotional costs at matching stages should play the role of forecasting its economic feasibility in determining whether to continue product development and ultimately to commercialize. The concept of cost relevant for this birth-control role is a prediction of full cost at a series of prospective volumes and corresponding technologies, and encompassing imputed cost of capital on intangible as well as tangible investment.

A second role is to establish a price floor which is also the threshold for selecting from candidate prices that which will maximize return on a new product investment over the long run.

For both jobs, the relevant concept is future costs, forecast over a range of volume, production technologies, and promotional outlays in the marketing plan.

Two categories of cost require separate forecasts and have quite different impacts on new-product pricing: (1) Production costs (including physical distribution), and (2) Persuasion costs, which are discretionary and rivalrous with price.

The production costs that matter are the future costs over the long run that will be added by making this product on the predicted scale (or scales) versus not making it. The added investment necessary to manufacture and distribute the new product should be estimated. Investment should include intangibles such as R&D, promotion, and launching outlays as well as increased working capital. Then the added costs of manufacturing and selling the product at various possible sales volumes should be estimated. It is important to calculate total costs (rather than unit costs) with and without the new product. The difference can then be assigned to the new product. Present overhead that will be the same whether or not the addition to the product line is adopted should be ignored. Future additions to overhead caused by the new product are alone relevant in pricing it. Two sets of cost and investment figures must be built up—one showing the situation *without* the new product and the other showing the situation *with* the new product added to the line, and at several possible volumes. High costs of pilot-plant production and of early small-scale production plants should be viewed as intangible capital investment rather than as the current operating costs. The losses of a break-in period are part of the investment on which a satisfactory return should be made.

Long-run future incremental costs, including costs of equity capital (i.e., satisfactory return on the added investment), supply the base line above which contribution profits of a new product should be maximized —not an impenetrable floor, but a calculation benchmark for optimization.

STRATEGY CHOICES

A major strategy decision in pricing a new product is the choice between (1) skimming pricing and (2) penetration pricing. There are intermediate positions, but the issues are made clearer by comparing the two extremes.

Skimming Pricing. Some products represent drastic improvements upon accepted ways of performing a service or filling a demand. For these products a strategy of high prices with large promotional expenditure in the early stages of market development (and lower prices at later stages) has frequently proved successful. This can be termed a "skimming-price" policy. There are four main reasons for its success:

1. Sales of the product are likely to be less sensitive to price in the early stages than when the product is "full-grown" and competitive imitations have appeared. In the early stages, the product usually has so few close rivals that cross elasticity of demand is low. Promotional sensitivity is, on the other hand, quite high, particularly for products with high unit prices, since it is difficult for the customer to value the service of the product.
2. Launching a new product with a high price is an efficient device for breaking the market up into

segments that differ in price elasticity of demand. The initial high price serves to skim the cream of the market that is relatively insensitive to price. Subsequent price reductions tap successively more elastic sectors of the market. This pricing strategy is exemplified by the systematic succession of editions of a book, sometimes starting with a $50 limited personal edition and ending up with a 75-cent paperback book.

3. A skimming policy is safer, or at least it appears so. Facing an unknown elasticity of demand, a high initial price serves as a "refusal" price during the stage of exploration. How much costs can be reduced as the market expands and as the design of the product is improved by increasing production efficiency with new techniques is difficult to predict.
4. High prices frequently produce a greater dollar volume of sales in the early stages of market development than are produced by low initial prices. When this is the case, skimming pricing will provide funds to finance expansion into the larger volume sectors of a given market.

Penetration Pricing. Despite its many advantages, a skimming-price policy is not appropriate for all new product problems. Although high initial prices may maximize profits during the early stages of product introduction, they may also prevent sales to many of the buyers upon whom you must rely for a mass market. The alternative is to use low prices as an entering wedge to get into mass markets early. This may be termed penetration pricing. Such an approach is likely to be desirable under any of these conditions:

First, when sales volume of the product is very sensitive to price, even in the early stages of introduction.

Second, when it is possible to achieve substantial economies in unit cost of manufacturing and distributing the product by operating at large volume.

Third, when a product faces threats of strong potential competition very soon after introduction.

Fourth, when there is no "elite" market—that is, no class of buyers willing to pay a higher price to obtain the newest and the best.

While a penetration pricing policy can be adopted at any stage in the product's life cycle, this pricing strategy should always be examined before a new product is marketed at all. Its possibility should be explored again as soon as the product has established an elite market. Sometimes a product can be rescued from premature death by adoption of a penetration price after the cream of the market has been skimmed.

One important consideration in the choice between skimming and penetration pricing at the time a new product is introduced is the ease and speed with which competitors can bring out substitute products. If you decide to set your initial price low enough, your large competitor may not feel it worthwhile to make a big investment for slim profit margins. The speed with which your product loses its uniqueness and sinks from its sheltered status to the level of just another competitive product depends on several factors:

1. Its total sales potential. A big potential market entices competitive imitation.
2. The investment required for rivals to manufacture and distribute the product. A big investment barrier deters invasion.
3. The strength of patent and know-how protection.
4. The alertness and power of competitors.

Although competitive imitation is almost inevitable, the company that introduces a new product can use price to discourage or delay the introduction of competitive products. Keep-out prices can be achieved quickly by penetration pricing.

Pricing in Maturity. To price appropriately for later stages in the cycle of competitive maturity, it is important to be able to tell when a product is approaching maturity. When the new product is about to slip into the commodity category, it is sometimes desirable to reduce real prices promptly as soon as symptoms of deterioration appear. Some of the symptoms of degeneration of competitive status toward the commodity level are:

1. Weakening in brand preference. This may be evidenced by a higher cross elasticity of demand among leading products, the leading brand not being able to continue demanding as much price premium as initially without losing position.

2. Narrowing physical variation among products as the best designs are developed and standardized. This has been dramatically demonstrated in automobiles and is still in process in television receivers.

3. The entry in force of private-label competitors. This is exemplified by the mail-order houses' sale of own-label refrigerators and paint sprayers.

4. Market saturation. The ratio of replacement sales to new-equipment sales serves as an indicator of the competitive degeneration of durable goods, but in general it must be kept in mind that both market size and degree of saturation are hard to define (e.g., saturation of the radio market, which was initially thought to be one radio per home and later had to be expanded to one radio per room).

5. The stabilization of production methods, indicated by slow rate of technological advance, high average age of equipment, and great uniformity among competitors' introduction technology.

PROMOTION AND DISTRIBUTION

Promotion. Closely related to pricing is promotional strategy. An innovator must not only sell his product, but frequently he must also make people recognize their need for a new *kind* of product. The problem is one of "creating a market."

Initial promotion outlays are an investment in the product that cannot be recovered until some kind of market has been established. The innovator shoulders the burden of educating consumers to the existence and uses of the product. Later imitators will never have to do this job; so if the innovator does not want to be simply a benefactor to his future competitors, he must make pricing plans to earn a return on all his initial outlays before his pricing discretion evaporates.

The basic strategic problem is to find the right mixture of price and promotion to maximize long-run profits. A relatively high price may be chosen in pioneering stages, together with large advertising and dealer discounts, and the plan may be to get the promotion investment back early; or low prices and lean margins may be used from the very outset in order to discourage potential competition when the barriers of patents and investment in production capacity, distribution channels, or production techniques become inadequate.

Channels of Distribution. Choice of channels of distribution should be consistent with strategy for initial pricing and for promotional outlays. Penetration pricing and explosive promotion call for distribution channels that promptly make the product broadly available. Otherwise advertising is wasted or mass-market pricing stymied. Distribution policy also concerns the role the dealer is to play in pushing a given product, the margins he must be paid to induce this action, and the amount of protection of territory and of inventory required to do so.

Estimation of the costs of moving the new product through the channels of distribution to the final consumer must enter into the pricing procedure, since these costs govern the factory price that will result in a specified final price. Distributive margins are partly pure promotional costs and partly physical distribution costs. Margins must at least cover the distributors' costs of warehousing, handling, and order taking. These costs are similar to factory production costs in being related to physical capacity and its utilization; i.e., fluctuations in production or sales volume. Hence these set a floor to trade-channel discounts. But distributors usually also contribute promotional effort—in point-of-sale pushing, local advertising, and display—when it is made worth their while. These pure promotional costs are more optional.

Distributors' margins are best determined by study of distributors' alternatives. This does not mean that the distributor gross margin on a given product must be the same as that of rival products. It should instead produce a competitive rate of return on the distributors' investment (in inventory, shelf space and sales capacity).

SUMMARY

Pricing new products is an art. The important determinants in economic pricing of pioneering innovations are complex, interrelated, and hard to forecast. Experienced judgment is required in pricing and repricing the product to fit its changing competitive environment. This judgment may possibly be improved by some pricing precepts suggested by the preceding analysis:

1. Corporate goals must be clearly defined. Pricing a new product is an occasion for rethinking them. This chapter has assumed that the overriding corporate goal is long-run profit maximization; e.g., making the stock worth the most by maximizing the present worth, at the corporation's cost of capital, of its per-share earnings.

2. Pricing a new product should begin long before its birth. Prospective prices, coupled with forecast costs, should play the decisive role in product birth control.

3. Pricing a new product should be a continuing process of bracketing the truth by successive approximations. Rough estimates of the relevant concepts are preferable to precise knowledge of historical irrelevancies.

4. Costs can supply useful guidance in new-product pricing, but not by the conventional wisdom; i.e., cost-plus pricing. Three categories of costs are pertinent: those of the buyer, those of the seller, and those of the seller's rivals. The role of cost differs among the three, as does the concept of cost that is pertinent to that role: different costs for different purposes.

5. The role of cost is to set a reference base for picking the most profitable price. For this job the only costs that are pertinent to pricing a new product on the verge of commercialization (i.e., already developed and tested) are incremental costs; the added costs of going ahead at different plant scales. Costs of R&D and of market testing are now sunk and hence irrelevant.

6. The pricing implications of the changing economic status and competitive environment of a product must be recognized as it passes through its life cycle from birth to obsolescence. This cycle, and the plans that are made to influence it, are of paramount importance for pricing policy.

7. The product should be seen through the eyes of the customer and priced just low enough to make it an irresistible investment in view of his alternatives as he sees them. To estimate successfully how much a given product is worth to the prospect is never easy, but it is usually rewarding.

8. Customers' rate of return should be the main consideration in pricing novel capital goods. Buyers' cost savings (and other earnings) expressed as a return on his investment in the new product are the key to predicting the price sensitivity of demand and to pricing profitably.

9. The strategic choice between skimming and penetration pricing should be based on economics. The skimming policy—i.e., relatively high prices in the pioneering stage, cascading downward thereafter—is particularly appropriate for products whose sales initially are comparatively unresponsive to price but quite responsive to education. A policy of penetration pricing—i.e., relatively low prices in the pioneering stage in anticipation of the cost savings resulting from an expanding market—is best when scale economies are big, demand is price sensitive, and invasion is threatened. Low starting prices sacrifice short-run profits for long-run profits and discourage potential competitors.

BIBLIOGRAPHY

Dean, Joel, *Managerial Economics,* Prentice-Hall, Englewood Cliffs, N.J., 1951 (especially pp. 419–424).

Harper, Donald, *Price Policy and Procedure,* Harcourt, Brace & World, New York, 1966.

Mulvihill, D. F.., and S. Paranka, *Price Policies and Practices: A Source Book in Readings,* Wiley, New York, 1967.

Thompson, G. Clark, and M. M. MacDonald, "Pricing New Products," *Conference Board Record,* National Industrial Conference Board, New York, 1964.

CASES

NOEL-JOANNA, INC.

This southern California-based company manufactures a variety of infant products, including blankets, sleeping bags, and infant seat comforters. Despite its austere beginnings, Noel-Joanna products are now sold in many prestige stores, such as Bloomingdales and Neiman-Marcus. With recent cost increases, consideration was being given to a price increase for the infant seat comforters—the firm's major product line.

LEE'S MARKETS

This chain of fourteen grocery stores is located in a large city in the northeastern part of the United States. As a family-owned business, the chain traditionally charged high prices but offered superior products and good service. Faced with increasing pressures from discount stores and discount warehouses, the chain is undertaking a change in pricing policies to remain competitive.

INDUSTRIAL SUPPLY CORPORATION

Industrial Supply Corporation of Jacksonville, Florida, manufactured and sold various types of rubber and plastic products for industrial use, including hoses, belts, couplings, and gaskets. Additionally, the company distributed specialty lines of safety equipment and hardware items to industrial customers. Management was considering a competitor's offer to divide territories.

TWIN PEAKS NATIONAL BANK

Located in Ohio, Twin Peaks National Bank was in the process of reviewing its pricing policies for its "All-in-One Account." Comparing the different services and prices at other banks was the responsibility of the Vice President of Marketing. Of key concern was whether the charges for the All-in-One Account could be raised without endangering the bank's market share.

TRI-CITY BALLET ASSOCIATION

The Tri-City Ballet Association is a nonprofit community ballet company with a rocky financial history. Cost overruns, unpredictable grant allocations, performance revenue deficits, and a lack of long-run financial planning face the Association.

NOEL-JOANNA, INC.

Connie Jarvis and Barbara Heinz, owners of Noel-Joanna, Inc. (NoJo), were in the process of reviewing the price of their "infant seat comforter" (see exhibit 1). This was the first product they had made back in 1970, and it still was their number one seller—accounting for nearly 40 percent of company sales. Cost increases, as well as the products established position in the market, made them believe that a price increase might be in order. Yet, they did not want to overprice the comforter, and they were concerned that a change in the existing price might affect not only its sales, but the sales of other lines as well. As Mrs. Jarvis noted:

We built this company on the basis of the infant seat comforter. It was well accepted right from the start and is now sold in many of the finer department stores such as Neiman-Marcus in Dallas, Marshall Fields in Chicago, Bloomingdales in New York City, and Bullock's in southern California. Our other product lines came as a result. All along, we have tried to preserve an image of high quality, and we don't want to change that.

Since the comforter is so well accepted, Barbara thinks we could raise price with no problem. It certainly would improve our profits if sales didn't fall off. I'm concerned that they might. We haven't changed price for over two years now, and our customers and the store buyers may resist. The comforter is our most popular item, and any problem with it could hurt the other products. Our doll accessories line would not be affected, but that only accounts for about 10 percent of sales. It's the other baby products, including the comforter, that worry me.

This case was prepared by Professor Dennis H. Tootelian, California State University, Sacramento. Photos courtesy of Noel-Joanna, Inc.

COMPANY HISTORY

Noel-Joanna, Inc., manufactured lines of baby products and doll accessories which were sold through sales representatives to department and specialty stores throughout the United States. The company was formed under rather modest circumstances in 1970 in southern California. The owners created the comforter for their own babies, and other mothers in the neighborhood saw and liked it, Mrs. Heinz recalled:

Our friends kept reminding us what a great idea it was. They would come over and say they saw somebody who liked our infant seat comforters. Pretty soon we began to think, "If everybody likes them so much, why not sell them commercially?"

First we made six and took them to a nearby baby store. They sold quickly, so we figured we might as well go big! We made more comforters and took them to Bullock's in Santa Ana. The buyer agreed to order a dozen at $2 each, and we were on our way.

By going to various baby stores in southern California, Mrs. Jarvis and Mrs. Heinz developed about ten accounts in the first six months of business. Most were small stores, however, and sales in the first year totaled only $200. Toward the end of the first year, they added a second product—a crib comforter. This was suggested by a buyer for another Bullock's store. In NoJo's third year of operation, the first big sale was made—for $2,000 to Bullock's in downtown Los Angeles. Sales in that year exceeded $60,000 and continued upward as shown in exhibit 2.

By October 1973 (the company's fiscal year was such that it was in its fourth year of operation), NoJo expanded its market to include all of California and Arizona and Nevada. Several other products were added to their baby line, and plans were made during that time to use additional sales representatives for the South, Midwest, and East.

Just before Christmas in 1973, an agent in Dallas was commissioned to represent NoJo in four southern states. In the next ten months a New York representative was added, and the entire line was being sold in Alaska, Hawaii, Puerto Rico, Canada, and Mexico. By 1978, the NoJo lines were carried in

EXHIBIT 1
The Infant Seat Comforter

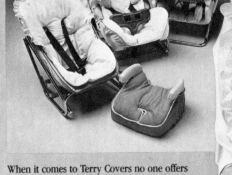

EXHIBIT 2
NoJo Sales

Year	Sales
1971	$ 200*
1972	1,000*
1973	60,000*
1974	100,000*
1975	176,980
1976	404,545
1977	566,382
1978	785,029

*Approximate sales levels. Company records were unavailable for these time periods.

the better stores in most major cities, including New York, Cleveland, Dallas, Atlanta, Denver, Chicago, San Francisco, Los Angeles, and Miami.

NOJO PRODUCTS

NoJo manufactured two main lines of products. The comforter (or "terry cover") is shown in exhibit 1. Doll accessories were added in 1975, as were spin-offs of several baby items including sleeping bags and pillows, as well as unique items such as all-fabric backpacks and purses, and a "toothfairy pillow." Despite their growth in popularity, however, the doll accessories continued to account only for approximately 10 percent of NoJo sales.

Of the baby products, the two infant seat comforters were by far the most popular. Although the fabric patterns and colors varied widely, the main difference between the two models was that one had a rickrack border and the other an eyelet border, with the latter being considerably more expensive. Although the comforters were designed initially to slip over plastic infant seats—somewhat of a staple product for infant care and feeding—they served many other uses as well. Since their functional value was to protect against cold, hard plastic, they served equally well over the seats of baby strollers, car seats, high-chair seats, and any other chairlike structures.

In addition, the comforter was aesthetically pleasing. The bright colors were considered cheery, and provided the opportunity to create an overall baby decor. As Mrs. Heinz commented:

I believe we initiated the trend for a coordinated nursery, with comforters, bumper pads, sheets, pillows, canopies, and diaper stackers that match. It's a nice opportunity to give the nursery a coordinated look. People are having babies later in life, and they are willing to spend more money to prepare a nursery.

As an overall product strategy, NoJo was committed to bringing out new lines on a relatively frequent basis as well as changing the designs of existing items. Mrs. Jarvis commented on their efforts:

It has become really difficult to come up with cute new ideas for baby products. Actually, what we have done recently was to expand our market to older children. One of our newer products, the Toothfairy Pillow, is more for children between the ages of four and six. This has sold really well. It is a novelty item and there is nothing like it on the market.

The other problem we have had to deal with is changing the patterns for our existing baby products—especially the comforter. We have found that many people receive these as gifts from baby showers and birthdays. Surprisingly, however, most have more than one. After they use the gift for a while, they typically buy a spare to use when the other is being washed, or simply to change colors. We search the fabric mills all the time to find new and interesting fabric patterns. In a normal year, we may use eight to ten new patterns instead of using the same ones over again.

One key is to use a "neuter" design since that's the way about 90 percent of all infant gifts are purchased. The look has to be for either a boy or a girl. The other requirement is good quality fabric and yarn. These comforters have to look like they are well made since we are partly appealing to the grandmother market, and they can tell quickly if the filler and material are good enough.

PURCHASING AND MANUFACTURE

All purchasing was done by Mrs. Jarvis and Mrs. Heinz. This was conducted directly with the fabric mills through their offices in the various merchandise marts located across the United States. Manufacturing of all products was handled at the NoJo plant in southern California by thirteen full-time seamstresses and some others on a part-time basis. Although production is quite labor-intensive, the wages have not been as much of a problem as the material costs, as Mrs. Jarvis noted:

> *I can remember when we could get the material at retail stores cheaper than we can buy now directly from the mills. This year alone, fabric costs went up 15 percent!*
>
> *One of the problems is that we don't buy in very large quantities since we like to change patterns frequently. By going this way, we cannot take advantage of some attractive quantity discounts. On the other hand, we don't want to make 10,000 comforters with all the same pattern. That would cut into the repeat and spare buying. I think the department store buyers also are impressed with the great diversity and change, too. After all, that creates "new" products for them to merchandise.*

DISTRIBUTION AND PROMOTION

NoJo products were sold through department and specialty stores in the baby and doll sections. Although the owners had considered discount outlets as a source of possible sales, they decided that it did not fit into the image they wanted to convey. Additionally, they were afraid that such a distribution structure would create price competition among retail outlets and thereby hurt overall department store sales.

As such, the main selling effort was made by NoJo sales representatives located in Los Angeles, San Francisco, Dallas, Atlanta, Columbus (Indiana), Tensleep (Wyoming), Denver, Chicago, Kansas City (Missouri), Minneapolis, and New York City. These representatives had exclusive territories and received commissions of 10.2 percent on sales in their areas. Their contacts were, of course, with store buyers.

To assist the representatives in their selling functions, NoJo advertised in various trade publications, as in the example shown in exhibit 1. In addition, they supplied various fliers and brochures. The brochure in exhibit 3 shows a NoJo product tie-in with a children's story book.

PRICING

Typically, the prices charged for various baby products would be marked up 100 percent by the retail store—for example, the $4 comforter would carry a retail price of $8. These margins were attractive to buyers for the retail stores and helped stimulate sales. Overall company costs and financial data are presented in exhibit 4.

The comforter itself had originally sold for $4 at the retail level, and over a span of five years doubled in price. At the request of Mrs. Jarvis and Mrs. Heinz, a few of the sales representatives altered the standard price to stores to measure any differences in sales. The results of this six-month experiment are shown in exhibit 5. The cost structure for the comforter is shown in exhibit 6.

FUTURE

In assessing the pricing question, Mrs. Jarvis stated:

> *We're not really sure what we want to do with the price of the comforter. We have tried to maintain a mark-up of at least 35 percent on this item since it contributes so greatly to overall revenues and profits. If we don't increase price, our margin falls, and if we do increase price I'm afraid our sales may taper off. We could lose out either way if we are not careful.*

With the end of their fiscal year approaching, the owners agreed that some decision must be made. They were about to print new brochures and fliers and meet with their sales representatives. They decided that they had to finalize their pricing plans.

EXHIBIT 3
Trade Publication Advertising

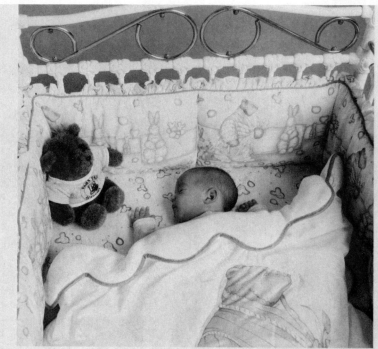

NoJo's exclusive Last Elegant Bear Bumper and Cuddle Me Comforter™

Abiner Smoothie is
The Last Elegant Bear
A new American Classic by Dennis Kyte

The Book & Color Book
By Simon & Schuster

**Infant Bedding
and Accessories**
By Noel Joanna Inc.

Bedding and Bath Ensembles
By Fieldcrest

Plush Toys
By GUND

Boy's Sleepwear
By Tom & Jerry Boys Wear

Girls Sleepwear
By Laura Dare

**Men's Robes, Pajamas
and Night Shirts**
By Knothe

Giftware
By Sigma / Deldan

NOEL JOANNA INC.

One Mason, Irvine, California 92718 (714) 770-6303 (800) 854-8760

CASE

EXHIBIT 4
Noel-Joanna Inc.
Income Statements

Income Summary

	1978	1977	1976
Sales	$785,029	$566,382	$404,545
Cost of Goods Sold*	560,195	389,832	272,170
Gross Profit	223,834	176,550	132,375
Selling Expenses†	88,914	72,989	53,877
Gen. & Admin. Expenses**	81,196	57,129	62,024
Net Income Before Taxes	$ 54,724	$ 46,432	$ 16,474

*See Schedule A
†See Schedule B
**See Schedule C

Schedule A—Cost of Goods Sold

	1978	1977	1976
Materials & Labor:			
Fabric	$258,384	$164,847	$110,541
Polyester	58,036	36,524	23,074
Thread & Zipper	55,128	35,359	22,148
Labels	5,041	3,430	2,024
Shipping	8,963	8,914	8,031
Freight	16,078	11,931	8,716
Labor	125,751	102,371	80,109
Occupancy Costs:			
Rent of Building	$ 22,408	$ 15,555	$ 8,879
Property Taxes	987	837	327
Insurance	7,502	6,028	1,693
Repairs & Maintenance	156	329	545
General Factory Expenses	1,761	3,707	6,083
Total Cost of Goods Sold:	$560,195	$389,832	$272,170

Schedule B—Selling Expenses

	1978	1977	1976
Sales Commissions	$ 80,073	$ 57,771	$ 41,264
Telephone	4,219	4,924	4,115
Sales Promotion & Travel	4,622	10,294	8,498
Total	$ 88,914	$ 72,989	$ 53,877

(*continued on next page*)

EXHIBIT 4 (*continued*)

Schedule C—General and Administrative Expenses

	1978	1977	1976
Officers' Salaries	$ 27,500	$ 16,500	$ 22,500
Payroll Taxes	2,641	1,945	1,166
Office Supplies	6,238	5,729	6,621
Automobile	15,730	12,860	10,808
Printing	6,185	5,438	5,869
Legal and Accounting	1,500	1,000	1,000
Other Taxes & Licenses	1,201	1,097	1,180
Advertising	5,891	4,421	4,036
Interest Expenses	9,775	4,965	3,963
Depreciation	853	469	502
General Adm. Expenses	3,682	2,705	4,379
Total	$ 81,196	$ 57,129	$ 62,024

Balance Sheets

	1978	1977	1976
ASSETS:			
Current Assets			
Cash	$ 10,132	$ 8,763	$ 16,005
Trade Receivables	81,320	72,637	53,307
Inventories	126,021	92,137	57,639
Prepaid Expenses	6,735	4,414	7,623
Total	$224,208	$177,951	$134,574
Fixed Assets			
Machinery	$ 21,368	$ 15,685	$ 12,766
Office Equipment	5,792	4,093	4,211
Total	$ 27,160	$ 18,678	$ 16,977
TOTAL ASSETS	$251,368	$197,729	$151,551
LIABILITIES:			
Current Liabilities			
Accounts Payable	$ 71,830	$ 56,935	$ 30,823
Payroll Taxes	5,010	3,022	1,463
Interest & Other Taxes	10,361	7,779	4,798
Sales Commissions	18,381	9,865	4,969
Long-Term Debt—Current	13,601	14,741	16,620
Accrued Wages	16,910	14,599	11,597
Payable to Officers	20,000	14,075	8,420
Total	$156,093	$121,016	$ 78,690
Long Term Notes:	26,591	27,543	30,165
TOTAL LIABILITIES	$182,684	$148,559	$108,855
CAPITAL:			
Capital Stock	$ 1,000	$ 1,000	$ 1,000
Retained Earnings	$ 67,684	$ 48,170	$ 41,696
Total	$ 68,684	$ 49,170	$ 42,696
TOTAL LIABILITIES & CAPITAL	$251,368	$197,729	$151,551

EXHIBIT 5
Price Adjustment Results

	Wholesale Price*		Volume of Sales†	
Test Number	801	2301	801	2301
1	$4.00	$5.50	18,362	14,211
2	3.50	5.50	24,318	9,423
3	3.50	4.50	19,681	17,284
4	4.50	6.00	17,631	13,299
5	5.00	6.50	15,097	8,681
6	5.50	7.50	9,631	4,102

*Retail price would be based on 100 percent markup on cost.

†Volume is in units sold.

EXHIBIT 6
Infant Seat Comforter Cost Structure

	Model 801	Model 2301
Material:		
Fabric	$ .81	$ .81
Polyester	.36	.36
Thread	.04	.06
Rickrack/Eyelet	.10	.38
Yarn	.30	.30
Labor:	.65	1.36
Package & Shipping:	.20	.20
Total Direct Cost	$2.46	$3.47

LEE'S MARKETS

Tom Lee, general manager of Lee's Markets, was in the process of reviewing the operations of the grocery chain he managed. A number of changes had taken place within the last year, and he was not sure that the methods he had been using to keep control over the stores, and especially the new pricing policies, were still appropriate. Reflecting on the recent developments, he noted:

This is a family-owned business, and my father, my uncle, and two of my brothers wanted to expand our market area and the number of grocery stores we had. Although none of them are active in the grocery business, they are my elders and I had little choice but to accept their wishes. In the last year, we have grown much faster than I would have liked, but it was their decision. In our family, tradition and age carry considerable weight when it comes to making business decisions.

This case was prepared by Professor Dennis H. Tootelian, California State University, Sacramento.

In any event, we now have three more stores, and I need to reassess our pricing methods. Because of the big discount food warehouses moving into our area, we have decided to compete more on a price basis than we ever have before. That was a tough decision for our family to make. Historically, we have stayed away from price competition, preferring to offer superior quality and service, and expecting our customers to pay a little extra for that. Now, with the lower prices, we have to watch our stores' costs more closely as well as the prices and services offered by our competitors. this means more work and greater possibility of error. With the margins we are now operating on, a small increase in costs or a mistake in pricing too low will wipe out our profits. On the other hand, if we price even a little too high, we can be left behind by the big chains and discounters.

HISTORY

Lee's Markets is a chain of fourteen grocery stores located in a large city in the northeastern United States. Tom Lee is the third of four sons of Mr. M. Lee, a Chinese immigrant who came to the United States in the early 1920s. After working in grocery stores for several years, Mr. M. Lee started his own store and two years later formed a partnership with his brother, Kim, when the latter came to the United States.

By the late 1950s, the Lee brothers owned four grocery stores and a Chinese restaurant. Mr. M. Lee took over the management of the grocery stores and Mr. Kim Lee managed the restaurant. When they later added a series of specialty Oriental food stores, they incorporated the business under one family-owned corporation, Lee Brothers, Inc.

Although not all of the children of the two founders became active in the corporation, several sons and cousins eventually took over facets of the operation. Mr. M. Lee remained the president of the corporation and Kim Lee continued to be active as its vice president and treasurer.

As more family members became involved in the business, decisions were made to expand the scope of the grocery stores, the restaurant, and the specialty outlets. Over the years, Lee Brothers, Inc., slowly became the holding company for a chain of twelve grocery stores, three restaurants, and seven specialty food outlets. The most significant growth in the grocery section, however, came last year with the addition of two new stores and the development of plans for another. Historically, the family had never approved the addition of more than one store in two years.

ORGANIZATION

According to Tom Lee, the corporation was organized and managed on a strict basis of tradition and hierarchical order. Family harmony was regarded as the most important criterion for decision-making, with the wishes of the more senior members of the family given considerably more weight than those of the younger members. The actual organizational structure is shown in exhibit 1.

The corporation's board of directors was composed of the nine oldest members of the family. Although the board met formally only twice per year, consultations were made on an individual basis with the two founders whenever one of the section managers deemed it necessary.

Each section manager was free to make any decision regarding his section, so long as it did not affect any other section. In instances where actions would have an overlapping influence, the founders were consulted. Mr. M. Lee and Mr. Kim Lee would decide if the possibility of dissension existed among members of the family pertaining to the decision. If so, contact would be made with other members of the board. As Tom Lee noted:

While this process makes it cumbersome to act quickly on some matters, it helps to keep the family together. Usually if my brothers and cousins are consulted on matters that might affect them, they try their best to help me, and I do the same for them. When we have serious disagreements about things, it is generally understood that we will continue talking until there is unanimous agreement. I remember once that this took nearly twenty-four hours. Those discussions concerned the change in pricing policies for our markets. I held out for a long time on that decision.

Each section of the corporation was organized in a different manner, depending on the preferences of the general manager and the needs of the business. Mr. Tom Lee established the organization for Lee's Markets, shown in exhibit 2, early in his nine years as general manager of the grocery store section.

Each of the fourteen stores had a manager who was responsible for the operations of the store, including hiring of personnel, maintaining desired levels of sales and inventories, and preparing accounting reports.

Directly managing the operations of the fourteen stores were two supervisors who each oversaw seven stores. Company policy was that the supervisors would visit each of their seven stores on a daily basis, collect sales reports for the previous day, and check the general operations of the store. This included discussing operations with clerks and getting feedback from customers, monitoring inventory levels, evaluating store maintenance and general layout, and resolving any disputes between the manager and employees.

Mr. Tom Lee's primary responsibilities included

CASE

EXHIBIT 1
Lee Brothers, Inc.
Organization Chart

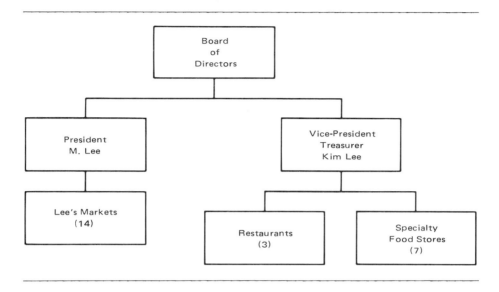

EXHIBIT 2
Lee's Markets
Organization Chart

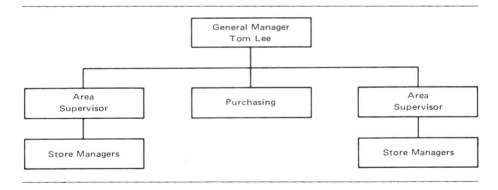

monitoring the supervisors by discussing store activities with them at the end of each day, resolving any problems they could not handle, dealing with suppliers, setting prices, analyzing sales and profits, and planning in general. Mr. Lee typically reported the performance of the grocery stores to the treasurer of the corporation on a daily basis, and to his father and uncle twice a week. Mr. Lee's wife was in charge of the accounting activities for the grocery store section, preparing weekly sales reports and quarterly financial statements used by both her husband and the officers of the corporation.

Purchasing for the grocery stores was handled by three department managers: the meat manager, the produce manager, and the grocery manager. The managers of the departments would make purchases only when there was agreement between the store managers and the supervisors. When there were disputes between the store managers and the supervisors—typically regarding lines to carry or the amount of inventory to keep on hand—Mr. Tom Lee would intercede to resolve the problems. In nearly all instances, he would insist on agreement before proceeding. As he noted:

I want my store managers and supervisors to understand that they have to work together, and not be constantly at each other's throats. When they argue about something, I make them sit down and discuss it until they work out an agreement. Occasionally, this takes a long time, but I feel it is the best way.

The managers of the meat, produce, and grocery departments were responsible for ordering merchandise as efficiently as possible, and for keeping track of who ordered what. This centralization of ordering helped keep costs low, ensured that merchandise quality would be consistent, and controlled overall inventory levels. In many instances, an order from one store could be filled out of excess inventory from another. From an accounting stand-point, such transactions would be handled in much the same manner as if the store were receiving an order from an outside supplier, so the profitability of individual stores could be monitored.

THE MARKET

Because Lee's Markets were in virtually all areas of the city, the target markets and competitive conditions varied considerably from store to store. Generally, however, the older stores tended to be in lower income areas where there were greater percentages of young families and senior citizens. Commonly, these were situated close to the center of the city, which had become somewhat depressed. Most of the newer stores were located along the outer edges of the city in areas primarily populated by middle-income families and middle-aged parents.

Just as the types of customers varied greatly, so did the competition faced by individual stores. Mr. Lee felt that stores located closer to the center of the city did not confront the same quality of competition that faced those in the outer areas. He commented:

The stores in the center of town compete mostly with small "mom and pop" grocery stores and some small and very old chains. Even though our stores are old, they have been well-maintained or remodeled, and typically are bigger than those of the chains. We can compete very well here.

Mr. Lee believed that the intensity and quality of competition were considerably greater in the outlying areas, where 65 percent of Lee's Markets were located. New, large, chain supermarkets and discount food warehouses had entered these areas and competed aggressively for market position. As Mr. Lee noted:

The board of directors felt that we were being hurt badly in this market since the national chains and discount warehouses have used price as a competitive weapon. They have consistently undercut our prices, even during our weekly advertised specials. The board was afraid that as customers became more price sensitive we would lose out, and be viewed as a high-priced store. Eventually, this could hurt us in the inner-city areas as well.

In addition to the national chain supermarkets and discount warehouses located in the city, there were three local food chains. One chain was larger than Lee's Markets with fifteen outlets, but was not considered to be an especially strong competitor. Its stores were poorly maintained and merchandised and were considered to have below-average meats and produce. The other local chains had eight and eleven outlets respectively, and were somewhat more aggressive. Their size, however, made it more difficult for them to compete on a price basis, and their meats and produce were not considered to be equal to those offered by Lee's Markets. According to Mr. Lee:

We offer excellent quality meats and produce. And, we try to give the most attentive and friendly service possible. These are areas where we can really outshine the competition.

STORE OPERATIONS

Of great concern to Mr. Lee from a competitive standpoint were inventory and labor. He considered these to be the most critical aspects of internal grocery store operation. Accordingly, he tried to maintain close control over each store's inventory levels and labor costs. Without this control, he did not believe that Lee's Markets could compete with the larger chains.

Based on the size of each store and its sales history, Mr. Lee set a general range of inventory for the store and tried to keep it at or below that level. This was done on the basis of dollars in inventory rather than the number of units. He indicated that he did not care much about the quantity of inventory; it was the dollars committed that were important from a cost-control perspective.

With central ordering, Lee's Markets also had a warehouse from which its own trucks distributed to the individual stores. Mr. Lee thought that this was both good and bad. While the process made it easier to purchase in larger quantities—and therefore at lower prices—Lee's Markets had only one truck available for deliveries. Although the routing of deliveries had been determined by Mr. Lee, it had not been changed for several years. As new stores were added to the chain, they were pieced into the existing routing system. As a result, there were occasional stockouts which required special deliveries during the off-hours. This was especially costly, averaging $100 per special delivery for both labor and truck expense. However, Mr. Lee doubted that an entirely new routing plan would be any more effective and felt that it might even be counterproductive:

If we start changing our deliveries, we mess up the cycles that every store has come to rely upon. I

don't want to confuse people—I'd rather spend an extra $100, even if this happens twice a week.

The other aspect of internal operations that was of great concern to Mr. Lee was the cost of labor. The Grocery Store section employed nearly 130 checkers and stock clerks, and 35 butchers—all of whom were unionized. The amount of money paid for labor occasionally bothered Mr. Lee:

I know that the quality of our employees is crucial to the success of Lee's Markets. We have always emphasized quality products and friendly service. But it still hurts me to see how much money we have to pay in wages, especially for unproductive time. It literally costs us over a dollar every time one of them drinks a cup of coffee or goes to the bathroom.

To control the costs of labor, Mr. Lee had repeatedly asked the supervisors to watch for opportunities to reduce the number of employees or the number of hours employees worked. He emphasized the use of part-time employees as a way to schedule personnel more precisely around peak periods:

I have tried to get the store managers to use more part-time employees and schedule them only during the busy periods. But they complain that the problems encountered in using these people outweigh the benefits in cost savings. I may have to get tougher about this. You can talk nicely to some people and get things done, but with others you almost have to use a stick. Since we do not have any manager-types in the stores other than the actual store manager, they (the store managers) don't want the added burdens of closely supervising their employees. But that's part of their jobs. That's what I pay the managers to do. They tell me that we cannot offer quality products and friendly service, and get by with a little less labor at the same time. I think they are just avoiding the issue.

MARKETING

The marketing practices used by Lee's Markets centered primarily on local newspaper advertising, point-of-purchase displays, customer service, and various pricing techniques. Until recently, the greatest attention went to weekly newspaper advertising. Like most other stores in the city, Lee's Markets ran weekly sales, and promoted them in two-page advertisements in two local newspapers. To get full use of the newspaper advertising, small portions of space were devoted to the items available at the seven specialty outlets which carried nothing but Oriental foods. This joint advertising had been a policy of the board of directors because they wanted to gradually combine the two sections into one unit.

Newspaper advertising, however, was rather drastically reduced once the decision was made by the board to compete on a price basis. They felt that the advertisements were too expensive, and that it was no longer desirable to tie together the specialty outlets with the discount orientation of Lee's Markets.

Instead of full-page advertising, therefore, Mr. Lee decided to use small ads, approximately one-eighth page, to remind customers that Lee's Markets had "made across-the-board price reductions." In addition, leaflets about the new pricing program were to be distributed. The leaflets contained coupons for select merchandise as an inducement to customers to come into the market. Mr. Lee felt that since the board would not authorize newspaper advertising as it had in the past, the leaflets would be the best way to reach customers in the immediate geographic area surrounding each store—especially the primary target markets.

Complementing the limited advertising efforts, Mr. Lee planned to devote more attention to in-store promotions. As he noted:

I spend about 25 percent of my time visiting the stores, stocking and remerchandising the shelves. This is one part of the business that I really enjoy. It gives me a chance to be a little creative with each store. Adjusting displays here and there can make a big difference in terms of sales. This is something that the chains usually don't do, and the discount warehouses cannot do. It also gives me an opportunity to talk to the customers and determine if they are getting good service from our employees. In the last year, I fired three

employees who customers said were discourteous. That will not happen in one of my stores.

Certainly the biggest change that had taken place was the conversion to more of a discount store orientation. Having lowered prices by an average of 8 percent, Mr. Lee set a policy of having his prices two to three cents lower on 90 percent of the items also carried by the competing chains. Previously, Lee's Markets had been 3 to 4 percent higher on most merchandise, especially meats and produce (see exhibit 3). In some areas where competiton was especially keen, Mr. Lee had the store managers publicize the differences in prices on the leaflets they were distributing.

Although he did not agree with the board's decision regarding this change in strategy, he resigned himself to its implementation:

I still do not like the idea of price reductions because we have always emphasized quality and service. I'm not sure we can continue to provide the same quality meats and produce over the long term as we are going to have to compete aggressively on a price basis. I'm not even sure that customers believe that we offer lower prices. Besides, we now have to continually monitor the prices being charged by our competitors. This has put greater pressure on our store managers and supervisors. The added responsibility will sooner or later take its toll on them. We may have to add more supervisors or a managerial level below that of the store manager. Either way, this will be an added cost that we must account for while simultaneously reducing prices. I only hope that we can increase sales volume enough to cover this. Our early returns seem to indicate that this strategy may be successful, but it's too early to tell. It may just be a novelty at this point.

To test the results of the price changes, Mr. Lee took a sample of merchandise and set different prices on the goods in each of five stores he considered to have similar customers. In monitoring prices and quantities demanded over a relatively brief period of time, Mr. Lee prepared the chart shown in exhibit 4. Store A was used for control purposes, so no changes were made in merchandise prices.

CASE

EXHIBIT 3
Sample Price Comparisons
(as a percentage of Lee's Markets old prices)

Item	Lee's Markets		National Chain (Average)	Local Chain (Average)	Discount Warehouse (Average)
	Old Price	New Price			
Meats:					
Ground Chuck (lb)	100%	99%	96%	91%	98%
New York Steak (lb)	100	91	94	102	90
Boneless Round Steak (lb)	100	91	97	92	90
Whole Fryer (lb)	100	96	95	93	89
Center Cut Pork Chops (lb)	100	95	95	95	96
Produce:					
Head Lettuce (ea)	100%	97%	102%	100%	99%
Tomatoes (lb)	100	100	103	98	100
Apples (lb)	100	92	94	92	89
Oranges (lb)	100	92	94	92	89
Brussel Sprouts (lb)	100	85	101	93	90
Potatoes (10 lb)	100	90	95	85	85
Grocery:					
Canned Peaches (29 oz)	100%	93%	92%	90%	91%
Canned Green Beans (16 oz)	100	94	93	90	91
Cannel Whole Beets (16 oz)	100	87	93	96	90
Canned Sliced Pineapple (15¼ oz)	100	90	97	97	88
Cheese Spread (5 oz)	100	89	103	100	90
Canned Pieces & Stems Mushrooms (4 oz)	100	89	102	100	86
Canned Chicken Noodle Soup (10½ oz)	100	96	93	91	90
Crackers (11½ oz)	100	94	90	92	94
Long Grain Rice (42 oz)	100	97	98	102	97
Cereal—Childrens (11 oz)	100	99	93	94	95
Pancake Flour (32 oz)	100	89	105	95	91
Sugar (5 lb)	100	95	95	92	85
Bottled Salad Dressing (8 oz)	100	88	102	101	85
Frozen Orange Juice (12 oz)	100	95	94	98	91
Coffee (2 lb)	100	96	95	97	93
Peanut Butter (18 oz)	100	96	99	102	90
Shortening (48 oz)	100	98	96	93	90
Bread (1 lb)	100	98	97	98	85
Margarine (1 lb)	100	90	99	97	85
Eggs (1 dozen)	100	96	96	96	85

Prices in Store B were discounted in the same manner as that used in the original change to a discount strategy, as shown in exhibit 3. In Store C, the prices of meats were lowered, while the prices of produce were raised. Just the opposite strategy was employed in Store D. Finally, Store E used a mixture of higher and lower prices. Although Mr. Lee realized that his merchandise sample was not truly representative of all product lines carried, he believed that it presented a reasonable facsimile of market conditions.

CASE

EXHIBIT 4
Lee's Markets
Sample of Prices & Quantities Demanded

	Store A Price	Store A Quan.	Store B Price	Store B Quan.	Store C Price	Store C Quan.	Store D Price	Store D Quan.	Store E Price	Store E Quan.
MERCHANDISE										
Meats (per lb.)										
Ground Chuck	$1.59	1400	$1.57	1450	$1.47	1700	$1.98	1100	$1.89	1050
Whole Fryer	$0.65	2800	$0.59	3300	$0.55	4100	$0.71	2100	$0.69	2700
Produce										
Lettuce (ea.)	$0.79	500	$0.76	510	$0.81	440	$0.52	750	$0.62	600
Potatoes (10 lb.)	$1.09	625	$0.98	815	$1.19	600	$0.88	1150	$1.29	500
Apples (lb.)	$0.65	1100	$0.59	1500	$0.71	1000	$0.49	1700	$0.79	900
Grocery										
Canned Peaches	$0.84	110	$0.78	165	$0.83	110	$0.71	185	$0.88	95
Canned Beans	$0.76	230	$0.69	240	$0.49	410	$0.55	330	$0.78	220
Chicken Soup	$0.52	285	$0.49	315	$0.47	330	$0.39	510	$0.55	270
Sugar (5 lb.)	$1.27	150	$1.19	170	$1.15	165	$1.09	180	$1.31	140
Coffee (2 lb.)	$3.95	105	$3.79	100	$4.29	70	$3.68	95	$4.49	65
Margarine (lb.)	$0.82	240	$0.74	320	$0.89	230	$0.69	450	$0.98	100

FINANCE

Nearly all of the financial matters relating to Lee Brothers, Inc., were managed by Mr. Kim Lee and his daughter, Mary. On a daily basis, Ms. Lee was responsible for monitoring the corporation's cash balance and ensuring that all excess funds were properly invested. Although separate records were kept for each grocery store (see exhibit 5), restaurant, and specialty food outlet, all of the funds were pooled into a central account. In this way, funds could be diverted from one activity to another with Mr. Kim Lee's approval. And it was believed that the corporation as a whole was in a better position than any one section by itself to secure favorable terms on any necessary long-term financing.

Condensed financial statements are presented in exhibits 6 and 7. Over the years, Mr. Kim Lee had maintained that the corporation would not borrow money unless it became absolutely necessary. He reasoned that if his children and those of his brother realized that most of their wealth was tied up in the

EXHIBIT 5
Lee's Markets
Sales by Stores
(in hundreds of dollars)

Store*	Last Year	Two Years Ago	Three Years Ago
1	$1,578	$1,336	$1,231
2	1,262	1,103	1,002
3	1,147	1,038	1,010
4	1,025	1,212	1,406
5	1,419	1,199	998
6	1,699	1,312	1,321
7	1,273	1,025	1,011
8	1,435	1,230	1,012
9	1,456	1,218	1,121
10	901	850	799
11	914	879	849
12	710	666	—
13	535	—	—
14	422	—	—

*By order of when opened, from oldest to newest.

EXHIBIT 6
Lee's Markets
Income Statements
(in hundreds of dollars)

	Last Year (14 Stores)	Two Years Ago (12 Stores)	Three Years Ago (11 Stores)
Sales			
Meat	$3,156	$ 2,985	$ 3,057
Produce	2,366	1,818	1,529
Grocery	10,254	8,177	7,174
Total	$15,776	$12,980	$11,760
Cost of Sales	$13,001	$10,596	$ 9,442
Gross Profit	$ 2,775	$ 2,384	$ 2,318
Expenses			
Salaries & Wages	$ 1,437	$ 1,118	$ 1,041
Rent	331	279	235
All Other	159	175	171
Total	$ 1,927	$ 1,572	$ 1,447
Net Profit Before Taxes	$ 848	$ 812	$ 871

EXHIBIT 7
Lee's Markets
Balance Sheet
(in hundreds of dollars)

Current Assets	
Cash	$ 345
Inventory	1,086
Other	82
Total	$1,513
Fixed Assets	$2,698
Total Assets	$4,211
Current Liabilities	$1,258
Long Term Liabilities	400
Total Liabilities	$1,658
Net Worth	$2,553

corporation, they would be more likely to take the business seriously. While at times this slowed the growth of various sectors of the business, his position in the family gave him the right to set policy.

FUTURE

In reflecting on the future, Mr. Tom Lee was wondering how the expansion and changes in pricing strategy might affect the grocery stores. Both of the supervisors recommended that the prices set for Lee's Markets be reduced even further, possibly 2 percent to 3 percent more, to gain a better advantage over the chains. This added to Mr. Lee's existing concern about the wisdom of the change in price strategy instituted by the board. He felt that if he had to continually modify store prices, his present management processes would also have to be changed in order for the markets to maintain a competitive edge in pricing over the long term.

INDUSTRIAL SUPPLY CORPORATION

The Industrial Supply Corporation (ISC) of Jacksonville, Florida, processed and sold various types of industrial rubber or plastic products, including belting, hoses, couplings, gaskets, and sheets. In addition, they distributed specialty lines of safety equipment and hardware to industrial customers within a radius of approximately 150 miles from Jacksonville.

While the rubber lines had been consistently profitable, profits on safety equipment—alarms, barricades, instruments, signs, and restraining equipment as well as protective gear for hands, feet, eyes, ears, face, and body—had been disappointing. Moreover, ISC's lines of industrial hardware—tools, bits, blades, fasteners, abrasives, adhesives, coatings, brushes, and material-handling devices—had never been profitable (see exhibits 1 and 2). However, Mr. James Powell, age forty-six, president and majority stockholder of ISC, was optimistic about 1978. In his words:

Today we've got a profitable rubber operation, a borderline safety division, and a losing hardware division. It's time to digest the growth. If we add any new resources, it should only be in the areas of market research and strategy. I believe our new organization plus our computerized information system will help us develop and accomplish an intelligently conceived marketing plan for 1978. I expect safety to show overall profit this year, and hardware should break even.

On the other hand, Mr. Powell's optimism was tempered by his concern about territorial rights, especially in the highly profitable rubber lines. Several

This case was prepared by Professor Leete A. Thompson, California State University, Sacramento.

distributors in the Southeast had tacitly divided markets to avoid cutthroat competition, but the extent and nature of such agreements was not always certain, nor was Mr. Powell certain of ISC's best strategy. Recently, when an Orlando distributor Mr. Powell had once tried to buy out had called to discuss sharing rights in "border cities," Mr. Powell had referred him to Ron Whitehill, ISC's vice-president and general manager, without any particular recommendation, but with his blessings to investigate. Mr. Powell said:

It's a form of collusion, and I recognize this. It takes such an enormous investment in the industrial rubber business that I'm not sure we could survive if we had to compete on a day-to-day basis with X (a major tire and rubber manufacturer) distributors or the private distributors with whom they maintain supply contracts. In this case, I'm satisfied that the man who called has no designs on the Jacksonville market, but I do think there's room for some dialogue about border markets.

HISTORY

James Powell, a successful land developer for a large real estate firm, had purchased Jacksonville Rubber Company in 1968. The $180,000 price seemed to be reasonable in view of the firm's potential, and he wanted to be his own boss. He recalled:

Although they (the real estate firm) made a number of concessions to keep me, and I wasn't unhappy there, I really wanted a show of my own. Well, I got one, but a guy like me who knew absolutely nothing about rubber or industrial distribution was on a very steep learning curve. At first, I placed myself in as many different situations as possible to learn what we were and what we ought to be. I started reading industry magazines, attending seminars, talking with other distributors, and...

One of the first things I decided was that the company image as a retail rubber goods store had to change. The store was downtown, where customers dropped in off the street and clerks

EXHIBIT 1
Industrial Supply Corporation

Income Statements as of November 30
(in thousands of dollars)

	1977	1976	1975	1974	1973
Rubber:	$1,579	$1,504	$1,336	$1,343	$1,168
Cost of Goods Sold	972	957	836	858	761
Selling & Administrative Expense	525	442	419	415	362
Interest Expense	31	25	21	8	5
Net Profit	$ 51	$ 80	$ 60	$ 62	$ 40
Safety Equipment:					
Sales	$ 747	$ 595	$ 570	$ 393	$ 68
Cost of Goods Sold	488	432	404	299	51
Selling & Administrative Expense	252	171	178	125	23
Interest Expense	15	10	9	3	1
Net Profit	$ (8)	$ (18)	$ (21)	$ (34)	$ (7)
Hardware:*					
Sales	$ 694	$ 561	$ 373		
Cost of Goods Sold	499	395	256		
Selling & Administrative Expense	233	163	114		
Interest Expense	14	9	5		
Net Profit	$ (52)	$ (6)	$ (2)		

Consolidated Income Statements as of November 30
(in thousands of dollars)

	1977	1976	1975	1974	1973
Sales (net)	$3,020	$2,660	$2,279	$1,736	$1,236
Less Cost of Goods Sold	1,959	1,784	1,496	1,157	812
Gross Profit	$1,061	$ 876	$ 783	$ 579	$ 424
Selling & Administrative Expense	1,010	776	711	540	385
Interest Expense	60	44	35	11	6
Net Profit Before Tax	$ (9)	$ 56	$ 37	$ 28	33
Federal Income Tax		16	10	†	†
Net Profit After Tax	$ (9)	$ 40	$ 27	$ 28	33

*Hardware line added in 1975.

†In 1973 and 1974 the firm was still a sole proprietorship, called Jacksonville Rubber Company. The firm was incorporated under its present name in 1975, and its profits became subject to federal income tax at that time.

filled penny ante orders. You can't expect to grow that way. So we moved to a warehouse, dropped some of the retail rubber items. and put salesmen in the field. We also started closing the doors from noon until one o'clock every day. Orders got larger right away.

I tried to grow faster by negotiating a merger with other rubber distributors. That just didn't work out. Then I figured, why not sell more things to the people we already know. A man from Atlanta sold me on the potential of safety equipment to go with the rubber gloves and

EXHIBIT 2
Industrial Supply Corporation
Consolidated Balance Sheets as of November 30
(in thousands of dollars)

	1977	1976	1975	1974	1973
ASSETS					
Cash	$ 1	$ 11	$ 1	$ 1	$ 1
Receivables (net)	349	276	243	376	147
Inventories	738	532	479	327	256
Prepaid Expenses	45	28	38	9	5
Current Assets	$1,133	$847	$761	$713	$409
Motor Vehicles (net)	$ 3	$ 2	$ 4	$ 6	$ 6
Furniture & Equipment (net)	59	42	38	13	14
Leasehold Improvements	15	12	12	13	14
Other Assets	58	52	45	15	10
TOTAL ASSETS	$1,268	$955	$860	$760	$453
LIABILITIES					
Accounts Payable	$ 170	$138	$130	$297	$113
Notes Payable	637	366	346	137	17
Contracts Payable	20	17	13	—	—
Accrued Expenses	59	43	23	43	4
Accrued Interest	6	4	4	—	5
Accrued Taxes	12	25	19	26	5
Current Liabilities	$ 904	$593	$535	$503	$144
Long Term Notes	49	38	41	—	80
TOTAL LIABILITIES	$ 953	$631	$576	$503	$224
NET WORTH					
Common Stock	$ 257	$257	$257	—	—
Retained Earnings	58	67	27	—	—
Equity	$ 315	$324	$284	$257*	$229*
TOTAL LIABILITIES & NET WORTH	$1,268	$955	$860	$760	$453

*In 1973 and 1974 the firm was a sole proprietorship called Jacksonville Rubber Company. The firm was incorporated under its present name in 1975, and common stock was issued at that time.

clothing we handled, so I hired him to set up a safety division in 1972.

Through 1974, Mr. Powell had emphasized long-range growth at the expense of profits. He explained:

I wanted size, stability, and enough perpetual energy to make the firm function no matter who was running it. If my total objective had been profits, then a lot of things might have been different. I determined not to get involved in staff detail any more than I absolutely had to—to stay in the role of a manager. As a result, I acquiesced to some mistakes in the interest of letting people grow.

In 1975, he decided to concentrate more on attaining profitability. A line of industrial hardware was added because of its high markup and because it could be sold to existing customers. The enlarged firm was incorporated under its present name, Industrial Supply Corporation, and its facilities were moved to a modern industrial park on the outskirts of Jacksonville.

THE ORGANIZATION

In 1978, ISC was managed by an executive committee consisting of Mr. Powell, president, Ron Whitehill, vice-president and general manager, and Don Rouse, vice-president of finance. The latter two were minority stockholders in the corporation. The operating division managers reported to the vice-president and general manager (see exhibit 3). Mr. Whitehill, age forty, a former Goodrich salesman, held a college degree in education, but most of his working life had been spent in the rubber industry. He explained the authority relationships thusly:

Jim (Powell) is a real estate expert...a good financial man...a great guy.... I only left Goodrich because of him. But he often said he had no intention of learning the difference between a hose and a conveyor belt. Me, I like the smell of rubber.

Jim and I reached a decision one evening last October based on my understanding of what the customer wants and my ability to project and predict. That was the approach. His financial ability and my sales ability form a good working relationship. It provides me with latitude I didn't have in a large corporation. Now that Don (Rouse) is taking over more of Jim's responsibilities in finance, the three of us have to share and solve some problems by more dialogue, but it's coming along. Typically, we three meet at least once a week with the division managers. We call this the operations committee.

Don Rouse, age thirty-two, was the newest member of the executive committee, but his influence was expanding. Although he was a CPA and had advanced to a position of audit supervisor for the Miami office of a "Big 8" accounting firm, he joined ISC in 1975 because it offered him an opportunity to move into the area of his primary interest—

management information systems. Upon his recommendations, purchasing and inventory control had been centralized under his control. He also was in charge of accounting, finance, and credit. More recently, he had convinced Mr. Powell to install a Distronics computerized system.

Mr. Powell was considering still further changes in the organizational structure and its authority relationships. As he said:

I turned over responsibility for running the company on a day-to-day basis, operationwise, to Ron (Whitehill). Don (Rouse) is moving pretty fast. We've been struggling with it to define where responsibilities are and are not... there are still some unclear areas. But we have good relationships, and we'll resolve them with a clear understanding of just what I want to stay involved in and what I don't. I don't want to let it all go—just a certain portion of it—so we're working to define just what that is....

Mr. Whitehill and Mr. Rouse each expressed the feeling that Mr. Powell would eventually seek new ventures, and perhaps sell control of the company to them. According to Don Rouse:

Sometimes he [Mr. Powell] seems to get restless. He's still a real estate man at heart. He wants more time with his family too. His wife's into art. He's got horses, goats, two youngsters, and a pretty big boat calling for his attention. If we get a chance, I think Ron and I could make a go of it.

THE DISTRONICS SYSTEM

The Distronics system, installed in 1977, already was being implemented. Some accounting records had been computerized; forecasting, purchasing, credit, and inventory control models were being set up; and a complex cost-price matrix for each product was in the developmental stage. The matrix employed LIFO valuation of inventory to compute each product's cost; it added the appropriate markup, then discounted the price to reflect savings in handling, shipping, and billing various-size lots which customers ordered. If the system worked properly, customers

EXHIBIT 3
Industrial Supply Corporation
Organization Chart

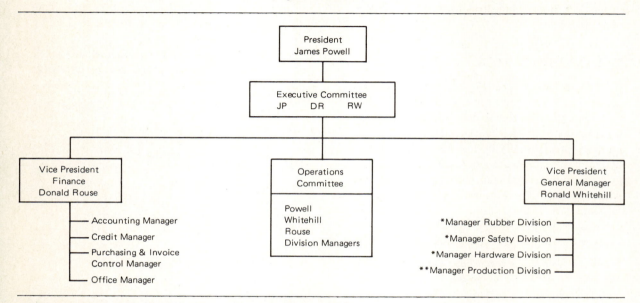

*Salesmen report to the Rubber, Safety, and Hardware Division Managers.
†Receiving, shipping, and shop workers report to the Production Division Manager.

would be allowed different quantity discounts on each item of each order rather than a discount based on total order size. According to Mr. Rouse, some items might no longer be discounted at all.

Distronics also was expected to help ISC reduce purchasing and inventory costs by 15 to 25 percent. Most of the 12,000 products inventoried would be reordered according to an economic order quantity model. In the past, salesmen had insisted upon small purchasing orders without regard for their cost. On some occasions, salesmen even had quoted their customers larger discounts for quantity orders than purchasing received from suppliers.

While the safety and hardware lines consisted of "pick and pull" items, all purchased for resale, about 75 percent of the rubberline purchases had "value added" by ISC's production division. In general, the production manager tended to fabricate more than an order called for and place the excess in inventory.

With the purchasing and inventory control functions centralized, economic production lot sizes as well as economic order lot sizes could be determined, so better correlation of inventory with demand was anticipated.

Still another Distronics program was expected to set credit limits for each customer. While most buyers complied with ISC's 1/10 net/30 sales terms, those who were unable to pay within thirty days had been carried routinely for thirty to sixty additional days without interest charges. As a result, ISC had sometimes been forced to borrow up to the bank's limit of 80 percent on accounts receivable, plus 60 percent of inventories, and pay 3 percent or more above the prime interest rate. It was believed that use of the Distronics credit model would help reduce both credit losses and borrowing costs.

Mr. Powell was enthusiastic about Distronics:

I'm very excited about it. It will put us far ahead of anybody locally. It's also consistent with my idea of making the organization self-sustaining. It might even help us evaluate other business opportunities.

PRODUCTION

ISC's profitability depended heavily upon sales of rubber and plastics products, and much of the products' appeal lay in ISC's expert processing Processing the belting involved slicing huge rolls of fabricated rubber into desired widths on a "slitter," cutting these widths to proper length, then either lacing and cleating each one or vulcanizing the strip into an endless belt. Hoses were cut and processed to order on electric swedgers and banding machines. Some fabrication work was done at customer sites, particularly when precise fitting to stationary equipment was essential. Repair work constituted a significant portion of the shop activity, too.

A number of the production operations required skill as well as precision, so it took at least nine months to train a shop worker. For example, elevator belting, such as that used in conveyors, had to be punched by hand with uniformly spaced holes, at a cost of $15 per hour. Belt cleating also involved much hand labor. An unskilled or careless worker could easily ruin a belt costing up to $400.

Bob Jamison, the production manager, supervised production as well as shipping and receiving. Although he had been with ISC less than a year, he was eager to improve production efficiency. He elaborated:

This is a quality shop. We try to instill pride in doing a good job so that nothing goes out that's questionable. In fact, maybe we're a little too quality conscious....

We're just beginning to grow. If I didn't feel that way, I wouldn't have taken the job here. We'll have to replace some of the hand labor. A $4,700 belt hole puncher would soon pay for itself now. Also, we could save by buying a sonic cleating machine, although the $20,000 cost would have to be written off over two or three years. With growth, we can lengthen production runs and start

carrying larger inventories. Ron (Whitehill) seems willing to go along with such improvements, but I'm not so sure about Mr. Powell or Don Rouse.

CUSTOMERS

ISC customers ranged in size from small farmers and machine shops to nationally known industrial firms. About 65 percent of the sales volume was obtained within a seventy-mile radius of Jacksonville, and almost 100 percent of the customers lived within one hundred miles. The primary customers were original equipment manufacturers (OEMs), several of whom placed large orders for rubber and safety items. Smaller manufacturers, contractors, and government agencies bought in smaller but sometimes significant quantities. According to Mr. Whitehill:

We have 3,000 accounts, but we really want to deal with only about 900 of them. They pay their bills on time, give us lead time, and order in larger quantities. I'm not suggesting that we forget the other 2,100, but we don't make much effort to seek their business. Too much of it is walk-in or phone-in, and we don't even pay commissions on that.

COMPETITION

Each of ISC's three marketing divisions operated under somewhat different competitive conditions. None made any effort to sell in the Tampa-St. Petersburg, Orlando, or Kennedy Space Center areas, primarily because of the competition. Mr. Whitehill explained:

We stay out of their territories, and they stay out of ours, so we aren't harpooning each other's customers. I'n not sure about the legalities of this "gentlemen's agreement," but it's pretty well defined. Partly, it's based on how far away a firm can give adequate service to industrial customers. Thirty or forty miles makes a big difference in ability to give fast service.

Rubber division competition varied from city to city. Even though smaller fabricators and distributors posed a problem in "border areas," Mr. Whitehill was of the opinion that ISC could compete with them. He argued:

> We see fabrication and custom service as our "knack." Our prices are right and our processing is superior. I'm not even sure we need to risk trouble by territorial agreements with suppliers of our size.

Competition from the big *X* Tire and Rubber Company from which ISC purchased such raw materials as hoses, belting, and gaskets was due to *X* outlets in some of the cities, and this severely restricted ISC's territorial expansion. Mr. Whitehill explained:

> We have 55 or 60 percent of the industrial rubber product sales in the cities we service. The X Tire and Rubber Company gives us lower prices than we can get anywhere else, and I'm convinced they'll continue to cooperate as long as we stay out of their outlets' territories.
>
> The trouble is, we need to expand geographically. Manufacturing isn't increasing all that fast around here. Even agriculture is losing ground to housing in Florida. We've considered opening a branch plant in Georgia or South Carolina, where industry is booming. X doesn't have outlets near all the good locations.

The hardware division faced competition of a different nature. Not only were many of the items sold by local merchants; the suppliers' manufacturing agents often called on ISC's customers. Exclusive agency contracts were almost impossible to obtain from manufacturers of tools, bits, blades, fasteners, adhesives, abrasives, or paints. Mr. Whitehill conceded:

> There are six or eight local competitors who specialize in such different things as "power transmission." They offer specialized service, have larger inventories, and buy in larger lots. I'd guess our market there is about 10 percent. We just haven't found our niche.

Competition in safety products was somewhat less severe than that in hardware. Brand names were not as well established. Exclusive dealerships were easier

to obtain. Fewer local distributors carried a wide line of safety equipment. As Mr. Whitehill saw the situation:

> In safety equipment our "knack" is selling specialized service. We are the largest distributor in our area.

Despite his reservations about the hardware division, Mr. Whitehill did see some distinct advantages in ISC's broad product line. He remarked:

> I don't know of another house like ours in all of northern Florida. Some companies we were doing a good job with five years ago in belting, hose, gaskets, etc., now buy their safety equipment and hardware from us as well.

SALES POLICIES

Salesmen were selected by Mr. Whitehill after being screened by the Klein Test and by personal interviews with at least two ISC executives. Those selected were sent to a Dale Carnegie course designed to improve their selling techniques, then trained by accompanying a major supplier's salesman on his route. Typically, the process took a total of approximately nine months.

A total of sixteen salesmen—eight in the field, six on the phones, and two at the counter—were employed. Each field salesman handled fifty to seventy-five accounts, 15 or 20 percent of which were considered "primary." Commissions were 10 percent on all gross sales above a base minimum. Top producers earned $25,000, while the average salesman in the field earned about $16,000 per year.

Since 1976, ISC salesmen had specialized by product as well as by geographical area. Such specialization emphasized expert customer service in each product line and allowed ISC to sell a customer those portions of its total line not reserved to a competitor in that territory. While Mr. Whitehill recognized the value of specializing, he noted that two or three salesmen sometimes called on a single customer and, since each salesman sold only one division's lines, a shortage of inventory in a single line might mean no offsetting sale by that salesman to that customer. He was hopeful that the Distronics system would help avoid shortages as well as reduce expenses to a point where higher salesmen compensation could be paid.

Unfortunately, turnover of salesmen had been rising. In 1977, two left voluntarily and four were terminated because they failed to meet sales quotas. Mr. Powell insisted that salesmen must "earn their existence." In the past, salesmen had been placed in new territories and subsidized until they could build a following. This was touch-and-go in hardware. Mr. Whitehill was working on a plan to split and realign territories. Failing that, he saw no alternative but to reduce the number of salesmen.

Salesmen were assisted by advertising, including large displays in the yellow pages of major cities' telephone books, plus frequent special mailers sent to established customers. The mailers, which called attention to new or improved products or products not normally purchased by the customer, were addressed to individual executives in each company— e.g., the safety director, purchasing agent, or production manager.

Salesmen had been allowed a certain amount of discretion in quoting prices. Individual items sold for as little as 50¢ to as much as $400, but the customized nature of some products made their pricing difficult. In the hardware and safety lines, manufacturers' suggested list prices rarely were followed. Instead, pricing varied with market conditions and the discounts ISC received from its suppliers. Unfortunately, customers sometimes received different quotes from different ISC persons. It was hoped that the Distronics system would soon identify unprofitable lines as well as unprofitable transactions.

THE FUTURE

President Powell was counting on high enough sales and profits in 1978 to set the stage for 1979. Both he and Mr. Whitehill were forecasting sales of $5 million within five years provided that certain problems could be resolved.

Mr. Whitehill cautioned that, while economies and better systems might improve profitability, sales in the present territories were unlikely to grow rapidly.

In his view, the threatened energy shortage would curtail some customers' operations; manufacturers, upon whom ISC depended for sales, were not increasing much in the area; and ISC was unlikely to get a much larger share of its limited market, even if more tacit agreements to share markets were negotiated. Instead, he thought that growth depended upon consolidating present lines and opening branch plants. In his view:

> We can get closer to the customer by branch operations. I see the need for branches by 1979. The competition is doing it. If we get there first, we can forestall competition by pricing, good service, and quality rubber products.

Don Rouse, on the other hand, believed that diversification was the answer to growth, and he was forecasting ISC sales of $10 million in five years by the following strategy:

> We have talked about entering the machinery end of hardware. Plumbing, pumps, and construction equipment should sell well. Even rubber manufacturing could be broadened easily. Then look at hardware. Most of our hardware is for maintenance or repairs. We could add janitorial supplies. If people here will open their eyes and use Distronics, we can set up profitable lines that will sell and drop those that won't.

Mr. Powell saw the establishment of sales dominance and increased profit margins as the way to growth. He spoke of buying out competitors in territories not served by ISC, and of further agreements to share "border area" markets, rather than of adding branch rubber processing branches. For the present, at least, he saw little value in expanding the product lines. He was, he said, shooting for sales of $3.9 million in 1978, with profits in excess of $100,000, and he planned few expenditures to do it. Tentatively, he had decided to raise his own salary from $35,000 to "about $50,000" for the coming year. If his negotiations with some Tampa and Orlando firms proved successful, he expected to enter one or both of those markets and exceed his forecast substantially.

TWIN PEAKS NATIONAL BANK

On February 2, 1976, Mr. James Clark, vice president in charge of marketing, Twin Peaks National Bank, received a telephone call from the president of the bank, Mr. Frank Horman, regarding the bank's All-in-One Account. Mr. Horman mentioned that he had been looking at the different services that the bank offered. Mr. Horman indicated that he was contemplating changes in pricing policies for the bank's services that would increase the bank's profitability without jeopardizing its market share. Mr. Horman felt that since Twin Peaks National Bank had the lowest price of all competitors for the All-in-One type account that he would like a review of the All-in-One Account to determine if a change in pricing or service should be made.

After the telephone conversation with Mr. Horman, Mr. Clark met with the product manager, Mr. Joe Will, who was in charge of the All-in-One Account and the marketing research manager, Mr. Steve Hale, to explain Mr. Horman's concern regarding the pricing policy for the All-in-One Account. Mr. Will had worked with the account since its inception in July 1973. Mr. Hale had started with the bank in 1974 and had formulated some data on the All-in-One Account.

Mr. Will felt that Mr. Hale should conduct further research on the customer demographies in order to evaluate the service since its inception to determine if the All-in-One Account had met the objectives that were initially set up for the program. The three managers decided to meet again at a later date to make a recommendation on any change that could be

This case was prepared by Professor Subhash C. Jain, University of Connecticut and Professor Iqbal Mathur, University of Pittsburgh.

made to the account to increase the bank's profitability without affecting Twin Peaks' market share.

BACKGROUND

The Twin Peaks National Bank was the lead bank in the Twin Peaks Holding Corporation which had 12 other banks located in the state of Ohio. The Holding Company was the eighth largest in the state with total assets of $1.4 billion. Twin Peaks National Bank was the second largest in Frank County, which had a population of 900,000. Twin Peaks had been primarily a wholesale bank serving commercial customers and correspondent banks throughout the state. However in 1960, management recognized the opportunity in the retail market and the bank opened its first branch and then proceeded to its present level of 33 branches located in prime market areas in the county. In keeping with the changing needs of the retail customer, Twin Peaks was the first bank in the community to introduce a package account. This was called the All-in-One Account, consisting of seven banking services with a single charge per month.

The package included the following:

> Write all the checks you want for a $2 monthly fee.
> Free personalized checks.
> A Passbook Savings Account with $1 deposited by the bank.
> Ten percent rebate of the finance charge on qualifying installment loans.
> Free traveler's checks.
> A 24-hour bank at the automated banking machines.
> Overdraft protection with checking reserve. Lets you write a check for more money than you have in your checking account, up to your credit line.

The exclusiveness of the All-in-One Account lasted for six months until other banks in town introduced their package accounts. Exhibit 1 shows the services and charges of the various banks in the community.

EXHIBIT 1
Package Comparison

	Twin Peaks	Bank 1	Bank 2	Bank 3	Bank 4
Price	$2.00	$2.50	$2.75	$2.25	Free*
Checks included	Yes	Yes	Yes	Yes	No
Charge card	Yes	Yes	Yes	Yes	No
24-hour banking	Yes	Yes	Yes	Yes	No
Identification card	Yes	Yes	Yes	Yes	No
Savings	$1.00	$2.50	0	$1.00	No
Installment loan rebate	10%	0.50% add†	Average month**	0.50% add†	No††
Safe deposit box included	No	Yes	No	No	No
Overdraft demand deposit	Yes	Yes	Yes	Yes	No
Official checks	No	Yes	No	No	No
Travelers checks	Yes	Yes	No	Yes	No
Check cashing	Yes	Yes	Yes	Yes	No
Money orders	No	Yes	No	Yes	Yes
Budget	No	Yes	No	No	No

*$100 minimum deposit required.

†The regular add-on interest rate is reduced by 0.50 percent (from 6 percent add-on to 5.50 percent, for example).

**The rebate is equal to the average interest paid per month during the time period of the loan.

††Regular rates are comparable to rates of the other banks after deducting their rebates.

Source: Company records.

ALL-IN-ONE ACCOUNT GROWTH

When the All-in-One Account was introduced in July 1973, it was projected that by the end of the third year there would be 10,000 All-in-One Accounts. This projection was based on a review of the previous three years and the highest percentage rate change was used. Regular savings account growth was projected at 160 percent of the regular demand deposit accounts outstanding at year-end. Checking reserve accounts were projected at 15 percent annual growth which compared to a growth of 14.3 percent in the prior year.

The success of the All-in-One Account is shown in exhibit 2, which illustrates the actual growth of the All-in-One Account and related accounts as compared with the growth without the All-in-One Account and related accounts using the above assumptions.

ALL-IN-ONE ACCOUNT IMPACT ON MARKET SHARE

Using weekly Federal Reserve Bank data and averaging weeks into months, Twin Peaks' market share was compared with the other two major banks within Frank County. The figures were available for regular savings, MasterCard, and checking reserve. Exhibits 3, 4, and 5 indicate that the bank's market share increased each year since the inception of the All-in-One Account. Exhibit 6 was developed by utilizing a survey taken by the bank's Research Department to show the impact of the All-in-One Account on the total demand deposit accounts as well as the new demand deposit accounts market.

EXHIBIT 2
Number growth of All-in-One—Related Accounts

	Year-end number of accounts					Number change				Percent change			
	1971	1972	1973	1974	1975	71-72	72-73	73-74	74-75	71-72	72-73	73-74	74-75
Scenario 1— with All-in-One													
All-in-One	0	0	6,180	18,931	30,500	n.a.*	6,180	12,751	11,569	n.a.	0%	206.3%	61.1%
Regular DDA†	54,082	57,321	63,344	72,118	82,427	3,239	6,023	8,774	10,309	6.0%	10.5	13.9	14.3
Regular savings	80,475	90,311	102,557	116,566	133,244	9,836	12,246	14,009	16,678	12.2	13.6	13.7	14.3
MasterCard	46,264	47,150	58,063	63,158	70,000	886	10,913	5,095	6,842	1.9	23.1	8.8	10.8
Checking reserve	6,900	7,884	14,028	27,417	40,000	984	6,144	13,389	12,583	14.3	77.9	95.4	45.9
Scenario 2—without All-in-One (control)													
Regular DDA	54,082	57,321	62,193	67,479	73,215	3,239	4,872	5,286	5,736	6.0	8.5	8.5	8.5
Regular savings	80,475	90,311	99,509	107,966	117,114	9,836	9,198	8,457	9,148	12.2	10.2	8.5	8.5
MasterCard	46,264	47,150	52,864	57,357	62,233	886	5,714	4,493	4,876	1.9	12.1	8.5	8.5
Checking reserve	6,900	7,884	9,067	10,427	11,991	984	1,183	1,360	1,564	14.3	15.0	15.0	15.0

Note: Regular DDA control projected based on review of 1969–70, 1970–71, and 1971–72 percent changes of 7.2, 8.5, and 6, respectively. Then arbitrarily selected highest of the three (8.5 percent). Regular savings control projected by assuming that it would run 160 percent of regular DDA numbers outstanding. MasterCard control projected by assuming that it would run 85 percent of regular DDA numbers outstanding. Checking reserve control projected by arbitrarily selecting an annual percent change of 15 percent which is slightly higher than the 14.3 percent rate experienced one year prior to All-in-One.

*n.a. = not applicable.

†DDA = Demand deposit account (checking).

Source: Company records.

EXHIBIT 3
Market Shares: Regular Savings

	Share of market				Share of market increase			
	1972	1973	1974	1975	1972	1973	1974	1975
Twin Peaks	28.9	29.2	29.5	30.3	33.1	33.6	34.0	34.3
Other	71.1	70.8	70.5	69.7	66.9	66.4	66.0	65.7

Source: Federal Reserve Bank data.

EXHIBIT 4
Market Shares: Frank County MasterCard Cards

	Share of market				Share of market increase			
	1972	1973	1974	1975	1972	1973	1974	1975
Twin Peaks	20.92	21.99	22.68	23.68	23.7	25.8	24.1	44.6
Other	70.08	78.01	77.32	76.32	76.3	74.2	75.9	55.4

Source: Federal Reserve Bank data.

EXHIBIT 5
Market Shares: Overdraft Checking

	Share of market			Share of market increase	
	1972	1973	1974	1973	1974
Twin Peaks	29.3	27.7	34.3	11.8	67.8
Bank 1	31.6	34.0	32.7	57.4	25.9
Bank 2	39.0	38.0	33.0	30.8	6.3

Source: Federal Reserve Bank data.

EXHIBIT 6
Market Shares: Demand Deposit Accounts

	New account market		General market	
	3/73	3/75	11/73	2/75
Twin Peaks	27.9	38.8	29.1	35.4
Bank 1	34.9	37.6	29.1	31.7
Bank 2	37.2	23.5	41.8	32.9

Source: Company records.

RETENTION OF ACCOUNTS

A major objective of the All-in-One Account was the cross-selling of bank services. The assumption was that the more services a bank customer had, the harder it would be for him to leave the bank. Net growth was determined as follows: Acquisition – Attrition = Net growth. The bank's performance in reducing the number of closed accounts increased its net growth.

Exhibit 7 shows the attrition rate for demand deposit and savings accounts since 1972. Their retention performance had allowed Twin Peaks to have a positive increase (14.3 percent versus 13.9 percent) in overall acquisition rate in 1975 even though the percentage of open rate decreased from 1974.

EXHIBIT 7
Attrition Rate for Selected Product Lines, 1971–1975

	Regular demand deposit accounts					Regular savings accounts			
	Opened	Closed	Accounts outstanding	Attrition rate*		Opened	Closed	Accounts outstanding	Attrition rate*
1971			54,082					80,475	
1972	14,654	11,415	57,321	21.1		28,314	18,478	90,311	23.0
1973	18,347	12,324	63,344	21.5		31,977	19,731	102,557	21.8
1974	20,771	11,997	72,118	18.9		35,964	21,955	116,566	21.4
1975	22,298	11,989	82,427	16.6		37,910	21,232	133,244	18.2

*Calculated as a percentage of previous year's outstanding.
Source: Company records.

CUSTOMER SURVEY

A survey of 3,997 All-in-One Accounts was made in order to determine the customer demographics and evaluate the service and its components. This was accomplished through the mailing of a questionnaire and the investigating of the account activity through the Central Information File for these customers. A total of 2,278 replied for a 57 percent return, which represented 11.3 percent of the total All-in-One Accounts.

The All-in-One Account service had attracted the young, highly educated white-collar worker with above average income. Specifically, the predominant characteristics were:

41 percent are 25–34 years of age.
19 percent are 35–44 years of age.
49 percent have a college degree.
67 percent are white-collar workers.
47 percent have income of $15,000 or more.
59 percent were Twin Peak conversions.

The mail-out survey indicated that 59 percent of the All-in-One Account customers were conversions from existing Twin Peaks checking account holders.

An additional 18 percent of the customers switched from other Frank County banks. This was followed by 13 percent new moves, 6 percent change in marital status, 4 percent other, and 3 percent additional account and first account. Analysis was done on the 18 percent of the customers who

EXHIBIT 8
All-in-One—Most Important Features

Attribute	Percent mentioned
Price	62%
Checking reserve	59
Free checks	46
24-hour banking	32
Unlimited checking	31
10% loan rebate	22
Traveler's checks	20
No minimum balance DDA	10
MasterCard	8
Convenience	2
Savings account dollars deposited	2
Easy to understand	1
No answer/no opinion	13

Source: Company records.

switched banks. Of these respondents, 25 percent switched for convenient location, 24 percent due to dissatisfaction at another bank, 24 percent based on the $2 price, and 21 percent due to the All-in-One package.

The participants in the survey were asked to give their opinions on the four most important features of the All-in-One Account. The most important feature turned out to be the price followed by checking reserve. The results of this open-end question are shown in exhibit 8.

ACCOUNT PROFITABILITY

The All-in-One Account study included the measurement of account activity through the CIF (Central Information File). Based on this measurement, the average All-in-One Account customer was then analyzed for profit/loss. The income and expense analysis (exhibit 9) shows that the average All-in-One Account customer contributed $19.09 before tax, profits and indirect overhead. If this analysis were applied to the 30,500 All-in-One Account customers the operating profit contributed from these accounts would be $582,245.00, which is $0.238 per share.

A review of this information showed that the All-in-One Account had tremendous impact on the growth of the bank's market share. It had accomplished all of the objectives set up in July 1973 when the service was first introduced. It had increased the cross-selling of the bank's services. It had proved to be a checking account that was unique versus other competitors'. It reduced the attrition rate of Twin Peaks' customers and it was a marketable service which reflected an aggressive retail-oriented corporate image that Twin Peaks desired to project.

Mr. Will and Mr. Hale agreed that the fee charged for the All-in-One Account was inelastic and since the service was still in its growth stage that a small change in price and/or service would not affect the demand for the All-in-One Account. They also felt that if a substantial change in price were made, a service should also be added to somewhat offset the price change. They recommended to Mr. Clark that he present the following proposals to Mr. Horman:

1. The All-in-One Account fee may be increased to $3 per month and a safe deposit box included.
2. The All-in-One Account fee may be increased to $2.50 per month with no additional service.
3. The All-in-One Account fee may be increased to $2.50 per month and the installment loan rebate reduced to 5 percent.
4. The All-in-One Account charge may be left at $2 with the installment loan rebate reduced to 5 percent.

EXHIBIT 9
Twin Peaks National Bank
Income and Expense Analysis
(account customer average for All-in-One)

Income:		
All-in-One fee	$ 24.00	
Installment loan	131.47	
MasterCard	24.34	
Checking reserve	12.45	
		$192.26
Expense:		
Traveler's checks	$ 0.27	
DDA*		
Operation cost	38.27	
Personal checks	4.29	
Savings:		
Operation cost	4.59	
Interest	34.59	
Installment:		
Operation cost	37.48	
Rebate	12.85	
MasterCard—operation cost	10.88	
Checking reserve—operation cost	1.56	
Cost of borrowed funds	13.78	
Bad debt:		
Installment (1%)	9.37	
Master Card (2%)	3.58	
Checking reserve (2%)	1.66	
		$173.17
Net contribution before tax to profit and indirect overhead		$ 19.09

*DDA = Demand deposit account.
Source: Company records.

TRI-CITY BALLET ASSOCIATION

The Tri-City Ballet was one of approximately 130 regional ballet companies in the United States. The company was sponsored by the Tri-City Ballet Association (TCBA), an incorporated nonprofit organization which contributed financial, administrative, and promotional support. The Association was governed by a board of directors who were elected by the membership of the organization for a one-year term. Mr. Roger Hector was serving as the president of the board of directors, and his wife, Christina, served as the ballet's artistic director. There were seventeen other directors on the board, and the association listed approximately 223 members on its roster, 15 of whom were business or corporate members. At the time of the case, two surveys had just been completed which were to be discussed at the next board meeting.

HISTORY

Mrs. Christina Hector had served as artistic director of the ballet since its founding twenty-five years ago. For the past fourteen years, the Tri-City Ballet Association had been a regional company under the auspices of the National Association for Regional Ballet. Mrs. Hector was a recognized and established leader in the ballet community at the local, regional, and national levels. As such, she had guided and directed the efforts of the organization, both in aesthetic and business activities since its inception.

Like many small, nonprofit performing arts organizations, the TCBA had a rocky financial history. Mrs. Hector explained that over the years there had been numerous times when the ballet company's

This case was prepared by Professor Ralph M. Gaedeke, California State University, Sacramento.

existence had been jeopardized by substantial deficits. Six years earlier the Tri-City Ballet Association had been incorporated as a nonprofit organization, and its board of directors had continued to make progress in the areas of growth and financial stability. Records indicated that the Ballet's budget had grown from $5,000 to a proposed figure of nearly $500,000 for the coming fiscal year (see exhibit 1).

This growth was certainly impressive. Yet the association continued to be plagued by cost overruns, unpredictable grant allocations, performance revenue deficits, staffing inadequacies, and a lack of dependable future sources of income. These problems were certainly not unique to arts organizations, yet their commonality did not make them any more palatable. But if financial issues had in the past ranked as the most pressing problem of this organization, its resolve to mitigate, if not alleviate this weakness, appeared to be one of the Tri-City Ballet Associations's greatest strengths.

EXHIBIT 1
Tri-City Ballet Association
Income & Expense Statement

	Last Year	Current Year
Revenue		
Ticket Sales	$400,000	$435,000
Grants, Endowments	10,000	11,500
Memberships	45,000	48,000
Fundraising Activities	5,000	5,300
Total Revenue	$460,000	$499,800
Expenses		
Rental of Community Center	$160,000	$185,000
Officers' Salaries	45,000	50,000
Dancers' Wages	245,000	260,000
Payroll Taxes	21,000	25,000
Costumes & Sets	8,500	8,000
Office Supplies	2,000	2,500
Printing	5,000	5,500
Advertising	5,000	5,500
Miscellaneous Expenses	2,500	3,000
Total Expenses	$494,000	$544,500

GOALS AND OBJECTIVES

The goals of the TCBA were stated in its annual Ballet brochure as follows:

To provide more opportunity for dancers to perform in a professional setting.

To invite guest choreographers to stage new ballets for the company.

To invite guest dancers to perform with the company.

To establish a subscription season.

To sell 800 season tickets.

To attain professional company status.

The first three goals were realized at the time of the case, but the last three goals had not been attained.

CURRENT STRENGTHS AND WEAKNESSES

The tenacious ability of the TCBA to survive twenty-five years as a viable and respected member of the local arts community pointed to the overall strength of this organization. Several weaknesses, however, limited the success the TCBA could enjoy. (Some of the notable strengths and weaknesses of the TCBA are listed in exhibit 2.)

THE INDUSTRY
Characteristics

Classical ballet was produced locally on a regular basis by two companies in the city. One of these companies had produced a single major performance in each of the last three years. The Tri-City Ballet had performed *The Nutcracker* during the Christmas season for many years. Normally, the Tri-City Ballet had at least one other major performance each year. Last year the Ballet presented the full-length ballet *Coppeli*, and a Repertoire Concert, as part of an arts series at the local university.

Approximately nineteen dance studios in the city advertised ballet instruction. Ballet classes were also

EXHIBIT 2
Strengths and Weaknesses of the TCBA

	Strengths	Weaknesses
Managerial	Board of directors consisted of dedicated, loyal, hardworking individuals. Good variety of professional skills represented. Apparent recognition of problems.	Organizational focus and direction weak. Lack of coordinated efforts hampered effective management of resources and future planning.
Market/ Market Information Mechanisms	Apparent abundance of potential customers with little local competition.	Naive marketing approach. No actual market data or information available.
Financial	Financially knowledgeable members on board of directors. Increased success with special grant and endowment funding.	Lack of long-run financial planning. Uncertain funding sources.

frequently offered as part of local park and recreation programs. Local chapters of the YWCA listed ballet classes in their curriculum and local colleges and universities did likewise. These business and community organizations performed paid recital programs on an irregular basis.

Trends

The ballet "industry" in the city was very small and showed little inclination toward expansion. The two companies which had survived over the years did so more on the strength of their dedicated leaders and enthusiastic young dancers than on the support of the local community. Explanations for this phenomenon frequently cited the city's proximity to a large metropolitan area that actively supported a number of noted professional and nonprofessional companies. Locally trained dancers had gone to these companies as well as to other national and international ballet organizations. It appeared that the city's ballet "industry" served as an early training ground for those dancers who would go on to "bigger and better things."

TRI-CITY'S POSITION

The Tri-City Ballet was the acknowledged leader in the city for classical art form. The Ballet was the only local dance company receiving support from the city's newspapers and was the only company mentioned in the local Chamber of Commerce literature.

It appeared unlikely that any serious local competition would surface in the near future. However, any attempt to compete with the professional companies located in the metropolitan area nearby seemed both unrealistic and unwarranted. Without downgrading or devaluing the important contributions of regional companies, their purposes seemed geared toward early training and experience programs.

THE MARKET

Research suggests that ballet is attended by certain customer types. Classical music and dance represent one distinct performing arts attendance type. One study suggested that this attendance type is characterized by the following variables:

Sociodemographic:
- Usually older people.
- More highly educated.
- Typically these events are more highly attended by teachers, agnostics, and Jews.

Attitudes:
- The more classical and music performances attended, the more critical of nonprofessional performers.

Beliefs
- Believe the government does not support the arts enough.
- Believe performing arts make life more interesting.
- Believe performing arts should be supported even if unprofitable.
- No longer believe their greatest achievements lie ahead of them.

- Believe things are changing too fast.
- Believe there is too much violence today.

The same research study suggested that people do not attend classical music and dance for the following reasons:

1. Lack of time to attend.
2. Believe that the performers are not professional enough.
3. Do not believe performances are too stuffy, but do believe movies are more entertaining and meaningful.
4. Do not believe that such events are relevant to everyday life.

According to the most recent census, 980,500 people were residing in the Tri-City area. Of this population, 290,896 women and 333,811 men were thirty-five years of age or older. This group was the target market which most frequently attended classical dance performances. The major productions of the Tri-City Ballet were, however, frequently youth-oriented story ballets, such as *The Nutcracker* and *Coppelia*.

The TCBA operated with limited factual knowledge of the market (see exhibit 3). The organization functioned as if the number of customers were unlimited even though it was consistently unable to meet its goals with respect to both funding and paid performances. (The one notable exception was the annual *Nutcracker* ballet.) Decisions concerning what programs to offer had been based on historical practice, gut feeling, and artistic requirements.

The Tri-City Ballet Association's market was segmented into two major components as shown in exhibit 4. One segment supported the ballet as an art form (the patrons) and the other segment supported the TCBA as a charitable enterprise (the philanthropists). Each of these segments had two subsegments—one contributed money, the other contributed time, professional skills, leadership and services. Although this segmentation model represented the realities of the market as they existed, there was lack of evidence that this breakdown was being used for planning, marketing strategies, or target marketing.

EXHIBIT 3
Tri-City Ballet Questionnaire and Responses

Number of questionnaires mailed: 75 (mailed to randomly selected members of the TCBA)

Number of questionnaires returned: 41 (55%)

Total
Responses

1. Are you aware that Tri-City has a regional ballet company in residence? Yes _41 (100%)_ No _0_   _41_

2. Referring to the ranges below, how much would you normally be willing to pay for tickets to a ballet performance by this local dance organization?

   Adult Price: $1-4.99 _4 (10%)_ $5-9.99 _27 (66%)_ $10-14.99 _8 (20%)_ $15 or more _2 (4%)_   _41_

   Child Price: $1-4.99 _16 (70%)_ $5-9.99 _6 (26%)_ $10-14.99 _0_ $15 or more _1 (4%)_   _23_

3. How far would you be willing to travel to see a local performance?

   Drive into Tri-City _____   24 (58%)

   Drive outside the City but inside the County   6 (15%)

   Outside the County but within 35 miles   11 (27%)

   I would not attend a performance   0   _41_

4. Assuming you are familiar with the Tri-City Ballet Association, how do you usually hear about their performances:

   Personal involvement with the organization   16 (19%)

   General mass media (TV, radio, newspaper, etc.)   20 (24%)

   Special media (arts newsletters, public TV, etc.)   19 (23%)

   Direct mail notification   23 (27%)

   Through personal acquaintances   5 (6%)

   No regular method   0

   I have never heard of this group   1 (1%)   _84_

5. Your age: Under 16 _0_   16-29 _1 (2%)_   30-49 _18 (44%)_   50 and over _22 (54%)_   _41_

6. Your sex: Female _31 (76%)_   Male _10 (24%)_   _41_

7. Your occupation: Student   1 (2%)

        Unemployed outside the home   10 (24%)

        Professional   17 (42%)

        Technical/Craft   2 (5%)

        Other   11 (27%)   _41_

8. Location of your residence:

   Live in Tri-City   12 (31%)

   Live in the County   20 (51%)

   Outside these areas   7 (18%)   _39_

9. Personal evaluation: How would you classify yourself?

   I consider myself a strong supporter of the performing arts.   28 (68%)

   I enjoy the arts, but do not actively support them by regularly attending ballet, symphony, opera, or theatre performances.   13 (32%)

   I do not support or enjoy the performing arts.   0   _41_

10. In the past year, how many *live* performances of the ballet have you attended? (These need not be limited to local performances.)

    None _7 (17%)_   1-5 _27 (67%)_   6-10 _5 (12%)_   11-15 _1 (2%)_   16 or more _1 (2%)_   _41_

EXHIBIT 4
Market Segmentation Model

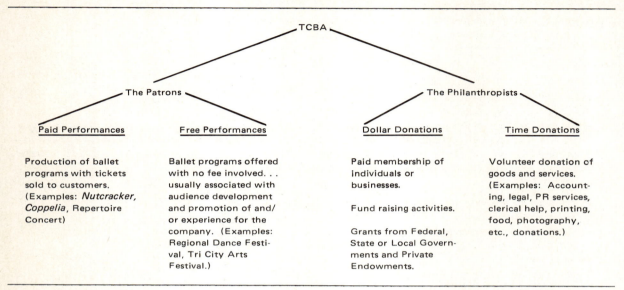

```
                              TCBA

          The Patrons                        The Philanthropists

  Paid Performances    Free Performances    Dollar Donations    Time Donations
```

Paid Performances	Free Performances	Dollar Donations	Time Donations
Production of ballet programs with tickets sold to customers. (Examples: *Nutcracker, Coppelia*, Repertoire Concert)	Ballet programs offered with no fee involved. . . usually associated with audience development and promotion of and/or experience for the company. (Examples: Regional Dance Festival, Tri City Arts Festival.)	Paid membership of individuals or businesses. Fund raising activities. Grants from Federal, State or Local Governments and Private Endowments.	Volunteer donation of goods and services. (Examples: Accounting, legal, PR services, clerical help, printing, food, photography, etc., donations.)

THE MARKETING MIX

Product Dimensions

The product of the Tri-City Ballet Association was defined by Mr. and Mrs. Hector as "the presentation of classical ballet for the appreciation and visual pleasure of the audience." Taking a somewhat broader view, the psychic satisfaction gained by those individuals who volunteered time or made monetary contributions could also be considered part of the "product."

The TCBA maintained its local leadership position in the performing arts field on the strength of its superior classical ballet performances. These ballets contributed to the community's willingness to support the organization's efforts to a greater extent than other local ballet groups.

Distribution Dimensions

The TCBA normally limited its paid performances to the Tri-City Metropolitan Area. These performances took place in the Community Center, which was centrally located.

Use of the Community Center auditorium did present some problems. The auditorium was unionized and expensive to rent. As a result, the break-even point of performances was frequently at a level unsupportable by revenues generated from ticket sales. Nevertheless, the TCBA's board of directors was reluctant to consider less expensive and less prestigious locations in the area, because these facilities did not lend themselves as well to ballet performance requirements.

Promotion Dimensions

Historically, promotional activities had been loosely organized and coordinated. Spasmodic attention coupled with little or no funding had handicapped a dynamic promotion strategy. Recently public relations and publicity functions were reorganized into a new public relations committee headed by a professional consultant who volunteered his time and service. A basic plan was developed for, presented to, and accepted by the board of directors of the TCBA (see exhibit 5). The leadership of the organization seemed pleased with the initial efforts of the committee.

EXHIBIT 5
Proposed Public Relations—Publicity Program of the TCBA

The purpose of this program is to create a broader base of community support for the Ballet.

I. Basic Plan

Here's how the basic plan works:

1. A schedule of regular media releases averaging 2–4 per month (during the season) will be initiated. A mailing list containing media outlets and personal and professional contacts will be determined and assembled by the public relations committee. Material to be used in the releases will be determined through regular meetings of the Ballet. Releases will be reviewed by the president before being submitted to the media. Special mailings as needed are also included.

2. A photo file will be started. The file will include black and white, and color shots of dancers, employees, and productions in all stages. In general all subject matter deemed important will be included. The file photos will be available for news release mailings and other projects.

3. An ongoing effort will be made to schedule feature articles and coverage whenever events and/or newsworthy items become available.

4. A "Name Dropper" service will be included. When something unique or unusual occurs it will be fed through personal contact to local newspaper columnists for possible mention. This service can also be used to announce meetings, programs, or other items of community interest.

5. Participation in community events will be encouraged in areas deemed beneficial. These may range from parades to various other events.

6. Special events of all sorts will be actively pursued during all times of the year. Appearances and demonstrations at shopping malls, schools, and other places of visibility will be made to the extent of the Company's availability.

7. Press conferences and parties preceding and following various events will be arranged with assistance from the public relations committee.

8. Wherever possible, a record of broadcast and newspaper coverage will be kept on file.

9. Educational programs for schools, parents, the business community, and the public in general will be supported and wherever possible arranged with the assistance of the board and guild members. Programs may take the form of slide shows, service organization presentations, ballet and set production workshops, and printed materials.

10. Preparation of annual reports, etc., for presentations to funding agencies will be undertaken by the public relations committee.

11. Other services as needed.

II. Yearly Brochure

The public relations committee will provide assistance, ideas, direction and guidance to various companies or art departments that are undertaking the preparation of any and all brochures for the Ballet.

The chief functions of PR to brochure development will be to make recommendations and provide copy or recommend copy direction.

III. Advertising

Since there is no specifically funded program and since most advertising is donated by the various media, this committee will stand by to serve in an advisory capacity.

Additional public service advertising will be sought and the development of television slides and public service announcement scripts will be prepared through this committee.

IV. Special Events—Fundraising

Although special events and fundraising are not the sole domain of any PR committee, both committees should work very closely together to ensure an efficient communications system.

Special events of all types and nature are highly encouraged. From the PR standpoint an active schedule of events, whether they serve to raise funds or simply greater public recognition, builds esteem and creates a "spirit" of participation.

Fundraising is the domain of the selected committee. The PR committee is able to assist with communications efforts and other aspects as needed. From time to time the PR committee should propose, initiate, and coordinate "new" fundraising events.

Price Dimensions

The stated goal of the TCBA was to achieve a zero balanced budget. To that end, pricing decisions were based on breakeven analysis, which attempted to cover production expenses with revenue generated through ticket sales.

Mr. Hector stated that for each production a budget was prepared, reviewed, and presented for approval. Ticket prices were determined by dividing the total projected production budget by the number of seats available (using a 60 percent attendance level). Assuming the production budget was not exceeded, paid attendance above 60 percent provided revenue which could be used for audience development projects, costume repair or replacement, repertoire expansion, and so on. Attendance below the 60 percent break-even point required deficit funds which were generated by fund-raising activities, one time endowments, or increased membership contributions.

The Tri-City Ballet did not offer discounted tickets for performances. However, limited price discrimination was practiced. Seating location provided a method for establishing a range of ticket prices. Although there was no price discount, ballet association members were normally offered tickets in advance of general public offerings and, thereby, had access to preferential seating.

Memberships could be purchased in a range from $5 to $1,500 by private individuals, families, and business concerns. Fund-raising activities had contribution "prices" which were subjectively based on the particular event. Typically, costs were kept at a minimum, donations were solicited whenever possible and a "fair" price was established to generate as much income as possible.

The Community Center had a seating capacity of 2,500. The break-even level of 60 percent necessitated selling 1,500 seats. In the past year, the average ticket price to cover costs had been approximately $9.50. Because of seating location, actual prices ranged from $15 to $7.50 for both matinee and evening performances. It was expected that prices would have to increase slightly for the coming year.

Channel Strategies

Channel of distribution decisions are among the most critical decisions facing management because they affect all other marketing strategies and are often hard to change once they are set up. They involve relatively long-term commitments to other firms that perform various marketing functions in the distribution channel.

Many types of intermediaries and facilitating agencies assist the physical movement and transfer of ownership of a product from producer to customer. The major types of intermediaries (or "middlemen") are retailers, whosesalers, and agents. Facilitating agencies include advertising agencies, marketing research firms, financial institutions, transportation companies, storage firms, and insurance companies. Key functions that are performed by intermediaries and/or facilitators include: buying, selling, research, promotion, product planning, price planning, customer service, sorting, physical distribution, storage, financing, and risk-taking.

CHANNELS OF DISTRIBUTION

Channels of distribution for consumer or industrial goods may be direct or indirect. Traditional distribution patterns for consumer goods include the following arrangements:

Manufacturer–Consumer
Manufacturer–Retailer–Consumer
Manufacturer–Wholesaler–Retailer–Consumer
Manufacturer–Agent–Wholesaler–Retailer–Consumer

The direct channel, selling direct to the ultimate consumer, may involve door-to-door selling, mail order, or telemarketing. The most common channel for the distribution of consumer goods is one which links manufacturer to wholesaler to retailer.

Distribution patterns for industrial goods include the following channel arrangements:

Manufacturer–Industrial User
Manufacturer–Industrial Distributor–Industrial User
Manufacturer–Agent or Broker–Industrial User
Manufacturer–Agent or Broker–Industrial Distributor–Industrial User

Unlike consumer products, industrial goods are commonly distributed directly. This is because industrial buyers tend to be more concentrated and smaller in number, usually purchase larger quantities, and require more pre-sale and post-sale service. In the article, "The Role of the Industrial Distributor in Marketing Strategy," Frederick E. Webster notes that the industrial distributor's role in the manufacturer's marketing strategy is changing toward greater reliance on fewer, larger, and better-managed distributors. This change requires that suppliers commit resources to programs for enhancing the distributor's role, thereby improving the channel's effectiveness.

CHANNEL DESIGN

In designing distribution channels, producers have to choose between what is ideal and what is available. In some industries there are strong traditions for particular channel arrangements, which may be difficult to circumvent. In other cases, independent intermediaries may not be present or willing to add to their current assortment of goods. In short, choices open to the manufacturer may be limited.

The producer's choice of distribution channel depends significantly on the customer's purchasing habits and these also ultimately influence the channel design. Other factors which influence the design and/or modification of channels include:

- The number of customers and their geographic dispersion
- The buying volume of customers
- The nature of the product—its perishability, value, bulkiness, service requirements, and complexity
- The degree and extent of promotion considered necessary
- The availability of middlemen
- The producer's characteristics, size, financial resources, location to market, past experience, marketing objectives, and management capabilities
- The environment's characteristics—economic conditions, number and location of competitors, and laws and regulations.

DISTRIBUTION COVERAGE

Channels of distribution should be designed to provide the necessary intensity of market coverage. The channel has to offer the products or services when and where customers expect them. Intensive distribution aims to make products available in as many outlets as possible. Selective distribution attempts to use the most qualified and reputable middlemen to price and promote the product properly and provide post-sale service if needed. Exclusive distribution uses a limited number of distributors, who are granted exclusive distribution rights within a particular territory.

In the article, "Retail Strategy and the Classification of Consumer Goods," Louis P. Bucklin shows how the concept of shopping, convenience, and specialty goods may be updated and integrated with the idea of patronage motives. Classifying consumer goods and patronage motives results in three types of stores, namely, convenience stores, shopping stores, and specialty stores.

CHANNEL CONFLICT AND COOPERATION

Conflict and cooperation are both common in a channel of distribution. Conflict occurs when one channel member perceives the behavior of another member to be detrimental to the attainment of specific objectives, such as marketing control, profits, and other factors. Conflict needs to be resolved in such a way that all members in the distribution channel cooperate and act as a unified system.

Despite strong incentives for cooperation among the various members of a distribution channel, conflicts can arise from actions of either the manufacturer or the middleman. The forces leading to conflict and cooperation within marketing channels need to be addressed by all members of a channel in order to increase channel efficiency.

Bruce Malle explores the major forms of distributive conflict—horizontal competition, intertype competition, and vertical conflict—in the article, "Conflict and Cooperation in Marketing Channels." He confronts the question of who is and who should be the channel leader. Mallen notes that the mutuality of interest dictates that members of a channel will be best off under conditions of optimum cooperation, because cooperation leads to greater consumer and profit satisfaction.

PHYSICAL DISTRIBUTION

Physical distribution deals with the movement of products within firms and through marketing channels. The objective of physical distribution is to attain a balance between customer service level and distribution costs. This requires determining customer service standards pertaining to order-cycle time, inventory reliability, order constraints, and delivery of goods in undamaged condition, as well as determination of the total costs involved in providing a specified level of customer service.

Physical distribution decisions should be made using the systems approach, which requires that all elements of the physical distribution system be considered simultaneously. The individual components—inventory, transportation, warehousing, materials handling, and order processing—should be viewed as a total system. A change in any one component may impact the other components. The system's effectiveness will be greatest when individual components avoid suboptimization and work toward producing an overall greater level of output or lower level of cost.

The total-cost approach to physical distribution emphasizes that all components of physical distribution must be examined as a whole when considering changes in any one component. Cost trade-offs result, because various cost elements of a distribution system display characteristics which may put them in conflict with one another. For example, when the number of warehouses is increased or decreased, a firm faces trade-offs relating to inventory costs, order processing costs, and transportation costs. The objective of physical distribution is to minimize total costs while providing a specified level of customer service.

Frederick E. Webster, Jr.

The Role of the Industrial Distributor in Marketing Strategy

The industrial distributor is an important institution in the American marketing system, yet he has received little attention from researchers. Trade association surveys have generally yielded small responses and have often been designed primarily to promote the image of the industrial distributor. Changing census definitions of this position and conflicting definitions used by different trade associations have made it virtually impossible to analyze trends in industry sales volume, degrees of specialization, firm size, and the like.

Yet manufacturers who sell to other manufacturers, and the industrial distributor himself, have a vital interest in the pressures and trends affecting this marketing channel. This is especially true in the current environment of materials shortages, depressed industrial production, tight money, and rising costs, since the industrial distributor may offer the manufacturer major opportunities for improved marketing effectiveness and physical distribution efficiency.

In an attempt to get an in-depth look at the industrial distributor, a field study of distributors and manufacturers was conducted in the summer of 1975. This article discusses that study in light of what is currently known about industrial distributors. Special attention is given to the results of the survey, which produced several insights into both the role of the industrial distributor in manufacturers' marketing strategies and how the distributor and his relationship

Source: From the *Journal of Marketing,* Vol. 40 (July 1976), pp. 10–16. Reprinted by permission of the American Marketing Association.

The research on which this article is based was supported by grants from the Marketing Science Institute and the Tuck Associates Program. Fieldwork and data analysis were completed with the help of Research Assistants Francis P. Brown and J. William Dryden.

to his suppliers are changing. Some highlights of the findings are:

1. For manufacturers who have been using industrial distributors, there has been a trend toward increased reliance on the distributor for a larger portion of total sales and a broader variety of marketing functions.
2. The average size of the distributor appears to be increasing, and there is a trend toward greater product specialization in distributor operations.
3. Basically, however, the typical industrial distributor remains a small, independent business, owner-managed, with limited management competence and little or no long-range planning.
4. In some product areas where specialized distributors have become strong, the industrial distributor has gained more control of the marketing channel.
5. There is no single marketing strategy characteristic of those firms that rely heavily on industrial distributors. Some stress market coverage and product availability; others stress high product quality and technical service; there are both high-price and low-price strategies; and so on. However, the nature of the distributor organization and the relationship between distributor and supplier will reflect the manufacturer's marketing strategy.
6. As firms have increased their reliance on industrial distributors, they have also tended to increase the amount of support given the distributor in the form of sales training (both product knowledge and salesmanship training), technical support, advertising and sales promotion assistance, and, in several cases, increased margins.
7. Industrial distributors are generally of little or no use to their suppliers as sources of market information.
8. Among the most common issues in the distributor-supplier relationship are how to handle large accounts, required inventory stocking levels for the distributor, the quality of distributor management, overlapping distributor territories, size of distributor margins, and the philosophical question of whether the distributor's primary obligations and loyalty are to the customer or to the supplier.

THE INDUSTRIAL DISTRIBUTOR

The industrial distributor is a specific type of agent middleman who sells primarily to manufacturers. He stocks the products that he sells, has at least one outside salesperson as well as an inside telephone and/or counter salesperson, and performs a broad variety of marketing channel functions, including customer contact, credit, stocking, delivery, and providing a full product assortment. The products stocked include: *maintenance, repair,* and *operating* supplies (MRO items); *original equipment* (OEM) supplies, such as fasteners, power transmission components, fluid power equipment, and small rubber parts, which become part of the manufacturer's finished product; *equipment* used in the operation of the business, such as hand tools, power tools, and conveyers; and *machinery* used to make raw materials and semifinished goods into finished products.

There are three types of industrial distributors. *General-line distributors,* or "mill supply houses," stock a broad range of products and are often referred to as "the supermarkets of industry." *Specialist firms* carry a narrow line of related products such as bearings, power transmission equipment and supplies, or abrasives and cutting tools. The *combination house* is engaged in other forms of wholesaling in addition to industrial distribution; an example is the electrical distributor who sells to the construction industry and manufacturers as well as to retailers and institutions. The distinction between the first two types of industrial distributor has been blurred in recent years by a growing trend for general-line houses to develop specialist departments. Less common but also found is the situation where a specialist firm broadens it product offerings in order to provide more complete service to customers; for example, bearing specialists may move into the broader field of power transmission.

Although available data are, as noted, somewhat limited, the total volume of sales through industrial distributors was estimated at $23.5 billion for 1974.[1] A reasonable estimate of the total number of industrial distributors would be between 11,000 and 12,000, for an average firm with sales volume of around $2,000,000. General-line distributors are, on the average, slightly larger than specialists in terms of sales volume. General-line distributors also maintain somewhat larger inventories than specialists, roughly $500,000 as compared with $375,000. The total volume of sales through industrial distributors has been growing slightly faster than GNP for several years, and the total number of distributors has been decreasing slightly, so average distributor size has been increasing.

There has been a trend toward branching and chaining in recent years, but the typical firm is still independently owned, owner-managed, and operates from a single location. Although average annual sales volume per firm is increasing, the typical firm continues to serve a rather small geographic area, from a 25-mile radius or even less in areas of industrial con-

centration to 100 or 150 miles in sparsely populated areas. The size of the average order would be in the neighborhood of $120.

Each data source has a somewhat different method for categorizing the types of products handled by industrial distributors. A 1970 publication listed fifteen major product categories for industrial distributors; these ranged in size from 5,505 distributors of mechanics and power tools (and accessories) to 2,184 distributors of ferrous and nonferrous metals.[2] More recently, the American Supply & Machinery Manufacturers' Association (ASMMA) used the following twelve-category product classification in its survey of members' 1973 sales:

1. Abrasives
2. Cutting tools
3. Saws and files
4. Hand tools
5. Power tools and accessories
6. Threaded products
7. Wire rope, chain, and fittings
8. Fluid power systems and accessories
9. Power transmission equipment and supplies
10. Industrial rubber goods
11. Material handling equipment
12. All other

Since this classification was the latest available at the time the fieldwork for this study was planned, it was used as the basis for the sample selection. The ASMMA survey of 1974 sales, released in mid-1975, had a new Class 1, "chemicals including aerosols and lubricants; paints; tape; brushes," and abrasives had been absorbed into the "all other" category.

RESEARCH DESIGN

After extensive library research involving both academic marketing studies on the industrial distributor[3] and the trade literature, a field study was designed. This study was guided by four objectives:

1. To understand the role of the industrial distributor in manufacturers' marketing strategies and how this role is changing
2. To identify the major forces shaping the evolution of industrial distribution
3. To define the key issues in management of the distributor-supplier relationship, as seen by both parties
4. To define opportunities for enhancing the effec-

tiveness of the distributor in marketing strategy and for improving the distributor-supplier relationship

The initial stage of fieldwork involved a series of unstructured interviews with a convenience sample of eight industrial distributors in Vermont, New Hampshire, Rhode Island, Massachusetts, and Connecticut. The purpose of these interviews was to develop an understanding of the nature of distributor operations, to learn firsthand how the distributor views his relationship with his suppliers, and to further analyze the trends and pressures shaping industrial distribution as an industry.

When the distributor interviews were completed and analyzed, an interview guide was developed to direct field interviews with manufacturers. Constrained by the costs of travel and respondent availability, we selected a sample of 31 manufacturers to assure representativeness by product category, geographic location, and firm size and market position. These manufacturer respondents included the leading firms in each of the product categories and among them account for a major portion of the sales of most industrial distributors. Respondents were given the usual guarantee of anonymity, but it can be stated that the firms interviewed included those whose distributor policies are generally regarded as exerting major influence on the trade.

Interviews were conducted with one or more executives (titles included vice-president of marketing and sales, product manager, sales manager, and the like) responsible for distribution in companies in all the ASMMA product categories. Generally, three or four companies from each category participated, and an attempt was made to interview both firms who were market leaders and firms who were not dominant in the markets under investigation. Respondents' sales volumes in the product categories considered varied from $3 million to $420 million, market shares varied from 2 percent to 75 percent, and the volume of sales through distributors varied between 15 percent and 100 percent. Manufacturer interviews were conducted in four states: Massachusetts, Connecticut, New York, and Ohio. The sample is believed to be both broad and representative of firms selling through industrial distributors.

When manufacturer interviews had been completed, two specialist distributors, in bearings and fasteners, were interviewed to deepen our awareness of the specialist firm. So the total sample was ten distributors and 31 manufacturers in eight states, representing all ASMMA product categories.

THE DISTRIBUTOR'S ROLE IN MARKETING STRATEGY

The study found no single marketing strategy that characterized those manufacturing firms that depend heavily on the industrial distributor. Furthermore, the distributor's role varied as a function of several interrelated factors, including:

1. The manufacturer's marketing strategy and especially the basis on which he attempts to achieve a unique competitive advantage: quality, price, availability, applications, engineering and technical service, full line, technical product leadership, and the like
2. The strength of the manufacturer's market position, that is whether he is a market leader or a minor brand
3. The technical characteristics of the product, especially the presence of strongly differentiating product features among brands and the need to make technical judgments about the best response to customer requirements
4. The importance of immediate product availability to the customer or, conversely, the extent to which requirements can be forecasted and planned for

All of the products involved, however, are established products with broad and large demand. Industrial distributors generally lack the ability to aggressively develop markets for new products or to serve narrow market segments with specialized product needs. Even the specialist distributor in such product areas as bearings, power transmission equipment, or fasteners serves customers from a broad range of manufacturing industries.

It was also apparent that all companies using industrial distributors must maintain their own field sales forces as well. Typically, the salesperson's major function is to solicit orders from the distributor organization and to service and support it. This may involve frequent customer calls with distributors' salespeople, especially for technical service. In other cases, the manufacturer's salespeople are responsible for customer contact and order generation, with the distributor performing primarily a physical distribution function. Not uncommonly, the manufacturer's salespeople are responsible both for working with the distributor on most accounts and for giving direct service to large accounts.

Several major functions tended, in varying degrees depending on the market circumstances of the manufacturer, to characterize the role of the industrial distributor in the manufacturer's marketing strategy. These included: market coverage and product availability, market development and account solicitation, technical advice and service, and market information.

Market Coverage and Product Availability

The industrial distributor's key responsibility in all cases is to contact present and potential customers and to make the product available—with the necessary supporting services such as delivery, credit, and technical advice—as quickly as economically feasible. In some product areas, such as abrasives, market coverage and availability require that the manufacturer use as many as 1,000 general-line distributors. In other areas, such as fluid power equipment, 25 to 30 distributors may be adequate. The number of distributors required to cover the market and insure availability was seen to depend on several variables, most notably:

1. Total market potential and its geographic concentration
2. The manufacturer's current market share and the intensity of competition
3. Frequency of purchase and whether the product is an MRO item or an OEM item
4. Whether lack of availability could interrupt the customer's production process
5. Amount of technical knowledge required to sell or service the product
6. Extent of product differentiation, determining how important immediate availability is as a competitive variable.

Market Development and Account Solicitation

Although in most cases the distributor was responsible primarily for servicing existing demand, in some he also had major responsibility for soliciting new accounts and expanding the size of the market. For example, a manufacturer of saw blades depended on his distributors to solicit new business from potential customers whom the manufacturer had identified, after thorough and expensive market studies, in the distributor's assigned territory. Similarly, a manufacturer of pop rivets expected his distributors to aggressively solicit customers away from sheet metal screw manufacturers.

When the distributor takes on major responsibility for promoting the product line, it is likely to be a line that provides a large share of his total volume. In such circumstances, this responsibility often extends to sales promotion (especially direct mail) and advertising, in addition to field sales coverage.

Technical Advice and Service

Technical expertise is important for many products handled by industrial distributors. Even for product categories where the technology is rather stable, such as grinding wheels, the technical nature of the item is usually such that many customers need advice in determining optimum product specifications for a given application. Thus, the distributor's salespeople must have adequate product knowledge to render necessary assistance. In the case of grinding wheels, for example, minor differences in wheel composition can produce major cost differences in the grinding operation.

Market Information

The large majority of manufacturers interviewed reported that their distributors were of virtually no help as a source of market information. Notable exceptions were cases where a technical product was distributed mainly through specialists and where the manufacturer's line was over 50 percent of the distributor's volume. In such cases, the distributor's market scope is narrow enough to encourage development of some expertise and there is real incentive to be a true partner with the manufacturer in market development.

While the desire to protect competitively valuable information might have been a consideration for some distributors, in most cases the distributor did not have current or complete market data. Even where the distributor used electronic data processing (estimated to apply to less than one-third of all cases), the market analysis and planning function was virtually nonexistent.

ISSUES IN THE RELATIONSHIP

Direct Accounts

A perennial source of tension in the supplier-distributor relationship is the direct account issue. This issue usually arises when a major customer, often with multiple buying locations, threatens to do business with another manufacturer unless he receives a lower price than the manufacturer can provide through a distributor. In other cases, the customer may demand direct coverage to obtain better technical advice or because he wants the presumed recognition and higher service level of dealing direct.

Since such powerful accounts are often a major portion of the distributor's volume, the solution is usually a difficult one. Complicated commission or fee arrangements for the distributor's service on direct accounts may be negotiated, or the supplier may arbitrarily withdraw the account from the distributor. Only a minority of manufacturers have been able to steadfastly refuse to deal direct with major, national accounts.

Distributor Management

The owner-manager is not often a well-trained, professional manager. As a successful small businessman he may reach a point where he has little interest in opening new territories, soliciting new accounts, or developing new product lines. The distributor's lack of growth motivation was mentioned frequently as a source of frustration to the manufacturer who wished to improve his competitive position.

A related issue is the problem of management succession. The distributor owner-manager often is a one-man management show, and his retirement or death can seriously reduce the effectiveness of the distributorship. Suppliers attempt to deal with this issue by working with the distributor to assure smooth transitions and by having contract provisions for terminating the relationship if there is a change in ownership.

In general, the quality of distributor management is a pervasive issue. Lack of planning, inadequate financing, poor managerial and administrative control systems, cash flow problems, and haphazard inventory policies remain as common symptoms of inefficient management. Distributors often have inadequate information to determine product line profitability, order-processing costs, or optimum stocking levels.

Inventory Levels

It usually takes considerable persuasion to get distributors to increase inventory levels, a move that the manufacturer often sees as essential to effective customer service. One solution is to give increased profit margins; it is common for manufacturers to attempt to be among the most profitable lines stocked by their distributors. Reflecting the distributor's characteristically strained financial condition, the manufacturer may find it necessary to finance distributor inventory expansion by delayed billing, consignment sale, or even a cash loan. Often, the manufacturer's salesperson can demonstrate how larger inventories can improve the distributor's profitability.

Second Lines

Manufacturers cannot legally prohibit their distributors from carrying competing product lines. And most distributors want a second line in order to have a broader price range or to get a wider variety of product types. Quantity discounts for distributor purchases are one incentive used to encourage the distributor to concentrate his purchases in a single line. Some manufacturers compete for available distributors by positioning themselves as a second-line supplier, although this may lead to a "catch as catch can" distributor organization and leaves the distributor in control of the relationship.

The presence of second lines is especially annoying to those firms that make major investments in their distributors, as with training programs, market development expenses, and the like. Such commitments are made in an attempt to become the distributor's single most important and profitable line; second lines frustrate the achievement of those objectives.

Adding Distributors and Overlapping Territories

As markets and distributors change, existing distributor coverage patterns may prove inadequate. When it is determined that the existing distributor is incapable of covering his assigned territory, he may be replaced or a new distributor may be added. Since distributors seldom have uniform geographical limits to what they regard as *their* territories, overlapping territories may result. This may, in fact, be the conscious intention of the supplier if he determines that different distributors have strengths in different market segments.

Obviously, such arrangements can lead to considerable controversy, and most distributors will seek to avoid them. The manufacturer who persists in this practice clearly runs the risk of losing the older distributor, but it is a risk he often intentionally takes.

HOW THE RELATIONSHIP IS CHANGING

No dramatic shifts appear to be occurring in the nature of industrial distribution, but a number of trends are quite evident. Perhaps the most important trend is the development of specialist distributors in such product areas as bearings and fasteners. Related to this is the development of *chains* of distributors with common name and ownership doing business in multiple locations. In these cases, the presence of strong distributor organizations, combined with relatively undifferentiated products and greater technical expertise (as a result of product specialization), has led to increased market power and channel control for the distributor.

Some distributors are strengthening their relationships with end-user customers by offering systems purchasing contracts, subassembly and submanufacturing, and a variety of inventory- and purchasing-related services. These services can produce significant cost savings for the customer, while they improve the distributor's attractiveness to both the manufacturer and the end-user.

A number of forces are combining to improve the quality of distributor management. Distributors are becoming larger. The owner-manager is being joined by professional managers, especially in larger, publicly owned firms. Distributor associations and suppliers are offering a broad variety of programs aimed at improving distributor management. Some manufacturers believe that the specialist firms are likely to be more marketing oriented, not just selling oriented, in order to achieve the market penetration necessary to succeed with a reduced product range. There is a stronger profit orientation and a greater concern for the profitability of individual product lines.

Many manufacturers have actively reviewed their distributor policies and organizations in recent years. On balance, there is a clear trend toward *greater reliance on fewer, larger, and better-managed distributors.* The result is a weeding out of the weak, marginal distributor firms. A variety of market-related and economic forces have stimulated this process. Manufacturers faced with tight money, increased competition (often price competitors from overseas), and rapidly increasing transportation costs are forced to search hard for ways to increase physical distribution system efficiency and marketing program effectiveness.

Most manufacturers have developed a variety of training programs and supporting services to make the distributor as effective as possible, thus strengthening the distributor and the commitment to him. There is also greater emphasis on the distributor's market development and account solicitation functions. Thus, it appears that the trend will sustain itself for some years to come, producing larger, more effective, better-managed industrial distributors, who will perform a broader variety of functions for their suppliers. For the typical manufacturer, it will mean fewer but better distributors to work with a stronger, more

effective partnership. It will also be that much harder for firms who wish to move from direct sales and service coverage to find available and qualified distributors, since there will be fewer distributors and these will have stronger commitments to existing suppliers.

A final word of caution is in order. Even though the industrial distributor is becoming stronger and more effective, he still depends heavily on the manufacturer for his strength and effectiveness. The idea of *partnership* remains essential; when the manufacturer turns to the distributor for added help, he does not give up his own responsibility for effective marketing, nor can he expect the distributor to respond positively to all suggestions. Rather, he assumes new responsibilities for making the distributor more effective—through programs of product development, careful pricing, promotional support, technical assistance, and order servicing, and through training programs for distributor salespeople and management. This places increased responsibility on the manufacturer to make sure that *his* salespeople are well trained to implement these programs for the distributor organization. Developing and maintaining an effective relationship with the distributor should be regarded as the salesperson's primary responsibility.

CONCLUSION: DEVELOPING EFFECTIVE INDUSTRIAL DISTRIBUTORS

From this study a number of guidelines emerge for marketing managers who wish to strengthen their relationships with their industrial distributors.

First, it is impossible to define the distributor's role in marketing strategy if the marketing strategy is not clearly developed. The initial step in developing effective distributors must be a careful statement of the role of customer service, product availability, technical support, and price in the total product-market positioning of the firm. Then, the role of the distributor can be more carefully defined in terms of the functions he will be expected to perform and for which he will be compensated.

As this study has indicated, the role of the industrial distributor is likely to become more important for most suppliers in the future. However, the findings have also suggested that distributors are not generally effective as a source of market information or in aggressively marketing new products. Likewise, specific steps must be taken to insure distributor cooperation in any program of new account development.

Assuming that the supplier company already has an established distributor network, the second step is an assessment of the capabilities of those distributors for fulfilling their role. This "situation analysis" must be matched with the planned role of the industrial distributor, and specific programs must be developed for improving defined areas of weakness. In this analysis, the supplier should be especially sensitive to the role that his salespeople must play as the linking pin between marketing strategy and distributor effectiveness. Rather than bemoan the characteristic shortcomings of the industrial distributor (limited managerial competence and growth motivation, excessive customer orientation, etc.), the manufacturer should think in terms of a distributor-salesperson team. The salesperson's first function is to serve and strengthen the distributor, but he must also be able to supplement the distributor's competence in technical support, new account development, and so on. The trend toward distributor specialization may alleviate the need for technical support, but that should not be taken for granted.

Third, the supplier must assess the appropriateness of various policies guiding his relationship with distributors. Recent developments suggest that it may be desirable to help distributors finance higher levels of inventory. Special compensation arrangements may be necessary to encourage new account development. There may be an opportunity here to offset losses to the distributor caused by the supplier's need to re-capture certain major customers as direct accounts. This latter problem area may also be treated by developing special commission arrangements to compensate distributors for their willingness to continue to provide service to these direct accounts and to otherwise compensate them for the loss in revenue.

To summarize, greater reliance on distributors of increased size and importance will require that suppliers commit resources to programs for enhancing the distributor's role and improving his effectiveness. The key concept here is that of a partnership where the supplier tries to strengthen his distributors as independent businesses while at the same time supplementing their weaknesses with a strong "missionary" sales organization.

NOTES

1. *Industrial Distribution,* March 1975, pp. 31–38.

2. *Facts about Industrial Distribution,* a pamphlet copyrighted 1970 by *Industrial Distribution* magazine.

3. Two of the most important studies are: Robert D. Buzzell, *Value Added by Industrial Distributors and Their Productivity,* Bureau of Business Research Monograph 96 (Columbus: Ohio State University, 1959); and William M. Diamond, *Distribution Channels for Industrial Goods,* Bureau of Business Research Monograph 114 (Columbus: Ohio State University, 1963).

Louis P. Bucklin

Retail Strategy and the Classification of Consumer Goods

When Melvin T. Copeland published his famous discussion of the classification of consumer goods, shopping, convenience, and specialty goods, his intent was clearly to create a guide for the development of marketing strategies by manufacturers.[1] Although his discussion

Source: From the *Journal of Marketing,* Vol. 27 (October 1962), pp. 50–55.

involved retailers and retailing, his purpose was to show how consumer buying habits affected the type of channel of distribution and promotional strategy that a manufacturer should adopt. Despite the controversy which still surrounds his classification, his success in creating such a guide may be judged by the fact that through the years few marketing texts have failed to make use of his ideas.

The purpose of this article is to attempt to clarify some of the issues that exist with respect to the classification, and to extend the concept to include the retailer and the study of retail strategy.

CONTROVERSY OVER THE CLASSIFICATION SYSTEM

The starting point for the discussion lies with the definitions adopted by the American Marketing Association's Committee on Definitions for the classification system in 1948.[2] These are:

Convenience Goods: Those consumers' goods which the customer purchases frequently, immediately, and with the minimum of effort.

Shopping Goods: Those consumers' goods which the customer in the process of selection and purchase characteristically compares on such bases as suitability, quality, price and style.

Specialty Goods: Those consumers' goods on which a significant group of buyers are habitually willing to make a special purchasing effort.

This set of definitions was retained in virtually the same form by the Committee on Definitions in its latest publication.[3]

Opposing these accepted definitions stands a critique by Richard H. Holton.[4] Finding the Committee's definitions too imprecise to be able to measure consumer buying behavior, he suggested that the following definitions not only would represent the essence of Copeland's original idea, but be operationally more useful as well.

Convenience Goods: Those goods for which the consumer regards the probable gain from making price and quality comparisons as small compared to the cost of making such comparisons.

Shopping Goods: Those goods for which the consumer regards the probable gain from making price and quality comparisons as large relative to the cost of making such comparisons.

Specialty Goods: Those convenience or shopping goods which have such a limited market as to require the consumer to make a special effort to purchase them.

Holton's definitions have particular merit because they make explicit the underlying conditions that control the extent of a consumer's shopping activities. They show that a consumer's buying behavior will be determined not only by the strength of his desire to secure some good, but by his perception of the cost of shopping to obtain it. In other words, the consumer continues to shop *for all goods* so long as he feels that the additional satisfactions from further comparisons are at least equal to the cost of making the additional effort. The distinction between shopping and convenience goods lies principally in the degree of satisfaction to be secured from further comparisons.

The Specialty Good Issue

While Holton's conceptualization makes an important contribution, he has sacrificed some of the richness of Copeland's original ideas. This is essentially David J. Luck's complaint in a criticism of Holton's proposal.[5]

Luck objected to the abandonment of the *willingness* of consumers to make a special effort to buy as the rationale for the concept of specialty goods. He regarded this type of consumer behavior as based upon unique consumer attitudes toward certain goods and not the density of distribution of those goods. Holton, in a reply, rejected Luck's point; he remained convinced that the real meaning of specialty goods could be derived from his convenience goods, shopping goods continuum, and market conditions.[6]

The root of the matter appears to be that insufficient attention has been paid to the fact that the consumer, once embarked upon some buying expedition, may have only one of two possible objectives in mind. A discussion of this aspect of consumer behavior will make possible a closer synthesis of Holton's contribution with the more traditional point of view.

A Forgotten Idea

The basis for this discussion is afforded by certain statements, which the marketing profession has largely ignored over the years, in Copeland's original presentation of his ideas. These have regard to the extent of the consumer's awareness of the precise nature of the item he wishes to buy, *before* he starts his shopping trip. Copeland stated that the consumer, in both the case of convenience goods and specialty goods, has full knowledge of the particular good, or its acceptable substitutes, that he will buy before he commences his buying trip. The consumer, however, lacks this knowledge in the case of a shopping good.[7] This means that the buying trip must not only serve the objective of purchasing the good, but must enable the consumer to discover which item he wants to buy.

The behavior of the consumer during any shopping expedition may, as a result, be regarded as heavily dependent upon the state of his decision as to what he wants to buy. If the consumer knows precisely what he wants, he needs only to undertake communication activities sufficient to take title to the desired product. He may also undertake ancillary physical activities involving the handling of the product and delivery. If the consumer is uncertain as to what he wants to buy, then an additional activity will have to be performed. This involves the work of making comparisons between possible alternative purchases, or simply search.

There would be little point, with respect to the problem of classifying consumer goods, in distinguishing between the activity of search and that of making a commitment to buy, if a consumer always performed both before purchasing a good. The crucial point is that he does not. While most of the items that a consumer buys have probably been subjected to comparison at some point in his life, he does not make a search before each purchase. Instead, a past solution to the need is frequently remembered and, if satisfactory, is implemented.[8] Use of these past decisions for many products quickly moves the consumer past any perceived necessity of undertaking new comparisons and leaves only the task of exchange to be discharged.

REDEFINITION OF THE SYSTEM

Use of this concept of problem solving permits one to classify consumer buying efforts into two broad categories which may be called shopping and nonshopping goods.

Shopping Goods

Shopping goods are those for which the consumer *regularly* formulates a new solution to his need each time it is aroused. They are goods whose suitability is determined through search before the consumer commits himself to each purchase.

The motivation behind this behavior stems from circumstances which tend to perpetuate a lack of complete consumer knowledge about the nature of the product that he would like to buy.[9] Frequent changes in price, style, or product technology cause consumer information to become obsolete. The greater the time lapse between purchases, the more obsolete will his information be. The consumer's needs are also subject to change, or he may seek variety in his purchases as an actual goal. These forces will tend to make past information inappropriate. New search, due to forces internal and external to the consumer, is continuously required for products with purchase determinants which the consumer regards as both important and subject to change.[10]

The number of comparisons that the consumer will make in purchasing a shopping good may be determined by use of Holton's hypothesis on effort. The consumer, in other words, will undertake search for a product until the perceived value to be secured through additional comparisons is less than the estimated cost of making those comparisons. Thus, shopping effort will vary according to the intensity of the desire of the consumer to find the right product, the type of product and the availability of retail facilities. Whether the consumer searches diligently, superficially, or even buys at the first opportunity, however, does not alter the shopping nature of the product.

Nonshopping Goods

Turning now to nonshopping goods, one may define these as products for which the consumer is both willing and able to use stored solutions to the problem of finding a product to answer a need. From the remarks on shopping goods it may be generalized that nonshopping goods have purchase determinants which do not change, or which are perceived as changing inconsequentially, between purchases.[11] The consumer, for example, may assume that price for some product never changes or that price is unimportant. It may be unimportant because either the price is low, or the consumer is very wealthy.

Nonshopping goods may be divided into convenience and specialty goods by means of the concept of a preference map. Bayton introduces this concept as the means to show how the consumer stores information about products.[12] It is a rough ranking of the relative desirability of the different kinds of products that the consumer sees as possible satisfiers for his needs. For present purposes, two basic types of preference maps may be envisaged. One type ranks all known product alternatives equally in terms of desirability. The other ranks one particular product as so superior to all others that the consumer, in effect, believes this product is the only answer to his need.

Distinguishing the Specialty Good

This distinction in preference maps creates the basis for discriminating between a convenience good and a specialty good. Clearly, where the consumer is indifferent to the precise item among a number of substitutes which he could buy, he will purchase the most accessible one and look no further. This is a convenience good. On the other hand, where the consumer recognizes only one brand of a product as capable of satisfying his needs he will be willing to bypass more readily accessible substitutes in order to secure the wanted item. This is a specialty good.

However, most nonshopping goods will probably fall in between these two polar extremes. Preference maps will exist where the difference between the relative desirability of substitutes may range from the slim to the well marked. In order to distinguish between convenience goods and specialty goods in these cases, Holton's hypothesis regarding consumer effort may be employed again. A convenience good, in these terms, becomes one for which the consumer has such little preference among his perceived choices that he buys the item which is most readily available. A specialty good is one for which consumer preference is so strong that he bypasses, or would be willing to bypass, the purchase of more accessible substitutes in order to secure his most wanted item.

It should be noted that this decision on the part of the consumer as to how much effort he should expend takes place under somewhat different conditions than the one for shopping goods. In the nonshopping good instance the consumer has a reasonably good estimate of the additional value to be achieved by purchasing his preferred item. The estimate of the additional cost required to make this purchase may also be made fairly accurately. Consequently, the consumer will be in a much better position to justify the expenditure of additional effort here than in the case of shopping goods where much uncertainty must exist with regard to both of these factors.

The New Classification

The classification of consumer goods that results from the analysis is as follows:

Convenience Goods: Those goods for which the consumer, before his need arises, possesses a preference map that indicates a willingness to purchase any of a number of known substitutes rather than to make the additional effort required to buy a particular item.

Shopping Goods: Those goods for which the consumer has not developed a complete preference map before the need arises, requiring him to undertake search to construct such a map before purchase.

Specialty Goods: Those goods for which the consumer, before his need arises, possesses a preference map that indicates a willingness to expend the additional effort required to purchase the most preferred item rather than to buy a more readily accessible substitute.

EXTENSION TO RETAILING

The classification of the goods concept developed above may now be extended to retailing. As the concept now stands, it is derived from consumer attitudes or motives toward a *product*. These attitudes, or product motives, are based upon the consumer's interpretation of a product's styling, special features, quality, and social status of its brand name, if any. Occasionally the price may also be closely associated with the product by the consumer.

Classification of Patronage Motives

The extension of the concept to retailing may be made through the notion of patronage motives, a term long used in marketing. Patronage motives are derived from consumer attitudes concerning the retail establishment. They are related to factors which the consumer is likely to regard as controlled by the retailer. These will include assortment, credit, service, guarantee, shopping ease and enjoyment, and usually price. Patronage motives, however, have never been systematically categorized. It is proposed that the procedure developed above to discriminate among product motives be used to classify consumer buying motives with respect to retail stores as well.

This will provide the basis for the consideration of retail marketing strategy and will aid in clearing up certain ambiguities that would otherwise exist if consumer buying motives were solely classified by product factors. These ambiguities appear, for example, when the consumer has a strong affinity for some particular brand of a product, but little interest in where he buys it. The manufacturer of the product, as a result, would be correct in defining the product as a specialty item if the consumer's preferences were so strong as to cause him to eschew more readily available substitutes. The retailer may regard it as a convenience good, however, since the consumer will make no special effort to purchase the good from any particular store. This problem is clearly avoided by separately classifying product and patronage motives.

The categorization of patronage motives by the above procedure results in the following three definitions. These are:

Convenience Stores: Those stores for which the consumer, before his need for some product arises, possesses a preference map that indicates a willingness to buy from the most accessible store.

Shopping Stores: Those stores for which the consumer has not developed a complete preference map relative to the product he wishes to buy, requiring him to undertake a search to construct such a map before purchase.

Specialty Stores: Those stores for which the consumer, before his need for some product arises, possesses a preference map that indicates a willingness to buy the item from a particular establishment even though it may not be the most accessible.

The Product-Patronage Matrix

Although this basis will now afford the retailer a means to consider alternative strategies, a finer classification system may be obtained by relating consumer product motives to consumer patronage motives. By cross-classifying each product motive with each patronage motive, one creates a three-by-three matrix, representing nine possible types of consumer buying behavior. Each of the nine cells in the matrix may be described as follows:

1. *Convenience Store—Convenience Good:* The consumer represented by this category prefers to buy the most readily available brand of product at the most accessible store.
2. *Convenience Store—Shopping Good:* The consumer selects his purchase from among the assortment carried by the most accessible store.
3. *Convenience Store—Specialty Good:* The consumer purchases his favored brand from the most accessible store which has the item in stock.
4. *Shopping Store—Convenience Good:* The consumer is indifferent to the brand of product he buys, but shops among different stores in order to secure better retail service and/or lower retail price.
5. *Shopping Store—Shopping Good:* The consumer makes comparisons among both retail controlled factors and factors associated with the product (brand).
6. *Shopping Store—Specialty Good:* The consumer has a strong preference with respect to the brand of the product, but shops among a number of stores in order to secure the best retail service and/or price for this brand.
7. *Specialty Store—Convenience Good:* The consumer prefers to trade at a specific store, but is indifferent to the brand of product purchased.
8. *Specialty Store—Shopping Good:* The consumer prefers to trade at a certain store, but is uncertain as to which product he wishes to buy and examines the store's assortment for the best purchase.
9. *Specialty Store—Specialty Good:* The consumer has both a preference for a particular store and a specific brand.

Conceivably, each of these nine types of behavior might characterize the buying patterns of some consumers for a given product. It seems more likely, however, that the behavior of consumers toward a product could be represented by only three or four of the categories. The remaining cells would be empty, indicating that no consumers bought the product by these methods. Different cells, of course, would be empty for different products.

THE FORMATION OF RETAIL STRATEGY

The extended classification system developed above clearly provides additional information important to the manufacturer in the planning of his marketing strategy. Of principal interest here, however, is the means by which the retailer might use the classification system in planning his marketing strategy.

Three Basic Steps

The procedure involves three steps. The first is the classification of the retailer's potential customers for some product by market segment, using the nine categories in the consumer buying habit matrix to define the principal segments. The second requires the retailer to determine the nature of the marketing strategies necessary to appeal to each market segment. The final step is the retailer's selection of the market segment, and the strategy associated with it, to which he will sell. A simplified, hypothetical example may help to clarify this process.

A former buyer of dresses for a department store decided to open her own dress shop. She rented a small store in the downtown area of a city of 50,000, ten miles distant from a metropolitan center of several hundred thousand population. In contemplating her marketing strategy, she was certain that the different incomes, educational backgrounds, and tastes of the potential customers in her city meant that various groups of these women were using sharply different buying methods for dresses. Her initial problem was to determine, by use of the consumer buying habit matrix, what proportion of her potential market bought dresses in what manner.

By drawing on her own experience, discussions with other retailers in the area, census and other market data, the former buyer estimated that her potential market was divided, according to the matrix, in the proportions shown in table 1.

This analysis revealed four market segments that she believed were worth further consideration. (In an actual situation, each of these four should be further divided into submarket segments according to other possible factors such as age, incomes, dress size required, location of residence, etc.) Her next task was to determine the type of marketing mix which would most effectively appeal to each of these segments. The information for these decisions was derived from the characteristics of consumer behavior associated with each of the defined segments. The following is a brief description of her assessment of how elements of the marketing mix ought to be weighted in order to formulate a strategy for each segment.

TABLE 1
Proportion of Potential Dress Market
in Each Matrix Cell

Buying Habit	% of Market
Convenience store—Convenience good	0
Convenience store—Shopping good	3
Convenience store—Specialty good	20
Shopping store—Convenience good	0
Shopping store—Shopping good	35
Shopping store—Specialty good	2
Specialty store—Convenience good	0
Specialty store—Shopping good	25
Specialty store--Specialty good	15
	100

A Strategy for Each Segment

To appeal to the convenience store-specialty good segment she felt that the two most important elements
in the mix should be a highly accessible location and
a selection of widely-accepted brand merchandise. Of
somewhat lesser importance, she found, were depth
of assortment, personal selling, and price. Minimal
emphasis should be given to store promotion and
facilities.

She reasoned that the shopping store–shopping
good requires a good central location, emphasis on
price, and a broad assortment. She ranked store promotion, accepted brand names and personal selling
as secondary. Store facilities would, once again, receive minor emphasis.

The specialty store–shopping good market would,
she believed, have to be catered to with an excep-
tionally strong assortment, a high level of personal
selling and more elaborate store facilities. Less emphasis would be needed upon prominent brand
names, store promotions, and price. Location was of
minor importance.

The specialty store–specialty good category, she
thought, would require a marketing mix heavily emphasizing personal selling and highly elaborate store
facilities and services. She also felt that prominent
brand names would be required, but that these would
probably have to include the top names in fashion,
including labels from Paris. Depth of assortment
would be secondary, while least emphasis would be
placed upon store promotion, price, and location.

Evaluation of Alternatives

The final step in the analysis required the former
dress buyer to assess her abilities to implement any
one of these strategies, given the degree of competition existing in each segment. Her considerations
were as follows. With regard to the specialty store-
specialty good market, she was unprepared to make
the investment in store facilities and services that she
felt would be necessary. She also thought, since a considerable period of time would probably be required
for her to build up the necessary reputation, that this
strategy involved substantial risk. Lastly, she believed
that her experience in buying high fashion was somewhat limited and that trips to European fashion centers would prove burdensome.

She also doubted her ability to cater to the specialty store–shopping good market, principally because
she knew that her store would not be large enough to
carry the necessary assortment depth. She felt that
this same factor would limit her in attempting to sell
to the shopping store–shopping good market as well.
Despite the presence of the large market in this segment, she believed that she would not be able to
create sufficient volume in her proposed quarters to
enable her to compete effectively with the local
department store and several large department stores
in the neighboring city.

The former buyer believed her best opportunity
was in selling to the convenience store–specialty good
segment. While there were already two other stores in
her city which were serving this segment, she believed
that a number of important brands were still not
represented. Her past contacts with resources led her
to believe that she would stand an excellent chance
of securing a number of these lines. By stocking these
brands, she thought that she could capture a considerable number of local customers who currently were
purchasing them in the large city. In this way, she
believed, she would avoid the full force of local competition.

Decision

The conclusion of the former buyer to use her store
to appeal to the convenience store-specialty good segment represents the culmination to the process of
analysis suggested here. It shows how the use of the
three-by-three matrix of consumer buying habits may
aid the retailer in developing his marketing strategy.
It is a device which can isolate the important market
segments. It provides further help in enabling the

retailer to associate the various types of consumer behavior with those elements of the marketing mix to which they are sensitive. Finally, the analysis forces the retailer to assess the probability of his success in attempting to use the necessary strategy in order to sell each possible market.

NOTES

1. Melvin T. Copeland, "Relation of Consumers' Buying Habits of Marketing Methods," *Harvard Business Review,* Vol. 1 (April, 1923), pp. 282–289.

2. Definitions Committee, American Marketing Association, "Report of the Definitions Committee," *Journal of Marketing,* Vol. 13 (October, 1948), pp. 202–217, at p. 206, p. 215.

3. Definitions Committee, American Marketing Association, *Marketing Definitions* (Chicago: American Marketing Association, 1960), p. 11, 21, 22.

4. Richard H. Holton, "The Distinction Between Convenience Goods, Shopping Goods, and Specialty Goods," *Journal of Marketing,* Vol. 23 (July, 1958), pp. 53–56.

5. David J. Luck, "On the Nature of Specialty Goods," *Journal of Marketing,* Vol. 24 (July, 1959), pp. 61–64.

6. Richard H. Holton, "What is Really Meant by 'Specialty' Goods?" *Journal of Marketing,* Vol. 24 (July, 1959), pp. 64–67.

7. Melvin T. Copeland, same reference as footnote 1, pp. 283–284.

8. George Katona, *Psychological Analysis of Economic Behavior* (New York: McGraw-Hill Book Co., Inc., 1951), p. 47.

9. Same reference, pp. 67–68.

10. George Katona and Eva Mueller, "A Study of Purchase Decisions in Consumer Behavior," Lincoln Clark, editor, *Consumer Behavior* (New York: University Press, 1954), pp. 30–87.

11. Katona, same reference as footnote 8, p. 68.

12. James A. Bayton, "Motivation, Cognition, Learning—Basic Factors in Consumer Behavior," *Journal of Marketing,* Vol. 22 (January, 1958), pp. 282–289, at p. 287.

Bruce Mallen

Conflict and Cooperation in Marketing Channels

The purpose of this paper is to advance the hypotheses that between member firms of a marketing channel there exists a dynamic field of conflicting and cooperating objectives, that if the conflicting objectives outweigh the cooperating ones, the effectiveness of the channel will be reduced and efficient distribution impeded; and that implementation of certain methods of cooperation will lead to increased channel efficiency.

DEFINITION OF CHANNEL

The concept of a marketing channel is slightly more involved than expected on initial study. One author in

Source: L. George Smith, et al., *Reflections on Progress in Marketing* (Chicago: American Marketing Association, 1964), pp. 65–85. Reprinted by permission of the American Marketing Association.

a recent paper[1] has identified "trading" channels, "non-trading" channels, "type" channels, "enterprise" channels, and "business-unit" channels. Another source[2] refers to channels as all the flows extending from the producer to the user. These include the flows of physical possession, ownership, promotion, negotiation, financing, risking, ordering, and payment.

The concept of channels to be used here involves only two of the above-mentioned flows: ownership and negotiation. The first draws merchants, both wholesalers and retailers, into the channel definition, and the second draws in agent middlemen. Both, of course, include producers and consumers. This definition roughly corresponds to Professor Breyer's "trading channel," though the latter does not restrict (nor will this paper) the definition to actual flows, but to "flow-capacity." "A trading channel is formed when trading relations, making possible the passage of title and/or possession (usually both) of goods from the producer to the ultimate consumer, is consummated by the component trading concerns of the system."[3] In addition, this paper will deal with trading channels in the broadest manner and so will be concentrating on "type-trading" channels rather than "enterprise" or "business-unit" channels. This means that there will be little discussion of problems peculiar to integrated or semi-integrated channels, or peculiar to specific channels and firms.

CONFLICT

Palamountain isolated three forms of distributive conflict.[4]

1. Horizontal competition—this is competition between middlemen of the same type, for example, discount store *versus* discount store.
2. Intertype competition—this is competition between middlemen of different types in the same channel sector; for example, discount store *versus* department store.
3. Vertical conflict—this is conflict between channel members of different levels; for example, discount store *versus* manufacturer.

The first form, horizontal competition, is well covered in traditional economic analysis and is usually referred to simply as "competition." However, both intertype competition and vertical conflict, particularly the latter, are neglected in the usual micro-economic discussion.

The concepts of "intertype competition" and "distributive innovation" are closely related and require some discussion. Intertype competition will be divided into two categories; (a) "traditional intertype competition" and (b) "innovative intertype competition." The first category includes the usual price and promotional competition between two or more different types of channel members at the same channel level. The second category involves the action on the part of traditional channel members to prevent channel innovators from establishing themselves. For example, in Canada there is a strong campaign, on the part of traditional department stores, to prevent the discount operation from taking a firm hold on the Canadian market.[5]

Distributive innovation will also be divided into two categories; a) "intrafirm innovative conflict" and b) "innovative intertype competition." The first category involves the action of channel member firms to prevent sweeping changes within their own companies. The second category "innovative intertype competition" is identical to the second category of intertype competition.

Thus the concepts of intertype competition and distributive innovation give rise to three forms of conflict, the second of which is a combination of both: (1) traditional intertype competition, (2) innovative intertype competition, and (3) intrafirm innovative conflict.

It is to this second form that this paper now turns before going on to vertical conflict.

Innovative Intertype Competition

Professor McCammon has identified several sources, both intrafirm and intertype, of innovative conflict in distribution, i.e., where there are barriers to change within the marketing structure.[6]

Traditional members of a channel have several motives for maintaining the channel status quo against outside innovators. The traditional members are particularly strong in this conflict when they can ban together in some formal or informal manner—when there is strong reseller solidarity.

Both entrepreneurs and professional managers may resist outside innovators, not only for economic reasons, but because change "violates group norms, creates uncertainty, and results in a loss of status." The traditional channel members (the insiders) and their affiliated members (the strivers and complementors) are emotionally and financially committed to the dominant channel and are interested in perpetuating it against the minor irritations of the "transient" channel members and the major attacks of the "outside innovators."

Thus, against a background of horizontal and intertype channel conflict, this paper now moves to its area of major concern; vertical conflict and cooperation.

Vertical Conflict—Price

The Exchange Act. The act of exchange is composed of two elements: a sale and a purchase. It is to the advantage of the seller to obtain the highest return possible from such an exchange and the exact opposite is the desire of the buyer. This exchange act takes place between any kind of buyer and seller. If the consumer is the buyer, then that side of the act is termed shopping; if the manufacturer, purchasing; if the government, procurement; and if a retailer, buying. Thus, between each level in the channel an exchange will take place (except if a channel member is an agent rather than a merchant).

One must look to the process of the exchange act for the basic source of conflict between channel members. This is not to say the exchange act itself is a conflict. Indeed, the act or transaction is a sign that the element of price conflict has been resolved to the mutual satisfaction of both principals. Only along the road to this mutual satisfaction point or exchange price do the principals have opposing interests. This is no less true even if they work out the exchange price together, as in mass retailers' specification-buying programs.

It is quite natural for the selling member in an exchange to want a higher price than the buying member. The conflict is subdued through persuasion or force by one member over the other, or it is subdued by the fact that the exchange act or transaction does not take place, or finally, as mentioned above, it is eliminated if the act does take place.

Suppliers may emphasize the customer aspect of a reseller rather than the channel member aspect. As a customer the reseller is somebody to persuade, manipulate, or even fool. Conversely, under the marketing concept, the view of the reseller as a customer or channel member is identical. Under this philosophy he is somebody to aid, help, and serve. However, it is by no means certain that even a large minority of suppliers have accepted the marketing concept.

To view the reseller as simply the opposing principal in the act of exchange may be channel myopia, but this view exists. On the other hand, failure to recognize this basic opposing interest is also a conceptual fault.

When the opposite principals in an exchange act are of unequal strength, the stronger is very likely to force or persuade the weaker to adhere to the former's desires. However, when they are of equal strength, the basic conflict cannot so easily be resolved. Hence, the growth of big retailers who can match the power of big producers has possibly led to greater open conflict between channel members, not only with regard to exchange, but also to other conflict sources.

There are other sources of conflict within the pricing area outside of the basic one discussed above.

A supplier may force a product onto its resellers, who dare not oppose, but who retaliate in other ways, such as using it as a loss leader. Large manufacturers may try to dictate the resale price of their merchandise; this may be less or more than the price at which resellers wish to sell it. Occasionally, a local market may be more competitive for a reseller than is true nationally. The manufacturer may not recognize the difference in competition and refuse to help this channel member.

Resellers complain of manufacturers' special price concessions to competitors and rebel at the attempt of manufacturers to control resale prices. Manufacturers complain of resellers' deceptive and misleading price advertising, nonadherence to resale price suggestions, bootlegging to unauthorized outlets, seeking special price concessions by unfair methods, and misrepresenting offers by competitive suppliers.

Other points of price conflict are the paperwork aspects of pricing. Resellers complain of delays in price change notices and complicated price sheets.

Price Theory. If one looks upon a channel as a series of markets or as the vertical exchange mechanism between buyers and sellers, one can adapt several theories and concepts to the channel situation which can aid marketing theory in this important area of channel conflict.[7] For example, the exchange mechanism between a manufacturer as a seller and a wholesaler as a buyer is one market. A second market is the exchange mechanism between the wholesaler as a seller and the retailer as a buyer. Finally, the exchange mechanism between the retailer as a seller and the consumer as a buyer is a third market. Thus, a manufacturer—wholesaler—retailer—consumer channel can be looked upon as a series of three markets.

The type of market can be defined according to its degree of competitiveness, which depends to a great extent on the number of buyers and sellers in a market. Some possible combinations are shown in table 1.

A discussion of monopoly in a channel context may show the value of integrating economic theory with channel concepts.

If one channel member is a monopolist and the others pure competitors, the consumer pays a price equivalent to that of an integrated monopolist; and the monopolist member reaps all the channel's pure profits; that is, the sum of the pure profits of all channel members. Pure profits are, of course, the economist's concept of those profits over and above the minimum return on investment required to keep a firm in business.

Assume that the retailer is the monopolist and the others (wholesalers and manufacturers) are pure competitors, as for example, a single department store in an isolated town. Total costs to the retailer are composed of the total cost of the other levels plus his own costs. No pure profits of the other levels are included in his costs, as they make none by definition (they are pure competitors).

The retailer would be in the same buying price position, so far as the lack of suppliers' profits are concerned, as would the vertically integrated firm. Thus, he charges the same price as the integrated monopolist and makes the same profits.

If the manufacturer were the monopolist and the other channel members pure competitors, he would calculate the maximizing profits for the channel and then charge the wholesaler his cost plus the total channel's pure profits—all of which would go to him since the others are pure competitors. The wholesaler would take this price, add it on to his own costs, and the result would be the price to retailers. Then the retailers would do likewise for the consumer price.

TABLE 1
Classification of Economic Markets

Suppliers (sellers)	Middlemen (buyers)	Market situation
Pure competitor	Pure competitor	Pure competition
Oligopolist	Pure competitor	Oligopoly
Monopolist	Pure competitor	Monopoly
Pure competitor	Oligopsonist	Oligoposony
Pure competitor	Monopsonist	Monopsony
Oligopoly	Oligopsonist	Bilateral oligopoly
Monopolist	Monopsonist	Bilateral monopoly
Monopolist	Monopolist	Successive monopoly

Thus, the prices to the wholesaler and to the retailer are higher than in the first case (retailer monopoly), since the channel's pure profits are added on before the retail level. The price to the consumer is the same as in the first case. It is of no concern to the consumer if the pure profit elements in his price are added on by the manufacturer, wholesaler, or retailer.

Thus, under integrated monopoly, manufacturer monopoly, wholesaler monopoly, or retailer monopoly, the consumer price is the same; but the prices within the channel are the lowest with the retailer monopoly and the highest with the manufacturer monopoly. Of course, the nonmonopolistic channel members' pure profits are not affected by this intra-channel price variation, as they have no such profits in any case.

Vertical Conflict—Non Price

Channel conflict not only finds its source in the exchange act and pricing, but it permeates all areas of marketing. Thus, a manufacturer may wish to promote a product in one manner or to a certain degree while his resellers oppose this. Another manufacturer may wish to get information from his resellers on a certain aspect relating to his product, but his resellers may refuse to provide this information. A producer may want to distribute his product extensively, but his resellers may demand exclusives.

There is also conflict because of the tendency for both manufacturers and retailers to want the elimination of the wholesaler.

One very basic source of channel conflict is the possible difference in the primary business philosophy of channel members. Writing in the *Harvard Business Review,* Wittreich says:

> In essence, then, the key to understanding management's problem of crossed purpose is the recognition that the fundamental (philosophy) in life of the high-level corporate manager and the typical (small) retail dealer in the distribution system are quite different. The former's (philosophy) can be characterized as being essentially dynamic in nature, continuously evolving and emerging; the latter, which are in sharp contrast, can be characterized as being essentially static in nature, reaching a point and leveling off into a continuously satisfying plateau.[8]

While the big members of the channel may want growth, the small retail members may be satisfied with stability and a "good living."

ANARCHY[9]

The channel can adjust to its conflicting-cooperating environment in three distinct ways. *First,* it can have a leader (one of the channel members) who "forces" members to cooperate; this is an autocratic relationship. *Second,* it can have a leader who "helps" members to cooperate, creating a democratic relationship. *Finally,* it can do nothing, and so have an anarchistic relationship. Lewis B. Sappington and C. G. Browne, writing on the problem of internal company organizations, state:

> The first classification may be called "autocracy." In this approach to the group the leader determines the policy and dictates or assigns the work tasks. There are no group deliberations, no group decisions . . .
> The second classification may be called "democracy." In this approach the leader allows all policies to be decided by the group with his participation. The group members work with each other as they wish. The group determines the division and assignment of tasks . . .
> The third classification may be called "anarchy." In anarchy there is complete freedom of the group or the individual regarding policies or task assignments, without leader participation.[10]

Advanced in this paper is the hypothesis that if anarchy exists, there is a great chance of the conflicting dynamics destroying the channel. If autocracy exists, there is less chance of this happening. However, the latter method creates a state of cooperation based on power and control. This controlled cooperation is really subdued conflict and makes for a more unstable equilibrium than does voluntary democratic cooperation.

CONTROLLED COOPERATION

The usual pattern in the establishment of channel relationships is that there is a leader, an initiator who puts structure into this relationship and who holds it together. This leader controls, whether through command or cooperation, i.e., through an autocratic or a democratic system.

Too often it is automatically assumed that the manufacturer or producer will be the channel leader and that the middlemen will be the channel followers. This has not always been so, nor will it necessarily be so in the future. The growth of mass retailers is increasingly challenging the manufacturer for channel leadership, as the manufacturer challenged the wholesaler in the early part of this century.

The following historical discussion will concentrate on the three-ring struggle between manufacturer, wholesaler, and retailer rather than on the changing patterns of distribution within a channel sector, i.e., between service wholesaler and agent middleman or discount and department store. This will lay the necessary background for a discussion of the present-day manufacturer-dominated *versus* retailer-dominated struggle.

Early History

The simple distribution system of Colonial days gave way to a more complex one. Among the forces of change were the growth of population, the long distances involved, the increasing complexity of new products, the increase of wealth, and the increase of consumption.

The United States was ready for specialists to provide a growing and widely dispersed populace with the many new goods and services required. The more primitive methods of public markets and barter could not efficiently handle the situation. This type of system required short distances, few products, and a small population, to operate properly.

19th Century History

In the same period that this older system was dissolving, the retailer was still a very small merchant who, especially in the West, lived in relative isolation from his supply sources. Aside from being small, he further diminished his power position by spreading himself thin over many merchandise lines. The retailer certainly was no specialist but was as general as a general store can be. His opposite channel member, the manufacturer, was also a small businessman, too concerned with production and financial problems to fuss with marketing.

Obviously, both these channel members were in no position to assume leadership. However, somebody had to perform all the various marketing functions between production and retailing if the economy was to function. The wholesaler filled this vacuum and became the channel leader of the 19th century.

The wholesaler became the selling force of the manufacturer and the latter's link to the widely scattered retailers over the nation. He became the retailer's life line to these distant domestic and even more important foreign sources of supply.

These wholesalers carried any type of product from any manufacturer and sold any type of product to the general retailers. They can be described as general merchandise wholesalers. They were concentrated at those transportation points in the country which gave them access to both the interior and its retailers, and the exterior and its foreign suppliers.

Early 20th Century

The end of the century saw the wholesaler's power on the decline. The manufacturer had grown larger and more financially secure with the shift from a foreign-oriented economy to a domestic-oriented one. He could now finance his marketing in a manner impossible to him in early times. His thoughts shifted to some extent from production problems to marketing problems.

Prodding the manufacturer on was the increased rivalry of his other domestic competitors. The increased investment in capital and inventory made it necessary that he maintain volume. He tended to locate himself in the larger market areas, and thus, did not have great distances to travel to see his retail customers. In addition, he started to produce various products; and because of his new multi-product production, he could reach—even more efficiently—these already more accessible markets.

The advent of the automobile and highways almost clinched the manufacturer's bid for power. For now he could reach a much vaster market (and they could reach him) and reap the benefits of economics of scale.

The branding of his products projected him to the channel leadership. No longer did he have as great a need for a specialist in reaching widely dispersed customers, nor did he need them to the same extent for their contacts. The market knew where the product came from. The age of wholesaler dominance declined. That of manufacturer dominance emerged.

Is it still here? What is its future? How strong is the challenge by retailers? Is one "better" than the other? These are the questions of the next section.

Disagreement Among Scholars

No topic seems to generate so much heat and bias in marketing as the question of who should be the channel leader, and more strangely, who is the channel leader. Depending on where the author sits, he can give numerous reasons why his particular choice should take the channel initiative.

Authors of sales management and general marketing books say the manufacturer is and should be the chief institution in the channel. Retailing authors feel the same way about retailers, and wholesaling authors (as few as there are), though not blinded to the fact that wholesaling is not "captain," still imply that they should be, and talk about the coming resurrection of wholesalers. Yet a final and compromising view is put forth by those who believe that a balance of power, rather than a general and prolonged dominance of any channel member, is best:

The truth is that an immediate reaction would set in against any temporary dominance by a channel member. In that sense, there is a constant tendency toward the equilibrium of market forces. The present view is that public interest is served by a balance of power rather than by a general and prolonged predominance of any one level in marketing channels.[11]

John Kenneth Galbraith's concept of countervailing power also holds to this last view.

For the retailer:

In the opinion of the writer, "retailer-dominated marketing" has yielded, and will continue to yield in the future greater net benefits to consumers than "manufacturer-dominated marketing," as the central-buying mass distributor continues to play a role of ever-increasing importance in the marketing of goods in our economy....

...In the years to come, as more and more large-scale multiple-unit retailers follow the central buying patterns set by Sears and Penneys, as leaders in their respective fields (hard lines and soft goods), ever-greater benefits should flow to consumers in the way of more goods better adjusted to their demands, at lower prices.[12]

...In a long run buyer's market, such as we probably face in this country, the retailers have the inherent advantage of economy in distribution and will, therefore, become increasingly important.[13]

The retailer cannot be the selling agent of the manufacturer because he holds a higher commission; he is the purchasing agent for the public.[14]

For the wholesaler:

The wholesaling sector is, first of all, the most significant part of the entire marketing organization.[15]

...The orthodox wholesaler and affiliated types have had a resurgence to previous 1929 levels of sales importance.[16]

...Wholesalers have since made a comeback.[17] This revival of wholesaling has resulted from infusion of new management blood and the adoption of new techniques.[18]

For the manufacturer:

...the final decision in channel selection rests with the seller/manufacturer and will continue to rest with him as long as he has the legal right to choose to sell to some potential customers and refuse to sell to others.[19]

These channel decisions are primarily problems for the manufacturer. They rarely arise for general wholesalers....[20]

Of all the historical tendencies in the field of marketing, no other is so distinctly apparent as the tendency for the manufacturer to assume greater control over the distribution of his product....[21]

...Marketing policies at other levels can be viewed as extensions of policies established by marketing managers in manufacturing firms; and, furthermore....the nature and function can adequately be surveyed by looking at the relationship to manufacturers.[22]

Pro-Manufacturer

The argument for manufacturer leadership is production oriented. It claims that they must assure themselves of increasing volume. This is needed to derive the benefits of production scale economies, to spread their overhead over many units, to meet increasingly stiff competition, and to justify the investment risk they, not the retailers, are taking. Since retailers will not do this job for them properly, the manufacturer must control the channel.

Another major argumentative point for manufacturer dominance is that neither the public nor retailers can create new products even under a market-oriented system. The most the public can do is to select and choose among those that manufacturers have developed. They cannot select products that they cannot conceive. This argument would say that it is of no use to ask consumers and retailers what they want because they cannot articulate abstract needs into tangible goods; indeed, the need can be created by the goods rather than vice-versa.

This argument may hold well when applied to consumers, but a study of the specification-buying programs of the mass retailers will show that the latter can indeed create new products, and need not be relegated to simply selecting among alternatives.

Pro-Retailer

This writer sees the mass retailer as the natural leader of the channel for consumer goods under the marketing concept. The retailer stands closest to the consumer; he feels the pulse of consumer wants and needs day in and day out. The retailer can easily undertake consumer research right on his own premises and can best interpret what is wanted, how much is wanted, and when it is wanted.

An equilibrium in the channel conflict may come about when small retailers join forces with big manufacturers in a manufacturer leadership channel to compete with a small manufacturer–big retailer leadership channel.

Pro-Wholesaler

It would seem that the wholesaler has a choice in this domination problem as well. Unlike the manufacturer and retailer though, his method is not mainly through a power struggle. This problem is almost settled for him once he chooses the type of wholesaling business he wishes to enter. A manufacturers' agent and purchasing agent are manufacturer-dominated, a sales agent dominates the manufacturer. A resident buyer and voluntary group wholesaler are retail-dominated.

Methods of Manufacturer Domination

How does a channel leader dominate his fellow members? What are his tools in this channel power struggle?

A manufacturer has many domination weapons at his disposal. His arsenal can be divided into promotional, legal, negative, suggestive, and, ironically, voluntary cooperative compartments.

Promotional. Probably the major method that the manufacturer has used is the building of a consumer franchise through advertising, sales promotion, and packaging of his branded products. When he has developed some degree of consumer loyalty, the other channel members must bow to his leadership. The more successful this identification through the promotion process, the more assured is the manufacturer of his leadership.

Legal. The legal weapon has also been a poignant force for the manufacturer. It can take many forms, such as, where permissible, resale price maintenance. Other contractual methods are franchises, where the channel members may become mere shells of legal entities. Through this weapon the automobile manufacturers have achieved an almost absolute dominance over their dealers.

Even more absolute is resort to legal ownership of channel members, called forward vertical integration. Vertical integration is the ultimate in manufacturer dominance of the channel. Another legal weapon is the use of consignment sales. Under this method the channel members must by law sell the goods as designated by the owner (manufacturer). Consignment selling is in a sense vertical integration; it is keeping legal ownership of the goods until they reach the consumer, rather than keeping legal ownership of the institutions which are involved in the process.

Negative Methods. Among the "negative" methods of dominance are refusal to sell to possibly uncooperative retailers or refusal to concentrate a large percentage of one's volume with any one customer.

A spreading of sales makes for a concentrating of manufacturer power, while a concentrating of sales may make for a thinning of manufacturer power. Of course, if a manufacturer is one of the few resources available and if there are many available retailers, then a concentrating of sales will also make for a concentrating of power.

The avoidance and refusal tactics, of course, eliminate the possibility of opposing dominating institutions.

Suggestives. A rather weak group of dominating weapons are the "suggestives." Thus, a manufacturer can issue price sheets and discounts, preticket and premark resale prices on goods, recommend, suggest, and advertise resale prices.

These methods are not powerful unless supplemented by promotional, legal, and/or negative weapons. It is common for these methods to boomerang. Thus a manufacturer pretickets or advertises resale prices, and a retailer cuts this price, pointing with pride to the manufacturer's suggested retail price.

Voluntary Cooperative Devices. There is one more group of dominating weapons, and these are really all the voluntary cooperating weapons to be mentioned later. The promise to provide these, or to withdraw them, can have a "whip and carrot" effect on the channel members.

Retailers' Dominating Weapons

Retailers also have numerous domination weapons at their disposal. As with manufacturers, their strongest weapon is the building of a consumer franchise through advertising, sales promotion, and branding. The growth of private brands is the growth of retail dominance.

Attempts at concentrating a retailer's purchasing power are a further group of weapons and are analogous to a manufacturer's attempts to disperse his volume. The more a retailer can concentrate his purchasing, the more dominating he can become; the more he spreads his purchasing, the more dominated he becomes. Again, if the resource is one of only a few, this generalization reverses itself.

Such legal contracts as specification buying, vertical integration (or the threat), and entry into manufacturing can also be effective. Even semiproduction, such as the packaging of goods received in bulk by the supermarket can be a weapon of dominance.

Retailers can dilute the dominance of manufacturers by patronizing those with excess capacity and those who are "hungry" for the extra volume. There is also the subtlety, which retailers may recognize, that a strong manufacturer may concede to their wishes just to avoid an open conflict with a customer.

VOLUNTARY COOPERATION

But despite some of the conflict dynamics and forced cooperation, channel members usually have more harmonious and common interests than conflicting ones. A team effort to market a producer's product will probably help all involved. All members have a common interest in selling the product; only in the division of total channel profits are they in conflict. They have a singular goal to reach, and here they are allies. If any one of them fails in the team effort, this weak link in the chain can destroy them all. As such, all members are concerned with one another's welfare (unless a member can be easily replaced).

Organizational Extension Concept

This emphasis on the cooperating, rather than the conflicting objectives of channel members, had led to the concept of the channel as simply an extension of one's own internal organization. Conflict in such a system is to be expected even as it is to be expected within an organization. However, it is the common or "macro-objective" that is the center of concentration. Members are to sacrifice their selfish "micro-objectives" to this cause. By increasing the profit pie they will all be better off than squabbling over pieces of a smaller one. The goal is to minimize conflict and maximize cooperation. This view has been expounded in various articles by Peter Drucker, Ralph Alexander, and Valentine Ridgeway.

> Together, the manufacturer with his suppliers and/or dealers comprise a system in which the manufacturer may be designated the primary organization and the dealers and suppliers designated as secondary organizations. This system is in competition with similar systems in the economy; and in order for the system to operate effectively as an integrated whole, there must be some administration of the system as a whole, not merely administration of the separate organizations within that system.[23]

Peter Drucker[24] has pleaded against the conceptual blindness that the idea of the legal entity generates. A legal entity is not a marketing entity. Since often half of the cost to the consumer is added on after the product leaves the producer, the latter should think of his channel members as part of his firm. General Motors is an example of an organization which does this.

> Both businessmen and students of marketing often define too narrowly the problem of marketing channels. Many of them tend to define the term channels of distribution as a complex of relationships between the firm on the one hand, and marketing establishments exterior to the firm by which the products of the firm are moved to market, on the other . . . . . A much broader more constructive concept embraces the relationships with external agents or units as part of the marketing organization of the company. From this viewpoint, the complex of external relationships may be regarded as merely an extension of the marketing organization of the firm. When we look at the problem in

this way, we are much less likely to lose sight of the interdependence of the two structures and more likely to be constantly aware that they are closely related parts of the marketing machine. The fact that the internal organization structure is linked together by a system of employment contracts, while the external one is set up and maintained by a series of transactions, contracts of purchase and sale, tends to obscure their common purpose and close relationship.[25]

Cooperation Methods

But how does a supplier project its organization into the channel? How does it make organization and channel into one? It accomplishes this by doing many things for its resellers that it does for its own organization. It sells, advertises, trains, plans, and promotes for these firms. A brief elaboration of these methods follows.

Missionary salesmen aid the sales of channel members, as well as bolster the whole system's level of activity and selling effort. Training of resellers' salesmen and executives is an effective weapon of cooperation. The channels operate more efficiently when all are educated in the promotional techniques and uses of the products involved.

Involvement in the planning functions of its channel members could be another poignant weapon of the supplier. Helping resellers to set quotas for their customers, studying the market potential for them, forecasting a member's sales volume, inventory planning and protection, etc., are all aspects of this latter method.

Aid in promotion through the provision of advertising materials (mats, displays, commercials, literature, direct-mail pieces), ideas, funds (cooperative advertising), sales contests, store layout designs, push money (PM's or spiffs), is another form of cooperation.

The big supplier can act as management consultant to the members, dispensing advice in all areas of their business, including accounting, personnel, planning, control, finance, buying, paper systems or office procedure, and site selection. Aid in financing may include extended credit terms, consignment selling, and loans.

By no means do these methods of coordination take a one-way route. All members of the channel, including supplier and reseller, see their own organizations meshing with the others, and so provide coordinating weapons in accordance with their ability. Thus, the manufacturer would undertake a marketing research project for his channel, and also expect his resellers to keep records and vital information for the manufacturer's use. A supplier may also expect his channel members to service the product after the sale.

A useful device for fostering cooperation is a channel advisory council composed of the supplier and his resellers.

Finally, a manufacturer or reseller can avoid associations with potentially uncooperative channel members. Thus, a price-conservative manufacturer may avoid linking to a price-cutting retailer.

E. B. Weiss has developed an impressive, though admittedly incomplete list of cooperation methods (Table 2). Paradoxically, many of these instruments of cooperation are also weapons of control (forced cooperation) to be used by both middlemen and manufacturers. However, this is not so strange if one keeps in mind that control is subdued conflict and a form of cooperation—even though perhaps involuntary cooperation.

Extension Concept is the Marketing Concept

The philosophy of cooperation is described in the following quote:

> The essence of the marketing concept is of course customer orientation at all levels of distribution. It is particularly important that customer orientation motivate all relations between a manufacturer and his customer—both immediate and ultimate. It must permeate his entire channels-of-distribution policy.[26]

This quote synthesizes the extension-of-the-organization system concept of channels with the marketing concept. Indeed, it shows that the former is, in essence, "the" marketing concept applied to the channel area in marketing. To continue:

> The characteristics of the highly competitive markets of today naturally put a distinct premium on harmonious manufacturer-distributor relationships. Their very mutuality of interest demands that the manufacturer base his distribution program not only on what he would like from distributors, but perhaps more importantly, on what they would like from him. In order to get the cooperation of the best distributors, and thus maximum exposure for his line among the various market segments, he must adjust his policies to serve their best interest and, thereby, his own. In other words, he must put the principles of the marketing concept to work for him. By so doing, he will inspire in his customer a feeling of mutual interest and trust and will help convince them that they are essential members of his marketing team.[27]

TABLE 2
Methods of Cooperation as Listed[28]

1. Cooperative advertising allowances	19. Delivery costs to individual stores of large retailers
2. Payments for interior displays including shelf-extenders, dump displays, "A" locations, aisle displays, etc.	20. Studies of innumerable types, such as studies of merchandise management accounting
3. P.M.'s for salespeople	21. Payments for mailings to store lists
4. Contests for buyers, salespeople, etc.	22. Liberal return privileges
5. Allowances for a variety of warehousing functions	23. Contributions to favorite charities of store personnel
6. Payments for window display space, plus installation costs	24. Contributions to special store anniversaries
7. Detail men who check inventory, put up stock, set up complete promotions, etc.	25. Prizes, etc., to store buyers when visiting showrooms— plus entertainment, of course
8. Demonstrators	26. Training retail salespeople
9. On certain canned food, a "swell" allowance	27. Payments for store fixtures
10. Label allowance	28. Payments for new store costs, for more improvements, including painting
11. Coupon handling allowance	29. An infinite variety of promotion allowances
12. Free goods	30. Special payments for exclusive franchises
13. Guaranteed sales	31. Payments of part of salary of retail salespeople
14. In-store and window display material	32. Deals of innumerable types
15. Local research work	33. Time spent in actual selling floor by manufacturer, salesmen
16. Mail-in premium offers to consumer	34. Inventory price adjustments
17. Preticketing	35. Store name mention in manufacturer's advertising
18. Automatic reorder systems	

SUMMARY

Figure 1 summarizes this whole paper. Each person within each department will cooperate, control, and conflict with each other (notice arrows). Together they form a department (notice department box contains person boxes) which will be best off when cooperating (or cooperation through control) forces weigh heavier than conflicting forces. Now each department cooperates, controls, and conflicts with each other. Departments together also form a higher level organization—the firm (manufacturer, wholesaler, and retailer). Again, the firm will be better off if department cooperation is maximized and conflict minimized. Finally, firms standing vertically to each other cooperate, control, and conflict. Together they form a distribution channel that will be best off under conditions of optimum cooperation leading to consumer and profit satisfaction.

CONCLUSIONS AND HYPOTHESES

1. Channel relationships are set against a background of cooperation and conflict; horizontal, intertype, and vertical.
2. An autocratic relationship exists when one channel member controls conflict and forces the others to cooperate. A democratic relationship exists when all members agree to cooperate without a power play. An anarchistic relationship exists when there is open conflict, with no member able to impose his will on the others. This last form could destroy or seriously reduce the effectiveness of the channel.
3. The process of the exchange act where one member is a seller and the other is a buyer is the basic source of channel conflict. Economic theory can aid in comprehending this phenomenon. There are, however, many other areas of conflict, such as differences in business philosophy or primary objectives.
4. Reasons for cooperation, however, usually outweigh reasons for conflict. This has led to the concept of the channel as an extension of a firm's organization.
5. This concept drops the facade of "legal entity" and treats channel members as one great organization with the leader providing each with various forms of assistance. These are called cooperating weapons.
6. It is argued that this concept is actually the marketing concept adapted to a channel situation.
7. In an autocratic or democratic channel relationship, there must be a leader. This leadership has shifted and is shifting between the various channel levels.
8. The wholesaler was the leader in the last century, the manufacturer now, and it appears that the mass retailer is next in line.

FIGURE 1
Organizational Extension Concept

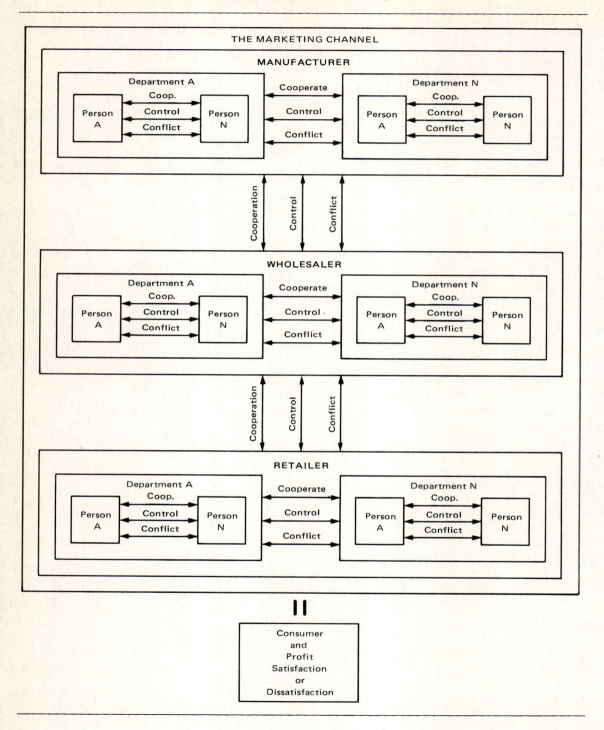

9. There is much disagreement on the above point, however, especially on who should be the leader. Various authors have differing arguments to advance for their choice.

10. In the opinion of this writer, the mass retailer appears to be best adapted for leadership under the marketing concept.

11. As there are weapons of cooperation, so are there weapons of domination. Indeed the former paradoxically are one group of the latter. The other groups are promotional, legal, negative, and suggestive methods. Both manufacturers and retailers have at their disposal these dominating weapons.

12. *For maximization of channel profits and consumer satisfaction, the channel must act as a unit.*

NOTES

1. Ralph F. Breyer, "Some Observations on Structural Formation And The Growth of Marketing Channels," in *Theory In Marketing,* Reavis Cox, Wroe Alderson, Stanley J. Shapiro, Editors. (Homewood, Illinois: Richard D. Irwin, Inc., 1964), pp. 163–175.

2. Ronald S. Vaile, E. T. Grether, and Reavis Cox, *Marketing In the American Economy* (New York: Ronald Press, 1952), pp. 121 and 124.

3. Breyer, *op. cit.,* p. 165.

4. Joseph C. Palamountain, *The Politics of Distribution* (Cambridge: Harvard University Press, 1955).

5. Isaiah A. Litvak and Bruce E. Mallen, *Marketing: Canada* (Toronto: McGraw-Hill of Canada, Limited, 1964), pp. 196–197.

6. This section is based on Bert C. McCammon, Jr., "Alternative Explanations of Institutional Change And Channel Evolution," in *Toward Scientific Marketing,* Stephen A. Greyser, Editor. (Chicago: American Marketing Association, 1963), pp. 477–490.

7. Bruce Mallen, "Introducing The Marketing Channel To Price Theory," *Journal of Marketing,* July, 1964, pp. 29–33.

8. Warren J. Wittreich, "Misunderstanding The Retailer," *Harvard Business Review,* May-June, 1962, p. 149.

9. The term "anarchy" as used in this paper connotes "no leadership" and nothing more.

10. Lewis B. Sappington and C. G. Browne, "The Skills of Creative Leadership," in *Managerial Marketing,* rev. ed., William Lazar and Eugene J. Kelley, Editors. (Homewood, Ill.: Richard D. Irwin, Inc., 1962), p. 350.

11. Wroe Alderson, "Factors Governing The Development of Marketing Channels," in *Marketing Channels For Manufactured Products,* Richard M. Clewett, Editor. (Homewood, Richard D. Irwin, Inc., 1954), p. 30.

12. Arnold Corbin, *Central Buying in Relation To The Merchandising of Multiple Retail Units* (New York, Unpublished Doctoral Dissertation at New York University, 1954), pp. 708–709.

13. David Craig and Werner Gabler, "The Competitive Struggle for Market Control," in *Readings in Marketing,* Howard J. Westing, Editor. (New York, Prentice-Hall, 1953), p. 46.

14. Lew Hahn, *Stores, Merchants and Customers* (New York, Fairchild Publications, 1952), p. 12.

15. David A. Revzan, *Wholesaling in Marketing Organization* (New York: John Wiley & Sons, Inc., 1961), p. 606.

16. *Ibid.,* p. 202.

17. E. Jerome McCarthy, *Basic Marketing* (Homewood, Illinois: Richard D. Irwin, Inc., 1960), p. 419.

18. *Ibid.,* p. 420.

19. Eli P. Cox, *Federal Quantity Discount Limitations and Its Possible Effects on Distribution Channel Dynamics* (Unpublished Doctoral Dissertation, University of Texas, 1956), p. 12.

20. Milton Brown, Wilbur B. England, John B. Matthews Jr., *Problems in Marketing,* 3rd ed. (New York: McGraw-Hill Book Co., Inc., 1961), p. 239.

21. Maynard D. Phelps and Howard J. Westing, *Marketing Management,* Revised Edition. (Homewood, Ill.: Richard D. Irwin, Inc., 1960), p. 11.

22. Kenneth Davis, *Marketing Management* (New York: The Ronald Press Co., 1961), p. 131.

23. Valentine F. Ridgeway, "Administration of Manufacturer-Dealer Systems," in *Managerial Marketing,* rev. ed., William Lazer and Eugene J. Kelley, Editors. (Homewood, Ill.: Richard D. Irwin, Inc., 1962), p. 480.

24. Peter Drucker, "The Economy's Dark Continent," *Fortune,* April 1962, pp. 103 ff.

25. Ralph S. Alexander, James S. Cross, Ross M. Cunningham, *Industrial Marketing,* rev. ed. (Homewood, Ill.: Richard D. Irwin, Inc., 1961), p. 266.

26. Hector Lazo and Arnold Corbin, *Management in Marketing* (New York: McGraw-Hill Book Company, Inc., 1961), p. 379.

27. Lazo and Corbin, *loc cit.*

28. Edward B. Weiss, "How Much of a Retailer Is the Manufacturer," in *Advertising Age,* July 21, 1958, p. 68.

CASES

PREMIER TITLE INSURANCE COMPANY

This Sacramento, California, company provides title insurance and escrow service to buyers and sellers of real estate. Management wants to expand its capacity to process orders by recentralizing operations and opening new branch offices in the Sacramento area.

QUALITY SHOWROOMS

This regional catalog showroom in the western part of the United States began as a jewelry store nearly fifteen years ago. Restructured as a catalog showroom nine years ago, Quality Showrooms has experienced solid growth despite more intense competition. Presently, management is considering the expansion of the showroom concept to other geographic areas, and the addition of different lines of merchandise to reduce the heavy dependence on jewelry.

ESQUIRE CLEANERS

Esquire Cleaners is one of the largest dry cleaners in the industry, with eighty-four franchised stores located in and around an Ohio metropolitan area. Partly due to the seasonality of sales, Esquire management is evaluating the possibilities of expanding services to include laundering sheets, towels, and the like, as well as uniform leasing. Of perhaps even greater concern, however, is Esquire's home delivery service for the metropolitan area, which has not been as profitable as expected.

THOMPSON RESPIRATION PRODUCTS

As a manufacturer of portable respirators and accessories, Thompson Respiration Products, Inc., was attempting to expand the distribution of its products into other midwestern and southern markets. Of particular concern was how to structure its channel of distribution, and what terms and conditions should be established for its dealer network.

ALASKA NATIVE ARTS & CRAFTS COOPERATIVE

The Alaska Native Arts & Crafts Cooperative is a nonprofit organization developed to facilitate the sale of native arts and crafts throughout Alaska. Based in Anchorage, the cooperative distributes native-made products to 120 villages and also sells them in its retail store in Anchorage. Presently, the management is reviewing its entire system for acquiring and selling merchandise.

PREMIER TITLE INSURANCE COMPANY

In April 1977, Mr. Carl H. Love, vice-president and manager of the Sacramento, California, division of Premier Title Insurance Company, was considering what recommendations he might make to the home office for increasing his division's output. The firm was eager to hold or increase its share of the Sacramento County title insurance and escrow service market—a market which was expected to grow rapidly. Although home prices were at an all-time high, prospective owners seemed eager to buy before prices rose even higher. Moreover, there was a surplus of mortgage credit in the community, and interest rates were not expected to frighten many buyers.

Mr. Love already had agreed that branch offices were needed in the rapidly growing Elk Grove (south), and Citrus Heights (northeast) sections of Sacramento County. Unfortunately, capacity of the title plant, which served all of Premier's Sacramento branches, was presently limited to 640 orders per month, and 633 orders already had been opened and 361 closed in the month of March. Even without new branch offices, future orders were likely to exceed the title plant's processing capacity. The lag between opening and closing an order ranged from fifteen to forty-five days, and present activity represented some rise in orders from the November and December lows; however, the high home sales of July and August were likely to result in far greater orders for escrow and title insurance later in the year.

TITLE INSURANCE

Title insurance is essential in almost all real estate purchases. A title insurance policy protects the buyer (and the lender, if there is a loan) against such risks

This case was prepared by Professor Leete A. Thompson, California State University, Sacramento.

as: liens or judgments against the property incurred by former owners; forged deeds; falsification of public records; previous conveyances of the property by persons who were of minor age, were mentally incompetent, or were under duress; and errors in surveying or describing the property.

The premium for title insurance is a one-time charge, paid at the closing of escrow, after the neutral third-party or escrow holder has received all necessary deeds, money, and instructions from the principals. In 1977, the amount of premium averaged $225 for a $40,000 sale or $446 for a $100,000 sale, but the premium varied somewhat depending upon:

1. The cost of searching the title, eliminating defects, and preparing the insurance policy
2. Possible claims against the title insurer for losses covered by the policy provision

A title company can insure directly, by carrying minimum reserves specified by the state insurance commissioner, or it can issue policies underwritten by a separate insurance company.

When a property owner enters into a contract to sell, he or his broker visits or telephones a branch office of the selected title company. Typically, the title company assigns a number to the order, sets up a file, and collects information (about the property, the seller, the buyer, and the broker), which it immediately relays to the main office. After a thorough search of the property's title history back to a "starter" (a previously issued title policy or preliminary report), the title company prepares a preliminary report and delivers it to the requesting party. This report contains all essential facts about who owns the property, what liens or encumbrances affect it, and conditions under which a title insurance policy would be issued.

Title plants must store comprehensive files of information on each parcel of real property in the county they serve. Usually they are located near the county court and tax offices for ready reference to records. However, the state insurance commissioner requires them to carry their own records of all county real estate transfers for at least five previous years. Such information may be stored in handwritten folios, in microfilm or microfiche files, or on computer tapes.

ESCROW SERVICE

When a buyer and seller enter into a contract to transfer real property, they typically ask a neutral third party to make the exchange of necessary documents, collect and disburse funds, deal with lenders, and account in a number of ways to principals in the transaction. In 1977, fees for this service averaged $95 per transaction.

Although issuing title insurance and performing escrow services are separate transactions, title insurance firms usually provide escrow services as a convenient and profitable adjunct. As a matter of fact, title insurance firms are likely to receive much of their business from conveniently located escrow offices.

PREMIER'S SACRAMENTO DIVISION

The issuance of title insurance policies was the principal business of Premier Title Insurance Company, which operated in forty-nine states and several foreign countries. The Sacramento division had been acquired in 1966 by the purchase of another title company's main offices and title plant, plus its two branch offices. By acquiring a title plant intact, copies of all documents affecting real estate transfers in the county back to the 1930s were immediately available, and the costly process of copying thousands of documents, covering at least five years, was avoided.

Premier's newly acquired title plant, plus those of most competitors in Sacramento, were located in a four-block area, less than a mile from the Sacramento County Courthouse, and within easy freeway access of existing or proposed branch offices.[1] By 1977, four Premier branches and a main office were in operation, and two additional offices were proposed (see locations in exhibit 1).

Premier, like its competitors, provided escrow service for transactions in which title insurance was likely to be involved and, even though they charged

separately for title insurance and escrow service, they attempted to sell them both as a package unless escrow personnel were overloaded with orders at the time.

The Sacramento division's organization is shown in exhibit 2. Mr. Love directed the division, with only minimal supervision from the regional vice-president, Mr. Don Berg. Policies, within broad home office guidelines, were formulated by Mr. Love and his executive committee of seven members. This committee, consisting of Mr. Love, Mr. Berg, Ms. Leeta McCurry, district public relations officer, and all four Sacramento branch office managers, met monthly. In these meetings they considered such matters as staffing, salaries, budgets, and marketing strategy for the division. Mr. Love decided matters of questionable title and attempted to minimize both title insurance and escrow losses. His judgment in such matters was backed by thirteen years' experience in the title industry. In addition, he engaged in personal selling and building goodwill with real estate brokers in the area.

In all, Premier employed sixty-five people, including thirty-one in escrow, thirty in title insurance activities, and four in public relations and business development. Each of the four branches employed a manager, an escrow officer, and one to four clerks. All title insurance employees and twelve of the escrow employees were housed in the main office in downtown Sacramento. The main-office escrow office was much like a separate branch, and the escrow manager there performed duties quite similar to those of a branch manager.

THE MAIN OFFICE

Premier's main office in Sacramento was crowded with files, machines, and employees. Title insurance employees, under the title plant manager, searched for evidence of titles, assessments, bonds, liens, and encumbrances. Escrow workers were busy verifying such things as addresses, existing and new lenders, termite inspections, buyer or seller instructions, expected dates of escrow closing, and financial details. Recruitment, selection, and training of employees was a continuing process—twenty-three had left and had been replaced since September 1975.

---

1. Most title firms underwrote title insurance for their own, or for sister firms in their own, organizations. Their underwriting operations made proximity to public records of real estate transactions most essential.

EXHIBIT 1
Premier Title Insurance Company Office Locations, Sacramento Division

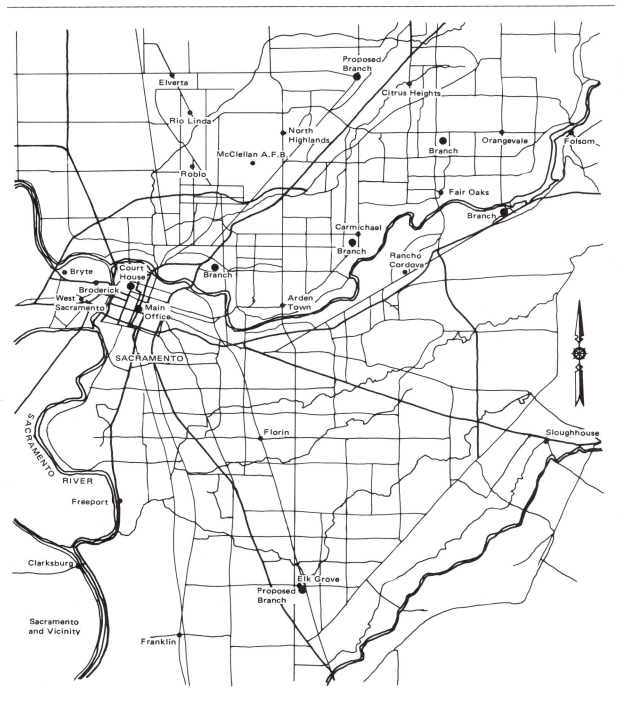

CASE

EXHIBIT 2
Premier Title Insurance Company
Sacramento Division
Organization Chart

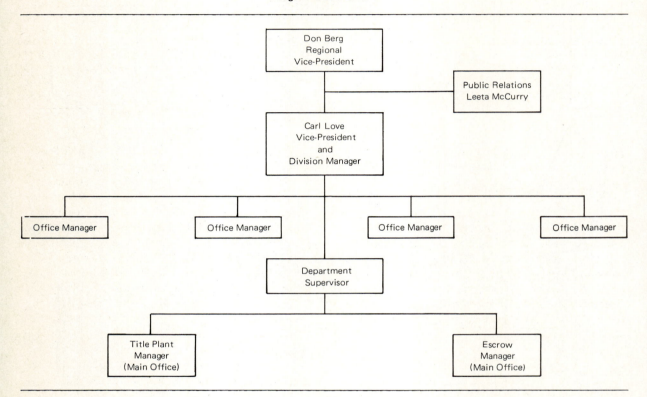

Work in the main office was detailed and meticulous. An overlooked bond or assessment against property, the transposition of a figure, or a typographical error, could lead to substantial company losses. Title records were posted in handwritten folios, and each posting had to be double checked. Typists used word processors with storage discs from which one could delete words, sentences, or paragraphs and instruct automatic retyping of documents with proper margins. It was hoped that all handwritten records would eventually be replaced and losses from errors would be eliminated. In 1976, title losses had been only 2.3 percent of the gross revenue (3.9 percent of gross title insurance revenues vs. 4 to 8 percent losses for the industry as a whole),[2] while losses on escrow operations had been minimal.

Main-office capacity was severely limited, but Mr. Love had been unsuccessful in his attempt to find larger quarters. The location was convenient, reasonable in cost, and close to competitors' title plants. There were no vacant offices of sufficient size in the immediate area; moreover, the cost of buying property in that area and demolishing structures on the property made it impractical to consider a new building. Preliminary studies suggested that

---

2. "The Costly Business of Title Insurance." *Business Week,* 31 October 1977, p. 113.

CASE

EXHIBIT 3
Real Estate Documents
Sacramento County Recordings

Document	1972	1973	1974	1975	1976
Deeds	30,490	30,529	25,521	31,047	38,172
Deeds of Title & Mortgage	22,516	21,165	19,352	24,654	33,050
Notices of Completion	3,095	2,698	2,350	2,546	3,111
Subdivision Maps	80	83	66	88	161
Totals	56,181	54,475	47,289	58,335	74,494
Percent Change		-3%	-13%	+23%	+28%

production costs for title insurance would rise as much as 15 percent if operations were moved to any outlying buildings presently available.

While main-office staff might be reduced by lengthening the period in which preliminary reports for title insurance were prepared, Mr. Love and the executive committee believed that issuing such reports in three to five days, rather than in the five to seven days allowed by competitors, attracted a significant amount of repeat business from real estate brokers. Executive committee opinions differed as to whether removal of escrow operations from the main office would be feasible.

THE MARKET

In 1977, Sacramento County's population approached 800,000 and was growing rapidly. The number of real estate document recordings had increased significantly in 1975 and 1976, after the 1974 recession (see exhibit 3). National trends in housing starts, particularly for multiple-dwelling units, appeared to be favorable. HUD had scheduled more projects in Sacramento than in either San Francisco or San Diego and as many as in Los Angeles for 1977.

In 1976, the volume of title business had ranged from 5,000 to 6,000 orders per month in Sacramento, and Premier had garnered approximately 11 percent of that market (see exhibit 4). Competition was expected to increase in 1977, for Transamerica had recently opened a new branch in Elk Grove, a new title firm was due to enter the market by midyear,

and existing firms were expected to open at least three new branch offices within the year.

Although Premier's main office contributed 35–40 percent of total revenue, much new business was received through branch offices, and location of such offices was critical. Premier plotted competitors' branch locations on an area map showing subdivisions, new housing starts, and real estate brokerage offices; they then located new branches in those areas having the highest concentrations of potential business. The proposed outlets in Elk Grove and Citrus Heights appeared to be essential in view of the fact that Mr. Love was under considerable pressure to increase the firm's orders by 20 percent, its market share by at least 2½ percent, and profits by 25 percent. The best means of increasing title insurance business seemed to be expansion of branch offices to handle escrow operations for real estate transactions, though escrow service, by itself, was less profitable than title insurance. A branch office incurred expenses of at least $5,900 per month ($650 rent, $4,500 salaries, and $750 other) in 1977. Such an office was expected to generate sixty-five to eighty escrow orders per month and thereby support itself by escrow income alone. However, rising labor and space costs might soon make it necessary to generate more orders just to break even. In 1976, all of Premier's Sacramento branches earned 10–12 percent on escrow income alone (see "Condensed Income Statement," exhibit 5).

Mr. Love was somewhat apprehensive about increasing or even maintaining Premier's market share. Of its competitors, "A" had increased its share by

EXHIBIT 4
Shares of Real Estate Title Insurance and Escrow Market—Sacramento, 1976

Name of Company	Number of Offices Sacramento County	Percent of Sacramento County Market
A	7	21%
B	9	18
C	9	18
D	8	12
Premier Title Insurance Co.	5	11
E	7	11
F	5	9
Totals	50	100%

EXHIBIT 5
Premier Title Insurance Company Condensed Income Statement, 1976

	Dollars	Percent
REVENUE:		
Title Insurance Premiums	$737,000	59%
Escrow Services	513,000	41%
Total Operating Revenue	$1,250,000	100%
EXPENSES:		
Salaries	$ 562,500	45.0%
Rent & Occupancy	86,300	6.9
Profit Sharing, Health & Life Ins.	86,200	6.9
Advertising	13,750	1.1
Public Relations	23,750	1.9
Travel Expense	13,250	1.1
General Office Expense	37,600	3.0
Utilities	30,200	2.4
Maintenance	12,700	1.0
Depreciation	6,250	.5
Insurance	6,100	.5
Professional Services	12,650	1.0
Losses and Bad Debts	28,750	2.3
Taxes	30,000	2.4
Total Expenses	$ 950,000	76.0%
Net Profits	$ 300,000	24.0%

6 percent within the past three years, while "B," "C," and "D" all had dropped from 3 to 6 percent of their shares. Although "E" was still a relatively small operation, it had grown more rapidly than any of the firms, and it seemed likely that it might surpass Premier in 1977 unless the latter could reverse the trend.

SALES METHODS AND PROMOTION

In practice, most buyers of title insurance relied upon the recommendations of real estate brokers or salesmen. Consequently, title firms tended to direct sales efforts toward real estate brokers. Real estate developers also were cultivated as customers. New subdivisions provided a steady source of business for six months to three years, with single title searches often being sufficient for the entire tract. Subdivision documents accounted for 15 percent of Premier's orders processed in 1976, although "bulk rate" discounts for title insurance had been allowed in most cases. One Premier specialist worked almost wholly with real estate developers.

"C" had promoted its "for sale by owner" or FSBO sales in 1976. Although it had garnered a substantial share of the FSBO market, Mr. Love believed it required more personal time and attention of title company staff and use of home office facilities, to deal with uninformed home owners.

The state real estate commissioner frowned upon heavy entertainment expenditures, and state antirebate regulations prevented title companies from purchasing office supplies, paying telephone or automobile leasing fees, or providing secretarial help for broker-customers. Consequently, Premier tried to maximize its personal calls and emphasize superior service. Expenditures for public relations were being limited to 2 percent, and they seldom spent more than 1 percent of gross revenues for advertising.

THE FUTURE

Mr. Love, as well as most members of his executive committee, were agreed that the Sacramento Division must quickly expand its capacity to process orders, but no one was certain as to how this should be accomplished. Mr. Berg was highly resistant to heavy building expenditures. He wondered if office efficiency couldn't be increased to accommodate additional sales. At least two of the branch managers thought that all escrow operations should be moved to the branch offices, thereby allowing more room in the main office for title insurance operations. Leases on two of the branch offices would expire in mid-1977, and the two branch managers thought that additional space for personnel and equipment to handle the added load would cost no more than $18,000 per year. Other office managers wondered if lowering quality standards for title insurance might not reduce time and cost per order enough to offset any increase in title insurance losses. They pointed out that service could be speeded up by doing less checking, and public relations would be enhanced. Finally, Ms. McCurry was inclined to favor more attention to insuring titles in housing tracts or on commercial real estate, since insuring either would require less title search time per dollar of premium than would insuring titles to private residences.

QUALITY SHOWROOMS

Quality Showrooms was a regional catalog showroom, founded nine years ago in the western part of the United States. Although the company was primarily a discount retailer of jewelry, it also carried consumer electronics, small appliances, and other gift items. The company had made drastic improvements in both sales and profits to recover from net losses in its early years of operation. Sales for the first six months of its current year, in fact, had already surpassed the previous year's total sales—reaching a level of nearly $13.8 million (see exhibits 1 and 2).

As she assessed the future of her company, however, Virginia Mann, president of Quality Showrooms, reflected on the performance of the business:

Although we've done quite well in jewelry, I'm afraid to rely on the jewelry industry for future growth. Our growth will have to be more balanced, coming from increasing volume in other areas. Or, we will have to continue to expand geographically.

Since most of her experience had been in fine jewelry, Ms. Mann was not certain how to ensure the continued success of the company in the face of mounting competition and higher costs of operations.

HISTORY OF THE COMPANY

Quality Showrooms was originally formed as Quality Jewelers by Gene Mann, Ms. Mann's brother, nearly fifteen years ago. The jewelry store had operated successfully in a relatively large building in the downtown area of a medium-size western city.

Ms. Mann had worked in her brother's store in its first two years before buying a full partnership interest. With the added capital, they both began

This case was prepared by Professor Dennis H. Tootelian, California State University, Sacramento.

thinking of either opening another jewelry outlet or developing a catalog showroom type of retail business. Before any of this could happen, however, her brother was killed in an automobile accident. Subsequently, Ms. Mann purchased her brother's half of the partnership from his estate.

Quality Jewelers grew slowly over the next two years, and Ms. Mann became concerned about the company's future. Accordingly, she decided to convert the store to a catalog showroom, and applied for and received a Small Business Administration loan in the amount of $140,000 to help her get Quality Showrooms started.

Since the floor space in the jewelry store was inadequate to carry and display a wider range of merchandise, Ms. Mann moved the store to a larger facility in the suburbs. To her surprise, jewelry sales increased even though the business evolved from a jewelry to a general merchandise store. During the next six years, Ms. Mann opened seven new showroom outlets, four of which were located in an adjacent state.

Catalog Showrooms

Since their beginning, catalog showrooms have become a significant factor in local markets. These outlets have grown rapidly, especially in the early years. From 1970 to 1979, for example, catalog showroom sales rose approximately 700 percent. Comparison of catalog showroom sales with those of other major retail outlets during the 1970s is shown in exhibit 3.

Catalog showrooms in general allow customers to pre-shop for a vast array of nationally-known merchandise. They also encourage in-home shopping by providing comparative price information—a "reference price" as well as the showroom's actual price is given along with a description, photograph, and stock number for each product. Product offerings, however, usually are limited to goods which are not radically affected by seasonal and fashion changes.

Other appealing characteristics of showrooms are name-brand merchandise and prices lower than those in most department stores. The high volume generated by this selling approach allows catalog merchandisers

CASE

EXHIBIT 1
Quality Showrooms
Condensed Income Statements

	Current 6 mos		Last Year		Two Years Ago	
	Dollars	Percentage of Sales	Dollars	Percentage of Sales	Dollars	Percentage of Sales
Net Sales	$13,739,842	100.0%	$13,682,095	100.0%	$12,941,858	100.0%
Cost of Sales	8,711,060	63.4	8,756,541	64.0	8,218,080	63.5
Gross Profit	5,028,782	36.6	4,925,554	36.0	4,723,778	36.5
Operating Expenses	3,750,977	27.3	4,542,455	33.2	4,309,639	33.3
Net Profit	1,277,805	9.3	383,099	2.8	414,139	3.2

EXHIBIT 2
Quality Showrooms
Condensed Financial Statements

ASSETS

Current Assets

Cash	$ 66,940
Accounts Receivable	29,679
Inventory	1,803,910
Prepaid Expenses	38,910
Total	$1,939,439

Fixed Assets

Automobile	$ 33,044
Equipment	362,081
Furniture/Fixtures	276,600
Improvements	407,601
Total	$1,079,326
TOTAL ASSETS	$3,018,765

LIABILITIES & CAPITAL

Current Liabilities

Notes Payable	$ 173,033
Current Portion, Long Term Debt	63,616
Accounts Payable	1,614,861
Accrued Expenses	205,538
Total	$2,057,048
Long Term Debt	$ 383,064
TOTAL LIABILITIES	$2,440,112
NET WORTH	$ 578,653
TOTAL LIABILITIES & CAPITAL	$3,018,765

to maintain profitability at an average markup of 25 percent compared with up to 35 percent for discount stores, and over 45 percent for department stores.

Most catalog showrooms stock everything from multi-carat diamond rings and stereo equipment to kitchen appliances and sporting goods accessories. Items shown in the catalogs typically are displayed one-of-a-kind on shelves for customer inspection with the actual merchandise stored in a warehousing room. Customers place orders at a sales counter and showroom employees bring the selected items from inventory to the counter.

The average size of a showroom is slightly over 20,000 square feet, of which 8.000 square feet are used for display and counters; the balance of the space is used for warehousing inventory. Approximately 45 percent of the newer outlets are free-standing buildings and nearly 35 percent are located in shopping centers.

The size and layout of these showrooms means that less staff is needed to police aisles and stock shelves. These and other cost efficiencies make showroom operations about 35 percent to 40 percent less costly to run than discount stores of comparable size and volume. Since most catalog showrooms are managed on the theory of low-margin—high-volume, they are able to demonstrate their price advantages to shoppers by underselling their non-showroom competitors, and still show significant levels of profit.

The primary form of advertising used by showroom companies has been the catalog. Typically, these are

CASE

EXHIBIT 3
Growth in Retail Sales in the United States
(billions of dollars)

Year	Catalog Showrooms Sales	Increase (Percent)	Discount Houses Sales	Increase (Percent)	Department Stores Sales	Increase (Percent)	Total Retail Sales	Increase (Percent)
1970	$1.03	—	$22.5	—	$38.3	—	$375.5	—
1971	1.22	18.4%	25.6	12.1%	42.8	11.7%	408.9	8.9%
1972	1.50	23.0	28.2	19.2	47.2	10.3	448.4	9.7
1973	2.00	33.3	31.5	10.5	51.5	9.1	503.3	12.2
1974	2.45	22.5	34.4	8.4	54.1	5.1	537.8	6.9
1975	3.00	22.4	38.0	9.5	57.4	6.1	584.4	8.7
1976	3.81	27.0	44.0	15.8	62.9	9.6	651.9	11.6
1977	4.68	22.8	47.0	6.4	71.5	13.7	708.3	8.7
1978	5.58	19.2	50.0	6.4				
1979	7.00	22.3						

Source: Journal of Marketing, Vol. 43 (Summer 1979), page 86.

mailed or distributed to potential customers in a showroom's trading area, or picked up by customers at the showroom. Seasonal direct-mail fliers, such as those sent out during the Christmas period, have also been commonly used. Many of the larger catalog showroom chains have used extensive amounts of newspaper and television advertising to promote name recognition. Nevertheless, the catalog has been the most critical element—and the most expensive, costing more than $2 each to produce and distribute.

Despite the continued growth of some catalog outlets, they face keen competition from combination supermarkets-drugstores-home centers, which offer customers the convenience of one-stop shopping. Some analysts also predict that catalog showrooms will double their sales of small appliances and consumer electronics in the next few years, but will suffer sales declines in other product areas—most notably jewelry. Overall, the experts believe that catalog companies could continue to be profitable so long as they retain the key ingredients to their past success: the right merchandise, low prices, attractive showrooms, good locations, and the ability to keep adequate inventory levels for items listed in the catalogs.

Market Characteristics

The typical market area for a Quality Showrooms outlet has been thought to consist of slightly below average household incomes, predominantly blue collar workers, and average age distributions and levels of unemployment. However, Ms. Mann did not believe that an outlet's primary buyers were necessarily those located closest to the showroom. She had attempted to locate outlets near freeways or other good access areas, so that people throughout the geographic area would consider the showrooms convenient.

To better define her "typical" customer, Ms. Mann hired an independent research firm to collect pertinent demographic data and other information on customer shopping habits. The study was based on a sample portion of one of the mailing lists used to distribute catalogs. This list was kept fairly current since it was needed to inform customers of new catalogs as they became available at the showrooms each October.

The mailing list was thought to be adequate, though not truly representative. Most notably, it did not contain names of tourists and occasional shoppers, who were important elements in the company's total sales. Nevertheless, Ms. Mann thought the list

EXHIBIT 4
Summary of Questionnaire Statistics

Question & Choices	Percentage of Responses	Range	Average
1. How first heard of Quality Showrooms			
a. Newspaper	15.9		
b. TV	5.7		
c. Someone Else	63.6		
d. Other	14.8		
2. Number of visits during last year		1–25	6.6
3. Number of purchases during last year		1–20	3.5
4. Primary purpose for shopping at Quality Showrooms			
a. Jewelry	42.4		
b. Sports	7.5		
c. Appliances	36.8		
d. Stereos/TV	7.5		
e. Other	5.7		
5. Primary reason for patronizing Quality Showrooms			
a. Price	79.4		
b. Convenience	5.2		
c. Location	5.2		
d. Range	8.2		
e. Service	1.0		
f. Other	1.0		
6. Main complaint with Quality Showrooms			
a. Inadequate Stock	49.3		
b. Inadequate Variety	13.4		
c. Little Assistance	23.9		
d. Other	13.4		
7. Approximate family income			
a. Below $10,000	12.3		
b. $10,000–$15,000	31.0		
c. $15,000–$20,000	26.0		
d. $20,000–$30,000	17.7		
e. Over $30,000	13.0		

contained the names of those most interested in Quality Showrooms. Summary results of the study are presented in exhibits 4, 5, 6, and 7.

While Quality Showrooms competed directly with larger national catalog showroom chains for customers, Ms. Mann broadly defined her competition as any store that carried comparable merchandise. In reviewing the market areas for the eight outlets, she tallied the average number of competitors for each showroom. This is shown in exhibit 8.

Ms. Mann thought that most of these competing stores were more aggressive in their promotional efforts than they were in their pricing. Accordingly, she tried to ensure that Quality Showrooms kept promotional costs down and prices low. While many other stores were considerably more visible and offered more variety in merchandise, Ms. Mann's outlets attempted to consistently beat their prices and use more aggressive in-store selling.

Concerning the market, Ms. Mann commented:

EXHIBIT 5
Relation of Family Income to Principal Product Shopped For

Primary Product Shopped For	Family Income Ranges			
	Below $10,000	$10,000– $15,000	$15,000– $20,000	Over $20,000*
Jewelry	55%	38%	43%	39%
Sporting Goods	14	7	5	7
Small Appliances	23	41	33	39
Stereos and TV		7	14	11
Other	9	7	5	4

*Combined $20,000–$30,000, and Over $30,000 Income Groups.

EXHIBIT 6
Relation of Family Income to Primary Reason for Shopping at Quality Showrooms

Primary Reason for Shopping	Family Income Ranges			
	Below $10,000	$10,000– $15,000	$15,000– $20,000	Over $20,000*
Price	71%	96%	56%	88%
Convenience	10		11	4
Location	5	11		
Range of Goods	10	4	17	8
Quality of Service			6	
Other	5			

*Combined $20,000–$30,000, and Over $30,000 Income Groups.

Our goal is to increase sales and profits by selling quality brand merchandise at lower prices. To determine if our prices are low, we regularly make comparisons of Quality Showrooms' prices with that of various other stores for standard brands in various product groups [see exhibit 9]. Normally, Quality Showrooms' prices are 10 percent to 40 percent less than our competitors in overall product groups. And even on individual items, it is unusual to find products that cost more in our stores.

We are in a very unique position since we're one of the few regional catalog showrooms in the area. We certainly want to expand our market. We have done well in jewelry so far and we need to retain our strength in this product category. But, we need to increase our business in other categories as well. Right now, we are protected by our strength in jewelry, but in time this could change. I am confident, though, that by selling top quality merchandise at low, competitive prices, we can keep a competitive edge over other retailers.

Company Operations

The catalog system employed by Quality Showrooms differed somewhat from the typical catalog operation. In many other outlets, the showrooms displayed only one of each item, along with its catalog number and price. To purchase an item, the customer wrote an order ticket and took it to an order pick-up area. At Quality Showrooms, not only was a cataloged item

EXHIBIT 7
Relation of Family Income To
the Number of Items Purchased During the Last 12 Months

Items Purchased	Family Income Ranges			
	Below $10,000	$10,000–$15,000	$15,000–$20,000	Over $20,000*
None	25%	15%	14%	8%
One	20	7	7	16
Two	10	19	14	20
Three	5	25	37	8
Four	10	11	21	8
Five	5	4		8
Six	15	15		12
Seven				12
Eight	5			
Nine				
Eleven			7	
Twelve				4
Thirteen	5			
Fifteen				4
Twenty +		4		

*Combined $20,000–$30,000, and Over $30,000 Income Groups.

EXHIBIT 8
Average Number of Competitors for
A Quality Showroom's Outlet

	Competitors per Outlet
National Catalog Showrooms	1.5
Regional/Local Catalog Showrooms	.5
National Department Stores	3.4
Regional/Local Department Stores	1.7
Supermarket-Drug Stores	4.3
Jewelers	5.7
Discount Stores	4.9

priced and displayed, but back-up merchandise was also on the shelf—in much the same manner as in department stores. In addition, Ms. Mann employed salespeople on the floor and a multi-site cash register system. Ms. Mann commented on the rationale behind this approach to catalog sales:

In contrast to most catalog showroom operations, which stress self-service, our floor is staffed with salespeople to assist our customers with their purchases. This procedure reduces lost sales due to customer reluctance to write order tickets. It also speeds up the transaction process and provides a touch of personal service to our customers. My sales staff can also promote alternative selections of merchandise if an item is out of stock. This is more expensive than the self-service approach, but it helps to separate us from the competition.

New catalogs were printed annually in September, just before the Christmas buying season. As soon as the catalogs were received by the showrooms in October, Ms. Mann's staff would mail postcards to customers indicating that the new catalogs had arrived. Upon presentation of the postcard, the customer received a copy of the catalog. This procedure allowed Ms. Mann to keep an up-to-date list of customers. Catalogs were also issued to walk-in customers upon request if they would sign up to be placed on the showroom's mailing list.

CASE

EXHIBIT 9
Price Variations Between Quality Showrooms and Some Competitors

Product Group	Extent to Which Prices Were Higher (Lower) Than Quality Showrooms			
	National Department Store	Regional Department Store	National Discount Chain	National Catalog Showroom
Electrical Appliances*				
Range	14–39%	4–43%	17–70%	(2.2)–15%
Average	25.5	27	38.4	5.3
Median	24.5	28	35.0	4.1
Audio Equipment**				
Range	7–35%	6–20%	9–46%	(7.1)–11%
Average	21.2	13	28.3	3.3
Median	10.0	13	29.0	4.8
Photography†				
Range	15–67%	1–45%	(2)–16%	(11.2)–4.8%
Average	37.6	19.1	4.3	(4.8)
Median	30.0	18.5	3.8	(4.0)
Watches††				
Range	20–58%	13–56%	7–32%	3.8–16.9%
Average	33.4	31.5	18.1	4.1
Median	22.0	30.5	16.2	8.7

*Includes Sunbeam, G.E., Oster, Waring, & Kitchen Aid
**Only Panasonic
†Includes Kodak, GAF, Polaroid, & Minolta
††Includes Lucien Piccard, Elgin, Gruen, & Hamilton

The 400 page catalog listed approximately five thousand items, of which 80 percent to 90 percent were stocked for the Christmas season. The merchandise in the catalog was divided into the following categories: rings, gold jewelry, watches, china-silver-crystal, gifts, clocks and lamps, luggage, electronics, photography, cookware, appliances, sporting goods, and juvenile (toys and games). Sales by category are shown in exhibit 10. Ms. Mann commented on the subject of catalogs:

The catalog is both a help and a hindrance to our business. It is beneficial because it allows us to purchase and sell merchandise at low prices. However, the problem is that we do not presently have adequate capital to sell the full range of goods offered in the catalog and because the

catalog creates the expectation that all merchandise listed is available for sale, we get numerous complaints from customers because items are not in stock. It's a problem we need to resolve before our reputation becomes one of carrying only limited lines—if this hasn't happened already.

Another unique aspect of Quality Showrooms was its policy regarding mail-order purchases. Although special orders of unstocked merchandise were not accepted, the showrooms accepted mail orders. And, depending on the size of the purchase, the showroom manager would decide whether to add a freight charge to the cost of the merchandise by sending it C.O.D. to the buyer, or to simply asborb the freight charges internally. Ms. Mann thought that mail orders accounted for less than 2 percent of sales:

EXHIBIT 10
Operating Statistics by Select Product Groups

Select Product Groups	Sales As Percentage of Total	Gross Profit As Percentage of Sales	Inventory As Percentage of Total	Inventory Turns
Diamonds	34.5	52.5	35.2	2.18
Watches	8.4	51.5	11.7	1.60
Stone Rings	7.6	69.1	7.9	2.14
Miscellaneous Gifts	10.4	85.0	8.7	N.A.
14K Gold Jewelry	7.7	47.4	12.6	1.36
Miscellaneous Jewelry	3.4	78.4	3.4	2.25
Small Appliances	13.0	87.2	6.8	N.A.
Crystal, Silver	9.3	59.0	10.7	1.95
Electronics	5.7	75.6	3.0	N.A.

This is one area that may help us to increase our distribution if more effort was put into it. Part of the problem is that mail orders involve considerable time and we are not sure what to do about the freight charges.

Ms. Mann estimated that 98 percent to 99 percent of her business was walk-in, and approximately 95 percent of the sales were for cash. In special instances, in-store credit was provided to preferred customers and friends of Ms. Mann and other key personnel. Additionally, Quality Showrooms had a policy of giving no cash refunds without a receipt and no cash refunds on charge sales. No exchange of any sort was allowed after seven days from the sale. Any merchandise returned due to defects, however, was accepted with a proof of purchase. In these instances, over-the-counter exchanges were made and the merchandise returned to the manufacturer. The only repair work conducted by Quality Showrooms was for jewelry.

Purchasing and Merchandising

Ms. Mann and the store managers selected most of the merchandise to be sold in the showrooms. All stores carried the same merchandise as shown in the catalogs, but some variations were allowed based on geographical differences.

Purchases were made by experience and by visually estimating which goods were moving and which were not. No formal inventory analyses were made except for tax purposes at the end of each year. All inventory control was conducted visually and each store manager ordered the quantities needed directly from designated suppliers. According to Ms. Mann, the company was hampered by its inability to purchase merchandise economically:

We would prefer to buy in small quantities to see which items will sell, and then later buy in larger quantities. But this is not possible because of the length of time it takes for shipments, and because we let showroom managers order for themselves. This can create real problems when manufacturers require minimum quantity orders. It does not create serious difficulties for the national showrooms, but it does for us. It makes it very hard at times to obtain the merchandise we need at prices that will allow us to retain our margins and be competitive. We have not centralized our purchasing because we have no warehouse capabilities, and our showrooms are relatively small—averaging 20,000 square feet—so they cannot keep large quantities of inventory. In addition, we simply do not have adequate capital to make large purchases and store them somewhere.

The retailing strategies that were used when the original showroom was first opened continued over the years. The physical arrangements of the stores, however, were not considered efficient. Furthermore, not all of the showrooms had the same layout—it varied slightly in each showroom.

Overall, Ms. Mann was not satisfied with the present merchandising:

The arrangements of our facilities are largely the result of rapid expansion and the key desire to find good locations. At times the facilities at these sites were only marginally acceptable, but we took them because of traffic flow, and so on. The increased sales we have had have now forced us to expand our merchandise lines, and especially the jewelry. Our showrooms are cramped and they look that way.

As a result of all of this, our departments do not flow well and the merchandise is not always displayed attractively. This hurts our gift sales and the impulse items that don't receive the emphasis that they should in terms of visual display.

Company Organization

Organizationally, Ms. Mann and her sister-in-law, Joyce Mann Denton, were president and vice president respectively. Ms. Mann's functions were primarily centered on setting company policy and overall planning. Ms. Denton worked directly with the showroom managers to oversee bookkeeping, sales, and store personnel. Each showroom had a manager, an assistant manager, and a merchandise manager. The manager had overall authority and responsibility for virtually every aspect of the showroom's operations. The assistant manager was in charge of the jewelry department, and the merchandise manager was responsible for all other departments in the showroom except bookkeeping and clerical. Those functions were the responsibility of the showroom manager (see exhibit 11).

Each store manager had the authority to purchase merchandise from a list of suppliers that had been approved by Ms. Mann and to handle all personnel matters. Operating hours for each showroom varied somewhat, and they were established by Ms. Mann. Ms. Denton and Ms. Mann worked together on store budgets, and set limits on the number of personnel any showroom could employ. According to Ms. Denton:

Our store managers basically are supposed to carry out the policies we set and make sure none of the employees or customers walk off with our merchandise. Virginia and I decide what to stock and in what quantities. And we set operating budgets for each showroom. We do ask the managers for their advice, but we make the actual decisions. It has been fairly easy so far since most of our sales have been in jewelry, and we pretty much know what to do in this area.

The Future

Despite her concerns about the company, Ms. Mann was optimistic about the future:

The most important single fact in our favor is the increase in population, which should be good for business. I see this as more opportunities for people to buy the products we sell. Furthermore, the general work force earns much more than they ever did before, so there will be more people with more money. With the convenience of catalog shopping, I think we can capture a fair share of our market.

Yet, she also expressed some reservations about how Quality Showrooms should be positioned:

In attempting to achieve long-term growth and profitability, we are considering expanding our product base to include an apparel line and more prestigious brands in existing lines. The addition of clothing, particularly since women are our major customers, would add considerable volume. Our quality jewelry and low prices will certainly bolster both traffic and volume for apparel.

However, this addition will depend on obtaining additional capital for inventory. Another problem is space. Expanding our product line would place a strain on the present store space, which seems to be in poor shape already.

We could try to find larger facilities in our current markets, I guess. If we do this, we may lose

CASE

EXHIBIT 11
Quality Showrooms
Organization Chart

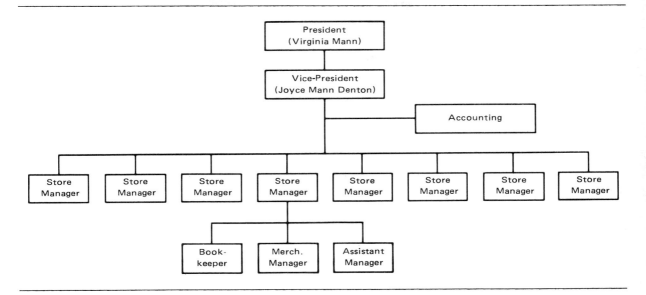

current customers. *Joyce thinks we should keep the lines we have and try to move our operations into the midwest. If we added a few showrooms there, we would have to localize them to suit their unique market needs and the physical facilities available. We have never given up that much control and it worries me a little.*

In reviewing the current conditions, Ms. Mann felt that she would have to make some decisions soon about what direction Quality Showrooms would take:

If I wait too long before taking some action, I'm afraid that we will lose our momentum. Besides, if we wait to long, the competition will take over.

ESQUIRE CLEANERS, INC.

Esquire Cleaners was one of the largest of the 24,000 firms in the professional dry cleaning industry in 1977. The industry was characterized by small, independently operated plants with annual sales ranging from $30,000 to $75,000. The number of firms which serviced one to perhaps a dozen branch outlets had increased; but these firms seldom had sales in excess of $400,000 per year. Approximately 5 percent of all firms in the industry were "package plants," connected with production facilities by either service or franchise agreements. Coin-operated self-service facilities had reduced professional laundry sales, but dry cleaning had continued to grow at a slow pace.

Esquire Cleaners' production facilities and administrative offices were housed in a modern 90,000-square-foot plant, located in an Ohio metropolitan area of more than one-half million people. In April 1977, Esquire employed 340 people, including those in sales and administrative positions, although employment tended to fall below that figure in the summer months.

Sales were made from eighty-four franchised stores as well as from the main plant counters. Approximately one-half of the stores were located in the home office city, while the remainder were scattered throughout the smaller cities and towns within a 75-mile radius. In 1977, customers in the metropolitan shopping area who preferred home pickup and delivery were being served by five retail truck routes, including one for rugs only and one for draperies only. With regard to such routes, Mr. William Garrard, president and sole owner of Esquire Cleaners, commented:

This case was prepared by Professor Leete A. Thompson, California State University, Sacramento.

In the past twelve years or so we haven't made a dime on the routes. They're my biggest headache, and at times I've felt like getting rid of them. Then I think of all that free advertising on the sides of the trucks and hate to think of losing them.

Mr. Garrard also was concerned about the seasonality of sales. Losses had been common in the third quarter of each year, in part because newspaper advertisements, special promotions, cents-off coupons, and price reductions had been offered to boost sales during the slow summer months. He explained:

We attempt to keep sales and production up in the summer for two reasons. First, it keeps our employee turnover costs to a minimum and employees stay happier. Second, it keeps the stores busy, which is important for us as well as for the store managers.

HISTORY

Esquire Cleaners was founded in 1952 by its present owner, William Garrard. The business began in a small, inefficient plant serving three stores and four routes. Mr. Garrard had started in the cleaning business in the late 1940s, running a retail route for another company. In his words:

They needed someone to take over a route which was doing poorly. Within three months I doubled the sales, and within six months they had to divide my route into three. I was only making a 10 percent commission, but it added up to between $150 and $190 a week—a lot of money in those days.

Primarily on the basis of his experience with pickup and delivery service, Mr. Garrard decided, in 1955, to concentrate entirely on route service. "I had a theory," Mr. Garrard said, "that routes were the way to go. Rents for stores would no longer be a problem and costs could be more easily controlled." As a result of this decision, Esquire grew from four routes to thirteen during the period from 1955 to 1961. "In 1962," recalled Mr. Garrard, "the union struck the plant, and I sent all the drivers on a two-week vacation. When the strike ended, some of the routemen didn't return. As a result, we lost some of our routes and were forced to turn to stores for more business."

Through the development of branch stores, sales increased rapidly until, finally, more plant facilities were needed. Construction of a new building was begun in 1969, financed primarily through a bank loan and Mr. Garrard's personal funds. Though the plant was not completed and ready for operations until the middle of 1970, Mr. Garrard began purchasing equipment for the new plant in 1968 because, he explained:

We were making good profits at the time. It was apparent we would probably suffer some losses in 1970 and possibly 1971. For that reason, I felt we needed to generate high depreciation against our present high profits in order to retain more cash in the business.

(See exhibits 1 and 2 for financial statements.)

SALES

Esquire's policy had been to: (1) maintain high quality in cleaning and finishing as well as in service, while at the same time (2) expand sales through creation of more branch stores. All of the work was done at the plant. As a result, the cleaning from the stores had to be transported daily to and from each store. The clothes were trucked in large vans, each of which was capable of carrying the cleaning for eight stores. Four trucks serviced the routes to the stores. For the branches in the immediate area, the garments were picked up and delivered twice daily. On the more distant stores, deliveries were made only once a day. Mr. Garrard commented:

Service is somewhat of a problem for us as far as time is concerned. We can't compete on a time basis with the package plant, since our normal service is two to three days with one day for specials. Personally, I feel most customers don't really need, nor wish, to have faster service. Most of the cleaners that do offer eight-hour service are either producing at lower standards of quality, or at a higher price, or both.

Mr. Garrard was always seeking to develop new services which would stimulate sales. Among those offered at Esquire were: (1) cleaning and pressing of all types of garments including suede or leather, formals, wedding gowns, fur coats, gloves, and hats; (2) cleaning of household goods such as blankets, quilts, pillows, spreads, tablecloths, draperies, upholstery, rugs, and sleeping bags; (3) laundering of shirts and pants; and (4) miscellaneous services such as dye work, mass cleaning by weight, waterproofing, monogramming, alterations, and repairs.

By 1976 sales were approaching $4 million. Most of these sales were being generated through the branch outlets. The sales area in which Esquire's branches were located was divided into three districts with one sales manager in charge of all stores within his district. It was the district sales manager's responsibility: (1) to place capable store operators in the branch outlets; (2) to see that they were trained properly; (3) to control any problems arising in the stores, including customer complaints which the store operator could not handle; and (4) to seek new locations.

The district sales managers operated from the main plant, but much of their time was spent on the road solving the various problems of the store clerks and checking on possible new locations. According to John Roberts, one of the district managers:

There are two necessities a branch outlet must have. First, the location must be good, that is, there must be traffic by the store and ample parking available. Second, the clerk behind the counter must be good with customers. He or she must be interested in serving the customer properly.

One of the most formidable problems faced by the district sales managers was maintaining adequate communication with managers in the stores. Almost all routine correspondence with stores was done through memos distributed by the van drivers. Said Mr. Roberts:

We try to discourage phone calls from the stores. If one store operator gets the habit of calling the

EXHIBIT 1
Esquire Cleaners, Incorporated
Statement of Income and Expenses
(in thousands of dollars)

	3 Months Ended 3/31/77	1976	1975	1974	1973	1972	1971	1970	1969	1968
Net Sales										
Plant and stores	$1,019	$3,779	$3,723	$3,403	$2,874	$2,520	$2,264	$1,737	$1,409	$1,262
Routes	45	177	193	195	158	144	153	149	134	113
Total net sales	$1,064	$3,956	$3,916	$3,598	$3,032	$2,664	$2,417	$1,886	$1,543	$1,375
Plant Expenses										
Salaries and wages	$ 350	$1,320	$1,289	$1,200	$ 997	$ 869	$ 802	$ 703	$ 533	$ 456
Payroll taxes	25	91	83	81	68	56	40	39	26	16
Compensation insurance	6	19	23	21	17	14	8	7	6	4
Sublet work	23	87	85	80	73	56	56	48	21	6
Solvents	14	49	45	45	38	36	42	33	25	23
Soaps and chemicals	25	85	85	85	66	60	51	46	42	43
Laundry supplies	20	66	78	69	71	54	38	36	17	16
Hangers and wrappings	35	125	106	103	90	96	73	76	45	47
Rents	82	377	362	360	342	322	295	192	98	62
Utilities	19	92	96	85	83	73	68	56	36	30
Repairs and maintenance	15	84	99	91	73	61	53	49	40	28
Insurance	19	60	58	52	43	37	30	20	21	15
Depreciation—machinery	21	102	100	97	93	87	94	94	63	36
Depreciation—leaseholds	13	54	54	55	55	57	56	45	13	14
Other expenses	15	101	90	93	69	61	65	78	36	30
Total plant expenses	$ 682	$2,712	$2,653	$2,517	$2,178	$1,939	$1,771	$1,522	$1,022	$ 826
Gross Operating Profit	$ 382	$1,244	$1,263	$1,081	$ 854	$ 725	$ 646	$ 364	$ 521	$ 549
Sales Expenses										
Salaries and wages	$ 77	$ 292	$ 326	$ 303	$ 248	$ 227	$ 215	$ 166	$ 125	$ 113
Payroll taxes	5	20	18	19	16	13	9	9	5	4
Compensation insurance	1	3	4	3	2	2	2	1	1	. . .
Gasoline, oil, etc.	8	35	34	33	26	25	19	17	13	14
Automotive repairs	5	31	26	25	20	26	20	18	15	11
Automotive depreciation	5	22	28	23	16	12	6	7	6	6
Advertising	43	180	168	160	100	126	116	88	79	73
Claims and adjustments	5	16	15	13	11	8	6	7	4	2
Supplies	. . .	11	13	17	19	10	10	6	4	2
Total sales expenses	$ 149	$ 610	$ 632	$ 596	$ 458	$ 449	$ 403	$ 319	$ 252	$ 225
Administrative Expenses										
Salaries and wages	$ 62	$ 198	$ 194	$ 163	$ 132	$ 112	$ 92	$ 61	$ 76	$ 87
Payroll taxes	2	6	5	5	5	4	3	2	1	1
Office supplies	3	10	9	9	9	4	8	6	3	3
Telephone	3	21	18	17	16	17	14	10	6	5
Taxes and licenses	7	34	32	29	22	20	8	24	24	13
Professional fees	1	13	8	15	7	5	7	4	5	4

(*continued on next page*)

EXHIBIT 1 (continued)

	3 Months Ended 3/31/77	1976	1975	1974	1973	1972	1971	1970	1969	1968
Promotion and travel	$ 1	$ 7	$ 11	$ 8	$ 3	$ 2	$ 9	$ 9	$ 11	$ 8
Dues and subscriptions	1	5	4	4	4	3	3	2	2	2
Depreciation	1	5	6	6	6	6	6	4	2	3
Interest expense	9	33	39	45	54	58	59	51	13	. . .
Profit sharing	12	53	63	. . .	. . .	. . .	. . .	. . .	. . .	. . .
Miscellaneous expense	2	20	29	20	12	11	19	17	3	7
Total administrative expense	$ 104	$ 405	$ 418	$ 321	$ 270	$ 242	$ 228	$ 190	$ 146	$ 133
Total sales and administrative expense	$ 253	$1,015	$1,050	$ 917	$ 728	$ 691	$ 631	$ 509	$ 398	$ 358
Net Operating Profit	$ 129	$ 229	$ 213	$ 164	$ 124	$ 34	$ 15	$ (145)	$ 123	$ 190
Other Income	12	57	43	54	47	50	34	24	2	4
Net Profit Before Taxes	$ 141	$ 286	$ 256	$ 218	$ 171	$ 84	$ 49	$ (121)	$ 125	$ 194
Provision for Federal Income Taxes	57	128	103	90	67	27	15	. . .	54	89
Net Income After Taxes	$ 84	$ 158	$ 153	$ 128	$ 104	$ 57	$ 34	$ (121)	$ 71	$ 105

EXHIBIT 2
Esquire Cleaners, Incorporated
Comparative Balance Sheets for Fiscal Years Ending December 31, 1968–1977
(in thousands of dollars)

	3 Months Ended 3/31/77	1976	1975	1974	1973	1972	1971	1970	1969	1968
ASSETS										
Current Assets										
Cash	$ 297	$ 103	$ 426	$ 227	$ 205	$ 143	$ 113	$ 48	$ 52	$ 302
Accounts receivable	151	182	78	106	98	69	84	64	28	18
Notes receivable	26	187	. . .	. . .	. . .	. . .	. . .	. . .	. . .	. . .
Tax refund claim	. . .	. . .	. . .	. . .	. . .	. . .	. . .	55**	. . .	. . .
Inventories*	41	42	40	39	38	39	32	31	39	34
Lease rental deposits	27	27	26	33	30	29	29	26	10	8
Prepaid insurance	19	19	17	15	14	7	5	9	. . .	2
Prepaid franchise tax	5	5	2	. . .	. . .	. . .	. . .	. . .	. . .	. . .
Other	3	4	4	4	5	6	9	15	7	20
Total current assets	$ 569	$ 569	$ 593	$ 424	$ 390	$ 293	$ 272	$ 248	$ 136	$ 384

(continued on next page)

EXHIBIT 2 (*continued*)

	3 Months Ended 3/31/77	1976	1975	1974	1973	1972	1971	1970	1969	1968
Fixed Assets										
Building	$1,081	$1,081	$1,081	$1,081	$1,081	$1,081	$1,081	$1,081	$ 956[†]	$ ...
Automotive equipment	184	184	166	153	103	96	90	82	82	67
Machinery	1,206	1,182	1,136	1,037	958	806	740	672	592	328
Office equipment	76	76	74	72	67	60	55	44	27	25
Leasehold fixtures	175	174	164	151	146	146	144	107	96	92
Signs	37	35	27	25	24	24	24	23	18	12
Total fixed assets	$2,759	$2,732	$2,648	$2,519	$2,379	$2,213	$2,134	$2,009	$1,771	$ 524
Less: Depreciation	1,433	1,422	1,279	1,093	922	765	610	487	420	337
Net fixed assets	$1,326	$1,310	$1,369	$1,426	$1,457	$1,448	$1,524	$1,522	$1,351	$ 187
Goodwill	21	21	21	21	21	21	21	21	21	21
Total assets	$1,916	$1,900	$1,983	$1,871	$1,868	$1,762	$1,817	$1,791	$1,508	$ 592
LIABILITIES										
Current Liabilities										
Accounts payable	$ 31	$ 16	$ 72	$ 78	$ 93	$ 56	$ 114	$ 135	$ 99	$ 18
Accrued payroll	125	122	109	96	79	52	38	24	40	29
Accrued insurance	1	3	7	6	6	5	4	6	4	2
Taxes payable[††]	122	147	156	143	113	66	44	26	77	106
Profit sharing	20	61	63	...	...	...	...	...	...	...
Interest payable	...	...	6	20	23	24	24	18	11	...
Bank payment	86	86	86	86	98	118	120	...	...	...
Total current liabilities	$ 385	$ 435	$ 499	$ 429	$ 412	$ 321	$ 344	$ 209	$ 231	$ 155
Long-Term Liabilities										
Bank loan	$ 134	$ 152	$ 222	$ 288	$ 350	$ 423	$ 513	$ 655	$ 515	$ ...
Notes payable	202	202	322	367	447	462	462	462	250	...
Total long-term liabilities	$ 336	$ 354	$ 544	$ 655	$ 797	$ 885	$ 975	$1,117	$ 765	$ ...
Capital										
Common stock	$ 502	$ 502	$ 502	$ 502	$ 502	$ 72	$ 72	$ 72	$ 72	$ 72
Retained earnings	693	609	438	285	157	484	426	393	460	389
Total liabilities and capital	$1,916	$1,900	$1,983	$1,871	$1,868	$1,762	$1,817	$1,791	$1,528	$ 616

*Inventories include only supplies and materials used in course of business. It includes no garments in process.

**Refers to loss in year 1970.

[†]Taxes include Federal income taxes, Federal and State payroll taxes, and State sales tax.

[††]New building under construction in 1969 but not complete until 1970. Prior to that time the company leased the plant in which the work was done.

plant about every little problem that comes up, our control clerk and the district managers may eventually waste 20 to 30 percent of their time talking on the telephone. Our job, as district managers—and Mr. Garrard stresses this often enough—is not to spend half the day looking for every lost garment we get a call on. Our true function is to see to it the stores are operating properly and to the best of their ability.

ORGANIZATION

With regard to the organization, Mr. Garrard said:

We have an organization chart, but it hasn't been upgraded in about six years. The only reason we have one at all is that some people feel they cannot get along without it. Personally, I don't believe in giving everyone the title of vice-president, and I'm sure there isn't one person in this plant who associates the word president with my name. Everyone, including Jerry Black, calls me Mr. Garrard, but that is as far as the formalities go.

Not too long ago, I used to be involved in virtually all the functions of this business. I used to install all the fixtures in the stores, but now Ed Vine does the installations. I still design the layout of every store, since floor space and rack space are critical and vary considerably from store to store.

Gerald Black, the general manager, had been with Esquire for twenty-one years. According to Mr. Garrard, sales was the only area in which Mr. Black was weak. This weakness had not caused many problems, however, as Mr. Black's responsibility centered around production. Under Mr. Black (see exhibit 3) were the plant manager, route manager, engineer, office manager, and the district sales managers. Mr. Black seldom exercised any authority over the district managers or the route manager. His usual activities involved conferring with Bill Rohn, the plant manager, to make sure that production was going smoothly and the work was getting out on schedule. "I think of myself," said Mr. Black, "as a troubleshooter. I'm always finding something for John Gill to work on. If he can't do it, I can. And if

I can't do the job, then Mr. Garrard can." In addition to these duties, Mr. Black hired all the production workers and purchased the supplies and materials for the plant. According to Mr. Garrard, "We don't use an inventory control system here, because we've been able to get along without one. But some day soon I'm afraid we'll be forced to adopt one."

Sales to the stores and routes were recorded in the office, which was run by Mrs. Burns. In addition, the office was in charge of payroll and handling calls from customers wishing pickup and delivery service or information about services and prices. Accounting was done by an outside firm. Mr. Garrard personally okayed every bill or invoice before payment with the exception of routine billings such as utilities and licenses. No attempt was made to forecast sales or budgets for future time periods.

The company did not employ a cost accounting system. In Mr. Garrard's words:

I'm primarily concerned with overall results. I try to determine how to price our services in order to make them profitable, but for many of my decisions there just isn't enough data available. I could probably rank everything we offer according to profitability, but I could never assign an exact percentage to each item.

THE ROUTES

Mr. Garrard had mixed feelings about the routes. Exhibit 4 shows route productivity. He complained:

Our route sales account for only a small portion of our total revenue. I would like to do a better business with the routes, but I can't seem to get them to produce. We even offer credit on small orders and take checks with reasonable identification. In fact, in the last couple of years, route sales have actually fallen. Turnover is a problem for us on our routes. Route number 1 and a route which was merged with it have had at least six men on it over the past ten years. The same men have held routes number 2 and number 3 since 1968, although their routes are the result of mergers. I've tried a number of modifications in salaries and commissions, and in 1976 I changed

EXHIBIT 3
Esquire Cleaners, Incorporated
Organization Chart

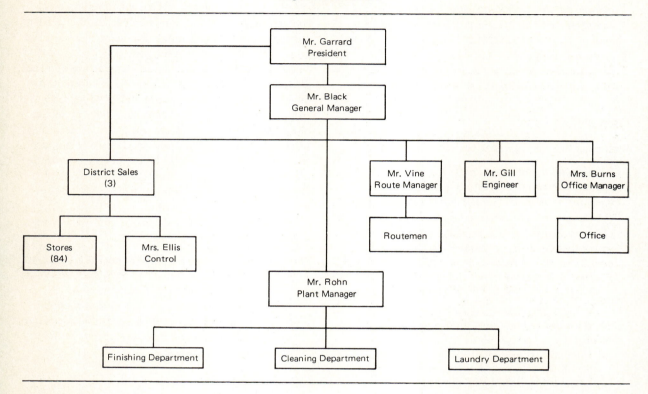

number 1 over to a franchise basis. The main thing is picking the right personnel. I used to pick all the store operators and all the routemen, but now I don't have time anymore.

Mr. Vine, the route manager, had been with Esquire Cleaners for about four years. He was considered by Mr. Garrard to be an excellent salesman, but somewhat lacking in managerial ability. Mr. Vine felt that the most important quality a good routeman could possess was the ability to sell and to please the customer. "You've got to cultivate customers in order to do well," said Mr. Vine. He continued,

If you fail your customer, he may take his cleaning to the firm around the corner and find out that it's less expensive. Some people argue that demand for call services are doomed, but I believe that in the future housewives will demand even more of the pickup and delivery service we offer. It's true that families have more cars at their disposal today than ever before. However, the traffic is becoming so congested in this city that the average housewife doesn't want to leave the house. Furthermore, it's really less expensive to have delivery service than it is to trade with one of the stores. The smart housewife can save more than the price differential in gas and oil savings—let alone the cost and

EXHIBIT 4
Esquire Cleaners, Incorporated
Route Sales

Year	Route Number and Sales in thousands of dollars[††]					Total Route	Route Sales % Total Sales
	1*	2	3	4**	5[†]		
1976	$30.3	$33.5	$54.8	$24.0	$35.0	$177.6	4.5%
1975	36.2	38.6	58.3	24.2	36.5	193.8	4.9
1974	37.0	39.8	68.0	22.5	27.5	194.8	5.5
1973	35.9	37.2	60.0	19.6	5.4	158.1	5.2
1972	34.4	36.3	54.3	18.6	—	143.6	5.4
1971	—	—	—	—	—	153.6	6.3
1970	—	—	—	—	—	148.8	7.9
1969	—	—	—	—	—	134.1	8.7
1968	—	—	—	—	—	112.4	8.3
1967	—	—	—	—	—	102.9	8.5
1966	—	—	—	—	—	97.1	9.4
1965	—	—	—	—	—	96.6	11.3

*On franchise basis since March 1976. Initially, the routeman did not buy the "inventory"—i.e., the cleaning in process. He was paid 23 percent on cash sales and 21 percent on charge sales. (Other routemen earn the greater of 22 percent of sales or $150 per week.) By March 31, 1977, three different routemen had held the franchise, and the current man was being paid 25 percent on cash sales and 21 percent on charge sales.

**Route 4 was exclusively for rugs.

[†]Route 5 was exclusively for draperies.

[††]Several routes had been consolidated into the four remaining routes prior to 1972. The drapery route was first started in mid-1973.

inconvenience of making the trip back and forth to the store. I know route service has declined nationally, but I sure can't see why.

Mr. Garrard determined that the costs associated with pickup and delivery service were about 15 percent greater than those for store service. This difference had risen somewhat since the 1960s due to higher fuel, truck, and routeman costs. Drivers complained so much that Mr. Garrard lowered pickup and delivery prices in 1967 to only 10 percent greater than store prices. In 1976, however, he again raised route prices to 15 percent above store rates.

In 1974, Mr. Garrard asked Mr. Roberts, who had helped with the routes before Vine became route manager, to make a study of the route sales. He found that, although route number 3 had well over 400

customers, other routes averaged 192 active customers each and approximately one-third of a routeman's calls resulted in a sale. He recommended prizes for building larger routes and higher guaranteed pay for the routemen. In return, routemen would agree to meet minimum standards for numbers of calls each week.

As a result of this study, Mr. Roberts and Mr. Garrard had discussed the possibility of using a radio-dispatched system for the retail routes. Each week an average of thirty-four telephone calls per route requested service and Mr. Garrard believed that a dispatching system would greatly increase both the requests and the sales per call for his routemen and thus make the entire operation more efficient and profitable. The installation of a radio system would cost at least $11,000 and increase expenses by $5,000 per year.

FUTURE PLANS

Mr. Garrard recalled:

At the time we built our plant, people thought I was crazy. No one thought I could ever use that much capacity. I don't hear comments like that anymore. In this business, as in any other competitive industry, you've got to move ahead. Some people feel our business is doomed by introduction of the "miracle" fabrics. I doubt that. Tests now show that they last longer when professionally cared for. I think we can always find services to perform economically for the customer, as long as he wears clothes.

Mr. Garrard was considering expanding into two new areas: (1) "flat work"—which consisted of laundering of sheets, towels, and the like; and (2) a "rental garment service"—in the form of leasing uniforms and other standard dress to large companies.

In reference to "flat work," Mr. Garrard observed that "we would need an additional 10,000 square feet of operating space if we decided to go into that area." He felt that the new space could be built onto the existing plant on some adjacent property presently owned by Esquire Cleaners. He estimated that such a building would cost approximately $15 per square foot, and that an investment of nearly $100,000 in capital equipment would be required. Mr. Garrard estimated that flatwork would increase sales about $45 a week per store and at least $50 to $75 a week for each route. "One advantage," stated Mr. Garrard, "in anything new we go into is our strong advertising power. People know our name and they associate it with quality."

THOMPSON RESPIRATION PRODUCTS, INC.

Victor Higgins, executive vice president for Thompson Respiration Products, Inc. (TRP), sat thinking at his desk late one Friday in April 1982. "We're making progress," he said to himself. "Getting Metro to sign finally gets us into the Chicago Market . . . and with a good dealer at that." *Metro,* of course, was Metropolitan Medical Products, a large Chicago retailer of medical equipment and supplies for home use. "Now, if we could just do the same in Minneapolis and Atlanta," he continued.

However, getting at least one dealer in each of

This case was written by Professor James E. Nelson and DBA Candidate William R. Woolridge, the University of Colorado.

these cities to sign a TRP Dealer Agreement seemed remote right now. One reason was the sizeable groundwork required—Higgins simply lacked the time to review operations at the well over 100 dealers currently operating in the two cities. Another was TRP's lack of dealer-oriented sales information that went beyond the technical specification sheet for each product and the company's price list. Still another concerned two conditions in the Dealer Agreement itself—prospective dealers sometimes balked at agreeing to sell no products manufactured by TRP's competitors and differed with TRP in interpretations of the "best efforts" clause. (The clause required the dealer to maintain adequate inventories of TRP products, contact four prospective new customers of physicians or respiration therapists per month, respond promptly to sales inquiries, and represent TRP at appropriate conventions where it exhibited.)

"Still," Higgins concluded, "we signed Metro in spite of these reasons, and 21 others across the country. That's about all anyone could expect—after all, we've only been trying to develop a dealer network for a year or so."

THE PORTABLE RESPIRATOR INDUSTRY

The portable respirator industry began in the early 1950s when polio stricken patients who lacked control of muscles necessary for breathing began to leave treatment centers. They returned home with hospital-style iron lungs or fiber glass chest shells, both being large chambers that regularly introduced a vacuum about the patient's chest. The vacuum caused the chest to expand and, thus, the lungs to fill with air. However, both devices confined patients to a prone or semiprone position in a bed.

By the late 1950s, TRP had developed a portable turbine blower powered by an electric motor and battery. When connected to a mouthpiece via plastic tubing, the blower would inflate a patient's lungs on demand. Patients could now leave their beds for several hours at a time and realize limited mobility in a wheelchair. By the early 1970s, TRP had developed a line of more sophisticated turbine respirators in terms of monitoring and capability for adjustment to individual patient needs.

At about the same time, applications began to shift from polio patients to victims of other diseases or of spinal cord injuries, the latter group existing primarily as a result of automobile accidents. Better emergency medical service, quicker evacuation to spinal cord injury centers, and more proficient treatment meant that people who formerly would have died now lived and went on to lead meaningful lives. Because of patients' frequently younger ages, they strongly desired wheelchair mobility. Respiration therapists obliged by recommending a Thompson respirator for home use or, if unaware of Thompson, recommending a Puritan-Bennett or other machine.

Instead of a turbine, Puritan-Bennett machines used a bellows design to force air into the patient's lungs. The machines were widely used in hospitals but seemed poorly suited for home use. For one thing, Puritan-Bennett machines used a compressor pump or pressurized air to drive the bellows, much more cumbersome than Thompson's electric motor. Puritan-Bennett machines also cost approximately 50 percent more than a comparable Thompson unit and were relatively large and immobile. On the other hand, Puritan-Bennett machines were viewed by physicians and respiration therapists as industry standards.

By the middle 1970s, TRP had developed a piston and cylinder design (similar in principle to the bellows) and placed it on the market. The product lacked the sophistication of the Puritan-Bennett machines but was reliable, portable, and much simpler to adjust and operate. It also maintained TRP's traditional cost advantage. Another firm, Life Products, began its operations in 1976 by producing a similar design. A third competitor, Lifecare Services, had begun operations somewhat earlier.

THE COMPETITION

Puritan-Bennett

Puritan-Bennett was a large, growing, and financially sound manufacturer of respiration equipment for medical and aviation applications. Its headquarters were located in Kansas City, Missouri. However, the firm staffed over 40 sales, service, and warehouse operations in the United States, Canada, United Kingdom, and France. Sales for 1981 exceeded $100 million while employment was just over 2,000 people. Sales for its Medical Equipment Group (respirators, related equipment, and accessories, service and parts) likely exceeded $40 million for 1981; however, Higgins could obtain data only for the period 1977–1980 (see exhibit 1). Puritan-Bennett usually sold its respirators through a system of independent, durable medical equipment dealers. However, its sales offices did sell directly to identified "house accounts" and often competed with dealers by selling slower moving products to all accounts. According to industry sources, Puritan-Bennett sales were slightly more than three fourths of all respirator sales to hospitals in 1981.

However, these same sources expected Puritan-Bennett's share to diminish during the 1980s because of the aggressive marketing efforts of three other manufacturers of hospital-style respirators: Bear Medical Systems, Inc., J. H. Emerson; and Siemens-Elema. The latter firm was expected to grow the most rapidly, despite its quite recent entry into the

EXHIBIT 1
Puritan-Bennett Medical Equipment Group Sales

	1977	1978	1979	1980
Domestic sales:				
Model MA-1:				
Units	1,460	875	600	500
Amount ($ millions)	8.5	4.9	3.5	3.1
Model MA-2:				
Units	—	935	900	1,100
Amount ($ millions)	—	6.0	6.1	7.8
Foreign sales:				
Units	250	300	500	565
Amount ($ millions)	1.5	1.8	3.1	3.6
IPPB equipment ($ millions)	6.0	6.5	6.7	7.0
Parts, service, accessories				
($ millions)	10.0	11.7	13.1	13.5
Overhaul ($ millions)	2.0	3.0	2.5	2.5
Total ($ millions)	28.0	34.0	35.0	37.5

Source: The Wall Street Transcript.

EXHIBIT 2
Lifecare Services, Inc., Field Offices

Augusta, Ga.	Houston, Tex.
Baltimore, Md.	Los Angeles, Calif.
Boston, Mass.	New York, N.Y.
Chicago, Ill.	Oakland, Calif.
Cleveland, Ohio	Omaha, Nebr.
Denver, Colo.	Phoenix, Ariz.
Detroit, Mich.	Seattle, Wash.
Grand Rapids, Mich.*	St. Paul, Minn.

*Suboffice.

Source: Trade literature.

U.S. market (its headquarters were in Sweden) and a list price of over $16,000 for its basic model.

Life Products

Life Products directly competed with TRP for the portable respirator market. Life Products had begun operations in 1976 when David Smith, a TRP employee, left to start his own business. Smith had located his plant in Boulder, Colorado, less than a mile from TRP headquarters.

He began almost immediately to set up a dealer network and by early 1982 had secured over 40 independent dealers located in large metropolitan areas. Smith had made a strong effort to sign only large, well-managed durable medical equipment dealers. Dealer representatives were required to complete Life Product's service training school, held each month in Boulder. Life Products sold its products to dealers (in contrast to TRP, which both sold and rented products to consumers and to dealers). Dealers received a 20 to 25 percent discount off suggested retail price on most products.

As of April 1982, Life Products offered two respirator models (the LP3 and LP4) and a limited number of accessories (such as mouthpieces and plastic tubing) to its dealers. Suggested retail prices for the two respirator models were approximately $3,900 and $4,800. Suggested rental rates were approximately $400 and $500 per month. Life Products also allowed Lifecare Services to manufacture a respirator similar to the LP3 under license.

At the end of 1981, Smith was quite pleased with his firm's performance. During Life Products' brief history, it had passed TRP in sales and now ceased to see the firm as a serious threat, at least according to one company executive:

We really aren't in competition with Thompson. They're after the stagnant market and we're after a growing market. We see new applications and ultimately the hospital market as our niche. I doubt if Thompson will even be around in a few years. As for Lifecare, their prices are much lower than ours but you don't get the service. With them you get the basic product, but nothing else. With us, you get a complete medical care service. That's the big difference.

Lifecare Services, Inc.

In contrast to the preceding firms, Lifecare Services, Inc., earned much less of its revenues from medical equipment manufacturing and much more from medical equipment distributing. The firm primarily resold products pruchased from other manufacturers, operating out of its headquarters in Boulder as well as from its 16 field offices (exhibit 2). All offices were stocked with backup parts and an inventory of respirators. All were staffed with trained service technicians under Lifecare's employ.

Lifecare did manufacture a few accessories not readily available from other manufacturers. These items complemented the purchased products and in the company's words, served to "give the customer a complete respiratory service." Under a licensing agreement between Lifecare and Life Products, the firm manufactured a respirator similar to the LP3 and marketed it under the Lifecare name. The unit rented for approximately $175 per month. While Lifecare continued to service the few remaining Thompson units it still had in the field, it no longer carried the Thompson line.

Lifecare rented rather than sold its equipment. The firm maintained that this gave patients more flexibility in the event of recovery or death and lowered patients' monthly costs.

THOMPSON RESPIRATION PRODUCTS, INC.

TRP currently employed 13 people, 9 in production and 4 in management. It conducted operations in a modern, attractive building (leased) in an industrial park. The building contained about 6,000 square feet of space, split 75/25 for production/management purposes. Production operations were essentially job shop in nature: skilled technicians assembled each unit by hand on work benches, making frequent quality control tests and subsequent adjustments. Production lots usually ranged from 10 to 75 units per model and probably averaged around 40. Normal production capacity was about 600 units per year.

Product Line

TRP currently sold seven respirator models plus a large number of accessories. All respirator models were portable but differed considerably in terms of style, design, performance specifications, and attendant features (see exhibit 3). Four models were styled as metal boxes with an impressive array of knobs, dials, indicator lights, and switches. Three

were styled as less imposing, "overnighter" suitcases with less prominently displayed controls and indicators. (Exhibit 4 shows the metal box design of the M3000 Minilung.)

Four of the models were designed as *pressure machines,* using a turbine pump that provided a constant, usually positive, pressure. Patients were provided intermittent access to this pressure as breaths per minute. However, one model, the MV Multivent, could provide either a constant positive or a constant negative pressure (i.e., a vacuum, necessary to operate chest shells, iron lungs, and body wraps). No other portable respirator on the market could produce a negative pressure. Three of the models were designed as *volume machines,* using a piston pump that produced intermittent, constant volumes of pressurized air as breaths per minute. Actual volumes were prescribed by each patient's physician based on lung capacity. Pressures depended on the breathing method used (mouthpiece, trach, chest shell, and others) and on the patient's activity level. Breaths per minute also depended on the patient's activity level.

Models came with several features. The newest was an assist feature (currently available on the Minilung M25 but soon to be offered also on the M3000) that allowed the patient alone to "command" additional breaths without having someone change the dialed breath rate. The sigh feature gave patients a sigh, either automatically or on demand. Depending on the model, up to six alarms were available to indicate a patient's call, unacceptably low pressure, unacceptably high pressure, low battery voltage/power failure, failure to cycle, and the need to replace motor brushes. All models but the MV Multivent also offered automatic switchover from alternating current to either an internal or an external battery (or both) in the event of a power failure. Batteries provided for 18 to 40 hours of operation, depending of usage.

Higgins felt that TRP's respirators were superior to those of Life Products. Most TRP models allowed pressure monitoring in the airway itself rather than in the machine, providing more accurate measurement. TRP's suitcase style models often were strongly preferred by patients, especially the polio patients

CASE

EXHIBIT 3
TRP Respirators

Model*	Style	Design	Volume (cc)	Pressure (cm. H$_2$O)
M3000	Metal box	Volume	300–3,000	+10 to +65
MV Multivent	Metal box	Pressure (positive or negative)	n.a.	–70 to +80
Minilung M15	Suitcase	Volume	200–1,500	+5 to +65
Minilung M25 Assist (also available without the assist feature)	Suitcase	Volume	600–2,500	+5 to +65
Bantam GS	Suitcase	Pressure (positive)	n.a.	+15 to +45
Compact CS	Metal box	Pressure (positive)	n.a.	+15 to +45
Compact C	Metal box	Pressure (positive)	n.a.	+15 to +45

Model	Breaths per minute	Weight (lbs.)	Size (ft.^{3})	Features
M3000	6 to 30	39	0.85	Sigh, four alarms, automatic switchover from AC to battery
MV Multivent	8 to 24	41	1.05	Positive or negative pressure, four alarms, AC only
Minilung M15	8 to 22	24	0.70	Three alarms, automatic switchover from AC to battery
Minilung M25 Assist (also available without the assist feature)	5 to 20	24	0.70	Assist, sigh, three alarms, automatic switchover from AC to battery
Bantam GS	6 to 24	19	0.75	Sigh, six alarms, automatic switchover from AC to battery
Compact CS	8 to 24	25	0.72	Sigh, six alarms, automatic switchover from AC to battery
Compact C	6 to 24	19	0.50	Sigh, four alarms, automatic switchover from AC to battery

Note: n.a. = not applicable.

*Five other models considered obsolete by TRP could be supplied if necessary.

Source: Company sales specification sheets.

who had known no others. TRP's volume models offered easier volume adjustments and all TRP models offered more alarms. On the other hand, he knew that TRP had recently experienced some product reliability problems of an irritating—not life threatening—nature. Further, he knew that Life Products had beaten TRP to the market with the assist feature (the idea for which had come from a Puritan-Bennett machine).

TRP's line of accessories was more extensive than that of Life Products. TRP offered the following for separate sale: alarms, call switches, battery cables, chest shells, mouthpieces, plastic tubing, pneumobelts and bladders (equipment for still another breathing method that utilized intermittent pressure on a patient's diaphragm), and other items. Lifecare Services offered many similar items.

EXHIBIT 4
The M3000 Minilung

EXHIBIT 5
TRP Dealer Locations

Bakersfield, Calif.	Salt Lake City, Utah
Baltimore, Md.	San Diego, Calif.
Birmingham, Ala.	San Francisco, Calif.
Chicago, Ill.	Seattle, Wash.
Cleveland, Ohio	Springfield, Ohio
Fort Wayne, Ind.	Tampa, Fla.
Greenville, N.C.	Tucson, Ariz.
Indianapolis, Ind.	Washington, D.C.
Newark, N.J.	
Oklahoma City, Okla.	Montreal, Canada
Pittsburgh, Pa.	Toronto, Canada

Source: Company records.

Distribution

Shortly after joining TRP, Higgins had decided to switch from selling and renting products directly to patients to selling and renting products to dealers. While it meant lower margins, less control, and more infrequent communication with patients, the change had several advantages. It allowed TRP to shift inventory from the factory to the dealer, generating cash more quickly. It provided for local representation in market areas, allowing patients greater feelings of security and TRP more aggressive sales efforts. It shifted burdensome paperwork (required by insurance companies and state and federal agencies to effect payment) from TRP to the dealer. It also reduced other TRP administrative activities in accounting, customer relations, and sales.

TRP derived about half of its 1981 revenue of $3 million directly from patients and about half from the dealer network. By April 1982, the firm had 22 dealers (see exhibit 5) with three accounting for over 60 percent of TRP dealer revenues. Two of the three serviced TRP products, as did two of the smaller dealers; the rest preferred to let the factory take care of repairs. TRP conducted occasional training sessions for dealer repair personnel but distances were great and turnover in the position high, making such sessions costly. Most dealers requested air shipment of respirators, in quantities of 1 or 2 units.

Price

TRP maintained a comprehensive price list for its entire product line. (Exhibit 6 reproduces part of the current list.) Each respirator model carried both a suggested retail selling price and a suggested retail rental rate. (TRP also applied these rates when it dealt directly with patients.) The list also presented two net purchase prices for each model along with an alternative rental rate that TRP charged to dealers. About 40 percent of the 300 respirator units TRP shipped to dealers in 1981 went out on a rental basis. The comparable figure for the 165 units sent directly to consumers was 90 percent. Net purchase prices allowed an approximate 7 percent discount for orders of three or more units of each model. Higgins had initiated this policy early last year with the aim of encouraging dealers to order in larger quantities. To date, one dealer had taken advantage of this discount.

Current policy called for TRP to earn a gross margin of approximately 35 percent on the dealer price for 1–2 units. All prices included shipping charges by United Parcel Service (UPS); purchasers requesting more expensive transportation service paid the difference between actual costs incurred and the UPS charge. Terms were net 30 days with a 1.5 percent service charge added to past due accounts. Prices were last changed in late 1981.

EXHIBIT 6
Current TRP Respirator Price List

| | Suggested retail | | Dealer price | | |
Model	Rent/month	Price	Rent/month	1–2	3 or more
M3000	$380	$6,000	$290	$4,500	$4,185
MV Multivent	270	4,300	210	3,225	3,000
Minilung M15	250	3,950	190	2,960	2,750
Minilung M25	250	3,950	190	2,960	2,750
Bantam GS	230	3,600	175	2,700	2,510
Compact CG	230	3,600	175	2,700	2,510
Compact C	200	3,150	155	2,360	2,195

Source: Company sales specification sheets.

CONSUMERS

Two types of patients used respirators, depending on whether the need followed from disease or from injury. Diseases such as polio, sleep apnea, chronic obstructive pulmonary disease, and muscular dystrophy annually left about 1,900 victims unable to breathe without a respirator. Injury to the spinal cord above the fifth vertebra caused a similar result for about 300 people per year. Except for polio, incidences of the diseases and injury were growing at about 3 percent per year. Most patients kept one respirator at bedside and another mounted on a wheelchair. However, Higgins did know of one individual who kept eight Bantam B models (provided by a local polio foundation, now defunct) in his closet. Except for polio patients, life expectancies were about five years. Higgins estimated the total number of patients using a home respirator in 1981 at 3,000 for polio, 6,500 for other diseases, and 1,000 for spinal cord injuries.

Almost all patients were under a physician's care as well as that of a more immediate nurse or attendant (frequently a relative). About 95 percent paid for their equipment through insurance benefits or foundation monies. About 90 percent rented their equipment. Almost all patients and their nurses or attendants had received instruction in equipment operation from respiration therapists employed by medical centers or by dealers of durable medical equipment.

The majority of patients were poor. Virtually none were gainfully employed and all had seen their savings and other assets diminished to varying degrees by treatment costs. Some had experienced a divorce. Slightly more patients were male than female. About 75 percent lived in their homes with the rest split between hospitals, nursing homes, and other institutions.

Apart from patients, Higgins thought that hospitals might be considered a logical new market for TRP to enter. Many of the larger and some of the smaller general hospitals might be convinced to purchase one portable respirator (like the M3000) for emergency and other use with injury patients. Such a machine would be much cheaper to purchase than a large Puritan-Bennett and would allow easier patient trips to testing areas, X-ray, surgery, and the like. Even easier to convince should be the fourteen regional spinal cord injury centers located across the country (exhibit 7). Other medical centers that specialized in treatment of pulmonary diseases should also be prime targets. Somewhat less promising but more numerous would be public and private schools that trained physicians and respiration therapists. Higgins had estimated the numbers at these institutions (see exhibit 8).

DEALERS

Dealers supplying homecare medical products (as distinct from dealers supplying hospitals and medical

<table>
<tr><td colspan="2">

EXHIBIT 7
Regional Spinal Cord Injury Centers

</td></tr>
</table>

Birmingham Ala.	Houston, Tex.
Boston, Mass.	Miami, Fla.
Chicago, Ill.	New York, N.Y.
Columbia, Mo.	Philadelphia, Pa.
Downey, Calif.	Phoenix, Ariz.
Englewood, Colo.	San Jose, Calif.
Fishersville, Va.	Seattle, Wash.

EXHIBIT 8
Potential Respirator Purchases

General hospitals (100 beds or more)	3,800
General hospitals (fewer than 100 beds)	3,200
Spinal cord injury centers	14
Pulmonary disease treatment centers	100
Medical schools	180
Respiration therapy schools	250

centers) showed a great deal of diversity. Some were little more than small areas in local drugstores that rented canes, walkers, and wheelchairs in addition to selling supplies like surgical stockings and colostomy bags. Others carried nearly everything needed for home nursing care—renting everything from canes to hospital beds and selling supplies from bed pads to bottled oxygen. Still others specialized in products and supplies for only certain types of patients.

In this last category, Higgins had identified dealers of oxygen and oxygen-related equipment as the best fit among existing dealers. These dealers serviced victims of emphysema, bronchitis, asthma, and other respiratory ailments, a growing market that Higgins estimated was about 10 times greater than that for respirators. A typical dealer had begun perhaps 10 years ago selling bottled oxygen (obtained from a welding supply wholesaler) and renting rather crude metering equipment to patients at home under the care of a registered nurse. The same dealer today now rented and serviced oxygen concentrators (a recently developed device that extracts oxygen from the air), liquid oxygen equipment and liquid oxygen, and much more sophisticated oxygen equipment and oxygen to patients cared for by themselves or by relatives.

Most dealers maintained a fleet of radio dispatched trucks to deliver products to their customers. Better dealers promised 24 hour service and kept delivery personnel and a respiration therapist on call 24 hours a day. Dealers usually employed several respiration therapists who would set up equipment, instruct patients and attendants on equipment operation, and provide routine and emergency service. Dealers often expected the therapists to function as a sales force. The therapists would call on physicians and other

respiration therapists at hospitals and medical centers, on discharge planners at hospitals, and on organizations such as muscular dystrophy associations, spinal cord injury associations, and visiting nurse associations.

Dealers usually bought their inventories of durable equipment and supplies directly from manufacturers. They usually received a 20 to 25 percent discount off suggested list prices to consumers and hospitals. Only in rare instances might dealers instead lease equipment from a manufacturer. Dealers aimed for a payback of one year or less, meaning that most products began to contribute to profit and overhead after 12 months of rental. Most products lasted physically for upwards of 10 years but technologically for only 5 to 6: every dealer's warehouse contained idle but perfectly suitable equipment that had been superseded by models demanded by patients, their physicians, or their attendants.

Most dealers were independently owned and operated, with annual sales ranging between $5 million and $10 million. However, a number had recently been acquired by one of several parent organizations that were regional or national in scope. Such chains usually consisted of from 10 to 30 retail operations located in separated market areas. However, the largest, Abbey Medical, had begun operations in 1924 and now consisted of over 70 local dealers. Higgins estimated 1981 sales for the chain (which was itself acquired by American Hospital Supply Corporation in April 1981) at over $60 million. In general, chains maintained a low corporate visibility and provided their dealers with working capital, employee benefit programs, operating advice, and some centralized purchasing. Higgins thought that chain organizations might grow more rapidly over the next 10 years.

THE ISSUES

Higgins looked at his watch. It was 5:30 and really time to leave. "Still," he thought, "I should jot down what I see to be the immediate issues before I go—that way I won't be tempted to think about them over the weekend." He took a pen and wrote the following:

1. Should TRP continue to rent respirators to dealers?
2. Should TRP protect each dealer's territory (and how big should a territory be)?
3. Should TRP require dealers to stock no competing equipment?
4. How many dealers should TRP eventually have? Where?
5. What sales information should be assembled in order to attract high quality dealers?
6. What should be done about the "best efforts" clause?

As he reread the list, Higgins considered that there probably were still other short-term-oriented questions he might have missed. Monday would be soon enough to consider them all.

Until then he was free to think about broader, more strategic issues. Some reflections on the nature of the target market, a statement of marketing objectives, and TRP's possible entry into the hospital market would occupy the weekend. Decisions on these topics would form a substantial part of TRP's strategic marketing plan, a document Higgins hoped to have for the beginning of the next fiscal year in July. "At least I can rule out one option," Higgins thought as he put on his coat. That was an idea to use independent sales representatives to sell TRP products on commission: a recently completed two-month search for such an organization had come up empty. "Like my stomach," he thought, as he went out the door.

ALASKA NATIVE ARTS AND CRAFTS COOPERATIVE, INC.

The artistry of Alaska natives grew out of a spontaneous urge which embraced many motives, none of which were monetary. The pre-European Alaskan native indulged his creative prowess in embellishments of his person, in recording the details of his unique and colorful culture, and in the symbolic expression of his religion. It didn't occur to these people to create such beauty to be sold. The marketing of native crafts before the advent of the

white man simply did not exist, as the native had no conception of payment for his art.

Because of the obvious and unavoidable impact of modern society upon the traditional native culture, the need of at least a minimal cash flow has become vital to the basic survival of these people. A man must have money for his snow machine or outboard motor in order to engage in subsistence hunting and fishing and money for oil to heat his home. Many rural natives who move to Alaska's urban communities lack the education and skills to adapt to a new life style. There is infrequent employment for those who seek to live in the isolated areas of their heritage; consequently, they have discovered that an important source of income is the sale of artistic creations and handcrafted items.

The survival of the Alaska Native Arts and Crafts Cooperative, the organization established over forty years ago to market the creative expression of the aboriginal population of Alaska, has been threatened by an operating deficit. Such important issues as the preservation of a magnificent but imperiled art form

This case was prepared by Professor G. Hayden Green of the University of Alaska and Professor Walter Greene, University of North Dakota.

versus the uplifting of a destitute and forgotten race are at stake in the formulation of the future of the Alaska firm.

BACKGROUND OF ALASKAN NATIVES

Throughout northwest Alaska and parts of Canada resides a large aboriginal population which includes numerous tribes of Indians, Eskimos, and Aleuts, referred to vernacularly as *natives*. These people have for generations endured some of the world's harshest climatic conditions. Many native inhabitants of the north still retain a relatively traditional subsistence life-style with hunting and fishing being the mainstay of their livelihood. The Bureau of Indian Affairs (BIA), federal and state agencies, and native leaders have, since the turn of the century, tried to reduce dependence of the natives upon seasonality and volatility of caribou migrations, salmon runs, mammal harvesting, and the public welfare system. This has proven to be no easy task.

Many of the northern villages are hundreds of miles from each other and as much as eight hundred miles from Anchorage, the state's major population center. The harbors are often frozen eight to nine months out of the year; and only the larger communities receive commercial air transportation, which is sporadic at best. The general level of education in many villages does not exceed that of grammar school, and housing conditions are some of the worst in the United States. Most of the smaller communities and even some of the larger communities do not have public sewers or water systems. These living conditions are compounded by winter temperatures of 50° to 60° below zero, and the sun only shines three to six months out of the year. Yet the Alaskan native holds fast to a life-style which has been traditional since man first crossed the land bridge from Asia (see exhibit 1).

BACKGROUND OF NATIVE ARTS AND CRAFTS

One of the areas upon which concerned groups have placed much hope for shifting total dependence on

subsistence living to a partial cash economy has been the development of the arts and crafts trade. These arts and crafts include ivory carving, basketry, skin sewing, dolls, and other traditional items. These products are not to be confused with curios and mass-produced knickknacks from Japan and Korea (marketed as cheap imitations), but are works of art, with an individuality of creativity and time-consuming detail that is reflected in their costliness as well as their quality (see exhibit 2).

HISTORY OF ARTS AND CRAFTS MARKETING

In the past, the purchasing of native crafts was done in a very casual manner. The common ways of selling work were through the local store manager (who would give, if not cash, food and trade goods in return) or through the local BIA teacher, or through bush pilots or local missionaries, or finally, through the seasonal tourists and professional trader-buyers. This marketing pattern was unsatisfactory for the craft people. Even today, professional traders seldom visit a particular village more frequently than once a month.

In 1936 a clearinghouse for native arts and crafts was formed under the sponsorship of the Bureau of Indian Affairs. The intent of the clearinghouse was to establish a marketing mechanism and maintain a central inventory of native arts and crafts. Juneau, the state capital, located in the southwestern part of Alaska and approximately 800 to 1000 miles south of some of these villages, was selected as the headquarters. It was chosen mainly for its port, which was on the regular run of the North Star, a ship that was the major source of transport in Alaska in those years. Articles were sent to Juneau on consignment, warehoused, and later marketed in retail and military stores throughout Alaska. This was an earnest attempt to resolve the natives' plight, but, as a whole, the program proved ineffective.

In 1956 the BIA reorganized the original clearinghouse and established a private, nonprofit cooperative, the Alaska Native Arts and Crafts Cooperative. The payment and marketing policy of the new organization remained the same as the original

EXHIBIT 1
Location of Principal Alaskan Native Groups

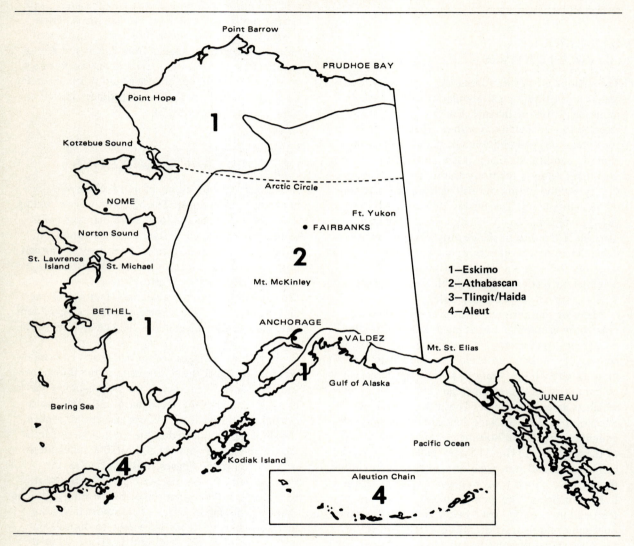

1—Eskimo
2—Athabascan
3—Tlingit/Haida
4—Aleut

establishment. ANAC was not truly serving in a marketing capacity, although this was to be one of its more vital functions when the organization was initiated. Instead, it continued to serve as a sort of clearinghouse for the crafts.

The managers of ANAC were not well-grounded in exactly what marketing is, as funds were not used for advertising or promotional activities. Indeed, when business became poor and funds short, the books show that expenditures for advertising and travel were cut. Although ANAC was another step forward in straightening out the crafts cash system, it was far from being a successful organization.

EXHIBIT 2
Samples of Craft Work

(continued on next page)

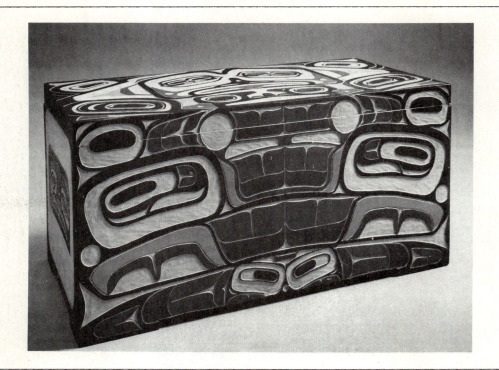

OPERATING HISTORY

In the first year of operation in 1936, ANAC's sales were $29,000. In 1938, the financial figure showed sales at $30,000. For the fiscal year 1939, the value of native arts and crafts rose to $98,000 and thereafter enjoyed a phenomenal rise until the mid-1940s. In part this was due to contracts with the U.S. Antarctic Expedition made in 1939 and 1940, and a number of contracts with the U.S. Army for the sewing of fur garments.

Annual reports give the peak value of native arts and crafts as $485,641 during the fiscal year 1945. Immediately thereafter there was a dramatic drop in the reported value of sales to a low of $101,133.43 in fiscal year 1946. This was attributed to the decline of military personnel in Alaska from a high of 152,000 to a low of only 19,000 in 1946.

During the mid-1950s and the 1960s, ANAC sales declined, inventories increased, and profits declined accordingly, a trend which continued through the 70s (see exhibit 3).

THE CONTROVERSY

During this more than forty-year period, Alaska was rampant with different groups who advocated multiple approaches to marketing the arts and crafts of the native population. Their divergent views compounded an already complex situation. Most of them were quite vociferous about their viewpoints. This field of battle had an inhibiting effect upon any spirit of conciliation and rapport. Understandably, little real communication has been established among these groups, since their primary concerns were their respective "causes."

EXHIBIT 3
Alaska Native Arts and Crafts Cooperative, Inc.
(Wholesale)

	Total Net Sales	Cost of Sales	Gross Profit	Operating & Selling Expenses	Net Operating Profit (Loss)	Total Other Income Expense	Net Profit & Losses
Representative Year 1970s	$133,800.59	$ 89,346.07	$44,454.52	$58,943.63	($14,489.11)	($7,029.71)	($21,518.82)
Representative Year 1960s	$130,395.23	$ 84,015.70	$46,379.53	$52,268.95	($ 5,889.42)	($7,960.71)	($13,850.13)
Representative Year 1950s	$181,799.49	$129,669.73	$52,129.76	$46,696.66	$ 5,433.10	$ 272.87	$ 5,705.97

There was one faction whose overriding aim was the preservation of native arts at all costs. These people felt that the real value of native art lay in the creation of superior objects by a few talented individuals. They esteemed these objects of art as potential museum pieces and deplored the intemperate production of pieces of lesser quality as a corruptive force within the creative community. The proponents of this viewpoint turned a deaf ear to the social injustice group who propounded that the ultimate issue here was the economic betterment of the native groups and that the preservation of the art as an issue was "low man on the totem pole." This group supported the community instituting a regular production-line facility for turning out commercialized versions of native crafts for the tourist trade.

There existed another element composed of a large percentage of politically active natives whose only concern seemed to be that, whatever the program instituted, it should be completely administered by natives. It is no mystery that these people frequently came into direct conflict with that group which advocated the hiring of qualified outside administrative leadership as the most efficient way of getting things done.

The question whether or not the native people even wanted an organization for marketing their goods looms ominously in the background. The answer to this question has not always been in the obvious positive vein that is expected. Some of the leading craftsmen themselves have expressed doubt in this regard.

THE NEW GENERAL MANAGER

This then was the situation when Henry Tiffany III was drafted by the board of directors of ANAC to serve as general manager of the firm and to implement some organizational changes in order to make it more responsive to the needs of Alaskan natives. Henry Tiffany came to Alaska from New York when he was in his early twenties and experienced success in construction and real estate investments. Through repeated association, due to the mobility demanded of him by his enterprises, he became sensitive to the social and environmental difficulties unique to the Alaskan natives. This concern, as well as a natural appreciation of fine crafts and a desire to see the art form preserved, led him to accept the position as general manager of ANAC. In accepting this post he stipulated that ANAC would sever its connection with the Bureau of Indian Affairs, a condition with which the federal agency concurred.

EXPANSION OF ANAC

After three months of research in the development of a long-range organizational plan, the directors met with the new general manager who presented to them the following proposal: ANAC would open and operate a retail outlet in Anchorage across the street from Alaska's largest hotel. The new retail outlet would include a showroom for direct sales to the public, and approximately half of the 2,000-square-foot store was set aside for craft demonstrations by the artists for the public.

At that time it was also decided that the policy of ANAC would be to encourage the creation of arts and crafts which aspired to the quality sought after by museums and exclusive art stores, and it would discourage the poorer quality of work or mass production of existing designs. Tiffany also proposed that ANAC would become involved in the training of its members and sponsoring of conferences, and in promotion to the public, in order to advance Alaskan crafts to acceptance as an art form.

With the approval of the board of directors, Henry Tiffany embarked on the program of expansion; and, in the ensuing months, he developed a cooperative relationship with over 120 villages statewide; and the buyer network was established in 12 of these villages. He moved the Juneau retail operation from the back of an old building to the Juneau retail center near the ferry system and the tourist trade. To accommodate the wholesale business, a loan was obtained for a 4,000-square-foot warehouse erected near the Anchorage Municipal Airport, at which time the wholesale operation was moved from Juneau to the new facilities.

The new general manager introduced the mechanics of a rebate system to reward craftsmen for superior work, whereby the buyers used a quadruplicate invoice upon which the buyer's and craftsman's names were recorded plus the item purchased. Where products sold for a higher price due to superior craftsmanship, the craftsman received a quality rebate. A system for providing craft supplies through the native stores was also introduced by Mr. Tiffany. In essence, ANAC was to provide a supply of craft materials to each village store on consignment in each village that contained an ANAC buyer. Between $300 and $500 was needed to supply the minimum requirements of each village.

The final and most critical element of the new program was the establishment of cash buyers in each of the craft-producing villages. The success of the rebate system and the craft supply system both hinged on having a good buyers' network. To establish such a network, it was proposed that an ANAC representative would visit each village to study the needs of the craftsman, establish a working relationship with the local governing council, study the community's social and economic base, and interview candidates who were interested in serving as ANAC buyers. The selection and existence of a buyer was completely voluntary and was determined by the local community leaders. It was agreed that most buyers would receive somewhere between 10 and 20 percent of the value of the items purchased. Each buyer was funded with cash ranging from between $200 and $1,500, to begin the purchases.

In addition to the expansion program, Tiffany undertook a personal campaign to educate the public in native arts and crafts—his goal ultimately being the preservation of the arts and the halting of imports and poor quality craftsmanship.

DEFICITS INCREASE AT ACCELERATED RATE

After several months of operation, deficits amassing and considerable creditor pressure ensuing, Henry Tiffany wrote the following memo to the ANAC board of directors.

During our expansionary period, operating deficits have continued to mount at an accelerated rate [see exhibits 4 and 5]. A major contributing force in this state of affairs is the buyer system. The system is operating at minimal efficiency due to multiple reasons. Many native buyers entered the program handicapped by both educational and cultural inadequacies. Many did not understand the record keeping system; consequently they are often unable to account for funds either by their presence or absence. Quality is often overlooked in the subjective viewpoint of the buyers, who are not capable of discerning the very best work from those pieces of less worth. Also, as a result of their cultural heritage, nepotism often sets in, which further adds to the problem of second-best material being occasionally purchased for top dollars.

Another contributing factor to the monetary deficits is that retail sales in the Anchorage store are not meeting sales objectives and projections. Although the Anchorage retail outlet is in a high foot-traffic district of Anchorage and located across from the state's largest hotel, its sales are

EXHIBIT 4
Alaska Native Arts & Crafts, Cooperative
Current Financial Statement
Retail Operation

ASSETS:

Current Assets			
Cash		$ 3,341.89	
Credit Cards & Layaways		525.68	
Accounts Receivable	$3,816.21		
Less RS. B/D	(1,166.58)	3,002.74	
Total		$ 6,870.31	
Inventories (See Schedule A)			
Arts & Crafts, Juneau		$ 27,449.80	
Craft Supplies, Juneau		1,332.75	
Arts & Crafts, Anchorage		32,310.55	
General Supplies		2,146.89	
Collection		26,195.80	
Total Inventories		$ 89,435.79	
Total Current Assets			$ 96,306.10
Other Assets			
Prepaid Expense		$ 2,319.85	
Clearing Account*		4,994.68	
Fixed Assets		18,531.57	
Deposits		50.00	
Investments		30,000.00	
Total Other Assets			$ 55,896.10
TOTAL ASSETS			$152,202.20

LIABILITIES AND CAPITAL:

Current Liabilities		$114,539.49	
Long-Term Liabilities		195,346.75	
Total Liabilities			$309,886.24
Membership Fees		$ 926.00	
Retained Earnings		(93,591.73)	
Loss From Operation (See Schedule C)		(65,018.31)	
Fees & Retained Earnings (Deficit)			($157,684.04)
TOTAL LIABILITIES AND CAPITAL			$152,202.20

*Includes Credit Card Discounts

disappointing. The problem is caused in part by the fact that the store has poor window visibility and gives the impression of being more of a museum than a retail business. Consequently, I recommend we move the store to a different section of Anchorage's downtown area—one more closely associated with the native community.

Figuring largely in the failure of the expansion program coming to fruition is the evolution of a conflict arising from the very system which it

EXHIBIT 5
Alaska Native Arts & Crafts, Cooperative
Current Financial Statement
Schedule C, Income vs. Expense
(Income Statement)

	Juneau To Date	Anchorage To Date
Sales, Arts & Crafts	$57,105.32	$91,840.56
Sales, Craft Supplies	2,319.22	
Repair Income	20.60	
Misc. Income	75.60	1,502.86
Returns & Allowance	(193.58)	(450.00)
Sales Discounts*	(2,428.60)	(1,621.00)
Sales Commission	(344.66)	(20.00)
Postage	—	68.00
Net Sales	$56,553.90	$91,320.42
Inventory Cost	(40,108.88)	(64,676.45)
Gross Profit	$16,445.02	$26,643.97
Expenses	48,264.60	59,842.10
Net Loss	($31,889.58)	($33,198.13)

*Includes Credit Card Discounts

doomed. The structure of ANAC is such that a larger volume of trade is essential to support the overhead incurred by the new warehouse and the two retail outlets. It has become apparent that enough quality artwork is not available to meet the sales volume needed to support such a system.

Consequently, and contrary to the ANAC marketing philosophy, inferior work would have to be purchased to infuse the operation with the cash flow necessary to its survival. I recommend we begin to nullify the policy of expansion and initiate the mechanics of contracting ANAC's exploratory tentacles of growth into a more compact and refined body of endeavor, the aims of which are more consistent with our original goals.

In an attempt to reverse the increasing deficit position, we should sell the Juneau retail store and move the merchandise in the wholesale warehouse to the Anchorage retail establishment and sell the warehouse. The warehouse should bring a price of $185,000, which will pay off the mortgage on it. A new buyer system must also be instituted.

The financial losses incurred by the firm are of a critical nature and immediate steps must be instituted to reverse the trend. However, we should not be discouraged, as ANAC is a very successful enterprise. In the early years of the formation of ANAC, our artists made, at best, a nominal wage. Today, a few artists earn a wage comparable to high-paying white-collar jobs in Anchorage, Alaska. A couple of artists have gained such national prominence that they have almost outgrown ANAC and are being courted by patrons of museums and establishments which exhibit the finest examples of American art.

Promotional Strategies

The development of an effective promotional program is vital to every organization. Having the right product at the right place with the right price will not result in a transaction unless the target market is made aware of the offer. The role of promotion is to make the target audience aware of the offer of an organization's products, services, or ideas, and to influence them to accept the offer.

PROMOTIONAL OBJECTIVES

The response sought from the target market is adoption of the organization's product. Before pursuing this objective, however, consideration must be given to the steps involved in the adoption process. The AIDA model and the "hierarchy-of-effects" model show buyers passing through several distinct stages before reaching the adoption stage.

The AIDA model shows four stages: *awareness, interest, desire,* and *action.* The "hierarchy-of-effects" model shows the buyer passing through *awareness, knowledge, liking, preference, conviction,* and *purchase.* These and other response hierarchy models show that the communicator must determine which stage his audience has already reached before he decides what and how to communicate. A promotional campaign needs to be developed that moves them to the next stage.

In the article, "A Model for Predictive Measurement of Advertising Effectiveness," Robert J. Lavidge and Gary A. Steiner show how advertising moves people up the six steps of the hierarchy-of-effects model. The authors stress that measurements of the effectiveness of advertising should provide measurements of changes at all levels of these steps, not only at purchase.

PROMOTIONAL MIX

The promotional mix consists of the communication tools that are used to move customers through the adoption process. The four major tools are advertising, sales promotion, publicity, and personal selling. Advertising consists of any form of paid, nonpersonal communication. Sales promotion consists of short-term incentives to encourage trial and purchase of a product or service. Publicity, like advertising, is a form of nonpersonal communication. Unlike advertising, it is not paid for by the sponsor. Personal selling is the process of informing prospective purchasers through personal communication.

Unfortunately, there is no single mix of promotional tools that will fit every product, service, or idea. As a consequence, several factors must be considered in developing a promotional strategy, including:

1. *Characteristics of the target market.* The number, geographic location, and type of customer (such as household vs. industrial), as well as the customer's stage in the adoption process, all influence the choice of promotional tools. Consumer goods companies devote most of their promotional funds to advertising, followed by sales

promotion, personal selling, and publicity. Industrial goods companies channel most of their funds to personal selling, followed by sales promotion, advertising, and publicity.

2. *The promotional budget.*   The size of an organization's promotional resources affects its preference in promotional tools. National and regional advertising and sales promotion are expensive. Even in local markets advertising rates for certain media may be beyond reach of organizations with limited budgets, so that more reliance is placed on publicity and word-of-mouth communication.

3. *The product's life cycle.*   Advertising has traditionally been the most important promotional method for consumer goods, while personal selling is typically the major promotional tool used in marketing industrial products and services. The adoption process provides the underlying rationale of the product life cycle. The effectiveness of specific promotional tools will vary depending on where the target market is in the adoption process, and this can depend on where the product is in its life cycle. For example, advertising and publicity are relied on heavily to bring about consumer awareness and knowledge—likely to be most significant in the first two stages of a product's life cycle—whereas sales promotion tools often play a significant role in the third stage of the cycle when lower cost methods of promotion are desired.

4. *The distribution strategy.*   The willingness of middlemen to participate in promotional activities can influence the relative emphasis placed on the various promotional tools, especially in deciding whether a company uses a "push" or "pull" strategy to create sales. A "push" strategy uses personal selling and trade incentives (price discounts, display allowances, sales contests) to convince middlemen that it is advantageous to carry a particular product. Personal selling and trade promotion are used to "push" the product through the distribution channel. A "pull" strategy calls for spending more of the promotional budget on advertising and sales promotion to build up consumer demand.

5. *Additional factors.*   Other factors which influence the promotional mix include the promotional strategies of competitors, availability of communication channels (personal and nonpersonal), and government regulations.

PROMOTIONAL BUDGET

Determining the size of the promotional budget is one of the most difficult aspects of the promotional strategy. "How much to spend?" is the question that has historically troubled organizations.

In the article, "Does Advertising Belong in the Capital Budget?", Joel Dean presents the economic case for an investment approach to the promotional budget. He addresses the question of whether advertising should be budgeted as an expense or as an investment. Dean notes that viewing promotion as an investment could bring dramatic changes in the decision-making, market-testing, measurements of effectiveness, and value judgments that are required to determine how much to spend on promotion.

Most organizations decide how much to spend on promotion by one of the following methods:

1. the "all you can afford" method;
2. the percentage-of-sales method;
3. the competitive parity method;
4. the objective-and-task method.

Using the "affordable" method, the promotional budget is established as a predetermined share of available financial resources. From the standpoint of effective marketing, this method is not sound because no correlation is made between available funds and promotional opportunities. The method may result in either spending too much or too little.

Setting the promotional budget based on a percentage of sales is a common method. A predetermined percentage of sales is used to determine the budget. While this method is very popular, especially among retailers, it leads to an appropriation that may not be based on promotional opportunities.

The competitive parity method, often used in conjunction with the percentage-of-sales method, is primarily based on the promotional outlays of competitors or other members of the industry. This method is questionable at best. It implies that competitors know what they are doing and that they have similar promotional objectives.

The objective-and-task method requires that an organization develop the promotional budget by deciding its specific promotional objectives, determining what tasks need to be accomplished, and then estimating the costs of performing the tasks. A major advantage of this method is that it forces management to consider what the promotional strategy should accomplish. Furthermore, specific objectives allow for measurement of promotional effectiveness. (See Lavidge and Steiner's article, "A Model For Predictive Measurement of Advertising Effectiveness.")

ADVERTISING STRATEGY

In general, an advertising strategy consists of the following steps:

1. Setting the advertising objectives—
   What are the communication objectives?
   (to inform, persuade, or remind?)
   What are the sales objectives?
2. Setting the advertising budget
3. Deciding on the message
4. Selecting the media—
   What should be the coverage?
   (number of potential customers reached)
   What should be the frequency?
   (number of times the message is transmitted)
5. Measuring the campaign's effectiveness.

SALES PROMOTION STRATEGY

The major decisions in determining a sales promotion strategy include:

1. Establishing objectives—
   Is it the objective to have an impact on consumers?
   Is it the objective to have an impact on channel members?
   Is it the objective to have an impact on the sales force?
2. Selecting the sales promotion tools—
   Coupons? Cents-off offers? Samples? Refunds? Games?
   Trade allowances? Display allowances? Cooperative allowances?
   Demonstrations? Point-of-purchase displays? Trade shows? Contests?
3. Developing the sales program—
   Conditions for participation
   Duration and timing of program
   Size of incentives
   Total sales promotion budget
4. Evaluating results

SELLING

Personal selling is one of the most ubiquitous and frequently used components of the promotional mix and usually accounts for the largest percentage of the promotional budget. It consists of personal communication and is therefore more flexible than advertising or sales promotion methods. Its major disadvantage is the cost of salaries, commission, and travel expenses.

In the article, "Comparison of Advertising and Selling," Harold C. Cash and W. J. E. Crissy discuss the similarities and differences between advertising and selling in terms of communication, perception, thought-processes, feelings, and degree of control. The authors provide specific suggestions for effective use of advertising by salespeople, as well as ways and means salespeople can employ to apprise management of the impact of the company's advertising efforts and ways of improving them.

The activities involved in the selling process vary among salespeople and different sales situations. However, many salespeople move through the following seven steps as they sell products:

1. Prospecting and qualifying
   (developing sales leads from various sources)
2. Pre-approach
   (gaining familiarity with the organization and those involved in buying)
3. Approach
   (making initial contact with the prospect)
4. Sales presentation
   (presenting information to arouse desire)
5. Handling objections
   (understanding reasons for objections and handling them effectively)
6. Closing the sale
   (getting the order)
7. Postsale followup
   (reinforcing customer's satisfaction in the seller)

To manage the sales force effectively, a number of decisions and activities are called for, including:

1. Establishing objectives for the sales force
2. Determining the size of the sales force
3. Recruiting and selecting qualified salespeople
4. Training the sales force
5. Motivating and compensating the sales force
6. Creating sales territories
7. Routing and scheduling salespeople
8. Supervising the sales force
9. Evaluating performance

Robert J. Lavidge and Gary A. Steiner

A Model for Predictive Measurements of Advertising Effectiveness

What are the functions of advertising? Obviously the ultimate function is to help produce sales. But all advertising is not, should not, and cannot be designed to produce immediate purchases on the part of all who are exposed to it. *Immediate* sales results (even if measurable) are, at best, an incomplete criterion of advertising effectiveness.

In other words, the effects of much advertising are "long-term." This is sometimes taken to imply that all one can really do is wait and see—ultimately the campaign will or will not produce.

However, if something is to happen in the long run, *something* must be happening in the short run, something that will ultimately lead to eventual sales results. And this process must be measured in order to provide anything approaching a comprehensive evaluation of the effectiveness of the advertising.

Ultimate consumers normally do not switch from disinterested individuals to convinced purchasers in one instantaneous step. Rather, they approach the ultimate purchase through a process or series of steps in which the actual purchase is but the final threshold.

Seven Steps

Advertising may be thought of as a force, which must move people up a series of steps:

1. Near the bottom of the steps stand potential purchasers who are completely *unaware of the existence* of the product or service in question.
2. Closer to purchasing, but still a long way from the cash register, are those who are merely *aware of its existence.*

Source: From the *Journal of Marketing,* Vol. 25, No. 6 (October 1961), pp. 59–62. Reprinted by permission of the American Marketing Association.

3. Up a step are prospects who *know what the product has to offer.*
4. Still closer to purchasing are those who have favorable attitudes toward the product—those who *like the product.*
5. Those whose favorable attitudes have developed to the point of *preference* over all other possibilities are up still another step.
6. Even closer to purchasing are consumers who couple preference with a desire to buy and the *conviction* that the purchase would be wise.
7. Finally, of course, is the step which translates this attitude into actual *purchase.*

Research to evaluate the effectiveness of advertisements can be designed to provide measures of movement on such a flight of steps.

The various steps are not necessarily equidistant. In some instances the "distance" from awareness to preference may be very slight, while the distance from preference to purchase is extremely large. In other cases, the reverse may be true. Furthermore, a potential purchaser sometimes may move up several steps simultaneously.

Consider the following hypotheses. The greater the psychological and/or economic commitment involved in the purchase of a particular product, the longer it will take to bring consumers up these steps, and the more important the individual steps will be. Contrariwise, the less serious the commitment, the more likely it is that some consumers will go almost "immediately" to the top of the steps.

An impulse purchase might be consummated with no previous awareness, knowledge, liking, or conviction with respect to the product. On the other hand, an industrial good or an important consumer product ordinarily will not be purchased in such a manner.

Different Objectives

Products differ markedly in terms of the role of advertising as related to the various positions on the steps. A great deal of advertising is designed to move people up the final steps toward purchase. At an extreme is the "Buy Now" ad, designed to stimulate immediate overt action. Contrast this with industrial advertising, much of which is not intended to stimulate immediate purchase in and of itself. Instead, it is designed to help pave the way for the salesman by making the prospects aware of his company and products, thus giving them knowledge and favorable attitudes about the ways in which those products or services might be of value. This, of course, involves movement up the lower and intermediate steps.

Even within a particular product category, or with a specific product, different advertisements or campaigns may be aimed primarily at different steps in the purchase process—and rightly so. For example, advertising for new automobiles is likely to place considerable emphasis on the lower steps when new models are first brought out. The advertiser recognizes that his first job is to make the potential customer aware of the new product, and to give him knowledge and favorable attitudes about the product. As the year progresses, advertising emphasis tends to move up the steps. Finally, at the end of the "model year" much emphasis is placed on the final step—the attempt to stimulate immediate purchase among prospects who are assumed, by then, to have information about the car.

The simple model assumes that potential purchasers all "start from scratch." However, some may have developed negative attitudes about the product, which place them even further from purchasing the product than those completely unaware of it. The first job, then, is to get them off the negative steps—before they can move up the additional steps which lead to purchase.

Three Functions of Advertising

The six steps outlined, beginning with "aware," indicate three major functions of advertising. (1) The first two, awareness and knowledge, relate to *information or ideas*. (2) The second two steps, liking and preference, have to do with favorable *attitudes or feelings* toward the product. (3) The final two steps, conviction and purchase, are to produce *action*—the acquisition of the product.

These three advertising functions are directly related to a classic psychological model which divides behavior into three components or dimensions:

1. The cognitive component—the intellectual, mental, or "rational" states.
2. The affective component—the "emotional" or "feeling" states.
3. The conative or motivational component—the "striving" states, relating to the tendency to treat objects as positive or negative goals.

This is more than a semantic issue, because the actions that need to be taken to stimulate or channel motivation may be quite different from those that produce knowledge. And these, in turn, may differ from actions designed to produce favorable *attitudes* toward something.

Functions of Advertising Research

Among the first problems in any advertising evaluation program are to:

1. Determine what steps are most critical in a particular case, that is, what the steps leading to purchase are for most consumers.
2. Determine how many people are, at the moment, on which steps.
3. Determine which people on which steps it is most important to reach.

Advertising research can *then* be designed to evaluate the extent to which the advertising succeeds in moving the specified "target" audience(s) up the critical purchase steps.

Table 1 summarizes the stair-step model, and illustrates how several common advertising and research approaches may be organized according to their various "functions."

Over-all and Component Measurements

With regard to most any product there are an infinite number of additional "subflights" which can be helpful in moving a prospect up the main steps. For example, awareness, knowledge, and development of favorable attitudes toward a *specific product feature* may be helpful in building a preference for the *line* of products. This leads to the concept of other steps, subdividing or "feeding" into the purchase steps, but concerned solely with more specific product features or attitudes.

Advertising effectiveness measurements may, then, be categorized into:

1. Over-all or "global" measurements, concerned with measuring the results—the consumers' positions and movement on the purchase steps.
2. Segment or component measurements, concerned with measuring the relative effectiveness of various *means* of moving people up the purchase steps—the consumers' positions on ancillary flights of steps, and the relative importance of these flights.

Measuring Movement on the Steps

Many common measurements of advertising effectiveness have been concerned with movement up either the *first* steps or the *final* step on the primary purchase flight. Examples include surveys to determine the extent of brand awareness and information and measures of purchase and repeat purchase among "exposed" versus "unexposed" groups.

Self-administered instruments, such as adaptations

TABLE 1
Advertising and Advertising Research Related to the Model

Related behavioral dimensions	Movement toward purchase	Examples of types of promotion or advertising relevant to various steps	Examples of research approaches related to steps of greatest applicability
CONATIVE —the realm of motives. Ads stimulate or direct desires.	PURCHASE ↑ CONVICTION	Point-of-purchase Retail store ads Deals "Last-chance" offers Price appeals Testimonials	Market or sales tests Split-run tests Intention to purchase Projective techniques
AFFECTIVE —the realm of emotions. Ads change attitudes and feelings.	PREFERENCE ↑ LIKING	Competitive ads Argumentative copy "Image" ads Status, glamor appeals	Rank order of preference for brands Rating scales Image measurements, including check lists and semantic differentials Projective techniques
COGNITIVE —the realm of thoughts. Ads provide information and facts.	KNOWLEDGE ↑ AWARENESS	Announcements Descriptive copy Classified ads Slogans Jingles Sky writing Teaser campaigns	Information questions Play-back analyses Brand awareness surveys Aided recall

of the "semantic differential" and adjective check lists, are particularly helpful in providing the desired measurements of movement up or down the middle steps. The semantic differential provides a means of scaling attitudes with regard to a number of different issues in a manner which facilitates gathering the information on an efficient quantitative basis. Adjective lists, used in various ways, serve the same general purpose.

Such devices can provide relatively spontaneous, rather than "considered," responses. They are also quickly administered and can contain enough elements to make recall of specific responses by the test participant difficult, especially if the order of items is changed. This helps in minimizing "consistency" biases in various comparative uses of such measurement tools.

Efficiency of these self-administered devices makes it practical to obtain responses to large numbers of items. This facilitates measurement of elements or components differing only slightly, though importantly, from each other.

Carefully constructed adjective check lists, for example, have shown remarkable discrimination between terms differing only in subtle shades of meaning. One product may be seen as "rich," "plush," and "expensive," while another one is "plush," "gaudy," and "cheap."

Such instruments make it possible to secure simultaneous measurements of both *global* attitudes and *specific* image components. These can be correlated with each other and directly related to the content of the advertising messages tested.

Does the advertising change the thinking of the respondents with regard to specific product attributes, characteristics or features, including not only physical characteristics but also various image elements such as "status"? Are these changes commercially significant?

The measuring instruments mentioned are helpful in answering these questions. *They provide a means for correlating changes in specific attitudes concerning image components with changes in global attitudes or position on the primary purchase steps.*

Testing the Model

When groups of consumers are studied over time, do those who show more movement on the measured steps eventually purchase the product in greater proportions or quantities? Accumulation of data utilizing the stair-step model provides an opporutnity to test the assumptions underlying the model by answering this question.

Three Concepts

This approach to the measurement of advertising has evolved from three concepts:

1. Realistic measurements of advertising effectiveness must be related to an understanding of the functions of advertising. It is helpful to think in terms of a model where advertising is likened to a force which, if successful, moves people up a series of steps toward purchase.
2. Measurements of the effectiveness of the advertising should provide measurements of changes at *all* levels on these steps—not just at the levels of the development of product or feature awareness and the stimulation of actual purchase.
3. Changes in attitudes as to specific image components can be evaluated together with changes in over-all images, to determine the extent to which changes in the image components are related to movement on the primary purchase steps.

Joel Dean

Does Advertising Belong in the Capital Budget?

Should advertising be budgeted as an expense or as an investment?

Advertising is now book-kept and budgeted as though its benefits were used up immediately, like purchased electricity. Management thinks about advertising as it is book-kept, as a current expense. The decision as to how much a corporation should spend

Source: From the *Journal of Marketing*, Vol. 30 (October 1966), pp. 15–21. Reprinted by permission of the American Marketing Association.

on persuasion is made by the same criteria as for materials used up in the factory—impact upon the current P&L. The advertising budget is part of the *operating* budget.

So far as is known, no corporation puts advertising in its capital budget. But maybe it belongs there. Several disinterested parties say so.

The stock market says it belongs there. It says the benefits derived from promotional outlays are just as capitalizable as the tangible assets that the bookkeeper does capitalize. It says this when Bristol Myers sells at ten times its book value.

Corporation presidents occasionally say it belongs there, especially when they evoke *investment* in advertising to justify poor current profits.

New entrants into an industry say advertising belongs in the capital budget. They say it by including the promotional outlays required to build brand-acceptance as an integral part of the total investment required to break into the business.

Antitrust economists say advertising belongs in the capital budget. They say it by viewing brand-acceptance, which is built up by promotion, as just as substantial a barrier to entry as the investment required in buildings and machinery.

It is just possible that the bookkeeper's guide to top-management thinking about advertising is wrong.

THE APPROACH

The plan of this article is, first, to find whether promotion is an investment; second, to consider how to optimize it if it is an investment; and third, to speculate on the probabilities that this novel approach, even if theoretically valid, will do any good.

The approach here to the problem of how much to invest in advertising is formal and objective, rather than intuitive. The premise is that the overriding goal of the corporation is to maximize profits. The viewpoint is that of an economist concerned with managerial finance.

This article is confined to the conceptual framework for deciding how much to invest in promotion. Measurement problems are not examined, nor the mechanics of application. The analysis is presented in terms of advertising, but is equally applicable to all forms of persuasion. Advertising is used as an example simply because it is the purest and most indisputable form of selling cost, and for many firms also the largest.

My thesis is as follows. Most advertising is, in economic essence, an investment. How much to spend on advertising is, therefore, a problem of investment economics. A new approach is required—economic and financial analysis of furturities. This approach focuses on future after-tax cash flows and centers on the profit-productivity of capital.

IS PROMOTION AN INVESTMENT?

To determine whether, as a matter of economics, outlays for advertising and other forms of promotion constitute an investment, rather than a current expense, is our first task.

So we must bravely face three basic questions concerning the economics of investment in corporate persuasion:

A. Precisely what is a business investment; how is it distinguished from a current expense?
B. Just what are promotional costs; how should they be distinguished from production costs?
C. What are the distinctive characteristics of promotional outlays: do they disqualify promotion for investment treatment?

A. Concept of Investment

What distinguishes a business investment from a current expense?

An investment is an outlay made today to achieve benefits in the future. A current expense is an outlay whose benefits are immediate. The question is not how the outlay is treated in conventional accounting, how it is taxed, or whether the asset is tangible or intangible. The hallmark of an investment is futurity.

B. Concept of Promotional Costs

Precisely what are promotional costs? How do they differ from production costs?

Promotional costs are outlays to augment the demand for the product—that is, to shift its price-quantity demand schedule upward, so that more will be sold at a given price. In contrast, production costs are all outlays required to meet this demand.

This different dividing line means that some costs which are conventionally classified as marketing costs, for example, physical distribution, are here viewed as part of production costs. It means also that some costs usually viewed as production costs, for example, inspection, are here viewed as promotional costs, even though they are incurred in the factory.

This is the cost-dichotomy needed for clear thinking about promotional investments. A clear idea of the purpose of an outlay is indispensable for a useful estimate of its effectiveness. Moreover, the criterion for optimization is quite different for production costs than for promotional costs. For production, it is sheer cost-minimization; for promotion, it is not cost-minimization but something much more intricate, as we shall see.

C. Distinctive Traits of Promotional Outlays

Do promotional investments differ from unimpeachable corporate investments in ways that make it impractical to manage them like true investments?

Promotional investments *are* different from traditional corporate investments—for example, capital tied up in machinery. The question is whether these differences call for a different intellectual apparatus for measuring productivity and rationing the firm's capital.

Promotional investments *are book-kept differently.* They are not capitalized and not depreciated. But this does not keep them from being investments. They tie up capital with equal inflexibility and do so with similar expectation of future benefits.

Promotional investments *are taxed differently.* Unlike acknowledged investments, they are deductible against income fully at the time of outlay, regardless of the delay of benefits. The fact that the tax collector is oblivious to promotional investments increases their productivity. Immediate tax writeoff of the entire outlay halves the investment after tax and steps up its true rate of return.

Promotional investments *are generally spread out over time* and usually can be adjusted in amount in relatively small steps. However, this is irrelevant in determining whether or not they are true investments.

Most promotional investments *have an indeterminate economic life.* Brand-acceptance "planted in the head" of a teenager by television may influence his purchases for 50 minutes or 50 years. But uncertainty of duration of the benefits does not make the promotional outlay any less an investment. The obsolescence-life of a computer is also quite uncertain.

Promotional investments *have multiple benefits* which can be reaped in optional ways. The profitability of augmented demand may be taken out either in higher prices or in larger volume. But this is not unique to promotional investments. Usually factory modernization not only saves labor, but also increases capacity and improves product-quality and employee morale.

Promotional investments *usually have irregular and diverse time-shapes in their benefits streams.* But this is a common characteristic of many tangible investments. Some oil wells, for example, come in as gushers, have an unexpected midlife rejuvenation from repressuring, and live out a tranquil old age as pumpers.

Promotional investments *have a benefit-stream which is difficult to measure and to predict.* But they share this characteristic with many forms of outlay conventionally classified as capital expenditures. Obsolescence of chemical-processing equipment, for example, is hard to predict, yet vitally affects its rate of return.

Promotional investments *are provocative;* they may induce rivals to retaliate. This adds to the difficulty of measuring and predicting benefits. Tangible investments, however, can also provoke competitors' reactions in ways that erode their profitability (for example, retail store modernization).

All this adds up to the fact that promotional investments *do* have unusual characteristics, different from many other investments that now fight for funds in the capital budget. However, these traits either are not distinctive, or if they are, do not destroy the essential investment-character of the promotional outlays.

All promotional outlays are now conventionally viewed exclusively as current expenses. Some are, if the time lag of benefits is sufficiently short; but others are instead true investments, because the delay in their benefits is substantial. Most promotion is a *mixture,* and the richness of the investment-mix varies over a wide range.

HOW TO OPTIMIZE INVESTMENT IN PROMOTION

Granted that much advertising is largely an investment in economic reality, how should a corporation determine how much it should invest in promotion? To solve this problem, we need answers to the following questions:

A. Does a satisfactory solution for the problem already exist?
B. Why has such an important problem remained unsolved?
C. To what corporate goal should the solution be geared?
D. How does promotion tie in to other ways of getting business?
E. What are the determinants of the productivity of capital invested in promotion?
F. What concepts of measurement are needed to calibrate productivity of capital?
G. What is the most appropriate yardstick of capital productivity for promotional investments?
H. How would rate-of-return rationing work for investments in corporate persuasion?

A. *Problem Unsolved*

Has the problem of how much a corporation should spend on advertising and other forms of persuasion been already satisfactorily solved?

The problem is important. The answer is crucial to the competitive success of many firms, and may involve vast expenditures.

In the future, it is likely to be even more vital. Depersonalized distribution, increased urbanization, rising consumer affluence, revolutionary advances in technology, and bigger economies of scale in some promotional media are dynamic forces which will make the decision as to how much to invest in promotion a jugular issue for many corporations in the next decade.

Surprisingly, this crucial problem is not yet solved. Despite yards of computer print-outs and millions of dollars spent on advertising research, most corporations do not really know whether their promotional outlays should be half or twice as large as they now are.

B. Reasons for Failure

Why has such an important problem remained unsolved? There are three main causes.

The first cause is *failure to acknowledge the importance of futurity*. The full impact of most promotional outlays upon demand is delayed, with associated uncertainty. Hence, the conceptual framework of analysis that management needs for solving this problem is the kind that is used in modern, sophisticated management of conventional corporate capital appropriations.

A second cause is *lack of a conceptual apparatus whose orientation is economic*. The problem of optimizing promotional investment is basically a matter of managerial economics, that is, balancing incremental promotional investment against predicted benefits, so as to augment sales most profitably.

The third cause of failure is *the difficulty of measuring the effectiveness of promotional outlays*. Their impacts on demand are diffused, delayed, and intricately interwoven with other forces. To make the kind of investment approach needed to produce practical benefits will require an open mind, fresh concepts, substantial research spending, and great patience.

C. Overriding Corporate Goal

What is the corporate goal to which the solution of optimum investment in promotion should be geared?

Promotional outlays, like other expenditures, should be judged in terms of their contribution to attainment of the corporation's objectives. Most companies have several goals, some of which conflict; but the solution for the problem of how much to invest in promotion should be geared primarily to the goal of profitability.

The master goal of the modern corporation should be maximum profits in the long run. More explicitly, it should be to maximize the present worth at the corporation's cost of capital of the future stream of benefits to the stockholder.

All other objectives—such as growth or market-share or eternal life—should be either intermediate or subsidiary to this overriding corporate objective.

D. Business-Getters

How does promotion relate to other ways of getting business?

A company has three ways to augment its sales: by cutting price, by spending more on promotion, and by bettering its product. The three members of the business-getting threesome pull together. But being alternatives, they are at the margin rivalrous substitutes.

The three reinforce each other in a complex symbiotic relationship. For a product that is superior to rivals in wanted ways, promotional outlays will be more effective than for an inferior product. A given amount and quality of promotion will produce more sales of a product priced in correct economic relationship to buyers' alternatives than for an overpriced product.

Each of the three business-getters can have delayed impacts and hence be a business investment. Their delayed and intertwining effects on sales, now and in the future, increase the problem of measuring the effects of promotional investment.

E. Determinants of Capital Productivity

What are the determinants of the productivity of capital invested in promotion?

These need to be identified to find out whether capital tied up in advertising will yield enough profits to earn its keep. Its yield must pay for the cost of this capital in the marketplace, or its opportunity costs in benefits passed up by not investing the money somewhere else.

The productivity of an investment in promotion is the relation of its earnings to the amount of capital tied up. This relationship requires explicit recognition of four economic determinants to be measured: (1) the amount and timing of *added investment;* (2) the amount and timing of *added earnings;* (3) the *duration of the earnings;* and (4) the *risks and imponderable benefits* associated with the project.

1. Added Investment. The appropriate investment base for calculating rate of return is the added outlay which will be occasioned by the adoption of a promotion project as opposed to its rejection.

The investment should include the entire amount of the original added outlay, regardless of how it is classified on the accounts. Any additional outlay for point-of-purchase displays or for distribution of samples to consumers should be included in the investment amount, as should future research expenses caused by the proposal.

The timing of these added investments has an important effect upon true profitability and should, therefore, be reflected in the rate-of-return computation.

2. Added Earnings. Concern with capital productivity implies, of course, that the company's goal is profits.

The productivity of the capital tied up is determined by the increase in earnings or savings, that is, net cash receipts, caused by making the investment as opposed to not making it. These earnings should be measured in terms of their after-tax cash or cash equivalents.

Only costs and revenues that will be different as a result of the adoption of the proposal should be included. The concept of earnings should be broad enough to encompass intangible and often unquantifiable benefits. When these have to be omitted from the formal earnings-estimates, they should be noted for subsequent appraisal of the project.

3. Durability of Earnings. The duration of the benefits from a promotional investment has a vital effect on its rate of return.

Economic life of promotion depends (a) on frequency of purchase; (b) on loyalty-life-expectancy, that is, longevity of customers; (c) on gestation period of the purchase decision; and (d) on erosion by the promotional efforts of rivals.

For advertising investments, durability is often the most difficult dimension of project value to quantify. But the problem cannot be avoided. Some estimate is better than none; and estimates can be improved by well-directed research.

4. Risks and Imponderable Benefits. Appraising the risks and uncertainties associated with a project requires a high order of judgment. It is only disparities in risk among projects which need to be allowed for, since the company's cost of capital reflects the overall risks. Although measurement of this sort of dispersion is difficult, some headway can sometimes be made by a necessarily arbitrary risk-ranking of candidate projects or categories of projects.

Most projects have some added benefits over and above the measurable ones. If excessive weight is given to these imponderables, then there is danger that rate-of-return rationing will occur. When a low rate-of-return project is preferred to a high one on the grounds of imponderable benefits, the burden of proof clearly should rest on the imponderables.

F. Concepts of Measurement

For calibrating these four determinants of return on investment, what concepts of measurement are needed? Four are particularly useful:

1. *Alternatives.* The proper benchmark for measuring added investment and the corresponding added earnings is the best alternative way to do it.

2. *Futurity.* Future earnings and future outlays of the project are all that matter.
3. *Increments.* Added earnings and added investment of the project alone are material.
4. *Cash flows.* After-tax cash flows (or their equivalents) alone are significant for measuring capital productivity.

1. Alternatives. There is always an alternative to the proposed capital expenditure.

The alternative may be so catastrophic that refined measurement is unnecessary to reject it; but in any case, the proper benchmark for the proposal is the next profitable alternative way of doing it.

2. Futurity. The value of a proposed capital project depends on its future earnings.

The past is irrelevant, except as a benchmark for forecasting the future. Consequently, earnings estimates need to be based on the best available projections. The outlays and earnings need to be estimated year by year over the economic life of the proposed promotion, and their time shape needs to be taken into account explicitly.

3. Increments. A correct estimate of both earnings and investment must be based on the simple principle that the earnings from the promotional proposal are measured by the total *added* earnings by making the investment, as opposed to *not* making it ... and that the same is true for the investment amount.

Project costs should be unaffected by allocation of existing overheads, but should reflect the changes in total overhead and other costs likely to result from the project. No costs or revenues which will be the same, regardless of whether the proposal is accepted or rejected, should be included and the same goes for investment.

4. Cash flows. To be economically realistic, attention should be directed exclusively at the after-tax flows of cash or cash equivalents which will result from making the promotional investment.

Book costs are confusing and immaterial. But taxes do matter, because advertising investments are favored over depreciable investments in after-tax rate of return.

G. Yardstick of Financial Worth

The productivity of capital in a business investment is the relationship between its earnings and the amount of capital tied up. To measure this productivity for promotional investments, we not only must have a correct conceptual framework of measurements, but also must choose the most appropriate yardstick of investment worth.

The concept of advertising as an investment already has some limited acceptance in new-product introduction. The measure of productivity of capital often used is the payout period—a crude yardstick. The cutoff criterion is also set rather arbitrarily to get the original outlay back in two years or three years. Such standards have no objective justification as compared with corporate cost of capital.

What is the best yardstick of economic worth for investments in persuasion? Clearly, the yardstick that is economically appropriate for investments in promotion is true profitability as measured by discounted-cash-flow analysis.

1. Discounted-Cash-Flow Analysis. The discounted-cash-flow (DCF) method is a new approach to measuring the productivity of capital and measuring the cost of capital.

The application is new, not the principle. Discounting has long been used in the financial community, where precision and realism are indispensable. The essential contributions of discounted-cash-flow analysis to management thinking about investment in promotion are three:

a. An explicit recognition that time has economic value—and hence, that near money is more valuable than distant money.
b. A recognition that cash flows are what matter—and hence, that book costs are irrelevant for capital-decisions except as they affect taxes.
c. A recognition that income taxes have such an important effect upon cash flows that they must be explicitly figured into project worth.

The discounted-cash-flow method has two computational variants.

The first is a rate-of-return computation, which consists essentially of finding the interest rate that discounts gross future after-tax cash earnings of a project down to a present value equal to the project cost. This interest rate is the rate of return on that particular investment.

The second variant is a present-value computation which discounts gross future after-tax cash earnings of all projects at the same rate of interest. This rate of interest is the company's minimum acceptable rate of return. This should be based on the company's cost of capital. Special risk should be reflected either by deflating project earnings or by adjusting the cutoff rate for projects of different categories of risk. The resulting present-value is then compared with the project cost investment. If the present value exceeds it, the project is acceptable. If it falls below, it is rejected.

In addition, projects can by this variant be ranked by various kinds of profitability indexes which reflect the amount or ratios of excess of present value over project cost.

Both variants of the discounted-cash-flow approach require a timetable of after-tax cash flows of investment and of gross earnings which cover the entire economic life of the project.

In practice, the timetable can be simplified by grouping years in blocks. For projects for which investment is substantially instantaneous and gross earnings are level, simple computational charts and tables can be used to estimate the discounted-cash-flow rate of return directly from estimated economic life and after-tax payback. For projects with rising or declining earnings streams, this conversion is more complex.

2. Superiorities of DCF. The discounted-cash-flow method of analysis is particularly needed for measuring the profitability of promotional investments, for two reasons.

First, the outlays are usually spread out. Second, benefits, mainly incremental profits from added sales in the future, are always spread out and usually have a non-level time-shape.

The superiorities of discounted-cash-flow analysis over rival yardsticks for measuring the productivity of capital in promotional investments are imposing:

a. It is economically realistic in confining the analysis to cash-flows and forgetting about book-allocations.
b. It forces guided thinking about the whole life of the project, and concentration on the lifetime earnings.
c. It weights the time-pattern of the investment outlay and the cash earnings, so as to reflect real and important differences in the value of near and distant cash-flows.
d. It reflects accurately and without ambiguity the timing of tax-savings.
e. It permits simple allowances for risks and uncertainties, and can be adapted readily to increasing the risk allowance over time.
f. It is strictly comparable to cost-of capital, correctly measured, so that decisions can be made quickly and safely by comparing rate of return and the value of money to the firm.

H. Rate-of-return Rationing

How should rationing of capital work for persuasion-investments?

Rate-of-return "battling" among capital proposals is the essence of capital rationing. The standard of minimum acceptable profitability should (after proper allowance for special risks and for imponderables) be the same for all, namely, the company's market cost-of-capital or its opportunity cost-of-capital, whichever is higher.

Market cost-of-capital is what the company probably will pay for equity and debt funds, on the average, over the future. For a large publicly-held company, this cost can be measured with adequate precision for rationing purposes. There is no better cutoff criterion.

Opportunity cost-of-capital is the sacrificed profit-yield from alternative investments. Only when a company refuses to go to market for funds can its opportunity costs stay long above market cost-of-capital.

PRACTICAL VALUES

Will putting advertising in the capital budget do any good?

Granted that as a matter of economic principle much advertising and other forms of promotional spending are investments...and granted also that conceptually correct and pragmatically proved techniques for optimizing investment outlays are available for promotional investment...the question is whether this sophisticated and powerful mechanism, applied to promotional investments, will have any practical value.

Most business investments are not made in ignorance of their probable impacts, whereas, many of the outlays for persuasion now are. Characteristically, the amount and timing of the effects of advertising are unknown. The duration of their impact on economic life is unknown, and the probabilities of effectiveness are also unknown. Quite possibly, attempting to estimate these unknowns cannot improve overall results.

The problem of how much to invest in promotion can be solved either by intuitive and perhaps artistic processes, or through a more formal and more systematic study of objective evidence. Quite possibly men of experience and good judgment can determine how much the corporation should invest in promotion by subjective judgment, regardless of whether advertising is formally put in the capital budget. This article is nevertheless confined to a consideration of ways in which sophisticated economic models and systematic quantitative study can help to find the appropriate size of the appropriation for corporate persuasion.

IN SUMMARY

1. Much advertising (and other corporate persuasion) is in economic reality partly an investment. The investment-mix varies over a wide spectrum.

2. Investments in promotion are different from conventional capital expenditures; but these distinctive characteristics do not disqualify promotion for investment treatment.

3. Profitability must be the basic measurement of the productivity of capital invested in promotion. Despite the multiplicity of conflicting corporate goals, the overriding objective for decisions or investment of corporate capital should be to make money.

4. The main determinants of profitability of an advertising investment that need to be estimated are the amount and timing of added investment and of added earnings, the duration of advertising effects and risks.

5. The measurement concepts of capital productivity that must be estimated are future, time-spotted, incremental, after-tax cash flows of investment outlays and of added profits from added sales.

6. Discounted-Cash-Flow (DCF) analysis supplies the financial yardstick most appropriate for promotional investments. By comparison, payback period, although widely used, has no merit.

7. Advertising belongs in the capital budget. Promotional investments should be made to compete for funds on the basis of profitability, that is, DCF rate of return.

8. The criterion for rationing scarce capital among competing investment proposals should be DCF rate of return. The criterion of the minimum acceptable return should be the corporation's cost of capital—outside market-cost or internal opportunity-cost, whichever is higher.

9. Putting advertising into the capital budget will not perform a miracle. Judgment cannot be displaced by DCF analysis and computers. But judgment can be economized and improved. The most that it can do is to open the way for a research approach which is oriented to the kind of estimates that are relevant and that will permit advertising investment in promotion to fight for funds on the basis of financial merit rather than on the basis of personal persuasiveness of their sponsor.

10. An investment approach to produce practical benefits will require fresh concepts, substantial research-spending, and great patience.

Harold C. Cash and W. J. E. Crissy

Comparison of Advertising and Selling

Advertising, like selling, plays a major role in the total marketing effort of the firm. The degree to which each is important depends upon the nature of the goods and the market being cultivated. In the industrial product field, personal selling is generally the major force. Here the nature of the goods often requires specific application information that is best presented in person by the salesman. The dollar value of the order generally makes it economically feasible to finance this more effective and expensive method of presentation. Comparable effort to sell a box of soap powder to the housewife would be a ridiculous extravagance. On the other hand, it is likely that personal selling will be used to get this consumer product into the channels of distribution—through the wholesaler or chain store buying organization.

The person-to-person two-way communication of personal selling makes it a superior means of selling every time. Advertising, by contrast, is only a one-way communication system and is necessarily generalized to fit the needs of many people. Where the unit value of the sale is small, however, advertising is more economical. For example, a full-page advertisement in an issue of *Life* magazine, which costs upward of $30,000, will deliver the message, at a rate of less than one-half cent per copy. And since, on an average, about four persons reach each copy, message exposure per reader is in the neighborhood of one-eighth cent per copy-reader. A full-color page advertisement provides exposure for about one-sixth cent per copy-reader. Of course, not every reader is likely to see a particular advertisement but even if only twenty-five per cent of the exposures capture attention, the cost is minute. Comparable costs of message delivery apply to radio, T.V. and other mass media. Recent figures indicate a total of $31.31 as the cost of a typical sales call when all expenses are considered.

The worth of the sales call and an advertising impression is not likely to be equal. If the prospect is serious and has sincere interest in the proposal, the sales call is definitely worthwhile. If, on the other hand, the prospect is not nearly ready to place an order, a reminder of the existence of the product or services in the form of an advertisement would have been more economical.

Generally speaking, advertising needs additional support, either through personal selling or through promotional activities, to effect the sale. In most cases, its basic function is in the demand-cultivation area. Hence it is more significant in the pre-transactional phase of marketing. There are, of course, instances where advertising alone makes the sale, as in the case of mail-order selling. This channel, however, represents only a very small volume of total sales in any year. To a lesser extent, advertising can help in the post-transactional area of demand-fulfillment by providing a rationalization to the purchaser after the buying decision has been made.

Advertising can be thought of in many ways. Perhaps, however, the most useful perspective to take is in terms of primary objectives. Most advertising is aimed at inducing purchase of a particular brand of product. Sometimes this is referred to as pre-selling, since the aim is to lead the person to the transactional stage even though the transaction itself is not accomplished. This type of advertising is essentially competitive.

There are many things that can be accomplished through advertising. Perhaps the most obvious is to create an awareness of, an interest in, or demand for a product. When fluoride was added to toothpaste, large-scale advertising was conducted to let customers know that the product was available. Concurrently, the sales organization obtained distribution in retail outlets so that customers could acquire the product. It is doubtful that many sales could be accomplished without the advertising program. The alternative to advertising would be to have retail store personnel personally sell the toothpaste to customers. This is not feasible because the unit sale is too low to support the salary and expense of a sales person. In this sense, advertising paves the way for the salesman because, without the promise of a huge advertising and promotion campaign, retailers would not cooperate in finding display space. It has been said, "Salesmen put products on shelves and advertising takes them off."

Less frequently, advertising is used to introduce an entirely new idea. The educational effort may be

Source: From the *Psychology of Selling,* Vol. 12 (Personnel Development Associates, Box 3005, Roosevelt Field Station, Garden City, N.Y. 11530), 1965.

underwritten by a single company or, where there are a number of producers in the field, it may be the cooperative effort of the industry. Here the advertising is designed to win for the industry a share of the customer's dollar. Again it is a pre-selling activity. Such advertising is often called "pioneering" as contrasted with "competitive" advertising.

Many advertisements are aimed at reinforcing the product name or brand in the minds of the buying public. This may be considered as reminder advertising. It is normally used when a product has a dominant share of the market and cannot expect to attain any marked increase in volume within the economic limits of the extra promotional cost.

Some advertisements are primarily designed to convey a favorable image of the company as a good firm with which to do business. This institutional or public relations advertising is used by public utilities and major corporations which have an important stake in gaining a favorable public acceptance.

It is not unusual for a single advertisement to attempt to achieve a combination of these objectives.

As was noted before, generally speaking, advertising plays a more significant role in the marketing of consumer goods than it does in the case of industrial products. This is particularly true with respect to contact with the end users. However, even consumer goods depend to a significant extent on personal selling to move them through the channels.

When the item represents a substantial outlay and when there are complexities to be explained to the prospect, obviously personal contact is both practical and necessary. Advertising for such goods, however, is often used in specialized media for the purpose of generating leads for the field sales force.

When goods flow through indirect channels, advertising grows in complexity. It may be used to cultivate demand on the part of the ultimate users through nationally distributed media. It may also be used in selected specialized media to encourage the various intermediaries to stock the merchandise.

When advertising is used with industrial products, it has different functions. As mentioned above, one function is to generate leads for salesmen. It is common for the advertisement to carry a coupon. When the coupon is received at the home office, it is relayed to the salesman covering that territory who then makes a sales call.

A second function of the advertising of industrial products is to keep the name of the company and product before the customers between sales calls. Good advertising also reassures a customer that he is buying from a good supplier. The advertising adds prestige to the product, the company, and the sales-

man, especially when it equals or excels that of competitors.

When a company has a substantial advertising program, salesmen can use tear sheets of the advertisements to good advantage. These can appropriately be shown to both prospects and customers. With prospects, consideration should be given to leaving copies of the advertisements as they create a feeling of stability and solidity with regard to the supplier. When prospects see advertisements, normally in the trade press, this paves the way for salesmen.

In a well organized and disciplined industrial sales force, there will be a similarity between the content of the advertisement and the sales presentation. Thus the advertisement and the sales call reinforce each other.

Many products must be used in a certain way to produce the desired results. Complaints arise when the product does not fulfill the salesman's claims. Advertising can carry instructions on using the product. This will help to insure satisfactory performance. If the product has already been used inappropriately, the advertising may cause the customer to understand the poor performance and give it another chance. In this way, it holds customers that might otherwise be lost.

SIMILARITIES AND DIFFERENCES BETWEEN ADVERTISING AND SELLING

From the viewpoint of communications, advertising and selling have much in common. Both must meet four criteria. They need to be *understandable, interesting, believable,* and *persuasive* if they are to achieve their purpose. There are, however, some noteworthy differences. Communication through advertising is one-way. In contrast, selling is uniquely two-way. There is an inherent weakness in advertising—"*noise.*" This is likely to be present in greater amounts in advertising than in the case of the sales interview where misunderstandings can be cleared up on the spot. Whatever the medium being used, advertising must compete with other messages. For example, in a magazine the ad competes with surrounding editorial copy. The message conveyed by the salesman does not compete with other messages, at least at the time of the presentation.

Advertising may be used to generate either primary or selective demand; for example, an industry group may collaborate on its advertising with a view to enlarging the total market. In contrast, selling is aimed invariably at selective demand, that is, preference for the products and services being sold by the particular company over those available from competitors.

From the standpoint of persuasion, a sales message

is far more flexible, personal, and powerful than an advertisement. An advertisement is normally prepared by persons having minimal personal contact with customers. The message is designed to appeal to a large number of persons. By contrast, the message in a good sales presentation is not determined in advance. The salesman has a tremendous store of knowledge about his product or service and selects appropriate items as the interview progresses. Thus the salesman can adapt his message to the thinking and needs of the customer or prospect *at the time of the sales call.* Furthermore, as objections arise and are voiced by the buyer, the salesman can treat the objections in an appropriate manner. This is not possible in advertising.

Company control over the advertising message is more complete than over a sales presentation. When an advertisement is prepared, it is submitted for the approval of all interested executives before it is released to the media. Thus there is little likelihood of any discrepancy between company policy and the content of the advertisement. In theory, salesmen receive training so that they understand the product or service and company policy. With the best possible training program, there are two possible sources of error or bases for deviation from the company doctrine. One is loss of memory. Salesmen just cannot remember everything they are told. Also, they may meet situations that are unforeseen, and their reaction may not be identical to what the company management would specify if the problem were referred to them.

There is little a prospect can do to avoid a well-planned advertising campaign. With the number of media available, he is almost certain to be exposed to one or more advertising messages. Buyers can refuse to see salesmen. When the salesman arrives at the premises of the buyer's company, he is subject to the will of the buyer as to whether he enjoys an interview. Thus, over a period of time, advertising will bring the product to the attention of persons who would be missed by salesmen.

Perceptual Similarities and Differences

In terms of perceptual process, there are also similarities. Both must penetrate the sensory mechanisms of the customer or prospect if they are to be effective. With both, careful selection of the stimuli to be presented is important. However, significant differences do exist from the standpoint of perception.

In selling, it may be possible to enlist not only the senses of vision and audition, but taste, smell, and the tactual senses as well. Time and space restraints on advertising limit the number and array of stimuli that

can be presented. In selling, it is possible to vary the stimuli and to apply them as the salesman deems appropriate. Actual time duration of an ad generally limits the opportunity to summate and reinforce the message. In contrast, during the sales interview, frequent repetition and reinforcement are possible. In most instances, advertising commands less full attention than does selling. This limits the number of concepts that can be conveyed and places a high premium on careful construction of the ad copy and selection of the illustrations. In the case of the "commercial" on radio or television, few opportunities for reinforcement are possible within the ad itself. The salesman, too, must have a well-planned presentation. However, it can be varied and adjusted as the sales interview progresses. Further, the salesman on the spot is able to re-arrest attention when he detects it is waning. This is not possible with an advertisement.

Cognitive Similarities and Differences

In terms of cognitive process, both advertising and selling are designed to induce favorable thoughts toward the company, its products and services, and its people. Both are aimed at conveying an image of *different* and *better vis-à-vis* competition. Advertising is far more limited than selling in influencing thought process. A relatively small number of ideas can be conveyed by an ad. There is no way to check on understanding. In the sales interview, the ideas and concepts can be tailored to the understanding of the prospect or customer. Because advertising employs mass media, the message must often be geared to the less sophisticated segment of the readership or audience. In contrast, the salesman who is effective gears his message to the sophistication of the person with whom he is conversing. Only to a limited extent can advertising carry the person exposed to the message through a reasoning process about the product or service. Instead, suggestion must be utilized.

In contrast, the salesman is able to employ suggestion or reasoning as the sales interview progresses, depending upon the perception of his message on the part of the customer or prospect. In the case of relatively complex products and services, the most that can be hoped for from advertising is a whetting of the prospect's appetite for more information. Questions can be raised but relatively few answers can be provided. In the case of those same goods and services, the salesman is able to cope with problems and questions at first hand. In fact, in some instances he plays an important role as a problem-solver for the prospective customer.

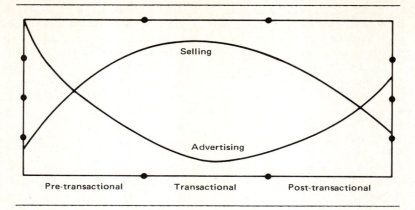

FIGURE 1
Relative Importance of Advertising and Selling Marketing Phase

Selling

Advertising

Pre-transactional   Transactional   Post-transactional

Feeling "State" Similarities and Differences

Advertising and selling both try to induce favorable feelings. In the case of selling the salesman himself becomes an important determiner of the customer's feeling "state" by the manner in which he conducts himself while he is with him. In advertising, too, it is important to induce a favorable feeling "state" or mood in order to provide more favorable receptivity to the message itself. This may be attempted directly within the ad by means of pleasant illustration, anticipatory enjoyment attending the use of the product, emotional words, phrases, analogies, and comparisons. This is accomplished less directly, where the medium permits it, by the entertainment bonus preceding and following the ad, as in the case of a television show or a radio program. In the case of the printed media, the surrounding editorial copy may be employed to set the mood. Even with these direct and indirect efforts, it is unlikely that any advertisement meets the objective of emotional reinforcement with all those who are exposed to the message. In fact, what may please one person may annoy another. Paradoxically, there is some research evidence from the radio field that if an ad doesn't please the person it is next best to have it annoy him rather than to leave him in a neutral feeling "state."

Selling, in contrast, has a tremendous advantage in the domain of feelings. The salesman in the first few seconds of face-to-face contact gauges the mood of the other person and adjusts his own behavior accordingly. Further, if he detects an unfavorable feeling "state" he may provide the other individual the opportunity to vent his feelings, or he may, in an extreme case, decide to withdraw and call on a more

favorable occasion. This option is not open to the advertiser.

Advertising permits the firm far less control over the ultimate buying decision than does selling. The person exposed to the ad may turn the page or spin the dial, or walk out of the room. In contrast, once a salesman has gained entry, if he is effective, he is likely to be able to make a reasonably full presentation of the sales message.

Transactional Similarities and Differences

If the market is viewed as having the three phases— *pre-transactional, transactional,* and *post-transactional,* it is evident that advertising fits mainly in the pre-transactional phase as a market-cultivating force. It may also enter into the post-transactional phase by providing a rationalization to the purchaser. Only in rare instances does it accomplish the transaction itself. In contrast, selling is of importance in all three phases (see figure 1).

Advertising may be viewed as readying the market for the salesman's personal efforts. Even with carefully selected media and well-conceived advertising, the strategy employed must be relatively general. In the case of selling, not only can strategy be formulated for each account and each decision maker in the account, but tactical adjustments can be made on the spot in order to influence those accounts.

SALESMAN'S USE OF ADVERTISING

Even though the salesman may not be directly involved in planning and formulating the advertising campaign of his firm, he certainly must be aware of the company's advertising plans, the media in which the advertisements are appearing, and the objectives that are being sought. If this information is not being furnished to him, it is legitimate for the salesman to request it. It can be very embarrassing to have a customer or prospect refer to an ad of which the salesman is unaware. The astute salesman is not only aware of his own company's ads, but he is also observant of the advertising done by competitors. The latter is often an important input for his own selling strategy.

Certainly if the demand cultivation of the company is to be coordinated, there must be a congruency between the content of the advertising and the salesman's presentations to customers and prospects.... Temporally, the exposure to the advertisements plus the periodic sales calls combine to reinforce the message. From a spatial summation standpoint the ads plus the sales messages bring to bear a varied array of stimuli on the customer and prospect.

Many companies accomplish this mutual reinforcement of advertising and selling by furnishing the sales force with selling aids, reprints, and tear sheets of advertisements from printed media. If this is done, the salesman has a direct means of reinforcing his oral presentation with advertising copy. Further, he is able to leave copies of ads as reminders to the persons called on.

When such ads are taken from prestige media they contribute to the building of a favorable image of the salesman's company. Sometimes local spot advertisements on radio and television make specific references such as "advertised in *Life* (or *Time*, or some other medium)" as an attempt to build up the prestige of the product and the company. The salesman accomplishes the same result with effective use of reprints and tear sheets.

The salesman is in a prime position to gauge the effectiveness of advertising. He is able to determine by inquiry how many of his customers and prospects have actually seen or heard the ad. By judicious questioning he also can learn of their reactions to the ads. This provides management useful feedback. He also may be able to suggest changes that will render the advertising more effective.

If suggestions are to be meaningful to management and the personnel who work on the advertising program, they must be in sufficient detail so that they can understand the reasoning of the salesman who submits them. They should include the following kinds of information:

1. Specific reasons why the campaign was not maximally successful. This should be supported by comments or behavior of customers and other interested parties, not merely an opinion of the salesman.
2. Sales figures which are directly related to the advertising campaign. If advertising mats are supplied, a comparison of the relative use of mats with those of other campaigns may be appropriate.
3. Comparisons can be made with competitive advertisers in the local area. In this case, samples of the competitive advertising should be submitted along with comments.

The foregoing observations should relate primarily to large scale print or broadcast media. In the case of dealer aids and point-of-purchase materials, the salesman is in an even stronger position to offer sound criticism. He can give first-hand reports of the ease with which display stands could be erected. He can report dealers' reactions to the materials and, even better, tally the actual use of the materials. When the materials have not been well received, he can inquire into the reasons for the poor reception and pass the information through the proper channels. It is perfectly proper for a salesman to state his opinion as well as the data he has collected, but to preserve his intellectual honesty and make his ideas more useful to management and advertising personnel he should indicate which ideas are his own and which are opinions or behavior of dealers and customers.

Salesmen who wish to have their ideas considered should find out when advertising campaigns are in a formative stage and submit their ideas so that they can be considered before the final ideas have been selected for development.

Lead Generators

Advertising containing a coupon or a request to write to a box number or to phone may be a useful lead-generating device for the salesmen. An important caution: such leads must be carefully screened before an appreciable investment of time and effort is made. A recent study of leads generated through reader service cards in a trade magazine indicated that only ten to twelve per cent were bona fide prospects for the goods offered. The remainder were curiosity seekers, literature collectors, and high school students.

In some sales situations, an added value expected by the reseller is assistance from the salesman with his own advertising. In such instances, the salesman must be knowledgeable on the actual principles, methods, and techniques of advertising. Usually, however, if this is a job duty, his firm furnishes instructional materials and specimen ads for use directly or with some modification. To the extent that the salesman can convince the customer of the worthwhileness of advertising, he is likely to generate increased profitable business for himself. Some firms encourage their intermediaries to advertise by sharing the costs. When this is the policy, it becomes even more imperative for the salesman to be astute in his recommendations. He is investing his company's money in the suggestions he makes. Ideas expected of him may range from choice of media, size of advertisement, frequency of inset, optimum time, to coordination of the advertising with other promotional efforts.

Where indirect channels are employed, the salesman may be able to use his firm's national advertising program as a potent force in his sales presentation. He can demonstrate as a *value added* that his company is applying a powerful, demand-generating force on the ultimate user which will develop increased business for all intermediaries. This is the "push-pull" effect. In this connection, if the salesman has information concerning an impending campaign, this can become a means of creating increased business in anticipation of likely demand. Inadequate inventory or "stock-out" can be translated into a loss of profit for the reseller as well as an attendant loss of good will by not having the merchandise available when the customer wants it.

SALESMEN'S ATTITUDES TOWARD ADVERTISING

A company's emphasis on advertising will vary depending on the nature of the product, the price, and the distribution of its customers. Salesmen's attitudes will vary with the relative importance of selling and advertising in the promotional mix. One common finding, however is that salesmen tend to become critical of their own company's advertising.

In some instances, salesmen, especially those handling industrial goods, feel too much money is spent on advertising. There is no point in discussing this problem, except in a specific instance. It can be pointed out that a salesman in his territory seldom has all the facts necessary to decide on the proper ratio of advertising and selling. It may be that he is entitled to more facts but that is an internal management decision, not one for outsiders. The best assumption for a salesman to make is that his company has established sound marketing objectives and has selected the right tools to achieve them. If the salesman feels differently, he should offer constructive criticism or, in the extreme case, consider seeking other employment. (Few salesmen have any idea of the cost of advertising per prospect. While the figures cited earlier in this chapter apply to consumer mass media, the cost per reader of industrial media is not too much greater.)

The content of advertising messages is often criticized by salesmen. As salesmen are face to face with customers and prospects every day, they are in a good position to gauge the impact of the firm's advertising. This does not mean they should compose the advertising because, as in the case of the amount of advertising, the company may have some objectives not known to the salesmen. It may wish to use part of the budget to promote what the salesmen feel is a minor rather than a major product in the line. This could very well happen if the salesmen are not informed on the profitability of each item in the line. In any event, each salesman should back up the company advertising, because however little immediate value he sees in it, he is in a stronger position supporting the advertising than opposing it.

Another area of possible disagreement between salesmen and management may be the media used. When the number of available advertising and promotional media is considered (T.V., radio, magazines [general and trade], newspapers, direct mail, transportation [car cards], outdoor, point of purchase, and sampling), it is not surprising that there may be disagreement. Indeed, there have probably been prolonged and exhaustive discussions within the management group before the media decision was reached. There are specialists in advertising agencies to help in selecting appropriate media. The likelihood of salesmen making constructive suggestions in this area of advertising is minimal except for some local conditions which may not have come to the attention of those making the final decision.

SUMMARY

Advertising and selling play major roles in the total marketing effort of the firm. Advertising, however, focuses mainly on market cultivation, though it sometimes plays a part in the actual transaction, and with some frequency, in the post-transactional aspect of the marketing program. The most useful way for the salesman to view advertising is in terms of its three key objectives—to induce an intention to purchase, to keep the product or brand in conscious awareness in the market place, and to project a favorable image of the firm. Similarities and differences between advertising and selling are discussed in terms of communication, perception, thought-process, feelings, and degree of control. Specific suggestions are made for effective use of advertising by the salesman, as well as ways and means the salesman can employ for apprising his management of the impact of the company's advertising efforts, and for suggesting ways of improving them.

CASES

SUNRISE HOSPITAL

Sunrise Hospital in Las Vegas, Nevada, has embarked on a promotional campaign to increase weekend use of hospital facilities. Because weekends are traditionally an under-utilized time period, management has advertised a variety of contests and cash rebates for patients who are admitted on Fridays or Saturdays, hoping to draw candidates for elective treatments and surgery to enter on those days.

THE COURTYARD

As one of the more exclusive restaurants in a major eastern state capital, The Courtyard has catered to the upper echelon of society and to politicians. Relying on word-of-mouth advertising, the restaurant has been quite successful. However, management is currently considering changing that policy since competition has become more intense and the restaurant has lost some of its appeal.

INLAND OCEANS, INC.—BIG SURF

Big Surf is a manmade lake and beach area in Tempe, Arizona—on the outskirts of Phoenix. Specifically designed machinery at the back of the lake operates to create five-foot waves, large enough for surfing. The company has created a simulated inland ocean to appeal to surfers, rafters, swimmers, and sunbathers. Its promotional campaign is under reconsideration by company management.

ATLANTIC INDUSTRIAL SUPPLY

As a fabricator and industrial supply distributor, Atlantic Industrial Supply had enjoyed steady growth in revenue but not in net profits. The president of the company, Mr. Richards, was disturbed about the bottom line and initiated various organizational changes. In addition, changes were made in the company's sales force and sales territories were realigned.

ARIZONA SOCCER CAMP (PART B)

Having begun a youth-oriented soccer camp in Orme, Arizona, in 1978, Arizona Soccer Camp opened a second facility in the Tucson area three years later. Faced with increased competition, management is in the process of reviewing its operations and its current situation. Special concerns have been expressed over the market potential and how to promote the camp in a manner that would distinguish it from other youth activities.

SUNRISE HOSPITAL: A CASE IN INNOVATIVE MARKET STRATEGY

PRESENT

David R. Brandsness, a young dynamic administrator at Sunrise Hospital, turned in his swivel chair and stared out over the hospital parking lot and pondered some thoughts. He had just looked at figures that indicated that the hospital was underutilized on the weekends. The figures, in part, revealed that the 486 beds at Sunrise had only 60 percent occupancy on weekends, compared with turnaway business on weekdays. This was a recurrent problem. David Brandsness muttered in frustration, "Our weekend census is below 300 and I know that by Tuesday night we will be turning patients away." Brandsness wondered aloud, "How can we have increased utilization of our outstanding equipment and skilled personnel on weekends which will eventually result in a reduction of patient costs and allow us to offer health services at the lowest rates of any private acute care hospital in Las Vegas?"

BACKGROUND

Sunrise Hospital is a fully accredited private acute care hospital with a licensed capacity of 486 beds. Since it opened in 1958, it has shown a consistent growth in both capacity and census (see exhibit 1).

These expansions have been accompanied by the development of an extensive range of ancillary services designed to meet both inpatient and outpatient

This case was prepared by Dr. Henry A. Sciullo, Dr. Eddie H. Goodin, and Dr. Philip E. Taylor. Dr. Sciullo and Dr. Goodin are members of the faculty at the University of Nevada, Las Vegas. Dr. Taylor is a member of the faculty at Princeton University.

demands. As a result of these programs, the hospital's share of the Las Vegas market has grown to approximately 46 percent of the total patient days recorded for the first half of 1976 and this growth is expected to continue.

MARKET DEMOGRAPHICS

Over the past fifteen years the population of Clark County (Las Vegas), Sunrise Hospital's primary service area, has grown 162 percent for a compound annual growth rate of 7.12 percent. It is the largest and fastest growing county in the state of Nevada and projections indicate it will continue to grow at a 5 percent rate through 1985, adding approximately 188,000 residents in that ten-year span (see exhibit 2).

A recent survey of 5,584 admissions to Sunrise Hospital revealed the geographic dispersion shown in exhibit 3.

MARKET SHARE

Perhaps the most important measure of Sunrise Hospital's success is that its average daily census has increased at an 8 percent compound average rate between 1972 and 1975 (263 average daily census to 363 average daily census, respectively), while total patient days recorded for all Las Vegas hospitals has grown at a compound rate of 4.74 percent. Sunrise Hospital has grown to dominate the Las Vegas market, as indicated in exhibit 4.

EXHIBIT 1
Sunrise Hospital Bed Capacity

Year	Bed Additions	Licensed Capacity	Average Daily Census	
1958	—	62	—	
1961	66	128	82	
1963	14	142	117	
1965	174	316	124	
1972	170	486	263	(55% occupancy)
1976	—	486	353	(74% occupancy)

EXHIBIT 2
Population Growth of Clark County (Las Vegas)*

Year	Population
1960	127,016
1970	273,288
1975	332,497
1980	435,000
1985	520,000

*Clark County Regional Planning Council.

EXHIBIT 3
Geographic Dispersions of Patients Admitted to Sunrise Hospital

Residence	Number of Admissions	Percent
Clark County (Las Vegas)	5,127	92.0%
Other Nevada	88	1.5
Other States and Foreign	369	6.5
Total	5,584	100.0%

Sunrise has achieved the present market position by aggressively marketing its services to the medical and general community. Recent innovations, such as a satellite outpatient testing center, twenty-four-hour pharmacy, and a laboratory pickup and delivery service for physicians' offices, are indicative of some of the marketing efforts.

As Sunrise Hospital's market share approaches the 50 percent level it gives a significant degree of stability to the operations. The broad base of support required to sustain this dominance indicates that Sunrise is not overly dependent on any single group of physicians and can continue to exercise leadership in providing medical services over a broad range of specialties.

Sunrise Hospital has always been a financially stable operation. Some factors which have contributed to this success are:

1. The maintenance of a prestigious position as "the hospital" in Las Vegas
2. The relatively low (35 percent) number of governmental reimbursement type patients

MEDICAL STAFF

The history of the Sunrise Hospital medical staff can be classified into three phases. At its inception, the primary support of Sunrise Hospital came from general practitioners, a limited number of internists, and less than six general surgeons. During the 1960s, a concentrated effort was made to attract specialists. This effort was primarily directed, in the initial stages, toward internists and subsequently moved on to other areas, including the subsurgical specialties.

The medical staff consists of 403 members. Of this total, over 50 percent are located within a one-mile radius of Sunrise Hospital. Another major concentration of physicians is located between Sunrise Hospital and Southern Nevada Memorial Hospital or a distance of less than four miles. These physicians, like most physicians in Las Vegas, have multiple hospital staff memberships. Approximately seventy physicians limit their practice to Sunrise exclusively.

PRESENT

David Brandsness took his eyes off the parking lot and got up from his chair and declared, "Why didn't I think of this before?" He thought to himself, other industries such as hotels and airlines offer special rates during certain times of the week to achieve overall efficiency, so why shouldn't an investor-owned hospital do the same?

After a careful economic analysis by his staff, David Brandsness announced a revolutionary new health care policy: cash rebates for patients admitted on Fridays and Saturdays. The program would guarantee a 5.25 percent cash rebate on the total hospital bill of every patient admitted to Sunrise Hospital on Fridays and Saturdays.

Mr. Brandsness stressed that the rebate program "will be paid directly to the patient by Sunrise Hospital and will have no effect on insurance claims." If a patient is admitted on a Friday or Saturday, and is confined for a week, a month or longer, the patient

EXHIBIT 4
Comparative Market Data

Hospitals	Licensed Beds	Percent of Total	1973	1974	1975	1976
Hospital A	211	16%	9%	10%	11%	11%
Hospital B	278	21	27	26	23	22
Sunrise	492	38	43	45	45	46
Hospital C	269	20	15	13	16	16
Hospital D	62	5	6	6	5	5
Total	1,312	100%	100%	100%	100%	100%

will receive a cash rebate covering the entire length of stay. Mr. Brandsness further stressed that the rebates "will amount, in all cases, to 5.25 percent of the entire hospital bill—not just for Fridays and Saturdays."

Within eight months the program had boosted weekend occupancy by between 15 and 30 percent and more than 2,200 patients had received $190,000 in rebates for an average of more than $85 per patient. One of the largest amounts paid to a patient under the program was a juvenile involved in an auto accident whose bill totaled over $22,000. The insurance company provided 100 percent coverage, thus paying the entire bill, the Sunrise Hospital rebated $1,164 to the patient.

Almost everyone was most happy with the plan. Doctors, who in the past were only "on call" on the weekends, now found themselves on the job. Doctors and nurses knew from the start that they would have to work a seven-day week. The biggest critic of the program, however, had been the insurance industry, distressed that rebates go to patients instead of insurers. Other hospitals in the area seemed skeptical of the whole idea.

The rebate program was abruptly stopped by Sunrise Hospital after 11 months of operation. Mr. David Brandsness stated that the "revolutionary" case rebate plan was suspended because large insurance companies were keeping the 5.25 percent patient-intended rebate for themselves. However, Mr. Brandsness said the hospital is pursuing legal action and intends to reinstate the program when possible.

"The rebate worked far better than we expected," he said, adding that Sunrise made no price increases in the 11 months since the program began. "I don't know of another hospital in the western United States that can say that." Mr. David Brandsness said the rebates amounted to $350,000 for patients coming in on Friday and Saturday.

He said the insurance companies believed that since they were insuring the patients, they should be the beneficiaries of the rebate. But Brandsness said that wasn't true because it was hospital profits that were to be redistributed to the patients and not insurance money. What eventually killed the program he said, was the insurance companies deducting the rebate themselves before they paid expenses to the hospital. Some companies, he charged, even conspired to get patients to boycott the hospital.

Mr. David Brandsness said hospitals must be allowed to initiate any cost-cutting innovations they can and not be hampered by outmoded concepts in hospital administration. "The health industry just tends to move at a slower rate...other companies have offered rebates and felt no repercussions," he said.

Mr. David Brandsness now had to face the same problem over again, i.e., how to get potential patients to check in on Friday or Saturday. In January 1977, Mr. David Brandsness announced that a drawing would be offered to those patients who check in on Friday or Saturday. The winner of the drawing, to be held on Monday, would win an all expense paid vacation for two worth $4,000 to the vacation spot selected. There would be a drawing every Monday—fifty-two weeks a year—for those patients who checked in the previous Friday or Saturday. Mr. David Brandsness hoped this new idea would be as successful as the cash rebate without the repercussions from the insurance companies.

THE COURTYARD

As Carl Hegwith, co-owner of the Courtyard, reflected on the current crises, he was uncertain how to proceed:

Everybody told us to open for lunch. They said that by dinner time, we would have cracked the nut (covered all costs). What we would take in during the dinner hours would be gravy. But this expansion has created a whole new set of problems. The way we generated and retained our clientele does not appear to be working now. In this business, you can be the hot spot one day, and be on the outside looking in on the next.

The Courtyard was one of the most successful restaurants in this major eastern city. For the last decade, it had been a favorite gathering place for politicians and the city's elite. Initially, the restaurant was only open for dinner, but after nine years of operation, Mr. Hegwith and Mr. Albert Copeland (Mr. Hegwith's partner) reorganized the restaurant and began serving lunch. However, soon after opening for the noon hours, the owners felt that they had to take some action if they were to maintain the restaurant's high status and level of quality—attributes that had originally made it so popular.

Accordingly, they hired a full-time maitre'd, Mr. Leo Newton. Prior to this, the owners had acted as maitre'd, alternating on successive evenings. Although such an arrangement had proven successful, Mr. Hegwith and Mr. Copeland felt that it was too constraining under the new conditions, and did not give them adequate time to oversee all of the operations needed for both lunch and dinner. As Mr. Copeland noted:

This case was prepared by Professor Dennis H. Tootelian, California State University, Sacramento.

We could do just fine as maitre'ds when we were only open in the evening hours. But now, we have no time to visit with our clientele, watch over the chef and his staff, and so on. Our success has been due to our excellent food and service; and, perhaps even more importantly, to the fact that we personally treat our clientele like royalty. Our whole approach to attracting customers has been oriented to cultivating VIP clientele, and then relying on word-of-mouth advertising. Our customers liked being greeted by name by the owners of the restaurant.

With the hiring of Leo as maitre'd, and the opening of some new restaurants, we have had some problems. The atmosphere is not the same, and our clientele has changed somewhat.

COMPANY HISTORY

The Courtyard was established nearly twelve years ago, as the result of Mr. Copeland's idea of opening a cocktail lounge and restaurant in the center of the business district of the city, which was also the capital of the state. Although the land was expensive, he leased the property for forty years and invited Mr. Hegwith to join him as a full partner.

Mr. Copeland previously worked with Mr. Hegwith in managing a relatively small hotel in a nearby city. Both men had held a variety of jobs, but neither had any restaurant experience. Mr. Copeland originally felt that the downtown area did not have many truly unique restaurants. Accordingly, he began looking for an unusual building adequate for conversion to a restaurant. He was faced with several alternatives and decided on an old Victorian-style house that had since been sold by the city to a builder. Based on the building's attractiveness, suitability, and proximity to the capitol, he took a long-term lease on the premises.

Mr. Copeland and Mr. Hegwith decided to decorate the restaurant in a late 19th century theme and create an atmosphere of old-world dining. They wanted to preserve as much of the old house as possible and tried to minimize the remodeling of the rooms to accommodate an enlarged dining area. In keeping with the theme, they purchased a large number of antiques, including serving plates, trays, mirrors, frames, bars, bottles, and pictures. They accomplished this so successfully that the Courtyard became known not only as an elegant restaurant, but also as a place of interest to antique collectors.

To cover their heavy investment, the owners decided to open sections of the establishment as they became ready. Thus, they initially opened the main bar for cocktails only and toward the end of the first year, they added two service bars. In the middle of the second year, they started serving food. The original menu was very basic and simple, oriented to what they believed to be average taste.

Two years later, three private dining rooms downstairs were added. These were called the Cellars I, II, and III. Because of their privacy, intimacy, and exquisite setting, these rooms became favorites for exclusive parties hosted for and by politicians. In the next year, an open patio area—from which the Courtyard got its name—opened for dinner during the summer. This later became a favorite lunch area as well.

RESTAURANT PERSONNEL AND OPERATIONS

Starting with four employees, the Courtyard staff grew to over fifty part- and full-time employees (see exhibits 1 and 2). From the beginning, however, the restaurant never followed a rigid organizational structure. Mr. Copeland's idea was that everybody should be friendly with each other, and he believed that any type of restriction would curtail this friendliness. As he noted:

We have been doing extremely well without having to boss everybody around, so why change it? There may come a day when our organization will grow even more, and we will need a general manager to oversee the operations of the business office and the dining rooms and bars. But we have not reached that point yet.

As active partners, Mr. Copeland and Mr. Hegwith supervised all hiring and firing, and each would be available to assist Mr. Newton with maitre'd duties on alternate nights.

The bar had been informally managed by Mr. Jack Tredd, who had been an employee of the Courtyard for more than eight years. He was forty-two years old and had about ten years of experience as a bartender and manager of bar business. According to Mr. Copeland:

Jack is not the fastest bartender in town because he likes to talk too much. But he is very honest, meticulous, and has the house's welfare at heart at all times. Most importantly, I think he knows many of the top people in town. Some politicians and big business people in the community say that they just come in to see Jack. I'm not sure if that is really true, but he definitely has been good for public relations.

When hired as maitre'd, Mr. Newton was given the power to hire, fire, and make any other personnel changes he deemed necessary. Actual hiring and firing, however, still had to be cleared with either Mr. Copeland or Mr. Hegwith. Mr. Newton, forty-seven years old, had been in the restaurant business for more than twenty-seven years. He did not have formal training but had practical experience in virtually every facet of restaurant operations. He had worked in many fine restaurants in California, New York, and Washington, D.C.

Mr. Newton had worked for the Courtyard on one earlier occasion. He had been a temporary maitre'd for nearly one and one-half years when Mr. Copeland was ill, sharing maitre'd responsibilities with Mr. Hegwith on alternate nights. During that time, Mr. Newton took great care to befriend many of the city's most influential people. In a very short period, he became a celebrity of sorts, speaking to numerous clubs and professional organizations, and making appearances on local radio and television shows. The main theme of his appearances centered on how to select a restaurant, and how to rate its quality of food and service.

The reaction of employees to Mr. Newton's hiring was less than enthusiastic, however. There had been a 50 percent turnover of waiters and nearly 80 percent turnover of busboys since he arrived. One waiter who had been with the Courtyard for several years commented:

CASE

EXHIBIT 1
Organizational Chart of the Courtyard

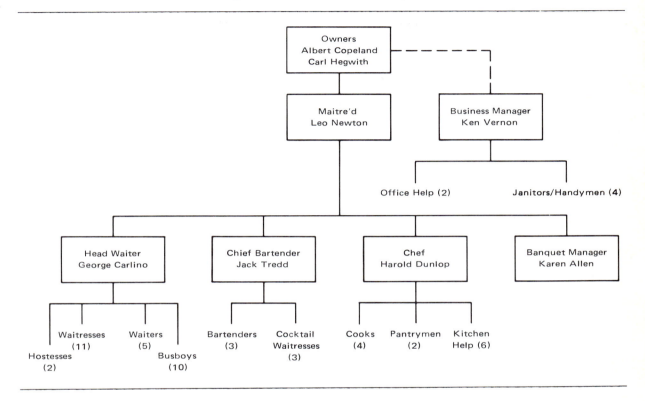

EXHIBIT 2
The Courtyard Staffing

Lunch

Waiters/Waitresses	6
Bartenders	2
Hostesses	2
Busboys	4

Dinner

Waiters*	9
Busboys*	6
Bartenders	2
Cocktail Waitresses	2

*One waiter and one busboy added for banquets.

Leo might know everybody in town and may have a good mind for the technical aspects of the restaurant business, but he sure doesn't know how to handle people. He can be very abrasive to employees. The morale around here is as low as I've ever seen it, and most employees do not feel secure in their jobs. That's why so many left; with a history of working at the Courtyard, you can get a job in many of the other restaurants in town. All of this has resulted in poorer customer service here. Before Leo arrived, our waiters knew who most of the important people were and made sure that they were well taken care of. Now that those employees are gone, our clientele simply don't get the same recognition and service that they were used to and that they came here for in the first place.

Mr. Harold Dunlop, the chef, was in his early fifties, and had over thirty years of experience cooking. He had been trained in Paris and New York and had come to the Courtyard over three years ago. Mr. Dunlop indicated that he and Mr. Newton frequently disagreed on restaurant policies:

The only thing Leo is concerned about is the number of people we serve. He does not take into consideration the size of the kitchen, the menu, and the timing of the parties. Yesterday, for example, he had booked two parties for lunch. Twenty in one group and twenty-five in the other; and both were set for 12:30, our busiest time. He let them order off of the regular menu instead of setting the menu in advance, and this created havoc. Timing of meals in instances like that is very difficult, and the quality of the lunches was not as good as it would have been if I had been informed and the menu selection limited. Unfortunately, this has happened on several occasions.

The banquet rooms were informally managed by Ms. Karen Allen, who had been employed by the Courtyard for six years. In reflecting on the working conditions, Ms. Allen noted:

Things are changing at the Courtyard. The quality parties are decreasing while the quantity of people being served has increased. We used to set the menu for private parties and most of the time we served exquisite gourmet dinners. Now, we seem to be doing more basic lunches and prime rib dinners. The clientele we are drawing for banquets seem to be looking for package deals with price a critical factor. Historically, price has been of little concern to our customers. The Cellar rooms are designed for a very special segment of the market, those who do not worry about expenses but want to have elegant atmosphere and unique food and wine. We still get the politicians and lobbyists, and the business parties, but not to the extent that we have in the past.

PHYSICAL LAYOUT

The main dining room had a capacity of 95 to 105 people per sitting, depending on whether tables were combined for larger parties. There were twenty-eight tables, eight of which were specifically for parties of two, and two tables seating six to eight. The remaining eighteen tables could be arranged in any desired combination. This offered maximum flexibility for seating arrangements.

Attached to this dining room was a service bar, which had an approximate seating capacity of thirty-five people. The layout of the restaurant is shown in exhibit 3.

The main bar had a Gay 90s design and originally was open from 6:00 PM to 2:00 AM, Monday through Saturday. Recently, however, the owners had decided to open it for lunches and private parties. Mr. Newton thought that the overflow from the main dining areas provided enough business to justify the bar's use for dining as well as for cocktails.

The three private dining rooms downstairs (Cellars I, II, and III) had seating capacities of ten to fifty people. Cellars I and II were the largest and had private bars which could be set up for special parties.

The owners and Mr. Newton felt that one of the restaurant's biggest attractions was the outside dining area. The courtyard had a capacity of eighty people. Arranged with twenty tables, each capable of seating four, the area was somewhat crowded. According to one lobbyist:

I like the courtyard area, but the tables are too close together. Assume that I'm talking to some legislators over lunch. Do you think I want to be heard by people at tables next to me? The trouble with the courtyard is that they have placed too many tables in it to accommodate the growing number of customers. There just isn't much privacy anymore. Besides, it's too well lighted, and some legislators don't like to be seen with lobbyists.

RESTAURANT OFFERINGS

The original menu used by the Courtyard had been very simple. In the fourth year of operation, however, Mr. Dunlop and Mr. Copeland had radically altered the food selection. Since that time, only minor changes had been made.

The current menu consisted of some American

EXHIBIT 3
Layout of the Courtyard

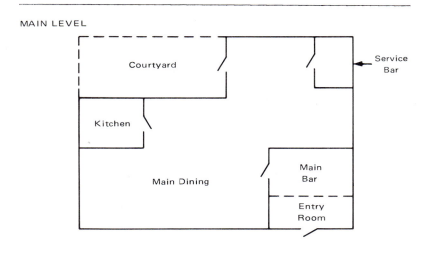

MAIN LEVEL

Courtyard

Service Bar

Kitchen

Main Bar

Main Dining

Entry Room

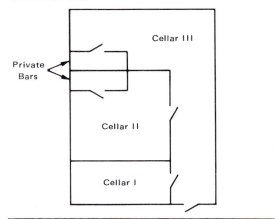

LOWER LEVEL

Cellar III

Private Bars

Cellar II

Cellar I

cuisine and an assortment of continental and flaming dishes. Most lunches and dinners were prepared in the kitchen, but the flaming entrees were prepared in the kitchen and then flamed by the waiters at the table. This required each waiter to have a knowledge of flaming dishes, and had caused some problems with the high turnover of personnel. Some complaints had been received about the quality of the flaming entrees,

and on one occasion, the busboy who assisted the waiter caught his jacket on fire.

The luncheon menu was very simple, and designed for quick service. All lunch items were prepared in the kitchen, and waitresses were used to serve the food. Mr. Newton adhered to a policy originally established by the owners, that women would serve lunch, and men would serve evening meals.

A new dessert menu was created by Mr. Newton soon after he was hired. It consisted of some standard favorites and some unique flaming desserts prepared at the table. While this added some attraction to the dining area, it also aggravated the problem of inexperienced personnel.

The wine list maintained by the Courtyard was one of the most extensive in the city. Mr. Newton insisted on making all wine selections for the restaurant, and had received numerous compliments on the wines available for lunch and dinner. Although such a wide selection of domestic and imported wines was expensive to keep in stock, Mr. Newton believed that it was essential if the Courtyard was to maintain a high-class clientele.

MARKETING PRACTICES

Following Mr. Copeland's theory that "the best advertising for restaurants is word-of-mouth," the Courtyard seldom advertised. It maintained a small advertisement in the Yellow Pages of the local telephone directory, but did no newspaper or television promotion. Over the years, the Courtyard had received extensive publicity in the local newspapers, so Mr. Copeland and Mr. Hegwith felt that they did not need to do much more. Recently, however, other restaurants had been receiving more attention—especially newer ones that also catered to the higher income clientele.

Each Christmas, the Courtyard sent attractive cards to each of its preferred customers. Inside each card was a replica of a silver dollar, which was good for a free drink at the restaurant throughout the holiday period. Mr. Copeland estimated that about 25 percent of these tokens were redeemed by customers.

The Courtyard's customers were predominantly professional people: high level state employees, politicians, lobbyists, and owners of successful business concerns in the city. Importantly, business fluctuated directly with legislative sessions, which tended to run from November through July. The busiest evenings were Mondays, Tuesdays, and Wednesdays since legislators were in the city on those days. Saturday nights were very popular, but Saturday patrons consisted mainly of nonlegislative clientele.

On the average, the Courtyard served 85 people for lunch, and 155 people for dinner. On some Saturdays, the restaurant served as many as 250 people for dinner.

Originally, the Courtyard was not affiliated with any credit card system. In the fourth year of operation, however, Mr. Copeland decided to accept most major nongasoline credit cards, and to offer an in-house credit system as well. At the most recent count, there were approximately 2,250 customers who had been approved for this in-house credit card. Mr. Copeland and Mr. Hegwith believed that their own credit card system was a good promotional device, and it did increase return business.

THE COMPETITION

The Courtyard's direct competition came from three other fine restaurants located a few blocks away. All four restaurants had almost identical menus and prices. Their principal differences were in their decor and atmosphere. The three competing restaurants featured more modern decor whereas the Courtyard retained its old-style dining theme, and had the outside eating area. The owners thought that those were significant advantages, especially the outdoor eating.

Two years ago, a high-fashion cocktail lounge and luncheon restaurant opened. It featured live entertainment, which none of the other restaurants in the area offered. This directly reduced the volume of the Courtyard's bar and after-dinner business. However, once the novelty wore off, the impact was believed to be negligible.

In assessing the competition, Mr. Copeland noted:

The more restaurants that open, the better it will be for us. It will bring more people out, and we'll get our share of the new business. Besides, none of the restaurants can directly compete with us because we are so well established. That's why we don't need to advertise.

Mr. Hegwith, however, was not as optimistic as his partner:

Even though all of these restaurants have somewhat different types of atmosphere, I'm still convinced

EXHIBIT 4
Income Statements
(hundreds of dollars)

	Last Year	Two Years Ago	Three Years Ago
Gross Revenues			
Food	$ 963	$ 865	$625
Bar	412	371	294
Total	$1,375	$1,236	$919
Cost of Goods	466	389	285
Gross Profit	$ 909	$ 847	$634
Expenses			
Selling Expenses	$ 376	$ 228	$173
Administrative Expenses	429	342	327
Total	$ 805	$ 570	$500
Net Profit Before Taxes	$ 104	$ 277	$134

EXHIBIT 5
Quarterly Income Statements for Lunch
(hundreds of dollars)

	1st Quarter	2nd Quarter	3rd Quarter	4th Quarter
Sales				
Food	$35	$40	$53	$37
Bar	12	17	24	14
Total	$47	$57	$77	$51
Cost of Goods	16	24	33	17
Gross Profit	$31	$33	$44	$34
Expenses				
Selling Expenses	$35	$34	$37	$36
Administrative Expenses	10	11	11	11
Total	$45	$45	$47	$47
Net Profit	($14)	($12)	($ 3)	($13)

that they will adversely affect us to at least some degree. Most of them advertise pretty heavily in the local papers, and they keep their names out in front of the public. We haven't been doing that for the last year or so.

The newest restaurant in the area was opened by two former employees of the Courtyard. After being dismissed by Mr. Newton, they opened a restaurant featuring a menu and wine list comparable to those of the Courtyard. The new restaurant's staff was made up primarily of ex-Courtyard employees, and Mr. Hegwith thought that they had a reasonably strong following.

FINANCIAL POSITION

Income statements for the last three years are shown in exhibit 4. Exhibit 5 contains quarterly income statements for lunches. Only recently did Mr. Copeland and Mr. Hegwith find that the lunch period was not profitable. Yet, they were not sure that adequate time had been given for "the word to spread" about the Courtyard's being open for lunch.

THE FUTURE

In reviewing their current situation, Mr. Copeland and Mr. Hegwith could not decide on what action, if any, they should take. Both agreed that the most recent financial statistics were disturbing. Mr. Copeland, however, thought that it was too early for any drastic changes.

Mr. Hegwith, on the other hand, had a somewhat different attitude:

We have made some fundamental mistakes in my opinion. We lost a lot of good people, and some are now competing with us. There was a lot of controversy following Leo's hiring. Before Leo was hired, we had a very unique following. Our customers tended to have exquisite taste and unlimited budgets. It was not unusual for our clientele to spend as much as $75 for a meal and drinks.

Leo's contention was that these people would tie up a table for the entire evening, and reduce the number of turns we could get. I pointed out to him that there was a trade-off between quality and quantity, but he disagrees. As you go to high volume, the amount spent for dinner will decrease, and the high spenders may go elsewhere if they feel rushed.

I think the Courtyard is beginning to appeal more to the mass market than the city's elite. Yet, we are not going after them in the traditional ways, which include heavy advertising. Our approach of using personalized service is great for

the upper-class clientele, but it is hard to maintain for larger volumes of customers. Ideally, I'd like to spend some money on advertising, say $15,000 to $20,000, and keep the high-class image of our restaurant intact. It's kind of scary to think about changing our style and image now. Who would appeal to the VIPs? Maybe Leo and Jack would quit and start a restaurant of their own for this group. That would be disastrous for the Courtyard.

INLAND OCEANS, INC. —BIG SURF

For most people, surfing in the desert is highly unlikely. However, Phil Dexter found a way to make this a possibility.

In 1969, Dexter and the Phoenix, Arizona, consulting firm, Sergent, Hauskins & Beckwith, convinced Clairol that their idea to construct an inland ocean for surfing was technically possible and profitably attractive. Later that year, a $2.5 million complex, called Big Surf, was constructed in Tempe, Arizona.

Big Surf is a twenty-acre recreation facility that has over 600 feet of sandy beach and palm trees surrounding a pump-filled, 500,000 gallon reservoir. Perfect five-foot-high waves are produced every fifty seconds, providing a 350-foot-long ride to the beach.

The huge reservoir is 20 feet wide, 160 feet long, and 47 feet high and holds the water and the hydraulic head that creates the waves. Fifteen modified tainter gates, which open and close in two to three seconds, release about 70,000 gallons of water through the nine-foot-deep narrow end of a keyhole-shaped lagoon. As illustrated in exhibits 1

This case was prepared by Dr. Charles H. Patti, Arizona State University.

and 2, the lagoon's four-inch-thick reinforced concrete floor has a three-foot-high baffle directly in front of the gate portals, which deflects the sudden discharge and creates the wave. The perfect wave begins to spill about 75 feet from the base of the reservoir wall and surfers catch it at this point.

In addition to the surfing and swimming facility, Big Surf also has a 300-foot water slide, a food and drink concession, an equipment rental service (for surfboards, rubber rafts, etc.), locker facilities, pinball arcade, and a surf shop that sells swimwear, sunglasses, suntan oil, etc.

In late 1971, a small group of investors formed a corporation, Inland Oceans, Inc., and purchased Big Surf from Clairol. In addition to assuming control and management of Big Surf, Inland Oceans began formulating plans for establishing franchises for other surf centers.

THE MARKET

Big Surf is located in one of the country's fastest growing metropolitan areas. Between 1960 and 1974, the population of the Phoenix area increased 45 percent. Dispelling the erroneous notion that Phoenix is "where old people go to retire," the median age is 24.6 years, with more than one-third of the household heads under 35 years.

Because of its warm, dry climate, Phoenix is a popular leisure and recreation area. Many of the area's leisure activities revolve around water. Phoenix has nearly 25,000 private swimming pools and 4,500

EXHIBIT 1
Big Surf's Oil-to-Water Hydraulic System

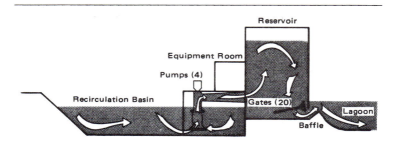

EXHIBIT 2
Big Surf's Water Return System

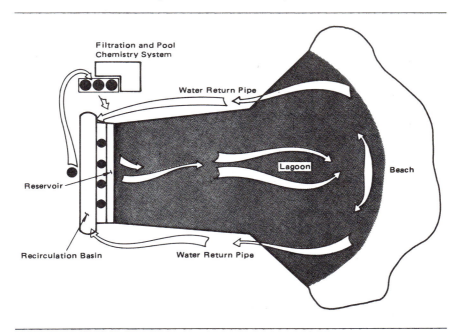

public and commercial pools (apartments, motels, etc.). In a ninety-day period, 51 percent of the area's population go boating or swimming at least once.

The Phoenix age profile is also custom-made for Big Surf's expectations that the bulk of regular customers would be in the under-twenty-one group. Since 1971, the under-twenty-one group has continued to represent the bulk of the Big Surf customers and is still considered the primary market. The next most important target market for Big Surf is the young marrieds (through age 29) with one or two small children. These two groups constitute 52.8 percent of the Phoenix metro area population.

Another target market for Big Surf is organizations. Big Surf offers an attractive recreation facility for any group with 25 to 10,000 members. Educational, religious, political, social, community service, and commercial organizations are among those that have rented the entire Big Surf facility for private parties.

BIG SURF PROMOTION

Since the opening of Big Surf in 1969, a number of promotional tools and techniques have been used to create awareness and stimulate attendance. In 1969 and 1970, Clairol relied primarily on publicity and advertising. News releases, press kits, open houses, and promotional literature were all used to inform potential customers that Big Surf was a new and unique facility that offered an exciting recreation activity. Clairol also used advertising extensively to encourage attendance by offering a variety of special promotions. Exhibit 3 presents an example of one of Big Surf's newspaper advertisements.

Most of this early advertising and publicity emphasized the surfing activity and there was a concentrated effort to attract a portion of the 26,000 student population of nearby Arizona State University. While it is difficult to assess the effectiveness of Clairol's early promotion, Inland Ocean's management felt that Clairol's large advertising expenditures and comprehensive publicity efforts contributed heavily to making Big Surf known as one of Arizona's recreation attractions.

Between 1971 and 1972, several developments took place which altered the direction of Big Surf's promotional program. The new owners, Inland Oceans, Inc., assumed complete control of Big Surf. They felt that most of the "awareness" communications task has been accomplished through the promotional efforts of Clairol; therefore, advertising expenditures were reduced substantially. In 1972, total spending for advertising and publicity was $63,000—less than a third of 1970 and 1971 expenditures.

Also, attendance data indicated that Big Surf was

EXHIBIT 3
1970 Newspaper Advertisement for Big Surf

not attracting the college market. Despite numerous promotions aimed at the college market, high school teenagers and young families were identified as the primary source of customers. Consequently, advertising directed to the college market was minimized and more high school and "family-oriented" promotional themes were initiated.

Finally, customer research and attendance data indicated a growing interest in the Big Surf facility but a declining interest in surfing. This increased interest in the overall water facility was substantiated by rental equipment receipts which showed a 40 percent increase in rubber raft rentals and a 25 percent decrease in surfboard rentals.

Many of the trends and developments of 1971 and 1972 continued in 1973 and 1974. A 1971 survey of Big Surf customers showed that swimming was the preferred activity for 81.5 percent of all visitors, rafting was second (57.4 percent), and surfing was third (14.6 percent). In a small study done in the fall of 1974, customer responses to the question, "What is your favorite Big Surf activity?" showed the following results:

Activity	% of Respondents
Rafting	46.7
Swimming	34.9
Surf slide*	7.0
Surfing	6.3
Other	5.1

*The surf slide was added in 1973

Also, increased use of Big Surf by families encouraged Inland Oceans to pursue this market more aggressively and during 1973 and 1974 more advertising was directed to family promotions (see exhibit 4).

As shown in exhibit 5, it was also during 1973–1974 that group sales began to represent a significant portion of Big Surf's total attendance. Groups were reached primarily by direct mail and inquiries about rental of the facility were then completed by telephone or personal call by a Big Surf representative to the interested group.

CURRENT SITUATION

In formulating his plans for the 1975 season, Mr. Kenneth Runkel, Big Surf's advertising manager, prepared the following information:

EXHIBIT 4
1975 Big Surf Advertisement
Promoting Family Night

A. Target markets (in order of importance):
1. preteens and teenagers (75 percent of the visitors to Big Surf are ages nine to nineteen)
2. young marrieds (household head under thirty) with children
3. organizations
4. college students
B. Advertising theme: Big Surf is a unique, action-oriented recreation facility that offers an oceanside beach atmosphere in a desert environment.
C. Advertising budget: $60,000 (excluding direct mail and publicity)
D. Advertising objectives:
1. to build preference for Big Surf as a recreation alternative among the primary target market
2. to interest young marrieds with children in Big Surf
3. to increase awareness among local organizations of Big Surf as a group activity facility

As exhibit 6 indicates, Big Surf has used most of the major advertising media during the past two years. In the past, the selection of media has been determined by the limitations of the size of the budget and management's "feelings" about the relative effectiveness of an individual medium.

CASE

EXHIBIT 5
Big Surf Attendance

Month	1971 Total	1971 Group	1972 Total	1972 Group	1973 Total	1973 Group	1974 Total	1974 Group
February	—	N/A	—	N/A	121	—	1,090	—
March	8,383		29,782		2,242	911	11,065	410
April	21,419		28,887		17,837	2,359	42,257	2,786
May	19,765		24,894		28,688	17,665	51,341	23,205
June	27,411		34,281		48,225	17,184	55,157	10,798
July	39,129		50,712		43,367	7,529	55,730	7,969
August	37,703		40,577		40,977	11,014	58,028	11,709
September	15,309		13,814		12,950	3,344	12,812	2,903
October	—		—		—	—	—	—
Totals	169,119		222,947		194,407	60,006	287,480	59,780
Number of operating days	141		152		142		144	
Average daily attendance	1,199		1,467		1,369		1,996	

EXHIBIT 6
Big Surf Advertising Media Expenditures

Medium	1973	1974
Television	$33,317	$ —
Radio	13,154	19,096
Newspapers	15,557	8,904
Totals	$62,028	$28,000

ATLANTIC INDUSTRIAL SUPPLY

Atlantic Industrial Supply, a fabricator and industrial supply distributor, grew from $1.2 million to over $3 million in sales between 1979 and 1983. The president of the company, Mr. Dean Richards, assessed 1982 as the most exciting sales year in the ten-year history of the company. In commenting about the position of the "bottom-line," however, the president stated:

We've got to increase the profitability of the company in 1984. We were looking for it in 1983 and 1982 and just didn't get it. We've got to do it in 1984. Otherwise it gets harder and harder to sell the company. We can't just keep going further and further in debt.

HISTORY

Mr. Richards had been a successful rancher and real estate developer. The company he worked for had offered him several attractive positions when his most recent project was completed, but he wanted to be his own boss. When he bought Atlantic Rubber Supply in 1973 for $220,000, he was actually looking for a job. In his words:

I knew absolutely nothing about industrial distribution. To learn the business, I placed myself into as many different situations as I could so I could benefit from what the industry was doing. I started reading industry magazines, attending industry seminars, talking to other distributors, formulating ideas and opinions and translating that back into what our company was.

This case was prepared by Professor Ralph M. Gaedeke, California State University, Sacramento.

An attempt to merge his company with another industrial supplier was disrupted by a fire that almost destroyed the other company's business. Instead of merging or expanding the rubber business, Richards decided to take a different marketing approach.

We decided then to become more things to the people that we already knew. We took our clothing, footwear, and gloves out of our rubber company and added eye, head and face protection. We hired another manager and set up a separate division—the Safety Equipment Company.

I promised myself, when I bought the company ten years ago, not to get involved in staff functions any more than I absolutely had to; to stay in the role of a manager. As a result, I paid a very, very dear price in terms of the bottom line of the corporation. I acquiesced to a lot of mistakes in the interest of letting people grow that conceivably would not have been made had I made the decisions myself. If my total objective was profits, many of the things that were done in the last ten years would not have happened. But my objective was growth, stability, and perpetual energy within the organization. No matter who was running the company, it would still function.

In 1981 Mr. Richards decided to look for stronger profitability and to no longer sacrifice the bottom line for corporate growth and personnel training. The company added industrial hardware, moved to an industrial park site, and was renamed Atlantic Industrial Supply.

ORGANIZATION

The Contractor Supply Division was created in 1982 with the purchase of all the inventory of a local contractor supply company. The purchase was initiated by the manager of the supply company, who was made manager of the division. Mr. Richards described the manager, Rob Parnell forthrightly.

He's a dynamic guy, an abrasive fellow. He's not an organization man. I perceived some of this when I met him but overestimated my ability and my company's ability to get him to adjust to our ways. We went through six tough months while the organization was coming apart at the seams. This guy was just tearing down everything that we had ever done—our standards, values, and systems. He brought into the company a different viewpoint on how you should treat people, how much work you should get out of them, whether you should fire them or not fire them. His was more of a despotic than a democratic approach.

This period was described as a crisis for the company during which changes took place that modified the company's organizational charts. (These charts are shown in exhibits 1 and 2; operating structure and brief job descriptions are shown in exhibit 3.) Mr. Parnell was made general manager of the entire company. Mr. Michael Fergeson was brought in as vice president in charge of finance. In addition, there were complications from the financial decline, and the organization's structure was again modified as shown in exhibit 4. Mr. Richards explained:

I've turned responsibility for running the company on a day-to-day basis over to Rob and we've been struggling with it since then—to define what those responsibilities are and what they are not. There are still some unclear areas. But I'm confident, because of the kind of relationship that Rob, Michael and I have, that over a reasonable period of time we'll resolve the majority of them, and that there will emerge a clearer understanding of just what I want to stay involved in and what I don't. It's hard for Rob to take over the organization, and it's hard for me to let it go when I don't want to let it all go. I just want to let a certain portion of it go, and we're struggling to define just what that is.

In describing Mr. Richards' relinquishment of daily operational matters and Mr. Parnell's assumption of the role of general manager, Mr. Parnell explained:

In reality the overall operations of the company became mine with a decision Dean and I reached one evening last year, based on my ability to better understand what the customer wants. I have the product knowledge, as opposed to Dean, who came into this business from ranching and real estate. Dean is a good financial guy, a great guy. I only left Goodyear because of him, he's top notch. Obviously, he made the decision a long time ago that he really had no intention of learning the difference between a piece of hose and a piece of conveyor belt. It wasn't of interest to him, but it was very much of interest to me. I like the smell of rubber.

That's been the approach—his financial ability and my sales ability have gone along together and formed a fairly good working relationship. The relationship has provided a lot of latitude, which is what I didn't have in a large corporation. I wanted to try some things which I just couldn't do during my time. Michael is taking over some of Dean's responsibilities as they relate to finance. There are still a lot of problems and questions which must be solved by the three of us.

A review of operating committee meetings for the previous two and one-half years revealed much about how the company responded to day-to-day operational, planning, and controlling problems. These meetings had been held frequently, typically weekly, in numerous locations and at varying times.

All managers were expected to attend and report on subjects addressed to them in the agenda distributed prior to the meeting. The agenda items consisted of "follow-up" and "new business" topics ranging in complexity from a "no smoking" policy to new catalog development. Although policy was not formulated in the operations committee meetings, procedures and methods were initiated, discussed, and established at these sessions.

PRODUCTION

Although Atlantic Industrial Supply acted primarily as a distributor of industrial supplies, the company was also involved in adding value (mostly belting and hosing) to existing products in the fabrication department of the Rubber Division. The fabrication process was largely job-shop oriented; that is, making products to a particular customer's specifications. Fabrication did not occur in either the Safety or

EXHIBIT 1

Atlantic Industrial Supply—Formal Organization Chart

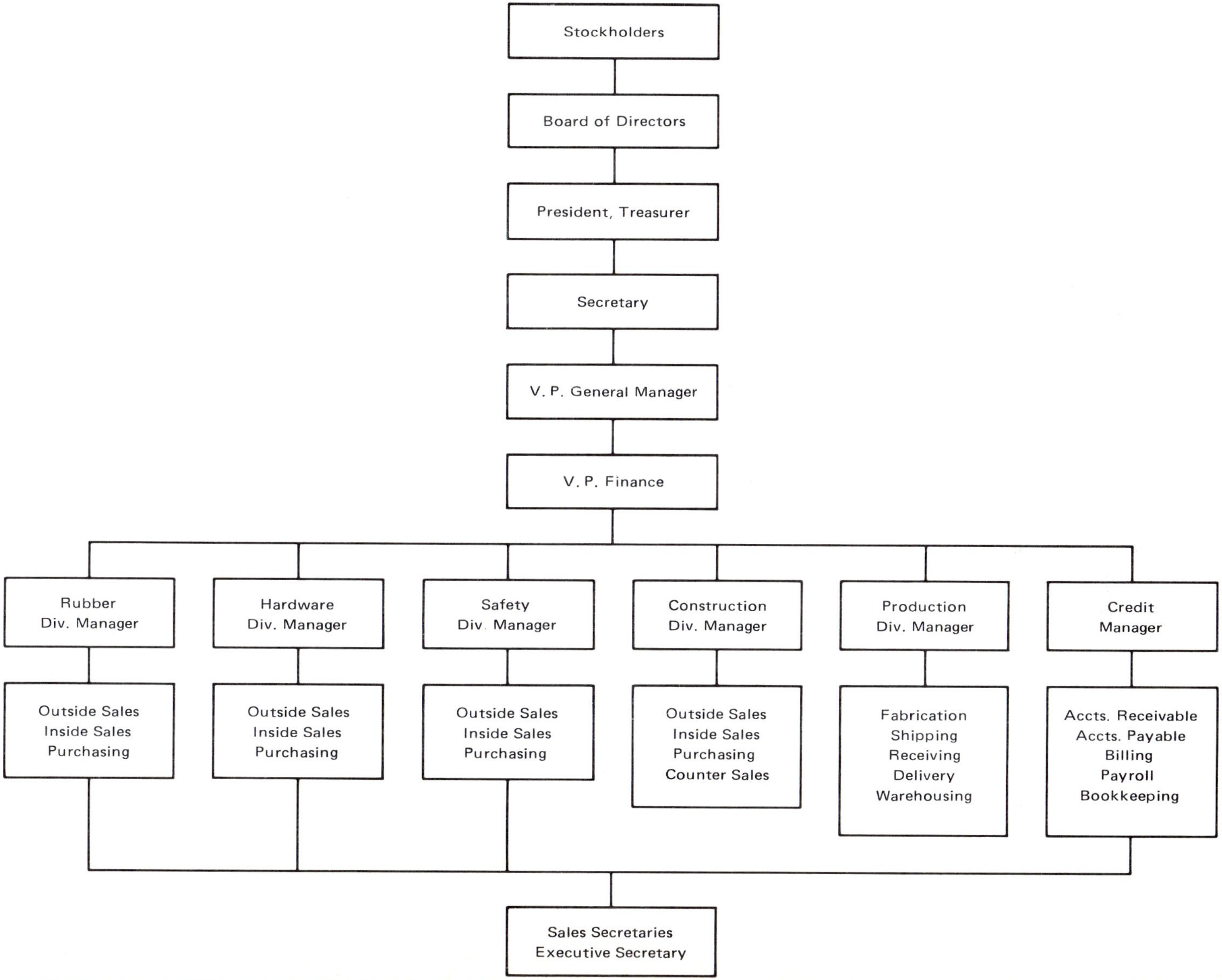

CASE

EXHIBIT 2
Atlantic Industrial Supply
Functional Organization

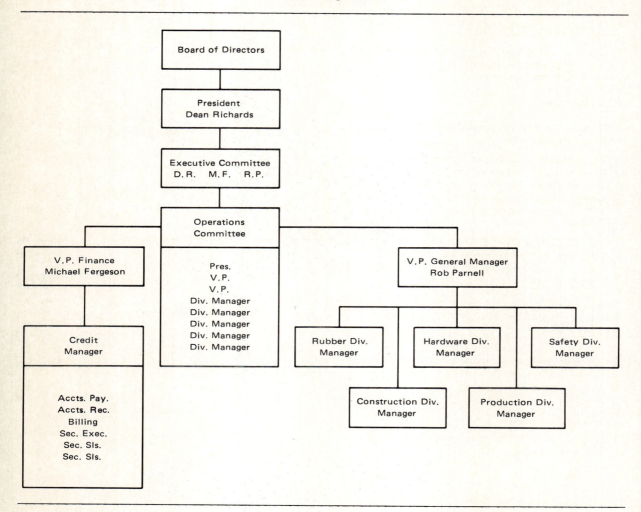

CASE

EXHIBIT 3
Atlantic Industrial Supply
Operating Structure and Job Descriptions

The Operating Structure

To carry out its major functions, the Company is divided into six departments, each of which is supervised by a manager. These units consist of four marketing or product divisions—Rubber, Safety, Hardware, and Construction—and one Production Division and an Accounting Department.

Product Divisions

Each product division is responsible for the purchasing, pricing and sales of its products. The sales force of each is divided into three separate functions:

1. Outside Sales: Field salespeople travel throughout the trade area on predetermined call schedules. They promote the Company, its products, and its services, and help customers to solve operating problems.
2. Telephone Sales: These salespeople handle incoming phone orders and inquiries and assist the outside salespeople.
3. Counter Sales: These salespeople service customers who choose to do business at the plant. They also assist in a variety of other functions, such as telephone sales, counter sales, will-call, inventory counts, and the pricing and costing of completed invoices.

The Product Divisions have been kept separate so that the sales force of each will become more specialized in knowledge of its own product line, resulting in better customer service.

Production Division

The Production Division coordinates its activities closely with those of the four product divisions. It is responsible for the timely delivery to the customer of all orders in the proper condition and quantity. This responsibility requires that the members of the Production Division:

1. promptly notify the marketing divisions of stock shortages so that new orders may be placed with suppliers;
2. receive and shelve merchandise for all of the product divisions;
3. locate, pack, cut, and/or fabricate all of the items required to fill an order;
4. package attractively the products in each order and ship or deliver them to the customer.

Accounting Department

The Accounting Department's functions include such activities as credit, accounting, record keeping, and personnel record changes for all of the divisions.

Administration

The administration of the Company is headed up by three key members of the management team: the president, the vice-president, general manager, and the vice-president, finance. These three persons form the executive committee, which coordinates the operations of the Company in pursuing overall long-range corporate objectives. The members of the executive committee, along with the managers of each division, make up the operations committee. The operations committee deals more with the day-to-day problems facing the Company and sets short-run goals and operating policies designed to move the Company toward its long-range objectives.

(Exhibit 3 continues on next page)

EXHIBIT 3 (*continued*)

Typical Jobs Performed

Below is a list and a short description of the typical job functions performed by the Company's personnel.

PRESIDENT.
Provides overall corporate strategy, planning, financing leadership and management evaluation.

VICE-PRESIDENT, GENERAL MANAGER
Provides leadership, coordination and assistance to all division managers in procedures, personnel training, goal setting and goal attainment. Develops an overall marketing strategy for the Company's products in conjunction with each product division.

VICE-PRESIDENT, FINANCE
Assists in corporate financing and evaluation of corporate performance, supervises all accounting functions, and acts as personnel officer.

PRODUCT DIVISION MANAGER
Provides leadership to all personnel assigned to his division in purchase, inventory control and sale of industrial products.

PRODUCTION DIVISION MANAGER
Provides division leadership and coordinates all activities related to the receiving, warehousing, manufacturing, fabricating, repairing, delivery, and shipping of product sales and services.

ADVERTISING MANAGER
Designs, coordinates, and directs comprehensive corporate advertising and promotion activities. Presently this function is handled by the President.

PERSONNEL OFFICER
Develops and maintains personnel information and records on each of the Company's employees; handles problems relating to personnel matters, and is responsible for developing company policies relating to personnel.

PURCHASING AGENT
Coordinates inventory control of his division's products by keeping records of the merchandise ordered by his division and its customers, by maintaining contact with present suppliers, by seeking out new suppliers as alternative sources of products when necessary, by evaluating and recording price changes in the division's products, and by handling problems in delivery of products to the customer.

MARKETING SERVICES REPRESENTATIVE
Develops a comprehensive knowledge of his assigned accounts and territory and pursues a sales servicing plan of the products assigned to him to sell.

INSIDE SALES COORDINATORS
Provide a high level of sales information and service to customers over the telephone and through the mail, and provide coordination of services with those of the Marketing Services Representatives.

COUNTER SALES COORDINATORS
Provide over-the-counter service to the general public in retail sales by supplying information about the Company's products and assembling and pricing of orders.

RECEIVING PERSONNEL
Record the receipt of products from suppliers and inform the appropriate product division of such receipt.

MANUFACTURING AND FABRICATION PERSONNEL
Alter, assemble, manufacture, or fabricate existing products to meet the specifications required by an individual customer.

WAREHOUSE AND STORAGE PERSONNEL
Properly and efficiently store the products carried by the Company so they are easily and quickly accessible, and informs the Product Divisions when the level of items stocked becomes low.

SHIPPING AND DELIVERY PERSONNEL
Insure prompt delivery or shipment of the products ordered by a customer.

EXHIBIT 4

Atlantic Industrial Supply
Modified Organization Chart

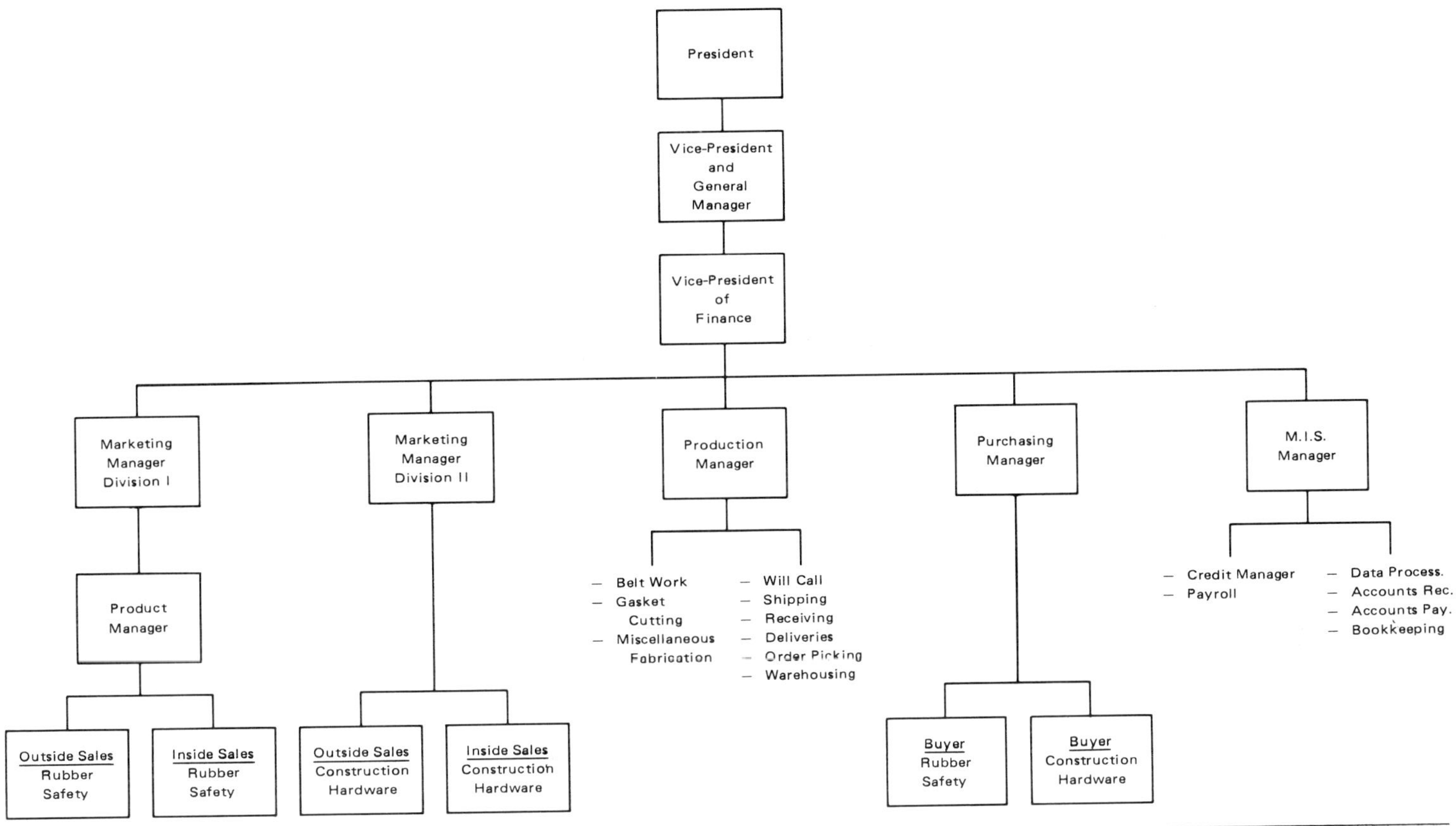

President

Vice-President and General Manager

Vice-President of Finance

Marketing Manager Division I
- Outside Sales Rubber Safety
- Product Manager
  - Inside Sales Rubber Safety

Marketing Manager Division II
- Outside Sales Construction Hardware
- Inside Sales Construction Hardware

Production Manager
- Belt Work
- Gasket Cutting
- Miscellaneous Fabrication
- Will Call
- Shipping
- Receiving
- Deliveries
- Order Picking
- Warehousing

Purchasing Manager
- Buyer Rubber Safety
- Buyer Construction Hardware

M.I.S. Manager
- Credit Manager
- Payroll
- Data Process.
- Accounts Rec.
- Accounts Pay.
- Bookkeeping

Hardware Divisions, as these were composed of products described as "pick and pull" items. The only exception to this was a line of rainwear made to company specifications in Taiwan for the Safety Division.

MARKETING
Characteristics of Consumers

Atlantic Industrial Supply serviced approximately 3,000 accounts, ranging in size from small farmers and machine shops to large industrial equipment manufacturers. Rob Parnell identified AIS's primary customers as original equipment manufacturers (OEMs). He felt that the company's "ability to work with OEMs in solving problems in various evolutionary stages" had helped establish AIS's strong reputation among local OEMs.

AIS also served manufacturers in the mobile home industry; city, county and state agencies; PVC pipe extruders; and various construction contractors. Mr. Parnell estimated that 90 percent of all business with city, county, and state agencies was done on a bid basis, but that less than 10 percent of AIS's total business relied on bidding.

One of the company's marketing policies was to concentrate on the company's largest customers and attempt to increase their sales. Mr. Parnell explained:

We have 3,000 accounts but really only want to deal with 900 of them. They pay their bills on time, give lead time, and buy large quantities. I am obviously not suggesting we forget the other 2,100 accounts, but we do not concentrate on them. It is walk-in and phone-type business and we don't pay commissions on it. Little effort is made to seek their business or we would go broke.

Product Line

As an industrial distributor, AIS served the needs of industrial customers by providing a wide variety of products and services. In 1983, the company's industrial products fell into four broad groups, and two marketing divisions had been formed to handle their distribution: Marketing Division I, comprising Rubber and Safety, and Marketing Division II,

Hardware and Construction. In 1982, Rubber comprised 50 percent of sales, Safety had 22 percent, Hardware 21 percent and Construction 7 percent; in 1975 the figures were 55 percent, 22.5 percent, and 22.5 percent respectively. (The Construction division was just beginning operations.) Sales were expected to steadily decrease in Rubber products, reflecting the growth of competition in the area. While both the Safety and Construction divisions were increasing in sales, the Hardware division was not progressing as management had hoped. Mr. Parnell attributed this to an initial lack of expertise in entering the field and difficulty in identifying a competitive advantage or "knack." He explained:

Our specialty in Rubber is offering a high quality product, either through redistributing it or creating new products out of existing products. We see fabrication as our 'knack' in this area and we see it growing, as it is very profitable.

In Safety, our 'knack' is aimed at personal protection only. We are not involved in safety equipment. Most companies offer a full line of personal protection and equipment together but AIS is doing well by offering personal protection only. Entering the equipment end of safety does not appear feasible—although I might get an objection to that from Dean Richards.

In the Construction division, AIS emphasized prompt delivery by distributing through stocked vans. Sales in 1981 were only $75,000, but were expected to increase to $900,000 in 1984. "It was tough to break into construction," said Mr. Parnell, "but we have a very experienced guy who helped us. He brought twenty years of experience in contracting with him to the company. This allowed us to quickly penetrate the market."

Selling and Advertising Practices

AIS salespeople specialized by geographical area as well as by product. Marketing Division I aimed its sales efforts at a wide variety of markets, while Marketing Division II aimed its products at a specific market. There were a total of sixteen salespeople—eight in the field, six inside on the telephone, and two inside at counter sales. A typical salesperson would handle 160 to 175 accounts, of which 30 were considered primary.

Salespeople were selected by the vice president of marketing in conjunction with the two division managers, in an interview session, after an initial screening of applicants. The company used the Klein test in addition to the personal interview to evaluate sales potential. Salespeople were sent to a Dale Carnegie course designed to improve selling technique, and were then trained in-house and by manufacturing representatives from AISs major suppliers. Nine months was the estimated time to effectively train a salesman.

Mr. Parnell had established a sales goal of $100,000 in sales for each employee in 1984, up from $72,000 in 1983. For 1984, projected sales were $3,880,000 and gross dollar profits were $1,297,000. The general manager felt such goals were instrumental in controlling expenses; if they were not met, corrective action would have to be taken. In 1983, four employees were terminated when it was felt that sales did not justify their existence. Mr. Parnell remarked:

Thus far, AIS has not been that profitable. I see that changing this year as a result of better expense control—that is, working and building a (sales) territory and then splitting it instead of putting a man into a territory and subsidizing him until he develops it—realignment of sales territories, better handling of inventory, proper placement of people, asking people to work harder than they ever thought possible, and not replacing a person until there is absolutely no other way.

The total advertising budget was $21,000 for 1983 and $50,000 for 1984. This included yellow page advertisements in telephone directories and special product mailers sent to established customers. The mailers were aimed at particular individuals within a company (safety director, maintenance personnel, purchasing agent, and contractors) as part of the effort to produce more sales from existing primary accounts.

FINANCE

Mr. Michael Fergeson, CPA, was vice president in charge of the financial affairs of the company. He was also responsible for the management information system which had been installed in 1983.

The operating results of the last five years showed the effects of the company's growth and acquisition policies (see exhibits 5 and 6). AIS used its inventory and accounts receivable as the basis for its short-term financing. The bank was willing to loan the company up to 80 percent of its accounts receivable at the prime interest rate plus 3 percent, and up to 60 percent of its inventory at the prime interest rate plus 4 percent. The projected cash flow schedule for fiscal year ending November 1983 showed that this line of credit would be needed, plus another $37,000. The necessary loans totaled $9,070,140 for the entire year with no one month exceeding $862,000 of short-term financing.

PROFITABILITY

Mr. Fergeson felt that the immediate goal of the company was to become profitable. In the past there had been a policy of "growth for growth's sake," but the emphasis had switched to net profitability. Mr. Fergeson cited an example of the growth policy of the past by saying that in 1982 there had been initially six outside salespeople, of whom only two were profitable. Despite this, AIS had added three more salespeople with their acquisition of the construction accessory line. These three salespeople were unprofitable during 1982.

But there was now a different attitude toward decisions. Profitability was recognized as being necessary in order to finance future growth and increase financial leverage. There was more attention being paid to operating costs, and the company was attempting to cover the same sales area with fewer people. Mr. Fergeson predicted an increase in net income because of sales growth and because of management's determination to keep fixed costs, such as salaries, at their present level. Salaries accounted for 60 percent of the company's operating expenses. This spreading of fixed costs over larger sales revenues, plus the savings from inventory control as a result of

EXHIBIT 5
AIS Statement of Consolidated Income
Fiscal Year Ending November 30

	1983	1982	1981	1980	1979
Net Sales and Revenues	$3,007,072	$2,680,936	$2,240,420	$1,734,558	$1,227,343
Costs and Expenses:					
Cost of sales	1,945,838	1,805,909	1,445,384	1,126,583	809,686
Selling, administrative					
expenses, etc.	1,009,699	775,843	711,237	539,838	384,547
Interest expense	59,380	43,778	34,702	11,328	6,157
Total Costs and Expenses	$3,014,917	$2,625,530	$2,191,323	$1,677,749	$1,200,390
Income (loss) before taxes					
and extraordinary items	(7,845)	55,406	49,097	56,809	26,953
Loss on sale of capital equipment			12,256		
Taxes on income	730	15,718	9,516	21,963	3,756
Net Income or Loss	($ 8,575)	$ 39,687	$ 27,325	$ 34,846	$ 23,197

implementing a computerized system, formed the basis for Mr. Fergeson's expectations for greater profitability. He saw the need to continue to grow in order to utilize the base they had developed.

INDUSTRY AND COMPETITION

The industry was highly competitive—hence, the great reliance on outside salespeople. The company was well known throughout its trade area. AIS had a broader line of products than any of its local competitors. Management felt that in its sales area, AIS had 55–60 percent of the market in rubber goods, 40 percent of the sales in safety equipment items, 10 percent in hardware and tools, and 15 percent in construction accessories. AIS was the largest distributor of safety products in the primary trade area.

Its main competition was local, but not necessarily locally owned. Competition for sales in the rubber segment was from both local firms and large regional firms. In the three other product segments there was competition from small, specialized local firms. These firms were able to offer the customer a larger inventory of a specialized product line, a better price

on some items because of bulk buying, and in some cases, more product knowledge.

In 1982, AIS had sought to overcome its occasional disadvantage in product knowledge by having some of its salespeople specialize in single product areas. As Mr. Fergeson saw it, this decision had advantages and disadvantages. He felt that this change in selling procedure was more costly. Since many of their customers purchased from more than one product line, more salespeople were now involved with each customer. However, dividing the areas allowed each salesperson to offer the customer greater product knowledge. Mr. Fergeson felt that AIS's competence now was in product knowledge, sales ability, and in knowing and being able to meet customer needs.

THE FUTURE

Mr. Richards discussed the company's immediate future by explaining:

The year 1984 should be a very exciting one, as well as the most successful one in the history of the corporation. I believe that we now have an organizational structure that will permit us to

CASE

EXHIBIT 6
AIS Consolidated Balance Sheets
Fiscal Year Ending November 30

	1983	1982	1981	1980	1979
ASSETS					
Current Assets					
Cash	$ 500	$ 11,014	$ 500	$ 500	$ 500
Accounts/r-net	348,939	276,405	242,908	376,350	147,432
Inventory	738,322	532,110	478,728	327,006	256,287
Prepaid expenses	45,318	27,615	38,773	8,554	4,938
Total Current Assets	$1,133,079	$847,144	$760,909	$712,410	$409,157
Property and Equipment, less depreciation					
Autos and truck	$ 2,910	$ 1,648	$ 3,846	$ 6,179	$ 5,523
Furniture and equipment	58,622	41,699	37,700	13,246	13,992
Leasehold improvements	15,470	12,630	11,714	12,769	14,513
Total property and equipment	$ 77,002	$ 55,977	$ 53,260	$ 32,194	$ 34,028
Other Assets	$ 57,605	$ 52,310	$ 46,292	$ 15,668	$ 10,203
TOTAL ASSETS	$1,267,686	$955,431	$860,461	$760,272	$453,388
LIABILITIES					
Notes	$ 637,217	$366,191	$346,205	$137,049	$ 17,455
Contracts	19,614	16,627	12,827	—	—
Accounts	169,625	138,338	129,784	296,911	112,923
Accrued expenses	59,101	42,593	23,337	42,969	3,773
Taxes	12,611	25,674	19,452	26,093	4,327
Accrued interest	5,668	3,541	3,892	—	5,493
Total Current Liabilities	$ 903,837	$592,964	$535,497	$503,022	$143,971
Long term notes	$ 48,162	$ 38,205	$ 40,388	—	$ 80,000
TOTAL LIABILITIES	$ 951,999	$631,169	$575,885	$503,022	$223,970
CAPITAL					
Stock outstanding	$ 120,709	$120,709	$120,709	$120,709	$120,709
R/E	194,979	203,553	163,867	136,541	108,708
Total owners equity	$ 315,688	$324,262	$284,576	$257,250	$229,417
TOTAL LIABILITIES AND O/E	$1,267,686	$955,431	$860,461	$760,272	$453,388

develop, pursue, and accomplish an intelligently conceived marketing plan. As the president of the company, I would like to see the corporation rededicate itself to accomplishing this goal with our present resources. If we are to devote any new or additional amount of resources (time, money, and people) during this coming year, it should only be in the area of market research and strategy planning.

I see 1984 as a year in which we gather together our present resources and gradually strengthen the company by clearly demonstrating, not only to ourselves, but also to our customers, suppliers, lenders, and other business associates, that we can accomplish a great deal with the resources already at our disposal.

Given the attainment of these objectives for 1984, the corporation will clearly be in an excellent position to again consider reaching out into such areas as new products, markets, divisions, branches, etc.

Mr. Fergeson was interested in looking into diversifying into janitorial supplies, power transmission supplies, plumbing supplies, pumps and machinery, and concrete accessories. He also considered expansion of their rubber manufacturing division feasible.

In speculating on future sales, a variety of estimates were made. Mr. Richards felt sales would not top $5 million in the next 5 years. In contrast, Mr. Fergeson felt that AIS could grow to $10 million because their sales area was increasing.

As for possible branch operations, there was a wide divergence of opinion. Mr. Fergeson felt that the long-range goals of the company included branches.

He cited definite advantages to local branches and indicated:

I see a need for this because the competition is doing it. The industrial products industry has so many lines that our major competitors are specialty houses. We get closer to the customer by having our salespeople specialize in particular product divisions, but branch operations will enable us to get even closer to our customers. Without branching, I believe that in five years it would be doubtful that AIS would exist. I see our market area shrinking as more competitors enter, and you can only forestall competitors with pricing, good service, and quality for so long. It is difficult unless you are an established part of the local community.

In predicting the future of branch operations, President Richards remarked:

The way our markets have been growing, there will be a lot of temptations for our people to want to branch out; to establish branches in outlying areas. For the most part those kinds of branches will be marginal, at best. The kinds of opportunities that I can see in the future are not very dynamic.

The company's future direction was ultimately intertwined with the president's decision to divest himself of daily managerial responsibilities to devote more time to higher-level corporate activities and other pursuits. Both Mr. Fergeson and Mr. Parnell expressed optimism about the future of AIS, despite the company's inability to sustain a profit thus far. Mr. Fergeson expressed the feeling that Mr. Richards was ready for a new venture and hoped that together with Mr. Parnell he would one day control the ownership of Atlantic Industrial Supply.

ARIZONA SOCCER CAMP (B)

In 1978, Ron Walters, Alan Meeder, and Steve Gay opened the Arizona Soccer Camp at Orme School in Orme, Arizona. In 1981, a second facility was opened at Cochise Community College. This new location is south of Tucson, near Douglas, Arizona. Since 1978, Steve Gay has removed himself from the partnership, leaving Meeder and Walters to make critical decisions about the product, price, place, and promotion of the Arizona Soccer Camp. Presently, a new situation faces Meeder and Walters. Changes have occurred in the public's enthusiasm toward soccer and in the types of lifestyles pursued. Competition has increased, the profile of the Arizona soccer camper has changed in many respects, and the financial status of the Arizona Soccer Camp has reflected these changes. Meeder and Walters feel that a total reassessment of the camp's environment is necessary to determine the future directions of the camp.

CHANGES IN SOCCER ENTHUSIASM

Soccer has become the world's most popular sport. Marilyn Wellemeyer, writing in *Fortune* magazine, has estimated that 1.5 billion people watched the 1982 World Cup on television.[1] To the international media, the World Cup soccer playoffs are equivalent to the Olympics, and multinational firms have been quick to obtain marketing rights in anticipation of the World Cup profits. Marketing rights give a company in a particular field the exclusive right to the promotion of a product, trademark, or intangible within a certain medium and for a particular event. In the March 1, 1982 issue of *Advertising Age,* M. Thompson-Noel cited Coca-Cola, Seiko, and

This case was prepared by Richard F. Beltramini, John Schlacter, and Nancy De Rogatis, all of Arizona State University. Copyright Richard F. Beltramini, 1983.

Gillette as those who secured marketing rights for the 1982 World Cup.

Despite international fervor, professional soccer in America is struggling. Fan support is low and many teams are going bankrupt. In *Maclean's,* Hal Quinn noted that the North American Soccer League (NASL) clubs lost a total of $30 million in 1981.[2] Ten NASL teams have folded in the past two years, and four more are expected to require new ownership and capitalization by 1983.

The situation has been called a "depression" by John Kerr, executive director of the NASL Players' Association, who noted that, "At the beginning of the season there were two hundred players with pro experience unemployed." One reason for pro soccer's demise is the changing consumption patterns in the United States. The *Federal Reserve Bulletin* shows that discretionary income, stated in 1972 dollars, has increased by $142 billion in the past five years. However, there seems to have been a change in the consumption patterns of many consumers. Consumers have become less willing to part with their hard-earned dollars. Furthermore, ticket prices have increased to meet rising costs. Examples of these costs include player acquisitions, player salaries and operating expenses such as transportation costs. Despite the decrease in fan support for professional soccer, amateur soccer has increased in popularity in America. Wellemeyer reports that amateur soccer is the fastest growing team sport in this country.[3] This increased interest in amateur soccer can be seen at all age levels.

Evidence indicates that soccer participation is high among youths. For example, Dallas youths are playing more soccer than baseball and football combined. Thirteen years ago, in New York, the Long Island Junior Soccer League was founded; currently 100,000 youths actively participate in its leagues.[4]

On the college level, the National Collegiate Athletic Association has announced that currently more colleges have varsity soccer teams than football teams.[5] Soccer clubs are also prevalent on most college campuses.

Adults are also becoming active soccer participants. The Parks and Recreation Department in Mesa, Arizona, has three soccer leagues. The Arizona State

Adult Men's Soccer League has a total of sixty participants. The Coed League has twelve teams of fifteen players each, and the Men's League consists of eight teams of fifteen players each. In total, there are 360 participating adults. Soccer participation has grown steadily in Mesa and the Parks and Recreation Department anticipates adding more soccer fields to its facilities within the next five years.

The U.S. Soccer Federation (USSF) is the United States division of the Federation International Football Association. This organization consists of both pro and amateur soccer players of all ages. The USSF sets the rules of soccer in America. All soccer players in America are encouraged to register as members, and the USSF, headquartered in New York, reports that registrations have been growing by 20 percent a year for the past several years.

CHANGES IN LIFESTYLES

Lifestyle is a common reason why most residents are attracted to Arizona. Exhibit 1 shows that the sports participation and outdoor enthusiast categories ranked high among all categories in a 1980 survey by Western Savings and Loan Association for the Phoenix Metropolitan Statistical Areas. This report indicated that a large segment of the Scottsdale population is highly sports oriented, with over 20,000 of these households reporting themselves as sports participants. More than 25,000 of the Tempe households reported that they lead lifestyles heavily involved in family, sports, and social activities. These figures decline somewhat for residents in the central city of Phoenix. Still, a high proportion of these residents consider themselves to be outdoor enthusiasts. Thirty-eight percent of the Mesa residents surveyed reported lifestyles that are heavily involved in sports participation. Almost fifty percent of the Glendale residents surveyed categorized themselves as outdoor enthusiasts. Thirty-nine percent are sports participants; thirty-seven percent are sports fans.

The fact that a large number of Phoenix area residents' leisure activities are recreational in nature is supported by another study. A report from Phoenix Newspapers, Inc., noted that 69 percent of those households surveyed reported swimming as a leisure activity in which they have participated within the last twelve months. Exhibit 2 shows that 45 percent indicated that they had been bicycling and 32 percent indicated that they had been jogging. Very vigorous sports such as racquetball were most popular with younger adults. These figures indicate that a large proportion of Phoenix area residents enjoy and participate in outdoor activities.

CHANGES IN THE COMPETITION

When Meeder and Walters originally assessed the external environment in 1978, the soccer camp market had been untapped. At that time, no soccer boarding camps were in existence in Arizona, and only one soccer day camp was operating. Since 1978, both direct and indirect competition have increased considerably. Although the Arizona Soccer Camp is the only soccer boarding camp in the area, several day camps have begun operations. Boarding camps provide sleeping arrangements for campers while day camps do not. Both types of soccer camps can be considered as directly competing in that both provide training to improve soccer skills.

The Phoenix Infernos are a professional soccer team in Phoenix, Arizona, whose Soccer Camp '82 boasted 960 participants in the twenty-four sessions. These three-hour, one-week sessions were conducted in the morning and afternoon. Both boys and girls could participate and both advanced and beginning sessions were offered. This camp distinguished itself by offering soccer balls, T-shirts, autographed bumper stickers, camp attendance certificates, and $25 discounts on Inferno season tickets to all camp participants. The total cost for each one-week session was $85. There were ten players to every Inferno coach with four coaches available at all times. The one-week session consisted of three hours each day, in either the morning or afternoon.

Phoenix Inferno players also coach at competing youth soccer camps. The cosponsored Arizona State University and Tempe Soccer Club 1982 Clinics are examples. Phoenix Inferno players were heavily advertised and helped the camp to draw one hundred and fifty youths.[6] Two clinics were offered, with each lasting four hours each day for a week. A $100 cost

CASE

EXHIBIT 1
Lifestyles in Maricopa County

	Metro	Glendale	Phoenix	Tempe	Mesa	Scottsdale
Population	5,577,300	113,900	852,800	123,600	328,300	107,400
Lifestyles						
Socially active	45%	47%	42%	56%	40%	56%
Family oriented	42	58	39	57	43	42
Church oriented	41	38	37	44	48	40
Outdoor enthusiast	38	47	38	46	39	38
Sports participant	38	39	32	56	38	48
Sports fan	34	37	22	49	29	43
Arts involved	16	10	15	27	11	25
Entertainment	13	10	13	26	10	14
Civically involved	10	—	—	10	—	14

Source: Western Savings & Loan Association, *Forecast* 1980.

included all instruction plus lunches for each participant.

A third competitor is the Tucson Pro Soccer Camp, located in Tucson, Arizona. It has been operating for three years. Because of its location, this camp directly competes with Meeder's and Walters' camp at Cochise College. The Tucson camp is headed by Wolfgang Weber, head coach for the Arizona Youth Soccer Association, and features half-day instruction for five days at a cost of $50 per player. The number of sessions has varied from year to year, as have the camp sites, but Weber advertises one coach for every ten players and a sixty space limit for each week. In 1982, Weber offered three sessions, with one week devoted entirely to girls. The "girls' only" session was a first for the Tucson Pro Soccer Camp, but with a turnout of fifty girls, Weber plans to continue this session in 1983. Although all other sessions have been coeducational, Weber reports that each year 90 percent of the players have been boys and that the majority of the players have been between the ages of eight and eleven. Boys and girls between the ages of seven to seventeen are eligible to attend the camp. The Tucson Pro Soccer Camp does not offer different skill level sessions, but does group the children according to skill level, size, and age on the first day of each session. Weber feels that there is

EXHIBIT 2
Household Leisure Activities in Phoenix
Past 12 Months

Activity	Percent	Number of Adults	Median Age
Bicycling	45%	505,400	35.5
Racquetball	19	208,400	29.0
Swimming	69	776,200	34.4
Running/Jogging	32	354,100	31.0
Amateur Sports Event	31	340,800	34.2
Professional Sports Event	26	295,500	36.1

Source: Phoenix Newspapers, Inc., *Inside Phoenix 1982.*

a good market to support an expansion. He reached this conclusion after participating as a soccer coach in the 1982 Arizona State University Soccer Camp. Weber's camp directly competes with the Arizona Soccer Camp.

The Arizona Soccer Camp indirectly competes with other youth programs that do not emphasize soccer. The Tempe YMCA, located in Tempe, Arizona, is one example of the various programs that are available for youths. This YMCA offers two

EXHIBIT 3
Youths in Arizona

Age	Arizona	Maricopa County	Yavapai County
7–9	130,313	69,639	2,655
10–13	174,898	94,254	3,760
14	44,675	23,969	989
15	47,962	25,926	1,055
16	49,303	26,596	1,156

Source: Summary Data of the 1980 Census of Population.

EXHIBIT 4
Number of Youths Playing Soccer

Year	Estimated Number of Youth Soccer Players	AYSA Registrations in Arizona	AYSA Registrations in Maricopa County
1978	20,000	10,000	4,000
1979	30,000	15,000	7,000
1980	40,000	18,000	9,000
1981	45,000	22,000	12,000
1982	50,000	25,000	14,000

Source: Kay Seuss, President of Arizona Youth Soccer Association, interview, November 7, 1982.

summer camps. One of these is located in Mayer, Arizona. It emphasizes horseback riding and arts and crafts for twelve- to fifteen-year-olds. A second camp is located in Prescott, Arizona. Eight- to thirteen-year-olds are encouraged to attend this camp. Swimming, arts and crafts, riflery, and horseback riding are the planned activities for these campers. A fee of $135 covers all expenses for seven days at either camp. Transportation by bus is provided to all campers at no extra charge.

The summer program offered by the Phoenix Parks and Recreation Department is another type of opportunity available to youths. Special summer courses, ranging from acting to swimming to dancercize, are available for all ages. The price for most courses is under $30. Courses are scheduled for one hour each day, three days a week for eight weeks. There is usually one teacher for every ten students. Courses are available in the afternoons and evenings.

These examples indicate that both direct and indirect competition are present. Meeder and Walters must consider this fact when determining the future direction of the Arizona Soccer Camp.

CHANGES IN YOUTH SOCCER PARTICIPANTS

The *Summary Data of the 1980 Census of Population* shows that there are 447,141 youths in Arizona between the ages of seven and sixteen (see exhibit 3). It is estimated that 50,000 youths in Arizona are soccer players. This number has doubled from 25,000 soccer players in 1978. The Arizona Youth Soccer Association (AYSA) is the largest youth soccer organization in the state, with 25,000 registered players in 1982. AYSA President Kay Seuss feels that their organization is representative of the youth soccer population. She says that the popularity of soccer among youths has grown tremendously in the past five years but sees a declining interest in the game.

> *Soccer's growth rate among youths in Arizona has slowed since 1980. The market may be saturated but I really feel that economic conditions have caused the decline in our registrations. Parents have become less willing to spend their dollars on a soccer program for their children.*

AYSA has registered approximately 50 percent of all Arizona youth soccer players each year (see exhibit 4), and they have consistently found the largest age group to be ten- to thirteen-year-olds. Three quarters of all participants each year have been boys and Seuss feels this is representative of the total Arizona youth soccer population. The majority of all registrations are from the Phoenix Metropolitan area, with the largest percentage of these coming from Northwest Phoenix. Seuss cites a larger youth population in this area as the explanation for this phenomenon. Strong soccer participation can also be found in the Tucson and Sierra Vista areas.

EXHIBIT 5
Participant Characteristics

Year	Total Children	Total Boys	Total Girls	Total Returning Boys	Total Returning Girls	Campers with Basic Skills	Campers with Advanced Skills	Campers with Very Advanced Skills
1978	112	112	0	12	0	112	0	0
1979	255	255	0	70	0	255	0	0
1980	432	382	50	160	0	277	155	0
1981	551	481	70	125	25	396	155	0
1982	603	546	57	125	23	363	185	55

Source: Company Records

CHANGES IN ARIZONA SOCCER CAMP PARTICIPANTS

The type of participant attracted to the Arizona Soccer Camp has changed throughout the years. These changes are illustrated in exhibit 5. As can be noted from these statistics, no advanced skill sessions were offered to boys until 1980. These sessions have been sold out every year since that time. Fifty girls were attracted to the first coeducational session in 1980. In 1981, the number increased, but in 1982, fewer girls attended the sessions. Advanced skill sessions were offered to girls in 1982 and thirty-five enrolled.

With the introduction of both girls' and boys' advanced sessions and a boys' very advanced (select) session, the number of participants in the basic skills level declined. The statistics indicate a possible trend toward growing demand for advanced sessions and slowing demand for fundamental sessions.

Meeder and Walters recommend that all first-time campers enroll in the beginning skills session. Those who have already attended this session and who are between the ages of ten to sixteen are placed in the advanced session. Male soccer enthusiasts who have completed the advanced session and are between eleven and seventeen-years-old may enroll in the boys select session. Exceptions are made when coaches recommend that a youth be placed at a particular skill level. Walters notes that campers usually cooperate with this system, "Campers want to enroll at the right skills level so that they can participate on a competitive basis with the other kids."

Throughout the years, skill level has been closely related to the age of the participant. For those with basic skills, 50 percent of the campers have traditionally been between the ages of eight to ten years. Most predominant in the advanced skill sessions have been the twelve-year-olds. Thirteen- to sixteen-year-olds were most often found enrolling in the select session in 1982.

FINANCIAL CHANGES

Financial expenses have increased since the camp first opened in 1978. Fortunately, these increases and the inflation rate have been offset by the growing number of children attending the camp each year.

Examining the variable costs for the Arizona Soccer Camp one sees that the cost-per-coach for one week has increased from $125 in 1978 to $350 in 1982. The cost of one nurse has increased from $100 in the first year of camp operations to $300 in 1982. Meeder and Walters offered to pay all expenses for counselors in 1980 but incurred an additional expense in 1982 when they agreed to let the children of counselors attend the camp at no charge. Exhibit 6 shows a year-by-year progression of the variable payroll costs.

Fixed costs have also increased throughout the years. While rental costs have averaged a 10 percent increase each year, Cochise College facilities have consistently remained $10-per-child less expensive than the facilities at Orme School. Insurance has increased by 1 percent each year and advertising has

CASE

EXHIBIT 6
Changes in Variable Costs

Year	Cost per Counselor	Cost per Coach	Cost per Nurse
1978	$ 0.00	$125.00	$100.00
1979	0.00	150.00	100.00
1980	78.00	200.00	300.00
1981	78.00	275.00	300.00
1982	100.00	350.00	300.00

Source: Company Records

EXHIBIT 7
Profit/Loss for the Arizona Soccer Camp

Year	Profit/Loss
1978	(2,626)
1979	4,365
1980	12,457
1981	11,650
1982	14,500

Source: Company Records

increased approximately 5 percent each year. Legal and accounting services have increased in cost to $900 in 1982. The previous cost for these services was $500. Office and video expenses have remained constant. Video expenses include the cassettes, equipment, and processing costs associated with taping scrimmages at the camp.

Profits declined sharply from 1979 to 1980. Exhibit 7 shows that profits remained stable in 1981 but have recently turned upward.

In the near future, Meeder and Walters are considering hiring an independent consultant to handle the marketing and promotion of their product. It is anticipated that $500 per month will pay for the salary and promotional materials of this consultant. How this money will be allocated has not been determined. Meeder and Walters are currently faced with the problem of financing this expenditure, as there is no reserve fund. Immediate cash flow may be generated through pre-registration, or Meeder and Walters may tap their personal funds until the regular registration period when cash flow improves. It is hoped that the increased revenue from greater promotion will more than offset the cost and expenses of the consultant. Should this not occur, Meeder's and Walters' profits may decline again in 1983.

Throughout the years, modifications have been made in the product, price, place, and promotional strategy for the Arizona Soccer Camp. Meeder and Walters feel they must reassess these decisions as they look toward new developments and question their future directions.

THE PRODUCT AND RESPONSES TO CHANGE

Meeder and Walters realize that their product offering has many attributes, but they are in disagreement as to the salient features relative to the markets served. Meeder believes that they are marketing soccer skills improvement and quality instructors. Walters believes that their product is a vacation for the parents away from the children, a social camp experience for the youths, and high quality sports competition. Meeder and Walters realize that they must decide on the most relevant product attributes for the target markets they select.

A look at the daily camp schedule (exhibit 8) reveals both social and competitive skill aspects of the camp. Considerable free time is scheduled each day for the participants. Friendships that develop on the soccer field may become closer during free recreational periods. The majority of the day, however, is devoted to sports competition in the form of soccer scrimmages and skill drills. The daily format for the Arizona Soccer Camp has not been changed since 1978 because Meeder and Walters have found the schedule well-liked by all campers.

One component of the schedule which has changed considerably since 1978 is the soccer skills sessions. Boys' fundamental sessions were the only sessions available until 1980, at which time an experimental boys' advanced session was organized. In this same year, a coeducational course was also offered. In 1982, both an advanced girls' and boys' select session

EXHIBIT 8
Daily Camp Schedule

8:00 A.M.	Breakfast and view videotape of previous night's scrimmage
9:00 A.M.	Skill demonstrations and drills
11:00 A.M.	Free recreation time
12:00 NOON	Lunch and free time
2:00 P.M.	Skill demonstrations and drills
5:30 P.M.	Evening scrimmage and one game is videotaped
9:00 P.M.	Snacks
10:00 P.M.	Lights out

were added. Exhibit 9 indicates the years when specific sessions were offered. It can be seen that the Arizona Soccer Camp has become somewhat more diversified in recent years.

Another part of the Arizona Soccer Camp's product offering is the quality of instructors. Meeder and Walters emphasize the teaching aspect of their camp and therefore prefer to employ coaches and professional players with teaching experience. This is another aspect of the product that has not changed since the camps began operations in 1978 and 1980.

EXPANSIONS IN CAMP LOCATIONS

In 1978, the Arizona Soccer Camp ran a one-week session at Orme School. Since that time, both the number of sessions offered and the number of camp locations have been expanding.

Orme School

Orme School is a private boarding school located about ninety miles north of Phoenix (see exhibit 10). Located on a 40,000-acre ranch, its facilities include five soccer fields, a recreational room, and a swimming pool. This facility accommodates one hundred and fifty campers at one time. Because the cooks at Orme School live on the premises throughout the year, they have been providing meals each summer for the campers. The cost of the meals has been included in the rental fee for the facilities. Meeder and Walters have been renting this facility for three weeks each summer for the last three years. In 1979, the facilities were rented for two weeks; in 1978, one week was rented at Orme School. Meeder and Walters are contemplating renting five weeks for Summer 1983. Orme School has been most successful in attracting campers from Maricopa County and especially from the Phoenix Metropolitan area. Exhibit 11 indicates that more children are currently being attracted from Tempe and Scottsdale than in the past, while the opposite pattern exists for Phoenix and Glendale participants.

EXHIBIT 9
Types of Sessions Offered

Year	Coed Fundamental Sessions	All Boys Fundamental Sessions	Boys Advanced Sessions	Girls Advanced Sessions	Boys Select Sessions
1978		X			
1979		X			
1980	X	X	X		
1981	X	X	X	X	X

Source: Company Records

EXHIBIT 10
Camp Locations

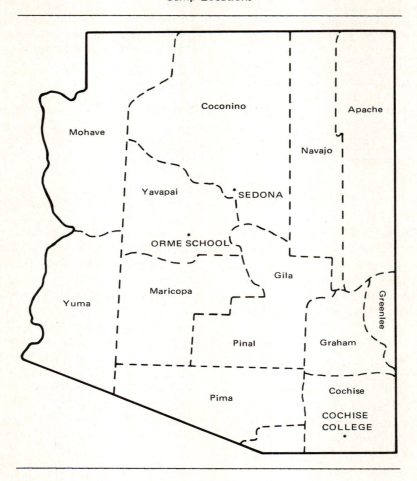

COCHISE COLLEGE

Cochise College is located southeast of Phoenix near Douglas, Arizona. Its facilities include three soccer fields, an Olympic-size pool, modern dorms, and a large gym where indoor soccer can be played. This facility can accommodate 110 campers at one time. Meeder and Walters have been renting these facilities for three weeks each summer for the past two years. Of the 220 campers to attend Cochise in 1982, 80 percent were from Tucson (see exhibit 12). The remainder of the children came from Phoenix and Sierra Vista areas. Some children were attracted from New Mexico. Although fairly close for Tucson and Sierra Vista residents, Cochise College is a five-hour drive for Phoenix residents. To promote this location with Phoenix residents, Meeder and Walters are considering developing a new marketing strategy. If enough campers are interested, a bus will be chartered in 1983 to transport campers from Phoenix to Cochise. One concern is that this convenience may draw campers from the Orme School facility. If this were to occur, Meeder and Walters may defeat their original purpose of attracting new campers. However,

EXHIBIT 11
Profile on Campers Attending Orme School

Year	Percentage of Campers from Phoenix, Glendale	Percentage of Campers from Tempe, Scottsdale Mesa, Chandler	Percentage of Campers from Other Areas
1978	90%	10%	10%
1979	90	10	10
1980	90	10	10
1981	70	20	10
1982	60	30	10

Source: Company Records

EXHIBIT 12
Profile on Campers Attending Cochise College

Year	Percentage of Campers from Tucson	Percentage of Campers from Douglas, Sierra Vista, New Mexico	Percentage of Campers from Phoenix Area
1981	80%	10%	10%
1982	80	10	10

Source: Company Records

since the rent at Cochise is $10 per child less expensive, Meeder and Walters might enjoy a greater profit margin at this camp site. Since Cochise College has expressed a willingness to rent more weeks to the Arizona Soccer Camp, it might be very profitable to entice potential Orme School campers to Cochise.

Sedona

Meeder and Walters have recently been presented with the opportunity to purchase forty acres of land directly adjacent to and currently owned by the Valley Verde School, a private school in Sedona, Arizona. The expectation would be that a portion of the acreage could be developed into a permanent site for the Arizona Soccer Camp. The camp would require twenty acres of this land. There are several investment options available to Meeder and Walters. They could buy all forty acres, develop them, and then sell off the land they do not need, or others could invest in and develop the land after which time Meeder and Walters could buy the needed twenty acres. The latter would require an initial investment of $80,000. While the site is being constructed, the current Valley Verde facilities could be rented. However, Valley Verde does not have a swimming pool or soccer fields. To return their original investment in the land, Meeder and Walters would have to operate the camp for ten to twelve weeks each summer for several years, in addition to the current weeks of operation at Cochise and Orme School.

Walters and Meeder are concerned that the present population will not support this investment.

PROMOTIONAL PROGRAMS

Since its inception five years ago, the Arizona Soccer Camp has conducted a series of promotional programs. Direct mail has been utilized each year to inform and interest potential campers. As shown in exhibit 13, approximately three thousand brochures have been printed and mailed each year. Registration materials have been included in the direct mail package for convenience. As an incentive, the Arizona Soccer Camp has offered a free camp picture to all campers who make their full tuition payments during pre-registration. Thirty percent of the campers each year take advantage of this offer.

Ron Walters has been responsible for generating mailing lists for the direct mail campaign. In 1978 and again in 1979, he secured the Tempe YMCA and West Town Soccer Club mailing lists. By the end of 1982, Walters had mailing lists accounting for the names of 30,000 soccer enthusiasts; however, whenever possible, Walters delivers the brochures directly to the clubs to decrease mailing costs. These clubs include the Rose Land Soccer Club in Phoenix, the Moon Valley Soccer Club in Phoenix, the Arcadia Soccer Club in Phoenix, the Tempe YMCA, and the West Town Soccer Club in Glendale, Arizona. Walters

CASE

EXHIBIT 13
Direct Mail Promotional Program

Year	Number of Brochures Printed	Number of Newsletters	Percentage of Pre-Registrations	Costs for All Printing
1978	3,000	125	30%	$1,400.00
1979	3,000	275	30	1,600.00
1980	3,000	450	30	1,800.00
1981	3,000	575	30	1,800.00
1982	3,000	625	30	2,500.00

Source: Company Records

feels additional sources may still be available. A bulk mailing permit has been used to mail brochures at ten cents each.

In addition to the brochure, the Arizona Soccer Camp has sent out newsletters to returning campers. The purpose of the newsletter is to further promote the Arizona Soccer Camp and to inform past campers about the recent accomplishments of their coaches. The newsletter is mailed in the fall of each year. It is sent by first class mail. The cost associated with this mailing is shown in exhibit 14.

During the summer of 1982, Club Med and the Arizona Soccer Camp co-sponsored the First Annual Skills Contest and Drawing. The two grand prizes were free vacations for the entire families of the winners. The vacations included air transportation from Phoenix, accommodations, meals, entertainment, and various sports activities at Club Med's newest resort location in Ixtapa, Mexico. A special feature was that the vacation package included soccer coaching in Ixtapa by two Phoenix Inferno soccer players. The vacation package was offered to all Arizona Soccer families at a total cost of $527 per child twelve years and under and $708 per adult.

The promotional budget for each year can be seen in exhibit 15. The categories of advertising, postage, and office expense make up the promotional budget. The advertising and office expense allocations must cover all printing and artwork costs for the brochures and newsletters. Because direct mail is expensive, Meeder and Walters have been questioning its effectiveness.

EXHIBIT 14
Mailing Costs for Newsletters

Year	Number of Newsletters Mailed	Total Cost for Mailing
1978	112	$ 1.80
1979	255	10.50
1980	432	31.50
1981	551	35.10
1982	603	36.40

Source: Company Records

EXHIBIT 15
Promotional Budget

Year	Budget
1978	$1,390.00
1979	2,825.00
1980	3,655.00
1981	3,830.00
1982	3,865.00

Source: Company Records

As Meeder and Walters consider the future they are faced with a number of questions:

1. What markets should be targeted and what is the potential of these markets?

CASE

2. What attributes of the offering are most important to each of the defined target markets, and how does the Arizona Soccer Camp rate on these attributes relative to the competition?
3. Should the Arizona Soccer Camp seek a single, permanent location? Should it seek ownership or continue renting facilities at Cochise and Orme? Is some combination of the above feasible?
4. How can the Arizona Soccer Camp promote to its markets most effectively and efficiently? What should be its message?
5. What is an appropriate pricing strategy given the nature of the camp's competition and its present cost structure?
6. Where do additional marketing opportunities lie?

NOTES

1. Marilyn Wellemeyer, "New Recruits for the Most Popular Sport," *Fortune,* 2 November 1981, p. 163.
2. Hal Quinn, "Hard Times for the Game of the Decade," *Maclean's,* 7 June 1982, p. 42.
3. Wellemeyer, "New Recruits for the Most Popular Sport."
4. Steve Bernheim, "Youth Soccer: Long Island's Fertile Crop," *Soccer Corner,* June 1980, pp. 29–30.
5. Wellemeyer, "New Recruits for the Most Popular Sport."
6. Jo Miller, Men's Soccer Club representative, Arizona State University personal interview, October 18, 1982.

Marketing Assessment and Control

Sound marketing programs are critical to the long-term survival and success of nearly all firms. The marketing effort is one of the firm's most expensive activities and is its direct link to the consumer. Accordingly, if the program is not properly developed and executed, considerable sums of money can be wasted and the firm's revenue-generating capabilities can be seriously hampered. This issue is addressed in the article by Leland L. Beik and Stephen L. Buzby, "Profitability Analysis by Market Segments."

To ensure that the marketing program is working properly, it is important that it be periodically evaluated and controlled. In this way, the marketing manager can take whatever corrective action may be warranted to bring the firm's performance in line with its established goals.

IMPLEMENTING THE MARKETING PROGRAM

Synthesizing all of the facets of the firm's marketing activities into an integrated whole is no small task. Because the process can be complex and time-consuming, portions of the program are often assigned to different individuals. As a result, the final marketing program can be disjointed unless precautions are taken to mold the various strategies created into a single unit. Typically, the process involves the following series of steps:

1. Review the goals of the firm to ensure that they are still appropriate.
2. Develop specific objectives for the marketing program that lead to the achievement of the firm's goals.
3. Determine the amount of resources to be committed to the marketing effort in terms of time, money, personnel, and material.
4. Review the potential and desirability of the selected target market(s).
5. Review the product, price, channel, and promotion strategies to ensure that they are appropriate and complement each other.
6. Establish a method for monitoring the results of the marketing program as it progresses through the fiscal period.
7. Develop contingency plans in case some of the vital activities prove to be unsuccessful.

Implementing a successful marketing program requires the careful blending of people, time, and money. Without all three of these resources, the chances of making the program successful are substantially diminished. The people needed to make a program work properly include both those within the firm and those in the firm's channel of distribution. Internally, production and sales personnel are critical elements of the program's implementation. The products must be made to predetermined standards on a timely and cost-efficient schedule, and the sales personnel must be trained to present the product in the best manner possible.

The timing of the firm's marketing program is often overlooked as a key variable. Yet, even the best marketing program will not succeed if the timing is not right. The production effort, the sales force, the promotional effort, and the efforts of the members of the channel of distribution must be coordinated with near pinpoint precision if the program is to achieve its full potential.

The firm also must commit adequate financial resources to the marketing effort. Because a marketing program is hard to evaluate and deals with many intangibles, some marketing managers have difficulty gaining needed financial support. As a result, they find themselves with too little funding to give the program a chance to work properly. Insufficient product testing or quality control, inadequate promotional support, and skimpy middleman support are common problems associated with having insufficient funds to implement the program in the most effective manner.

CONTROLLING THE MARKETING PROGRAM

Despite all the care that may go into the development and implementation of a marketing program, controls still must be established and the program monitored throughout the fiscal period. James M. Hulbert and Norman E. Toy's article, "A Strategic Framework for Marketing Control," describes the control process. Market conditions can change rapidly, making adjustments to the program essential if the firm is to achieve its goals. In addition, the complexity of the marketing effort makes it likely that some errors will be made during the formulation of the various strategies—errors that must be corrected along the way.

Maintaining control over every facet of the firm's marketing program can be a very time-consuming and expensive process. Accordingly, it often is desirable to maintain close control over only the target market and the four elements of the marketing mix. Critical issues include:

1. whether the product remains attractive to the target market, and the needs of its consumers have not changed;
2. whether the product still satisfies the needs of the target market;
3. whether the price being charged is appropriate for the value received and remains within the target market's capability to pay;
4. whether the methods of distributing products to consumers are satisfactory and cost-effective;
5. whether the promotion adequately reaches the target market and does so in a cost-efficient manner.

MARKETING AUDITS

To monitor the program's effectiveness during the course of the fiscal period, several types of audits can be conducted. These are described in the article by Philip Kotler, William Gregor, and William Rodgers, entitled, "The Marketing Audit Comes of Age." The first type is the cost-oriented audit, which may be directed either to all of the costs incurred for the marketing program, or to only a limited number of expense items.

As would be expected, full cost audits involve examining every expense item of the firm that directly relates to the marketing program. Generally, this includes the costs of purchasing, production, promotion, and personal selling. Other, more indirect costs may or may not be included in this type of audit, depending on the objectives of the marketing manager in conducting the audit.

Limited function audits, on the other hand, may not cover all of these expense areas. Typically, they will deal more directly with the actual marketing efforts involved with target market analyses and marketing mix expenses. Under most circumstances, limited function audits are preferred since they are less time consuming and expensive. Only in instances where the firm is experiencing serious cost-control problems is the full cost audit essential.

The second major type of audit is the revenue-oriented audit. As the name implies, these audits focus on the income-generating capabilities of the marketing program. Special concerns here are whether the product is still attractive to the target market and how the other elements of the marketing mix serve to enhance the product's desirability and sale-ability.

Like cost-oriented audits, revenue audits can either be full or limited in function, depending on the needs of the marketing manager. While full revenue audits cover all aspects of the firm's ability to generate sales dollars and/or units of sales, the limited function audits tend to isolate only the key areas. These would include monitoring of sales by such factors as geographic area, salespersonnel, and product.

In many instances, it is important to tie the cost and revenue-oriented audits together into a profit-oriented audit. This may entail nothing more than comparing the revenue-generating capacity of the program to the cost incurred. When viewed from this perspective, the profitability of the marketing program can be brought into sharper focus. To the extent that the firm is attempting to achieve some desired level of profitability, this type of audit and control process is considered the most appropriate.

Care must be taken in the judicious use of marketing audits so that they will be cost effective and achieve the desired results. The entire control process should be directed to ensuring that the marketing program leads the firm to achieving its goals. To the extent that marketing audits are disruptive or overly expensive to conduct, they are counterproductive. The audit and any other control devices used by the marketing manager must themselves be periodically evaluated to make sure that a satisfactory monitoring system is maintained over the marketing program.

Leland L. Beik and Stephen L. Buzby

Profitability Analysis by Market Segments

By tracing sales revenues to market segments and relating these revenues to marketing costs, the marketing manager can improve and control his decision making with respect to the firm's profit objective.

First expressed by Smith in 1956, the concept of market segmentation has since been elaborated in many different ways.[1] It has recently been defined by Kotler as "... the subdividing of a market into homogeneous subsets of customers, where any subset may conceivably be selected as a market target to be reached with a distinct marketing mix."[2] The underlying logic is based on the assumption that:

> ... the market for a product is made up of customers who differ either in their own characteristics or in the nature of their environment in such a way that some aspect of their demand for the product in question also differs. The strategy of market segmentation involves the tailoring of the firm's product and/or marketing program to these differences. By modifying either of these, the firm is attempting to increase profits by converting a market with heterogeneous demand characteristics into a set of markets that although they differ from one another, are internally more homogeneous than before.[3]

The concept of market segmentation may be used for strategic alignment of the firm's productive capacities with its existing and potential markets. By analyzing market needs and the firm's ability to serve those needs, the basic long-run policies of the firm can be developed. Through choice of target segments, competition may be minimized; through selective cultivation, the firm's competitive posture may be greatly improved.

Source: From the *Journal of Marketing*, Vol. 37 (July 1973), pp. 48–53. Reprinted by permission of the American Marketing Association.

For both strategic and tactical decisions, marketing managers may profit by knowing the impact of the marketing mix upon the target segments at which marketing efforts are aimed. If the programs are to be responsive to environmental change, a monitoring system is needed to locate problems and guide adjustments in marketing decisions. Tracing the profitability of segments permits improved pricing, selling, advertising, channel, and product management decisions. The success of marketing policies and programs may be appraised by a dollar and cents measure of profitability by segment.

Managerial accounting techniques have dealt with the profitability of products, territories, and some customer classes; but a literature search has revealed not one serious attempt to assess the relative profitability of market segments.[4] Although the term "segment" has a history of use in accounting, this use implies a segment of the business rather than a special partitioning of consumers or industrial users for marketing analysis. Even when classifying customers, accounting classes are formed by frequency and size of order, location, credit rating, and other factors, most of which are related to controlling internal costs or to assessing financial profit.[5]

After indicating the value for marketing decision making, this article will delineate a framework for cost accounting by market segments. An industrial product example is constructed to demonstrate the process and to spell out the features of the contribution approach to cost accounting as applied to accounting for segment profitability. Further discussion extends the concept to a consumer situation and specifies difficulties that may attend full-scale application of the technique. The expectation is that the technique will better control marketing costs and improve marketing decisions.

MARKET SEGMENTATION AND ITS UTILITY

To have value for managerial judgments, Bell notes that market segments should: (1) be readily identified and measured, (2) contain adequate potential, (3) demonstrate effective demand, (4) be economically accessible, and (5) react uniquely to marketing effort.[6] For present purposes, the key criterion for choosing the bases for segmenting a given market is the ability to trace sales and costs to the segments defined. Allocating sales and costs is the most stringent requirement and limitation of profitability accounting as used to support marketing decisions.

Among the many possible bases for market segmentation, the analysis can be accomplished using widely recognized geographic, demographic, and socio-economic variables.[7] Many of these, such as geographic units and population or income figures, provide known universe classifications against which to compare company sales and cost performance. Other bases of segmentation such as buyer usage rate, expected benefits, or psychological or sociological characteristics of consumers typically require research to match their distribution, directly or indirectly, with company sales and costs.

Given proper segmentation, separate products (or channels or other elements of the marketing mix) can serve as the primary basis for cost and revenue allocation. Knowledge of profit by segments then contributes directly to decisions concerning the product line and adjustment of sales, advertising, and other decision variables. The process is illustrated in the following industrial example.

A matrix system can be developed as part of marketing planning to partition segments for profitability analysis.[8] A company with lines of computers, calculators, and adding machines might first divide its market into territories as in the upper section of figure 1. The cell representing adding machines in the eastern market might next be sorted by product items and customer classes. The chief product preference of each company class is noted by an important benefit segmentation within the cells of the lower section of figure 1.

Since the segments react differently to product variations and other marketing activities, it is advantageous to isolate profit by product for each market segment. Using this information, the marketing manager can specifically tailor product policies to particular market segments and judge the reaction of segments to increased or decreased marketing efforts over time. Decision adjustments and control of marketing costs interact to improve product line management directly and other decisions indirectly.

In theory, segment profitability analysis is worthwhile only where decisions adjusting the marketing mix add incremental profits that exceed the costs of the extra analysis. In practice, information concerning the profitability of marketing decisions has been so sparse that the analysis is likely to be profitable where allocations to market segments are approximate and fail to approach theoretical perfection.

MARKETING COST ANALYSIS

In its simplest form, marketing cost analysis relates the cost of marketing activities to sales revenues in order to measure profits. A profit and loss statement must be constructed for any marketing component (e.g., product, channel) being analyzed. The approach consists of dividing the firm's basic costs (e.g., salaries, rent) into their functional categories (e.g., selling, advertising). The functional category amounts are then assigned within the appropriate marketing classifications.

The actual form of the profit and loss statements will depend upon the nature of the company being analyzed, the purpose of the marketing analysis, and the records available. The form of statement will also depend upon the accounting technique used to assign costs to the marketing components under study. One

FIGURE 1
Matrix Breakdown by Products and Segments

	West	South	North	East
Computers				
Calculators				
Adding Machines				

	Banks	Mfg. Firms	Small Retailers
Full Keyboard	Value Accuracy		
Deluxe Ten Key		Value Speed	
Basic Ten Key			Value Low Price

TABLE 1
TABLE 1
Product Productivity Analysis—Contribution Approach

	Company Total	Full Keyboard	Deluxe Ten Key	Basic Ten Key
Net Sales	$10,000	$5,000	$3,000	$2,000
Variable Manufacturing Costs	5,100	2,500	1,375	1,225
Manufacturing Contribution	$ 4,900	$2,500	$1,625	$ 775
Marketing Costs				
Variable:				
Sales Commissions	450	225	135	90
Variable Contribution	$ 4,450	$2,275	$1,490	$ 685
Assignable:				
Salaries—Salesmen	1,600	770	630	200
Salary—Marketing Manager	100	50	25	25
Product Advertising	1,000	670	200	130
Total	$ 2,700	$1,490	$ 855	$ 355
Product Contribution	$ 1,750	$ 785	$ 635	$ 330
Nonassignable				
Institutional Advertising	150			
Marketing Contribution	$ 1,600			
Fixed-joint Costs				
General Administration	300			
Manufacturing	900			
Total	$ 1,200			
Net Profits	$ 400			

might use a full-cost approach, assigning both direct and indirect costs across the marketing classifications on the best available bases. Alternatively, one might use a direct-cost approach and assign direct costs only, avoiding arbitrary assignment of fixed or overhead costs. Most marketing sources have utilized the full- and direct-cost approaches.

A third costing approach is better suited to the needs of the marketing manager and the requirements of analysis by market segments. Essentially, it is an adaptation of the contribution approach to preparing financial statements.[9] Table 1 presents a simplified illustration of how the contribution approach can be adapted to break out product profitability for adding machines in the eastern market.

First, all of the variable nonmarketing costs have been assigned to products. These costs represent non-marketing dollar expenditures which fluctuate, in total, directly in proportion to short-run changes in the sales volume of a given product. Similarly, variable marketing costs have been deducted to produce variable product contribution margins identical to those which would result from a direct costing approach.

The remaining marketing costs have been broken down into two categories—assignable and nonassignable. The assignable costs represent dollar expenditures of a fixed or discretionary nature for which reasonably valid bases exist for allocating them to specific products. For example, the assignment of salesmen's salaries in table 1 might be based on Sevin's recommendation to use "selling time devoted to each product, as shown by special sales-call reports or special studies."[10] The marketing manager's salary could be assigned on the basis of personal records indicating the amount of time devoted to the management of each product. Product advertising would be assigned by reference to the actual amount spent on advertising each product.

The use of the actual dollar level of sales was purposely avoided in choosing the allocation bases for the assignable costs in table 1. Horngren, among others, has stated that when dealing with fixed or discretionary costs, "The costs of efforts are independent of the results actually obtained, in the sense that the

TABLE 2
Segment Productivity Analysis—Contribution Approach

	Company Total	Full Keyboard Bank Seg.	Nonseg.	Deluxe 10-Key Mfg. Seg.	Nonseg.	Basic 10-Key Retail Seg.
Net Sales	$10,000	$3,750	$1,250	$2,550	$450	$2,000
Variable Manufacturing Costs	5,100	1,875	625	1,169	206	1,225
Mfg. Contribution	$ 4,900	$1,875	$ 625	$1,381	$244	$ 775
Marketing Costs						
Variable:						
Sales Commissions	450	169	56	115	20	90
Variable Contribution	$ 4,450	$1,706	$ 569	$1,266	$224	$ 685
Assignable:						
Salaries—Salesmen	1,600	630	140	420	210	200
Salary—Marketing Manager	100	38	12	19	6	25
Product Advertising	1,000	670	-0-	200	-0-	130
Total	$ 2,700	$1,338	$ 152	$ 639	$216	$ 355
Segment Contribution	$ 1,750	$ 368	$ 417	$ 627	$ 8	$ 330
Nonassignable						
Institutional Advertising	150					
Marketing Contribution	$ 1,600					
Fixed-joint Costs						
General Administration	300					
Manufacturing	900					
Total	$ 1,200					
Net Profits	$ 400					

costs are programmed by management, not determined by sales."[11]

The nonassignable marketing costs represent dollar expenditures of a fixed or discretionary nature for which there are no valid bases for assignment to products. Consequently, institutional advertising has not been assigned to the products to avoid confounding the product profitability margins which would result from the arbitrary allocation of this cost. Since the primary purpose is calculating marketing related product contribution margins, the remaining nonmarketing costs can be taken as a deduction from the total marketing contribution margin to produce a net profit figure for the firm.

Although the preceding example was purposely simplified, the framework is sufficiently flexible to handle different objectives and more complex problems. If the firm in table 1 were a single product firm, for example, the three customer classes (banks, manufacturers, and retailers) could easily be substituted for primary emphasis in place of the products. The analysis would differ only through variations in the treatment of fixed, variable, and assignable costs required by the new objective. That assignability changes with objective may be illustrated by the fact that product advertising costs can often be assigned to products but rarely to customer classes.

To aid in handling more complex problems, a discussion of common bases for assigning a wide range of marketing costs may be found in Sevin.[12] In some instances, the approach can be further improved by application of mathematical programming to assign costs to the marketing components.[13] Budgetary data and marketing lags could also be introduced up-grade the analysis.[14]

COSTING BY SEGMENTS

In particular, the framework of the contribution approach may be applied to costing by segments. Table 2 extends the product analysis of table 1. Recall that the segments are partitioned by territorial, customer class, and product benefit criteria although the primary customer class names are used to identify segments in the table. Instead of tracing the sales of each product to all three customer classes, one simplifying device is to identify the primary benefit sought by a customer class as segment sales and to combine sales of the given product to the other customer classes as nonsegment sales. For example, sales of the full-keyboard adding machine to banks become segment sales, while sales to large manufacturing firms or to retailers are nonsegment sales. This device is appropriate where nontarget sales are expected to be minimal; otherwise more columns can be added to the table.

Where sales revenues can be traced directly to customers, customer classes, and territories and where marketing costs can be similarly traced, the analysis is straightforward. Where the less tangible benefit segmentation is used, sales analysis or marketing research must measure the degree to which benefits are related to each customer class. If sales analysis shows that banks purchase 75% of the full-keyboard sales because they value accuracy while manufacturers and retailers account for the remaining 25%, both revenues and sales commissions may be prorated accordingly. This allocation is employed in table 2.

To illustrate a few marketing implications, it might be noted that over one-half of the full-keyboard profit contribution actually comes from nonsegment sales rather than from the primary target segment. The nonsegment profitability results in part from low personal selling and absence of advertising costs. An opportunity possibly exists in further promotion, perhaps to large manufacturing firms. Had the table completed the analysis for purchases of full-keyboard machines by manufacturers and retailers, the actual segment of opportunity could be pinpointed. If institutional or other possible sales proved substantial during further classification, a new segment of opportunity might be identified.

Quite obviously, the eastern banking segment has a low profit contribution considering the level of marketing effort expended. Table 2 deals with one sample area and product class, and a comparison with other area banking segments might prove enlightening. Perhaps marketing costs could be reduced in the eastern segment if sales were up to par. Or if sales were comparatively low, marketing effort (price, personal selling, advertising) could be reallocated to meet competition more effectively.

Similar analysis can be applied to the manufacturing and retailing segments of table 2, and to the territories and products not incorporated in the present illustration. The advantage over standard sales analysis is that a profit rather than a volume measure is applied and that variations in marketing costs and sales response are taken into account.

MARKETING PRODUCTIVITY: CONSUMER SEGMENTS

The previous example has been simplified so that minimum tables serve to explain the technique. Segment analysis becomes complex as more than two or three criteria are used for partitioning and as additional criteria are considered for different classes of marketing decisions. A further example adds realism and extends the concept to a consumer situation.

A company that sells snowmobiles is likely to have some special channel problems. To control channel management, meteorological data permit primary and secondary snow belts to be mapped across the U.S. and Canada. Sales analysis or research could show how to allocate purchases among consumers in major metropolitan, city, town, and rural areas. Further analysis could determine patronage among department stores, automotive dealers, farm equipment dealers, marinas, and other classes of outlets. Sales to resorts for rentals might be included as a segment or analyzed separately. Finally, the several analyses could map sales into geographical units. Segmenting by snow conditions, population density, outlets patronized, and dwelling area and then allocating revenues and costs to the segments would point outlet selection and channel adjustments toward the more profitable outlets in favorable population and snow-belt locations.

By collecting and analyzing warranty card information, snowmobile purchasers could be classified as to family life cycle, social status, or other variables. This data would probe the profit potential of appealing to young families, selected social classes, or possibly even to hunters, sailing enthusiasts, and other outdoors people. Dates on the warranty cards would help adjust the timing of promotions in advance of the snow season or to balance the pre-Christmas advertising in line with purchase habits of its customer segments. Having targeted promotion on the basis of past data, current warranty card information, and revenue and cost information, the profitability of each target segment could be determined.

Analyzing the profitability of advertising or price decisions involves special problems in tracing sales and costs. If segments have been defined on tangible bases, say area and dealer patronage, the difficulty might be overcome by setting up an experiment.[15] Variations of advertising messages, local media, and possibly price would serve as treatments in segments matched to control other variables. Recording segment revenues and treatment costs would constitute a profit measure of selected advertising and/or price decisions. Experiments may thus be used with segment cost analysis to plan corporate marketing programs.

MANAGERIAL IMPLICATIONS

Given responsible means of partitioning market segments, major elements of the marketing mix may be segregated for analysis using the contribution approach to cost accounting. An example has been employed to show how segment profitability can be measured for items in a product line thereby contributing directly to product management decisions. By analyzing the profit and loss statements for the costs of other marketing efforts, additional adjustments can be made in other decisions such as personal selling and advertising. A further example has indicated how channel and other marketing management problems can be similarly gauged by a profit measure for a consumer product and consumer segments.

Several major problems have to be met in applying costing techniques to market segments. One difficulty is choosing productive bases for segmentation, and limiting analysis to a manageable number of bases is another. Although some bases are obvious from experience, they remain product specific, and criteria for choice are not fully developed. Another major problem is obtaining data for the less tangible modes of segmentation, particularly data that permit assignment of sales revenues and costs in accord with each base used for segment definition.

Recognizing and solving problems, however, often leads to further improvements. For example, many of the behavioral applications to marketing imply use in segment analysis but are difficult to relate to other marketing variables on any basis other than judgment. As limitations of source data are overcome, profit accounting by segments may add to the marketing utility of behavioral advances.

Costing by market segments promises improvement in marketing efficiency by way of better planning of expenditures and control of costs. Upon documenting reasons for today's soaring marketing costs, Weiss comments over and over that marketing costs are resistant to sophisticated cost analysis and that marketing cost controls are inadequate in modern corporations.[16] Although not calculated to stem such pressures as inflation, cost accounting by market segments can control selling, advertising, packaging, and other marketing costs in relation to profit potentials. Perhaps even greater value stems from the potential ability to fine-tune product offerings and other marketing decisions to the requirements of well-defined consumer segments. As part of the material regularly supplied to marketing managers, market segment profitability analysis could easily become a key compo-

nent of marketing information systems of the future.

NOTES

1. Wendell R. Smith, "Product Differentiation and Market Segmentation as Alternative Marketing Strategies," *Journal of Marketing,* Vol. 21 (July 1956), pp. 3–8; and James F. Engel, Henry F. Fiorillo, and Murray A. Cayley, eds., *Market Segmentation: Concepts and Applications* (New York: Holt, Rinehart and Winston, Inc., 1972).

2. Philip Kotler, *Marketing Management,* Second Edition (Englewood Cliffs, New Jersey: Prentice-Hall, Inc., 1972), p. 166.

3. Ronald E. Frank, "Market Segmentation Research: Findings and Implications," in *Applications of the Sciences in Marketing Management,* Frank M. Bass, Charles W. King, and Edgar A. Pessemier, eds. (New York: John Wiley & Sons, Inc., 1968), p. 39.

4. Closest to the present analysis and perhaps the best summary of the state of the art is Charles H. Sevin, *Marketing Productivity Analysis* (New York: McGraw-Hill Book Company, 1965).

5. Robert B. Miner, "Distribution Costs," in *Marketing Handbook,* Albert W. Frey, ed. (New York: The Ronald Press Company, 1965); see especially pp. 23–17 and 23–32.

6. Martin L. Bell, *Marketing: Concepts and Strategy,* Second Edition (Boston: Houghton Mifflin Company, 1972), p. 185.

7. See William M. Weilbacher, "Standard Classification of Consumer Characteristics," *Journal of Marketing,* Vol. 31 (January 1967), p. 27.

8. See William J. E. Crissy and Robert M. Kaplan, "Matrix Models for Marketing Planning," *MSU Business Topics,* Vol. 11 (Summer 1963), p. 48. The matrix "targeting" treatment is also familiar to readers of basic marketing texts by E. J. McCarthy or G. D. Downing.

9. See Charles R. Horngren, *Cost Accounting: A Managerial Emphasis,* 2nd ed. (Englewood Cliffs, New Jersey: Prentice-Hall, Inc., 1967); and Ralph L. Day and Peter D. Bennett, "Should Salesmen's Compensation be Geared to Profits?" *Journal of Marketing,* Vol. 26 (October 1962), pp. 6–9.

10. Same reference as footnote 4, p. 13.

11. Same reference as footnote 9, p. 381.

12. Same reference as footnote 4, chapter 2.

13. William J. Baumol and Charles H. Sevin, "Marketing Costs and Mathematical Programming," in *Management Information: A Quantitative Accent,* Thomas Williams and Charles Griffin, eds. (Homewood, Illinois: Richard D. Irwin, Inc., 1967), pp. 176–190.

14. Richard A. Feder, "How to Measure Marketing Performance," in *Readings in Cost Accounting, Budgeting, and Control,* 3rd ed., W. Thomas Jr., ed. (Cincinnati, Ohio: South-Western Publishing Co., 1968), pp. 650–668.

15. Same reference as footnote 4, chapters 6, 7, and 8.

16. E. B. Weiss, "Pooled Marketing: Antidote for Soaring Marketing Costs," *Advertising Age,* Vol. 43 (November 13, 1972), pp. 63–64.

James M. Hulbert and Norman E. Toy

A Strategic Framework for Marketing Control

The decade of the 1960's led many companies down the primrose path of uncontrolled growth. The turbulence of the 1970's has drawn renewed attention to the need to pursue growth selectively, and many companies have been forced to divest themselves of businesses which looked glamorous in the 1960's, but faded in the 1970's. Simultaneously with this reappraisal has come a much more serious focus on problems of control—a concern with careful monitoring and appraisal to receive early warning on businesses or ventures that are suspect.

Yet, despite the extent to which control is stressed by authors,[1] there does not exist a generally agreed upon strategic framework for marketing control, and there has been little successful integration of concepts in marketing strategy and planning with those of managerial accounting. In particular, the work of the Boston Consulting Group,[2] the results of the PIMS study,[3] and a variety of other sources[4] have stressed the importance of market share objectives in marketing strategy, coincidentally emphasizing the need to know market size and growth rate and thus the importance of good forecasts. Typically, however, procedures for marketing control have not been related to these key parameters. (Incredibly, market size is sometimes even omitted from marketing plans according to one knowledgeable author.)[5]

In this article we seek to remedy that state of affairs by outlining a strategic framework for marketing control. Using the key strategic concepts discussed above, we first present a framework for evaluating marketing performance versus plan, thus providing a means for more formally incorporating the marketing plan in the managerial control process.

The plan, however, may well provide inappropriate

Source: From the *Journal of Marketing,* Vol. 41 (April 1977), pp. 12–20. Reprinted by permission of the American Marketing Association.

criteria for performance evaluation, especially if there have been a number of unanticipated events during the planning period. A second stage of this article, therefore, is to provide a means of taking these kinds of planning variances into account, so as to provide a more appropriate set of criteria for performance evaluation. Two conceptual developments are shown as Part I and Part II of the Appendix.

PERFORMANCE VS. PLAN

In figure 1 we show the results of operations for a sample product, *Product Alpha,* during the preceding period. In the analysis which follows, we shall focus on analysis of variances in profit contribution. As we discussed elsewhere,[6] an analysis of revenue performance is sometimes required; the procedure here is analogous. Organizationally, one of the results we would like to achieve is to be able to assign responsibility, and give credit, where due.

A variety of organizational units were involved in the planning and execution summarized in figure 1, and an important component of control activity is to evaluate their performance according to the standards or goals provided by the marketing plan. We should also note, however, that the type of analysis we shall discuss has limited potential for diagnosing the causes of problems. Rather, its major benefit is in the identification of areas where problems may exist. Determining the factors which have actually caused favorable or unfavorable variances requires the skill and expertise of the manager.

The unfavorable variance in contribution of $100,000, for *Product Alpha* could arise from two main sources:[7]

1. Differences between planned and actual quantities (volumes).
2. Differences between planned and actual contribution per unit.

Differences between planned and actual quantities, however, may arise from differences between actual and planned total market size and actual and planned market share (penetration) of that total market. The potential sources of variation between planned and actual contribution, then, are:

1. Total market size.
2. Market share (penetration).
3. Price/cost per unit.

This format for variance decomposition permits assignment into categories which correspond to key strategy variables in market planning.[8] The analysis proceeds as follows.

FIGURE 1
Operating Results for Product Alpha

Item	Planned	Actual	Variance
REVENUES			
Sales (lbs.)	20,000,000	22,000,000	2,000,000
Price per lb ($)	0.50	.4773	0.227
Revenues	10,000,000	10,500,000	500,000
Total Market (lbs.)	40,000,000	50,000,000	10,000,000
Share of Market	50%	44%	(6%)
COSTS			
Variable cost per lb ($)	.30	.30	—
CONTRIBUTION			
Per lb ($)	.20	.1773	.0227
Total ($)	4,000,000	3,900,000	(100,000)

Price-Quantity Decomposition

In order to measure volume variance with the standard yardstick of planned contribution per unit, actual quantity is used to calculate the price/cost variance. (This procedure is standard accounting practice.) To be more concise, we utilize the following symbols:

S — share of total market
M — total market in units
Q — quantity sold in units
C — contribution margin per unit

We use the subscript "a" to denote *actual* values, and "p" to denote *planned* values. The subscript "v" denotes *variance*. Thus the price/cost variance is given by

$$(C_a - C_p) \times Q_a = (.1773 - .20) \times 22,000,000$$
$$= -\$500,000;$$

and the volume variance is given by

$$(Q_a - Q_p) \times C_p = (22,000,000 - 20,000,000) \times .20$$
$$= \$400,000.[9]$$

The sum of these contribution variances therefore yields the overall unfavorable contribution variance of $-\$100,000$ shown in figure 1.

Penetration—Market Size Decomposition

The second stage of the analysis is the further decomposition of the volume variance in contribution into the components due to penetration and total market size. Figure 2 is helpful in the exposition of the analysis.

As a first step, we should like to explain differences in quantities sold $(Q_a - Q_p)$, where actual and planned quantities are the product of the market size times share $(Q_a = S_a \times M_a$, and $Q_p = S_p \times M_p)$. From figure 2, rectangles I and II are clearly assignable to share and market size, respectively. Rectangle III, however, is conceptually more complex.

We argue that discrepancies in forecasting market size should be evaluated using the standard yardstick of planned share, just as the dollar value of the quantity variance is measured using the standard of planned contribution. Thus, actual market size is used to calculate share variance, while both share and forecast components (which together comprise the quantity variance) are measured using planned contribution. This procedure is also consistent with recommended accounting practice.[10]

Then the variance in contribution due to share is given by

$$(S_a - S_p) \times M_a \times C_p$$
$$= (.44 - .50) \times 50,000,000 \times .2$$
$$= -\$600,000;$$

and the market size variance is given by

$$(M_a - M_p) \times S_p \times C_p$$
$$= (50,000,000 - 40,000,000) \times .5 \times .2$$
$$= \$1,000,000.$$

The sum of the market size and share variances yields the overall favorable volume variance in contribution of $\$400,000$ derived in the previous section.

We may now summarize the variances which in total constitute the overall variance as follows:

FIGURE 2
Variance of Total Market Size vs. Share

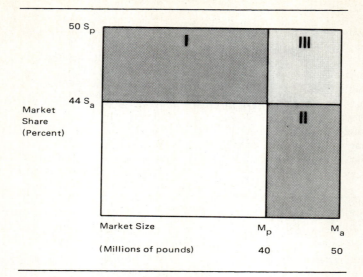

Market Share (Percent)

50 S_p

44 S_a

I III II

Market Size

(Millions of pounds)

M_p M_a

40   50

Planned profit contribution	$4,000,000
Volume variance	
Share variance (600,000)	
Market size variance 1,000,000	
	400,000
Price/cost variance	(500,000)
Actual profit contribution	$3,900,000

Interpretation

Conceptually, variances may occur because of problems in forecasting, execution, or both. In using the results of the analysis for performance evaluation, however, responsibility will have to be assigned. Generally, variances in total market size, for example, will be viewed as the responsibility of the market forecasting group.

Share or penetration variances present a more difficult case. They may arise due to incorrect forecasts of what "expected performance" should be, or due to poor performance itself. Apportioning responsibility in this case clearly necessitates managerial judgment. However, where marketing and sales personnel participate in the development of market share objectives, or where share declines relative to previous performance, the burden of proof is more likely to fall on the operating unit rather than on a separate planning or forecasting group.

Responsibility for price variances may also be difficult to assign. For example, prices may be seriously affected by changes in market or general economic conditions beyond the control of the operating group but which should have been foreseen by forecasters or planners. On the other hand, prices are an integral part of the marketing mix, and variances may well indicate problems in marketing or selling tactics.

With these considerations in mind, we may now review the results of the variance analysis:

First, *the favorable volume variance of $400,000 was in fact caused by two larger variances cancelling each other out. And while one of these variances was positive, the other negative, both are undesirable! By not achieving planned share of market, we lost $600,000 in profit contribution.*

The loss of market share may be due to poor planning, poor execution, or both . . . and managerial judgment is the key factor in diagnosing the causes of this discrepancy.

This unfavorable share variance was more than compensated for—or so it appears—by the $1,000,000 positive contribution variance due to the fact that the market turned out to be much larger than was forecast. This variance is unequivocally the responsibility of the forecasting group, though whether or not they should have been able to foresee the expansion is an issue which the manager must decide.

However, this nominally favorable variance is, in

fact, a danger signal. *We seriously underestimated the size of the market, which was 25% greater, at 50 million pounds, than the forecast (40 million pounds).* As the dominant competitor, we have lost market share in what is apparently a fast-growing market, the kind of error which can soon lead to loss of competitive position.[11]

In this instance, then, the share/size decomposition of the volume variance serves to emphasize the importance of good planning—and good information for planning—in terms directly related to two crucial variables in strategy design. This form of decomposition, we submit, generates considerably more useful insight into issues of marketing control *than isolation of only the volume variance, which is much less clearly interpretable.*

The final variance component is the unfavorable price variance of $500,000. Again, interpretation is the job of the manager. However, we should note that the accounting procedures used here (and generally) treat price and volume variances as if they were separable. *Yet, for the vast majority of products and services, demand is price-elastic to some degree so that variances in total revenue are the combined result of the interaction, via the demand function, of unit prices and quantities.*

In this example, for instance, the lower levels of prices may well have been an important factor in expanding industry and company demand. Nonetheless, the fact remains that failure to attain planned price levels led to a $500,000 decrease in actual versus planned profit contribution. The reasons for this variance may lie with performance (e.g., poor tactics) or planning (e.g., inaccurate forecasts).

Diagnosis and responsibility assignment procedures will be explored in more detail in the following section.

MONDAY MORNING QUARTERBACKING

A crucial issue, which we have thus far skirted, is the appropriate criterion for performance evaluation. This is a basic yet nagging problem underlying the whole area of strategic control. In the foregoing analysis, for example, we assumed that the marketing plan provides an appropriate set of criteria. The objectives therein are usually derived after considerable participation, discussion, and negotiation between interested parties,[12] and may well represent the most appropriate set of criteria that are available, at least at the beginning of the planning period.

In many companies, however, performance during the previous planning period serves as an additional set of evaluation criteria. In fact, the search for more "objective" criteria for performance evaluation led to the origins, at General Electric, of the PIMS project and the subsequent "par" criterion.[13]

The facts are, of course, that the marketing plan—which we used as our criterion—is generally based upon the best information which is available on an *ex ante* basis. The conditions which are manifest during the planning period, however, may be vastly different from those envisaged at the time of plan development. In some company planning systems, some of these changes may be encompassed by contingency planning, while in others the plan is updated when major environmental changes occur.[14] In many other instances the plan is not updated—at least in any formal way.[15]

Nonetheless, irrespective of the comprehensiveness of systems to provide flexibility in plans, when the time arrives to review performance, most marketing managers use some *ex post* information. In other words, the criteria of evaluation—implicitly or explicitly—are generally "what performance should have been" under the circumstances which actually transpired. Nor is this "Monday morning quarterbacking" undesirable, for it is eminently more sensible than blind adherence to a plan which is clearly outdated by violation of planning assumptions.[16]

For example, supply may be affected unexpectedly; a major competitor may drop out of the market—or an aggressive new competitor may enter; or demand may have an unexpected change—e.g., because of weather. Either of these would likely change the appropriate par market share for the company. The purpose of this second stage of the analysis, therefore, is to provide a variance decomposition which permits comparison of performance versus the criterion of "what should have happened under the circumstances."

Naturally, there are inherent dangers in such a process. Re-opening the issue of what constitutes an appropriate criterion for performance evaluation may mean opening a Pandora's Box. Equally clearly, however, there are frequently occasions when unforeseen events can significantly affect what target performance should be. In such instances, it is surely preferable that any adjustment process be systematic and orderly, explicit and visible.

Using "Expert" Information

Continuing with our previous operating results, then, let us construct the scenario which occurred during the planning period, using the *ex post* information which would be available to the marketing manager at the time of performance review:

1. A new competitor—Consolidated Company—entered the market early in the year. The competitor was a large, well-financed conglomerate, which used an aggressive promotional campaign and a lower price to induce trial purchase.
2. A fire in the plant of a European manufacturer led to totally unforeseeable foreign demand for one million pounds of *Product Alpha*.

With a small amount of additional work by the manager, we may now develop an appropriate *ex post* performance analysis. For example, the fact that the new competitor was quite prepared to subsidize his entry into our market out of his other operations was an important cause of the price deterioration, and also guaranteed that he would "buy" a share of market sufficient for him to run his new plant at close to standard capacity. At the same time, this aggressive entry and the price competition which ensued was an important factor in further expanding total industry demand.

In quantitative terms Consolidated's effective mean selling price for the year was $0.465 per lb. We had forecast an industry mean of $0.495 and a price for our own product of $0.475, and we realized $0.4773 per lb. Competitive intelligence informed us that Consolidated's new plant had a capacity of only 1.33 million pounds so that its inability to supply more set a lower limit for market prices, above that of Consolidated's introductory price.

We now reconstruct the discrepancy between conditions forecast at the time of planning and the conditions which subsequently prevailed.

Market Share

As noted, our intelligence estimates indicated that Consolidated's capacity would be 1.33 million pounds. Our historical market share had hovered around 50% for some time, so that *everything being equal,* we might expect that 50% of Consolidated's sales would be at our expense. However, knowing that we were (a) the dominant competitor and (b) the premium-price competitor, we also know that we were the most vulnerable to a price-oriented competitive entry. Consequently, we used as a planning assumption the supposition that 60% of Consolidated's sales would be at our expense. That is, we assumed that .6 × 1.33 million pounds, or 800 thousand pounds of sales volume which we would otherwise have obtained, would be lost to Consolidated. Thus, we had the following two conditions:

If no entry: forecast market share equal to 20.8 ÷ 40 = 52%

With entry: forecast market share equal to 20 ÷ 40 = 50%

Since we were certain that Consolidated would enter early in the year, we used the latter assumption. However, while our intelligence estimates on the size of Consolidated's plant were excellent, we did not glean the information that they would use 3-shift operation rather than two shifts which have been standard practice for the industry. As a result Consolidated's effective standard capacity was raised from 1.33 to 2.0 million pounds. Under these conditions, then, assuming the 60% loss rate holds, we should have expected to lose .6 × 2.0 or 1.2 million pounds to Consolidated, rather than 800,000 lbs. Thus, with perfect foresight we *should have* forecasted a market share of 19.6 ÷ 40, or 49%.

Price

We had forecast an industry mean price of $0.495 per pound, and planned for a net price to us of $0.50 per pound. This $.005 per pound premium had been traditional for us because of our leadership position in the industry, with slightly higher quality product and excellent levels of distribution and service.

The actual industry mean price was $0.475 per pound, and our net mean price was $0.4773, so that we only received a premium of $0.0023 per pound.[17] Here, then, we have some basis for separating the planning variance from the performance variance.

Although the basis for this distinction again involves managerial judgment, for present purposes we assume that the planning group should have foreseen that Consolidated's entry would be based on a low price strategy which would lead to an overall deterioration in market prices. On the other hand, our selling and marketing tactics were responsible for the deterioration in our price premium.

Market Size

Finally, there was no possibility that our planning group could have foreseen the European fire, and it would be demonstrably unfair to hold them responsible for this component of the variance.

On the other hand, the remainder of the market expansion should have been foreseen, and the responsibility should be assigned to them. Their failure in this regard was no doubt related to the oversight in the pricing area, for it seems entirely plausible that demand was more price elastic than we had realized, and the price decrease brought a whole new set of potential customers into the market.

Variance Decomposition

The full *ex post* decomposition using this information is displayed in figure 3.[18] To simplify the exposition, we employ a third subscript, "r" which indicates the standard which "should have been"—in other words, the plan as revised by *ex post* information. A number of useful insights are generated by the tableau.

The first issue is the nature of planning variances, which is somewhat counter-intuitive. Consider, for example, the planning variance in market share—a negative $98,000. What this is really telling us is that, considering only this factor in isolation, our planned market share was set unrealistically high, and that adjusting for this factor alone would have implied planning for a total contribution of $4,000,000 less the $98,000, or $3,902,000. Conversely, however, positive (or favorable) planning variances are in fact undesirable and represent, potentially, opportunity losses.

For example, the $900,000 favorable planning variance in market size, which is responsible for the fact that overall variance is favorable, represents lost profit contribution due to the fact that we had not correctly anticipated the market growth rate (given, of course, that there were no short-run capacity constraints). The $88,200 performance variance in market size is viewed as unassignable in this instance. We have decided that the planners could not have foreseen the foreign demand, and that we don't feel it should be assigned to sales.

Similar issues arise with the price variance. The planning group's failure to correctly predict market prices is responsible for the bulk of the price variance. However, there is no way that this component might have been recovered; it simply indicated the fact that our plan was subsequently shown by events to be unrealistic in its price expectations. In contrast, the failure of the marketing department to maintain our traditional price premium is reflected in the unfavorable performance variance in price of $60,000.

Again, however, we should point out that the most important element of the analysis is the market size/market growth rate issue. Picture the poor salesmen as they operate during the planning period. They know they are feeling some price pressure, to which, as we have seen, marketing responded. However, they also know that their quantity of sales is up—22 million pounds of product versus a planned amount of 20 million pounds.

Thus, it is entirely feasible that our salesmen were not pushing that hard, since they appeared to be having a banner year, handsomely exceeding their monthly volume quotas and prior periods' performance. In fact, during this period we were frittering away our market position through our ignorance of the rate at which the market had expanded.

However, accurate and timely industry sales statistics, in combination with a flexible planning system which could readily incorporate these data in a revised plan and set of sales quotas, would preempt a problem which, by the time we recognized it, had developed into a fair-sized disaster. While market information is always important, it truly takes on new meaning for the company competing in a high-growth market.

Finally, we should note that the aggregate variances for quantity (including share and market size) and price/cost shown in figure 3 do not agree with those developed in the first part of the article. The reason is, of course, that there are now two possible criteria or yardsticks against which to compare actual results: the original plan (subscripted "p") and the revised plan (subscripted "r").

Following the conceptual development of Part II of the Appendix, therefore, we have used what we believe to be the soundest analysis. Alternative decompositions, which permit the retention of identical aggregate variances to the preliminary "versus plan" comparison are possible, but their conceptual framework is less defensible.

SUMMARY

To be useful to the marketing manager, a framework for control should be related to strategic objectives and variables and, whenever possible, should permit assignment of responsibility for differences between planned and actual performance. The procedures described in this article utilize the key strategic variables of price, market share, and market size as a framework for marketing control.

The framework was first used to analyze marketing performance vs. plan, decomposing quantity variance into components due to under- or overachievement of planned market share and over- or under-forecasting of market size. Then, recognizing that the plan may well not constitute an adequate criterion for evaluation, we extended the example to illustrate how *ex post* information might be utilized to develop more appropriate evaluative criteria, which permitted isolation of the planning and performance components of the variance.

FIGURE 3
Export Performance Evaluation: Analysis of Contribution

Item	Composition	Type of Variance		Variance Totals	Reconciliation
		Planning Variance	Performance Variance		
PLANNED CONTRIBUTION					$4,000,000
QUANTITY VARIANCE					
SHARE					
Planning Variance	$(S_r-S_p) \cdot M_r \cdot C_p = (.49-.50)$ $\times 49,000,000 \times .20$	(98,000)			
Performance Variance	$(S_a-S_r) \cdot M_a \cdot C_r = (.44-.49)$ $\times 50,000,000 \times .18$		(450,000)		
Total				(548,000)	
MARKET SIZE					
Planning Variance	$(M_r-M_p) \cdot S_p \cdot C_p$ $= (49,000,000-40,000,000)$ $\times .5 \times .20$	900,000			
Performance Variance	$(M_a-M_r) \cdot S_r \cdot C_r$ $= (50,000,000-49,000,000)$ $\times .49 \times .18$		88,200		
Total				988,200	
TOTAL QUANTITY VARIANCE					440,200
PRICE VARIANCE					
Planning Variance	$(C_r-C_p) \cdot Q_r = (.18-.2)$ $\times 24,010,000$	(480,200)			
Performance Variance	$(C_a-C_r) \cdot Q_a = (.1773-.18)$ $\times 22,000,000$		(60,000)		
Total				(540,200)	
TOTAL PRICE VARIANCE					(540,200)
TOTAL PLANNING VARIANCE		321,800			
TOTAL PERFORMANCE VARIANCE			(421,800)		
TOTAL VARIANCE				(100,000)	
ACTUAL CONTRIBUTION					$3,900,000

While there is evidently a considerable amount of managerial judgment involved in the decomposition procedure, marketing planning and control has never been exactly bereft of managerial judgment. There is nothing radical about the procedure, which simply recognizes that it is not always possible to update and modify plans to reflect changing conditions, but that such changes may nonetheless be taken into account in appraisal and evaluation via *ex post* revision of the plan.

The example we worked with also indicates the dangers of not continuously monitoring markets and revising plans and objectives, particularly when market conditions are fluid. In such markets, good tracking procedures[19] and responsive tactics are essential for any company seeking to maintain or increase its market position. The importance of marketing control—so long a stepchild—will surely increase in the years ahead. The markets of the late 1970's will differ considerably from those of the 1960's, and pressures of costs and competition will force companies to be more effective in performance appraisal and evaluation.

APPENDIX
Part I: Variance Decomposition—Comparison with Plan

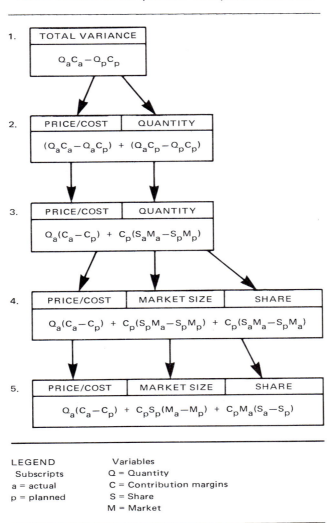

1. **TOTAL VARIANCE**

$$Q_a C_a - Q_p C_p$$

2. **PRICE/COST** | **QUANTITY**

$$(Q_a C_a - Q_a C_p) + (Q_a C_p - Q_p C_p)$$

3. **PRICE/COST** | **QUANTITY**

$$Q_a(C_a - C_p) + C_p(S_a M_a - S_p M_p)$$

4. **PRICE/COST** | **MARKET SIZE** | **SHARE**

$$Q_a(C_a - C_p) + C_p(S_p M_a - S_p M_p) + C_p(S_a M_a - S_p M_a)$$

5. **PRICE/COST** | **MARKET SIZE** | **SHARE**

$$Q_a(C_a - C_p) + C_p S_p(M_a - M_p) + C_p M_a(S_a - S_p)$$

LEGEND — Variables
Subscripts
a = actual   Q = Quantity
p = planned   C = Contribution margins
   S = Share
   M = Market

APPENDIX
Part II: Variance Decomposition—Use of *Ex Post* Information

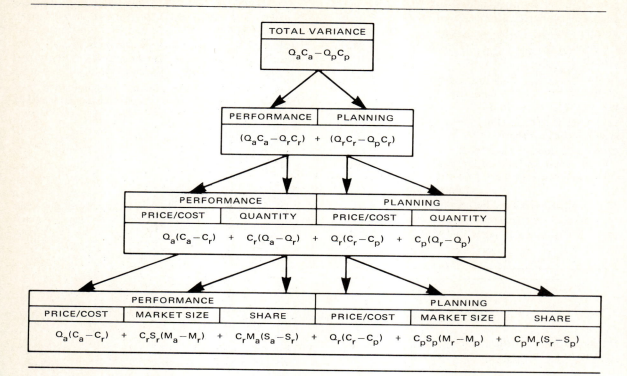

LEGEND

Subscripts

a = actual
p = planned
r = revised

Variables

Q = Quantity
C = Contribution margins
S = Share
M = Market

Notes

1. See, for example, V. H. Kirpalani and Stanley S. Shapiro, "Financial Dimensions of Marketing Management," *Journal of Marketing,* Vol. 37 No. 3 (July 1973), pp. 40–47; David J. Luck and Arthur E. Prell, *Marketing Strategy* (Englewood Cliffs, N.J.: Prentice-Hall Inc., 1968); Philip Kotler, *Marketing Management: Analysis, Planning and Control* (Englewood Cliffs, N.J.: Prentice-Hall Inc., 1972).

2. Boston Consulting Group, *Perspectives on Experience* (Boston: Boston Consulting Group, 1968); see also, Patrick Conley, "Experience Curves as a Planning Tool," in S. H. Britt and H. W. Boyd, eds., *Marketing Management and Administrative Action* New York: McGraw-Hill, 1974), pp. 257–68; William E. Cox, "Product Portfolio Strategy: A Review of the Boston Consulting Group Approach to Marketing Strategy," in *Proceedings,* 1974 Marketing Educators' Conference (Chicago: American Marketing Association), pp. 465–70.

3. Sidney Schoeffler, Robert D. Buzzell and Donald F. Heany, "Impact of Strategic Planning on Profit Performance," *Harvard Business Review,* Vol. 52 (March-April 1974), pp. 137–45; Robert D. Buzzell, Bradley T. Gale and Ralph G. M. Sultan, "Market Share—A Key to Profitability," *Harvard Business Review,* Vol. 53 (January-February 1975), pp. 97–106.

4. See Bernard Catry and Michel Chevalier, "Market Share Strategy and the Product Life Cycle," *Journal of Marketing,* Vol. 38 No. 4 (October 1974), pp. 29–34; C. Davis Fogg, "Planning Gains in Market Share," *Journal of Marketing,* Vol. 38 No. 3 (July 1974), pp. 30–38.

5. F. Beaven Ennis, *Effective Marketing Management* (New York: Association of National Advertisers, 1973), pg. 11.

6. James M. Hulbert and Norman E. Toy, "Control and the Marketing Plan," paper presented to the 1975 Marketing Educators' Conference of the American Marketing Association.

7. To simplify this example, no variances in either variable costs or marketing program costs are included.

8. (For algebraic exposition, see Appendix, Part I.)

9. Algebraically, we have:

$$(C_a - C_p)Q_a + (Q_a - Q_p)C_p$$
$$= C_aQ_a - C_pQ_a + C_pQ_a - C_pQ_p$$
$$= C_aQ_a - C_pQ_p$$

10. "Report of the Committee on Cost and Profitability Analyses for Marketing," *Accounting Review,* Supplement to Vol. XLVII (1972), pp. 575–615.

11. Boston Consulting Group, *Perspectives on Experience,* same as reference 2 above.

12. John A. Howard, James M. Hulbert and John U. Farley, "Organizational Analysis and Information System Design: A Decision Process Perspective," *Journal of Business Research,* Vol. 3.

13. Schoeffler, Buzzell and Heany, same as reference 3 above.

14. Ennis, same as reference 5 above, pg. 57.

15. Noel Capon and James M. Hulbert, "Decision Systems

Analysis in Industrial Marketing," *Industrial Marketing Management,* Vol. 4, 1975, pp. 143–60.

16. Joel S. Demski, "An Accounting System Structured on a Linear Programming Model," *The Accounting Review,* Vol. 42 (October 1967), pp. 701–12.

17. Some judgment is evidently involved here. Percentage differentials might well be used instead of absolute differentials.

18. For algebraic exposition, see Appendix, Part I.

19. John U. Farley and Melvin J. Hinich, "Tracking Marketing Parameters in Random Noise," in *Proceedings,* 1966 Marketing Educators' Conference.

The authors acknowledge the support of the Faculty Research Fund of the Columbia University Graduate School of Business, and the helpful comments of Professors Masai Nakanishi and Gordon Shillinglaw. Early drafts of this article were written while Prof. Hulbert was visiting at the Graduate School of Management, University of California, Los Angeles.

Philip Kotler, William Gregor and William Rodgers

The Marketing Audit Comes of Age

Comparing the marketing strategies and tactics of business units today versus ten years ago, the most striking impression is one of marketing strategy obsolescence. Ten years ago U.S. automobile companies were gearing up for their second postwar race to produce the largest car with the highest horsepower. Today companies are selling increasing numbers of small and medium-sized cars and fuel economy is a major selling point. Ten years ago computer companies were introducing ever-more powerful hardware for more sophisticated uses. Today they emphasize mini- and micro-computers and software.

It is not even necessary to take a ten-year period to show the rapid obsolescence of marketing strategies.

Source: Reprinted from the *Sloan Management Review,* Vol. 18, No. 2 (Winter 1977), pp. 25–43, by permission of the publisher. Copyright © 1977 by the Sloan Management Review Association. All rights reserved.

The growth economy of 1950–1970 has been superseded by a volatile economy which produces new strategic surprises almost monthly. Competitors launch new products, customers switch their business, distributors lose their effectiveness, advertising costs skyrocket, government regulations are announced, and consumer groups attack. These changes represent both opportunities and problems and may demand periodic reorientations of the company's marketing operations.

Many companies feel that their marketing operations need regular reviews and overhauls but do not know how to proceed. Some companies simply make many small changes that are economically and politically feasible, but fail to get to the heart of the matter. True, the company develops an annual marketing plan but management normally does not take a deep and objective look at the marketing strategies, policies, organizations, and operations on a recurrent basis. At the other extreme, companies install aggressive new top marketing management hoping to shake down the marketing cobwebs. In between there must be more orderly ways to reorient marketing operations to changed environments and opportunities.

ENTER THE MARKETING AUDIT

One hears more talk today about the *marketing audit* as being the answer to evaluating marketing practice just as the public accounting audit is the tool for evaluating company accounting practice. This might lead one to conclude that the marketing audit is a new idea and also a very distinct methodology. Neither of these conclusions is true.

The marketing audit as an idea dates back to the early fifties. Rudolph Dallmeyer, a former executive in Booz-Allen-Hamilton, remembers conducting marketing audits as early as 1952. Robert J. Lavidge, President of Elrick and Lavidge, dates his firm's performance of marketing audits to over two decades ago. In 1959, the American Management Associations published an excellent set of papers on the marketing audit under the title *Analyzing and Improving Marketing Performance,* Report No. 32, 1959. During the 1960s, the marketing audit received increasing mention in the lists of marketing services of management consulting firms. It was not until the turbulent seventies, however, that it began to penetrate management awareness as a possible answer to its needs.

As for whether the marketing audit has reached a high degree of methodological sophistication, the answer is generally no. Whereas two certified public accountants will handle an audit assignment using approximately the same methodology, two marketing auditors are likely to bring different conceptions of the auditing process to their task. However, a growing consensus on the major characteristics of a marketing audit is emerging and we can expect considerable progress to occur in the next few years.

In its fullest form and concept, a marketing audit has four basic characteristics. The first and most important is that it is *broad* rather than narrow in focus. The term "marketing audit" should be reserved for a *horizontal (or comprehensive) audit* covering the company's marketing environment, objectives, strategies, organization, and systems. In contrast, a *vertical (or in-depth) audit* occurs when management decides to take a deep look into some key marketing function, such as sales force management. A vertical audit should properly be called by the function that is being audited, such as a sales force audit, an advertising audit, or a pricing audit.

A second characteristic feature of a marketing audit is that it is conducted by someone who is *independent* of the operation that is being evaluated. There is some loose talk about self-audits, where a manager follows a checklist of questions concerning his own operation to make sure that he is touching all the bases.[1] Most experts would agree, however, that the self-audit, while it is always a useful step that a manager should take, does not constitute a *bona fide* audit because it lacks objectivity and independence. Independence can be achieved in two ways. The audit could be an *inside audit* conducted by a person or group inside the company but outside of the operation being evaluated. Or it could be an *outside audit* conducted by a management consulting firm or practitioner.

The third characteristic of a marketing audit is that it is *systematic.* The marketing auditor who decides to interview people inside and outside the firm at random, asking questions as they occur to him, is a "visceral" auditor without a method. This does not mean that he will not come up with very useful findings and recommendations; he may be very insightful. However, the effectiveness of the marketing audit will normally increase to the extent that it incorporates an orderly sequence of diagnostic steps, such as there are in the conduct of a public accounting audit.

A final characteristic that is less intrinsic to a marketing audit but nevertheless desirable is that it be conducted *periodically.* Typically, evaluations of company marketing effort are commissioned when sales have turned down sharply, sales force morale has fallen, or other problems have occurred at the company. The fact is, however, that companies are thrown into a crisis partly because they have failed to review their assumptions and to change them during good times. A marketing audit conducted when things are going well can often help make a good situation even better and also indicate changes needed to prevent things from turning sour.

The above ideas on a marketing audit can be brought together into a single definition:

> A marketing audit is a *comprehensive, systematic, independent,* and *periodic* examination of a company's—or business unit's—marketing environment, objectives, strategies, and activities with a view of determining problem areas and opportunities and recommending a plan of action to improve the company's marketing performance.

WHAT IS THE MARKETING AUDIT PROCESS?

How is a marketing audit performed? Marketing auditing follows the simple three-step procedure shown in figure 1.

Setting the Objectives and Scope

The first step calls for a meeting between the company officer(s) and a potential auditor to explore the nature of the marketing operations and the potential value of a marketing audit. If the company officer is convinced of the potential benefits of a marketing audit, he and the auditor have to work out an agree-

FIGURE 1
Steps in a Marketing Audit

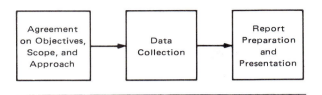

ment on the objectives, coverage, depth, data sources, report format, and the time period for the audit.

Consider the following actual case. A plumbing and heating supplies wholesaler with three branches invited a marketing consultant to prepare an audit of its overall marketing policies and operations. Four major objectives were set for the audit:

- Determine how the market views the company and its competitors.
- Recommend a pricing policy.
- Develop a product evaluation system.
- Determine how to improve the sales activity in terms of the deployment of the sales force, the level and type of compensation, the measurement of performance, and the addition of new salesmen.

Furthermore, the audit would cover the marketing operations of the company as a whole and the operations of each of the three branches, with particular attention to one of the branches. The audit would focus on the marketing operations but also include a review of the purchasing and inventory systems since they intimately affect marketing performance.

The company would furnish the auditor with published and private data on the industry. In addition, the auditor would contact suppliers of manufactured plumbing supplies for additional market data and contact wholesalers outside the company's market area to gain further information on wholesale plumbing and heating operations. The auditor would interview all the key corporate and branch management, sales and purchasing personnel, and would ride with several of those salesmen on their calls. Finally, the auditor would interview a sample of the major plumbing and heating contractor customers in the market areas of the two largest branches.

It was decided that the report format would consist of a draft report of conclusions and recommendations to be reviewed by the president and vice-president of marketing, and then delivered to the executive committee which included the three branch managers. Finally, it was decided that the audit findings would be ready to present within six to eight weeks.

Gathering the Data

The bulk of an auditor's time is spent in gathering data. Although we talk of a single auditor, an auditing team is usually involved when the project is large. A detailed plan as to who is to be interviewed by whom, the questions to be asked, the time and place of contact, and so on, has to be carefully prepared so that auditing time and cost are kept to a minimum. Daily reports of the interviews are to be written up and reviewed so that the individual or team can spot new areas requiring exploration while data are still being gathered.

The cardinal rule in data collection is not to rely solely for data and opinion on those being audited. Customers often turn out to be the key group to interview. Many companies do not really understand how their customers see them and their competitors, nor do they fully understand customer needs. This is vividly demonstrated in figure 2 which shows the results of asking end users, company salesmen, and company marketing personnel for their views of the importance of different factors affecting the user's selection of a manufacturer. According to the figure, customers look first and foremost at the quality of technical support services, followed by prompt delivery, followed by quick response to customer needs. Company salesmen think that company reputation, however, is the most important factor in customer choice, followed by quick response to customer needs and technical support services. Those who plan marketing strategy have a different opinion. They see company price and product quality as the two major factors in buyer choice, followed by quick response to customer needs. Clearly, there is lack of consonance between what buyers say they want, what company salesmen are responding to, and what company marketing planners are emphasizing. One of the major contributions of marketing auditors is to expose these discrepancies and suggest ways to improve marketing consensus.

Preparing and Presenting the Report

The marketing auditor will be developing tentative conclusions as the data comes in. It is a sound procedure for him to meet once or twice with the company officer before the data collection ends to outline some initial findings to see what reactions and suggestions they produce.

FIGURE 2
Factors in the Selection of a Manufacturer

Factor	All Users Rank	Company Salesmen Rank	Company Non-Sales Personnel Rank
Reputation	5	(1)	4
Extension of Credit	9	11	9
Sales Representatives	8	5	7
Technical Support Services	(1)	△3	6
Literature and Manuals	11	10	11
Prompt Delivery	[2]	4	5
Quick Response to Customer Needs	△3	[2]	△3
Product Price	6	6	(1)
Personal Relationships	10	7	8
Complete Product Line	7	9	10
Product Quality	4	8	[2]

Source: Marketing and Distribution Audit, A Service of Decision Sciences Corporation, p. 32. Used with the permission of the Decision Sciences Corporation.

When the data gathering phase is over, the marketing auditor prepares notes for a visual and verbal presentation to the company officer or small group who hired him. The presentation consists of restating the objectives, showing the main findings, and presenting the major recommendations. Then, the auditor is ready to write the final report, which is largely a matter of putting the visual and verbal material into a good written communication. The company officer(s) will usually ask the auditor to present the report to other groups in the company. If the report calls for deep debate and action, the various groups hearing the report should organize into subcommittees to do follow-up work with another meeting to take place some weeks later. The most valuable part of the marketing audit often lies not so much in the auditor's specific recommendations but in the process that the managers of the company begin to go through to assimilate, debate, and develop their own concept of the needed marketing action.

MARKETING AUDIT PROCEDURES FOR AN INSIDE AUDIT

Companies that conduct internal marketing audits show interesting variations from the procedures just outlined. International Telephone and Telegraph, for example, has a history of forming corporate teams and sending them into weak divisions to do a complete business audit, with a heavy emphasis on the marketing component. Some teams stay on the job, often taking over the management.

General Electric's corporate consulting division offers help to various divisions on their marketing problems. One of its services is a marketing audit in the sense of a broad, independent, systematic look at the marketing picture in a division. However, the corporate consulting division gets few requests for a marketing audit as such. Most of the requests are for specific marketing studies or problem-solving assistance.

The 3M Company uses a very interesting and unusual internal marketing plan audit procedure. A marketing plan audit office with a small staff is located at corporate headquarters: The main purpose of the 3M marketing plan audit is to help the divisional marketing manager improve the marketing planning function, as well as come up with better strategies and tactics. A divisional marketing manager phones the marketing plan audit office and invites an audit. There is an agreement that only he will see the results and it is up to him whether he wants wider distribution.

The audit centers around a marketing plan for a product or product line that the marketing manager is preparing for the coming year. This plan is reviewed at a personal presentation by a special team of six company marketing executives invited by the marketing plan audit office. A new team is formed for each new audit. An effort is made to seek out those persons within 3M (but not in the audited division) who can bring the best experience to bear on the particular plan's problems and opportunities. A team typically consists of a marketing manager from another division, a national sales manager, a marketing executive with a technical background, a few others close to the type of problems found in the audited plan, and another person who is totally unfamiliar with the market, the product, or the major marketing techniques being used in the plan. This person usually raises some important points others forget to raise, or do not ask because "everyone probably knows about that anyway."

The six auditors are supplied with a summary of the marketing manager's plan about ten days before an official meeting is held to review the plan. On the audit day, the six auditors, the head of the audit office, and the divisional marketing manager gather at 8:30 A.M. The marketing manager makes a presentation for about an hour describing the division's competitive situation, the long-run strategy, and the planned tactics. The auditors proceed to ask hard questions and debate certain points with the marketing manager and each other. Before the meeting ends that day, the auditors are each asked to fill out a marketing plan evaluation form consisting of questions that are accompanied by numerical rating scales and room for comments.

These evaluations are analyzed and summarized after the meeting. Then the head of the audit office arranges a meeting with the divisional marketing manager and presents the highlights of the auditor's findings and recommendations. It is then up to the marketing manager to take the next steps.

COMPONENTS OF THE MARKETING AUDIT

A major principle in marketing audits is to start with the marketplace first and explore the changes that are taking place and what they imply in the way of problems and opportunities. Then the auditor moves to examine the company's marketing objectives and strategies, organization, and systems. Finally he may move to examine one or two key functions in more detail that are central to the marketing performance of that company. However, some companies ask for less than the full range of auditing steps in order to obtain initial results before commissioning further work. The company may ask for a marketing environment audit, and if satisfied, then ask for a marketing strategy audit. Or it might ask for a marketing organization audit first, and later ask for a marketing environment audit.

We view a full marketing audit as having six major components, each having a semiautonomous status if a company wants less than a full marketing audit. The six components and their logical diagnostic sequence are discussed below. The major auditing questions connected with these components are gathered together in Appendix A at the end of this article.

Marketing Environment Audit

By marketing environment, we mean both the *macro-environment* surrounding the industry and the *task environment* in which the organization intimately operates. The macro-environment consists of the large scale forces and factors influencing the company's future over which the company has very little control. These forces are normally divided into economic-demographic factors, technological factors, political-legal factors, and social-cultural factors. The marketing auditor's task is to assess the key trends and their implications for company marketing action. However, if the company has a good long-range forecasting department, then there is less of a need for a macro-environment audit.

The marketing auditor may play a more critical role in auditing the company's task environment. The task environment consists of markets, customers, competitors, distributors and dealers, suppliers, and marketing facilitators. The marketing auditor can make a contribution by going out into the field and interviewing various parties to assess their current thinking and attitudes and bringing them to the attention of management.

Marketing Strategy Audit

The marketing auditor then proceeds to consider whether the company's marketing strategy is well-postured in the light of the opportunities and problems facing the company. The starting point for the marketing strategy audit is the corporate goals and objectives followed by the marketing objectives. The auditor may find the objectives to be poorly stated, or he may find them to be well-stated but inappropriate given the company's resources and opportunities. For example, a chemical company had set a sales growth objective for a particular product line at 15 percent. However, the total market showed no growth and competition was fierce. Here the auditor questioned the basic sales growth objective for that product line. He proposed that the product line be reconsidered for a maintenance or harvest objective at best and that the company should look for growth elsewhere.

Even when a growth objective is warranted, the auditor will want to consider whether management has chosen the best strategy to achieve that growth.

Marketing Organization Audit

A complete marketing audit would have to cover the question of the effectiveness of the marketing and sales organization, as well as the quality of interaction between marketing and other key management functions such as manufacturing, finance, purchasing, and research and development.

At critical times, a company's marketing organization must be revised to achieve greater effectiveness within the company and in the marketplace. Companies without product management systems will want to consider introducing them; companies with these systems may want to consider dropping them, or trying product teams instead. Companies may want to redefine the role concept of a product manager from being a promotional manager (concerned primarily with volume) to a business manager (concerned primarily with profit). There is the issue of whether decision-making responsibility should be moved up from the brand level to the product level. There is the perennial question of how to make the organization more market-responsive including the possibility of replacing product divisions with market-centered divisions. Finally, sales organizations often do not fully understand marketing. In the words of one vice-president of marketing: "It takes about five years for us to train sales managers to think marketing."

Marketing Systems Audit

A full marketing audit then turns to examine the various systems being used by marketing management to gather information, plan, and control the marketing operation. The issue is not the company's marketing strategy or organization per se but rather the procedures used in some or all of the following systems: sales forecasting, sales goal and quota setting, marketing planning, marketing control, inventory control, order processing, physical distribution, new products development, and product pruning.

The marketing audit may reveal that marketing is being carried on without adequate systems of planning, implementation, and control. An audit of a consumer products division of a large company revealed that decisions about which products to carry and which to eliminate were made by the head of the division on the basis of his intuitive feeling with little information or analysis to guide the decisions. The auditor recommended the introduction of a new product screening system for new products and an improved sales control system for existing products. He also observed that the division prepared budgets but did not carry out formal marketing planning and hardly any research into the market. He recommended that the division establish a formal marketing planning system as soon as possible.

Marketing Productivity Audit

A full marketing audit also includes an effort to examine key accounting data to determine where the company is making its real profits and what, if any, marketing costs could be trimmed. Decision Sciences Corporation, for example, starts its marketing audit by looking at the accounting figures on sales and associated costs of sales. Using marketing cost accounting principles,[2] it seeks to measure the marginal profit contribution of different products, end user segments, marketing channels, and sales territories.

We might argue that the firm's own controller or accountant should do the job of providing management with the results of marketing cost analysis. A handful of firms have created the job position of marketing controllers who report to financial controllers and spend their time looking at the productivity and validity of various marketing costs. Where an organization is doing a good job of marketing cost analysis, it does not need a marketing auditor to study the same. But most companies do not do careful marketing cost analysis. Here a marketing auditor can pay his way by simply exposing certain economic and cost relations which indicate waste or conceal unexploited marketing opportunities.

Zero-based budgeting[3] is another tool for investigating and improving marketing productivity. In normal budgeting, top management allots to each business unit a percentage increase (or decrease) of what it got last time. The question is not raised whether that basic budget level still makes sense. The manager of an operation should be asked what he would basically need if he started his operation from scratch and what it would cost. What would he need next and what would it cost? In this way, a budget is built from the ground up reflecting the true needs of the operation. When this was applied to a technical sales group within a large industrial goods company, it became clear that the company had three or four extra technical salesmen on its payroll. The manager admitted to the redundancy but argued that if a business upturn came, these men would be needed to tap the potential. In the meantime, they were carried on the payroll for two years in the expectation of a business upturn.

Marketing Function Audit

The work done to this point might begin to point to certain key marketing functions which are performing poorly. The auditor might spot, for example, sales force problems that go very deep. Or he might observe that advertising budgets are prepared in an arbitrary fashion and such things as advertising themes, media, and timing are not evaluated for their effectiveness. In these and other cases, the issue becomes one of notifying management of the desirability of one or more marketing function audits if management agrees.

WHICH COMPANIES CAN BENEFIT MOST FROM A MARKETING AUDIT?

All companies can benefit from a competent audit of their marketing operations. However, a marketing audit is likely to yield the highest payoff in the following companies and situations:

- *Production – Oriented and Technical – Oriented Companies.* Many manufacturing companies have their start in a love affair with a certain product. Further products are added that appeal to the technical interests of management, usually with insufficient attention paid to their market potential. The feeling in these companies is that marketing is paid to sell what the company decides to make. After some failures with its "better mousetraps," management starts getting interested in shifting to a market orientation. But this calls for more than a simple declaration by top management to study and serve the customer's needs. It calls for a great number of organizational and attitudinal changes that must be introduced carefully and convincingly. An auditor can perform an important service in recognizing that a company's problem lies in its production orientation, and in guiding management toward a market orientation.

- *Troubled Divisions.* Multidivision companies usually have some troubled divisions. Top management may decide to use an auditor to assess the situation in a troubled division rather than rely solely on the division management's interpretation of the problem.

- *High Performing Divisions.* Multidivision companies might want an audit of their top dollar divisions to make sure that they are reaching their highest potential, and are not on the verge of a sudden reversal. Such an audit may also yield insights into how to improve marketing in other divisions.

- *Young Companies.* Marketing audits of emerging small companies or young divisions of large companies can help to lay down a solid marketing approach at a time when management faces a great degree of market inexperience.

- *Nonprofit Organizations.* Administrators of colleges, museums, hospitals, social agencies, and churches are beginning to think in marketing terms, and the marketing audit can serve a useful educational as well as diagnostic purpose.

WHAT ARE THE PROBLEMS AND PITFALLS OF MARKETING AUDITS?

While the foregoing has stressed the positive aspects of marketing audits and their utility in a variety of situations, it is important to note some of the problems and pitfalls of the marketing audit process. Problems can occur in the objective-setting step, the data collection step, or the report presentation step.

Setting Objectives

When the marketing audit effort is being designed by the auditor and the company officer who commissioned the audit, several problems will be encountered. For one thing, the objectives set for the audit are based upon the company officer's and auditor's best *a priori* notions of what the key problem areas are for the audit to highlight. However, new problem areas may emerge once the auditor begins to learn more about the company. The original set of objectives should not constrain the auditor from shifting his priorities or investigation.

Similarly, it may be necessary for the auditor to use different sources of information than envisioned at the start of the audit. In some cases this may be because some information sources he had counted on became unavailable. In one marketing audit, the auditor had planned to speak to a sample of customers for the company's electro-mechanical devices, but the company officer who hired him would not permit him to do so. In other cases, a valuable new source of information may arise that was not recognized at the start of the audit. For example, the auditor for an air brake system manufacturer found as a valuable source of market intelligence a long-established manufacturers' representatives firm that approached the company after the audit had begun.

Another consideration at the objective-setting stage of the audit is that the management most affected by the audit must have full knowledge of the purposes and scope of the audit. Audits go much more smoothly when the executive who calls in the auditor either brings the affected management into the design stage, or at least has a general introductory meeting where the auditor explains his procedures and answers questions from the people in the affected business.

Data Collection

Despite reassurances by the auditor and the executive who brought him in, there will still be some managers in the affected business who will feel threatened by the auditor. The auditor must expect this, and realize that an individual's fears and biases may color his statements in an interview.

From the onset of the audit, the auditor must guarantee and maintain confidentiality of each individual's comments. In many audits, personnel in the company will see the audit as a vehicle for unloading their negative feelings about the company or other individuals. The auditor can learn a lot from these comments, but he must protect the individuals who make them. The auditor must question interviewees in a highly professional manner to build their confidence in him, or else they will not be entirely honest in their statements.

Another area of concern during the information collection step is the degree to which the company executive who brought in the auditor will try to guide the audit. It will be necessary for this officer and the auditor to strike a balance in which the executive provides some direction, but not too much. While over-control is the more likely excess of the executive, it is possible to undercontrol. When the auditor and the company executive do not have open and frequent lines of communication during the audit, it is possible that the auditor may place more emphasis on some areas and less on others than the executive might have desired. Therefore, it is the responsibility of both the auditor and the executive who brought him in to communicate frequently during the audit.

Report Presentation

One of the biggest problems in marketing auditing is that the executive who brings in the auditor, or the people in the business being audited, may have higher expectations about what the audit will do for the company than the actual report seems to offer. In only the most extreme circumstances will the auditor develop surprising panaceas or propose startling new opportunities for the company. More likely, the main value of his report will be that it places priorities on ideas and directions for the company, many of which have already been considered by some people within the audited organization. In most successful audits, the auditor, in his recommendations, makes a skillful combination of his general and technical marketing background (e.g., designs of salesman's compensation systems, his ability to measure the size and potential of markets) with some opportunistic ideas that people in the audited organization have already considered, but do not know how much importance to place upon them. However, it is only in the company's implementation of the recommendations that the payoff to the company will come.

Another problem at the conclusion of the audit stems from the fact that most audits seem to result in organizational changes. Organizational changes are a common outcome because the audit usually identifies new tasks to be accomplished and new tasks demand people to do them. One thing the auditor and the executive who brought him in must recognize, however, is that organizational promotions and demotions are exclusively the executive's decision. It is the executive who has to live with the changes once the auditor has gone, not the auditor. Therefore, the executive should not be lulled into thinking that organizational moves are any easier because the auditor may have recommended them.

The final problem, and this is one facing the auditor, is that important parts of an audit may be implemented incorrectly or not implemented at all, by the executive who commissioned the audit. Non-implementation of key parts of the audit undermines the whole effectiveness of the audit.

SUMMARY

The marketing audit is one important answer to the problem of evaluating the marketing performance of a company or one of its business units. Marketing audits are distinguished from other marketing exercises in being *comprehensive, independent, systematic,* and *periodic.* A full marketing audit would cover the company's (or division's) external environment, objectives, strategies, organization, systems, and functions. If the audit covers only one function, such as sales management or advertising, it is best described as a marketing function audit rather than a marketing audit. If the exercise is to solve a current problem, such as entering a market, setting a price, or developing a package, then it is not an audit at all.

The marketing audit is carried out in three steps: developing an agreement as to objectives and scope;

collecting the data; and presenting the report. The audit can be performed by a competent outside consultant or by a company auditing office at headquarters.

The possible findings of an audit include detecting unclear or inappropriate marketing objectives, inappropriate strategies, inappropriate levels of marketing expenditures, needed improvements in organization, and needed improvements in systems for marketing information, planning, and control. Companies that are most likely to benefit from a marketing audit include production-oriented companies, companies with troubled or highly vulnerable divisions, young companies, and nonprofit organizations.

Many companies today are finding that their premises for marketing strategy are growing obsolete in the face of a rapidly changing environment. This is happening to company giants such as General Motors and Sears as well as smaller firms that have not provided a mechanism for recycling their marketing strategy. The marketing audit is not the full answer to marketing strategy recycling but does offer one major mechanism for pursuing this desirable and necessary task.

APPENDIX A
Components of a Marketing Audit

THE MARKETING ENVIRONMENT AUDIT

I. Macro-Environment

Economic-Demographic
1. What does the company expect in the way of inflation, material shortages, unemployment, and credit availability in the short run, intermediate run, and long run?
2. What effect will forecasted trends in the size, age distribution, and regional distribution of population have on the business?

Technology
1. What major changes are occurring in product technology? In process technology?
2. What are the major generic substitutes that might replace this product?

Political-Legal
1. What laws are being proposed that may affect marketing strategy and tactics?
2. What federal, state, and local agency actions should be watched? What is happening in the areas of pollution control, equal employment opportunity, product safety, advertising, price control, etc., that is relevant to marketing planning?

Social-Cultural
1. What attitudes is the public taking toward business and toward products such as those produced by the company?
2. What changes are occurring in consumer life styles and values that have a bearing on the company's target markets and marketing methods?

II. Task Environment

Markets
1. What is happening to market size, growth, geographical distribution, and profits?
2. What are the major market segments? What are their expected rates of growth? Which are high opportunity and low opportunity segments?

Customers
1. How do current customers and prospects rate the company and its competitors, particularly with respect to reputation, product quality, service, sales force, and price?
2. How do different classes of customers make their buying decisions?
3. What are the evolving needs and satisfactions being sought by the buyers in this market?

Competitors

1. Who are the major competitors? What are the objectives and strategy of each major competitor? What are their strengths and weaknesses? What are the sizes and trends in market shares?
2. What trends can be foreseen in future competition and substitutes for this product?

Distribution and Dealers

1. What are the main trade channels bringing products to customers?
2. What are the efficiency levels and growth potentials of the different trade channels?

Suppliers

1. What is the outlook for the availability of different key resources used in production?
2. What trends are occurring among suppliers in their pattern of selling?

Facilitators

1. What is the outlook for the cost and availability of transportation services?
2. What is the outlook for the cost and availability of warehousing facilities?
3. What is the outlook for the cost and availability of financial resources?
4. How effectively is the advertising agency performing? What trends are occurring in advertising agency services?

MARKETING STRATEGY AUDIT

Marketing Objectives

1. Are the corporate objectives clearly stated and do they lead logically to the marketing objectives?
2. Are the marketing objectives stated in a clear form to guide marketing planning and subsequent performance measurement?
3. Are the marketing objectives appropriate, given the company's competitive position, resources, and opportunities? Is the appropriate strategic objective to build, hold, harvest, or terminate this business?

Strategy

1. What is the core marketing strategy for achieving the objectives? Is it a sound marketing strategy?
2. Are enough resources (or too much resources) budgeted to accomplish the marketing objectives?
3. Are the marketing resources allocated optimally to prime market segments, territories, and products of the organization?
4. Are the marketing resources allocated optimally to the major elements of the marketing mix, i.e., product quality, service, sales force, advertising, promotion, and distribution?

MARKETING ORGANIZATION AUDIT

Formal Structure

1. Is there a high level marketing officer with adequate authority and responsibility over those company activities that affect the customer's satisfaction?
2. Are the marketing responsibilities optimally structured along functional, product, end user, and territorial lines?

Functional Efficiency

1. Are there good communication and working relations between marketing and sales?
2. Is the product management system working effectively? Are the product managers able to plan profits or only sales volume?
3. Are there any groups in marketing that need more training, motivation, supervision, or evaluation?

Interface Efficiency

1. Are there any problems between marketing and manufacturing that need attention?
2. What about marketing and R&D?
3. What about marketing and financial management?
4. What about marketing and purchasing?

MARKETING SYSTEMS AUDIT

Marketing Information System

1. Is the marketing intelligence system producing accurate, sufficient, and timely information about developments in the marketplace?
2. Is marketing research being adequately used by company decision makers?

Marketing Planning System

1. Is the marketing planning system well-conceived and effective?
2. Is sales forecasting and market potential measurement soundly carried out?
3. Are sales quotas set on a proper basis?

Marketing Control System

1. Are the control procedures (monthly, quarterly, etc.) adequate to insure that the annual plan objectives are being achieved?
2. Is provision made to analyze periodically the profitability of different products, markets, territories, and channels of distribution?
3. Is provision made to examine and validate periodically various marketing costs?

New Product Development System
1. Is the company well-organized to gather, generate, and screen new product ideas?
2. Does the company do adequate concept research and business analysis before investing heavily in a new idea?
3. Does the company carry out adequate product and market testing before launching a new product?

MARKETING PRODUCTIVITY AUDIT

Profitability Analysis
1. What is the profitability of the company's different products, served markets, territories, and channels of distribution?
2. Should the company enter, expand, contract, or withdraw from any business segments and what would be the short- and long-run profit consequences?

Cost-Effectiveness Analysis
1. Do any marketing activities seem to have excessive costs? Are these costs valid? Can cost-reducing steps be taken?

MARKETING FUNCTION AUDITS

Products
1. What are the product line objectives? Are these objectives sound? Is the current product line meeting these objectives?
2. Are there particular products that should be phased out?
3. Are there new products that are worth adding?
4. Are any products able to benefit from quality, feature, or style improvements?

Price
1. What are the pricing objectives, policies, strategies, and procedures? To what extent are prices set on sound cost, demand, and competitive criteria?

2. Do the customers see the company's prices as being in line or out of line with the perceived value of its offer?
3. Does the company use price promotions effectively?

Distribution
1. What are the distribution objectives and strategies?
2. Is there adequate market coverage and service?
3. Should the company consider changing its degree of reliance on distributors, sales reps, and direct selling?

Sales Force
1. What are the organization's sales force objectives?
2. Is the sales force large enough to accomplish the company's objectives?
3. Is the sales force organized along the proper principle(s) of specialization (territory, market, product)?
4. Does the sales force show high morale, ability, and effort? Are they sufficiently trained and incentivized?
5. Are the procedures adequate for setting quotas and evaluating performances?
6. How is the company's sales force perceived in relation to competitors' sales forces?

Advertising, Promotion, and Publicity
1. What are the organization's advertising objectives? Are they sound?
2. Is the right amount being spent on advertising? how is the budget determined?
3. Are the ad themes and copy effective? What do customers and the public think about the advertising?
4. Are the advertising media well chosen?
5. Is sales promotion used effectively?
6. Is there a well-conceived publicity program?

Notes

1. Many useful checklist questions for marketers are found in C. Eldridge, *The Management of the Marketing Function* (New York: Association of National Advertisers, 1967).

2. See P. Kotler, *Marketing Management Analysis, Planning and Control* (Englewood Cliffs, N.J.: Prentice-Hall, Inc., 1976), pp. 457–462.

3. See P. J. Stonich, "Zero-Base Planning—A Management Tool," *Managerial Planning,* July-August 1976, pp. 1–4.

CASES

J & H HEATING AND AIR CONDITIONING

J & H Heating and Air Conditioning, located in a major northwestern city, was by far the city's largest firm engaged in the sale, installation, and service of furnaces, air conditioners, air purifiers, and related equipment. The owners were in the process of reviewing past operations and trying to decide on the future marketing strategies.

ALLIED PALLET COMPANY

Allied Pallet Company is one of five major producers of pallets in the northwestern part of the United States. Considered to be a producer of lower-priced, lower-quality pallets, Allied had experienced declining sales for the past two years. Currently, the management is reviewing the entire operation of the company to determine what improvements can be made in its performance.

PARK PHARMACIES

Park Pharmacies is a holding company for three drug stores located in the northeastern part of the United States. Founded by two pharmacists, the three stores are quite different from each other in design, organization, and marketing orientation. Although the two older stores, each managed by one of the partners, have been successful, the third store has been operated by a manager and has experienced considerable difficulties. At the present time, the partners are considering how to build sales and profits for the third pharmacy.

PACIFIC ART MUSEUM OF LAS POSITAS

The Pacific Art Museum has had a colorful history since its founding in 1869. Because the museum was a department of the city of Las Positas, it did not depend on admissions revenues or donations. Nevertheless, joint control between the city and the Pacific Art Museum Association resulted in significant jurisdictional problems.

J & H HEATING AND AIR CONDITIONING

J & H Heating and Air Conditioning was established in a major northwestern city in 1968 by Jerry and Hank Anderson. Starting as sole proprietors, the brothers built the business to the point where it presently had thirty employees and annual sales of nearly $700,000 (see exhibits 1 and 2). Their principal activities pertained to the sale, installation, service and repair of furnaces, air conditioners, air purifiers, and other related equipment.

Although they both felt that the firm has been successful, they recognized that improvements could be made and that plans should be developed for the future. It was concerning the long run that the brothers disagreed most. Jerry, sixty-one years old, had three sons, two of whom worked for the company and had an interest in taking over at a future point. Hank, fifty-five years old, on the other hand, had two daughters who had no interest in the firm whatsoever.

Consequently, in their planning they had to deal with immediate profits and returns as well as those for the long term. Both realized this was a problem and knew they had to make appropriate trade-offs for the good of the company. They were unsure, however, of what actions they should take in terms of expansion, contraction, and modifications to improve efficiency.

HISTORY

Jerry and Hank Anderson had considerable experience in the heating and air conditioning field. Jerry had begun thirty-seven years ago as a door-to-door solicitor for a local branch office of Area Manufacturing, Inc., a major producer of furnaces. Within five years, he

This case was prepared by Professor Dennis H. Tootelian, California State University, Sacramento.

had become one of the branch's three top salesmen, and after another five years had been promoted to branch manager. By the time Jerry was forty-five, he was division manager and was responsible for nearly 125 branch offices in the Midwest. Each branch typically had annual sales ranging between $75,000 and $350,000.

Hank Anderson began working for the same company nearly thirty years ago. Also starting as a door-to-door solicitor, he contintued in that capacity while his brother was branch manager. When Jerry was promoted to district manager, Hank assumed the branch manager position. After two years, Hank was also promoted to a district manager's position in the Southeast.

By 1967, both missed working together and wanted to return to the Northwest. Area Manufacturing was at that time experiencing financial difficulties, which contributed to their decision to quit and form J & H Heating and Air Conditioning. Since both had served as salesmen and branch managers in the city, they felt they knew the market, as well as the technical aspects of the business.

In forming J & H, they each invested $2,000 and were issued fifty shares of stock at $40 per share. Later that year, they gave two shares of stock apiece to an attorney as partial payment for legal services rendered. Although he did own four shares, he seldom participated in any management decision-making processes.

Concerning the overall development of J & H Heating and Air Conditioning, Jerry Anderson commented:

> Hank and I often reminisce about the early days when we both were salesmen and then when I was his boss. We are very close and it really hurt when I was moved to the Midwest. When Hank went to the Southeast I think we both moped around for weeks.
>
> Actually, the whole thing was good for both of us. We learned a lot about the business when we worked for Area. It had very conservative policies with respect to marketing programs. There was, for example, no advertising and only one product line—a high quality, high-priced unit that eventually was priced out of the market. At first it was easy

CASE

EXHIBIT 1
J & H Heating and Air Conditioning
Income Statements

		Last Year		Two Years Ago		Three Years Ago
Income						
(1)	Equipment Sales		$602,449		$444,300		$311,248
	Less:						
	Cost of Goods Sold	$103,621		$ 67,862		$ 67,293	
	Installation Expense	51,208		45,510		41,334	
	Installers Expense	63,257	218,086	56,507	169,879	47,040	155,667
	Gross Profit		$384,363		$274,421		$155,581
(2)	Furnace Cleaning Sales		$ 89,222		$ 90,144		$113,272
	Less:						
	Supplies	$ 4,275		$ 1,465		$ 3,719	
	Operators Expenses	44,053	48,328	46,759	48,224	55,857	59,576
	Gross Profit		$137,550		$138,368		$172,848
(3)	Service & Repair Income		5,271		6,653		11,224
	Total Gross Profit		$527,184		$419,442		$339,653
Expenses						
	Selling Expenses (Schedule A)	$251,467		$214,843		$193,900	
	General and Administrative Expense (Schedule B)	253,048		183,601		140,032	
	Total Expenses		$504,515		$398,444		$333,932
Net Profit Before Taxes			$ 22,669		$ 20,998		$ 5,721

Schedule A—Selling Expenses

	Last Year	Two Years Ago	Three Years Ago
Advertising	$ 5,469	$ 2,338	$ 3,879
Cleaning System Materials and Repairs	26,569	22,195	24,569
Bridge and Dump Expenses	482	313	481
Permits	1,591	1,447	1,044
Equipment Rental*	15,042	9,273	15,889
Sales Commission and Salaries	190,966	163,280	139,858**
Sales Expenses	9,359	13,156	8,180
Unrecovered Salesmen's Advances	1,982	2,841	—
Total	$251,467	$214,843	$193,900

*Used when demand for services was in excess of equipment capability.

**Commission structure was different in this year. Lower commissions were offered on equipment sales.

(*exhibit 1 continues on next page*)

EXHIBIT 1 (*continued*)
Schedule B—General and Administrative Expenses

	Last Year	Two Years Ago	Three Years Ago
Taxes & Licenses	$ 15,442	$ 14,894	$ 15,256
Pension Fund	1,836	1,994	1,740
Dues & Subscriptions	1,272	1,037	1,487
Legal & Accounting Fees	2,479	2,344	3,454
Utilities	1,970	1,587	1,534
Insurance Expense	14,458	10,594	9,017
Rental of Premises	4,859	2,954	4,261
Office Salaries	27,975	24,936	23,729
Officer Salaries	137,600	88,495	57,741
Building Maintenance & Supplies	3,885	1,681	1,601
Credit Investigation	170	318	122
Telephone	11,088	7,990	9,252
Travel	2,078	2,021	955
Employee Bonuses & Vacation Pay	26,423	13,794	7,281
Loss from Bad Debts	643	7,235	1,829
Interest Expense	266	51	—
Miscellaneous	604	676	773
Total	$253,048	$182,601	$140,032

to sell because it was so much better than the others and people would pay the price. Now they want only reasonable quality and a lower price.

Anyway, Hank and I enjoy working together. Over the years since J & H was started, we have complemented each other well.

ORGANIZATION

The organization chart for J & H Heating and Air Conditioning is presented in exhibit 3. Jerry Anderson, president of the corporation, was responsible for operations, installation, and service and repairs. Hank Anderson was vice-president and primarily responsible for sales. Despite the formal structure, however, either brother could act in both capacities and often did when it was convenient.

Working directly for Jerry Anderson was the office manager, Bill Martinson, who had been with the company since 1971. He was responsible for the furnace cleaning crews, the repairmen, and the general office operations including the bookkeeping and

purchasing. Depending on the volume of business, J & H employed anywhere between two and four furnace and air conditioning installers. Since Jerry Anderson believed that the quality of their work affected company image, he wanted to oversee their activities directly:

If the installers mess up, we are out of business! Once the word gets out that we cannot install a furnace properly, how can they believe we can service them? There is no question but that this work directly affects sales—so I want it to be right.

Hank Anderson organized the selling function by employing a service sales manager, Jack Harley, and a unit sales manager, Andrew Payson. Mr. Harley was responsible for selling the company's furnace cleaning service and had six salespeople, two of whom worked part-time. Mr. Payson was charged with selling furnaces, air conditioners, air cleaners, and vacuum cleaners, He employed eight salespeople, all of whom were full-time employees.

CASE

EXHIBIT 2
J & H Heating and Air Conditioning
Balance Sheet

	Last Year	Two Years Ago
ASSETS:		
Current		
Cash	$ 51,558	$ 65,148
Accounts Receivable		
Equipment Sales & Repair	19,658	22,358
Furnace Cleaning	1,791	1,038
Employee Advances	4,922	3,291
Inventory	30,414	32,083
Prepaid Expenses & Miscellaneous	8,986	5,535
Total	$117,329	$129,453
Fixed (Net of Depreciation)		
Trucks	$ 5,065	$ 3,836
Office Equipment	1,479	2,076
Building	61,386	—
Land	30,886	—
Total	$ 98,816	$ 5,912
TOTAL ASSETS	$216,145	$135,365
LIABILITIES:		
Current		
Accounts Payable	$ 12,204	$ 14,510
Employee Payroll	12,770	10,366
Employee Benefits (Vacation & Bonus)	6,647	6,257
Officers Salaries	29,846	40,926
Withholding Taxes & Sales Taxes	4,475	5,568
Federal & State Income Tax Payable	7,238	6,745
Mortgage Payable—Current Portion	7,260	—
Total	$ 80,440	$ 84,372
Long Term		
Notes Payable to Officers	$ 18,990	—
Mortgage Payable	45,053	—
Total	$ 64,043	—
TOTAL LIABILITIES	$144,483	$ 84,372
CAPITAL:		
Capital Stock	$ 2,000	$ 2,000
Retained Earnings	69,662	48,993
Total	$ 71,662	$ 50,993
TOTAL LIABILITIES & CAPITAL	$216,145	$135,365

EXHIBIT 3
J & H Heating and Air Conditioning
Organization Chart

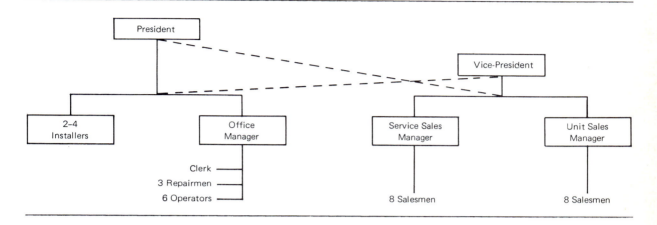

GENERAL OPERATIONS

J & H's operations consisted primarily of three activities: furnace cleaning, service and repairs, and equipment installation. Scheduling of furnace cleaning was arranged by the office manager. Mr. Harley received the cleaning sales slips from his salespeople and turned them over to Hank Anderson for service. Once noted, they were passed on to Mr. Martinson, who then called the customers to make service appointments. An attempt was made to schedule jobs by areas to minimize crosstown travel. Depending on the size of the jobs and their locations, one operator could clean as many as three to four furnaces a day. The cleaning operators were paid a commission of between $12 and $18 per furnace, depending on its condition and size.

Service and repairs were typically handled by one of the repairmen who reported to Mr. Martinson. This business usually resulted from "no heat" calls ("furnace not working properly"), which often came late at night or early in the morning. While day calls were passed directly to the repairmen, the night calls went to the brothers who had their home telephones listed as "emergency numbers." Depending on the

location, the time, and other circumstances, they either went out themselves or called a repairman. There was no set policy, and both considered it a necessary evil. Hank Anderson noted:

Jerry and I hate to go out on these calls, but I think they are a source of considerable business. Although our repairmen are paid a straight salary, we always hate to call them in the middle of the night to do the "dirty work." I guess this is just part of the business.

All equipment installation was performed by the installers. An attempt was made to have equipment placed and operating within one week from the date of the sale. Although they typically worked alone, at times a job required two installers which then made other scheduling difficult and additional installers were hired. Since all were union employees, extra personnel were usually available when needed. Mr. Martinson also scheduled installations in much the same manner as he did service calls. The only difference was that he reported each completed installation immediately to Jerry Anderson. Installers were paid a union wage plus a differential for overtime.

PRODUCTS

According to Hank Anderson, their business was oriented to service:

We are in the business of selling home comfort and cleanliness. All our product lines revolve around that fact. That was one of the problems with the company Jerry and I worked for–they sold a furnace rather than comfort.

Our products and services consist of six main lines: furnace cleaning, furnace service and repair, furnace replacement, air conditioning installation and service, electric air cleaner installation and service, and installation of built-in vacuum cleaning systems.

J & H's furnace cleaning service included vacuum cleaning of all warm air and cold air return ducts, cleaning the furnace, and spraying the duct system with insecticide. The company also serviced and repaired furnaces and sold and installed replacement furnaces. No attempt was made to sell to the new home market. While J & H cleaned, serviced, sold, and installed air conditioners also, activity in this market was negligible due primarily to the mild summer temperatures.

The second most significant part of J & H's sales consisted of installation and service of electronic air cleaners. When one of these devices was installed in the cold air return duct of a central heater system, virtually all solid particles were removed from the air electronically. The overall result was an appreciable reduction in the house cleaning effort since all airborne dust particles were removed. It also provided a more pleasant living environment by removing smoking and cooking odors.

Finally, rounding out their "comfort and cleanliness" line was a central vacuum cleaner system. The motor and collector bag was typically placed in the home's basement or garage. Plastic pipe was installed below the floor from the collector to floor sockets in various rooms of the house. The units themselves were built by a large manufacturer to J & H's specifications.

The breakdown of the types of equipment sold is presented in exhibit 4. Approximately 60 percent

EXHIBIT 4
Breakdown of Equipment Sales
(average over 10 years)

Equipment	Percent of Dollar Volume
Furnaces	60%
Air Cleaners	30%
Vacuum Cleaners	10%
Air Conditioners	Negligible

of the furnaces sold by J & H were oil fired, which were somewhat higher in price than gas furnaces. Originally the Andersons planned to buy furnaces from Area. Because of Area's financial difficulties, however, they decided to buy from a nationally known manufacturer under an exclusive distribution agreement. While they did carry other lines, this one brand accounted for about 90 percent of their oil furnace sales. The types of furnaces carried are listed in exhibit 5.

SALES

All sales were made through J & H's service sales and unit sales departments. The service sales department was responsible for door-to-door sales of furnace cleaning. A normal price range was between $60 and $150 for this service and the salesman received a 20 percent commission. The furnace cleaning sales made by each are shown in exhibit 6.

EXHIBIT 5
Furnaces (Installed)

Capacity (BTU's)	Brand	Fuel	Price
98,000	National	Oil	$1,031
100,000	National	Gas	784
100,000	Regional	Gas	952
125,000	National	Oil	1,177
185,000	Regional	Oil	1,718
200,000	Regional	Gas	1,107

EXHIBIT 6
Furnace Cleaning Sales
(typical month)

Salesman		Percent of Monthly Sales
A	. . . .	47%
B	. . . .	22%
C	. . . .	22%
D	. . . .	3%
E	. . . .	3%
F	. . . .	3%

EXHIBIT 7
Commission on Equipment Sales

Type of Equipment	Percent Commission
Central Vacuum Cleaner	35%
Electronic Air Cleaner	30%
Furnace	20%
Air Conditioners	20%

The unit sales department was responsible for all equipment sales and repairs. While cleaning furnaces, the operators took note of any potential equipment repair or sale business, and reported it to the unit salesman who inspected all furnaces after they were cleaned. This was a standard source of equipment sales. Additional equipment sales and repairs resulted from the "no heat" calls. These were transferred directly to unit salesmen who then referred them to repairmen.

The salesmen were paid a commission on the various equipment as shown in exhibit 7. A 5 percent commission was also paid to salesmen from service sales when equipment sales resulted from their cleaning contacts.

Jerry Anderson believed that about one in ten cleaning sales ultimately led to an equipment sale. Very few equipment sales were thought to be the result of a customer seeking out J & H Heating and Air Conditioning. Accordingly, little was spent on promotion, except for a small advertisement in the yellow pages of the telephone directory.

According to Hank Anderson, J & H's primary problem in sales was convincing customers of the need for its service. Based on his many years of experience, Hank felt that it was not the housewife, but the husband, who had to be sold. Under such circumstances, sales generally were becoming more concentrated in the evenings and Saturdays. The sales force, however, tried to maintain as much as possible an eight to five weekday schedule.

COMPETITION

In the local area there were over one hundred heating and air conditioning businesses listed in the telephone directory. Of that number, the great majority were one- or two-person operations offering limited services, primarily to the "no heat" repair calls. Most, furthermore, operated out of their homes, had minimum overhead, little invested in the business, and worked for less than union wage. Promotional efforts were heavily concentrated in yellow pages advertising. Jerry Anderson estimated that these "backyard operators" accounted for between 10 to 15 percent of all local business.

A second group of competitors were those tied in with the major oil companies. Approximately 60 percent of all local homes were heated by oil furnaces, although a definite trend from oil to gas furnaces in new home construction was evident. A similar trend, even though less significant, was occurring in the replacement furnace business.

This switch from oil to gas forced many oil companies to become more active in promoting their products. As a result, a number of J & H's competitors were either partly or wholly owned by these large firms. The heating and air conditioning firms not only provided repair and installation service, but also sold oil to the customers. In fact, they were primarily heating oil dealers. They did not promote their other products very intensively, but were able to use furnace cleaning and minor repairs as loss leaders in order to promote the sale of oil. J & H's two largest competitors had such tie-ins. These firms as a whole accounted for about 30 percent of all sales.

In the local market, J & H Heating and Air Conditioning was by far the largest, accounting for between 55 percent and 60 percent of all sales. Both Jerry and Hank Anderson attributed this to the fact that they were known for honest, high quality work, because they were one of the oldest such firms in the city. Although their market share had eroded somewhat from 70 percent in 1975, they felt it was the normal result of competition, particularly from competitors tied to major oil companies.

FUTURE

In light of the changing trends and the fact that so much of their business was tied in to furnace sales, Jerry Anderson was beginning to wonder whether the firm should become more diversified. Hank, on the other hand believed there were many internal inefficiencies to be remedied before any consideration should be given to expansion. He thought that competition over time would become much more intense and only those firms with low-cost operations could withstand possible price wars.

Although they agreed that both could be accomplished, perhaps simultaneously, they were unsure of where to start. They decided that whatever actions they took, however, had to be consistent with their history of quality and respectability.

ALLIED PALLET COMPANY

Seated in a small conference room the three partners in Allied Pallet Company were discussing the firm's current position. Over the last year, the company's sales had stagnated and profits had declined appreciably. In summarizing the situation, Gary Williams, Allied's president, noted:

I believe we are nearing a crisis point. Sales are slowing down, profits are off, and payables to the lumber company are way up. I'd hate to take a loss on this business, but I won't pour a lot more money into it. Either we turn it around or we close it down and all suffer.

This case was prepared by Professor Dennis H. Tootelian, California State University, Sacramento.

COMPANY HISTORY

Located in the suburbs of a small city in the Northwest, Allied Pallet Company's operations were limited primarily to the manufacturing and wholesale distribution of wooden pallets—platforms upon which various types of items can be stacked (see exhibit 1).

Allied Pallet Company had been founded nearly four years ago by Mr. Richard Davies, who had previously been employed as a superintendent in a local woodworking company. Since he did not have enough money to establish the business on his own, he borrowed $25,000 from a bank, relatives and friends, and put up $5,000 of his own savings. During the next year, he took on a partner, Frank Glenn. For the first two years of business together, Mr. Davies and Mr. Glenn maintained a policy of putting all of the money they could back into the business. They worked long hours and handled management matters and a large amount of the clerical work themselves in order to keep expenses to a minimum.

At the end of the two years, Mr. Davies and Mr. Glenn reached the point where they were unable to purchase necessary raw materials for their daily operations either with cash or on credit. Neither sales

CASE

EXHIBIT 1
A Two-Way Pallet

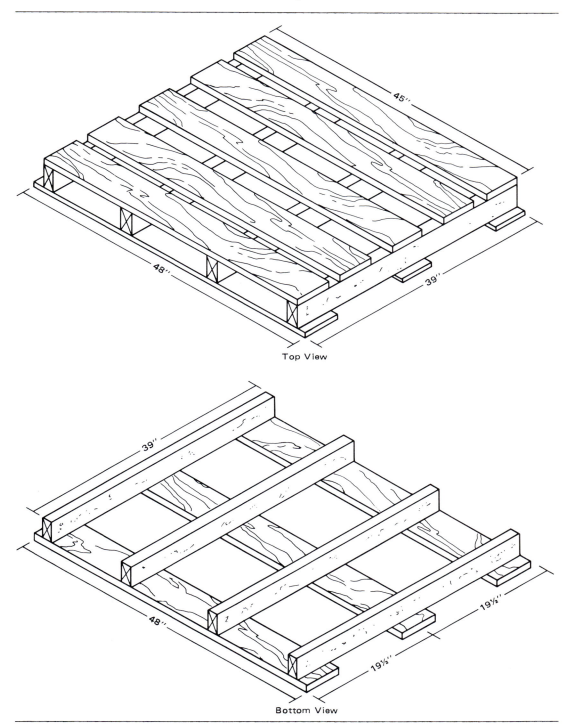

Top View

Bottom View

nor profits were meeting their expectations. Sluggish sales, increases in the company's liabilities to a local lumber firm which had given them a line of credit, and personality conflicts between the partners, made Mr. Davies decide to sell his share of the business. To absolve himself from debt, he turned his interest in the business over to Gary and Paul Williams, owners of Williams Lumber—the lumber company that had extended Allied the line of credit.

Williams Lumber was a large, successful wholesale company with three offices in a two-state area, and a good reputation within the industry. Its aggressive pricing policies, coupled with extensive financial reserves, made Williams Lumber one of the more respected firms in the Northwest.

Soon after taking over Mr. Davies' share of the business and becoming an equal partner with Mr. Glenn, Gary and Paul Williams assigned Mr. Donald Powell to manage their interests in Allied Pallet Company. Mr. Powell had been managing one of the sales offices for Williams Lumber and had been a trusted employee for many years. The Williams brothers asked Mr. Powell to investigate the business and render an opinion as to whether it would be best to continue operations or shut the business down and absorb the losses. At that time, Allied Pallet owed Williams Lumber nearly $105,000, and the brothers did not want to risk more money.

After making his review, Mr. Powell indicated that the business could be profitable if it were managed properly. Sales volume had been built largely on the basis of successful price competition. But operating expenses, customer services, and product quality had not been controlled as well as they should have been. With good management, Mr. Powell believed that sales could quickly surpass $15,000,000, with profits of between $100,000 and $200,000. Based on this assessment, Gary and Paul Williams decided to continue the business.

PALLETS

Pallets can be classified into three groups: expendable, general purpose, and special purpose. Expendable pallets are typically used for one-trip hauling and stay with the merchandise that is being shipped. About 75 percent of all pallets are expendable, and by their very nature, their design and construction are matters of negotiation between the pallet manufacturer and the customer. Expendable pallets are the lowest grade, and can be made from any species of wood which will support the product from the point of loading to the final destination.

General purpose pallets, on the other hand, are reusable, and can be made in standard design and construction. Overall, they account for approximately 15 percent of the total demand for pallets. Special purpose pallets, as their name implies, are designed to meet the specifications of the customer. In these instances, the buyer will have particular needs for design and construction depending on the merchandise to be shipped or the manner in which it is to be stored. Special purpose pallets account for the remaining 10 percent of pallet sales.

Although there can be many variations in the construction of wooden pallets, they typically are categorized by design and style. The design of pallets is based on the ways in which forklifts or hand trucks can enter the pallet. Two-way pallets allow entry from two sides only, in opposite directions. Four-way pallets permit entry on all four sides, and because of their construction are considerably more expensive to manufacture. Mr. Powell believed that four-way pallets were about 30 percent more expensive to produce and that they accounted for only about 30 to 40 percent of the markets Allied had targeted.

The style of pallet refers to the number of "decks" it has. A single-face pallet has only one flat side, that being the top surface. Double-face pallets have both top and bottom decks, and are considerably more expensive because of the added material and labor involved in their production. Mr. Powell estimated that 85 percent of the market was for single-face pallets, due to the fact that double-face pallets cost nearly 70 percent more to produce.

The key factors involved in the manufacture and sale of pallets are the type, size, and quality. The type and size are directly related to the amount of wood needed. The quality is related to both the type of wood used, and the amount of labor expended. As shown in exhibit 2, materials and labor were the primary cost factors for Allied Pallets.

EXHIBIT 2
Percentage Cost Distribution
(First six months)

Month	Lumber	Labor	Misc*	Total Costs
January	41.8	32.7	25.5	100.0
February	52.9	24.2	22.9	100.0
March	53.1	23.3	23.6	100.0
April	53.6	19.8	26.6	100.0
May	49.9	23.9	26.2	100.0
June	49.4	21.5	29.1	100.0

*Includes telephone, gasoline, payroll taxes, nails, etc.

THE MARKETPLACE

Allied Pallet Company was typical of most pallet manufacturers. Companies in this industry did little advertising, nor did they attempt to promote their brands of pallets. Usually, they developed their own customers by presenting their products, offering service, and—most importantly—providing very competitive prices.

There were some differences in quality of production among the manufacturers. Allied was considered to be a producer of low- to medium-quality pallets, but the company provided reasonably timely customer service (that is, Allied met delivery dates for the finished pallets).

There were four other major competitors in Allied's market area. One competitor, Apex Manufacturing, produced better quality pallets, although it often had problems meeting its time commitments for delivery. The other manufacturers made lower quality pallets, but generally were known for more prompt delivery—often a critical factor in the buyer's decision. Summary descriptions of the manufacturers are shown in exhibit 3.

Most manufacturers were partnerships or closely held corporations with relatively limited financial resources. Generally, the industry was stratified into three layers: (1) companies that were financially able to make pallets exclusively for governmental agencies; (2) companies with sufficient financial resources to handle both government and private contracts of moderate size; and (3) companies that survived on a job-order basis because they were financially unable to handle moderate-to-large private contract or government jobs due to the initial capital outlay necessary. Allied Pallet was in the third of these layers.

Mr. Paul Williams commented on Allied's position, and the industry as a whole:

The pallet business is just coming into its own again, and there will be tremendous demand for pallets from this point on. We feel that if we are to gain the number one position, we have to increase our sales and reduce our labor costs and fixed expenses. If we do all this, we think that we can realize a good profit.

Small and medium-size firms tend to compete on a price basis, while the larger manufacturers emphasize product quality and service. This is what we intend to do, as well as keep our prices competitive. The people who are buying pallets are reaching the point where they know they are going to have to pay to get the kinds of pallets they want. This opens the door for most of the pallet plants who, up until this point, were doing very poorly. However, there are not too many left because the profits have been so low. This is especially true for expendable pallets, where the demand is also the greatest.

According to Mr. Powell, selling the pallets is handled in a rather informal way. He noted:

We all work together as a family, so to speak. If anybody here or with Williams Lumber hears of an order or inquiry in the field, it will be passed on to us so we can check it out. We generally try to find out what a firm is looking for, how many pallets they want to buy, and the level of quality they demand. From there, we decide whether to bid for the job. If we get the contract, we make the pallets. It's as simple as that.

COMPANY ORGANIZATION AND MANAGEMENT

The organizational structure of Allied Pallet Company was quite direct. Gary Williams was the president of the company, Paul Williams was treasurer, Frank

EXHIBIT 3
Competitor Characteristics

	Major Competitors*				
	Apex	Brown	Western	U.S.	Allied
Target Market					
Government	X	X		X	
Large, Private	X		X		
Small, Job-order	X	X	X	X	X
Type of Pallet Sales					
Expendable	50	80	70	75	90
General	20	15	20	10	5
Specialized	30	5	10	15	5
Company Image/Rating					
Quality of Product	High	Low	Low	Medium	Low
Timing for Delivery	Fair	Good	Good	Fair	Fair
Price	High	Low	Medium	Medium	Low

*Major Competitors: Apex Manufacturing; Brown Pallet Company; Western Pallet Company; U.S. Pallet Company; Allied Pallet Company.

Glenn was plant manager, and Donald Powell was general manager.

Although Gary Williams was the president of Allied, Mr. Powell had the authority to do nearly anything he wanted. The main consideration was whether the action was in the best interests of the business, and if it served to reduce the debt Allied had to Williams Lumber. As Mr. Powell commented:

My function is to work for Williams Lumber and Allied, in that order. I handle the sales, but there is no buying, no selling, or anything without my authorization. My decisions are temporary, however, when they involve major purchases or sales. In those instances, Gary will come in for the final approval or disapproval. Major financial decisions are always made by Gary. Sometimes Frank gets a little annoyed with this arrangement, since he is an equal partner in the business. But there is not much he can do about it. Gary and Paul can close this place up any time they want, and all I have to do is suggest they do and the business dies. I think that is what really irks Frank the most.

MARKETING

Mr. Powell and two employees were responsible for all of the selling efforts of Allied Pallet. Most of the selling was conducted through telephone solicitations to contacts they had made over the years. Like Mr. Powell, the two salesmen had considerable experience in the lumber industry, but not in pallet manufacturing or sales. One salesman had been with Allied for two years, and the other for eleven months.

Allied maintained boldfaced name prints in the "Lumber" section of the yellow pages of telephone directories in several of the larger cities in which it did the majority of its business. The company did no other advertising.

Approximately 65 percent of Allied's business was generated from contacts with past customers and acquaintances. In addition, both salesmen routinely called various potential users of pallets—such as food processors, warehouses, and manufacturers. These "cold calls" accounted for approximately 25 percent of sales. The remaining sales primarily came from unsolicited orders, usually from buyers who had met Mr. Glenn at various lumber conventions. Neither

Mr. Powell nor the two salesmen attended industry conventions, believing them to be too costly and a waste of time. As Mr. Powell noted:

> We let Frank go to the conventions under the banner that he is representing us. Actually, I think Gary and Paul put up with it just to humor him since he is part owner. I like it because it gets him out of the office here.

Although Mr. Powell was not certain how other pallet manufacturers generated their sales, he assumed all operated in much the same manner. The only exception was Apex Manufacturing, which was generally believed to be more aggressive in seeking out new customers than any other pallet manufacturer. Its six salespeople did extensive research on potential clients, including visits to their plants if necessary. Mr. Powell felt this was due to the heavy volume of speciality pallets produced by Apex.

VIEWS OF THE COMPANY

Mr. Gary Williams volunteered a number of comments about Allied's problems:

> In the past three years, we have undergone a 10 to 20 percent loss of business because of mismanufactured items. We have also lost internal profits through extra labor costs involved in picking up the mismanufactured items and resupplying the proper pallets. Overall, we have had to go out and resell our customers on Allied, and that takes time away from developing new business.
>
> In order to develop a business today, you have to develop a product that can be utilized by the end consumer. To do this, you have to develop a product that is well designed and manufactured. Then you have something you can offer a customer. This is one of the problems we have had in our business up to now. Frank has never been schooled in customer requirements and customer needs regarding shipping and consistent quality. Our pallets run from high to low quality, and about 90 percent of the time near low.

In response to questions about Allied Pallet Company, John Slasson, the accountant for both

Allied and Williams Lumber, made the following comments:

> A classic example of the kind of problems Allied has occurred only last week. Frank decided to have one of our trucks repaired. It cost $1,100 to make the necessary repairs and the truck has a book value of only $750. Because the truck is so old, it has virtually no market value left. It seems that Frank will make a decision to purchase some materials or buy some machinery, even though this is technically Don's area of authority. However, Gary and Paul usually will go along with the decision with no further study or evaluation. They are tired of fighting with Frank. Besides, he is their partner.
>
> There has been no outline or projection of what we want to do, and what we should accomplish as far as the growth of the business is concerned. We just keep making and selling pallets as best we can.
>
> Allied pruchases its lumber and other raw materials through Williams Lumber, and pays a little higher price than it would on the open market. But, because Allied is not a good credit risk, most suppliers want payment in advance or on delivery. So, I think Gary and Paul are justified in charging higher prices for the added risks involved. Unfortunately, lumber and other raw materials have increased significantly in price, but the wholesale prices on expendable pallets have not increased proportionally.

Mr. Powell summarized Allied's condition:

> Once you develop an account, if you do a proper job in manufacturing and servicing the buyer, you should be able to keep it with you. If you do a good job in manufacturing, selling, and servicing, you are automatically going to have a product that is reasonably priced. All of this is not happening in our company.
>
> We have several large accounts. One of those has been mistreated in my opinion. The pricing structure is too high relative to the quality of pallet we are producing. They have paid top dollar for, at times, a very poor pallet. The only reason we were able to get by with it was that they had a

CASE

EXHIBIT 4
Condensed Financial Statements

	1st 6 Months	Last Year	Two Years Ago
Gross Sales	$4,503,000	$9,078,000	$12,298,000
Costs of Sales	2,477,000	4,663,000	6,734,000
Gross Profit	$2,026,000	$4,415,000	$ 5,564,000
Fixed Expenses	236,000	502,000	603,000
Variable Expenses	1,773,000	3,899,000	4,919,000
Net Profit Before Taxes	$ 17,000	$ 14,000	$ 42,000

fellow there that was a good friend of Frank's. He overlooked some of the deficiencies we had in our product. As of about ten months ago, this man quit. The company has a new management team that is demanding better quality, lower prices, and better service. We may lose this account if we don't do a better job.

Unfortunately, Frank really does not know how to handle the production side of this business. I know that he is a partner in the company, and that he has a lot of contacts. Sometimes, I think that he knows everybody in the industry, because when I talk to prospective customers, they always ask about Frank. But he has not been able to keep the product quality up and the labor costs down. This is killing us.

Mr. Glenn also reviewed the events leading up to the current situation and he commented:

Everything changed when Richard Davies left the company. Gary and Paul had been good for us in terms of supplying the materials and the credit. But as partners, they aren't so great. They are seldom around since they have the lumber company. I think their prime concern is to get Allied's debt to them paid off. After that, they probably won't care what happens to the business.

Overall, I'm not too happy with the situation here. Even though I own one-half of the business, I'm treated like another employee. They came in

EXHIBIT 5
Allied Pallet Company
Balance Sheet
(in hundreds of dollars)

Current Assets	
Cash	$ 18
Accounts Receivable	338
Inventory	190
Prepaid Expenses	7
Other	3
Total	$556
Fixed Assets	
Land	$ 19
Building	33
Machinery	38
Other	12
Total	$102
Total Assets	$658
Current Liabilities	
Notes Payable	$ 2
Accounts Payable	369
Accrued Taxes and Expenses	138
Total	$509
Owners' Equity	$149
Total Liabilities and Equity	$658

and just took over. It's degrading to have to get clearance from Don to do things. Occasionally, I don't even ask, partly to see what their reactions will be.

I think the complaints about the quality of our pallets are exaggerated. We have never tried to be the best; that isn't our primary market. Still, I don't see Gary, Paul, or Don coming down here in the plant and building pallets.

FUTURE

Although the current situation did not appear very promising, Allied had enjoyed some reasonable amounts of success financially (see exhibits 4 and 5). Of particular concern to both Gary and Paul Williams was how to increase sales and keep costs as low as possible. In the last several months, industry sales of pallets had increased substantially, and were expected to continue upward for at least the near future. Mr. Glenn, in fact, had completed negotiations with an old friend for Allied to make $150,000 worth of expendable pallets. While this caused a serious argument with Mr. Powell over who was responsible for the selling, both Gary and Paul Williams were happy to have the contract.

Despite this rather modest success, all three partners realized that Allied had serious organizational and financial problems. Mr. Glenn thought one way to improve the situation was to begin to focus more on other types of pallets. Mr. Powell did not think this wise until the quality of manufacturing could be improved, and because they were still selling a substantial volume of expendable pallets. Gary and Paul Williams were unsure of what direction the business should take, but both wanted to take some action rather than let Allied continue as it had.

PARK PHARMACIES, INC.

After losing their third manager in four years, Jerry Smith and Jeff Montgomery were reassessing their operating practices for Park Pharmacies, Inc., a holding company for three drug stores they owned and managed. The corporation had remained profitable over the years, but it seemed to Mr. Smith that although they were working harder, company sales and profits were stagnating. And, with the personnel problems in their third store, the frustrations were becoming tiresome. As Mr. Smith noted:

We have been in business for over fifteen years now, and have done reasonably well. But, I'm getting tired of all the work, the crises, and the frustrations of third-party billing (where payments were made by insurance companies and the government). Worst of all, I don't think that I'm getting any richer.

This case was prepared by Professor Dennis H. Tootelian, California State University, Sacramento.

CASE

HISTORY

Park Pharmacies, Inc., was founded nearly sixteen years ago in a relatively large community in the northeastern United States. Mr. Smith, president of Park Pharmacies, Inc., and Mr. Montgomery, its vice-president and treasurer, initially began working together as partners of Smith's Drugs, their first community-oriented pharmacy, soon after graduating from pharmacy school together. Three years later, they purchased Medico Pharmacy, a medical pharmacy, and incorporated Park Pharmacies as a holding company for both stores. For the next nine years, Mr. Smith managed Smith's Drugs while Mr. Montgomery managed Medico Pharmacy.

After accumulating a sizeable net worth, Park Pharmacies, Inc., at Mr. Smith's insistence, purchased a third pharmacy and called it "Jay's Drugs." This store was located in a less desirable area of the community, and had been previously owned by a friend of Mr. Montgomery's. Although the store had been reasonably successful before acquisition by Park Pharmacies, the previous owner had begun to let the business deteriorate in the few years preceding his retirement. While Mr. Montgomery was content with two stores and did not want the added burdens of rejuvenating this pharmacy, Mr. Smith was eager for the challenge and the opportunities for added growth and profits.

ORGANIZATION

The organizational structure of Park Pharmacies, Inc., is shown in exhibit 1. Mr. Smith served as president of the corporation and manager of Smith Drugs; Mr. Montgomery served as the corporation's vice-president and treasurer, and as manager of Medico Pharmacy. They believed that the duties of the president would be about as time-consuming as those of the vice-president and treasurer, therefore balancing out their work.

Because neither man wanted to manage two stores at once, they hired a manager for Jay's Drugs. Ron Karle was the last of a series of managers they had employed in that capacity. After the owners fired the first manager because they caught him taking merchandise from the store, the next manager

(Ms. Ames) and the next (Mr. Karle) quit due to what they considered to be undesirable working conditions.

Mr. Karle was especially vocal about what he thought to be the problems in managing this pharmacy:

Even though my duties as manager and pharmacist were fairly clear, either Mr. Smith or Mr. Montgomery would occasionally stop by and check what I was doing. Quite often they would make conflicting recommendations and I really did not know what to do then.

For example, Jerry would want me to promote the store more aggressively, using fliers and in-store sales programs, and to have my staff use more aggressive selling techniques. Jeff would come in and see this and hit the roof. He would tell me that such practices were unprofessional and should be stopped immediately. You'd think that after all the years they have been in business together, they would understand each other's methods of operation. Instead, they would come in, tell me different things, and evidently never talk about it to each other.

I became very frustrated trying to balance their orders. I can make almost the same amount of money as an employee pharmacist, actually only about $2,000 less, and it's just not worth the headaches. Besides, this store tends to cater to very low income clientele. These people are hard for me to deal with, especially with all the Medi-Care claims processing (the state-operated health care program for welfare and other recipients). Each store does its own billing to insurance companies and to the state under the Medi-Care program. We also had considerable problems with shoplifting, and we were robbed twice this year by drug addicts. It just wasn't worth the additional $2,000.

As Mr. Karle noted, each pharmacy was managed independently of the others. Since they were nearly seven miles apart, Mr. Smith and Mr. Montgomery felt that they were not competing with one another for customers, so they could operate autonomously. By doing this, they could each run their store as they saw fit, avoiding some of the common problems

CASE

EXHIBIT 1
Park Pharmacies, Inc.
Organization Chart

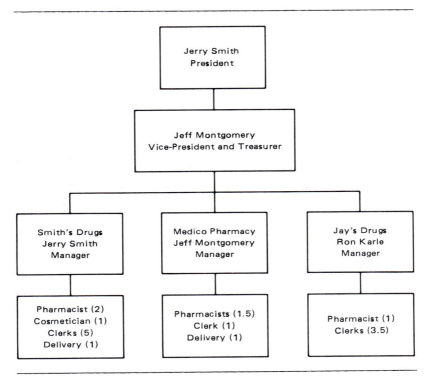

associated with partnerships. Not wanting to cause any new troubles, they agreed when they purchased Jay's Drugs that each would take an interest in overseeing its operations on a time-available basis. They left the day-to-day operations to the pharmacist-manager. Normally, Mr. Smith would stop by the store once a week, and Mr. Montgomery once every three weeks.

THE MARKET

Located in a city of nearly 350,000 people, the three pharmacies faced moderate to intense competition from both chain and independent drug stores located nearby. Within the city there were seventeen chain drug outlets, over forty independent pharmacies, and out-patient pharmacies in the four local hospitals (see exhibits 2 and 3).

Smith's Drugs faced the greatest amount of competition, since three chain stores and two independent pharmacies were located within two miles of the store. Being well established, however, the pharmacy was thought to have a loyal clientele, who were older and had higher incomes. Accordingly, these customers were not considered to be especially price sensitive or overly concerned with comparing chain store prices with those of Smith's Drugs. Mr. Smith believed that his customers were primarily interested in service and in-store credit rather than price. Although the store's growth had slowed down as new competition entered the area and the total population in the immediate area declined, both

EXHIBIT 2
Selected Demographics of the Market Area

	Smith's Drugs	Medico Pharmacy	Jay's Drugs
Age			
Under 21	9%	12%	16%
21 to 35	17	23	31
36 to 50	24	28	19
51 to 64	31	26	18
65 or older	19	11	16
Income (thousands of dollars)			
Under 10	5%	9%	16%
10 to 20	11	23	35
21 to 35	29	33	32
36 to 50	33	21	15
Over 50	22	14	2
Sex			
Female	56%	49%	59%
Male	44	51	41
Employment			
Blue Collar	19%	24%	39%
White Collar	47	42	21
Professionals	21	25	10
Unemployed	5	4	14
Other*	8	5	16

*Includes retired

Mr. Smith and Mr. Montgomery thought that the store was doing very well.

Medico Pharmacy was situated in a medical center located near one of the larger hospitals in the city. Being the only pharmacy in the center gave Medico Pharmacy a significant advantage. However, there were four other independent pharmacies and one chain outlet located within 1.5 miles. While Mr. Montgomery considered convenience to be a critical factor in selecting a pharmacy among those operating within his area, other pharmacies had been competing more on price since the chain store moved into the area. Mr. Montgomery, however, refused to do this because he considered price cutting to be unprofessional. As he noted:

If customers are going to patronize Medico Pharmacy strictly because we offer the lowest prices, I don't want them. After all, how long will they remain our customers? I'll tell you—just until one of the other pharmacies offers them a better deal. There's no future in that type of activity. I offer my customers good service and convenience, and I expect them to pay for it. And, they do!

Jay's Drugs was located on the outskirts of the city in a relatively depressed area, along with one chain and two independent pharmacies. Incomes tended to be lower and a significant level of unemployment was evident. A greater percentage of this store's customers were under the Medi-Care and other third-party programs than in either Smith's Drugs or Medico Pharmacy. As Mr. Karle commented:

Under third-party programs, our fees are limited to the ingredient cost of the drug plus a set fee. Prescriptions that are not under these programs earn us considerably more money, about double the fee paid by the insurance companies and the state. With all of the paperwork I have to do for this, and the delays we often have in receiving payments (averaging forty days on third-party claims for payment), we have a tough time making a profit. These programs only account for about 15 percent of Smith's Drugs' total revenues, and 30 percent of those for Medico Pharmacy. For us, they represent about 60 percent of total revenues. Even though we have a lot of floor space, our nonprescription sales represent only 25 percent of total revenue. These people do not buy our merchandise. I think they prefer to go to the chain stores instead, where they think they can get lower prices.

MARKETING

The marketing programs used in the three pharmacies differed greatly, reflecting the attitudes of the store managers. The most consistently aggressive efforts were conducted by Mr. Smith for Smith's Drugs. Of the 3,800 square feet of floor space, approximately 2,500 square feet were devoted to nonprescription merchandise. Mr. Smith made certain that he carried a wide range of merchandise, and used weekly newspaper advertising with specials on selected nonprescription items. The full-time cosmetician and all other personnel were well-trained in personal selling. Accordingly, Mr. Smith felt that he could compete with both the independent pharmacies and the chains in terms of both products and services (see exhibit 3). However, he thought that the chains could offer lower prices if they were willing to take lower profit margins.

To complement his other marketing efforts, Mr. Smith also was involved in various civic activities. Although he did this partly for personal enjoyment, he also felt that the publicity and goodwill he generated for the store were quite important:

> If I want the community to support my store, I have to support the community. It's important for people to get to know me, and for me to get to know them.

In contrast to Smith's Drugs, Medico Pharmacy received almost no marketing effort. With only 1,000 square feet of space, 400 of which were available for nonprescription merchandising, Mr. Montgomery did not think it was wise to aggressively promote the pharmacy. Since nearly 80 percent of the pharmacy's revenues came from prescription sales, he preferred to maintain a highly professional image—which meant no marketing effort other than a well-maintained store. Nearly all of Mr. Montgomery's marketing efforts were directed to cultivating good relations with physicians in the medical center. He believed that good rapport with the physicians would prompt them to recommend Medico Pharmacy when they wrote prescriptions. Medico Pharmacy's product and service offerings are shown in exhibit 3.

The most sporadic of all marketing efforts was undertaken by Jay's Drugs. In the fourteen months that Mr. Karle managed the store, he implemented several marketing programs that Mr. Smith had used successfully for Smith's Drugs. However, these were only moderately successful. While the store had nearly 4,500 square feet of floor space, not all of the 3,500 square feet of nonprescription space was stocked. Mr. Karle had suggested that the store seek a postal station for the unused area, but neither Mr. Smith nor Mr. Montgomery could decide whether it was worth the money and effort.

COMPANY OPERATIONS

Since Mr. Smith and Mr. Montgomery ran their own individual stores, there was very little in the way of standardized procedures. Mr. Montgomery worked closely with the corporation's accountant, and insisted that there be separate financial statements for each of the three stores, so that they could evaluate individual performance. Mr. Smith and Mr. Montgomery met formally on the third Thursday of every other month to review store activities. Aside from this, they managed their stores as if they were not under central ownership.

Smith's Drugs employed two pharmacists, a cosmetician, three clerks, and one part-time delivery person. Although Mr. Smith felt that he did not always need two pharmacists, his community service work often kept him away from the store. Accordingly, he preferred to be free from those duties except during peak times. On those occasions when he was not in the store, the pharmacist on duty would be in charge. During the evening hours, the senior clerk would have such duties since no pharmacist would be working. Store hours were 9:00 A.M. to 9:00 P.M., Monday through Saturday. The pharmacy was open 9:00 A.M. to 6:00 P.M., Monday through Friday. Since all employees were paid straight hourly wages, there were no financial incentives for managing the store during the times when Mr. Smith was away. He believed that the prestige of being store manager was adequate.

Store operations at Medico Pharmacy were much simpler. The pharmacy was open from 9:00 A.M. to 6:00 P.M., Monday through Friday. Mr. Montgomery ordinarily remained in the store throughout that time, even during normal lunch hours. He employed a delivery person on a part-time basis, and a semi-retired pharmacist during times he had to be away from the pharmacy.

Jay's Drugs employed a pharmacist-manager, one full-time pharmacist, and three clerks. Because so many of its prescriptions were third-party (and therefore carried low profit margins), delivery service

EXHIBIT 3
Competitor Profile

	Store	Chains			Independents			

A. For Smith's Drugs

	Smith's	1	2	3	1	2	3	4
Product Offerings								
Prescriptions	X	X	X	X	X	X		
Non-Rx drugs	X	X	X	X	X	X		
Cosmetics	X	X	X	X		X		
Greeting cards	X	X	X	X		X		
Gifts/notions	X	X	X	X	X			
Photographic		X		X				
Service Offerings								
Medication records	X	X		X	X	X	X	X
Consultations	X	X	X	X	X	X	X	X
Emergency Rx					X	X	X	
In-Store credit	X							
Delivery	X				X	X	X	X

B. For Medico Pharmacy

	Medico	1	2	3	1	2	3	4
Product Offerings								
Prescriptions	X	X			X	X	X	X
Non-Rx drugs	X	X			X	X	X	X
Cosmetics		X			X		X	
Greeting Cards		X			X	X		X
Gifts/notions		X					X	
Photographic								
Service Offerings								
Medication records	X	X			X	X	X	X
Consultations	X	X			X	X	X	X
Emergency Rx					X		X	
In-Store credit	X					X		
Delivery	X					X		X

C. For Jay's Drugs

	Jay's	1	2	3	1	2	3	4
Product Offerings								
Prescriptions	X	X			X	X		
Non-Rx drugs	X	X			X	X		
Cosmetics		X			X	X		
Greeting Cards	X	X			X			
Gifts/notions	X	X						
Photographic	X							
Service Offerings								
Medication records	X	X			X	X		
Consultations	X	X			X	X		
Emergency Rx						X		
In-Store credit								
Delivery								

EXHIBIT 4
Park Pharmacies, Inc.
Income Statements by Pharmacy
(for the current year)

	Smith's Drugs	Medico Pharmacy	Jay's Drugs
Sales			
Prescription	$399,800	$497,500	$235,500
Nonprescription	433,200	55,500	78,500
Total	$833,000	$553,000	$314,000
Cost of Goods Sold	566,400	382,900	197,800
Gross Margin	$266,600	$170,100	$116,200
Expenses			
Manager's salary	$ 40,500	$ 40,500	$ 24,000
Employees wages	116,300	49,200	59,000
Advertising	22,500	3,000	5,400
Rent	19,400	25,100	14,200
All other	38,900	29,600	9,500
Total	$237,600	$147,400	$112,100
Net Profit Before Taxes	$ 29,000	$ 22,700	$ 4,100

was not offered. Both Mr. Smith and Mr. Montgomery felt that the costs of delivery (estimated to be $1.50 each) were too high to justify this service, and that delivery costs could not be passed on to store customers as an added charge. Store hours were 9:00 A.M. to 7:00 P.M., Monday through Saturday. The store manager, unlike other employees, was paid a straight salary. In addition to the management responsibilities for hiring and firing, the manager was expected to fill in as a backup pharmacist during peak times. Typically, the manager would work 5.5 days per week and receive $2,000 more in salary than the employee pharmacist earned in hourly wages for a month.

FINANCIAL POSITION

As Mr. Smith and Mr. Montgomery reviewed the financial statements for each pharmacy (see exhibits 4, 5, and 6), it became apparent that the businesses had not grown to the extent that Mr. Smith had hoped. Although both Smith's Drugs and Medico Pharmacy had always been profitable, the former generated considerably more sales and profits than did the latter. Nevertheless, the owners divided the profits equally, and tried to maintain a policy of retaining 20 percent of the net profits before taxes in the company. Believing that the acquisition of Jay's Pharmacy would increase their sales to $2 million and profits to $75,000, Mr. Smith expected Park Pharmacies, Inc., to continue to grow—possibly with the purchase of another pharmacy.

Mr. Montgomery, on the other hand, seemed quite content with the level of sales and the income he was receiving. Although he agreed that the profitability of the corporation was not up to expectations, he noted that the business still provided him with a comfortable living. However, he did express one major concern:

Despite the fact that I am happy with my income from the business, I am worried about the future need for more money. Smith's Drugs is getting pretty old, and will need some extensive modernization within the next two years. I expect that this will cost approximately $55,000. And, I

CASE

EXHIBIT 5
Park Pharmacies, Inc.
Condensed Income Statement
(for last three years)

	This Year	Last Year	Two Years Ago
Sales			
Prescription	$1,132,800	$1,080,000	$1,000,000
Nonprescription	567,200	560,000	540,000
Total	$1,700,000	$1,640,000	$1,540,000
Cost of Goods	1,147,100	1,070,000	1,030,000
Gross Margin	$ 552,900	$ 570,000	$ 510,000
Expenses	497,100	480,000	457,000
Net Profit Before Taxes	$ 55,800	$ 90,000	$ 53,000

EXHIBIT 6
Park Pharmacies, Inc.
Balance Sheet

	Smith's Drugs	Medico Pharmacy	Jay's Drugs
ASSETS			
Current Assets			
Cash	$ 30,000	$ 32,000	$ 9,800
Accounts Receivable	32,000	31,000	37,800
Inventory	130,000	88,000	87,000
Other	11,000	6,000	3,000
Total	$203,000	$157,000	$137,600
Fixed Assets			
Fixtures & Equipment	$ 31,000	$ 14,000	$ 18,000
TOTAL ASSETS	$234,000	$171,000	$155,600
LIABILITIES			
Current Liabilities			
Accounts Payable	$ 59,200	$ 42,500	$ 53,000
Notes Payable	16,500	6,000	2,000
Accrued Expenses	28,000	4,300	16,000
Total	$103,700	$ 52,800	71,000
Long Term Liabilities			
Notes Payable	26,000	4,000	22,000
Total Liabilities	$129,700	$ 66,800	$ 93,000
Net Worth	$104,300	$104,200	$ 62,600
TOTAL LIABILITIES & NET WORTH	$234,000	$171,000	$155,600

would like to have a new computer for my store. Jerry has a new one, and I would like to put the present one I have in the other store and get a new one for myself. This may cost somewhere around $20,000. When we take these expenditures into account, we don't have all the money we think we do. Neither of us particularly likes to borrow money, so we could have some trouble here.

THE FUTURE

In considering Mr. Smith's comments regarding the problems they were facing, Mr. Montgomery was both concerned and amused:

Jerry was the one who wanted to jump into the "Jay's" deal. I was reluctant to change the good thing we had going; I just wanted to keep everything the way it was. He wanted to grow and

get rich and be the big businessman. Unfortunately, I don't think that we can sell Jay's Drugs without losing a lot of money.

Before even considering the possibility of selling Jay's Drugs, Mr. Smith wanted to review the entire operation of Park Pharmacies, Inc. He knew that the poor operating performance of Jay's Drugs over the past four years would make it very difficult to sell the store. Furthermore, he did not want to give up, feeling that there must be ways to solve the problems they faced:

I don't think we have done all that we could to make Jay's successful. Our advertising hasn't been consistent and the store is not well merchandised. Some of the strategies I have used in my store should work well in Jay's, but Jeff has not agreed. The effect has been a sporadic effort and the operating results show this to be true.

PACIFIC ART MUSEUM OF LAS POSITAS

The Pacific Art Museum of Las Positas had been the municipal art museum of Las Positas since 1885. It served a metropolitan population of approximately one million and a regional population of two and a half million as a general art museum. In the permanent collections were major holdings in old master drawings, nineteenth-century American paintings, and European paintings and sculpture of the fifteenth through nineteenth centuries. Other noteworthy collections included Oriental ceramics, nineteenth-century American decorative arts, and a growing collection of American contemporary art.

This case was prepared by Professor Ralph M. Gaedeke, California State University, Sacramento.

The museum regularly mounted special temporary exhibits; sponsored educational programs, classes, lectures, films and other events; and arranged numerous concerts and other performances which took place in the gallery building.

HISTORY

The museum was started in 1869 as the private collection of Judge Samuel Winthrop. The gallery building was intended to serve two purposes. One purpose was to house the art collection he was acquiring. The second purpose was to provide a cultural and recreational center for the family. (The gallery building included such rooms as a ballroom and a library on the main floor and a bowling alley in the basement.)

Judge Winthrop also supported Western American artists and collected their work. Upon his death in 1875, Mrs. Margaret Winthrop carried on her husband's dream, establishing the finest collection in the West. The art gallery frequently was opened to generate funding for worthy causes and often was opened to the public without charge. At an exhibition to raise funds for the California Museum Association (CMA), Mrs. Winthrop announced her intent to give the gallery to CMA. To insure that the gallery would always be open for the public's use, the plan was changed to deed the property and contents to the city of Las Positas. The city would have joint trusteeship of the gallery with CMA.

Under the 1885 Deed of Gift, CMA and the city would jointly name the board of directors of the gallery and formulate its policies. The city was "to hold and keep said property both real and personal forever; to care for and maintain the same in good repair, order and condition," in accordance with the deed of gift. This arrangement had remained in effect with only slight modification. In 1959 the Pacific Art Gallery Association was formed to support the museum in raising funds for programs, exhibitions, art acquisition, and facilities construction, a task that neither the city nor CMA was doing on any regular basis.

To facilitate a more coordinated effort of activity on behalf of the museum, the two associations began efforts to merge, eventually forming the Pacific Art Museum Association (PAMA). This was not an easy accomplishment. PAMA and the city petitioned the court to modify the deed of gift to allow the new association to jointly govern the museum with the city. Under this petition the name of the museum was changed to the Pacific Art Museum of Las Positas.

The museum's character had been shaped by the activities and interests of the gallery directors. The museum's first director, W. F. Jackson, to some extent set the course the museum has taken. Jackson was director for fifty years and, during that period, the gallery and its contents did not receive any renovative attention and in some instances items deteriorated from lack of proper care. While other West Coast galleries were forming and expanding their collections, the Pacific Museum did little other than display its collection.

Only since the 1950s had the museum embraced a positive educational program on a wide scale. Most of this change could be attributed to two factors: one, the formation of the Pacific Art Gallery Association;

and two, the selection of gallery directors with professional gallery experience and education.

GOALS

Recognizing that the museum's potential far outstripped the restricted facilities available to it for exhibitions, permanent display, and public activities, the joint board of trustees in 1975 adopted a ten-year plan called the "1985 Plan," which set the following goals for the museum:

1. to make the museum truly the visual arts resource center of the valley region with the best permanent collections, special exhibitions, small one-man or thematic exhibitions, innovative educational programs and introductory exhibits, contemporary art, and the finest of regional and nationally known crafts always on display;
2. to develop an integrated support program of films, lectures, and other educational activities, both in the museum and in the "field," related to the museum's collections and exhibitions, providing support for the visual arts programs of community schools and institutions of higher education;
3. to create an endowment for acquisitions which would permit planned and careful growth of the collections.

To achieve these goals, a three point agenda was developed:

1. the restructuring of the governance of the museum to provide a unified basis for fund raising and policy decisions;
2. the structural renovation and restoration of the original (1871–73) gallery building, and its designation as a national center for the study of Victorian art, with all aspects of art and design in the nineteenth and early twentieth century on display or available for research and study;
3. the construction of new facilities contiguous to the present museum with modern facilities for the display of the permanent collections; a special study and display area for master drawings and prints; an auditorium for films, lectures and

concerts; a kitchen and public cafeteria; staff offices; and increased storage space.

The first point of the plan had been accomplished by the merger of the California Museum Association and the Pacific Art Gallery Association (PAGA) to form the Pacific Art Museum Association (PAMA). The second point, restoration of the original gallery building, was nearing completion in early 1979.

The third point called for a $4.7 million building program. This point of the plan had been delayed because members of the joint board were waiting to take action until it was determined what would be done with the "Annex," which made up part of the current facilities.

ORGANIZATION

The structure of the museum's organization, as shown in exhibit 1, reflected its history as well as the participation of municipal government. At the time of the case, the joint board of directors set policy for the museum and did the primary job of selecting the gallery director and curator (these positions were exempt from civil service procedures). However, the gallery director and curator were formally hired by the city manager and, as the gallery director stated, "serve at his pleasure." The museum was a department of the city and was responsible for following its policies and procedures. The city provided funds for the staff and maintenance of the gallery and collections. The museum also received funds through various county, state and federal grants and aid programs.

The Pacific Art Museum Association served the museum in a joint trustee relationship with the city and provided assistance in the form of gifts and services. One major service has the docent program. This program furnished qualified guides for the museum. They gave tours complete with accounts of history and background on the buildings and exhibits. An extension of this was a slide tour that was taken to area schools.

FUNCTIONS

The functions of the museum as stated in its budget transmittal letter were:

(1) to display works of art for the benefit of the public; (2) to maintain and preserve works of art in its possession; (3) to provide public appreciation through education, professional interpretation, acquisition of works of art and organization of exhibitions devoted to various aspects of the fine arts.

The museum provided the community with a variety of art experiences. Displays of items in the permanent collections were rotated since lack of exhibition space allowed only a small portion to be on display at any one time. The museum's staff developed exhibits from the permanent collections to be shown locally and exchanged with other museums. They also organized and developed joint exhibitions with other museums.

The staff researched items in the permanent collections and those items under consideration for acquisition. The intent of this research was to develop a collection of quality pieces and an overall consistency of collection content. The research also was used in developing educational programs and documentation of exhibits.

FACILITIES

At the time of this case, the museum complex consisted of three structures; the original gallery building was constructed in 1871–73 and continued to serve as the hub of the museum's activities. It was undergoing complete structural renovation and restoration as an architectural landmark. The R. A. Herold Wing, constructed in 1969, provided additional space to display the permanent collection and flexible display facilities for temporary exhibitions.

The Annex was the major exhibition space from around 1921 until 1970. In 1970 the structure was closed to the public because it was found to be unsafe. The Annex had been the Winthrop's residence, but it had lost all architectural distinction as a result of the conversion in the 1920s. With its closing the museum lost close to 50 percent of its exhibition space. At the time of the case, plans for the Annex were uncertain. PAMA did not want to start raising funds until they knew what the final "complex" would consist of (they also were anxious for a

EXHIBIT 1
Museum Organization Chart

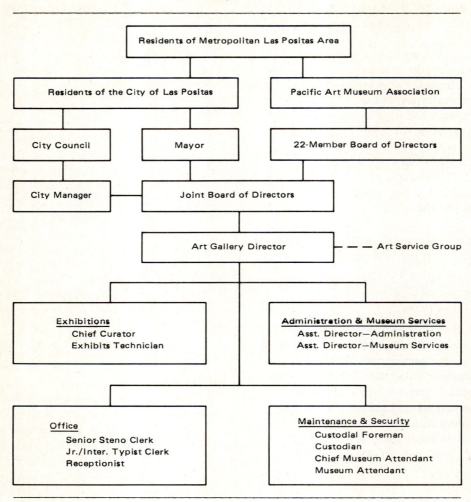

long-term commitment of support from the city council). PAMA, the joint board, and the gallery director wanted to see the Annex demolished and a new structure built in its place. However, the city council had made no decision because of protests from people interested in restoring the building. In 1979, two plans were being evaluated to form a joint plan between the museum's "1985 Plan" and one for preserving the building from the Historical Preservation Board. If the joint plan was adopted, the

Annex would be restored to its 1870s condition and used to house memorabilia and artifacts of the Winthrops and their era.

VISITORS

A survey conducted in 1977–78 showed that the museum attracted visitors from a wide area. However, 88 percent of the visitors lived within a 2-hour driving radius of the museum. Residents of the city accounted for 34 percent of the visitors, while residents of Las Positas County accounted for another 24 percent. An additional 30 percent of those attending came from the northern part of the state and the San Tomás Bay area.

Attendance at the museum had been around 100,000 visitors per year during the first half of the 70s (exhibit 2). Because of the permanent closing of the Annex and temporary closing of the original gallery, the museum had of necessity reduced its offerings—displaying less of the permanent collection and hosting fewer exhibitions—and was experiencing a corresponding decline in attendance.

The museum's attraction of visitors was not adversely affected by other galleries or performing arts organizations. The gallery director commented that:

When people become interested in the arts, they tend to become interested in a wide range, increasing their attendance and donations to the arts. So instead of dividing a pie, the various organizations, as they acquire new members, tend to enlarge the pie and everyone's share.

However, the "pie" had not been enlarged by funding from government sources. While the number of organizations promoting the arts had increased, the funds available from local government had not. Recent tax limitations on Las Positas County had caused it to reduce its support of almost all cultural activities; 1977-78 funding had been $50,665, while 1978-79 funding was only $5,000.

FUNDING

The museum, because it was a department of the city, had a basic source of operating funds that did not depend on admissions revenues or donations. For the fiscal years 1973-1978, the city budgeted the amounts shown in exhibit 3. The budget covered staff salaries, maintenance of the gallery and collections, and general operating costs of keeping the museum open.

The finance department of the city had conducted an internal audit of the museum in 1975. Based on findings of this audit, certain procedures were

EXHIBIT 2
Pacific Art Museum of Las Positas
Attendance for Selected Years

Year	Attendance
1970–71	104,593*
1971–72	100,926
1972–73	105,619
1973–74	109,430
1974–75	106,450
1975–76	94,774
1976–77	87,292**
1977–78	**

*Annex closed to public, no estimated date of reopening or replacement.

**Original gallery section closed for renovation until 1979.

changed to improve cash receipts and general financial control of the museum. One finding pointed out a major cause of the museum's weak financial control, namely a lack of clear organizational jurisdiction guidelines between: (1) the CMA; (2) the mayor of the city of Las Positas; (3) the gallery joint board; (4) the gallery director acting on behalf of the city manager. According to the audit report,

has resulted in a weak system of financial control and management. Resources are flowing from many sources in and around the gallery and nowhere is there a written statement of financial responsibility.

PAMA had its own budget which it developed and funded. It provided limited funding for the purchase of art for the museum and for some exhibitions. It also provided the major part of the art education offered to the community at large via its docent program.

The museum and PAMA have received funds through various grants for the arts. Planned exhibits at the museum have relied on resources of the collection and annually sponsored events by PAMA, the Kingsly Art Club and the Creative Arts League.

Although PAMA provided some funding, the gallery director had no control over PAMA's budget, and so had no permanent, set budget item for

EXHIBIT 3
City's Museum Budget
(1973–78)

Item	1973–74	1974–75	1975–76	1976–77	1977–78
Employee Services	$203,590	$249,064	$254,589	$292,278	$284,637
Other Services and Supplies	60,792	72,547	102,732	108,587	102,406
Equipment	2,262	3,340	1,635	1,442	539
Capital Improvements	100,000	30,000	—	—	—
Total	$366,644	$354,951	$358,596	$420,307	$387,582

exhibitions or acquisitions. Most funds for these activities of the museum were generated from donations and/or matching grants.

While the gallery director had no control over PAMA's budget or projects, PAMA greatly affected the museum. The gallery director expressed the relationship between the museum staff and PAMA as a sharing of joint facilities and the desire to expand the public's interest in art. PAMA did not provide general funds for the museum's use, but gave specific gifts and exhibitions.

The city's relationship with the museum had been basically supportive. The city generally funded the museum adequately and specified no performance requirements on which future funds depended. At the same time, the gallery director felt that there was a difference of opinion on what the museum was to do. He felt that the city did not understand the importance of research or the need for research facilities at the museum.

THE CITY'S POSITION

Historically the Las Positas mayor and city council had tended to be indifferent to the museum's activities. The gallery directors shaped the activities of the museum during its first 75 years. The formation of PAGA was a major change that improved the museum's concern for the general public. By the early 70s, forces were afoot to change the nature of the joint board to have wider community representation.

At the time of this case, the mayor, because of his interest in the city's cultural activities, had not been indifferent to the museum's activities. He had taken active responsibility as co-trustee and had emphasized that the museum was a department of the city. When reorganization of the museum's support associations came to a standstill in 1977 (reorganization efforts had been going on for almost 10 years), he took action to see that wider community representation on the joint board took place. He sent the following letter to the associations and city departments concerned:

At the recent PAGA Board meeting you announced the planned reformation of the California Museum Association as a "fait accompli." This surprised me since I was under the impression that CMA was to further discuss the proposal before acting.

Since your change is in my opinion, insufficient and guaranteed to lead to more confusion in gallery management, I can only conclude that further discussions are not contemplated, nor would they be productive.

Therefore, I see no alternative than for the city to begin to assert its full authority over the management of the Pacific Art Gallery. In that regard the following actions have been taken:

1. To see that no action regarding the trust property is taken without my prior consent.
2. To accept no gifts to the Pacific Art Gallery which are subject to the terms of Mrs. Winthrop's deed without my prior consent.
3. To indicate on the agenda of all future joint board meetings which items are subject to the

terms of the deed of trust. The joint board will only consider those items properly before it.

Second, there will be no further meetings of the joint board unless I, or my designated voting representative, are present. CMA, of course, can meet by itself. However, the practice of taking action without my approval will no longer occur.

Third, I have directed West Dillion, City Treasurer, to disperse no funds held in the name of the gallery, CMA or the joint board without my permission.

Fourth, I hereby rescind approval of the action allowing money in the building fund to be held by the CMA. Such funds are controlled by the joint board and therefore should be deposited with the City Treasurer and subject to the joint board action.

Please feel free to contact me if you have any questions.

The mayor said that the letter was considered to be hostile, but it precipitated the reorganization and formalizing of responsibilities of the various groups.

As for the future, the mayor was concerned about the museum's lack of interest in its "administrative activities." While the staff handled the creative activities of the museum very well, he felt there was a lack of understanding of the importance of departmental administrative duties on their part. He thought this might be corrected by making the museum part of the Parks and Recreation Department. Some of the old problems of the museum had been corrected, he felt, by selecting "professional museum directors." One example he cited was, "the first real inventory was done and now we don't have valuable paintings laying on the basement floor rotting!"

PACIFIC ART MUSEUM ASSOCIATION

The president of the Pacific Art Museum Association felt that a primary objective for the museum's future was to firmly define the various parties' responsibilities and functions. PAMA and the mayor would have to work closely together on this matter. The general areas had been defined by a "letter of agreement" that needed to be translated into day-to-day working terms.

The reorganization forming PAMA had been a step in the right direction. Because of the deed of gift, the museum would probably never have the type of organizational structure that might be viewed as normal or typical by other museums. Nevertheless, the president felt that reorganization and delineation of duties made the museum's structure a workable one.

The association did not feel that it could start raising funds for the new facilities until it knew what those facilities would be. The fund-raising plan outlined in the "1985 Plan" called for contacting contributors in stages. The first group consisted of approximately 1500 "key donors," major individual benefactors, board members, and foundations. This group would provide a major part of the necessary funds. The president thought that it would be a waste of time to contact this group without complete plans. He did not see how PAMA could expect an individual to contribute thousands of dollars to build "something" at "sometime" for the gallery.

As for developing an endowment fund for acquisitions or exhibitions, the president could not see any particular need for this. "Under the 'letter of agreement' the joint board members are specifically responsible for raising funds," the president stated, and "the director is responsible for day-to-day operations."

Contributor Index